LET'S GO

PAGES PACKED WITH ESSENTIAL INFORMATION

"Value-packed, unbeatable, accurate, and comprehensive."

—The Los Angeles Times

"The guides are aimed not only at young budget travelers but at the independent traveler; a sort of streetwise cookbook for traveling alone."

—The New York Times

"Unbeatable; good sight-seeing advice; up-to-date info on restaurants, hotels, and inns; a commitment to money-saving travel; and a wry style that brightens nearly every page."

—The Washington Post

THE BEST TRAVEL BARGAINS IN YOUR BUDGET

"All the dirt, dirt cheap."

—People

"Let's Go follows the creed that you don't have to toss your life's savings to the wind to travel—unless you want to."

—The Salt Lake Tribune

REAL ADVICE FOR REAL EXPERIENCES

"The writers seem to have experienced every rooster-packed bus and lunar-surfaced mattress about which they write."

—The New York Times

"[Let's Go's] devoted updaters really walk the walk (and thumb the ride, and trek the trail). Learn how to fish, haggle, find work—anywhere."

—Food & Wine

"A world-wise traveling companion—always ready with friendly advice and helpful hints, all sprinkled with a bit of wit."

—The Philadelphia Inquirer

A GUIDE WITH A SPIRIT AND A SOCIAL CONSCIENCE

"Lighthearted and sophisticated, informative and fun to read. [Let's Go] helps the novice traveler navigate like a knowledgeable old hand."

—Atlanta Journal-Constitution

"The serious mission at the book's core reveals itself in exhortations to respect the culture and the environment—and, if possible, to visit as a volunteer, a student, or a teacher rather than a tourist."

—San Francisco Chronicle

LET'S GO PUBLICATIONS

TRAVEL GUIDES

Australia
Austria & Switzerland
Brazil
Britain
California
Central America
Chile
China
Costa Rica
Eastern Europe
Ecuador
Egypt
Europe
France
Germany
Greece
Hawaii
India & Nepal
Ireland
Israel
Italy
Japan
Mexico
New Zealand
Peru
Puerto Rico
Southeast Asia
Spain & Portugal with Morocco
Thailand
USA
Vietnam
Western Europe

ROADTRIP GUIDE

Roadtripping USA

ADVENTURE GUIDES

Alaska
Pacific Northwest
Southwest USA

CITY GUIDES

Amsterdam
Barcelona
Boston
Buenos Aires
London
New York City
Paris
Rome
San Francisco
Washington, DC

POCKET CITY GUIDES

Amsterdam
Berlin
Boston
Chicago
London
New York City
Paris
San Francisco
Venice
Washington, DC

LET'S GO

HAWAII

JESSICA LANE LUCIER EDITOR
EVELYN Z. HSIEH ASSOCIATE EDITOR

RESEARCHER-WRITERS
PHILIP R. EISELE   **DANIELLE M. O'KEEFE**
WILLIAM E. JOHNSTON   **CLAIRE J. SAFFITZ**

ELISSA C. REIDY MAP EDITOR
R. DEREK WETZEL MANAGING EDITOR

ST. MARTIN'S PRESS ❧ NEW YORK

HELPING LET'S GO. If you want to share your discoveries, suggestions, or corrections, please drop us a line. We appreciate every piece of correspondence, whether it's a postcard, a 10-page email, or a coconut. Visit Let's Go at **http://www.letsgo.com,** or send email to:

> feedback@letsgo.com
> Subject: "Let's Go: Hawaii"

Address mail to:

> Let's Go: Hawaii
> 67 Mount Auburn St.
> Cambridge, MA 02138
> USA

In addition to the invaluable travel advice our readers share with us, many are kind enough to offer their services as researchers or editors. Unfortunately, our charter enables us to employ only currently enrolled Harvard students.

Maps by Let's Go copyright © 2009 by Let's Go, Inc.
Maps by David Lindroth copyright © 2009 by St. Martin's Press.

Distributed outside the USA and Canada by Macmillan.

ISBN-13: 978-0-312-38579-8
ISBN-10: 0-312-38579-X
Fifth edition
10 9 8 7 6 5 4 3 2 1

Let's Go: Hawaii is written by Let's Go Publications, 67 Mount Auburn St., Cambridge, MA 02138, USA.

Let's Go® and the LG logo are trademarks of Let's Go, Inc.

ACKNOWLEDGMENTS

TEAM HAWAII THANKS: Our fabulous ⬛RWs, for making our jobs not only possible but entertaining and worth it (and for desktop pictures). ⬛**Derek,** for the daily check-in, cool-out. ⬛**Elissa,** for love from Mapland. ⬛**Prod,** for having all the answers. ⬛**Julia,** Pandora, and snack drawers for making the office a nice place to be.

JESSIE THANKS: ⬛**Evelyn,** for being older, wiser, and generally better but having the sense of humor to deal with the rest of us. ⬛**Julia,** for being the greatest person on the planet with whom to share a desk, minus that Yankees affiliation. ⬛**Derek,** for trying to disguise his "Jessie-you-are-insane" look. ⬛**Elissa,** for being fab. ⬛**Claire** for sarongs, ⬛**Beamer** for stories, ⬛**Danielle** for MAUIhaha marginalia. My wonderful ⬛**family** for making my East Coast summer a good one. ⬛**Mom,** ⬛**Dad,** ⬛**Dani,** and ⬛**Jake,** for being the absolute best people to go home to.

EVELYN THANKS: Jessie, for patiently enduring many a "Can I ask you a question?" and going above and beyond. Julia, for rounding out the tropical trifecta with class n' sass n' Fluff. Both, for debunking Hahvahd myths. Derek, for keeping it real (aka low-stress). Elissa, for map clarity. Will, for being on the ball. Trow inhabitants for making a happy home. CBCGB for being the perfect place to edit and being filled with people who kept me sane.

ELISSA THANKS: Jessie, for her boundless energy and endless supply of baked goods; Evelyn for putting up with my disorderly stacks of maps; Danielle, Claire, Beamer, and Will for their humor and precision; Gretch's sighs and eclectic noises; Becca for secret glances and giggles; Illiana for insect lollipops; Derek for dealing with all the estrogen. A special thanks to ⬛**Prince** for making doves cry. Bump that.

Editor
Jessica Lane Lucier
Associate Editor
Evelyn Z. Hsieh
Managing Editor
R. Derek Wetzel
Map Editor
Elissa C. Reidy
Typesetter
Jansen A. S. Thurmer

LET'S GO

Publishing Director
Inés C. Pacheco
Editor-in-Chief
Samantha Gelfand
Production Manager
Jansen A. S. Thurmer
Cartography Manager
R. Derek Wetzel
Editorial Managers
Dwight Livingstone Curtis,
Vanessa J. Dube, Nathaniel Rakich
Financial Manager
Lauren Caruso
Publicity and Marketing Manager
Patrick McKiernan
Personnel Manager
Laura M. Gordon
Production Associate
C. Alexander Tremblay
Director of IT & E-Commerce
Lukáš Tóth
Website Manager
Ian Malott
Office Coordinators
Vinnie Chiappini, Jennifer Q. Wong
Director of Advertising Sales
Nicole J. Bass
Senior Advertising Associates
Kipyegon Kitur, Jeremy Siegfried,
John B. Ulrich
Junior Advertising Associate
Edward C. Robinson Jr.

President
Timothy J. J. Creamer
General Manager
Jim McKellar

HOW TO USE THIS BOOK

INTRODUCTORY MATERIAL. The first chapter, Discover Hawaii, will introduce you to the Hawaiian islands and get you primed for an unforgettable adventure. Additionally, our Suggested Itineraries make planning your trip a no-brainer.

ESSENTIALS. All the practical information involved in traveling can get downright pesky. Flip here for a quick and easy guide to Hawaii, including advice on getting there, getting around, finding a place to stay, and staying safe.

LIFE AND TIMES. The answers to all your burning questions. Why do so many Hawaiian words sound the same? Who was Kamehameha the Great? What's the deal with Spam? History, culture, music—you name it. It's all here.

GREAT OUTDOORS. Want to know how to cut through camping red tape, stay safe in the wilderness, or where the best beaches are for all your favorite activities? We're giving it to you, dear reader, in one convenient location.

COVERAGE. A chapter is dedicated to each main Hawaiian island—Oahu, the Big Island, Maui, Molokai, Lanai, and Kauai. Info on the "Other Islands"— Kahoolawe, Niihau, and the NW Hawaiian Islands—is in Life and Times.

ARTICLES AND FEATURES. Throughout this book you'll find sidebars and longer articles—built in reading material for waiting in line or sitting by the campfire. You can read researchers' tales **From the Road,** learn about volunteer opportunities in **Giving Back,** discover **Hidden Deals** and worthy **Big Splurges,** and much more. Don't miss the book's **scholarly articles:** the scoops on studying volcanoes from a student who did so (p. 77) and expert information on Hawaii's invasive species (p. 95).

SOLO TRAVELERS. All of our accommodations and transportation information is geared toward options for the solo traveler; we do report on accommodations for travelers in larger groups, but the default is one person.

APPENDIX. The Hawaiian islands have a language all their own. In our glossary, we've included many common words and phrases to help you avoid sounding like a tourist, as well as climate, measurement, and culinary information.

PRICES AND RANKINGS. We list establishments in order of value from **best** to **worst.** Our favorites have earned the **Let's Go thumbs-up** (☒). Since the best value may not mean the lowest price, we have incorporated a system of price ranges for food and accommodations. Each listing is followed by a price icon (**❶-❺**); see p. XII for a price range breakdown. Any $ sign you see denotes US$.

TIP BOXES. Tip boxes provide a wealth of information, from the smallest "didn't you know..." tip to pointers that can make or break your vacation (or at least part of it). Boxes with other icons contain warnings and further resources.

FINALLY. Remember to put down this guide once in a while and strike out on your own—Hawaii is full of more surprises than any book can cover.

CONTENTS

DISCOVER HAWAII.................. 1
When to Go 1
What to Do 2
Island Overviews 2
LIFE AND TIMES 14
History 14
People 21
The "Other" Islands 23
Culture 26
ESSENTIALS 38
Planning Your Trip 38
Safety and Health 45
Getting to Hawaii 50
Getting around Hawaii 53
Keeping in Touch 58
Accommodations 60
Specific Concerns 63
Other Resources 66
BEYOND TOURISM 67
A Philosophy for Travelers 67
Volunteering 68
Studying 71
Working 73
A Volatile Classroom 77
THE GREAT OUTDOORS 78
Land 78
Flora and Fauna 80
Camping in Hawaii 82
Wilderness Safety 87
Outdoor Activities 91
Useful Resources 94
Organized Adventure Trips 94
Aliens in Hawaii 95
OAHU 96
Honolulu 98
Waikiki 129
Central Oahu 144
Southeast Oahu 150
Waimanalo 153
Windward Coast 155
Kailua 155
Kaneohe and the Windward Coast 162
North Shore 168
Waimea and Sunset Beach 168
Haleiwa 172

Waialua and Mokuleia 178
Leeward Coast 181
THE BIG ISLAND.................187
Kailua-Kona 189
South Kona 199
Kau And Ka Lae 205
Hawaii Volcanoes National Park 210
Puna 218
Volcano 219
Pahoa 221
Hilo 226
Saddle Road 234
Mauna Kea 235
Mauna Loa 237
Hamakua Coast 238
Honokaa 240
Waipio Valley 243
Waimea 245
North Kohala 249
Hawi And Kapaau 249
South Kohala 255
MAUI 258
West Maui 260
Lahaina 261
Kaanapali 274
Honokowai, Kahana, and Napili 276
Kapalua and Beyond 278
Central Maui 280
Kahului and Wailuku 280
South Maui 288
Maalaea 288
Kihei 290
Wailea 297
Makena and Beyond 298
North Shore 299
Paia 302
Haiku 306
Hana 308
Kipahulu Valley and Oheo Gulch
(Haleakala National Park) 312
Upcountry Maui 313
Kula 313
Polipoli Spring State Recreation
Area 317
Haleakala National Park 318
Makawao 323

MOLOKAI 326
  Kaunakakai 329
  Central Molokai 334
  Kalaupapa Peninsula 334
  Kamakou Preserve 336
  Kalae and Kualapuu 338
  Hoolehua 341
  East of Kaunakakai 342
  Western Molokai 347
  West End Beaches 349
LANAI................................350
  Lanai City 352
KAUAI 361
  East Shore 361
  Wailua 371
  Waipouli 377
  Kapaa 379
  North Shore 383
  Kilauea 383
  Hanalei 386
  Haena 391

Na Pali Coast 395
  Kalalau Trail 396
  West of Kalalau 399
South Shore 399
  Poipu 400
  Koloa 406
West Shore 407
  Kalaheo 408
  Kalaheo to Waimea 410
  Waimea 413
  Waimea Canyon State Park 416
  Kokee State Park 417
  Kekaha 421
APPENDIX 423
  Climate 423
  Measurements 423
  Language 424
  Phrasebook 424
  Local Food and Drink 426
INDEX 427
MAP INDEX 436

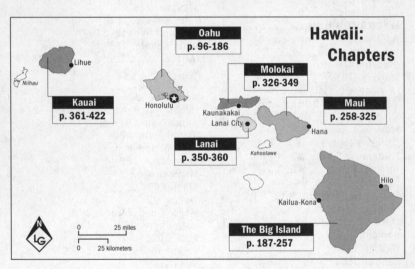

Hawaii:
Chapters

Oahu
p. 96-186

Molokai
p. 326-349

Kauai
p. 361-422

Maui
p. 258-325

Lanai
p. 350-360

The Big Island
p. 187-257

Lihue

Niihau

Honolulu

Kaunakakai
Lanai City

Hana

Kahoolawe

Hilo

Kailua-Kona

N
LG

0   25 miles

0   25 kilometers

RESEARCHER-WRITERS

Philip "Beamer" Eisele
The Big Island

A freshly graduated Government major with a passion for (dare we say, obsession with) brews, Beamer took the Big Island by force. From kava to cameramen, nightly camping to cliff-jumping, the B-Man kept his editors laughing (and maybe a bit worried). With a commitment to authentic island lifestyle and an appreciation for deadlines, Beamer infused his features and coverage with his friendly, adventurous perspective.

Will Johnston
Kauai and Molokai

A Social Studies major from Montana, Will went from one adventure to the next on the hills and shores of Kauai and Molokai. From tackling the entire Kalalau Trail to scoping out vegetarian delicacies, Will braved sunburns, car trouble, and the untamed wilderness to deliver snappy prose and timely information.

Danielle O' Keefe
Maui and Lanai

Holy eyelashes! This is one classy lady. A turbulent start did not prevent this recent graduate from delivering factual, flawless, and fresh copy (when in doubt, alliterate) on both Maui and Lanai. Though her editors may have missed a few of this aspiring (and inspiring) film director's many movie references, they treasured the Staten Island native's witty, whimsical, and wise thoughts.

Claire Saffitz
Oahu

Claire could have written the Oahu chapter on her own; saying this RW is competent is a criminal understatement. A History and Literature student, Claire tackled Oahu (yes, that's right—all of it) with style and grace. From circus rooms to free dinners to severe sunburns, this thoughtful, hard-working writer delivered prose that was a joy to edit.

CONTRIBUTING WRITERS

Katherine Thompson was the Editor of *Let's Go: Germany 2005* and a Managing Editor for the 2006 series.

Michael Bassford is a 1999 Harvard graduate and now teaches high school science in Honolulu.

Michael Judge is a 2005 Harvard graduate and now teaches high school science in Honolulu.

Hawaii

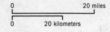

0   20 miles

0   20 kilometers

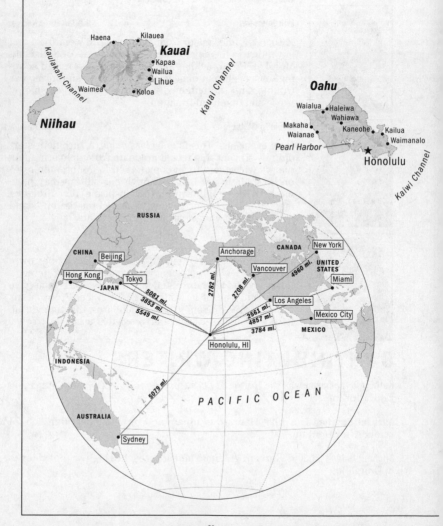

PACIFIC OCEAN

Kaulakahi Channel

Haena   Kilauea

Kauai

Kapaa
Wailua
Waimea   Lihue
Koloa

Niihau

Kauai Channel

Oahu

Waialua   Haleiwa
Wahiawa
Makaha   Kaneohe   Kailua
Waianae   Waimanalo
Pearl Harbor

Honolulu

Ka'iwi Channel

RUSSIA

CHINA   Beijing   Anchorage   CANADA   New York

Hong Kong   Vancouver   4960 mi.   UNITED
STATES
Tokyo   Miami
JAPAN   5081 mi.   2782 mi.   2708 mi.   Los Angeles
3853 mi.   2561 mi.
5549 mi.   4857 mi.   Mexico City
3784 mi.   MEXICO

INDONESIA   Honolulu, HI

5079 mi.

AUSTRALIA   PACIFIC OCEAN

Sydney

X

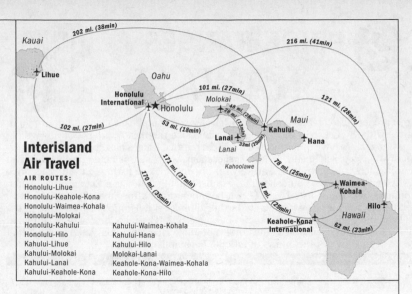

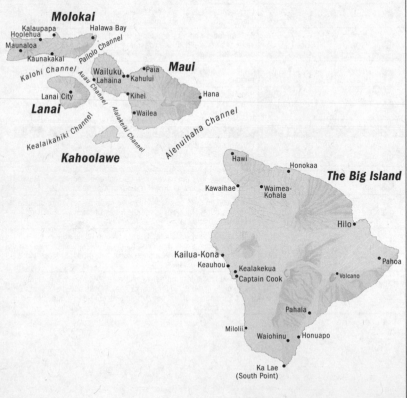

PRICE RANGES ❸ ❹
HAWAII
❶ **❷** **❺**

Our researchers list establishments in order of value from best to worst, honoring our favorites with the Let's Go thumbs-up (📖). Because the best *value* is not always the cheapest *price*, we have incorporated a system of price ranges based on a rough expectation of what you will spend. For **accommodations,** we base our range on the cheapest price for which a single traveler can stay for one night. Read listings carefully, as price diversity can sometimes be misleading; establishments listed as a ❶ can offer higher-end options, and those listed as a ❺ can be much more affordable if you room with a friend (or a few). For **restaurants** and other dining establishments, we estimate the average amount one traveler will spend in one sitting. The table below tells you what you'll *typically* find in Hawaii at the corresponding price range, but keep in mind that no system can allow for the quirks of individual establishments.

ACCOMMODATIONS	RANGE	WHAT YOU'RE *LIKELY* TO FIND
❶	under $25	Campgrounds and dorm rooms, both in hostels and universities. Expect bunk beds and a communal bath. You may have to provide or rent towels and sheets.
❷	$25-65	Upper-end hostels or lower-end hotels. You may have a private bath, or there may be a sink in your room and a communal shower in the hall.
❸	$66-110	A small room with a private bath. Should have decent amenities, such as phone and TV. Breakfast may be included. Many B&Bs are in this range.
❹	$111-150	Similar to a ❸, but may have more amenities or be closer to the beach.
❺	$151 and up	Resorts, large hotels, or upscale chains; almost always near the beach. If it's a ❺ and it doesn't have the perks you want, you've paid too much.

FOOD	RANGE	WHAT YOU'RE *LIKELY* TO FIND
❶	under $8	Probably street food or a fast-food joint, but also university cafeterias and bakeries (yum). Usually takeout, but you may have the option of sitting down.
❷	$8-12	Sandwiches, pizza, appetizers at a bar, or low-priced entrees. Most ethnic eateries are a ❷. Either takeout or a sit-down meal.
❸	$13-16	Mid-priced entrees, seafood, and exotic pasta dishes. More upscale ethnic eateries. Since you'll have the luxury of a waiter, tip will set you back a little extra.
❹	$17-20	A somewhat fancy restaurant. Entrees tend to be heartier or more elaborate, but you're really paying for decor and ambience. Few restaurants in this range have a dress code, but some may look down on T-shirts and sandals.
❺	$21 and up	Your meal might cost more than your room, but there's a reason— it's something fabulous, famous, or both. Slacks and dress shirts may be expected. Offers foreign-sounding food and a decent wine list. Don't order a PB&J.

DISCOVER HAWAII

Welcome to Hawaii, America's paradise. Since Hawaii became the US's most exotic state in 1959, millions of people have been allured by the islands' charm—they've sunbathed on its spectacular white, black, golden, green, and red sand beaches, become smitten with Hawaiian culture and the forgivably tacky aloha shirts, felt the awesomeness of active volcanoes, and succumbed to the 50th state's laid-back lifestyle. Hawaii's six major islands have so many facets that it is impossible to explore them all in one trip.

The beauty of the remote trails, verdant wilderness, and dramatic cliffs of Kauai—Hawaii's oldest and arguably most majestic island—is unrivaled. Maui unveils its elegance on the road to Hana, one of the most beautiful drives in the world, or from the lonely summit of Haleakala National Park. The Big Island brandishes its raw and rugged side at Hawaii Volcanoes National Park and the Waipio and Pololu Valleys. On Oahu, tan or learn to surf at Waikiki's wide beaches; at night, hit up the glamorous clubs and free beachside hulas and movies. Oahu's North Shore, the domain of professional surfers, serves as a pleasant escape from the touristy areas elsewhere on the island. Molokai and Lanai remain a Hawaii without stoplights or many paved roads, where street addresses are largely irrelevant and life is best taken slowly.

Even without the historic temples and palaces to see, the legends to absorb, the waves to surf, the bays to snorkel in, and the whales to watch, the essence of Hawaii's appeal may still be that it's accessible, yet exotic, paradise: part of the US, yet decidedly independent. You will come back for the beaches, lava, hula, hikes, and, above all, for the intangible allure of the islands. Along every coast there is a more secluded stretch of sand, and beyond each stunning vista an even more breathtaking view. The diversity of land, people, and culture ensures that, in Hawaii, the journey never ends.

FACTS AND FIGURES

STATE POPULATION: 1,275,194.

LOWEST RECORDED TEMPERATURE (UNDER 3000FT. ALTITUDE): 56°F.

STATE MOTTO: *Ua mau ke ea o ka aina i ka pono.* (The life of the land is perpetuated in righteousness.)

ETHNICITIES: Hawaii is one of only four US states in which non-Hispanic whites do not form a majority. It is also the state with the largest percentage of Asian Americans and people of mixed race.

CAPITAL: Honolulu.

TOTAL NUMBER OF ISLANDS AND ATOLLS: 137.

OFFICIAL LANGUAGES: English and Hawaiian.

UNOFFICIAL STATE FISH: *Humuhumunukunukuapuaa* (Hawaiian triggerfish).

MAJOR EXPORTS: Coffee, macadamia nuts, pineapple, and sugarcane—yum!

STATE SPAM CONSUMPTION RATE: Over 18,000 cans per day.

WHEN TO GO

How soon can you leave? With year-round temperatures rarely straying far from 80°F, Hawaii's climate is always welcoming. Even the hotter summer months are cooled by trade winds, and the ocean averages a pleasant 75°F. Though wind and rainstorms are more common in winter, they usually pass through the islands quickly and without incident. Hawaii's mountainous regions and valleys are often rainy and damp, though weather is localized and beachgoers are almost always able to find sunny patches on the drier, leeward sides of the islands. Depending on the focus of your vacation, there may be specific times when you should travel. Winter is surf season, when hardcore board riders and their groupies make the pilgrimage to Oahu's North Shore for the biggest waves of the year. Families with young children should consider a summer vacation, when swimming conditions are generally safer and plenty of other kids are guaranteed to be playing in the surf. Whale-watching season (January-March) and wind-surfing season (June-August) might also affect traveling decisions. Hawaii has two high seasons, December through April and June through August, so budget travelers might book a cheaper accommodation during the other months. Plane tickets are consistently expensive though a search in September might yield a deal.

WHAT TO DO

It is far less difficult to find things to do in Hawaii than to find time in which to do them. Hundreds of miles of winding trails, deep valleys, canyons, swamps, windswept crater floors, and lava-scarred land await. There's plenty of sand and surf to occupy the beach bum and enough frozen concoctions to fill the nights. Hawaii takes sports to a new level. Across the islands, there are athletes and travelers toeing the edge and pushing the limits of what is possible. Yet adventure sports aren't just for the future Ironman—for every grueling hike, there's a leisurely one, and for every big surf beach, there's a handful of "learning" beaches. Whatever your level of expertise, Hawaii has you covered.

And if the Mai Tais aren't slowing you down, Hawaii's historical sights, tours, and museums might. Throughout the islands, Hawaii's local culture remains a vivid backdrop, wooing travelers with colorful tales, local island grinds, and a genuinely welcoming attitude. The evidence of Hawaii's storied past is everywhere, from the 25 million artifacts that are meticulously maintained in the Bishop Museum to petroglyphs etched into rock throughout the islands. Every landmark, be it valley, rock, mountain, or cave, has a story behind it. The Menehune (legendary laborers) supposedly have had a hand in the creation of everything, and ancient Hawaiian kings had more stomping grounds and battlefields than we could possibly record. These glimpses into the Hawaiian lifestyle might leave you with more than just a tan from your trip to the islands.

ISLAND OVERVIEWS

OAHU

Oahu (p. 96) is where old meets new. Known as "the gathering place," this island joins natural wonders with modern luxuries, a storied past with a bright, productive future. This juxtaposition between the indigenous and the urban might be surprising. Hike down a lush mountainside in the **Honolulu Mauka Trail System** (p. 127), just minutes away from the cityscape of Hawaii's major metropolis, **Honolulu** (p. 98). Sunbathe all day on the quiet beaches of the **Windward Coast** (p. 155) then dance all night in **Waikiki** (p. 129).

When it comes to outdoor activities on Oahu, surfing reigns supreme. Every year, countless people catch their first waves at **Baby Queen's** (p. 129) in Waikiki, while many others perfect their technique on other beaches. The winter months bring mammoth waves to the **North Shore** (p. 168) and the Leeward Coast's **Makaha Beach** (p. 185), so naturally they also bring surf junkies, roaming the globe in search of the perfect wave. The rest of the island is also not without appeal. **Kailua Beach** (p. 160), with its constant breeze, is a windsurfer's paradise, and on the eastern coast, **Sandy Beach** (p. 152) and **Makapuu** (p. 153) are to bodyboarding what the North Shore is to surfing. Oahu is also the site of the only Royal Palace on US soil, **Iolani Palace** (p. 116), built by King Kalakuala, and the **Aliiolai Hale** (p. 117), which housed the legislature and Supreme Court of the Hawaiian Kingdom. The **Polynesian Cultural Center** (p. 166) performers dance Tahitian hula and demonstrate Samoan fire-making skills. This centerpiece of the Hawaiian island is also its major tourist destination, but you can hardly blame the hordes who visit.

HAWAII, OR "THE BIG ISLAND"

To avoid confusion with the name of the state, the island of Hawaii (p. 187) is called "Hawaii's Big Island," and what an appropriate name it is. Bigger than all of the other Hawaiian Islands combined, its sheer size can be humbling. **Mauna Kea** (p. 235), the world's largest sea mountain, and **Kilauea** (p. 213), the world's most active volcano, only add to the intimidation factor. You'll find 11 of the world's 13 climatic zones within this island's shores. The Big Island offers opportunities for on-land adventures, with mountain biking on Mauna Kea as well as biking, horseback riding, and ATVing in the **Waipio Valley** (p. 243). Snorkelers will delight in the underwater sights of **Kealakekua Bay** (p. 203) and **Lapakahi State Historical Park** (p. 252). The Big Island is also the site of the most extreme event of them all—the Ironman Triathlon, held in October.

Home to numerous ancient Hawaiian *heiau* (temples), the birthplace of King Kamehameha I, and the landing spot for the first European missionaries, the Big Island is also an important place to learn about Hawaiian history. **Hilo** (p. 226), hosts the state's biggest and most prestigious hula festival, the **Merrie Monarch Hula Festival** (p. 232). The **Puuhonua O Honaunau National Historical Park** (p. 205) is a reconstructed 180-acre village that was the home of Kona's *alii* (royalty). **Mookini Luakini Heiau** (p. 252) is one of Hawaii's oldest and most sacred religious sites, where kings would pray and make human sacrifices to Ku, the god of war. Though not the place for the resort-hopper, the Big Island's offerings are sure to astound the intrepid traveler.

MAUI

The second largest Hawaiian island has a smaller population than you'd expect, making Maui (p. 258) popular with visitors who are looking for sophisticated diversions and amenities in the small, intimate towns peppered throughout the island. Maui has been able to stave off the rampant development of Oahu while maintaining more accessible attractions than some of its more remote neighboring islands. From **beaches** that have repeatedly been voted among the best in the world to the scenic heights of **Haleakala Crater** (p. 318) to the countless waterfalls along the drive to **Hana** (p. 308), a visit to "The Magic Isle" is sure to astound. Maui beckons adventurers, though many Maui adventures require less heartiness than those of the Big Island and Kauai. Helicopter tours run out of **Kahului** (p. 280), dolphin- and whale-watching cruises leave from **Maalaea** (p. 288), and snorkel trips to **Molokini** are popular in **Kihei** (p. 290). **Paia** beaches (p. 302) are prime surfing and windsurfing spots, and within **Haleakala National Park**

TOP TEN LIST

BEST ADVENTURES BY SEA

Your trip to Hawaii won't be complete without a day on the beach or time in the water: Hawaii has 750 mi. of coastline, waters that contain 70% of the reefs in the US, and perfect conditions for a slew of watersports.

1. Maui: Snorkel in the **Aquarium** (p. 299), a large natural cove in the **Ahihi-Kinau Natural Area Reserve** located on a lava cape away from the crowds.
2. Oahu: Kiteboard—or learn how to—on the gorgeous and windy **Kailua Bay** (p. 160).
3. The Big Island: Bodysurf at the often overlooked **Papalokea Green Sands Beach** (p. 208).
4. Maui: Windsurf off Paia at **Hookipa Beach** (p. 305).
5. Maui: Sail from Kihei out to **Molokini Crater** (p. 294) for unparalleled snorkeling.
6. Oahu: Surf on world-class waves at one of several **North Shore** beaches (p. 170).
7. Kauai: Spelunk through the frigid water of the wet caves in **Haena State Park** (p. 395).
8. Oahu: Swim or snorkel next to hundreds of brightly colored fish in **Hanauma Bay** (p. 150).
9. Molokai: Kayak along the **North Shore Sea Cliffs** (p. 347), and view untouched valleys and the longest ocean-terminating waterfall in the world.
10. Kauai: Marvel at the fiery sunset from blissfully remote **Polihale Beach** (p. 422).

(p. 318), several companies offer bike tours. The surf spot **Jaws** (p. 307) is known for its immense waves that are too big to tackle without motorized assistance—surfers have jet skis tow them in.

Though Maui has grown commercial, the identity of the island community remains strong and is constantly evolving. The island provides some of the best opportunities for visitors to learn actively about Hawaii's past and present. **Maui's Iao Valley State Park** (p. 286) is a battlefield where Kamehameha I won a victory over the rival king of Oahu, and its **Iao Needle**, a 2250 ft. natural stone pillar, is named after the phallus of sea god Kanalou. **Maui Nei** (p. 269) leads a historical tour of the once thriving whaling port of **Lahaina** (p. 261) from a Native Hawaiian perspective. The **Hana Cultural Center** (p. 312) preserves Hawaiian history and culture with unique quilts and woodcarvings.

MOLOKAI

Little Molokai (p. 326) is known for its easygoing pace set among unscathed surroundings. Known as the most "Hawaiian" of the islands—thanks to nearly half of its population being of native ancestry—Molokai has been able to preserve its rural lifestyle due to its *aloha aina*, or love of the land. This island without stoplights is Hawaii's fifth largest, though only 38 mi. long and 10 mi. wide. Visitors can relax with friendly locals and also enjoy the island's history. Molokai is the birthplace of hula and celebrates the dance every year with the **Ka Hula Piko Festival** (p. 349). It also has the second-largest temple grounds in Hawaii, **Iliiliopae Heiau** (p. 344). The *heiau*'s flat stone surface rivals the size of a football field and was allegedly the site of human sacrifices. Molokai has plenty for the outdoorsy type as well. Snorkel at the Hawaii's largest white sand beach, **Papohaku** (p. 349) or kayak along the world's largest sea cliffs on the **North Shore** (p. 347). Head to this, the "Friendly Isle," for both a chance at adventure and lesson in relaxation.

LANAI

If you're looking for quiet isolation, Lanai (p. 350) is the island for you. The former Dole pineapple plantation has become a luxurious destination for the wealthy and the wealthier, with two extravagant, secluded resorts and championship golf courses. However, this small, friendly island has much to offer those on a more limited budget as well. **Manele Bay** (p. 359) is home to Lanai's best beach and only campsite. Rugged, untamed Lanai is accessible by 4WD or ATV on the **Munro Trail** (p. 357), from which views of neighboring islands Maui, Molokai, Kahoolawe (p. 23), Oahu, and the Big Island are possible. Lanai also has two well-preserved collections of petroglyphs at **Shipwreck Beach** (p. 358) and **Kukui Point** (p. 359) on the way to Manele Bay. The rocky, lunar landscape of the **Garden of the Gods** (p. 357), or **Keahikawelo,** is both steeped in legend and great for off-roading. Home to the authentically slow pace of life and hospitality that makes Hawaii famous, Lanai is an ideal place to spend a Hawaiian vacation.

KAUAI

"The Garden Isle" is purposefully named. Kauai (p. 361), the northernmost island in the Hawaiian chain, is marked with sharp mountain spires, lush valleys, and jagged cliffs, all draped in a canopy of emerald. Welcome to the nature freak's paradise. The crunchy granola type, rather than the party animal, will find this island most rewarding, though anyone would be hard pressed not to enjoy Kauai's stunning scenery. Beginners can get an introduction to the art of surfing on **Hanalei's** (p. 386) gentle waves. Advanced hikers and kayakers navigate the **Na Pali Coast** (p. 395) and snorkelers drift happily among the native fish at **Tunnels Beach** (p. 393). The adventurer can spend days exploring **Waimea Canyon** (p. 416), the "Grand Canyon of the Pacific" and sleeping under the stars on the island's multiple state parks. Even the sunbathers in **Poipu** (p. 400) enjoy spectacular views, though they hardly work as hard for them.

Though Kauai's natural wonders take the cake, we'd be remiss not to mention the island as a cultural destination as well. Kauai has strong ties to its past. **Polihale Cliff** (p. 422) was a jumping point of souls where the spirits of the dead would spring away from the earth into the blazing sun. The **Wailua River Basin** (p. 374) was the vacation spot of the *alii* (royalty) and maintains seven of their sacred *heiau* (temples) today. Kauai is also the location of the first American possession in Hawaii, the offshore **Mokuaeae Rock** (p. 386), though you wouldn't know it from the spirit of the island's inhabitants. The people of Kauai are fiercely proud of their heritage. From the numerous sacred sites preserved on Kauai to the island-wide aversion to commercialization, the "Garden Isle" is a great place to venture for a taste of real island life.

⚑LET'S GO PICKS

BEST PLACE TO HANG TEN: Learn to surf or just wipe out big time at **Waikiki Beach** (p. 138), where the gentle rollers make every wave a party wave.

BEST COLLECTION OF HAWAII'S HISTORY: The **Bishop Museum** (p. 122) in Honolulu holds nearly 25 million works of art and artifacts from Hawaii's history.

BEST PLACE TO TEST YOUR METTLE: The **Ironman Triathlon,** a grueling three-part trial, held each year in Kailua-Kona (p. 189).

MOST ROMANTIC SUNRISE: Atop **Sweetheart Rock lookout** (p. 360) in Hulopoe Beach Park on Lanai.

BEST PLACE TO FEEL PELE'S FURY: The lava flows of **Kilauea,** the most active volcano in the world, on the Big Island (p. 213).

SWEETEST TESTAMENT TO A FRUIT: The **Dole Plantation Gardens** (p. 149) on Oahu, a shrine to that famed island fruit, the pineapple.

BEST WAY TO WATCH THE SUN DISAPPEAR BENEATH THE WAVES: Reclining on the dunes of **Polihale State Park** (p. 422) on Kauai.

BEST PLACE TO CRACK A NUT: Purdy's **Macadamia Nut Farm** (p. 339), Molokai's most hospitable farm.

OAHU (1 WEEK)

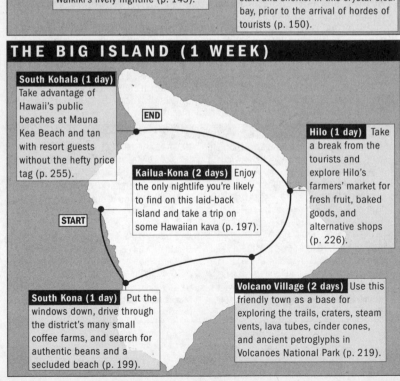

North Shore (2 days) Hang ten, or just watch the professionals do so, at Sunset Beach while enjoying the slow pace and friendly atmosphere of surfer country (p. 168).

Kaneohe (1 day) Spend a day on the Windward Coast wandering through rainforests, gardens, and cultural centers (p. 162).

END

Waimanalo (1 day) Get aquainted with aloha by wandering the streets of this small, relaxed town, or take a shave ice down to the beach (p. 153).

START

Honolulu (1 day) Take a day to explore the museums and historical sites in downtown Honolulu and Chinatown (p. 116).

Waikiki (1 day) Reserve a night (and perhaps the morning after) for Waikiki's lively nightlife (p. 143).

Hanauma Bay (1 day) Get an early start and snorkel in this crystal-clear bay, prior to the arrival of hordes of tourists (p. 150).

THE BIG ISLAND (1 WEEK)

South Kohala (1 day) Take advantage of Hawaii's public beaches at Mauna Kea Beach and tan with resort guests without the hefty price tag (p. 255).

END

Hilo (1 day) Take a break from the tourists and explore Hilo's farmers' market for fresh fruit, baked goods, and alternative shops (p. 226).

Kailua-Kona (2 days) Enjoy the only nightlife you're likely to find on this laid-back island and take a trip on some Hawaiian kava (p. 197).

START

South Kona (1 day) Put the windows down, drive through the district's many small coffee farms, and search for authentic beans and a secluded beach (p. 199).

Volcano Village (2 days) Use this friendly town as a base for exploring the trails, craters, steam vents, lava tubes, cinder cones, and ancient petroglyphs in Volcanoes National Park (p. 219).

MAUI (1 WEEK)

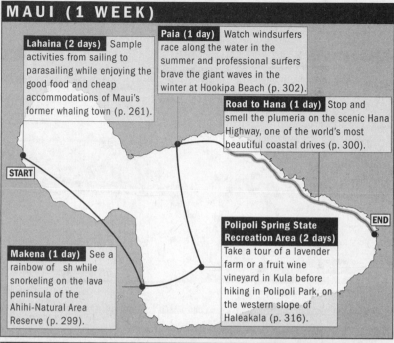

Lahaina (2 days) Sample activities from sailing to parasailing while enjoying the good food and cheap accommodations of Maui's former whaling town (p. 261).

Paia (1 day) Watch windsurfers race along the water in the summer and professional surfers brave the giant waves in the winter at Hookipa Beach (p. 302).

Road to Hana (1 day) Stop and smell the plumeria on the scenic Hana Highway, one of the world's most beautiful coastal drives (p. 300).

START

END

Makena (1 day) See a rainbow of sh while snorkeling on the lava peninsula of the Ahihi-Natural Area Reserve (p. 299).

Polipoli Spring State Recreation Area (2 days) Take a tour of a lavender farm or a fruit wine vineyard in Kula before hiking in Polipoli Park, on the western slope of Haleakala (p. 316).

KAUAI (1 WEEK)

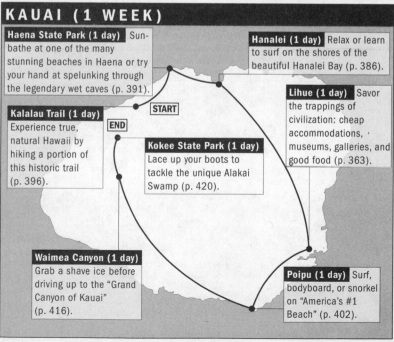

Haena State Park (1 day) Sunbathe at one of the many stunning beaches in Haena or try your hand at spelunking through the legendary wet caves (p. 391).

Hanalei (1 day) Relax or learn to surf on the shores of the beautiful Hanalei Bay (p. 386).

Lihue (1 day) Savor the trappings of civilization: cheap accommodations, museums, galleries, and good food (p. 363).

Kalalau Trail (1 day) Experience true, natural Hawaii by hiking a portion of this historic trail (p. 396).

START

END

Kokee State Park (1 day) Lace up your boots to tackle the unique Alakai Swamp (p. 420).

Waimea Canyon (1 day) Grab a shave ice before driving up to the "Grand Canyon of Kauai" (p. 416).

Poipu (1 day) Surf, bodyboard, or snorkel on "America's #1 Beach" (p. 402).

OFF THE TOURIST BEATEN PATH (2 WEEKS)

Kilauea Watch spinner dolphins during a quiet day at the beach in this eclectic and peaceful North Shore community (p. 383).

Kauai (4 days)

Kaapa Hang out with many of Kauai's residents in this independent, free-spirited town and save a few bucks at the only two hostels on the island (p. 379).

Molokai (3 days)

Kauai

Koloa Soak up the sun and a sense of Hawaiian pride in this, Hawaii's oldest sugar town (p. 406).

Moomomi Preserve Hike through the preserve to reach some of the most pristine beaches on the island (p. 341).

The B

Maui (3 days)

Kahekili Highway Get behind the wheel for this heart-pounding drive around the West Maui Mountains, stopping at beaches, blowholes, and charming towns (p. 279).

Halawa Valley Check out the site of Molokai's first settlement, as well as the magnificent Moaula and Hipuapua Falls (p. 345).

Paia Bare it all at the small secluded beach of Paia Bay, one of Maui's unofficial nude beaches (p. 305).

Kula Meander through the many gardens and art galleries in this small upcountry town on your way to Haleakala (p. 313).

Molokai

Maui

North Kohala Get away from the crowds and still enjoy great meals in the Big Island's North Shore towns, Hawi and Kapaau (p. 249).

Kaunakakai Take in a Little League game and some organic produce in this easy-going town (p. 329).

Lapakahi State Historical Park Visit this ancient Hawaiian sacred healing ground and enjoy the phenomenal snorkeling in the park's cove (p. 252).

The Big Island

ig Island (4 days)

Ka Lae Trek over lava rocks and off-road to Papakolea Green Sand Beach and get rewarded by the unusually beautiful sand (p. 208).

Puna Dance, meditate, and generally find your center with locals in Pahoa, Puna's unspoiled hippie center (p. 221).

DISCOVER

BACK TO NATURE (2 WEEKS)

Kokee State Park Hike the Awaawapuhi Loop and revel in the sites of the Na Pali Coast, only otherwise accessible by boat (p. 419).

Kauai (6 days)

Kilauea Point National Wildlife Refuge Look, but don't touch, Hawaii's endangered *nene* goose and various other bird species making their home on Mokuaeae Rock (p. 386).

Kauai

Poipu Commune with Hawaii's native flora and sea turtles at the McBryde and Allerton Gardens and Lawai Kai Beach (p. 404).

Garden of the Gods Experience the garden's awesome and eerie rock formations, best seen in the late afternoon (p. 357).

Kalalau Trail Experience the world-famous trail fully by hiking and camping its entire length. (p. 396).

Lanai (2 days)

Iao Valley State Park
Stand in awe of the West Maui mountains and the enormous 2250ft. Iao Needle, in this ancient, sacred place (p. 286).

Kihei Snorkel the sunken crater Molokini and get up-close and personal with some of the rarest aquatic life in the world (p. 294).

Maui (3 days)

Haleakala National Park Hike the ridge of the enourmous crater of Haleakala, large enough to hold the island of Manhattan, and see a once-in-a-lifetime sunset (p. 318).

Akaka Falls State Park Venture throught lush rainforest and check out the park's orchids, bamboo groves, and two spectacular waterfalls (p. 239).

Lanai

Maui

Munro Trail Reach Lanai's highest peak and view the surrounding islands by off-roading this wild trail (p. 357).

Waipio Valley Explore this verdant valley on horseback or by foot and hit up the waves at Waipio Beach as a reward (p. 243).

The Big Island

Hawaii Volcanoes National Park Bike, hike and camp on the cinder cones and glowing lava flows of the world's most active volcano, Hawaii's Kilauea (p. 210).

The Big Island (3 days)

HAWAIIANA AND MORE (2 WEEKS)

Oahu (5 days)

Haleiwa Check out some pretty cool surfboards at the North Shore Surf and Cultural Museum, quite possibly the world's most laid-back museum (p. 172).

Wahiawa Indulge that pineapple craving and get lost in the world's largest maze on the Dole Plantation (p. 149).

Leeward Coast Catch a Native Hawaiian spiritual ceremony at the authentically restored Kaneaki Heiau (p. 186).

Oahu

Honolulu Peruse the world's best collection of ancient Pacific Island artifacts at Honolulu's Bishop Museum (p. 122).

Pearl Harbor Historical Sites Pay your respects at these poignant memorials while you elbow aside the tourists and history buffs (p. 144).

Maui (3 days)

Molokai (2 days)

Ka Lae Taste-test at incredibly friendly and totally organic Purdy's Macadamia Nut Farm in Central Molokai (p. 339).

Kalaupapa Peninsula Take a sobering tour of this infamous former leper colony (p. 334).

Hana Wander through Hana's Kahanu Gardens and visit the Piilanihale Heiau, the largest remaining ancient structure in Hawaii (p. 311).

Molokai

Mauna Kea Stargaze perched on the slopes of the world's largest sea mountain, Mauna Kea, at the Onizuka Center for International Astronomy (p. 235).

Lahaina Learn about the rich history of Lahaina through the eyes of Maui Nei, an award-winning grassroots organization (p. 269).

Maui

Maalaea See hundreds of endangered humpback whales on one of the Pacific Whale Foundations eco-friendly and educational tours (p. 288).

Holualoa Roam through this former coffee town, now the Big Island's art epicenter (p. 199).

The Big Island

South Kona Visit St. Benedict's Painted Church, the closest thing to a Gothic cathedral on Hawaii, while exploring the coffee plantations of South Kona (p. 205).

Kau Pilgrimage to the immaculately maintained Nechung Dorje Daryang Ling, a stunning Buddhist temple (p. 209).

The Big Island (4 days)

LIFE AND TIMES

Hawaii is known as a land of unparalleled beauty. From the glistening sands of the islands' beaches to the lush rainforests above sea level and the expansive coral jungles below, Hawaii's natural marvels astound. Yet the state's people are as remarkable as their stunning, natural backdrops. A rich, complicated history has created the diverse and unique inhabitants of the islands today. Though a part of the United States, Hawaii has a history, language, and culture all its own. Hawaii is one of the few places in the world where there is no ethnic or racial majority. This diversity creates a land with unique food, dress, etiquette, and art, making this remote archipelago as culturally rich as its continental counterparts. Moreover, the spirit of aloha (love) generated for both the people and the land on Hawaii isn't a gimmick—it is a palpable sentiment. Though tourist traps abound on a trip to Hawaii, spending a bit more time with the Hawaiian people and learning about their rich history, travelers will learn to appreciate Hawaii for what it is—a beautiful place full of beautiful people.

HISTORY

EARLY HISTORY (AD 500-1778)

The original inhabitants of the Hawaiian islands are believed to have been descendants of Asiatic peoples who migrated over land and water, eventually arriving in the Central Pacific, although accounts vary and none are certain. **Polynesian voyagers** from the Marquesas were probably the first to discover the islands, landing near Ka Lae on the Big Island around AD 300-600. Hawaii shares linguistic and cultural heritage with the other islands of the Polynesian Triangle, an ancient Pacific Region which included the islands now known as Easter Island and New Zealand.

Tahitians were the next group to reach Hawaii, arriving between AD 1000-1200. These new arrivals likely conquered and enslaved the Marquesans. The Tahitians had a profound influence on Hawaiian history, bringing their language, customs, government, and religion to the islands. A Tahitian priest known as Paao founded the *kahuna nui* (high priest) line around 1175, initiating a new system of rule that lasted for several hundred years. One *alii nui*, the most powerful *alii* (royal) of the region, headed each island and distributed land to the chiefs below him in a feudal system. Plots of land took the form of *ahupuaa*, triangular slices running from the mountains in the centers of the islands to the seashore. The *alii* also collected taxes from the *makaaina*. The *alii* were believed to have been chosen by the gods, and they served as a link between the people and the deities they worshipped. Below the *alii* and the priest class were the *makaaina* (commoners) and a third class of citizens known as *kaua*. The *kaua* were most often those who had broken *kapu* (taboo) and had neither rights nor property. These early Hawaiians used little writing and preserved most of their history in chants, known as *mele*. Much of Hawaiian history was lost as *kahuna* and other storytellers died.

REDISCOVERY AND WESTERN TRADE (1778-1872)

THE BRITISH ARE COMING

The first known European to arrive in the Hawaiian Islands was **Captain James Cook,** who happened upon the islands in 1778 during his third and final quest for the Northwest Passage. After only a brief stop in Hawaii, which he dubbed the **Sandwich Islands** in honor of his patron, the Earl of Sandwich, Cook sailed north. Cook and his crew are credited with bringing Western plants and animals to the islands, as well as, unfortunately, venereal disease.

About a year later, on his way back from Alaska, Cook once again spotted the Hawaiian islands, this time landing on the Big Island. Cook and his men were welcomed and allowed to trade with the islanders, departing after two weeks of festivities, only to meet fierce storms that severely damaged their vessels. After being at sea for a week, they returned to Kealakekua Bay, but their second welcome was not as warm as the first. The Hawaiians helped themselves to items from Cook's ships in exchange for the supplies and gifts that they had given the British sailors a few weeks earlier. Cook and a small party of his men went ashore to take the island chief hostage and demand the return of their possessions (in particular, a small ship) but the plan went awry; Cook and several of his men were killed in a skirmish with the Hawaiians on Valentine's Day 1779. Some debate has arisen regarding the true manner of Cook's reception; see **Additional Resources** (p. 36) for further reading.

The next large influx of whites did not come until about 40 years later, when Christian missionaries arrived from America to convert Hawaiians. The short-lived hula ban (about 14 years long), condemned as a heathen dance, was indicative of the Christian influence on the island. Many Hawaiians adopted the Protestant faith from 1820 to 1840.

KAMEHAMEHA THE GREAT

At the time of Cook's discovery, the islands were under the rule of a number of warring kings. Eventually, in 1810, a royal from the Big Island, **Kamehameha,** succeeded in uniting the islands; he reigned for nine peaceful years.

During Kamehameha's reign, the export of highly prized **sandalwood** to China increased, facilitating trade with other nations, most notably the US and Britain. In 1819 the first whaling ships arrived in Kealakekua Bay. The **whaling industry** became profitable for the Hawaiian economy, but Western influence was to prove detrimental to the islands. Even as Kamehameha was creating peace and a strong culture, *haoles* (foreigners) were quietly undermining his progress.

1778
Captain Cook "discovers" Hawaii and names it the Sandwich Islands.

1803
The first horse is introduced to Hawaii from California.

1813
Spanish explorers introduce coffee and pineapple to Hawaii.

1822
First cockroach appears in Hawaii, species *Pycnoscelus surinamensis.*

LIFE AND TIMES

THE KAMEHAMEHA DYNASTY

1825
After Kamehameha II's untimely death, his nine-year-old brother, Kauikeaouli, ascends to the throne as Kamehameha III.

With the death of Kamehameha in 1819, power passed to his son, **Kamehameha II,** also known as **Liholiho.** History suggests, however, that Kamehameha the Great's favorite wife, Kaahumanu, may have been the real force behind the throne. At Kaahumanu's behest, Liholiho overthrew the ancient *kapu* system by allowing men and women to eat at the same table and ordering the destruction of *heiau* (temples) and idols. Liholiho also became the first Hawaiian king to venture off of the islands. In 1823, he and Queen Kamamalu made their first and only official state visit to England, where they both contracted measles and died shortly thereafter.

1830
Hula dancing is forbidden by Kaahumanu, the Queen Regent.

After his death, Kamehameha's second son, Kauikeaouli, **Kamehameha III** (1813-1854), became king. Only nine years old when he received the crown, Kamehameha III was raised amidst the changing Hawaiian culture. His actions during his reign are emblematic of this cultural transformation. In 1839, Kamehameha III introduced the **Declaration of Rights,** which is regarded as the Hawaiian Magna Carta. The Declaration of Rights served as the preamble for the Constitution of 1840, which ended Hawaii's days as an absolute monarchy. Eight

1835
The first permanent sugar plantation is started at Koloa, Kauai.

years later, in 1848, Kamehameha III enacted **The Great Mahele** (division), effectively ending the traditional feudal style of land ownership. True to its name, the edict divided land between the *alii* (royals) and the *makaaina* (commoners), and provided the first legal basis for private land ownership. The division opened the door for the purchase of land not only by previously disenfranchised Native Hawaiians, but also by *haoles* (Caucasians) and commercial investors.

EMERGING INDUSTRY (1840-1940)

SUGAR AND PINEAPPLES

The release of land 1848 coincided with the beginning of the decline of the whaling industry and a subsequent movement toward the development of agriculture. The tropical crops of sugar and pineapple rapidly became a natural source of profit. By the end of the 19th century, sugar and pineapple planta-

1851
Hawaii's first permanent dentist, Dr. John Mott Smith, takes up residence on Oahu.

tions run by American businessmen had overtaken much of Hawaii's land, and the crops were the two most important sources of revenue for the Hawaiian economy. The first sugar plantation in Hawaii, the **Koloa Plantation** on Kauai, was founded in 1835, initiating an explosion in the sugar industry; mills soon began to appear all over the islands. In 1850, the Hawaiian legislature approved the hiring of immigrant laborers from Japan, China, the Philippines, and Portugal to work in the booming industry. The inhabitants of today's Hawaii reflect the diversity of these immigrant laborers.

The massive Hawaiian pineapple industry began as a one-man operation, but today Hawaii produces one third of the world's commercial supply of pineapples. In 1901, James D. Dole built a pineapple cannery near Wahaiwa, on Oahu, marking the start of the **Hawaiian Pineapple Company,** also known as **Dole.** In 1922, Dole purchased the island of Lanai for the purpose of large-scale production; by 1950, his was the largest pineapple company in the world. Pineapples were the state's second-biggest industry until the mid-1940s. Dole was eventually bought out by the **Castle & Cooke** company, which still owns much of Lanai. Today, both Dole and Castle & Cooke are privately held companies.

1871
The first hotel is built in Honolulu and tourism begins.

ANNEXATION AND AMERICAN INFLUENCE (1875-1900)

THE END OF THE MONARCHY

David Kalakaua (1836-1891) was elected king in 1874. He began his reign with a tour of the United States in 1881, the first time a Hawaiian king had visited the mainland US. Kalakaua was proud of Hawaiian culture and promoted traditional Hawaiian customs and heritage at home and abroad. He reintroduced hula and wrote the lyrics for the Hawaiian national anthem, *"Hawaii Ponoi,"* which is now the state song.

1880
Hula is reinstated by Kalakaua, the second legislature-elected king.

Under Kalakaua's reign the **Reciprocity Treaty of 1875** was passed, foreshadowing the annexation of Hawaii. Under the treaty, Hawaiian sugar was admitted tax-free into the US, and in return a number of American products could enter the islands duty-free. The treaty gave Hawaiian sugar a favorable position in US markets, however, it consolidated American economic supremacy in Hawaiian trade and strengthened the influence of American interests in the kingdom.

1881
The first macadamia nuts are introduced to Hawaii.

In 1887, Kalakaua signed the **Bayonet Constitution,** which revised Kamehameha V's Constitution of 1864. Kalakaua signed the constitution under threat of armed disturbance and much of his power was transferred to his cabinet. The new constitution granted Americans and other foreigners with at least one year of residency in Hawaii the right to vote if they paid taxes and pledged to honor the constitution. The act enfranchised foreign businessmen, cementing their influence in the islands, while neglecting poor populations.

The controversy over the constitution and struggle for political power under Kalakaua carried over into the reign of his sister, **Queen Liliuokalani** (1838-1917). Hawaii's last monarch and only reigning queen ascended to the throne in 1891 following the death of her brother. In 1893, Liliuokalani recommended a new Hawaiian constitution, seeking to empower herself and Native Hawaiians. Queen Liliuokalani, slowed by ministers who feared a backlash from the white business community, failed to move quickly enough to ratify the proposals to expand suffrage to the common people. In the meantime, the **Annexation Club,** a group of white plantation

1893
Queen Liliuokalani is deposed in a US-backed coup; a provisional government is established under Sanford B. Dole.

1900
Great Chinatown fire; 7000 become homeless.

1907
What is today known as University of Hawaii at Manoa is founded.

1924
The "Hanapepe Massacre" occurs during a Filipino strike in Kauai; 20 are killed.

1935
The first trans-Pacific flight from San Francisco to Hawaii takes 21½ hours.

1941
Pearl Harbor in Oahu is attacked; the US enters WWII.

1941-1945
During WWII, Spam is first introduced to Hawaii.

owners, held a secret meeting to discuss the proceedings in government. The group formed a Committee of Public Safety that planned for troops to take control of Iolani Palace and other government buildings, set up a provisional government, and put forth a bid for US annexation.

AMERICAN RULE BEGINS

Queen Liliuokalani abdicated her throne to avoid bloodshed, and the provisional government gained power in 1893, due in large part to the force and manipulations of the Annexation Club. US President Grover Cleveland sent **James Blount** to investigate the conditions of the overthrow of the monarchy. Blount's report indicated that the majority of Hawaiians had not favored the move, and that American plantation owners had incited the revolt in order to further their own business interests. Blount charged that the illegal overthrow of Liliuokalani resulted from pressure by revolutionary leaders and US Minister **John L. Stevens.**

The annexation advocates succeeded in establishing a provisional government headed by Sanford B. Dole in 1894, despite President Cleveland's subsequent attempts to restore Queen Liliuokalani to her throne. Liliuokalani was arrested and imprisoned for eight months in Iolani Palace in 1895 after she was accused of attempting a counterrevolution.

In 1898, under President Cleveland's successor, William McKinley, a joint resolution of the US Congress approved **official annexation** of Hawaii. Native Hawaiians protested the action silently by boycotting the ceremonies. The islands were made a **US territory** in 1900, with Dole as governor.

WORLD WAR II (1941-1945)

A DAY THAT WILL LIVE IN INFAMY

In 1941, Europe and Asia were embroiled in the horrors of **WWII.** The US had yet to be drawn into the war, though engagement seemed inevitable. Sensing this, the Japanese continued their aggressive regional expansion throughout the Pacific. One of the few obstacles left in their way was the sizable American fleet that lay within striking distance of the South Pacific—the fleet based at **Pearl Harbor,** Hawaii.

At 7:55am on December 7, 1941, Japanese planes swooped down to the military base at Pearl Harbor, initiating a surprise strike that shook the US from isolationism. The Japanese targeted the seven US battleships moored in the harbor and aimed to cripple American military strength in the Pacific. Of the seven battleships, the **USS Arizona** suffered the most severe damage. One of the bombs fell through the steel decks, detonating stored ammunition; the twisted hull of the ship remains as a poignant monument to the 1177 crewmen who lost their lives. In total, the attack took the lives of 2388 American military personnel and civilians and propelled the US into conflict in both the Pacific and European theaters.

HAWAII'S ROLE IN THE PACIFIC THEATER

Following the attack at Pearl Harbor, Hawaii continued to serve as a base for military operations in the Pacific. The next notable clash in the Pacific islands was the **Battle of Midway** in June of 1942. The battle—a victory for the US—was a turning point for the American forces in the Pacific.

Hawaiian citizens stepped up to take part in the war effort. Some civilians participated in domestic defense and administration. Island-born Japanese served as language interpreters for the military. Many others took up arms. Among these was a contingent of Japanese Americans who were discharged from the Hawaii Territorial Guard, most likely as a result of paranoia regarding those of Japanese descent. About 1400 of these Hawaiian men banded together to form the **100th battalion,** the most decorated battalion of the war. They fought valiantly in the European theater and suffered heavy casualties, earning the nickname the **"Purple Heart Regiment."**

War continued to rage in the Pacific for several months after the European theater ended on **V-E Day** (Victory in Europe), May 8, 1945. The Pacific theater closed with the Japanese surrender on **V-J Day** (Victory in Japan), September 1, 1945, following the bombing of Hiroshima and Nagasaki.

THE ALOHA STATE (1945-1970)

THE QUESTION OF STATEHOOD

The move to statehood had been considered since the overthrow of the monarchy, but for nearly 50 years statehood proposals were defeated. A number of reasons, including opposition from southern states, distance, and concerns about the destruction of traditional Hawaiian ways of life, prevented Hawaii from entering the union.

One proposal for Hawaiian statehood was presented as part of a combined bill for both Hawaiian and Alaskan statehood. The combination complicated the congressional political processes during the debate of the plan, and progress stalled. Hawaiians favored the move to statehood and in 1954 over 110,000 islanders signed a petition urging Congress to act. Hawaii and Alaska were eventually put on separate bills, and in 1959 Hawaii became the **50th US state.**

THE GROWTH OF TOURISM

Advances in air travel and increased investment in the islands during WWII helped to expand Hawaii's tourism industry. Once Hawaii became a state, it was marketed on the mainland as the **"American Paradise,"** and tourists flocked to experience it. By the 1970s, tourism had a firm position as the state's top industry, surpassing the military.

1946
A tsunami hits Hilo, killing over 100 people.

LIFE AND TIMES

1960
Hawaii's star—the 50th—is added to the US flag on July 4.

1967
1 million tourists visit Hawaii for the first year in history.

1969
Television series "Hawaii Five-O" begins.

A HAWAIIAN RENAISSANCE (1970-1990)

HAWAIIAN HOMELANDS

A resurgent pride for authentic Hawaiian ways arrived in the 1970s. This Hawaiian activism was focused on *aloha aina* (love for the land). A key element was the movement to fulfill the claims of the **Hawaii Homestead Homes Act,** passed a half-century earlier in 1919. The act promised 200,000 acres for farmland and housing development to those who were at least half Native Hawaiian. Red tape had hindered the doling out of benefits. Hawaiians protested the backlog of requests, culminating in a near-riot on a Hilo airport runway in 1978.

The tiny island of Kahoolawe became a focal point for another struggle. The US Navy seized the island at the start of WWII to use it as a training area, but failed to return it at the end of the war. The island lay littered with military wreckage until the formation of **Project Kahoolawe Ohana** in 1976. Kahoolawe Ohana challenged the Navy and government by carrying out a series of occupations, bringing national attention to the movement. Kahoolawe Ohana settled a federal suit against the Navy in 1980 with a Consent Decree that allowed access to the island for educational, scientific, and cultural purposes. More about Kahoolawe is on page p. 23.

1976
The *Hokulea* canoe makes a round-trip voyage to Tahiti.

In 1993, the Hawaii State Legislature established the **Kahoolawe Island Reserve,** consisting of the island proper and all the waters around it in a 2 mi. radius. The area was preserved solely for Native Hawaiian cultural, spiritual, environmental, and historical purposes; commercial usage is strictly prohibited. Congress also passed a law requiring the Navy both to return the island to the state and to conduct a cleanup and environmental restoration of the area.

HOKULEA

On May 1, 1976, a double-hulled canoe, the kind that brought the first Polynesians to Hawaii, departed from the islands on an overseas voyage re-creating the route of those ancient mariners. The vessel, the **Hokulea** ("star of gladness"), was named in honor of Hawaii's zenith star. The crew traversed the seas in 33 days, relying only upon the stars and ocean currents as guides. When they arrived in Tahiti, more than 17,000 spectators were waiting to greet them.

1992
Hurricane Iniki, the most destructive hurricane in a century to hit Hawaii, pummels Kauai.

The voyage was not only a physical triumph, but a cultural one, creating a focal point for Hawaiian pride. After its successful journey, the vessel was taken to schools throughout Hawaii and used as an educational tool to promote knowledge of Hawaiian heritage. A second voyaging canoe, **Hawaiiloa,** was completed and launched in 1993. Both are powerful testaments to the efforts of Hawaiians to recover their native traditions.

HAWAII TODAY (1990-PRESENT)

TOO LITTLE, TOO LATE?

In the late 90s, there were perfunctory moves made to rectify the injustices of Hawaii's past. Both Dole's Iwilei pineapple cannery and the last sugar plantation on the Big Island closed in 1992 and 1995, respectively, ending more than a century of worker exploitation. In 1993, Congress passed the **"Apology Resolution,"** which formally apologized to Native Hawaiians for the overthrow of the monarchy in 1893 and for the deprivation of rights to self-determination.

1994
The first regularly scheduled Hawaiian-language news broadcast is presented on public radio.

THE NEW MILLENNIUM

The US Supreme Court case of **Rice v. Cayetano** (2000) was another seminal event in shaping the rights of Hawaiians. The ruling declared that the restriction of eligible voters to Native Hawaiians in the Office of Hawaiian Affairs trustee elections violated the 15th Amendment. The conclusion was seen as a blow to the recognition of Native Hawaiians as it did not privilege their native status over other residents. The issue of ethnicity regulations gained another dimension in 2002, when **Kamehameha Schools** admitted a non-Hawaiian student to their Maui campus. Kamehameha Schools were set up in 1883 by Bernice Pauahi Bishop, the great-granddaughter of Kamehameha the Great. The schools were set up to educate children of indigenous descent, who were traditionally disadvantaged. Controversy erupted over the schools' admissions policies, which have limited the acceptance pool to students of Hawaiian blood; critics alleged that the schools' racial exclusion was a violation of civil rights law. A lawsuit addressing this concern was settled out of court in 2008, and the schools were allowed to continue admissions preferences toward Native Hawaiians.

Debates in this vein continue as Hawaii grapples with its multi-faceted identity as a sacred homeland for its indigenous population, a uniquely multiethnic society unlike any other state, and a major tourist destination bringing both revenue and traffic to its serene landscape.

2002
First edition of *Let's Go: Hawaii* is published.

2005
Hawaiian-born golf prodigy Michelle Wie turns professional at age 15.

LIFE AND TIMES

PEOPLE

DEMOGRAPHICS

The people of Hawaii are world-famous for their spirit of aloha. This attitude of acceptance is characterized by warmth, generosity, humility, and patience.

The secret to Hawaiian harmony may lie in the fact that Hawaii is one of the few places in the US, and perhaps the world, where there is no racial or ethnic majority. The state population of 1.29 million (2006) is 25% white (haole), 10% Hawaiian, 40% Asian, 2% black, and 22% multiracial. This racial mixing is due to a complex history of immigration. The largest single group of immigrants, about a third, is thought to have come from southern Japan and Okinawa. When sugar was king, others migrated from the Philippines and southern China as well as from Europe and the US mainland. Though pure Polynesian Hawaiians have dwindled in number (fewer than 10,000), about one fifth of the population of Hawaii has native Hawaiian blood. The fact that about 40% of marriages on Hawaii are interracial contributes to this continuity. Hawaiians also have the longest average lifespan residents of any US state: 79.8 years.

LANGUAGE

English is spoken universally on all of the islands. **Olelo Hawaii,** the Hawaiian language, belongs to a family of Polynesian languages which also includes Tahitian, Maori, Tumotuan, and Rarotongan. Hawaiian is distinctive for its reduplication, apparent in words like *wikiwiki* (fast), its application of glottal stops, its single guttural letter (k), and the prolific use of vowels. A general rule of thumb when speaking Hawaiian is to produce every vowel: the Likelike Hwy. is pronounced "LEE-kay-LEE-kay." It is also important to remember that Olelo Hawaii does not use the letter "s," even for plural forms.

Olelo Hawaii was a strictly oral language until the arrival of Captain James Cook in 1778 and the Protestant missionaries who flocked to the island after him. The missionaries' goal was to teach islanders to read the Bible, so they set about giving the language a written form. What emerged was a 12-letter alphabet that became the official **writing system** of the Hawaiian government.

When Hawaii was annexed by the US in 1898, **English** became the state's official language. In 1899, Hawaiian was banned from all schools. *Olelo Hawaii* dwindled to near-extinction until the 1970s, when a Hawaiian cultural renaissance rekindled interest in the language. In 1978, *Olelo Hawaii* again became an official language of the state of Hawaii (along with English), and it remains the only Native American language that is officially used by a state government. By 1987, public schools were teaching the language, and the number of speakers continues to grow today.

Hawaii's unofficial language is **Hawaiian Creole English (HCE).** A byproduct of Hawaii's tremendous diversity, HCE, commonly known as **"pidgin,"** is an other-than-standard English which developed as a means of communication for business transactions between people who spoke different languages. The dialect integrates elements from Hawaiian, English, Chinese, Japanese, and several other languages. Although it is primarily used by teenagers, pidgin is incorporated in nearly every Hawaiian's daily conversations. While Native Hawaiians often appreciate attempts by visitors to speak *Olelo Hawaii*, it is inadvisable for visitors to try to speak pidgin, as it is usually considered condescending.

Hawaiian language often utilizes two symbols, the **glottal stop,** ', (or *'okina* in Hawaiian) and the **macron** (*kahakō*). The glottal stop is sometimes utilized in Hawaiian words like *Hawai'i* and *O'ahu*, indicating a short break in pronunciation, and can sometimes change the meaning of the word. English orthography does not use the letter and often Native Hawaiians also omit it from their writing. It is advocated mainly by teachers of Hawaiian as a second language and by linguists. The macron marks that a vowel is a double or long vowel in phonetic terms. Similar to the *'okina*, the *kahakō* is only used sporadically in written Hawaiian and is often not pronounced in conversation. For more reading on language in Hawaii, see **Additional Resources,** p. 36.

RELIGION

Prior to contact with the West, the religion of Polynesian Hawaiians was **polytheistic**. Hawaiians believed that all natural phenomena were controlled by the gods, whose aid and protection they sought through offerings and worship. Particularly in times of trouble, sacrifices—sometimes even human sacrifices—would be made in order to appease the gods and to encourage them to look upon the people with favor. Every home had a *kuaaha* (altar) where families worshipped their *aumaka* (guardian deities). *Akua* (greater gods) were worshipped in more complex ceremonies in **heiau** (open-air temples), which were presided over by **kahuna** (priests). Among the *akua* are: **Kane,** god of creation; **Ku,** god of war; **Lono,** god of peace, fertility, rain, and sports; **Kanaloa,** god of the ocean; and **Pele,** goddess of fire, who lives in Kilauea Volcano.

Life in ancient Hawaii was governed by the system of **kapu** (taboo) meaning literally, "obey or die." Every aspect of the early Hawaiians' daily life was regulated by this strict set of rules and customs. *Kahuna* wielded considerable power and were responsible for enforcing the *kapu*. Among their other responsibilities were healing, canoe building, and leading the islands' chiefs in elaborate religious ceremonies carried out in meticulous detail, since the slightest deviation from *aha* (perfection) would incur the wrath of the gods.

After the death of Kamehameha I around 1820, just before the arrival of missionaries from the West, the congregation of the ancient Hawaiians dissolved. *Heiau* were destroyed, and the *kapu* was abolished, making way for the new religion—Christianity—that was soon to arrive. Elements of this earlier belief system persist in Hawaii today, however, and many people, locals and tourists alike, still make offerings to Pele and other deities in attempts to win their favor. The ancient faith bequeathed to today's Hawaii myths rich in accounts of the deities and today survives chiefly as fascinating folklore.

As one would expect, religion in Hawaii today is as varied as its colorful and diverse population. Christianity, Judaism, Buddhism, Hinduism, and a variety of other beliefs exist peacefully together. Travelers will have no difficulty finding services to meet their spiritual needs, regardless of their faith. For more reading on religion in Hawaii, see **Additional Resources,** p. 36.

THE "OTHER" ISLANDS

KAHOOLAWE

LAND. Kahoolawe is 7 mi. southwest of Maui and the smallest of Hawaii's eight major islands. Low elevation on Kahoolawe prevents much precipitation and the entire island is relatively dry. Kahoolawe's sloping northern and western coasts were heavily populated by feral goats and sheep until 1988. Overgrazing by these animals destroyed the plant cover, causing massive soil erosion. The silt eroded into the water and killed much of the coral around its coast.

HISTORY. Early Hawaiians inhabited Kahoolawe 1000 years ago in fishing and farming settlements. Kahoolawe was a renowned training ground for *kahuna* (priests), and the island is home to hundreds of *heiau* (temples) and shrines.

Starting in 1778, criminals who had been exiled from Maui were sent to Kahoolawe, where they managed to subsist by raiding Maui and Lanai. The island's population dwindled, and it was the site of two failed sheep ranches.

The day after Pearl Harbor was attacked, the US Navy appropriated the entire, now unpopulated, island and began using it for bombing practice. Kahoolawe holds the distinction of being the most bombed island in the Pacific both during and after WWII. After the war, the island was supposed to be returned to the Hawaiian people, but to maintain control over it, President Eisenhower signed an executive order placing the island under the authority of the Secretary of the Navy. The order mandated the island be restored to a habitable condition once it was no longer needed.

In 1976, Hawaiians formed the Protect Kahoolawe Ohana Coalition (known as the Ohana) which was dedicated to opposing the bombing of Kahoolawe and demanding its return to the Hawaiian people. The Ohana also filed suit demanding the return of the island on environmental and religious grounds. The suit was settled in 1980, when the government allowed visitors to the island for cultural, educational, religious, or scientific purposes and Kahoolawe was added to the National Register of Historic Places. This, however, did not stop the bombing and, in the early 1980s, the US offered allies use of Kahoolawe for bombing exercises. This prompted an outcry from groups in Great Britain, Australia, New Zealand, and Japan. The international media attention generated by protests and several occupations of Kahoolawe staged by the Ohana eventually led to a cessation of bombing. Since then, the Ohana has brought over 5000 visitors to Kahoolawe. In addition, several trails have been cleared and a few religious sites have been re-dedicated.

In 1990, President George Bush issued a memorandum directing the military to cease using Kahoolawe as a weapons range. The Kahoolawe Island Conveyance Commission was created to coordinate the return of Kahoolawe and its surrounding waters to the state and the Hawaiian people. The commission held public hearings and conducted research, eventually outlining cleanup measures that would make Kahoolawe habitable. In November 1993, Congress prohibited all military activity on Kahoolawe and set aside $400 million for a 10-year cleanup. The same year, Hawaii established the Kahoolawe Island Reserve, declaring the island and the surrounding water closed to the public. In May 1994, the island was returned to Hawaii, and the Kahoolawe Island Reserve Commission was established to preserve the island's archaeological, historical, and environmental resources.

TODAY. The goals of the 10-year cleanup plan that expired November 11, 2003, proved too lofty. The Navy intended to clear all surface debris, make the land reasonably safe for human access, re-vegetate the island with native species, clear hiking trails, and construct camping and educational facilities. Although much of the island is reasonably safe for closely controlled visits by the Ohana and their guests, the vision of true public access remains out of reach. The Navy has hired a California firm to complete the cleanup. If you want to visit, contact the Protect Kahoolawe Ohana (www.kahoolawe.org) and ask about joining a trip. The trips have a religious and cultural focus and are primarily for Hawaiian residents. For further reading, see **Additional Resources,** p. 36.

NIIHAU

LAND. Niihau, 18 mi. southwest of Kauai, is the smallest of the inhabited islands, and the westernmost of the eight major islands. Niihau averages a mere 12 in. of rain per year, giving it a flat, arid landscape. This grassy lowland is well suited for the grazing herds on the island, which outnumber the island's 160 residents. Niihau is also home to Hawaii's only natural lake, Lake Halulu.

HISTORY. Niihau was never conquered by Kamehameha I during his campaign to unite the islands, but in 1810 it joined his kingdom on its own volition. In 1863, a woman named Elizabeth Sinclair moved to Honolulu, where Kamehameha V offered to sell her land on Oahu stretching from Honolulu Hale to Diamond Head. Sinclair did not think it was suitable for grazing and instead purchased the island of Niihau along with all of its inhabitants for $10,000 in gold. There Sinclair established the Niihau Ranch, where she enlisted the island's residents and her family to raise livestock. After she died in 1892, her grandson, Aubrey Robinson, took over. The highly isolated island owes its nickname, "The Forbidden Isle," to the fact that visitor entrance to the island has been highly restricted by residents since that time.

Niihau is famous for intricate shell leis that Native Hawaiian women have made for hundreds of years from tiny *laiki*, *kehelelani*, and *momi* seashells that wash ashore during the winter months. Many of these beautiful necklaces have been treasured heirlooms and can fetch up to the thousands.

TODAY. Niihau is still owned by the Robinson family, and descendants of Elizabeth Sinclair managed the ranch until its closure in 1999. With the unemployment rate close to 100%, the island was finally forced to open its doors to outsiders. Tourists can now visit the islands through a number of expensive excursions, from helicopter tours to hunting safaris.

Even today, the only electricity on the island is produced by privately owned generators. There are also no telephones, no paved roads, and only one school, which goes up to eighth grade. High school students must commute to Kauai or Oahu. Hawaiian is the primary language on Niihau, and the inhabitants are committed to preserving traditional Hawaiian culture. Residents are known for their insularity, widespread rejection of modern conveniences, and staunch opposition to Western ways. Residents are free to come and go as they please, though most stay on the island.

NORTHWEST HAWAIIAN ISLANDS

LAND. The Northwest Hawaiian Islands are an archipelago of small islands and coral atolls that stretch a thousand miles across the Pacific, starting 150 mi. northwest of Kauai. The islands and the surrounding water constitute the Northwest Hawaiian Islands Coral Reef Ecosystem Reserve, the largest protected area in the US, covering 131,800 sq. mi. The ecosystem of the Northwest Hawaiian Islands contains over 70% of the coral reef in US waters and 7000 marine species, half of which are unique to the island chain. The Hawaiian monk seal, loggerhead turtle, hawk bill turtle, leatherbackp. 36 sea turtle, and green sea turtle are among the endangered species that have habitats.

About 1400 monk seals live on the islands; the largest breeding colony is on French Frigate Shoals, or Mokupapapa Island. Necker Island, or Mokumanamana Island, is the top of the oldest-known active volcano in the chain. Numerous *heiau* (temples) indicate that it was once frequented by Native Hawaiians. Laysan Island, or Kauo, is notable for its nesting birds and salty lagoon. Kure Atoll, or Kanemilohai, named after Pele's brother, is the most distant island. Next to it are the Midway Islands, or Pihemnau, the best-known island group.

HISTORY. Evidence of an ancient human presence exists on the islands; agricultural terraces have been found on a few and artifacts found on other islands suggest that they were used for religious purposes only. In 1885, King Kalakaua had a wooden house built and stocked with provisions on the distant Kure Atoll for anyone who became stranded. In 1903, part of the trans-

Pacific cable was laid on Midway, drawing people to the island to manage the station. Midway became a national defense area in 1941 and served as a naval base through WWII. The Battle of Midway, one of the most important battles of WWII's Pacific Theater, took place on the island in June 1942. It was a victory for US forces that turned the tide of war in their favor (p. 18). Midway remained a naval base until it was made a National Wildlife Refuge by the US Fish and Wildlife Service in 1996.

TODAY. The National Oceanic and Atmospheric Administration's (NOAA) National Ocean Service manages the Coral Reef Reserve, conducting scientific research for fisheries and protected species and documenting and removing marine debris from the islands and reefs. Meanwhile, the US Fish and Wildlife Service manages and protects the two wildlife refuges of the islands. These organizations, together with the State of Hawaii Department of Land and Natural Resources, US National Park Service, University of Hawaii, Bishop Museum, and the Hawaii Maritime Center, among others, have participated in multiple and wide-ranging research projects on and around the islands. Learn about their projects at www.hawaiianatolls.org. The Midway Islands housed an ecotourism resort until 2002, when it closed due to lack of profit. For more info, contact the Midway Atoll National Wildlife Refuge, P.O. Box 50167, Honolulu, HI 96850 (☎808-674-8237; www.fws.gov/midway/).

CULTURE

FOOD

In many ways, the confluence of backgrounds and ethnicities that make up Hawaii's unique population is most evident in local culinary offerings. Most popular dishes combine elements of several cultures and incorporate unique island ingredients. Much like Hawaii residents, island fare is unpretentious and low-key; anything that isn't beach-friendly is immediately suspect.

The epitome of local cuisine is the **plate lunch.** Plate lunches are available almost everywhere in Hawaii, from roadside stands to fast-food chains. The meal is a descendant of the Japanese plantation worker's **bento,** a boxed lunch of rice, meat, and pickled vegetables. A typical plate lunch is a combination of two scoops of white rice, one scoop of macaroni salad, and an entree. For the entree, most places offer an overwhelming array of choices. At the very least, expect Japanese teriyaki or *katsu*, Korean short ribs, Filipino *adobo*, Chinese soy sauce chicken, hamburgers, and chili. Quantity often trumps quality in this island comfort food—most plate lunches can feed two people.

Many other local favorites have been taken from outside cultures and adapted over the years. **Saimin** is a noodle soup dish developed in and unique to Hawaii. Inspired by Japanese *udon*, Chinese *mein*, and Filipino *pancit*, *saimin* was developed during Hawaii's plantation era. It is a soup dish of soft wheat egg noodles served in hot *dashi* (stock from Japanese bonito fish or shrimp). Same as Japanese ramen (which is often incorrectly called *saimin* by locals), *saimin* noodles tend to crinkle when cooked. *Saimin* is so common that even McDonald's offers a fast-food version. **Crack seed,** residents' preferred snack, is a generic term that refers to preserved fruit that have been cracked or split with the seed or kernel partially exposed as a flavor enhancement. Crack seed was brought to Hawaii by Chinese plantation workers. Many generations of Hawaiian children have flocked to neighborhood crack seed shops for after- school snacks. The little stores are packed with island delicacies— Japanese rice crackers (*arare*), coconut candy, and dried squid—in addition to the huge glass jars filled with varieties of crack seed.

Other local treats were once imported but have been fully embraced by Hawaii. Japanese immigrants supposedly brought **shave ice** to the islands during the plantation era, and it has been an island favorite every since. According to legend, the treat was created by an ancient Japanese *shogun* (general) who liked to snack on snow from Mt. Fiji. Often confused with the mainland snow cones, shave (not shaved) ice in Hawaii is much finer and thus absorbs the flavors rather than letting them sink to the bottom, earning the jealousy of countless sticky-fingered mainlanders. Modern toppings include the basic flavored syrups as well as fancier options such as ice cream, condensed milk, shaved *li hing mui* (salty plum), and azuki beans. **Spam,** the lovable spiced ham in a can, rounds out any true Hawaiian's diet. After the US military introduced Spam during WWII, islanders quickly incorporated the food into their cooking. "The Hawaiian steak" is often cooked, giving it a different taste than mainlanders are used to. Despite mainland conceptions of Spam as pedestrian and unappealing, islanders are addicted. Hawaii now boasts the highest Spam consumption in the States (over 6.7 million cans per year). **Spam musubi,** sticky rice topped by Spam and wrapped in dried seaweed, is one of the most popular forms of the food's preparation. **Poi** is another unique island dish. Made out of pounded taro root, poi is a thick, purplish-gray paste past down from Native Hawaiian's Polynesian ancestors. Lacking a strong flavor, poi's unfamiliar consistency and appearance make it an acquired taste. Locals swear by it, however, and some even rave about its semi-magical healing powers. If you're going to give poi a try, make sure it's fresh—the poi is sweetest right after it's made.

In recent years, Hawaii-based chefs have developed a style of cooking they call **Hawaii Regional Cuisine.** Led by Sam Choy, Alan Wong, and Roy Yamaguchi, the chefs have taken advantage of Hawaii's unique ingredients to create a type of cuisine that honors Hawaii's diverse culture while meeting the highest culinary standards. Dishes include seared Hawaiian *ahi* with *lilikoi* shrimp butter and guava-smoked Kahua ranch lamb. Hawaiian Regional Cuisine has proved to be a culinary revolution on the island. Prized for its fresh ingredients, beautiful presentation, and creativity, it has not only raised the level of gourmet dining on the island but has also established Hawaii-grown products as some of the finest in the world. See **Additional Resources** (p. 36) for food festival dates.

LUAUS

Luaus began nearly 200 years ago as flagrant disregard for tradition or inspired forward progress, depending on how you see it. Under *kanawai*, the ancient Hawaiian system of laws, certain actions were *kapu* (forbidden). Women and men eating together was considered *kapu*. In addition, women were prohibited from eating many island delicacies. However, in 1819, King Kamehameha II held a huge feast, during which he ate with women. With that event, the ancient religious traditions died and the luau was born.

The luau takes its name from a dish prepared with young taro root leaves and coconut milk. Originally a celebration giving thanks to the gods, the luau has become one of the most well-known aspects of Hawaiian culture, almost synonymous with the term "party." Birthdays, anniversaries, and other significant events are marked by these feasts. The tourism industry has capitalized on the marketability of the luau and almost every major hotel offers its own version.

Historically, luau guests sat on woven mats laid on the floor and used their fingers to devour the feast. Many modern-day luaus are still held on the grass, though bigger celebrations might have tents and picnic tables. There is almost always some form of musical entertainment, whether it is a cousin strumming a guitar or an entire group complete with ukulele, steel guitar, and bass. The main focus of any luau is the traditionally prepared **kalua pig.** The meat is covered in ti or banana leaves and roasted in an *imu* (underground oven). When served, the meat is supplemented by other island dishes, such as poi, *poke* (raw, seasoned sashimi), and *lomi* salmon (salted salmon with tomatoes and Maui onions). The meal is finished with a dessert of *haupia* (coconut-arrow-root pudding), *kulolo* (coconut-taro pudding), pineapple, and coconut cake.

HAWAIIAN DRESS

On any given day, locals look beach-ready. The preferred style of dress often incorporates one or more of the following: slippers (plastic flip-flops), board shorts, other surf-inspired clothing, and anything aloha print. One of the most popular elements of Hawaiian dress, the **aloha shirt,** actually owes its inspiration to both Western and Asian cultures. Supposedly a descendant of the thick "thousand-mile" shirt worn by pioneers and missionaries, the aloha shirt came into its familiar form in the early 1930s when Waikiki tailor Ellery J. Chun began sewing brightly colored shirts for tourists out of old kimono fabrics. The style became common after Herbert Briner began mass-manufacturing the shirts in the late 1930s. During the 1950s, the aloha shirt craze spread to the mainland when audiences saw icons like Elvis Presley, John Wayne, and Frank Sinatra wearing them in feature films. Authentic aloha shirts worn by locals tend to be more muted in color, adorned with traditional Hawaiian quilt patterns and simple floral patterns. One technique for making modest aloha shirts is to print the pattern on the interior, "reverse print." Resulting in subtler pattern, these shirts are often mistaken for being worn inside-out. In response to the widespread mimicking of the aloha shirt, the Hawaii Chamber of Commerce ruled in the 1960s that a true aloha shirt must be made in Hawaii. Currently, the only company to design and produce shirts entirely in Hawaii is Reyn Spooner.

The aloha shirt has inspired what is known as **"aloha attire."** Popular for semi-formal occasions like weddings, birthday parties, and dinners, "aloha attire" typically implies aloha shirts for men and *muumuu*, a loose dress hung from the shoulder, for women. "Aloha attire" is also sported in business and government professions in Hawaii, being a more practical option in the Hawaiian heat than a suit and tie. It is rarely appropriate on Hawaii to attend functions in full evening wear—just throw on an aloha shirt and relax.

CUSTOMS AND ETIQUETTE

Hawaii residents place so much stock in the **aloha spirit** that there is an actual law in the Hawaii Revised Statutes that requires residents to abide by the spirit of ancient Hawaiians. And, for the most part, locals do. Smiles abound and islanders are quick to wave hello, usually in the form of **shaka,** a greeting made by extending the pinkie and thumb and curling up the middle three fingers of the right hand. It is especially popular with young people in Hawaii; the gesture is a way of saying, "hang loose" or, "relax." Easy-going driving in Hawaii is likely to surprise many visitors. Driving aggressively is one sure way to secure tourist status. No need to cut anyone off—a simple turn signal is likely to allow you access into another lane. Avoid using your horn except in emergencies.

In addition to shaka, the word **aloha** is also used extensively throughout the islands. Don't be afraid to use it to say hello; it's not regarded as corny. The **lei,** a garland of flowers, shells, leaves, or even candy, is a traditional Hawaiian symbol of love or friendship. Visitors entering and leaving Hawaii are often gifted with the fragrant necklaces. Leis are also given to mark special occasions like anniversaries, birthdays, and graduations.

While Hawaii is extremely laid-back, there are a few things that travelers should keep in mind. Hawaii is inhabited by an exceptionally diverse group of people, but the only people who are referred to as Hawaiian are those of Hawaiian blood. Except for Caucasians, anyone born in the islands is known as a local. The term *haole* (foreigner) is used to describe Caucasians is not necessarily offensive though it can be used by to denote general island incompetency. Residents who were born outside of Hawaii but have lived in the state for a long time are known as *kama aina* (children of the land).

Respect is key in Hawaiian culture. While this applies to the general spirit of aloha, it is especially important to treat sacred sites, such as *heiau* (temples), with appropriate consideration. On a more casual level, it is polite to remove your shoes when entering someone's home.

THE ARTS

ARCHITECTURE

Hawaii's architecture reflects its varied past. **Heiau** are remnants of ancient Hawaiian religion. These simple structures were built to honor the gods and typically consist of altars and taboo houses enclosed by lava or limestone walls. Many still stand today, albeit in varying stages of disrepair, and there have been initiatives to restore them to their original states.

Plantation-style houses are another throwback to Hawaii's past. Built to house immigrant workers from China, Japan, and the Philippines, the houses were grouped in villages. They stood on lava rock foundations and featured single-wall construction and cedar shingle roofs. The plantation-style commercial structures of this era were much more elaborate, often consisting of multiple buildings grouped around a courtyard. The main building would sometimes be modeled in mainland style, with wide canopies. The **Honolulu Hale** and the **Hawaii State Public Library** are prominent examples of this design.

Along with Christianity, missionaries also brought a more ostentatious style of architecture. The American Florentine Iolani Palace, the only example of American Florentine architecture in the world, and Gothic structures like Saint Andrew's Cathedral were built in the late 19th century and strongly reflect Western influences. The 1990s saw the construction of Hawaii's first true skyscrapers, including **First Hawaiian Center,** Hawaii's tallest building. Most residential houses in Hawaii have been built with regard to the islands' tropical climate. They are typically low, airy structures that were built with an eye to the cooling trade winds. Though some critics doubt the cohesion of Hawaiian architecture, contemporary styles certainly reflect the diverse architectural history of Hawaii. Constant reverence for Hawaiian symbolism and attention to abundant natural Hawaiian light are consistently included in current designs. For more reading on architecture in Hawaii, see **Additional Resources,** p. 36.

VISUAL ARTS

Hawaii has a rich and thriving art community. Along with numerous private galleries, Oahu has two notable art museums. **The Honolulu Academy of the Arts** (p.

120) celebrated its 80th birthday in 2007, and the museum houses a permanent stock of over 70,000 pieces, including a celebrated collection of Asian art. The less conventional **Contemporary Museum** (p. 121) has two locations on Oahu. Part of the organization's mission dictates that a significant portion of its exhibits must focus on art created in Hawaii. Maui, too, has a strong coalition of artists and art lovers. Each spring, the island hosts **Art Maui,** a prestigious exhibit of about 100 new works by Maui County artists.

Hawaiian art before the arrival of Captain James Cook in 1778 shares the themes of other Oceanic art from the period. Without metal or woven cloth, Native Hawaiians created of wood carvings, feather work, and petroglyphs. These art forms continue today as the Hawaiian renaissance persists.

Hawaii has inspired a number of extraordinary artists. Although prominent oil painter **John Young** died in 1999, he is remembered by a museum within the University of Hawaii. **Georgia O'Keeffe** (1887-1986) travelled to Hawaii in the late 1930s to escape a difficult divorce. She was revitalized by her three-month stay in Hawaii, which followed a two-year dry period. Prior to settling down in Honolulu, Paris-born **Jean Charlot** (1898-1979) worked as Diego Rivera's assistant in Mexico. During his time in Hawaii, Charlot applied the techniques he learned with Rivera to a number of fresco murals that can be seen in various Oahu locations. **Madge Tennent** (1889-1972) concentrated on capturing the beauty she saw in the Hawaiian people. She is best known for her oil paintings of Hawaiian women, many of which hang prominently in buildings around Honolulu. Other notable Hawaiian artists include watercolor artist **Hon-Chew Hee** (1906-1993), painter and printmaker **Yvonne Cheng** (born 1941), and potter and watercolor artist **Charles Higa** (born 1933).

Art takes on a practical form in Hawaii's distinctive quilts. After learning quilting techniques from New England missionaries, Hawaiian women translated the images from their daily lives onto fabric. The quilts, with their flower, leaf, and vine designs, are still popular today.

LITERATURE

As in the visual arts, the Hawaiian islands often served as inspiration to great writers. Early in his career, **Mark Twain** journeyed from San Francisco to Hawaii for a four-month stay that eventually helped him achieve his mammoth literary stature. Chronicles of his 1866 trip were published in the *Sacramento Union* and scholars hold that it was in Hawaii that Twain first began to develop his singular descriptive and interpretive style. Twain later compiled his personal and professional writings from this period into *Roughing It*. Intrigued by the islands and people of the Pacific, **Robert Louis Stevenson** explored Hawaii extensively and lived the last years of his life in Samoa. Much of his writing from that period is compiled in *Travels in Hawaii*. Jack London and Herman Melville also passed through the islands briefly and wrote about their travels. One of the most well-known novels about Hawaii, and perhaps one of the most monotonous, is James Michener's 1036-page epic titled, simply, *Hawaii*. A combination of fact and fiction, the book begins with the creation of the islands and follows their growth until the year 1955.

Nurtured by local enterprises, such as *Bamboo Ridge*, the journal of Hawaiian literature and arts, local writers are gaining exposure and critical acclaim. The leader of this generation of authors is Hawaiian-born novelist **Lois-Ann Yamanaka,** who tackles the themes of Asian-American families. Yamanaka's work addresses the reality of living in paradise; she eschews flowery words, aiming instead for authentic pidgin dialogue between her characters. Other authors who are a part of this reinvention of Hawaiian literature include **Milton Murayama, Darrell Lum, Sylvia Watanabe, Kathleen Tyau,** and **Nora Okja Keller.**

MUSIC

Hawaii has a rich musical tradition, both which were crucial in the development of modern pacific music. Traditional Hawaiian folk music is a huge part of the state's musical heritage and the music is largely religious in nature. The **mele** (chant) is often accompanied by percussion and dancing. From 1778 onward, Hawaii began a period of acculturation with the introduction of numerous styles of European music, including the *himeni* (hymns) introduced by Protestant missionary choirs and the string instruments of the Spanish-speaking *paniolo* (cowboys). Legends hold that the **ukulele** was introduced to Hawaii in 1879 by a Portuguese immigrant named **João Fernandes.** The islanders dubbed Fernandes's *cavaquinho* (also known as a *braguinha,* a type of guitar) a ukulele (literally, "jumping flea") because of the way the musician's fingers jumped across the strings of the instrument. The ukulele quickly gained popularity; even Hawaiian royalty became proficient. It became a symbol of Hawaiian beach culture during the 1920s and 30s, thanks to the **Waikiki Beachboys,** who serenaded locals and tourists with their ukuleles. The Waikiki Beachboys, not to be confused with the West Coast American group, included such renowned Hawaiian musicians as **Squeeze Kamana, Pua Kealoha,** and **Chick Daniels.**

Traditional Hawaiian musicians record songs almost entirely in Hawaiian and use the ukulele, **steel guitar,** and **slack key guitar** extensively. As legend has it, the steel guitar was developed on Oahu by local youngster **Joseph Kekuku** in the late 19th century. Kekuku's instrument was able to achieve a previously unthinkable range of sound and to this day remains a centerpiece of Hawaiian music. Contrary to legend, experts believe the guitar came to the islands via early 19th-century cowboys. However, Hawaiians developed the unique slack-key sound themselves. Hawaiian musicians round out the distinctive island sound with a guitar technique called slack key, or **ki hoal.** Literally, "loosen the key," this method of playing consists of relaxing the strings of an acoustic guitar and picking them with the fingers.

With the Hawaiian renaissance of the 1970s, traditional artists, such as **Israel "IZ" Kamakawiwoole** (1959-1997), the **Sons of Hawaii,** and **Kealil Reichel,** all experienced a boost in their popularity. The emergence of **Jawaiian,** a Hawaiian style of reggae music, in the 1980s coincided with the spread of reggae culture in Hawaii. Pop artist and surfer **Jack Johnson** also hails from Oahu, and the influence of laid-back North Shore culture permeates his popular music.

DANCE

The **hula** has long been a symbol of Hawaiian culture. The hula centers around the *mele* (chant) and the dance either dramatizes or comments on the *mele.* The dances and chants of ancient hula were an integral part of the Hawaiians' oral tradition. Through them, elders ensured that their traditions, customs, and history would live on in a younger generation. For a short period in the early 19th century, Christian missionaries convinced the reigning monarchs to outlaw the dance. However, all that changed when, in 1874, **King David Kalakaua** ascended to the throne. The new king, nicknamed the "Merrie Monarch," became hula's greatest patron, and during his rule, the dance flourished. The ukulele and the steel guitar were used to accompany dancers, who began wearing ti leaf skirts for the first time. Kalakaua is remembered each Easter in the **Merrie Monarch Festival** (p. 232), which showcases both ancient hula and the more modern versions that have developed.

FILM

Despite the difficulty of transporting film-making equipment, movie producers have never been able to resist Hawaii's allure. The islands are reputed to have made their on-screen debut as early as 1898, when a film crew shot footage of the tropical paradise during an 18hr. layover. Early Hawaiian films, such as **Honolulu Street Scene** (1898), were simple, silent films showing local life. In the early 1900s, Hawaii was used in numerous silent films, including **Hawaiian Love** and **The Shark God,** both made in 1913. The advent of "talkies" added a new dimension to Hawaiian-set films. In 1937, Bing Crosby starred in **Waikiki Wedding,** playing a crooning press agent for a pineapple cannery. The film's hit song, *"Sweet Leilani,"* garnered an Oscar and earned Crosby his first gold record.

Although WWII put filmmaking in Hawaii on hold for a few years, it also provided the industry with its most enduring subject: war. **From Here to Eternity** (1953) chronicled the days leading up to the Pearl Harbor attack, but it is probably best remembered for Burt Lancaster and Deborah Kerr's passionate embrace on the sand (and in the water) of Halona Cove. Kauai was used to film the musical **South Pacific** (1958), in which Mitzi Gaynor plays a love-struck Army nurse who tries, unsuccessfully, to wash a captivating man out of her hair. Elvis Presley gratified his adoring fans on Hawaii when he starred in 1961's **Blue Hawaii.** As an island boy back from the war, Presley spends much of the movie strumming the ukulele and wooing beach bunnies with his dance moves. The film yielded several musical hits, including *"Can't Help Falling In Love."*

Filmmakers switched gears in 1976, when Hawaii was featured in the blockbuster **King Kong.** Following the movie's release, Hawaii increasingly became the filming site of action-packed blockbusters. In 1980, George Lucas and Steven Spielberg joined forces to produce the first of the *Indiana Jones* series, **Raiders of the Lost Ark,** filmed partly in Kauai. Spielberg continued his blockbuster trend with **Jurassic Park** (1992), also filmed in Hawaii. The 1997 dino-sequel, **The Lost World,** features gorgeous shots of Kauai's lush scenery and boasted an opening weekend gross of over $92 million. Other crowd-pleasers filmed in Hawaii include **George of the Jungle** (1997) and **6 Days, 7 Nights** (1998).

Filmmaking in Hawaii shows no signs of stopping in the new millennium. In 2001, producer Jerry Bruckheimer let loose his biggest (and longest) film yet, the epic **Pearl Harbor.** The Hawaii Visitor's and Convention Bureau joined forces with Disney to market **Lilo & Stitch** (2002), a widely appreciated film about a young girl and an extraterrestrial fugitive set in the islands. The surfing flick **Blue Crush** (2002) features Kate Bosworth tackling Oahu's famous Bonzai Pipeline (see p. 170) and scoring points for female surfers everywhere. The state itself has capitalized on the premier filming conditions in Hawaii—the archipelago is home to the only state-owned and -operated studio in the country.

Hawaii hosts a few film festivals. The **Hawaii International Film Festival** began at the University of Hawaii at Manoa in 1981 as a means of cultural exchange between North America, Asia, and the Pacific. It is now a state-wide event. The **Maui Film Festival** (p. 287) is still in its infancy—it began in 2000—but it seems as if the event is around to stay.

TV SERIES

Hawaii has a long, successful history on television, beginning with the popular **Hawaii Five-O.** The show, filmed almost exclusively on Hawaii from 1968 to 1980, was one of the longest-running series on television. A daytime variety show featuring a local performer, **The Don Ho Show,** aired from 1976-1977. During the 80s, Tom Selleck charmed viewers across the nation as a dashing Hawaii-based private investigator in **Magnum, P.I.** The "Baywatch" cast packed up its itty-bitty wardrobe and suntan oil in 1999 to relocate from California to Hawaii. The new series, **Baywatch Hawaii,** lasted only two seasons. MTV's **The Real World: Hawaii** (1999) was the first in a series of reality TV shows to choose Hawaii as a backdrop. Soon to follow were **The Bachelor** (2002) and **Average Joe: Hawaii** (2004). Most recently, the four seasons of ABC's smash hit, **Lost,** were filmed on Oahu's North Shore. The 2hr. pilot for the series was one of the most expensive in television history, costing over $10 million.

SPORTS AND RECREATION

Watersports reign in Hawaii—some of the world's best surfing and windsurfing spots can be found here. Golf is the chosen sport of many tourists, and manicured greens are spread across the islands. Other popular activities include paddling, kayaking, snorkeling, surfing, scuba diving, swimming, bodyboarding, bodysurfing, hiking, and biking.

THE DIFFERENCE BETWEEN BOOGIE BOARDS AND BODYBOARDS. We'll let you in on a secret: they're the same thing. The good old mainland "boogie board" is a name that comes from the first mass produced body board, the "Morey 'Boogie' Board." That said, it is a bit derogatory to refer to them as boogie boards in Hawaii: boogie board has the connotation of little kids splashing around in half-foot waves that the serious and more hard-core body board avoids. It is considered touristy to exclaim, "Let's go boogie boarding, dude!" as opposed to saying, "Yo brah, see that barrel I got on my bodyboard? Brah, was nuts." Your training begins in this book—in our desire to be Hawaiian, we will use "bodyboard."

SURFING

Modern surfing was born in Hawaii, and the sport stays true to its homeland. There is no impeding continental shelf surrounding the islands to slow incoming waves, so they arrive huge and powerful on Hawaiian shores, creating magnificent, world-renowned surf. There are two surf seasons in Hawaii. Summer surf (May-Aug.) is generated by storms in the South Pacific and occurs on the southern shores of the islands. In the winter (Sept.-Apr.), storms in the northern Pacific create surf on the northern shores of the islands. The seasons' overlap allows for nearly year-round surfing.

The so-called "sport of kings" began as the ancient sport of *hee nalu* (wave-sliding) and was later perfected by the kings of Hawaii. The revival of interest in surfing in the early 20th century is attributed to Hawaii's **Duke Kahanamoku** (1890-1968). Kahanamoku, also known as "The Big Kahuna," was a talented swimmer, representing the United States at four Olympic Games between 1912 and 1924, winning three gold medals and two silvers to become Hawaii's first Olympic medalist. His first love was surfing, however, and he organized one of the first amateur surfing clubs in 1908. He is also credited for creating both windsurfing and wakeboarding on the islands.

Since then, the evolution of **board design** and material has made major changes to surfing, both as an activity and as a culture. The first boards were made of wood; their weight and lack of maneuverability was part of what limited the sport to certain physiques. The first big breakthrough in board design came in 1958 when construction changed to lightweight foam and fiberglass. A bottom fin also helped stabilize the new boards. These lighter, steadier boards made surfing more accessible to the general public. When surfing was introduced to

California it quickly gained popularity as both a sport and a culture, inspiring fashion, music, and movies in the 1950s and 60s.

Today, surfers use one of two types of boards: **long boards** (a traditional style that can be as long as 10-12 ft.) and **short boards.** Short boards are less than 9 ft. in length, are faster, and have better maneuverability. Although beginning surfers generally start off on long boards, most professional surfers use short boards, as they are better for riding larger waves. These surfboards often have two to three fins, called **thrusters,** which provide greater maneuverability. The addition of a **leash,** attached at the ankle, improved both the safety of surfing and its style. Before leashes were added, lost boards would collide with reefs and rocks as well, resulting in significant damage. With leashes, surfers can ride waves near rocks and reefs and try radical tricks with greater security.

 A SURFING STATE OF MIND. For many locals, surfing is not just an activity but a way of life. Surfers range from the hard-core professionals, to local bruddahs, to 9-5ers who keep a board on their car roof to catch a lunch-hour or post-work wave. While tourists are welcome to pick up a board and try their hand on a curl, don't expect to be inducted into surfer culture fresh off your first wave. Surfers are secretive about the best spots, have their own slang, and abide by their own code. A few tips on surfer etiquette for novice wave riders: never "drop in" on a wave. The surfer closest to the curl (the breaking part of the wave) has the right of way on that wave, and all other surfers should back out of it (failure to do so is dropping in). Be careful of body boarders and other surfers—collisions can cause serious injuries.

PADDLING

Outrigger canoe paddling is popular throughout Hawaii. The outrigger canoe differs from a regular canoe in that it has a rig, known as an outrigger, extending from one or both sides of the vessel. The outrigger acts to balance the hull of the boat. Early Hawaiians used the outrigger canoes extensively in their daily lives, and paddling eventually became a means of recreation.

Encouraged by King Kalakaua, paddling enthusiasts formed the first official outrigger club in 1908. **The Outrigger Canoe Club of Hawaii** was followed shortly after by Hui Nalu; there are now over 60 outrigger clubs throughout the islands. Canoe racing began in 1910, and formal regattas began in the 1940s. Paddlers are typically grouped into divisions by age. There is a separate junior season in late winter to ensure that younger athletes get as much attention as possible. Though paddling had previously been dominated by males, the number of women competing in the sport has increased steadily since the 1980s.

Sailing canoes are a variation on the outrigger canoes. Although not nearly as common as paddling, sailing canoe races have been gaining popularity. Each May, participants race the 75 mi. between Maui and Oahu in canoe sailing's most well-known, and still terribly obscure, competition, the **Steinlager Hoomanao Sailing Canoe Race.**

GOING THE DISTANCE

Laid-back lifestyle aside, Hawaii is home to hundreds of running events and triathlons, from 1 mi. fun runs to a 100 mi. ultra marathon on the Big Island. Among these is one of the world's most intense multi-sport events—the original **Ironman Triathlon.** Over 50,000 hopefuls from all 50 US states and over 50 countries compete to qualify for the event, held each October in Kona on the Big Island. Of these, 1500 are selected to compete in the grueling race. Competitors start with a 2.4 mi. ocean swim, follow with a 112 mi. bike race, and cap the whole thing off with a full 26.2 mi. marathon. The course is open for 17 hours; the record (8:04:08) was set by Luc Van Lierde in 1996. Over five million viewers worldwide tune in to watch the event each year.

Hawaii also has several official marathons. **The Honolulu Marathon,** held each December, is the 6th-largest marathon in the world. **The Maui Marathon,** held in March, is the oldest continuously held running event in Hawaii. Other marathons are the **Kilauea Volcano Marathon** in July, the **Kona Marathon** in June, and the **Big Island International Marathon** in March.

COLLEGE SPORTS AND FOOTBALL

Water polo, volleyball, and sailing are among the most popular high school and college competitive sports in Hawaii. The University of Hawaii at Manoa Warriors boast a nationally ranked sailing program, and the 2002 men's volleyball team were national champions. Since 1997, the **Hula Bowl All-Star Football Classic,** a game for potential professional players, has been held each year on Maui and the islands have long been home to the **NFL's Pro Bowl.** In addition, the fairly new **NCAA Hawaii Bowl** is played each year in Honolulu.

HOLIDAYS AND FESTIVALS

Jan.-Feb.: Chinese New Year. This celebration is best seen on Oahu, in Chinatown, where you'll be treated to a lion dance, fireworks, and an abundance of Chinese food.

Feb.: Maui's Whale Day Celebration. Family-friendly fun begins in Kihei, Maui.

Early Mar.: Honolulu Festival. Music, dance, and parades throughout the city.

Mar.: Kona Brewer's Festival. Nearly 30 breweries offer more than 60 types of beer at the Big Island's favorite brewery.

Mar. 26: Prince Kuhio Day. In celebration of the birthday of Prince Jonah Kuhio Kalanianaole, one of Hawaii's first delegates to Congress.

Apr. 15: Father Damien DeVeusteur Day. In celebration of Father Damien, the highly regarded Christian missionary to the Kalaupapa Peninsula leper colony. See p. 334.

Late Apr.: Merrie Monarch Festival. In Hilo. A week of cultural events culminating in Hawaii's most prestigious hula competition.

May 1: Lei Day. More fun than May Day. Also, more floral.

Late May: Taste of the Stars. This annual star studded event showcases the delectable creations from eighteen of Hawaii's premier resort and restaurant chefs. Chefs have included Roy Yamaguchi, Alan Wong, Russell Siu, Hiroshi Fukui, and many others.

Late May: Kauai Polynesian Festival. Food, entertainment, and crafts from the islands.

June 11: King Kamehameha Day. See p. 15 for information on Kamehameha the Great.

Mid-June: Maui Film Festival. In Wailea (see p. 287). Mainstream and indie film premieres under the stars, as well as culinary events.

Late June: Taste of Honolulu. An outdoor wine, food, and entertainment charity benefit.

July: Parker Ranch Rodeo. On the Big Island. Food, activities, and of course, rodeo events. Most popular rodeo on the island. See p. 248 for Parker Ranch info.

Aug.: Maui Onion Festival. Whalers Village (p. 274) hosts the Annual Maui Onion Festival featuring gourmet delights, celebrity chef demonstrations, and recipe contests.

Third Friday in Aug.: Statehood Day. See p. 17 for the history of Hawaii-US relations.

Sept.-Oct.: Aloha Festival. Hawaii's largest cultural festival, spanning 2 months and featuring events on all the major islands. US's only statewide multicultural celebration.

LIFE AND TIMES

Sept.: Sam Choy Poke Festival. The bounty of the sea takes center stage at this food festival reserved for seafood lovers. On the Big Island.

Late Oct.-Nov.: Kona Coffee Festival. A 10-day celebration of caffeination. Get pumped.

Oct. 31: Halloween in Lahaina. Trick-or-treat with over 30,000 revelers on Front Street.

Nov.: Hawaiian International Film Festival. State-wide. Screenings of (mostly) Pacific Rim films in various locations.

ADDITIONAL RESOURCES

THE GREAT OUTDOORS

A Field Guide to the Birds of Hawaii and the Tropical Pacific. Douglas Pratt (Princeton UP, 1987).

Hawaii: A Natural History: Geology, Climate, Native Flora and Fauna Above the Shoreline. Sherwin Carlquist (National Tropical Botanical Garden, 1994).

Hawaii's Best Hiking Trails. R. Smith & K. Chard (Hawaiian Outdoor Adventure, 2004).

Plants and Flowers of Hawaii. Seymour H. Sohmer (University of Hawaii Press, 1994).

Remains of a Rainbow: Rare Plants and Animals of Hawaii. David Littschwager, et al. (National Geographic Society, 2003).

HISTORY

A Concise History of the Hawaiian Islands. Phil Barnes (Petroglyph Ltd., 1999).

Aloha Betrayed. Noenoe K. Silva (Duke UP, 2004).

Ancient Hawaii. Herb Kane (Kawainui Press, 1998).

The Apotheosis of Captain Cook. Gananath Obeyesekere (Princeton UP, 1992).

The Betrayal of Liliuokalani: Last Queen of Hawaii 1838-1917. Helena Allen (Mutual Publishing, 1991).

Day of Infamy: The Classic Account of the Bombing of Pearl Harbor. Walter Lord (Owl Books, 2001).

Kahoolawe Na Leo o Kanaloa: Chants and Stories of Kahoolawe. Wayne Levin and Rowland B. Reeve, eds. (Al Pohaku Press, 1995).

Legendary Hawaii and the Politics of Place. Cristina Bacchilega (Penn UP, 2007).

Niihau: The Last Hawaiian Island. Ruth Tabrah (Booklines Hawaii Ltd., 1987).

CULTURE

The Aloha Shirt: Spirit of the Island. Dale Hope (Thames and Hudson Ltd., 2002).

Architecture in Hawaii: A Chronological Pictorial. Rob Sandler (Mutual Publishing Company: 1994).

The Food of Paradise: Exploring Hawaii's Culinary Heritage. Rachel Laudan (University of Hawaii Press, 1996).

Hawaiian Magic & Spirituality. Scott Cunningham (Llewellyn Publications, 2002).

Hawaiian Mythology. Martha Warren Beckwith (University of Hawaii Press, 1977).

Home in the Islands: Housing and Social Change in the Pacific. Jan Rensel and Margaret Rodman (University of Hawaii Press: 1997).

Illustrated Hawaiian Dictionary. Kahikahealani Wight (Bess Press, 2005).

The Seven Dawns of the Aumakua: The Ancestral Spirit Tradition of Hawaii. Moke Kapihea (Inner Traditions International, 2004)

FICTION AND TRAVEL NARRATIVES

A Hawaii Anthology. Joseph Stanton, ed. (University of Hawaii Press, 1997).

Blu's Hanging. Lois-Ann Yamanaka (Harper Perennial, 1998).

Comfort Woman. Nora Okja Keller (Penguin Books, 1998).

da word. Lee Tonouchi (Bamboo Ridge Press, 2001).

Growing Up Local: An Anthology of Poetry and Prose from Hawaii. Eric Chock, ed. (Bamboo Ridge Press, 1999).

Hawaii. James A. Michener (Random House, 1973).

Hawaii One Summer. Maxine Hong Kingston (University of Hawaii Press, 1998).

The House of Pride and Other Tales of Hawaii. Jack London (Classic, 1919).

Mark Twain's Letters From Hawaii. Mark Twain (University of Hawaii Press, 1975).

Roughing It. Mark Twain (Signet Classics, 1994).

Travels in Hawaii. Robert Louis Stevenson (University of Hawaii Press, 1991).

The Trembling of a Leaf. W. Somerset Maugham (Dixon-Price, 2002).

Wild Meat and the Bully Burgers. Lois-Ann Yamanaka (Harvest Books, 1997).

FILM

50 First Dates. (Dir. Peter Segal. Columbia Pictures, 2004.)

Blue Crush. (Dir. John Stockwell. Universal Studios, 2002.)

Blue Hawaii. (Dir. Norman Tauroq. 20th Century Fox, 1961.)

The Endless Summer. (Dir. Bruce Brown. Bruce Brown Films, 1966.)

Forgetting Sarah Marshall. (Dir. Nicholas Stoller. Universal Pictures, 2008.)

From Here to Eternity. (Dir. Fred Zinneman. Columbia TriStar, 1953.)

Gidget Goes Hawaiian. (Dir. Paul Wendkos. Columbia TriStar, 1961.)

Hawaii. (Dir. George Roy Hill. MGM, 1966.)

Lilo and Stitch. (Dir. David DeBlois and Chris Sanders. Disney, 2002.)

Molokai: The Story of Father Damien. (Dir. Paul Cox. Unapix, 1999.)

Pearl Harbor. (Dir. Michael Bay. Buena Vista, 2001.)

Step into Liquid. (Dir. Dana Brown. Lionsgate/Fox, 2003.)

Tora! Tora! Tora! (Dir. Fleischer, Fukasaku, Masuda. 20th Century Fox, 1970.)

Waikiki Wedding. (Dir. Frank Tuttle. Paramount, 1937.)

SPORTS

Becoming an Ironman. Kara Douglass Thom (Breakaway Books, 2002).

The Big Drop: Classic Big Wave Surfing Stories. John Long, ed. (Falcon Publishing, 1999).

Eddie Would Go: The Story of Eddie Aikau, Hawaiian Hero. Stuart Coleman (St. Martin's Griffin, 2004).

Girl in the Curl: A Century of Women's Surfing. Andrea Gabbard (Seal Press, 2000).

North Shore Chronicles: Big Wave Surfing in Hawaii. Bruce Jenkins (North Atlantic Books, 2005).

Sleeping in the Shorebreak and Other Hairy Surfing Stories. Don Wolf (Waverider Publications, 1999).

ESSENTIALS

PLANNING YOUR TRIP

ENTRANCE REQUIREMENTS
Passport (p. 40). Required for citizens of non-US countries.
Visa (p. 40). Required for citizens of non-US countries, but can be waived.
Inoculations (p. 47).
Work Permit (p. 40). Required for all foreigners planning to work in the US.

EMBASSIES AND CONSULATES

US CONSULAR SERVICES ABROAD

US EMBASSIES

Australia: Moonah Pl., Yarralumla, Canberra ACT 2600 (☎+61 2 6214 5600; http://usembassy-australia.state.gov).

Canada: 490 Sussex Dr., Ottawa, ON K1N 1G8. Mailing address: P.O. Box 866, Station B, Ottawa, Ontario K1P 5T1 Canada. (☎613-688-5335; http://ottawa.usembassy.gov).

Ireland: 42 Elgin Rd., Ballsbridge, Dublin 4 (☎+353 1 668 8777; http://dublin.usembassy.gov).

New Zealand: 29 Fitzherbert Terr., Thorndon, Wellington. (☎+64 4 462 6000; http://newzealand.usembassy.gov.) Mailing address: P.O. Box 1190, Wellington, New Zealand.

UK: 24 Grosvenor Sq., London W1A 1AE (2LQ for street; +☎44 020 7499 9000; www.usembassy.org.uk).

US CONSULATES

Australia: 553 St. Kilda Rd., **Melbourne** VIC 3004 (☎+61 3 9526 5900; fax 9510 4646); 16 St. George's Terr., 13th fl., **Perth** WA 6000 (☎+61 8 9202 1224; fax 9231 9444); MLC Centre, Level 10, 19-29 Martin Pl., **Sydney** NSW 2000 (☎+61 2 9373 9200; fax 9373 9125).

Canada: 615 Macleod Trail SE, Ste. 1000, **Calgary,** AB T2G 4T8 (☎403 266 8962; fax 264 6630); Ste. 904, Purdy's Wharf Tower II, 1969 Upper Water St., **Halifax,** NS B3J 3R7, mailing address P.O. Box 2130, CRO, Halifax, NS B3J 3B7 (☎902 429 2480, fax 423 6861); 1155 Rue St.-Alexandre, **Montréal,** QC H3B 1Z1, mailing address P.O. Box 65, Station Desjardins, Montréal, QC H5B 1G1 (☎514 398 9695; fax 398 0702); 2 Pl. Terrasse Dufferin, **Québec City,** QC G1R 4T9, mailing address B.P. 939, Québec City, QC G1R 4T9 (☎418 692 2095; fax 692-4640); 360 University Ave., **Toronto,** ON M5G 1S4 (☎416 595 1700; fax 595-5466); 1075 W. Pender St., **Vancouver,** BC V6E 2M6, mailing address P.O. Box 5002, Point Roberts, WA 98281 (☎604-685-4311, fax 685-7175).; 201 Portage Ave., Ste. 860, **Winnipeg,** MB, R3B 3K6 (☎204 940 1800, fax 940 1809).

Ireland: same as embassy; see above.

New Zealand: Citibank Building, 3rd fl., 23 Customs St. East, **Auckland,** Mailing Address: Private Bag 92022, Auckland (☎64 9 303 2724, fax 366 0870).

UK: Danesfort House, 223 Stranmillis Rd., **Belfast,** N. Ireland BT9 5GR (☎44 028 9038 6100; fax 9068 1301); 3 Regent Terr., **Edinburgh,** Scotland EH7 5BW (☎44 0131 556 8315; fax 557 6023).

CONSULAR SERVICES IN THE US

IN WASHINGTON, DC

Australia, 1601 Massachusetts Ave. NW, 20036 (☎202-797-3000; www.usa.embassy.gov.au). **Canada,** 501 Pennsylvania Ave. NW, 20001 (☎202-682-1740; www.canadianembassy.org). **Ireland,** 2234 Massachusetts Ave. NW, 20008 (☎202-462-3939; www.irelandemb.org). **New Zealand,** 37 Observatory Cir. NW, 20008 (☎202-328-4800; www.nzembassy.com). **UK,** 3100 Massachusetts Ave., 20008 (☎202-588-7800; www.britainusa.com/embassy).

IN HONOLULU, HI

Australia, Penthouse, 1000 Bishop St., 96813 (☎808-524-5050; www.dfat.gov.au/missions/countries/usha. html). **New Zealand,** 3929 Old Pali Rd., Honolulu, HI, 96817 (☎808-595-2200; plewis7777@hawaii.rr.com).

TOURIST OFFICES

The **Hawaii Visitors & Convention Bureau (HVCB)** oversees tourism and will provide brochures and facilitate orientation in Hawaii. The main office is located at 2270 Kalakaua Ave., Ste. 801, Honolulu, 96815 (☎800-464-2924; www.gohawaii.com).

Australia: Level 3, 11-17 Swanson Plaza, Belconnen ACT 2616 (☎+61 2 6228 6100; www.tra.australia. com). Open M-F 9am-5pm.

Canada: Consular Affairs Bureau, 125 Sussex Drive, Ottawa, ON K1A 0G2 (☎604-638-8300; www.voyage. gc.ca). Open M-F 9am-5pm.

Ireland: Dept. of Foreign Affairs, 80 St. Stephen's Green, Dublin (☎+353 1 478 0822; www.dfa.ie).

New Zealand: Ministry of Foreign Affairs and Trade, 195 Lambton Quay, Wellington (☎+64 4 439 8000; www.safetravel.govt.nz). Open M-F 10am-6pm. Mailing address: Ministry of Foreign Affairs, Private Bag 18 901, Wellington, New Zealand.

United Kingdom: Foreign Commonwealth Office, King Charles Street, London SW1A 2AH (☎0845 850 2829; www.fco.gov.uk).

TOP TEN LIST

HAWAII ON ZERO DOLLARS A DAY

Everyone's told you that Hawaii is an expensive place to visit. We've devoted this guide to proving the opposite. Below is the creme de la creme of our labor—the best free things in the islands.

1. All Islands: Go to the beach. You can go to the beach for free anywhere, but **Hawaiian beaches** are oh-so-much better.

2. Oahu: A free show at the **Honolulu Zoo** (p. 140) features live Hawaiian music and dance performances every W.

3. Molokai: Take a tour of **Purdy's Macadamia Nut Farm** (p. 339) and enjoy the free samples after you crack your first nut.

4. The Big Island: Attend a stargazing session at the **Onizuka Center** (p. 235) on Mauna Kea.

5. Kauai: Stroll the streets during **Art Night** (p. 411), when Hanapepe's galleries stay open late and offer food samples.

6. Maui: Try the Maui Blush at **Tedeschi Vineyard's** free wine tasting (p. 316).

7. Oahu: Stay put for a movie after a free hula show and torch-lighting ceremony at Kuhlo Beach's **Sunset on the Beach** (p. 138).

8. Maui: Take a self-guided **walking tour** (p. 261) through **Lahaina's** whaling past.

9. Oahu: Honolulu Academy of Arts admission (p. 120) is free on the 1st W of each month.

10. Oahu: Experience the poignant **Arizona Memorial** (p. 144) at Pearl Harbor.

DOCUMENTS AND FORMALITIES

PASSPORTS

REQUIREMENTS
Citizens of Australia, Canada, Ireland, New Zealand, and the UK need valid passports to enter the US and to re-enter their home countries. Returning home with an expired passport is illegal and may result in a fine.

NEW PASSPORTS
Citizens of Australia, Canada, Ireland, New Zealand, and the UK can apply for a passport at any passport office or at selected post offices and courts of law. Citizens of these countries may also download passport applications from the official website of their country's government or passport office. Any new passport or renewal applications must be filed well in advance of the departure date, though most passport offices offer rush services for a very steep fee. Note, however, that "rushed" passports still take up to two weeks to arrive.

PASSPORT MAINTENANCE
Photocopy the page of your passport with your photo as well as your visas, traveler's check serial numbers, and any other important documents. Carry one set of copies in a safe place, apart from the originals, and leave another set at home. Consulates also recommend that you carry an expired passport or an official copy of your birth certificate separate from other documents.

If you lose your passport, immediately notify the local police and your home country's nearest embassy or consulate. To expedite its replacement, you must show ID and proof of citizenship; it also helps to know all information previously recorded in the passport. In some cases, a replacement may take weeks to process, and it may be valid only for a limited time. Any visas stamped in your old passport will be lost forever. In an emergency, ask for immediate temporary traveling papers that will permit you to re-enter your home country.

VISAS AND WORK PERMITS

VISAS
Citizens of some non-English-speaking countries need a visa—a stamp, sticker, or insert in your passport specifying the purpose of your travel and the permitted duration of your stay—in addition to a valid passport to enter the US. Canadian citizens do not need to obtain a visa for admission; citizens of Australia, New Zealand, and most European countries (including the UK and Ireland) can waive US visas through the **Visa Waiver Program (VWP).** Visitors qualify if they are traveling only for business or pleasure (not work or study), are staying for fewer than 90 days, have proof of intent to leave (e.g., a return plane ticket), possess an I-94W form (arrival/departure certificate issued upon arrival), are traveling on particular air or sea carriers (most major carriers qualify—contact the carrier for details), and have no visa ineligibilities.

As of October 2004, visitors in the VWP must possess a **machine-readable passport** to be admitted to the US without a visa, although most countries in the VWP have been issuing such passports for some time and many travelers will not need new passports. **Children** from these countries who normally travel on a parent's passport will also need to obtain their own machine-readable passports. Additionally, as of June 2005, the following requirements are in place for the use of **biometric identifiers** as visa waivers: passports issued before October 26, 2005 do not require biometric identifiers, passports issued between October 26, 2005 and October 25, 2006 require either a digital photograph or an integrated data chip, and passports issued after October 26, 2006 require an integrated data chip. See http://travel.state.gov/visa for a list of countries participating in the VWP as well as the latest info on biometric deadlines.

For stays of longer than 90 days in the US, all foreign travelers (except Canadians) must obtain a visa. Travelers eligible to waive their visas who wish to stay for more than 90 days must receive a visa before entering the US.

Check entrance requirements at the nearest embassy or consulate of the US (p. 38) for up-to-date info before departure. Entering the US to study requires a special visa. For more information, see the **Beyond Tourism** chapter (p. 67).

WORK PERMITS

Admittance to a country as a traveler does not include the right to work, which is authorized only by a work permit. See the **Beyond Tourism** chapter (p. 67).

IDENTIFICATION

When you travel, always carry at least two forms of identification on your person, including a photo ID. A passport and a driver's license or birth certificate will usually suffice. Never carry all of your IDs together; split them up in case of theft or loss and keep photocopies in your luggage and at home.

STUDENT, TEACHER, AND YOUTH IDENTIFICATION

The **International Student Identity Card (ISIC),** the most widely accepted form of student ID, provides discounts on some sights, accommodations, food, and transportation; access to a 24hr. emergency help line; and insurance benefits for US cardholders (see **Insurance,** p. 48). Applicants must be full-time, secondary, or post-secondary school students and at least 12 years old. Because of the proliferation of fake ISICs, some services (particularly airlines) require additional proof of student identity.

The **International Teacher Identity Card (ITIC)** offers teachers the same insurance coverage as the ISIC and similar discounts. To qualify for the card, teachers must be currently employed and have worked a minimum of 18hr. per week for at least one school year. For travelers who are under 26 years old but are not students, the **International Youth Travel Card (IYTC)** also offers many of the same benefits as the ISIC. Each of these identity cards costs $22. ISICs, ITICs, and IYTCs are valid for one year from the date of issue. To learn more about ISICs, ITICs, and IYTCs, try www.myisic.com. Many student travel agencies (p. 50) issue the cards; for a list of issuing agencies or more information, see the **International Student Travel Confederation (ISTC)** website (www.istc.org).

The **International Student Exchange Card (ISEC)** is a identification card available to students, faculty, and children ages 12 to 26. The card provides discounts, medical benefits, access to a 24hr. emergency line, and the ability to purchase student airfares. An ISEC costs $25; call ☎800-255-8000 (in North America) or ☎480-951-1177 (anywhere else) for more info or visit www.isecard.com.

CUSTOMS

Upon entering Hawaii, you must declare certain items from abroad and pay a duty on the value of those articles if they exceed the allowance established by the US customs service. Goods and gifts purchased at **duty-free** shops abroad are not exempt from duty or sales tax; "duty-free" means that you won't pay tax in the country of purchase. Upon returning home, you must likewise declare all articles acquired abroad and pay a duty on the value of articles in excess of your home country's allowance. In order to expedite your return, make a list of any valuables brought from home and register them with customs before traveling abroad. It's a good idea to keep receipts for all goods acquired abroad.

MONEY

CURRENCY AND EXCHANGE

The currency chart below is based on August 2008 exchange rates between local currency and Australian dollars (AUS$), Canadian dollars (CDN$), European Union euro (EUR€), New Zealand dollars (NZ$), and British pounds (UK£). Check the currency converter on websites like www.xe.com or www.bloomberg.com for the latest exchange rates.

CURRENCY ($)		
AUS$ = US$0.91		US$ = AUS$1.10
CDN$ = US$0.95		US$ = CDN$1.05
EUR€ = US$1.54		US$ = EUR€0.65
NZ$ = US$0.72		US$ = NZ$1.39
UK£ = US$1.95		US$ = UK£0.51

As a general rule, it's cheaper to convert money in Hawaii than at home. While currency exchange will probably be available in your arrival airport, it's wise to bring enough foreign currency to last for at least 24-72 hours. When changing money abroad, try to go only to banks that have at most a 5% margin between their buy and sell prices. Since you lose money with every transaction, it makes sense to **convert large sums** at one time.

If you use traveler's checks or bills, carry some in small denominations (the equivalent of $50 or fewer) for times when you are forced to exchange money at poor rates, but bring a range of denominations since charges may be applied per check cashed. Store your money in a variety of forms; ideally, at any given time you will carry cash, traveler's checks, and an ATM and/or credit card.

TRAVELER'S CHECKS

Traveler's checks are one of the safest and most convenient means of carrying funds. American Express and Visa are the most recognized brands. Many banks and agencies sell them for a small commission. Check issuers provide refunds if the checks are lost or stolen, and many provide additional services, such as toll-free refund hotlines abroad, emergency message services and assistance with lost and stolen credit cards or passports. Traveler's checks are readily accepted in Hawaii. Ask about toll-free refund hotlines and the location of refund centers when purchasing checks, and always carry emergency cash.

American Express: Checks available with commission at select banks, at all AmEx offices, and online (www.americanexpress.com; US residents only). AmEx cardholders can also purchase checks by phone (☎800-528-4800). AmEx also offers the Travelers Cheque Card, a prepaid reloadable card. For purchase locations or more information, contact AmEx's service centers: in Australia ☎+61 2 9271 8666, in New Zealand +64 9 367 4567, in the UK +44 1273 696 933, in the US and Canada 800-221-7282; elsewhere, call the US collect at +1-336-393-1111.

ESSENTIALS

Visa: Checks available (generally with commission) at banks worldwide. For the location of the nearest office, call the Visa Travelers Cheque Global Refund and Assistance Center: in the UK ☎0800 895 078, in the US 800-227-6811; elsewhere, call the UK collect at +44 2079 378 091. Checks available in British, Canadian, European, Japanese, and US currencies, among others. Visa also offers TravelMoney, a prepaid debit card that can be reloaded online or by phone. For more information on Visa travel services, see http://usa.visa.com/personal/using_visa/travel_with_visa.html.

CREDIT, DEBIT, AND ATM CARDS

Where they are accepted, credit cards often offer superior exchange rates—up to 5% better than the retail rate used by banks and other currency exchange establishments. Credit cards may also offer services such as insurance or emergency help and are sometimes required to reserve hotel rooms or rental cars. **MasterCard** and **Visa** are the most frequently accepted; **American Express** cards work at some ATMs and at AmEx offices and major airports.

The use of ATM cards is widespread in Hawaii. Depending on the system that your home bank uses, you can most likely access your personal bank account from abroad. ATMs get the same wholesale exchange rate as credit cards, but there is often a limit on the amount of money you can withdraw per day (usually around $500). There is also typically a surcharge of $1-5 per withdrawal.

Debit cards are as convenient as credit cards but withdraw money directly from the holder's checking account. A debit card can be used wherever its associated credit card company (usually MasterCard or Visa) is accepted. Debit cards often also function as ATM cards and can be used to withdraw cash from associated banks and ATMs throughout Hawaii.

The two major international money networks are **MasterCard/Maestro/Cirrus** (for ATM locations ☎800-424-7787 or www.mastercard.com) and **Visa/PLUS** (for ATM locations ☎800-847-2911 or www.visa.com). Most ATMs charge a transaction fee that is paid to the bank that owns the ATM.

GETTING MONEY FROM HOME

If you run out of money while traveling, the easiest and cheapest solution is to have someone back home make a deposit to your bank account. Otherwise, consider one of the following options.

WIRING MONEY

It is possible to arrange a **bank money transfer,** which means asking a bank back home to wire money to a bank in Hawaii. This is the cheapest way to transfer cash, but it's also the slowest, usually taking several days or more. Note that some banks may only release your funds in local currency, potentially sticking you with a poor exchange rate; inquire about this in advance. Money transfer services like **Western Union** are faster and more convenient than bank transfers—but also much pricier. To find a Western Union, visit www.westernunion.com, or call in Australia ☎1800 173 833, in Canada and the US 800-325-6000, in the UK 0800 833 833. To wire money using a credit card (Discover, MasterCard, Visa), call in Canada and the US ☎800-CALL-CASH, in the UK 0800 833 833. Money transfer services are also available to **American Express** cardholders and at selected **Thomas Cook** offices.

COSTS

The cost of your trip will vary considerably, depending on where you go, how you travel, and where you stay. The most significant expenses will probably be your round-trip (return) **airfare** to Hawaii (see **Getting to Hawaii: By Plane,** p. 50). Before you go, spend some time calculating a reasonable daily **budget.**

STAYING ON A BUDGET

To give you a general idea, a bare-bones day in Hawaii (camping or sleeping in hostels, buying food at supermarkets) would cost about $40- 50; a slightly more comfortable day (sleeping in hostels/guesthouses and the occasional hotel, eating one meal per day at a restaurant, going out at night) would cost $70-90; and for a luxurious day, the sky's the limit. Don't forget to factor in emergency reserve funds (at least $200) when planning how much money you'll need.

TIPS FOR SAVING MONEY

Simple ways include searching out opportunities for free entertainment, splitting accommodation and food costs with fellow travelers, and buying food in supermarkets. **Camping** (p. 82) is a good way to save money in Hawaii. Bring a **sleepsack** (p. 82) to save on sheet charges in hostels and do your **laundry** in the sink. Museums often have certain days once a month or once a week when admission is free; plan accordingly. Many sights and museums offer reduced admission to students and youths with ISIC and IYTC (p. 41). Drinking at bars and clubs quickly becomes expensive.; it's cheaper to buy alcohol at a supermarket and imbibe before going out. That said, don't go overboard. Though staying within your budget is important, don't do so at the expense of your health or a great travel experience.

TIPPING AND BARGAINING

It is customary to tip waitstaff and cab drivers 15% (though especially poor or good service warrants tipping from 10-20%). Tips are usually not included in restaurant bills; a restaurant will tell you if gratuity is included. Porters expect at least a $2 per bag tip to carry your luggage. Except at flea markets or other informal settings, bargaining is generally frowned upon in Hawaii.

TAXES

In Hawaii, the state general excise tax is 4%, which is effectively identical to a sales tax and is levied on groceries also. Usually this tax is not included in the prices of items. There is an additional 0.5% surcharge in Honolulu. An accommodations tax of 7.25% applies to all rooms for fewer than 180 consecutive days; this tax is on top of the state general excise tax for a total of 11.25%. An arcane tax on rental cars is automatically factored into the price of a rental.

PACKING

Pack lightly: lay out only what you absolutely need, then take half the clothes and twice the money. **The Travelite FAQ** (www.travelite.org) is a good resource for tips on traveling light. The online **Universal Packing List** (http://upl.codeq.info) will generate a customized list of suggested items based on your trip length, the expected climate, your planned activities, and other factors. If you plan to do a lot of hiking, also consult **The Great Outdoors** (p. 78). Some frequent travelers keep a bag packed with all the essentials: passport, money belt, hat, socks, etc. Then, when they decide to leave, they know they haven't forgotten anything.

Luggage: If you plan to cover most of your itinerary by foot, a sturdy **internal frame backpack** is unbeatable. (For the basics on buying a pack, see p. 82.) In addition to your main piece of luggage, a **daypack** (a small backpack or courier bag) is useful.

Clothing: Dress in Hawaii is like the Hawaiian lifestyle—casual and laid-back. Almost everyone, from grandparents to preschoolers, swears by plastic flip-flops. Shorts and light T-shirts or tank tops will do for almost any occasion. However, if you're planning a trip to high altitudes, bringing warmer clothing is advisable. It is also a good idea to bring a light rain jacket. If you're hiking, sturdy shoes or hiking boots are a must.

Sleepsack: Some hostels require that you either provide your own linen or rent sheets from them. Save cash by making your own sleepsack: fold a full-size sheet in half the long way, then sew it closed along the long side and one of the short sides.

Converters and Adapters: In Hawaii, electrical appliances are designed for 120V. Visitors from the UK, Ireland, Australia, and New Zealand (who use 230V) will need to purchase a converter. An adapter (around $5) is always needed to make other plug types compatible with the 3-prong outlet found in the US. For more on all things adaptable, check out http://kropla.com/electric.htm.

First-Aid Kit: For a basic first-aid kit, pack bandages, a pain reliever, antibiotic cream, a thermometer, a multifunction pocketknife, tweezers, moleskin, decongestant, motion-sickness remedy, diarrhea or upset-stomach medication (Pepto-Bismol® or Imodium®), an antihistamine, sunscreen, insect repellent, and burn ointment.

Other Useful Items: For safety purposes, you should bring a **money belt** and a small **padlock.** Basic **outdoors equipment** (plastic water bottle, compass, waterproof matches, pocketknife, sunglasses, sunscreen, hat) may also be handy. Other things you're liable to forget include: an umbrella, sealable **plastic bags** (for damp clothes, soap, food, shampoo, and other spillables), an **alarm clock,** safety pins, rubber bands, a flashlight, earplugs, garbage bags, and a small calculator. A **cell phone** can be a lifesaver (literally) on the road; see p. 59 for information on acquiring one that will work in Hawaii.

Important Documents: Don't forget your passport, traveler's checks, ATM and/or credit cards, adequate ID, and photocopies of all of the aforementioned in case these documents are lost or stolen (p. 40). Also check that you have any of the following that might apply to you: a HI card (p. 60); travel insurance forms (p. 48); ISIC (p. 41).

SAFETY AND HEALTH

GENERAL ADVICE

In any type of crisis, the most important thing to do is **stay calm.** Your country's embassy abroad (p. 38) is usually your best resource in an emergency; registering with that embassy upon arrival in the country is a good idea. The government offices listed in the **Travel Advisories** box (p. 46) can provide information on the services they offer their citizens in case of emergencies abroad.

LOCAL LAWS AND POLICE

DRUGS AND ALCOHOL

As in the continental US, the drinking age in Hawaii is a **strictly enforced 21.** Young people should expect to be asked to show government-issued ID when purchasing any alcoholic beverage. In Hawaii, off-premises alcohol sales stop at 11pm while on-premises sales vary depending on the establishment. Drinking and driving is prohibited everywhere. **Never drive under the influence.** In Hawaii it is a crime to drive with a blood alcohol concentration (BAC) above 0.08%, a level that can be achieved with as few as two drinks in one hour. Hawaii has a **zero tolerance policy** for those under 21, with severe consequences for those found to have consumed *any* amount of alcohol. It is also illegal to have an open container of alcohol inside a car, even if you are not the driver and even if you are not drinking it. Those caught drinking and driving face fines, a suspended license, imprisonment, or all three.

Marijuana and narcotics such as heroin, cocaine, and methamphetamines are illegal in the US, and possession carries extremely harsh sentences. If you carry prescription drugs while you travel, it is important that you keep a copy of the prescription with you. A letter from your doctor is advisable if you carry large amounts of prescription drugs.

SPECIFIC CONCERNS

NATURAL DISASTERS
See **Great Outdoors,** p. 78.

TERRORISM
In light of the September 11, 2001 terrorist attacks in the eastern US, the US government infrequently puts the nation, and its territories, on an elevated terrorism alert. Hawaii has not had any attacks, or threats of attacks, but, like the rest of the US, the islands have taken necessary precautions. Allow extra time for airport security and do not pack sharp objects or more than 3 oz. of liquid in your carry-on luggage, as they will be confiscated. Monitor developments in the news and stay on top of any local, state, or federal terrorist warnings, but do not let fear of terrorism prevent you from enjoying your vacation. The box on travel advisories lists offices to contact and websites to visit to get the most updated list of your government's advisories about travel.

TRAVEL ADVISORIES. The following government offices provide travel information and advisories by telephone, by fax, or via the web:

Australian Department of Foreign Affairs and Trade: ☎+61 2 6261 1111; www.dfat.gov.au.

Canadian Department of Foreign Affairs and International Trade (DFAIT): ☎800-267-8376; www.dfait-maeci.gc.ca. Call for their free booklet, Bon Voyage...But.

New Zealand Ministry of Foreign Affairs: ☎+64 4 439 8000; www.mfat.govt.nz.

United Kingdom Foreign and Commonwealth Office: ☎+44 20 7008 1500; www.fco.gov.uk.

US Department of State: ☎888-407-4747; http://travel.state.gov. Visit the website for the booklet, A Safe Trip Abroad.

PERSONAL SAFETY

EXPLORING AND TRAVELING

To avoid unwanted attention, try to blend in as much as possible. Respecting local customs (in many cases, dressing more conservatively than usual) may ward off would-be hecklers. Familiarize yourself with your surroundings before setting out and carry yourself with confidence. Check maps in shops and restaurants rather than on the street. If you are traveling alone, be sure someone at home knows your itinerary and never tell anyone you meet that you're by yourself. When walking at night, stick to busy, well-lit streets.

There is no surefire way to avoid all the threatening situations that you might encounter while traveling, but a good **self-defense course** will give you concrete ways to react to unwanted advances. **Impact, Prepare,** and **Model Mugging** can refer you to self-defense courses in Australia, Canada, Switzerland, and the US. Visit their website at www.modelmugging.org for a list of nearby chapters.

If you are using a **car,** learn local driving signals and wear a seat belt. Children under 40 lb. should ride only in specially designed car seats, available for a small fee from most car-rental agencies. Study route maps before you hit the road and, if you plan on spending a lot of time driving, consider bringing spare parts. For long drives in desolate areas, invest in a cellular phone and a road-side assistance program (p. 55). Park your vehicle in a garage or well-traveled area and use a steering-wheel locking device in larger cities. Sleeping in your car is the most dangerous way to get your rest, and it's also illegal in many areas. For info on the perils of **hitchhiking,** see p. 57.

POSSESSIONS AND VALUABLES

Never leave your belongings unattended; crime can occur in even the most safe-looking hostel or hotel. Bring your own padlock for hostel lockers and don't ever store valuables in a locker. Be particularly careful on **buses** and **trains;** horror stories abound about determined thieves who wait for travelers to fall asleep. Carry your bag or purse in front of you where you can see it. Try to sleep on top bunks with your luggage stored above you (if not in bed with you) and keep important documents and other valuables on you at all times.

There are a few steps you can take to minimize the financial risk associated with traveling. First, **bring as little with you as possible.** Second, buy a few combination **padlocks** to secure your belongings. Third, **carry as little cash as possible.** Keep your traveler's checks and ATM/credit cards in a **money belt**—not a "fanny pack"—along with your passport and ID cards. Fourth, **keep a small cash reserve separate from your primary stash.** This should be about $50 sewn into or stored in the depths of your pack, along with your traveler's check numbers, photocopies of your passport, your birth certificate, and other important documents. **Never let your passport and your bags out of your sight.**

If you will be traveling with electronic devices, such as a laptop computer, check whether your homeowner's insurance covers loss, theft, or damage when you travel. If not, you might consider purchasing a separate insurance policy. **Safeware** (☎800-800-1492; www.safeware.com) specializes in covering computers and charges $90 for 90-day international travel coverage up to $4000.

PRE-DEPARTURE HEALTH

In your passport, write the names of any people you wish to be contacted in case of a **medical emergency** and list any allergies or medical conditions. Matching a prescription to a foreign equivalent is not always easy, safe, or possible, so, if you take **prescription drugs,** consider carrying up-to-date prescriptions or a statement from your doctor stating the medication's trade name, manufacturer, chemical name, and dosage. Be sure to keep all medication with you in your carry-on luggage. For tips on packing a **first-aid kit,** see p. 44.

IMMUNIZATIONS AND PRECAUTIONS

Travelers over two years old should make sure that the following vaccines are up to date: MMR (for measles, mumps, and rubella); DTaP or Td (for diphtheria, tetanus, and pertussis); IPV (for polio); Hib (for *haemophilus influenzae* B); and HepB (for Hepatitis B). For recommendations on immunizations and prophylaxis, consult the Centers for Disease Control and Prevention (CDC) in the US or the equivalent in your home country and check with a doctor.

INSURANCE

Travel insurance covers four basic areas: medical/health problems, property loss, trip cancellation/interruption, and emergency evacuation. Though regular insurance policies may well extend to travel-related accidents, you may consider purchasing separate travel insurance if the cost of potential trip cancellation, interruption, or emergency medical evacuation is greater than you can absorb. Prices for travel insurance purchased separately generally run about $50 per week for full coverage, while trip cancellation/interruption may be purchased separately at a rate of $3-5 per day, depending on length of stay.

Medical insurance (especially university policies) often covers costs incurred abroad; check with your provider. **Homeowners' insurance** (or your family's coverage) often covers theft during travel and loss of travel documents (passport, plane ticket, etc.) up to $500. **ISIC** and **ITIC** (p. 41) provide insurance benefits to US cardholders, including $100 per day of in-hospital sickness for up to 100 days and $10,000 of accident-related medical reimbursement (see www.isicus. com for details). **American Express** (☎800-338-1670) grants most cardholders automatic collision and theft car rental insurance.

USEFUL ORGANIZATIONS AND PUBLICATIONS

The American **Centers for Disease Control and Prevention** (CDC; ☎877-FYI-TRIP; www.cdc.gov/travel) maintain an international travelers' hotline and an informative website. Consult the appropriate government agency of your home country for consular information sheets on health, entry requirements, and other issues for various countries (see the listings in the box on **Travel Advisories,** p. 46). For quick information on health and other travel warnings, call the **Overseas Citizens Services** (from overseas ☎+1-202-501-4444, from US 888-407-4747; line open M-F 8am-8pm EST) or contact a passport agency, embassy, or consulate abroad. For information on medical evacuation services and travel insurance firms, see the US government's website at http://travel.state.gov/travel/abroad_health.html or the **British Foreign and Commonwealth Office** (www. fco.gov.uk). For general health information, contact the **American Red Cross** (☎202-303-4498; www.redcross.org).

STAYING HEALTHY

Common sense is the simplest prescription for good health while you travel. Drink lots of fluids to prevent dehydration and constipation and wear sturdy, broken-in shoes and clean socks.

ONCE IN HAWAII

ENVIRONMENTAL HAZARDS
See **Great Outdoors,** p. 78.

ESSENTIALS

INSECT-BORNE DISEASES
See **Great Outdoors,** p. 78.

FOOD- AND WATER-BORNE DISEASES
See **Great Outdoors,** p. 78.

OTHER INFECTIOUS DISEASES
The following diseases exist all over the world. Travelers should know how to recognize them and what to do if they suspect they have been infected.

Hepatitis B: A viral infection of the liver transmitted via blood or other bodily fluids. Symptoms, which may not surface until years after infection, include jaundice, appetite loss, fever, and joint pain. It is transmitted through unprotected sex and unclean needles. A 3-shot vaccination sequence is recommended for sexually active travelers and anyone planning to seek medical treatment abroad; it must begin 6 months before traveling. Hepatitis B is rare in Hawaii.

AIDS and HIV: For detailed information on Acquired Immune Deficiency Syndrome (AIDS) in Hawaii, call the 24hr. National AIDS Hotline at ☎800-342-2437. Note that, according to US law, people who are HIV positive may not legally enter the US unless they obtain special permission from the US embassy before traveling. Legislatures are working on removing this ban and it will likely be repealed in the near future. Contact the US consulate for more information.

Sexually transmitted infections (STIs): Gonorrhea, chlamydia, genital warts, syphilis, herpes, HPV, and other STIs are easier to catch than HIV and can be just as serious. Though condoms may protect you from some STIs, oral or even tactile contact can lead to transmission. If you think you may have contracted an STI, see a doctor immediately.

OTHER HEALTH CONCERNS

MEDICAL CARE ON THE ROAD
Medical services in Hawaii are accessible 24hr. at hospitals throughout the islands. Some more rural towns may be a short drive away from the nearest hospital, but for the most part, medical care is readily available. In an emergency, dial ☎**911** from any phone, and an operator will send out paramedics.

If you are concerned about obtaining medical assistance while traveling, you may wish to employ special support services. The **MedPass** from **GlobalCare, Inc.,** 6875 Shiloh Rd. East, Alpharetta, GA 30005 (☎800-860-1111; www.globalcare.net), provides 24hr. international medical assistance, support, and medical evacuation resources. The **International Association for Medical Assistance to Travelers** (**IAMAT;** US ☎716-754-4883, Canada 519-836-0102; www.iamat.org) has free membership and offers detailed info on immunization requirements and sanitation. If your regular insurance policy does not cover travel abroad, you may wish to purchase additional coverage (p. 48). Those with medical conditions (such as diabetes, allergies, epilepsy, or heart conditions) may want to obtain a **MedicAlert** membership ($40 per year), which includes an ID tag and a 24hr. collect-call number. Contact the **MedicAlert Foundation International,** 2323 Colorado Ave., Turlock, CA 95382 (☎888-633-4298, www.medicalert.org).

WOMEN'S HEALTH
Women traveling in unsanitary conditions are vulnerable to **urinary tract (including bladder and kidney) infections.** Over-the-counter medicines can sometimes alleviate symptoms, but if they persist, see a doctor. Vaginal yeast infections may flare up in hot and humid climates. Wearing loosely fitting trousers or a

ESSENTIALS

skirt and cotton underwear will help, as will over-the-counter remedies like Monostat or Gynelotrimin. Bring supplies from home if you are prone to infection, as they may be difficult to find on the road. Tampons, pads, and contraceptive devices are widely available, though your favorite brand may not be stocked—bring extras of anything you can't live without. **Abortion** is legal in the US, and information is available through Planned Parenthood of Hawaii (☎808-589-1156; www.plannedparenthood.org/hawaii).

GETTING TO HAWAII

BY PLANE

When it comes to airfare, a little effort can save you a bundle. Tickets sold by consolidators and standby seating are good deals, but last-minute specials, airfare wars, and charter flights often beat these fares. The key is to hunt around, be flexible, and ask about discounts. Students, seniors, and those under 26 should never pay full price for a ticket.

AIRFARES

Airfares to Hawaii are high throughout the year; holidays and the winter months are particularly expensive. Midweek (M-Th morning) round-trip flights run $40-50 cheaper than weekend flights, but they are generally more crowded and less likely to permit frequent-flier upgrades. Not fixing a return date ("open return") or arriving in and departing from different cities ("open-jaw") can be pricier than round-trip flights. Flights into Honolulu are most common and will almost always be less expensive than flights into cities on the islands.; consider flying into Honolulu and then connecting to your destination. Taking flights with layovers or stops can significantly reduce the price of your fare.

If Hawaii is only one stop on a more extensive globe-hop, consider a round-the-world (RTW) ticket. Tickets usually include at least five stops and are valid for about a year; prices range $1200-5000. Try **Northwest Airlines/KLM** (☎800-225-2525; www.nwa.com) or **Star Alliance,** a consortium of 16 airlines including United Airlines (www.staralliance.com).

Fares for round-trip flights to Honolulu from the US or Canadian east coast cost $760-1300 depending on when your flight is and how early you book it; from the US or Canadian west coast $500-1200; from the UK ₤700-1000; from Australia AUS$1200-3000; from New Zealand NZ$1500-4000.

BUDGET AND STUDENT TRAVEL AGENCIES

While agents specializing in flights to Hawaii can make your life easy, they may not spend the time to find you the lowest possible fare—they get paid on commission. Travelers holding ISICs and IYTCs (p. 41) qualify for discounts from student travel agencies. Most flights from budget agencies are on major airlines, but some may sell seats on less reliable chartered aircraft.

STA Travel, 5900 Wilshire Blvd., Ste. 900, Los Angeles, CA 90036 (24hr. reservations and info ☎800-781-4040; www.statravel.com). A student and youth travel organization with over 150 offices worldwide, including US offices in Boston, Chicago, Los Angeles, New York, Seattle, San Francisco, and Washington, DC. Ticket booking, travel insurance, and more. Walk-in offices are located throughout Australia (☎+61 3 9207 5900), New Zealand (☎+64 9 309 9723), and the UK (☎+44 8701 630 026).

The Adventure Travel Company, 124 MacDougal St., New York, NY 10021 (☎800-467-4595; www.theadventuretravelcompany.com). Offices across Canada and the US including Calgary, New York, San Diego, Seattle, and San Francisco.

USIT, 19-21 Aston Quay, Dublin 2, Ireland (☎+353 1 602 1906; www.usit.ie). Ireland's leading student/budget travel agency has 20 offices throughout Northern Ireland and the Republic of Ireland. Offers programs to work, study, and volunteer worldwide.

COMMERCIAL AIRLINES

The commercial airlines' lowest regular offer is the **APEX (Advance Purchase Excursion)** fare, which provides confirmed reservations and allows "open-jaw" tickets. Generally, reservations must be made seven to 21 days ahead of departure, with seven- to 14-day minimum-stay and up to 90-day maximum-stay restrictions. These fares carry hefty cancellation and change penalties (fees rise in summer). Book peak-season APEX fares early. Use **Expedia** (www.expedia.com) or **Travelocity** (www.travelocity.com) to get an idea of the lowest published fares, then use the resources outlined here to try to beat those fares. For useful information on Hawaii's airports, including a list of airlines that fly into Hawaii, go to www.state.hi.us/dot/airports.

FLIGHT PLANNING ON THE INTERNET. The Internet may be the budget traveler's dream when it comes to finding and booking bargain fares, but the array of options can be overwhelming. Many airline sites offer special last-minute deals on the web. Try **Hawaiian Airlines** (www.hawaiianair.com) or **go!** (www.iflygo.com). **STA** (www.statravel.com) and **StudentUniverse** (www.studentuniverse.com) provide quotes on student tickets, while **Orbitz** (www.orbitz.com), **Expedia** (www.expedia.com), and **Travelocity** (www.travelocity.com) offer full travel services. **Priceline** (www.priceline.com) lets you specify a price and obligates you to buy any ticket that meets or beats it; **Hotwire** (www.hotwire.com) offers bargain fares but won't reveal the airline or flight times until you buy. Other sites that compile deals include www.bestfares.com, www.flights.com, www.lowestfare.com, www.onetravel.com, and www.travelzoo.com.

SideStep (www.sidestep.com) and **Booking Buddy** (www.bookingbuddy.com) are online tools that can help sift through multiple offers; these two let you enter your trip information once and search multiple sites.

Air Traveler's Handbook (www.faqs.org/faqs/travel/air/handbook) is an indispensable resource on the Internet; it has a comprehensive listing of links to everything you need to know before you board a plane.

TRAVELING FROM NORTH AMERICA

Basic round-trip fares to Hawaii range from roughly $500-1500 (to Honolulu, $500-1100; to Hilo, Kahului, Kona, and Lihue $700-1200), depending on your departure city. Standard commercial carriers like American and United will probably offer the most convenient flights, but they may not be the cheapest, unless you snag a special promotion or airfare-war ticket.

Air Canada (☎888-247-2262; www.aircanada.com).

Alaska Airlines (☎800-252-7522, lines open 8am-3am; www.alaskaair.com).

Continental Airlines (☎800-523-3273; www.continental.com), also has a ticket office at Ala Moana Center, Ste. 2230, Honolulu, HI 96814 (M-Sa 9am-1:30pm, 2pm-5pm).

Hawaiian Airlines (☎800-367-5320, lines open 9am-3:30am; www.hawaiianair.com).

Northwest Airlines (☎800-225-2525; www.nwa.com).

TRAVELING FROM IRELAND AND THE UK

Flights from Ireland and the UK to Hawaii run ₤700-1000. Check these companies for the best fares:

Air Canada (☎+44 0871 220 1111, lines open M-F 8am-6pm, Sa 8am-4pm, Su 8am-3pm; www.aircanada.com).

Continental Airlines (☎+44 0845 607 6760; www.continental.com).

Lufthansa (☎+44 0871 945 9747; www.lufthansa.com).

TRAVELING FROM AUSTRALIA AND NEW ZEALAND

Flights from Australia and New Zealand range from $1200-2400 depending on when and where you fly. Try these airlines for the best rates:

Air New Zealand (☎+64 0800 737 000; www.airnewzealand. co.nz/default.htm).

Hawaiian Airlines (☎+61-300 669 106, open M-F 9am-5pm; www.hawaiianair.com).

Qantas Airlines (☎+61 13 13 13; www.qantas.com).

STANDBY FLIGHTS

Traveling standby requires considerable flexibility in arrival and departure dates. Companies dealing in standby flights sell vouchers rather than tickets, along with the promise to get you to your destination (or near your destination) within a certain window of time (typically 1-5 days). Vouchers can usually be bought for both one-way and round-trip travel. You may receive a monetary refund only if every available flight within your date range is full; if you opt not to take an available (but perhaps less convenient) flight, you can only get credit toward future travel. To check on a company's service record in the US, contact the **Better Business Bureau** (☎703-276-0100; www.bbb.org). Clients' vouchers will not be honored when an airline fails to receive payment in time.

TICKET CONSOLIDATORS

Ticket consolidators, or **"bucket shops,"** buy unsold tickets in bulk from commercial airlines and sell them at discounted rates. The best place to look is in the Sunday travel section of any major newspaper (such as *The New York Times*), where many bucket shops place tiny ads. Call quickly, as availability is extremely limited. Not all bucket shops are reliable, so insist on a receipt that gives full details of restrictions, refunds, and tickets, and pay by credit card (in spite of the 2-5% fee) so you can stop payment if you never receive your tickets. For more info, see www.travel-library.com/air-travel/consolidators.html.

TRAVELING FROM CANADA AND THE US

Some major consolidators are **Rebel** (☎800-732-3588; www.rebeltours.com), **Cheap Tickets** (www.cheaptickets.com), and **TravelHUB** (www.travelhub.com). *Let's Go* does not endorse any of these agencies. As always, be cautious; research companies before you hand over your credit card number.

GETTING AROUND HAWAII

BY PLANE

There are several interisland airlines, including **Hawaiian Airlines** (☎800-367-5320; www.hawaiianair.com), **go!** airlines (☎800-637-2910; www.iflygo.com), and **Island Air** (☎808-484-2222 on Oahu, 800-652-6541 on neighbor islands and North America; www.islandair.com). All offer competitive rates on interisland flights. One-way flights from Honolulu to the outer islands start around $65.

BY BUS

Public transportation on **Oahu** is generally safe, clean, and relatively convenient. With 93 routes criss-crossing the island and over 4200 bus stops, **The-Bus** (p. 98), 811 Middle St., Honolulu 96819 (☎808-848-5555, customer service 808-848-4500; www.thebus.org), can usually get you where you're going. Adult one-way fare is $2. Monthly passes ($40) can be purchased at various supermarkets and drugstores. The county of **Kauai** also maintains a decent bus system ($1.50 one-way). Schedules and other information are available at the **County of Kauai Transportation Office**, 3220 Hoolako St., Lihue, Kauai 96766 (☎808-241-6410; www.kauai.gov/Government/Departments/TransportationAgency/BusSchedules). The Big Island has a free bus service, **Hele-On,** which services the whole island. Routes run about once a day. Contact the **County of Hawaii Mass Transit Office**, 630 E. Lanikaula St., Hilo 96720 (☎808-961-8744; www.co.hawaii.hi.us/mass_transit/heleonbus.html). **Maui** has a new bus system with nine routes. The **Maui Bus** can be contacted at **County of Maui Department of Transportation,** 2145 Kaohu Street, #102, Wailuku, HI 96793 (☎808-871-4838; www.co.maui.hi.us/bus). One-way fare for most routes is $1, though the Kahului and Wailuku loops are free; monthly passes ($40) can also be purchased. Localized shuttle service can also be secured through **Speedishuttle** (☎877-242-5777; www.speedishuttle.com). **Molokai** and **Lanai** have no form of public transportation.

BY CAR

Though car rental can be expensive, driving is the best and most efficient way to get around in Hawaii. "U.S." (as in "U.S. 1") refers to US highways, and "Rte." (as in "Rte. 7") refers to state and local highways.

RENTING

Depending on which island you plan to visit, the business of renting a car varies. Molokai and Lanai have only a few car rental agencies. In addition, some areas all but demand 4WD (areas on Lanai, Molokai, Kauai, and the Big Island in particular). Rental agencies on these islands will limit the roads where you are allowed to drive and will not cover towing if you get stuck. In general, cheaper cars tend to be less reliable and harder to handle on difficult terrain. Less expensive 4WD vehicles tend to be more top-heavy and are more dangerous when navigating bumpy roads.

RENTAL AGENCIES

You can generally make reservations before you leave by calling major international offices in your home country. However, occasionally the price and availability information they give doesn't jive with what the local offices in your country will tell you. Try checking with both numbers to make sure you get the best price and accurate information. The local desk numbers are included in town listings; for home-country numbers, call your toll-free directory.

Car rental agencies fall into two categories: national companies with hundreds of branches, and local agencies that serve only one city or region. Generally, airport branches have more expensive rates. To rent a car from most establishments in Hawaii, you need to be at least 21 years old and have a major credit card. Some agencies require renters to be 25, and most charge those ages 21-24 an additional insurance fee around $25 per day. Small local operations occasionally rent to people under 21, but be sure to ask about the insurance coverage and deductible, and always check the fine print. Reserve a rental car in Hawaii far in advance; the 4WD vehicles go especially quickly.

NATIONAL AGENCIES

Alamo (☎800-462-5266; www.alamo.com) rents to those under 25 with a major credit card for about $25 per day. Locations on Oahu, Maui, Kauai, and the Big Island.

Budget (☎800-527-0700; www.budget.com) rents to those under 25 with a surcharge of $25 per day. Drivers between ages 21-24 are not permitted to rent luxury cars, mini vans, 12-passenger vans, specialty vehicles, full-size SUVs, or premium SUVs. Locations on Oahu, Maui, Kauai, the Big Island, and Molokai.

Dollar (☎800-800-3665; www.dollar.com) rents to those under 25 with a variable surcharge. Locations on Oahu, Maui, Kauai, the Big Island, Lanai, and Molokai.

Enterprise (☎800-261-7331; www.enterprise.com) rents to those under 25 with a variable surcharge. On Oahu, Maui, and the Big Island. A great option for longer rentals.

Hertz (☎800-654-3131; www.hertz.com). Policy for those under 25 varies by city. Locations on Oahu, Maui, Kauai, and the Big Island.

Thrifty (☎800-847-4389; www.thrifty.com) locations rent to those under 25 for varying surcharges. Locations on Oahu, Maui, Kauai, and the Big Island.

LOCAL AGENCIES

Hawaii also has a number of locally owned rental services. Be aware that their selection of vehicles may be more limited than that of national chains. Local car rental agencies are listed in the Transportation section of towns and cities.

AA Aloha Cars-R-Us (☎800-655-7989; www.hawaiicarrental.com). Researches the lowest rates for cars from major rental agencies. Also offers special Hawaii promotions.

Adventure Lanai Ecocentre (☎808-565-7373; www.adventurelanai.com). Rents 4WD vehicles and other gear on Lanai. Only car rental company that allows off-roading in their vehicles. Also rents a house.

Aloha Rent a Car (☎877-452-5642; www.aloharentacar.com). Maui-based.

Car Rentals in Hawaii (☎888-292-3307; www.carrentalsinhawaii.com). Travelers can search available rentals online.

Harper Car and Truck Rental (☎800-852-9993; www.harpershawaii.com). Two locations on the Big Island. Rents motor homes as well.

Kihei Rent A Car (☎800-251-5288; www.kiheirentacar.com). Family-owned business located in Kihei, Maui. Also a certified travel agency.

COSTS AND INSURANCE

Rental car prices start at around $35 a day from national and local agencies. Expect to pay more for larger cars and on the smaller islands. Many rental deals offer unlimited mileage, while others offer a limited number of miles per day with a surcharge per mile after that. Return the car with a full tank of gasoline to avoid high fuel charges. National chains sometimes allow one-way rentals (picking up in one city and dropping off in another). There is usually a minimum hire period and an extra dropoff charge of several hundred dollars.

Remember that if you are driving a conventional rental vehicle on an unpaved road in a rental car, you are almost never covered by insurance; ask about this before leaving the rental agency. Rental companies in Hawaii offer a variety of insurance plans to supplement your rental; these are not required to rent but are usually a smart decision. You can buy a **Collision Damage Waiver (CDW)**, which will waive the excess in the case of a collision. **Loss Damage Waivers (LDWs)** do the same in the case of theft or vandalism.

DRIVING PERMITS AND CAR INSURANCE

INTERNATIONAL DRIVING PERMIT (IDP)

If you plan to drive while in Hawaii, you must be over 18 and have a US driver's license or an International Driving Permit (IDP). Your IDP, valid for one year, must be issued in your own country before you depart. An application for an IDP usually requires one or two photos, a current license, an additional form of ID, and a fee. To apply, contact your home country's automobile association.

CAR INSURANCE

Most credit cards cover standard insurance. If you rent or borrow a car, you will need a **green card,** or **International Insurance Certificate,** to certify that you have liability insurance and that it applies abroad. Green cards can be obtained at car rental agencies, some travel agents, and some border crossings. Rental agencies may require you to purchase theft insurance.

ON THE ROAD

The majority of the main highways are easily navigable in a 2WD car. Other roads on the islands, however, are narrow, bumpy, and subject to erosion, rain damage, and closure due to close running lava flows. Check out **www.hawaiihighways.com** for up-to-date information about road conditions in Hawaii. Most out-of-state drivers will find that the biggest difference between driving in Hawaii and driving anywhere else is the friendliness of other drivers; speed limits are observed and driving aggressively will likely earn you the "stink eye" from locals. Hawaii's seat belt laws require all front seat occupants to buckle up, as well as back seat passengers under the age of 18. Violators of seat belt laws will be assessed a $92 fine. Gasoline (petrol) prices vary, but average about $4.20 per gallon in Honolulu and around $4.50 per gallon on the outer islands.

DRIVING PRECAUTIONS. Bring substantial amounts of water (a suggested 5L of water per person per day) for drinking and for the radiator. You should always carry a spare tire and jack, jumper cables, extra oil, flares, a flashlight, and heavy blankets (in case your car breaks down at night or in the winter). If you don't know how to change a tire, learn before heading out, especially if you are planning on traveling in deserted areas. If your car breaks down, stay in your vehicle and call a towing service (p. 56).

DANGERS

The roadways on **Oahu** are some of the easiest to navigate. Be careful in Honolulu and Waikiki, as many of the one-way streets are bustling with people.

ESSENTIALS

Some of Oahu's freeways and two-lane highways are narrow, winding and scenic (such as the H3 Freeway). Don't get behind the wheel if you're likely to take your eyes off the road for some sightseeing.

The main highway system through central **Maui** is easy to understand and well maintained, but expect a steady flow of traffic most of the time. The infamous road to Hana (p. 313), a 52-mi. stretch of road containing over 600 turns and 50 one-lane bridges, is both one of the most beautiful and most dangerous roads in the state. Roads beyond the town of Hana are even more difficult to negotiate. You won't need 4WD, just patience and alertness. Check with your rental car company about where they will allow you to drive.

Though a 4WD is not necessary for much of the **Big Island,** time and caution are crucial. The Big Island's main roads are two-lane highways, often narrow and winding, with no shoulder; do not underestimate how long it will take you to get around the island. Gas stations are fairly far apart, and in rural areas, they tend to close early in the day. Fill up at the first station you encounter when you start to run low. Most rental companies do not allow driving on Saddle Rd. because it is narrow and poorly maintained in areas.

Kauai's main roads are also narrow two-lane highways, often without shoulders. Avoid Lihue during the morning and late-afternoon—traffic clogs the narrow roads. 4WD is necessary for the more remote parts of the island and caution should be taken especially after heavy rain.

Driving on **Lanai** is some of the trickiest in the state. Be sure to have 4WD. Heavy rain frequently washes out roads, making them impassable. Ask about current driving conditions when you rent your car and always bring a map and plenty of supplies. Lanai's axis deer population outnumbers its human population (6000 to 2500). Always watch for deer, especially in the evening hours.

Molokai has only one main highway. The roads leading off the highway are not often traveled and heavy rain can sometimes make them impassable. Be sure to check with your rental car company about the driving conditions and watch for the occasional mongoose (small, brown, weasel-shaped animals).

CAR ASSISTANCE

In general, but especially on Molokai and Lanai, call your rental car company first if you need roadside assistance.

HAWAII-WIDE

AAA Hawaii, 1130 N. Nimitz Hwy. A170, Honolulu, Oahu 96817 (☎808-593-2221 for Oahu; 800-736-2886 for other islands; www.aaa-hawaii.com).

Allstate Motor Club (☎800-998-8697; www.allstatemotorclub.com). Roadside assistance all over Hawaii for members.

HAWAII COUNTY

A Eagle 24Hr. Towing, Kailua, Hawaii 96734 (☎808-263-2777). Serves Kailua-Kona.

Ken's Towing, 55 Kukila St., Hilo, Hawaii 96720 (☎808-959-3361). Serves Hilo area.

HONOLULU COUNTY

Godspeed Towing LLC, 98-867 D Kaonohi St., Aiea, Oahu 96701 (☎808-690-0351 or 808-216-8355; www.godspeedtowing.com). Serves much of Oahu.

Kuni's Automotive & Towing, 41-515 Poalima St., Waimanalo, Oahu 96795 (☎808-259-6699). Serves Upcountry Oahu.

Rudy's Towing, 45-381 Kaneohe Bay Dr., Kaneohe, Oahu 96744 (☎808-235-7761).

ESSENTIALS

KAUAI COUNTY

C Lee's Towing Service, 4320 Nawiliwili Rd., Lihue, Kauai 96766 (☎808-822-9133).

DK Towing, 4668 Hauaala Rd., Kapaa, Kauai 96746 (☎808-821-0200).

MAUI COUNTY

Campos Auto Body & Towing, 1191 Lower Main St., Wailuku, Maui (☎808-242-5831)..

Doctor Jim's Auto Repair, 3411 Haleakala Hwy., Makawao, Maui (☎808-572-6661).

Wreckx & Co Towing, 561 Kaiola St., Kihei, Maui (☎808-874-1920). Serves Kihei.

BY BOAT

Travel by boat between the Hawaiian islands has been a point of much controversy. The **Hawaii Superferry,** a luxurious 450ft. ferry, thought to be the largest aluminum ship ever built in the United States, was planned to be the first ferry to carry cars (up to 286), trucks, and 866 passengers between Honolulu, Oahu; Kahului, Maui; and Lihue, Kauai. The ferry has faced much opposition from both environmentalists concerned about the effect it will have on Hawaii's natural flora and fauna and from Hawaiian locals concerned about the loss of their traditional lifestyle. In Dec. 2007, the boat first began operating between Oahu and Maui; time will tell whether Kauai will follow suit. **Private companies** also operate ferries with routes between Maui and Lanai and Maui and Molokai.

Hawaii Superferry (☎877-443-3779; www.hawaiisuperferry.com). Daily service between Maui and Oahu; 2 routes run M, W, F, Su.

Discover Molokai (☎866-307-6524; www.molokaiferry.com). Daily service aboard the *Molokai Princess* and the *Maui Princess* between Lahaina Harbor on Maui and Kaunakakai Harbor on Molokai.

Expeditions Maui-Lanai Ferry (☎800-695-2624 or 808-661-3756; www.go-lanai. com). Multiple daily routes between Lanai and Lahaina and Maalaea Harbors.

BY MOPED

Mopeds are a popular mode of transport in parts of Hawaii, especially Waikiki and Honolulu. A full-day rental costs $24 to $30 and a week costs about $130.

A&B Moped, 3481 Lower Honoapiilani Hwy., Wailuku, Maui 96793. (☎808-669-0027).

Discount Moped Rentals, 1958 Kalakaua Ave., Honolulu, Oahu 96815. (☎808-941-3623).

Rent-Scootah, 74-5563 Kaiwi St., Kailua-Kona, Hawaii 96740. (☎808-329-3250).

BY THUMB

 LET'S NOT GO. *Let's Go* never recommends hitchhiking as a safe means of transportation, and none of this information is intended to encourage it.

Let's Go strongly urges you to consider the risks before you choose to hitchhike. Hitching means entrusting your life to a stranger and risking assault, sexual harassment, theft, and unsafe driving. For women traveling alone (or even in pairs), hitching is just too dangerous. Hitchhiking on the Hawaiian islands is illegal. Though it is common place and people regularly use this practice to get around, you can still be arrested for thumbing a ride along any road.

KEEPING IN TOUCH

BY EMAIL AND INTERNET

With plenty of Wi-Fi hot spots, connections in accommodations, and public library computers, it shouldn't be too difficult for the typical traveler to stay connected in Hawaii. **Internet cafes** and the occasional free Internet terminal at public libraries or universities are listed in the **Practical Information** sections of major cities. Increasingly, travelers find that taking their laptops on the road with them can be a convenient option for staying connected. Travelers with wireless-enabled computers can take advantage of an increasing number of Internet cafes and accommodations where they can get online for free or for a small fee in Hawaii. Websites like www.jiwire.com and www.wififreespot.com can help you find hotspots. For info on insuring your laptop, see p. 47.

WARY WI-FI. Wireless hot spots make Internet access possible in public and remote places. Unfortunately, they also pose **security risks.** Hot spots are public, open networks that use unencrypted, unsecured connections. They are susceptible to hacks and "packet sniffing"—ways of stealing passwords and other private information. To prevent problems, disable ad hoc mode, turn off file sharing and network discovery, encrypt your email, turn on your firewall, beware of phony networks, and watch for over-the-shoulder creeps.

BY TELEPHONE

CALLING HOME FROM HAWAII

Prepaid phone cards are a common and relatively inexpensive means of calling abroad. Each one comes with a Personal Identification Number (PIN) and a toll-free access number. To purchase prepaid phone cards, check online for the best rates; www.callingcards.com is a good place to start. Online providers generally send your access number and PIN via email. You can call home with prepaid phone cards purchased in Hawaii (see **Calling Within Hawaii,** below).

PLACING INTERNATIONAL CALLS. Dial:
1. The **international dialing prefix.** To call from Australia, dial 0011; Canada or the US, 011; Ireland, New Zealand, or the UK, 00.
2. The **country code** of the country you want to call. To call Australia, dial 61; Canada or the US, 1; Ireland, 353; New Zealand, 64; the UK, 44.
3. The **city/area code.** The city/area code for all of Hawaii is 808. When calling internationally, if the 1st digit is a zero (e.g., 020 for London), omit the zero when calling from abroad.
4. The **local number.**

Another option is to purchase a **calling card,** linked to a major national telecommunications service in your home country. Calls are billed collect or to your account. To call home with a calling card, contact the operator for your service provider in Hawaii by dialing the appropriate toll-free access number.

COMPANY	TO OBTAIN A CARD:	TO CALL ABROAD:
AT&T (US)	☎800-364-9292 or www.att.com	☎800-225-5288
Canada Direct	☎800-561-8868 or www.info-canadadirect.com	☎800-555-1111 or 800-646-0000
MCI (US)	☎800-777-5000 or www.minutepass.com	☎800-888-8000
Telecom New Zealand Direct	www.telecom.co.nz	☎800-248-0064, 800-659-0064, or 800-666-5494
Telstra Australia	☎+61 800 676 638 or www.telstra.com	☎888-464-0299

Placing a collect call through an international operator can be expensive, but may be necessary in case of an emergency. You can frequently call collect without even possessing a company's calling card just by calling its access number and following the instructions.

CALLING WITHIN HAWAII

The simplest way to call within the country is to use a coin-operated phone. Prepaid phone cards (available at convenience stores and newspaper kiosks), usually save time and money in the long run. Phone rates tend to be highest in the morning, lower in the evening, and lowest on Sunday and late at night.

CELLULAR PHONES

The international standard for cell phones is **Global System for Mobile Communication (GSM).** To make and receive calls in Hawaii you will need a GSM-compatible phone and a **SIM (Subscriber Identity Module) card,** a country-specific, thumbnail-sized chip that gives you a local phone number and plugs you into the network. Many SIM cards are prepaid, and incoming calls are frequently free. You can buy additional cards or vouchers (usually available at convenience stores) to "top up" your phone. For more information on GSM phones, check out www.telestial.com, www.orange.co.uk, www.roadpost.com, or www.planetomni.com. Companies like **Cellular Abroad** (www.cellularabroad.com) rent cell phones that work in a variety of destinations around the world.

 GSM PHONES. Just having a GSM phone doesn't mean you're necessarily good to go when you travel abroad. The majority of GSM phones sold in the United States operate on a different frequency (1900) than international phones (900/1800) and will not work abroad. Tri-band phones work on all three frequencies (900/1800/1900) and will operate through most of the world. Additionally, some GSM phones are SIM-locked and will only accept SIM cards from a single carrier. You'll need a SIM-unlocked phone to use a SIM card from a local carrier when you travel.

TIME DIFFERENCES

Hawaii has its own time zone—**Hawaii Standard Time (HST).** HST is 10hr. behind Greenwich Mean Time (GMT). It is 5hr. behind New York and Boston (6hr. behind during daylight saving time), 2hr. behind Vancouver and San Francisco, 3hr. ahead of Sydney, and 2hr. ahead of Auckland (NZ). Hawaii does not observe

Daylight Saving Time. The chart below gives the time in various cities around the world when it is midnight in Honolulu during the Daylight Saving months (second Sunday in March through the first Sunday in November).

MIDNIGHT	3AM	6AM	11AM	6PM	8PM
Honolulu	Vancouver Seattle San Francisco Los Angeles	Toronto Ottawa New York Boston	London (GMT)	China Hong Kong Manila Singapore	Sydney Canberra Melbourne

BY MAIL

SENDING MAIL HOME FROM HAWAII

Airmail is the best way to send mail home from Hawaii. Surface mail is by far the cheapest and slowest way to send mail. It takes one to two months to cross the Atlantic and one to three to cross the Pacific—good for heavy items you won't need for a while. These are standard rates for mail from Hawaii to:

Australia and New Zealand: Allow 4-7 days for regular airmail home. Letters up to 1 oz. cost $0.94; packages up to 0.5 lb. $7, up to 2 lb. $16.90.

Ireland: Allow 4-7 days for regular airmail home. Letters up to 1 oz. cost $0.94; packages up to 0.5 lb. $7, up to 2 lb. $16.90.

UK: Allow 4-7 days for regular airmail home. Letters up to 1 oz. cost $0.94; packages up to 0.5 lb. $7, up to 2 lb. $16.90.

Mainland: From overnight to 12 days. Letters: $0.42, packages up to 0.5 lb. $2.23-19.50, up to 2 lb. $2.58-25.65

SENDING MAIL TO HAWAII

Mail can be sent via General Delivery to almost any place in Hawaii with a post office. Address General Delivery letters like so:

Ivana Reeseeve Mail

General Delivery

City, HI zipcode, USA

The mail will go to a special desk in the central post office, unless you specify a post office by street address or postal code. It's best to use the largest post office, since mail may be sent there regardless. It is usually safer and quicker, though more expensive, to send mail express. Bring your passport (or other photo ID) for pickup; there may be a fee. If the clerks insist that there is nothing for you, have them check under your first name as well. *Let's Go: Hawaii* lists post offices in the **Practical Information** section for each city and most towns.

ACCOMMODATIONS

HOSTELS

Many hostels are laid out dorm-style, often with large single-sex rooms and bunk beds, although private rooms that sleep two to four are becoming more common. They sometimes have kitchens and utensils for your use, bike or moped rentals, storage areas, transportation to airports, breakfast and other meals, laundry facilities, and Internet. However, there can be drawbacks: some hostels close during certain daytime "lockout" hours, have a curfew, don't accept reservations, impose a maximum stay, or, less frequently, require that you do chores. In Hawaii, a dorm bed in a hostel will average around $20 and a private room around $35-50.

A HOSTELER'S BILL OF RIGHTS. There are certain standard features that we do not include in our hostel listings. Unless we state otherwise, you can expect that every hostel has no lockout, no curfew, free hot showers, some system of secure luggage storage, and no key deposit.

Joining the youth hostel association in your own country (listed below) automatically grants you membership privileges in **Hostelling International (HI)**, a federation of national hosteling associations. Non-HI members may be allowed to stay in some hostels, but will have to pay extra to do so. There are two HI hostels in Hawaii—one in Honolulu and one in Waikiki—both of which are popular, respectable, and tend to be cheaper than other hosteling options.

Australian Youth Hostels Association (AYHA), 422 Kent St., Sydney NSW 2000 (☎+61 2 9261 1111; www.yha.com.au). AUS$52, under 18 AUS$19.

Hostelling International-Canada (HI-C), 205 Catherine St., Ste. 400, Ottawa, ON K2P 1C3 (☎613-237-7884; www.hihostels.ca). CDN$35, under 18 free.

Youth Hostels Association of New Zealand Inc. (YHANZ), Level 1, 166 Moorhouse Ave., P.O. Box 436, Christchurch (☎+64 3 379 9970, in NZ 0800 278 299; www.yha. org.nz). NZ$40, under 18 free.

Youth Hostels Association (England and Wales), Trevelyan House, Dimple Rd., Derbyshire DE4 3YH (☎+44 8707 708 868; www.yha.org.uk). UK£16, under 26 UK£10.

Hostelling International-USA, 8401 Colesville Rd., Ste. 600, Silver Spring, MD 20910 (☎301-495-1240; www.hiayh.org). $28, under 18 free.

HOTELS

Several major hotel chains have multiple locations within Hawaii. **Outrigger** (☎800-688-7444; www.outrigger.com) trumps the competition with its sheer number of offerings. Between its upscale resorts and the more moderately priced sister chain **Ohana Hotels** (☎800-464-6262; www.ohanahotels.com), there are dozens of hotel options. Ohana offers myriad specials and packages, including discounts for seniors and military personnel. Call to inquire about promotions or see their website. **Hilton** (☎800-774-1500; www.hilton.com) has a resort on Oahu and one on the Big Island. **Sheraton** (☎888-625-5144; www.sheraton. com), which includes the **Westin** and **W** hotel chains, has locations on each of Hawaii's islands. Sheraton rates range from high to higher, depending on the island and location. **Best Western** (☎800-780-7234; www.bestwestern.com) and **Marriott** (☎888-236-2427; www.marriott.com) also maintain a number of locations throughout Hawaii. Hotel singles in Hawaii start around $65-90.

OTHER TYPES OF ACCOMMODATIONS

BED AND BREAKFASTS (B&BS)

For a cozy alternative to impersonal hotel rooms, B&Bs (private homes with rooms available to travelers) range from acceptable to sublime. In general,

B&Bs are a great and easy way to both experience the aloha spirit and to immerse yourself in island lifestyle. There are many B&Bs on Hawaii; rooms in B&Bs generally run anywhere between $50-150. Any number of websites provide listings for B&Bs; check out **Bed & Breakfast Inns Online** (www.bbonline. com), **InnFinder** (www.inncrawler.com), **InnSite** (www.innsite.com), **BedandBreakfast.com** (www.bedandbreakfast.com), or **BNBFinder.com** (www.bnbfinder.com). For Hawaii-specific B&B sites, check out **Hawaii's Best Bed & Breakfasts** (www. bestbnb.com), **Hawaii Island B&B Association** (www.stayhawaii.com), and **Bed and Breakfast Hawaii** (www.bandb-hawaii.com).

YMCAS AND YWCAS

Young Men's Christian Association (YMCA) and **Young Women's Christian Association (YWCA)** lodgings are usually cheaper than a hotel but more expensive than a hostel. Not all locations offer lodging; those that do are often located in urban areas. Many YMCAs accept women and families; some will not lodge those under 18 without parental permission.

YMCA of the USA, 101 N. Wacker Dr., Chicago, IL 60606 (☎800-872-9622; www. ymca.net). Provides a listing of the nearly 1000 Ys across the US and Canada, as well as info on prices and services.

YWCA of the USA, 1015 18th St. NW, Ste. 1100, Washington, DC 20036 (☎202-467-0801; www.ywca.org). Provides a directory of YWCAs across the US.

YMCA Canada, 42 Charles St. E, 6th fl., Toronto, ON M4Y 1T4 (☎416-967-9622; www. ymca.ca). Offers info on Ys in Canada.

HOME EXCHANGES AND HOSPITALITY CLUBS

Home exchange offers the traveler various types of homes (houses, apartments, condominiums, villas), plus the opportunity to live like a native and to cut down on accommodation fees. For more information, contact **HomeExchange.com Inc.,** P.O. Box 787, Hermosa Beach, CA 90254 (☎310 798 3864 or toll-free 800-877-8723; www.homeexchange.com) or **Intervac International Home Exchange** (☎800-756-4663; www.intervac.com).

Hospitality clubs link their members with individuals or families abroad who are willing to host travelers for free or for a small fee to promote cultural exchange and general good karma. In exchange, members usually must be willing to host travelers in their own homes; a small fee may also be required. **The Hospitality Club** (www.hospitalityclub.org) is a good place to start.

LONG-TERM ACCOMMODATIONS

Travelers planning to stay in Hawaii for extended periods of time may find it most cost-effective to rent an apartment. A basic one-bedroom (or studio) apartment in Honolulu will range $600-1100 per month. Besides the rent itself, prospective tenants sometimes are also required to front a security deposit (frequently one month's rent) and the last month's rent. Check with hostels, YMCAs, and condos for other long-term accommodation options. Look in the classifieds section of the *Honolulu Advisor* and other newspapers for options or check out websites like **Craigslist** (www.craigslist.org), **Sublet.com** (http:// hawaii.sublet.com), and **Subleaser** (www.subleaser.com/states/hawaii_sublet).

CAMPING

Why stay near the beach when you can stay on the beach? Camping is an economical and fun way to tour Hawaii, with most campsites charging around $5 for a permit. For all you need to know, see **Great Outdoors** (p. 78).

SPECIFIC CONCERNS

SUSTAINABLE TRAVEL

As the number of travelers on the road rises, the detrimental effect they can have on natural environments is an increasing concern. *Let's Go* promotes the philosophy of sustainable travel with this in mind. Through a sensitivity to issues of ecology and sustainability, today's travelers can be a powerful force in preserving and restoring the places they visit.

Ecotourism, a rising trend in sustainable travel, focuses on the conservation of natural habitats—mainly, on how to use them to build up the economy without exploitation or overdevelopment. Travelers can make a difference by doing advance research, by supporting organizations and establishments that pay attention to their carbon "footprint," and by patronizing establishments that strive to be environmentally friendly. For more local information about businesses that subscribe to and promote ecotourism see **www.hawaiiecotourism. org, www.alternative-hawaii.com,** and **www.earthfoot.org/us_hw.htm.** To get involved in ecotourism check out the section in our **Beyond Tourism** chapter (p. 67).

ECOTOURISM RESOURCES. For more information on environmentally responsible tourism, contact one of the organizations below:

Conservation International, 2011 Crystal Dr., Ste. 500, Arlington, VA 22202 (☎800-406-2306 or 703-341-2400; www.conservation.org).

Green Globe 21, Green Globe of, Verbenalaan 1, 2111 ZL Aerdenhout, the Netherlands (☎+31 23 544 0306; www.greenglobe.com).

International Ecotourism Society, 1333 H St. NW, Ste. 300E, Washington, DC 20005 (☎202-347-9203; www.ecotourism.org).

United Nations Environment Program (UNEP), 39-43 Quai André Citroën, 75739 Paris Cedex 15, France (☎+33 1 44 37 14 50; www.uneptie.org).

RESPONSIBLE TRAVEL

Your tourist dollars can make a big impact on your destinations. The choices you make during your trip can have powerful effects on local communities—for better or for worse. Travelers who care about the destinations and environments they explore should make themselves aware of the social, cultural, and political implications of their choices. Simple decisions such as buying local products, paying fair prices for products or services, and attempting to say a few words in the local language can have a strong, positive effect.

Hawaii has been a center of tourism for nearly a century, but that does not mean travelers should assume that they are always welcome. Although the aloha spirit is alive and well in Hawaii, some locals can resent tourists for the effect tourism has had on their native land. It is always important to show respect to everyone you encounter on your journeys through the islands; courtesy is paramount in Hawaiian culture. Hawaii's unique ecosystem is often affected by tourism as well, both positively and negatively. To learn more see **The Great Outdoors** (p. 78). If you are interested in learning more about opportunities to help preserve all things Hawaii, check out **Beyond Tourism** (p. 67).

TRAVELING ALONE

Traveling alone can be extremely beneficial, providing a sense of independence and a greater opportunity to connect with locals. On the other hand, solo travelers are more vulnerable targets of harassment and theft. If you are traveling alone, look confident, try not to stand out as a tourist, and be especially careful in deserted or very crowded areas. Stay away from areas that are not well lit. If questioned, never admit that you are traveling alone. Maintain regular contact with someone at home who knows your itinerary, and always research your destination before traveling. For more tips, pick up *Traveling Solo* by Eleanor Berman (Globe Pequot Press; $18), visit www.travelaloneandloveit.com, or subscribe to **Connecting: Solo Travel Network,** 689 Park Rd., Unit 6, Gibsons, BC V0N 1V7, Canada (☎604-886-9099; www.cstn.org; memberships $30-48).

WOMEN TRAVELERS

Women exploring on their own inevitably face some additional safety concerns. Single women can consider staying in hostels which offer single rooms that lock from the inside or in religious organizations with single-sex rooms. Always carry cash for a phone call, bus, or taxi. **Hitchhiking** is never safe for lone women. Look as if you know where you're going and approach older women or couples for directions if you're lost. Dress conservatively, especially in rural areas. Wearing a conspicuous **wedding band** sometimes helps to prevent unwanted advances. Your best answer to verbal harassment is no answer at all; feigning deafness, sitting motionless, and staring straight ahead at nothing in particular will usually do the trick. Memorize the emergency numbers in places you visit, and consider carrying a whistle on your keychain. A self-defense course will both prepare you for a potential attack and raise your level of awareness of your surroundings (see **Personal Safety,** p. 46).

GLBT TRAVELERS

Hawaii is one of the most progressive states when it comes to gay, lesbian, bisexual, and transgendered (GLBT) travelers, though more so in cities than in rural areas. Listed below are contact organizations and publishers that offer materials addressing some specific concerns. **Out and About** (www.planetout.com) offers a weekly newsletter addressing travel concerns and a comprehensive site addressing gay travel concerns. The online newspaper **365gay.com** also has a travel section (www.365gay.com/travel/travelchannel.htm).

> **Gay's the Word,** 66 Marchmont St., London WC1N 1AB, UK (☎+44 20 7278 7654; http://freespace.virgin.net/gays.theword). The largest gay and lesbian bookshop in the UK, with both fiction and non-fiction titles. Mail-order service available.
>
> **Giovanni's Room,** 345 S. 12th St., Philadelphia, PA 19107 (☎215-923-2960; www.queerbooks.com). An international lesbian and gay bookstore with mail-order service (carries many of the publications listed below).

ADDITIONAL RESOURCES: GLBT

Spartacus 2008: International Gay Guide. Bruno Gmunder Verlag ($33).

Damron Men's Travel Guide and *Damron Women's Traveller.* Damron Travel Guides ($18-24). Call ☎800-462-6654 or visit www.damron.com.

The Gay Vacation Guide: The Best Trips and How to Plan Them, by Mark Chesnut. Kensington Books ($15).

Gayellow Pages USA/Canada, by Frances Green. Gayellow Pages ($20). Publishes regional guides. Visit online at http://gayellowpages.com.

TRAVELERS WITH DISABILITIES

In large Hawaiian cities, most hotels and restaurants are wheelchair-accessible, though this may not be the case in smaller towns or rural areas. Wheelchair-accessible vans are available to rent in most places, as are wheelchairs. Call ahead to restaurants, museums, and facilities to find out if they are wheelchair-accessible. **Guide-dog owners** should inquire as to quarantine policies.

If you are planning to visit a national park or attraction in the US run by the **National Park Service** (☎888-467-2757; www.nps.gov), obtain a free **America the Beautiful Access Pass,** which is available at park entrances. The pass entitles disabled travelers and their families to free park admission and provides a lifetime 50% discount on all campsite and parking fees. For information on transportation availability in individual US cities, contact the local chapter of the **Easter Seal Society** (☎800-221-6827; www.easter-seals.org).

Accessible Journeys, 35 W. Sellers Ave., Ridley Park, PA 19078 (☎800-846-4537; www.disabilitytravel.com). Designs tours for wheelchair users and slow walkers. The site has tips and forums for all travelers.

The Guided Tour, Inc., 7900 Old York Rd., Ste. 114B, Elkins Park, PA 19027 (☎800-783-5841; www.guidedtour.com). Organizes travel programs for persons with developmental and physical challenges in Hawaii.

MINORITY TRAVELERS

Hawaii is a diverse place where no ethnic group stands out as an obvious minority. Caucasians may be uncomfortable with being called a *haole* (foreigner), but in general, if you treat the island and its inhabitants with respect, the same respect will be afforded to you. While there are relatively few people of African descent in Hawaii, racial prejudice against blacks is extremely rare.

DIETARY CONCERNS

With tons of fresh produce and widespread eco-friendly attitudes, Hawaii is a relatively easy place to find vegetarian options. Additionally, many restaurants are Asian or Asian-inspired and use noodles, rice, and vegetables. Just be sure to ask at each restaurant you visit. Visit the **Vegetarian Society of Hawaii** website (www.vsh.org) for more information on going veggie in Hawaii.

Travelers who keep kosher should contact synagogues in larger cities for information on kosher restaurants. In Hawaii, kosher restaurants and markets are limited outside of Honolulu. A good resource is the *Jewish Travel Guide,* ed. Michael Zaidner (Vallentine Mitchell; $18).

ESSENTIALS

OTHER RESOURCES

Let's Go tries to cover all aspects of budget travel, but we can't put everything in our guides. Listed below are books and websites that can serve as jumping-off points for your own research.

USEFUL PUBLICATIONS

Aloha from Hawaii (☎808-538-0330; www.aloha-hawaii.com).

Hawaii Magazine (☎808-534-1515; www.hawaiimagazine.com). Monthly magazine with features on restaurants, events, and community happenings.

Honolulu Magazine (☎808-537-9500; www.honolulumagazine.com). Articles on community figures and events.

WORLD WIDE WEB

Almost every aspect of budget travel is accessible via the web. In 10min. at the keyboard, you can make a hostel reservation, get advice on hot spots from other travelers, or find out how much a plane from Honolulu to Lihue costs.

LET'S GO ONLINE. Plan your next trip on our newly redesigned website, **www.letsgo.com.** It features the latest travel info on your favorite destinations, as well as tons of interactive features: make your own itinerary, read blogs from our trusty researcher-writers, browse our photo library, watch exclusive videos, check out our newsletter, find travel deals, and buy new guides. We're always updating and adding new features, so check back often!

THE ART OF TRAVEL

Backpacker's Ultimate Guide: www.bugeurope.com. Tips on packing, transportation, and where to go. Also tons of country-specific travel information.

How to See the World: www.artoftravel.com. A compendium of great travel tips, from cheap flights to self defense to interacting with local culture.

Travel Intelligence: www.travelintelligence.net. A large collection of travel writing by distinguished travel writers.

INFORMATION ON HAWAII

Alternative-Hawaii: www.alternative-hawaii.com. "Your guide to the path less traveled." Self-described ecotourism site with links to Hawaii's special places.

Best Places Hawaii: www.bestplaceshawaii.com. An online travel planner with a virtual island tour and information on attractions.

DaKine: www.dakine.net. The local's guide to Hawaii. Reviews of Oahu plate lunch and shave ice establishments. Local humor!

PlanetRider: www.planetrider.com. A subjective list of links to the "best" websites covering the culture and tourist attractions of Hawaii.

BEYOND TOURISM

A PHILOSOPHY FOR TRAVELERS

HIGHLIGHTS OF BEYOND TOURISM IN HAWAII

DISH UP MEALS at the **Honolulu Food Bank** (p. 70).

GUIDE TOURISTS on trails through **Volcanoes National Park** (p. 69).

SWIM WITH and research spinner dolphins off the coast of Oahu (p. 69).

ENCOUNTER true Hawaiian life by au pairing for a local family (p. 75).

FLIP TO our **"Giving Back"** sidebar features for even more regional Beyond Tourism opportunities (p. 238, p. 256, and p. 140).

As a tourist, you are always a foreigner. Sure, hostel-hopping and sightseeing can be great fun, but connecting with a foreign country through studying, volunteering, or working can extend your travels beyond tourist traps. At *Let's Go*, our goal is provide some suggestions which can serve as the springboards for such experiences. Instead of being that tourist asking for directions, you can be the one who gives them (and correctly!). Though understanding Hawaii like a local is likely out of reach, intimately interacting with the islands can lead to a much more personal, and meaningful, trip. All the while, you get the satisfaction of leaving Hawaii in better shape than you found it. (After all, it's being nice enough to let you stay.) It's not wishful thinking—it's Beyond Tourism.

From the sun-kissed sands of Waikiki to the awe-inspiring lava flows in Volcanoes National Park, Hawaii presents many unique opportunities for Beyond Tourism experiences. The tourism industry exploded during the past century; in 1927, there were about 17,000 people per year traveling to Hawaii, but by 2005, there were over 7.3 million. The dramatic rise in tourism created an interdependence among the economy, environment, and culture of Hawaii that is impossible to ignore. Since tourism has surpassed agriculture as the islands' preeminent economic force, it is important that travelers be aware and respectful of all that has made Hawaii the natural, remote destination it is today.

As a **volunteer** in Hawaii, you can unleash your inner superhero with projects as varied as saving native Hawaiian marine life from drift nets or helping preserve Hawaii's rich cultural heritage. This chapter is chock-full of ideas on how to get involved, whether you're looking to pitch in for a day or run away from home for a whole new life in Hawaiian activism.

The powers of **studying** abroad are beyond comprehension: it actually makes you feel sorry for those poor tourists who don't get to do any homework while they're here. Kilauea, the world's most active volcano, presents an unrivaled opportunity for intense study of all things geological; the University of Hawaii at Hilo is the only school in the country to offer a master's program in the study of indigenous languages; and the Pacific Island cultural studies and marine science programs are strong at the University of Hawaii at Manoa. Looking to do some research? Hawaii is an excellent arena for research in many areas, ranging from climate change, aquaculture, and species protection to genealogy, language development, and indigenous populations.

Working abroad immerses you in a new culture and can bring some of the most meaningful relationships and experiences of your life. Yes, we know you're on vacation, but these aren't your normal desk jobs. (Plus, it doesn't hurt that it helps pay for more globetrotting.) Many hostels will exchange room and board for short-term work cleaning or helping at the reception desk (p. 75). **Willing Workers on Organic Farms (WWOOF)** has a long list of organic farms on Hawaii that will give you the opportunity to help sustain the state's agriculture and earn some dough. Given its high turnover rate, the tourism industry, Hawaii's largest source of jobs, will likely be an available source of employment.

SHARE YOUR EXPERIENCE. Have you had a particularly enjoyable volunteer, study, or work experience that you'd like to share with other travelers? Post it to our website, www.letsgo.com!

VOLUNTEERING

Feel like saving the world this week? Volunteering can be a powerful and fulfilling experience, especially when combined with the thrill of traveling in a new place. Naturally, many volunteer programs focus on conserving the beauty of Hawaii's biodiversity and environment. Other opportunities exist for preserving and representing Hawaiian culture and supporting community services. Everything from gardening to clerical skills can be applied in the wide variety of ways to live out the *ohana* (family) spirit through volunteerism.

Most people who volunteer in Hawaii do so on a short-term basis at organizations that make use of drop-in or once-a-week volunteers. The best way to find opportunities that match your interests and schedule may be to check with **www.volunteerhawaii.org** and **www.volunteerzone.org,** or give particular organizations of interest a phone call. It is probably a good idea to have a human voice confirm the opportunity, as online listings may occasionally be out of date. As always, read up before heading out.

Those looking for longer, more intensive volunteer opportunities usually choose to go through a parent organization that takes care of logistical details and often provides a group environment and support system—for a fee. There are two main types of organizations—religious and secular—although there are rarely restrictions on participation for either. Websites like **www.volunteerabroad.com, www.servenet.org,** and **www.idealist.org** allow you to search for volunteer openings both in your country and abroad.

I HAVE TO PAY TO VOLUNTEER? Many volunteers are surprised to learn that some organizations require large fees or "donations," but don't go calling them scams just yet. While such fees may seem ridiculous at first, they often keep the organization afloat, covering airfare, room, board, and administrative expenses for the volunteers. (Other organizations must rely on private donations and government subsidies.) If you're concerned about how a program spends its fees, request an annual report or finance account. A reputable organization won't refuse to inform you of how volunteer money is spent. Pay-to-volunteer programs might be a good idea for young travelers who are looking for more support and structure (such as pre-arranged transportation and housing) or anyone who would rather not deal with the uncertainty of creating a volunteer experience from scratch.

SAVE THE TREES

Like an artistic masterpiece, Hawaii's breathtaking trails and sparkling beaches evoke wonder and awe. Also like pieces of art, this beauty is maintained by behind-the-scenes work and constant upkeep. Visitors can partake in this important task while enjoying the outdoors in a whole new way. Opportunities such as planting trees and cleaning parks and beaches exist for all age groups. Conduct research in biodiversity and volcanic geology or deliver office and website support—all tasks, small or large, can help contribute to keeping the islands beautiful. By learning and working, visitors may come to appreciate Hawaii's natural surroundings even more, if such a thing is possible.

Hawaii Sierra Club, P.O. Box 2577, Honolulu, HI 96803 (☎808-538-6616; www. hi.sierraclub.org). Seeks to improve natural resource management, clean up pollution, and protect biodiversity in Hawaii. It offers a service-trip program involving fence building, trail work, and noxious plant control, mixed with recreational activities.

Hawaii Volcanoes Park, P.O. Box 52, Hawaii National Park, HI 96718 (☎808-985-6000; www.nps.gov/havo). Various volunteer positions; some provide meals and dorm-style housing. A listing of all the volunteer positions offered by the park service in Hawaii can be found at www.nps.gov/gettinginvolved/volunteer/opportunities.htm?state=HI.

Hawaii Youth Conservation Corps (YCC), 46-148 Kahuhipa St., Ste. 201, Kaneohe, HI 96744 (☎808-247-5753; www.hawaiiycc.com). Runs programs, from June to July, on the islands of Oahu, Maui, Molokai, Kauai, and the Big Island for high school sophomores through college sophomores. Learn first-hand about conservation through field work and service learning projects. Participants receive a stipend and 3 college credits at the end of the program, if eligible. Under the auspices of Pono Pacific.

Malama Hawaii, 923 Nuuanu Ave., Honolulu, HI 96817 (www.malamahawaii.org). A coalition of 70 environmental and community organizations. Website updated often.

USGS Hawaiian Volcano Observatory (HVO), US Dept. of the Interior, US Geological Survey, Menlo Park, CA 94025 (http://hvo.wr.usgs.gov/volunteer). Assigns each volunteer researcher a support group and HVO staff member. Opportunities include work in geochemistry, seismology, geology, geodesy, electronics, carpentry, and website or library support. If you can commit to 3 months of work, free lodging and transportation will be provided. Volunteers should have a background in the physical sciences.

SAVE THE ANIMALS

Hawaiians have long shared their paradise with other species, and visitors can help protect the animals and their habitats to continue to ensure their coexistence. Marine life is a definite focus as Hawaiian shores teem with dolphins, seals, fish, turtles, and whales.

EarthTrust Windward Environmental Center, 1118 Maunawili Rd., Kailua, HI 96734 (☎808-261-5339; www.earthtrust.org). Occasionally needs unpaid interns for 2 months or longer in its efforts to protect marine life from drift nets or to research dolphins. Office support especially needed.

Hawaiian Humane Society, 2700 Waialae Ave., Honolulu, HI 96826 (☎808-946-2187; www.hawaiianhumane.org). Houses less exotic animals with no less needs. Accepts volunteers year-round. Walk a dog by the seashore or take a pet to the hospital.

Pacific Whale Foundation, 300 Maalaea Rd., Ste. 211, Wailuku, HI 96793 (☎808-249-8811; www.pacificwhale.org). An organization on Maui dedicated to marine conservation. Promotes appreciation of marine life such as the archipelago's humpback whales, Lanai's wild dolphins, and threatened coral reefs. Offers education and event positions.

Wild Dolphin Foundation, 87-1286 Farrington Hwy., Waianae, HI 96792 (☎808-306-3968; http://wilddolphin.org). Offers visitors the opportunity to work alongside marine biologists studying Oahu's spinner dolphins, whales, turtles, and coral reefs. There is no cost for the program, but it does not offer food, housing, or transportation.

COMMUNITY OUTREACH

More "traditional" service opportunities exist for those who want to support the community through administration, construction, and sorting foodstuffs.

Catholic Charities Hawaii, 200 N. Vineyard St., Ste. 200, Honolulu, HI 96817 (☎808-536-1794; www.catholiccharitieshawaii.org). Provides a range of social services.

Goodwill Industries of Hawaii, 2610 Kilihau St., Honolulu, HI 96819 (☎808-836-0313; www.higoodwill.org). Goodwill expects a minimum commitment of a month, 16hr. per week of retail store support; revenue goes to helping people with disabilities or other employment barriers find jobs. Volunteers can also help with donation drives.

Hawaii Food Bank, 2611 Kilihau St., Honolulu, HI 96819 (☎808-836-3600; www.hawaiifoodbank.org). Volunteers are needed year-round for data entry and inspecting, cleaning, and sorting food, especially for the annual food drive in Apr.

Honolulu Habitat for Humanity, 1136 Union Mall, Ste. 510, Honolulu, HI 96701 (☎808-538-7070; www.habitat.org). A non-denominational, non-profit group that builds affordable housing. There are affiliates on all of the other major islands as well.

ADVOCACY AND NATIVE HAWAIIAN RIGHTS

While legal or policy backgrounds are helpful, volunteers without experience can also participate in addressing issues affecting indigenous Hawaiians.

Council for Native Hawaiian Advancement, 1050 Queen St., Ste. 200 Honolulu, HI 96814 (☎808-596-8155; www.hawaiiancouncil.org). Offers internships in training and resource building, policy advocacy, and event services. Its mission is to serve Native Hawaiians in policy, economic, and community development.

Volunteer Legal Services Hawaii, 100 Honuakaha Bldg., 545 Queen St., Honolulu, HI 96813 (☎808-839-5200; www.vlsh.org). Invites attorneys, law students, and others to volunteer and help tackle the unmet legal needs of Hawaii's less fortunate residents.

CULTURAL PRESERVATION AND THE ARTS

Hawaii's rich cultural heritage is relayed to visitors and new generations alike through its museums, galleries, and cultural centers. Volunteers can work up front as docents and gallery greeters; those who prefer to remain behind the scenes can participate in always-needed office support.

East Hawaii Cultural Center, 141 Kalakaua St., Hilo, HI 96720 (☎808-961-5711; www.ehcc.org). Hosts art shows, concerts, and other cultural events, may need gallery sitters at one of its 3 public galleries.

Hawaii Theatre, 1130 N. Bethel St., Honolulu, HI 96813 (☎808-791-1314; www.hawaiitheatre.com). A historic landmark that looks for docents, backstage hands, gift shop attendants, and office help.

Hui Noeau Visual Arts Center, 2841 Baldwin Ave., Makawao, Maui, HI 96768 (☎808-572-6560; fax 808-572-2750; www.huinoeau.com). Hui Noeau also sponsors visiting artists, offers classes, and leads painting, photography, printmaking, jewelry, woodworking, and ceramics workshops for all ages, and offers volunteer positions. Volunteer information can be attained by e-mailing info@huinoeau.com.

Iolani Palace, P.O. Box 2259, Honolulu, HI 96804 (☎808-522-0821; www.iolanipalace. org). Relies on volunteers to work in the gift shop, lead tours, and greet guests.

Japanese Cultural Center, 2454 South Beretania St., Honolulu, HI 96826 (☎808-945-7633; jcch.com/volunteers.asp). Seeks to educate the public about the Japanese-American experience in Hawaii. Many options from archival work and oral history transcription to gallery help and office work.

FOR THE UNDECIDED ALTRUIST

Indecisive volunteers-to-be can be overwhelmed or excited by islands-wide databases that compile opportunities under an umbrella site. These sites offer search fields and multiple points of contact to help you get your feet wet.

Aloha United Way, 200 N. Vineyard Blvd., Ste. 700, Honolulu, HI 96817 (☎808-536-1951; www.auw.org). Umbrella organization for a variety of community-oriented programs.

Volunteer Hawaii (☎808-539-1951, ask for the Volunteer Hawaii administrator; www. volunteerhawaii.org/index.php). Maintains a listing of over 200 volunteer opportunities on the islands. Listings range from being an acupuncture assistant to helping with child literacy. Many organizations have low hourly commitments, but expect to spend 6 months to a year on a project.

Volunteer Zone, 2021 Pauoa Rd., Honolulu, HI 96813 (☎808-524-9343; www.volunteerzone.org). Founded to facilitate volunteering in Hawaii. Provides a free, searchable catalogue of volunteer opportunities on the islands in a variety of fields.

STUDYING

VISA INFORMATION. Foreign students who wish to study in the US must apply for either an **F-1 visa** (for full-time students enrolled in an academic or language program) or **M-1 visa** (vocational studies). Visas may be obtained at the US Embassy or Consulate in your country. Visit the Destination USA study abroad website (http://www.unitedstatesvisas.gov/studying. html) for current infromation on the process and a list of embassies and consulates. If English is not your native language, you will probably be required to take the Test of English as a Foreign Language (TOEFL) as part of the admission process. Contact TOEFL/TSE Publications, P.O. Box 6151, Princeton, NJ 08541 (☎609-771-7100; www.toefl.org).

It's hard to dread the first day of school when Hawaii is your campus and exotic restaurants are your meal plan. A growing number of students report that studying abroad is the highlight of their learning careers. If you've never studied abroad, you don't know what you're missing—and if you have studied abroad, you do know what you're missing. Either way, it's an awesome experience not to be missed.

Study-abroad programs range from basic language and culture courses to university-level classes, often for college credit. In order to choose a program that best fits your needs, research as much as you can before making your decision—determine costs and duration, as well as what kind of students participate in the program and what sorts of accommodations are provided. Back-to-school shopping was never this much fun.

UNIVERSITIES

Most university-level study-abroad programs are conducted in English. You can search **www.studyabroad.com** for various semester programs that meet your criteria, including your desired location and focus of study. If you're a college student, your friendly campus study-abroad office is often the best place to start.

The **University of Hawaii** (www.hawaii.edu) is composed of 10 independent university and community college campuses and five education centers throughout the islands. Students wishing to study in Hawaii may find it cheaper to enroll directly in one of the two major universities on Oahu and the Big Island (listed below), but check about obtaining college credit. While Honolulu is certainly the largest college town, you may find that the most rewarding study-abroad experiences in Hawaii occur in an off-campus research setting. Dining halls and college bars look less appealing when compared to beaches, coral reefs, rainforests, and volcanoes.

Hawaii Pacific University, 1164 Bishop St., Honolulu, HI 96813 (☎808-544-0200; www.hpu.edu). Offers 12 different masters programs, as well as hundreds of courses over the summer for anyone wishing to take a few classes.

Maui Community College, 310 Kaahumanu Ave., Kahului, HI 96732 (☎808-984-3500; http://maui.hawaii.edu). Has 2-year vocational and liberal arts degrees and 4-year programs. The Culinary Arts program and Maui Language Institute are particularly notable.

Sea Education Association (SEA), P.O. Box 6, Woods Hole, MA 02543 (☎800-552-3633; www.sea.edu). Students undertake coursework in oceanography, nautical science, and maritime literature and history, followed by a practical component of hands-on marine science and blue-water sailing in the Pacific Ocean. Students are full participants in the operation and navigation of a 134' brigantine with a scientific mission and ongoing student research projects. All programming is accredited and available for any major.

Study Abroad Hawaii, 25 New South St., #102, Northampton, MA 01060 (☎413-584-7639; www.studyabroadhawaii.com). An all-inclusive cultural and educational program takes place at various satellites of Hawaii Pacific University and includes excursions, tours, and luaus. Perhaps a bit gimmicky, Study Abroad Hawaii is still a good option for those looking for an introduction to Hawaii.

University of Hawaii at Manoa, 2500 Campus Rd., Honolulu, HI 96822 (☎808-956-8111; http://manoa.hawaii.edu). A research institution with close to 20,000 students has strengths in tropical agriculture, tropical medicine, oceanography, and Hawaiian, Pacific Island, and Asian studies and languages. Over 1000 graduate and undergraduate classes are offered over the summer. Airfare discounts are available. A program for high school students to earn college credit is also offered.

University of Hawaii at Hilo, 200 W. Kawili St., Hilo, HI 96720 (☎808-974-7414 or 800-897-4456; http://hilo.hawaii.edu). Specializes in the study of indigenous languages, volcanoes, astronomy, and marine science, and offers undergraduate liberal arts, professional, and graduate degrees. A summer session is also offered.

LANGUAGE SCHOOLS

Enrolling at a language school has two major perks: a slightly less rigorous course load and the ability to teach you exactly what those kids in Hilo are calling you under their breath. There can be great variety in language schools—independently run, affiliated with a larger university, local, international—but one thing is constant: they rarely offer college credit. Their programs are also good for younger high-school students who might not feel comfortable with older students in a university program. Due to the diverse nature of the islands, many excellent English language programs exist for Hawaii's residents and visitors. If you're looking for unique experience, try a Hawaiian language class. Some worthwhile organizations include:

Academia Language School, 1600 Kapiolani Blvd., Ste. 1215, Honolulu 96814 (☎808-946-5599; www.academiaschool.com). Offers English and TOEFL, TOEIC, and CLEP classes starting every week and ongoing classes in French, Japanese, and Spanish.

Culture Nature Communication, Universal English Academy, 75-167 Kalani St., Kailua-Kona 96740 (☎808-936-2179). The program offers homestay accommodations, a motivational English class, and some of the best activities and locations available on Hawaii's Big Island. This is a unique, small-town, from-the-heart program focused on creating deep enjoyment for language learning and communication.

Hawaii English Language Program (HELP), 1395 Lower Campus Rd. MC 13-1, Honolulu 96822 (☎808-956-6636; www.hawaii.edu/eslhelp). Offers 4- or 8-week programs in English on the UH Manoa campus and full-time TOEFL and TOEIC prep classes.

Institute of Intensive English, 2155 Kalakaua Ave., Ste. 700, Honolulu 96815 (☎808-924-2117; www.studyenglishhawaii.com/index.html). Offers both intensive and short-term English programs, TOEFL and TOEIC prep courses, and other specifically geared programs like "Business English" or "Travel English."

Ka Haka 'Ula O Ke'elikōlani College of Hawaiian Language, 200 W. Kawili St., Hilo 96720 (☎808-974-7339; http://www.olelo.hawaii.edu/khuok). The Hale Kuamo'o is the Hawaiian Language Center within Ka Haka 'Ula O Ke'elikolani, College of Hawaiian Language of the University of Hawaii at Hilo. Established by the Hawaii State Legislature in 1989, the center supports and encourages the expansion of the Hawaiian language as a medium of communication in education, business, government, and other contexts of social life in the public and private sectors of Hawaii and beyond.

WORKING

Nowhere does money grow on trees (though *Let's Go* researchers aren't done looking), but there are still some pretty good opportunities to earn a living and travel at the same time. As with volunteering, work opportunities tend to fall into two categories. Some travelers want long-term jobs that allow them to integrate into a community, while others seek out short-term jobs to finance the next leg of their travels. In the major tourist areas of Hawaii, work is often available on the staffs of hotels and resorts, or at local restaurants. Another possibility is to check with the national car rental agencies, which may have jobs on their lots that need to be filled. **Transitions Abroad** (www.transitionsabroad.com) also offers updated online listings for work over any time span.

MORE VISA INFORMATION. A work permit (p. 38) is required for all foreigners planning to work in the US. Your employer must obtain this document, usually by demonstrating that you have skills that locals lack. It may be up to you, however, to apply for an **Employment Authorization Document** to prove that you may work in the US. Friends in the US can sometimes help expedite work permits or arrange work-for-stay exchanges. Obtaining a worker's visa may seem complex, but it's critical that you go through the proper channels. Visit the **Destination USA** website for temporary workers (http://www.unitedstatesvisas.gov/business_temp.html) for more information on the process for acquiring a work permit.

Consult the help wanted sections of local newspapers for more listings—*Honolulu Star Bulletin* and *Hawaii Tribune Herald* on Oahu, *The Garden Island* on Kauai, *The Maui News* on Maui, and *West Hawaii Today* on the Big Island are helpful sources. For links to Hawaii **job banks,** check out **www. employmentspot.com/state/hi.htm** and **http://hawaii.gov/portal/employment,** as well as the classified sections of the aforementioned publications. Note that working abroad often requires a special work visa.

LONG-TERM WORK

If you're planning on spending a substantial amount of time (more than 3 months) working in Hawaii, search for a job well in advance. International placement agencies are often the easiest way to find employment abroad, especially for those interested in teaching. Although they are often only available to college students, **internships** are a good way to ease into working abroad. Many say the interning experience is well worth it, despite low pay (if you're lucky enough to be paid at all). Be wary of advertisements for companies claiming to be able get you a job abroad for a fee—often the same listings are available online or in newspapers. Try websites like **JobsHawaii** (www.jobshawaii.com), **Hawaii Careers** (www.hawaiicareers.com), and **Intern Abroad** (www.internabroad. com) for ideas. Some reputable organizations include:

All About Visiting Earth (AAVE), 2308 Fossil Trace Dr., Golden, CO 80401 (☎800-222-3595; http://www.aave.com/jobs.php). This program runs trips for teenage kids through Hawaii and is always looking for leaders. The jobs are for a large part of the summer and involve outdoor activities, community service, and working with teenagers.

Council on International Educational Exchange (CIEE), 300 Fore St., Portland, ME 04101 (☎207-553-4000 or 800-40-STUDY/407-8839; www.ciee.org). They don't just assist in study abroad but in teaching abroad as well. Tucked into their study-abroad listings is a resource for international internships. In addition, an entire branch of the CIEE is devoted to finding work in the USA.

TEACHING

While some private American schools offer competitive salaries, let's just say that teaching jobs abroad pay more in personal satisfaction and emotional fulfillment than in actual cash. Perhaps this is why volunteering as a teacher instead of getting paid is a popular option. Even then, teachers often receive some sort of a daily stipend to help with living expenses. In almost all cases, you must have at least a bachelor's degree to be a full-fledged teacher, although college undergraduates can often get summer positions teaching or tutoring. Hawaii is the only state with a single, unified school system and therefore getting a job through a public school is straightforward. There is currently a high demand for special education, math, and science teachers in Hawaii.

International Schools Services (ISS), 15 Roszel Rd., P.O. Box 5910, Princeton, NJ 08543 (☎609-452-0990; www.iss.edu). Hires teachers for more than 200 overseas schools, including in Hawaii and the rest of the US. Candidates should have teaching experience and a bachelor's degree. 2-year commitment is the norm.

Teachers-Teachers (www.teachers-teachers.com/hawaii/index.cfm), works specifically with Hawaii's Department of Education. In order to work in Hawaii's public schools you must have a bachelor's degree and agree to acquire a Hawaii teaching license.

AU PAIR WORK

Au pairs are typically women (although sometimes men) aged 18-27 who work as live-in nannies, caring for children and doing light housework in foreign countries in exchange for room, board, and a small stipend. One perk of the job is that it allows you to get to know Hawaii without the high expenses of traveling. Drawbacks, however, can include mediocre pay and long hours. Weekly stipends and salaries vary greatly in Hawaii depending on the number of hours worked and kids watched, but usually settle around $200 per week. Much of the au pair experience depends on the family with which you are placed. The agencies below are a good starting point for looking for employment.

AuPair in America, 37 Queen's Gate, London SW7 5HR, UK (☎+44 20 7581 7322; www.aupairamerica.com/info_hawaii.htm).

InterExchange, 161 6th Ave., New York City, NY 10013 (☎212-924-0446 or 800-AU-PAIRS/287-2477; www.interexchange.org).

GreatAuPair, 1329 Hwy. 395 N., Ste. 10-333, Gardnerville, NV 89410 (☎775-215-5770; www.greataupair.com).

SHORT-TERM WORK

Believe it or not, traveling for long periods of time can be hard on the wallet. Many travelers try their hand at odd jobs for a few weeks at a time to help pay for another month or two of touring around. Short-term work in exchange for room and board can be found at organic farms, B&Bs, and hostels across Hawaii. A popular option is to work several hours a day at a hostel in exchange for free or discounted room and/or board. Most often, these short-term jobs are found by word of mouth or by expressing interest to the owner of a hostel or restaurant. Due to high turnover in the tourism industry, many places are eager for help, even if it is only temporary. This is especially prevalent in Hawaii as tourism is the largest industry—hunt around hotels and restaurants for odd jobs. *Let's Go: Hawaii* lists temporary jobs of this nature whenever possible; look in the Practical Information sections of larger cities or see below.

Evie's Natural Food, 79-7460 Mamalahoa Hwy. 11 (☎808-322-0739), in Mango Court south of Kainaliu on the Big Island. A bulletin board lists current short-term work possibilities provided by the nearby Kona coffee industry. There are often farm jobs available that trade room and board for labor.

Kalani Oceanside Retreat, RR2 Box 4500, Pahoa, HI 96778 (☎808-965-0468, volunteer coordinator ext. 117; www.kalani.com). This retreat center for wellness, culture, and nature offers several programs in which visitors can volunteer for 2 weeks to 3 months. Meals, room and board, and other benefits are included for a fee.

Willing Workers on Organic Farms (WWOOF), 4429 Carlson Rd., Nelson, BC, VIL 6X3, Canada (☎250-354-4417; www.wwoofhawaii.org). Matches visitors with host farms. Program applicants are required to fill out a short form and pay a small fee ($20). They then receive a booklet of all the available hosts in their desired destination; travelers are expected to contact farms and arrange a situation with the host. Most volunteers stay at the farms for 1-3 weeks. There are WWOOF farms on 5 of Hawaii's islands: the Big Island, Kauai, Maui, Molokai, and Oahu.

HOSTELS

The following hostels offer the possibility of trading room and board for part-time work around the establishment in maintenance and housekeeping.

Backpackers, 59-788 Kamehameha Hwy., Waimea, HI 96731 (☎808-638-7838; http://backpackers-hawaii.com). Short-term work in exchange for room and board.

Banana Bungalow, 310 N. Market St., Wailuku, HI 96793 (☎800-846-7835; www.mauihostel.com). Call about the availability of short-term work.

Hostelling International Honolulu, 2323A Seaview Ave., Honolulu, HI 96822 (☎808-946-0591; www.hiayh.org). Contact Mrs. Akau Naki.

Kalani Oceanside Retreat, RR2 Box 4500, Pahoa, HI 96778 (☎808-965-7828; www.kalani.com) offers a 1 or 3 mo. volunteer program which provides a unique short-term work alternative working on a plantation.

Koa-wood, 75-184 Ala Ona Ona St., Kailua-Kona, HI 96740 (☎808-326-7018; www.alternative-hawaii.com/affordable/kona.htm). Occasionally needs inn help.

Pineapple Park Hostel, 7927 Pikake St., Pahoa, HI 96778 (☎877-800-3800; www.pineapple-park.com). Ask about trading a bed for a few hr. of housekeeping per week.

Waikiki Beachside Hostel, 2556 Lemon Rd., Ste. B101, Honolulu, HI 96815 (☎808-923-9566; www.hokondo.com). Offers short-term work in exchange for accommodations depending on availability and duration of stay. Longer stays preferred.

YMCA Camp Erdman, 69-385 Farrington Hwy., Waialua, HI 96791 (☎808-637-4615; www.camperdman.net). After completing a lengthy application process, travelers can work short-term in exchange for room and board.

FURTHER READING ON BEYOND TOURISM

Alternatives to the Peace Corps: A Guide of Global Volunteer Opportunities, edited by Paul Backhurst. Food First, 2005 (US$12).

The Back Door Guide to Short-Term Job Adventures: Internships, Summer Jobs, Seasonal Work, Volunteer Vacations, and Transitions Abroad, by Michael Landes. Ten Speed Press, 2005 (US$22).

Green Volunteers: The World Guide to Voluntary Work in Nature Conservation, by Fabio Ausenda. Universe, 2007 (US$15).

How to Get a Job in Europe, by Cheryl Matherly and Robert Sanborn. Planning Communications, 2003 (US$23).

International Job Finder: Where the Jobs Are Worldwide, by Daniel Lauber and Kraig Rice. Planning Communications, 2002 (US$20).

Live and Work Abroad: A Guide for Modern Nomads, by Huw Francis and Michelyne Callan. Vacation Work Publications, 2001 (US$20).

Volunteer Vacations: Short-Term Adventures That Will Benefit You and Others, by Doug Cutchins, Anne Geissinger, and Bill McMillon. Chicago Review Press, 2006 (US$18).

Work Abroad: The Complete Guide to Finding a Job Overseas, edited by Clayton A. Hubbs. Transitions Abroad, 2002 (US$16).

Work Your Way Around the World, by Susan Griffith. Vacation Work Publications, 2007 (US$22).

BEYOND TOURISM

a volatile classroom
studying in hawaii volcanoes national park

Once you're away from it, it's hard to remember the intensity of the heat. You can tell people, "Oh yeah, it was really hot. The lava was radiating about 900°F and the tropical sun was on our necks the entire time." But when you're out on the cliffs, sweating, trapped between the sun and the hotter-than-asphalt-in-August lava, you can see the heat in waves that blur the Pacific and smell it in the melting rubber of tourists' flip-flops. You can taste the heat in the sulfur-filled air, and once you're close enough, you can hear it, too: the crackling of tiny hardened lava flakes as they chip off the front of the flow. It sounds almost like fire, though it's far hotter and flames only flare up if someone throws *ohelo* berries on the lava as an offering to Pele.

We sleep at the Kilauea military campground, 200 ft. from the summit, and we eat and take classes in a schoolhouse farther down the mountain. We don't spend much time in the classroom; this is an intensive introduction to field methods in volcanism (Geology 471 at the University of Hawaii at Hilo), and we work on the mountain itself. Kilauea is the most active volcano in the world, and there's always something to measure, to watch, and to injure us. The University makes us sign forms saying we understand the danger of working on the mountain; the form lists more than 20 ways people have been killed or injured on the mountain, from the man who fell 30 ft. into a newly-formed crevice to the Boy Scouts pulled out to sea by a tsunami.

Reading about these accidents on our first day, it is hard to believe that these are dangers we're actually going to face. Then again we've all only read about volcanoes from the safety of our respective universities.

Our group of 18 includes geology students from England, Australia, Germany, and the US and a high school teacher. The subjects we learn about include seismology (recording earthquakes), physical volcanology (looking at landforms to understand past eruptions), deformation monitoring (measuring the movement of the volcano's flanks), and gas geochemistry (analyzing gases to map magma migration). To generate seismograms, we hike across the craters, stopping in the middle of each to deploy a seismometer. Only a matter of years ago, each of these craters held a lava lake; the slabs of rough black rock we walk over are younger than many of us. We pass streams of tourists also hiking the Kilauea Iki trail and wonder how many of them realize how recently this whole area was molten. They get the same views we do, smell the same stifling gases, develop similar tank-top tan lines—but the things they don't know are endless and fascinating.

We don gas masks and stand over glistening yellow crystals to collect sulfur emitted by one of the thousands of fumaroles that vent Kilauea's volcanic gasses. Even

"...there's always something to measure, to watch, and to injure us."

breathing through the masks, our mouths fill with the rotten egg taste of hydrogen sulfide. We love it, because we love the volcano. We love the early morning hikes, the tedious calibration of instruments, the state of being forever dirty with volcanic debris. We don't have the same fervor for the hours it takes to analyze our samples in lab, but once we walk outside again into the green humidity we remember that we are in Hawaii, and getting course credit for it.

Katherine Thompson attended the Field Methods in Volcanology course, through the Center for the Study of Active Volcanoes. In three weeks she received an unparalleled crash course in volcano monitoring, several burns (sun, wind, and lava), and coral cuts on her feet. She loved every minute of it.

THE GREAT OUTDOORS

You were warned about the concrete jungle of Waikiki; about the tangle of high-rise resorts, upscale stores, and more free hula shows than you could shake a stick at. But you braved its whirlwind of glitter and light, and survived it—nay, dominated it. Ready for a real adventure?

Hawaii has nearly 400,000 acres of national and state parks and hundreds of miles of trails along which you may be the only hiker. It has deserts where NASA astronauts have trained for moon landings, lush rainforests, rolling grasslands, 51 mi. of coastal reef, and over 110 species of fish that are found nowhere else in the world. It is a stopping point in winter for migratory whales that play, breach, and spout in the water. Some of the best and biggest surf breaks in the world are found on the North Shore of Oahu and attract top-notch, world-famous surfers at the height of the winter surf season.

If this guidebook is your atlas, think of this section as your compass, map legend, and index rolled into one. We'll tell you how to cut through camping red tape, point out some of the best places to go when you want to hit the surf, and, above all, show you how to keep safe while enjoying the outdoors.

LAND

GREAT OUTDOORS

Hawaii is located in the Pacific Ocean, about 2400 mi. (3900km) southwest of the coast of California. It is the most isolated populated landmass in the entire world. At approximately the same latitude as central Mexico, it is the southernmost US state and the 7th smallest in area, spanning 10,931 sq. mi. The archipelago stretches 2000 mi., making it the world's longest island chain, and it contains 132 islands and atolls, all of which are the result of volcanic activity. There are eight major Hawaiian islands, only seven of which are inhabited, and with the exception of the large but uninhabited Kahoolawe, most of the rest are too small to make human occupancy viable. Of the seven inhabited islands, six are frequented by visitors to the state and are known as the main islands.

THE MAIN ISLANDS

Hawaii (or **Hawaii's Big Island**), the youngest and largest of the Hawaiian islands, is home to three active volcanoes: Kilauea, Mauna Loa, and Hualalai. This means that Hawaii's Big Island is not only big, but that it's growing due to lava buildup. Kilauea has been erupting almost continuously since 1823, and visitors to the Hawaii Volcanoes National Park can observe the world's most active volcano's lava flows up close. Mauna Kea, a dormant volcano that last erupted 45,000 years ago, is the highest point in the state at an altitude of 13,796 ft. (4208m) above sea level. It is also the tallest sea mountain on Earth. The high cliffs along the northern and southeastern coasts of the Big Island create dramatic waterfalls. Additionally, the island's varied terrain and tradewinds make for a multifarious climate: the Big Island houses 11 of the world's 13 climate zones.

Maui is a "volcanic doublet," formed by two separate volcanoes that over-lapped. The isthmus between them is the reason why Maui is known as "The Valley Isle." The East Maui volcano, known as Haleakala, is considered dor-mant; its last eruption was in 1790. The remains of the West Maui volcano, eroded by rainfall and wind, are known as the West Maui Mountains. The fertile expanse between the two volcanoes is conducive to sugarcane cultivation, while much of the rest of the island is covered by rainforest. Maui is one of the four main Hawaiian islands that formed the much larger prehistoric island, **Maui Nui** ("great Maui"), which submerged about 200,000 years ago.

LAVA ME TENDER. When the volcanic substance made of liquid and solid rock remains below ground, it is known as **magma.** Once magma is exposed to the air, either through a volcanic eruption or a fissure in the earth, it becomes **lava.** The behavior of lava depends on its chemical composition. **Low silica lava,** which is common in Hawaii, flows and can travel for great distances. **High silica lava,** also called pyroclastics, explodes in ash or cinders when it leaves a volcano. In addition to having varying silica levels, Hawaiian lava generally comes in three forms:

Pahoehoe: Nearly all lava in Hawaii erupts as *pahoehoe*. Fast-flowing, it hardens into a smooth, rope-like solid because the outermost lava of a lava channel cools before the lava inside. Such a delay in solidification produces **lava tubes;** lava can flow within these tubes for long distances.

Pillow Lava: A type of *pahoehoe* lava, pillow lava forms when lava flows into the ocean. When the lava makes contact with water, a solid crust forms immediately. As more lava flows beneath the crust, the crust cracks and oozes "pillows," or blobs, of lava.

Aa: Some attribute the name of this form of lava to an old tale about Captain Cook walking barefoot across the lava, screaming, "Ah! Ah!" In actuality, the term means "to glow" in Hawaiian. Slow-moving *aa* lava is characterized by its rough and jagged appearance—its the reason why sturdy shoes are needed in Hawaii Volcanoes National Park. Its flows are thicker than those of the other forms of lava and have been known to pile up (sometimes to heights of over 100 ft.). *Pahoehoe* can become *aa* if it experiences an increase in viscosity—that is, if it cools or loses gas.

Molokai, another remnant of the prehistoric Maui Nui, has three distinct geographic regions: the mountainous east, the arid west, and the verdant central plain. The island also contains some of the world's tallest sea cliffs, which soar up to 3000 ft. above the ocean on Molokai's north shore.

Castle & Cooke Resorts owns 98% of **Lanai.** This monopoly of the island is a result of a history of commercial pineapple production—Castle & Cooke Resorts bought the aptly nicknamed "the Pineapple Island" from the Dole Food Company in 1985. Lanai is the only Hawaiian island from which five of the other main islands are visible. It was also once a part of Maui Nui as was the large but uninhabited island of Kahoolawe.

Fertile grounds are also found on **Oahu,** in the central valley between the Koolau Mountain Range and the Waianae Range. These ranges, Koolau in the east and Waianae in the west, run almost parallel to each other and are the result of two separate shield volcanoes. There are several smaller post-shield volcanic outcroppings scattered throughout the island, all of which are extinct. The most famous of these former craters is Diamond Head, an extinct volcanic crater on the southeastern coast. At 760 ft. in height and 3520 ft. in diameter, it's impressive, but it hasn't erupted in 150,000 years.

Kauai is home to the rainiest spot on earth, Mount Waialeale, which averages 460 in. (1143cm) of rain per year. Such heavy rainfall has succeeded in eroding parts of the mountains of Kauai, generating a number of impressive canyons. The most impressive of these is the 10 mi. long and 3500 ft. deep Waimea

Canyon, known as the "Grand Canyon of the Pacific." The northernmost and geologically oldest of the Hawaiian islands, Kauai is often called "The Garden Island," a nod to its lush natural beauty.

FLORA AND FAUNA

Hawaii is a natural marvel. Because the archipelago was never part of a larger landmass, none of the plants and animals that exist in Hawaii today originated there. It was not until after the lava cooled that tides, winds, and birds carried seeds to the islands. Later, when Polynesian settlers arrived in canoes, bringing plant and animal species from their native lands, much of the flora and fauna on Hawaii developed special adaptations to their new home. Today, most of the biota on Hawaii—over 3000 plants, 7000 insects, 1000 land snails, 1500 mollusks, 600 fish, 100 birds, 1 bat, and 1 seal—exist nowhere else in the world.

Since Hawaii's native plants and animals evolved in the absence of predators or competitors, they did not develop natural defenses like thorns or camouflage. As a result, many native species have been pushed to the brink of extinction by alien plants and animals that have been introduced to the islands in the past few hundred years. Considered the **endangered species** capital of the US, Hawaii has more endangered species per square mile and has lost a higher percentage of its endemic species than anywhere else on earth.

PLANTS

There are more than 3000 species of native plants in Hawaii, as well as a considerable number of non-native species. One hundred and thirty-nine different types of **ferns** cover Hawaii. These lush, green plants were some of the first to arrive on the islands, sprouting up on the cooled lava flows. Often the first life in fresh lava flow, **ohia lehua** is Hawaii's most abundant native tree. Highly distinctive, the ohia lehua can be identified by its crooked branches and red, pompom-like flowers. It can survive in numerous environments, including elevations from 1000 to 9000 ft. above sea level, and was a crucial hardwood used by ancient Hawaiians for temple idols, poi bowls, and spears.

Hawaii's second-most prominent native tree is the **koa**, which is also indigenous to the islands. Capable of growing up to 100 ft. tall, the koa has sickle-shaped leaves and yellow flowers clustered into puffballs. Ancient Hawaiians used the reddish wood of the koa tree to fashion canoes, surfboards, and weapons. The hard wood is highly sought-after today as a material for making household furniture. Cattle and other feral animals have destroyed thousands of acres of Hawaiian koa, but, fortunately, the tree is highly resilient and has thrived under recent reforestation programs.

The **Haleakala silversword,** a spherical flowering member of the sunflower (asteraceae) family that grows close to the ground, nearly became extinct in the 1920s due to grazing by goats and cattle. The silversword is still very rare due to its limited range; the only place in the world it can be found is on the Haleakala volcano on Maui. However, protection programs within the Haleakala National Park have saved the species from extinction. Its thin, spiny leaves are covered with tiny silver hairs, and at the end of its 15- to 50-year life span it produces a tall stalk covered with maroon blossoms.

The **ti plant,** called *ki* in Hawaii, was introduced to the islands by Polynesian settlers. Sacred to the fertility god, Lono, and the goddess of the hula, Laka, *ki* became a symbol of power and good luck in Hawaii. A member of the lily family, the ti plant has shiny green water-resistant leaves, which were used as roof thatching, decoration, and rain capes. *Ki* grows abundantly throughout Hawaii, thriving in areas of low elevation where moisture is plentiful.

Hawaii's state flower is the **yellow hibiscus** (*pua aloalo* or *mao hau hele*). Ubiquitous throughout the islands, there are five endemic species of hibiscus in Hawaii. These brightly colored tropical blossoms can measure up to a foot in diameter and have become a popular symbol of the state. **Orchids, plumeria, bougainvillea,** and **birds of paradise** are also commonly found in Hawaii. Sugarcane, pineapples, guavas, mangoes, papayas, coconuts, avocados, bananas, passion fruit, macadamia nuts, taro root, breadfruit, and ginger—the makings for the ultimate fruit salad—are all cultivated on Hawaii. The endangered **sandalwood** tree, famous for its aromatic oil, also grows on the islands.

ANIMALS

Hawaii has only two native mammals: the **Hawaiian monk seal** and the **Hawaiian hoary bat.** The hoary bat is most often found on the islands of Hawaii, Maui, and Lanai and is recognizable by its brown and white fur. Endangered since 1970, the prognosis for the bat's recovery from endangered status is good as it is able to adapt to alien vegetation. The fate for monk seals, however, looks less promising. Unlike most seals, Hawaiian monk seals are solitary animals. They are a very old species; experts believe that they have not evolved in 15 million years. They are primarily found in the remote regions of the Northwestern Hawaiian islands. Like many species native to Hawaii, they developed in the absence of predators and have few defense mechanisms. Today, with a dwindling population of around 1200, they are considered the most endangered marine mammal in the US. Because the survival of these gentle creatures remains precarious, it is crucial that visitors not disturb them. Please stay a safe distance away.

Humpback whales were among the first species to discover the joy of wintering in Hawaii. Each autumn they travel 3000 mi. from their arctic feeding grounds to the tropical waters, where they mate and give birth. Somewhere between 2000 and 5000 whales make the trip each year, a significant portion of the total North Pacific population. These baleen whales are known for their spectacular acrobatics and complex underwater mating songs. They are now an endangered species, as there are only between 15,000 and 20,000 worldwide (15-20% of the original population). Maui is the best island from which to see the whales, particularly between November and February.

Green sea turtles have nesting grounds along the Hawaiian islands and can often be seen by snorkelers directly offshore. These animals are also endangered, threatened by hunting, pollution, and human development—observe from a distance. Hawaiian waters are also home to 13 species of **toothed dolphins.** Spinner and bottlenosed dolphins are most common and can be observed playing the in waves of Hawaii's shores. Locals often refer to these animals as "porpoises," using "dolphin" to refer to the dolphin fish, *mahi mahi.*

There are an estimated 700 different species of fish in Hawaiian waters, many of which exist nowhere else. Impress your friends by naming Hawaii's unofficial state fish, the **humuhumunukunukuapuaa** (pronounced HOO-moo-HOO-moo-NEW-coo-NEW-coo-AH-poo-AH-ah), which is also known as the **reef triggerfish.** This tiny tropical fish is 8-9 in. long and has a trigger-shaped, blue-and-yellow dorsal fin and, according to the ancient Hawaiians, a snout like a pig. There are also about 40 different species of shark inhabiting Hawaiian waters. The most commonly seen near shore are **tiger sharks** (considered the most dangerous), **whitetip reef sharks,** and **hammerheads** (see **Wilderness Safety,** p. 87).

Hawaii's state bird, the highly endangered **nene,** or Hawaiian goose, is the rarest goose in the world—fewer than 900 exist in the wild. As they tend to nest low to the ground, their low numbers are in part attributed to predation by mongooses, as well as destruction of nests by pigs and cats. Capable of living up to 4000 ft. above sea level, most *nene* dwell on the slopes of volcanoes on the Big Island, though they can also be found on Maui and Kauai. Thought to be closely related to the Canadian goose, the *nene* developed long toes and reduced webbing on their feet for climbing on lava flows. The **mongoose** was introduced to Hawaii in the late 19th century in an attempt to exterminate the rats that were overrunning plantations. Unfortunately, this solution was ineffective, since rats are nocturnal and mongooses are diurnal. For more information on the plants and animals of Hawaii, see **Additional Resources,** p. 94.

CAMPING IN HAWAII

Oceanfront campsites afford travelers the opportunity to enjoy a million-dollar view at a fraction of the price of a hotel. Hawaii's temperate climate only adds to the appeal and ease of camping. Many county beach parks (p. 85) have areas set aside for camping, though some are better equipped than others. The number of campsites varies; some parks offer as few as four spots while others have up to 50. In addition, Hawaiian state parks (p. 84) are open year-round and issue permits for camping, lodging, and group day use for those who are at least 18. Contact the **Department of Land and Natural Resources, Division of State Parks,** P.O. Box 621, Honolulu 96809 (☎808-587-0300; http://hawaii.gov/dlnr), for permit availability and additional information. If you plan on camping, make sure to rent a car with a lockable compartment (not a soft-top Jeep) for your gear. Building a fire, where permitted, can be difficult due to lack of wood, so bring a stove for cooking and boiling water. Excellent resources for travelers planning on camping or spending time in the outdoors include the **Great Outdoor Recreation Page** (www.gorp.com), **Alternative Hawaii** (http://www.alternative-hawaii.com/index.html), and **Na Ala Hele** (www.hawaiitrails.org).

 LEAVE NO TRACE. Let's Go encourages travelers to embrace the "Leave No Trace" ethic, minimizing impact on natural environments and protecting them for future generations. Trekkers and wilderness enthusiasts should set up camp on durable surfaces. Cook stoves are safer and more eco-friendly than campfires, but if you must build a fire, keep it small and use only dead branches or brush. Bury human waste 4 in. deep and above the high water line and 150ft. away from water supplies and campsites. Bag trash and carry it out with you. For more detailed information, contact the **Leave No Trace Center for Outdoor Ethics,** P.O. Box 997, Boulder, CO 80306 (☎303-442-8222 or 800-332-4100; www.lnt.org).

CAMPING AND HIKING EQUIPMENT

WHAT TO BUY
Good camping equipment is both sturdy and light. North American suppliers tend to offer the most competitive prices.

GREAT OUTDOORS

Sleeping Bags: Most sleeping bags are rated by season; "summer" means 30-40°F (around 0°C) at night; "four-season" or "winter" often means below 0°F (-17°C). Areas of high elevation in Hawaii tend to get chilly at night; four-season bags are a safe bet to keep you cozy. Bags are made of **down** (warm and light, but expensive, and miserable when wet) or of **synthetic** material (heavy, durable, and warm when wet). Prices range $50-250 for a summer synthetic to $200-300 for a good down winter bag. **Sleeping bag pads** include foam pads ($10-30), air mattresses ($25-70), and self-inflating mats ($30-120). Bring a **stuff sack** ($5-20) to store your bag and keep it dry.

Tents: The best tents are freestanding (with their own frames and suspension systems), set up quickly, and don't generally require staking. Low-profile dome tents are the best of these. Worthy 2-person tents start at $100, 4-person start at $160. Make sure your tent has a rain fly, and seal its seams with waterproofer. Other useful items include a **battery-operated lantern,** a plastic **ground cloth,** and a nylon **tarp.**

Backpacks: Internal frame packs mold well to your back, have a lower center of gravity, and flex adequately to allow you to hike difficult trails, while **external frame packs** are more comfortable for long hikes over even terrain, as they carry weight higher and distribute it more evenly. Make sure your pack has a strong, padded hip belt to transfer weight to your legs. Some models are designed specifically for women. Any serious backpacking requires a pack of at least 4000 cu. in. (16,000cc), plus 500 cu. in. for sleeping bags in internal frame packs. Sturdy backpacks cost anywhere from $125-420. Your pack is one item you won't want to skimp on. On your hunt for the perfect pack, fill up a prospective model with something heavy, strap it on correctly, and walk around the store to get a sense of how the model distributes weight. Either buy a **rain cover** ($10-20) or store all of your belongings in plastic bags inside your pack.

Boots: Regular sneakers should be sufficient for all but the most hard-core hiking trails in Hawaii. If you buy boots, be sure to get ones with good **ankle support.** To spare yourself from blisters, break in boots several weeks before you go.

Other Necessities: Synthetic layers, like those made of polypropylene or polyester, and a pile jacket will keep you warm even when wet. A **space blanket** ($5-15) will help you to retain body heat and doubles as a ground cloth. Plastic **water bottles** are vital; look for shatter- and leak-resistant models. Carry **water purification tablets** for when you can't boil. Although some campgrounds provide campfire sites, you may want to bring a small **metal grate** or **grill.** For those places that forbid fires or the gathering of firewood, you'll need a camp stove (starting at around $50) and a propane-filled fuel bottle to operate it. Also bring a **first-aid kit, sunscreen, pocketknife, insect repellent,** and **waterproof matches** or a **lighter.**

WHERE TO BUY IT

The mail-order and online companies listed below offer lower prices than many retail stores. A visit to a local camping or outdoors store will give you a good sense of the look and weight of certain items.

Campmor, 400 Corporate Dr., P.O. Box 680, Mahwah, NJ 07430 (☎888-226-7667; www.campmor.com).

Discount Camping, 833 Main North Rd., Pooraka, South Australia 5095, Australia (☎08 8262 3399; www.discountcamping.com.au).

L.L. Bean, Freeport, ME 04033 (US and Canada ☎800-441-5713, UK 0800 891 297; www.llbean.com).

Mountain Designs, P.O. Box 824, Nundah, Queensland 4012, Australia (☎07 3856 2344; www.mountaindesigns.com).

Recreational Equipment, Inc. (REI), Sumner, WA 98352 (US and Canada ☎800-426-4840, elsewhere 253-891-2500; www.rei.com).

GREAT OUTDOORS

NATIONAL PARKS

Hawaii has two national parks: **Haleakala National Park** (p. 318) on Maui, and **Hawaii Volcanoes National Park** (p. 210) on the Big Island. Haleakala is the site of Haleakala Volcano, whose majestic summit above the cloud line has become a popular peak for watching magnificent sunrises. Rangers are actively engaged in the preservation of the park's fragile ecosystem, which includes the silversword and *nene* goose, two endangered species. Hawaii Volcanoes National Park encompasses both the most active volcano in the world, **Kilauea,** and the largest, **Mauna Loa.** There are miles of hikes through amazingly diverse ecosystems and awesome trappings of 70 million years of volcanic activity; you can even walk up to the slow-flowing active lava in the eastern rift zone.

HALEAKALA. Prepare for mosquitoes, sun, rain, and—if you are camping on Haleakala—cold and wind. Haleakala has two drive-in campgrounds, two wilderness campgrounds, and three wilderness cabins. No permits, reservations, or registration are necessary for the drive-in campgrounds. Permits are required for hike-in campsites and are issued the day of the hike for free on a first-come, first-served basis at Park Headquarters (open 8am-3pm). Permits are good for a maximum of three nights per month, with no more than two nights at any site. Cabin reservations are awarded by a monthly lottery. Apply three months in advance. See **Camping and Cabins,** p. 321, for more info.

HAWAII VOLCANOES. Volcanoes has two drive-in campgrounds; two backcountry tent sites; three backcountry shelters with tent sites, pit toilets, and water catchments; and three hike-in cabin locations. The drive-in campgrounds are free and permits, reservations, and registration are not required. Permits for backcountry sites are free and can be easily obtained from the Visitors Center on a first-come, first-served basis. Stays are limited to seven days per month and 30 days per year. Registration is required for backcountry camping. For more information, see p. 210 and their website, www.nps.gov/havo.

STATE PARKS

Camping at a state park requires a permit from the **Division of State Parks,** which maintains offices on Oahu, Maui, the Big Island, Kauai, and Molokai. The same fees and restrictions apply on each island. A **camping permit** is $5 per night per campsite, with a maximum of 10 people per site for a maximum of five nights. You are only allowed one permit per park within a 30-day period. (One exception is Na Pali Coast, which is $10 per person per night and has a 3-night max. stay.) You can apply in writing, by phone, or in person no earlier than one year in advance, unless noted otherwise below. The permit will be held at the office for pickup, or you can include a self-addressed, stamped envelope to have it mailed to you. If you decide to mail your request, be sure to include your name, address, and phone number, specify the dates and the park where you wish to camp, and give the names and some form of ID number (driver's license, passport, or Social Security number) of all campers. For further information visit the Hawaii State Parks website (www.hawaiistateparks.org) or call ☎808-587-0300. All parks are open seven days a week with exceptions noted below. All offices are open M-F 8am-3:30pm.

OAHU. Mail requests to P.O. Box 621, Honolulu 96809, or call ☎808-587-0300. Pick up or apply for permits in person at 1151 Punchbowl St., Rm. 131, Honolulu. Parks are open M-W and F-Su, and permit applications will be accepted no sooner than 30 days before the 1st day of camping. The **Friends of Malaekahana** (☎808-293-1736) manage cabins at Malaekahana; see p. 163 for more info.

PARK NAME	PAGE
Keaiwa Heiau State Recreation Area (4 10-person campsites)	p. 186
Malaekahana Campgrounds	p. 163
Sand Island State Recreation Area	p. 152

MAUI. Mail requests to 54 S. High St., Ste. 101, Wailuku 96793, or call ☎808-984-8109. Pick up or apply for permits in person at the same address. The cabins are $45 per night (1-4 people) and $5 per night for each additional person.

PARK NAME	PAGE
Polipoli Spring State Recreation Area (also has cabins)	p. 317
Waianapanapa State Park (also has cabins)	p. 311

MOLOKAI. Call or visit the **Maui Division of State Parks** at ☎808-984-8109, or go to the caretaker's office at the entrance to the park to attain permits.

PARK NAME	PAGE
Palaau State Park	p. 340

THE BIG ISLAND. Mail requests to P.O. Box 936, Hilo 96721, or call ☎808-974-6200. Pick up or apply for permits in person at 75 Aupuni St., Hilo. Reservations taken 8am-noon. A-frame cabins are $20 per night. Six-person cabins are $45 per night for one to four people, and $5 per night for each additional person.

PARK NAME	PAGE
Kalopa State Recreation Area (also has cabins)	p. 242
Hapuna Beach State Recreation Area (cabins only)	p. 256
Mackenzie State Recreation Area	p. 225
Mauna Kea State Recreation Area (4 6-person cabins)	p. 235

KAUAI. Mail requests to 3060 Eiwa St., Rm. 306, Lihue 96766, or call ☎808-274-3444. Pick up or apply for permits at same address. Special restrictions apply to camping on the Na Pali Coast; visit the Hawaii State Parks website (www.hawaiistateparks.org) for more information. Kokee State Park also has 12 cabins managed by **Kokee Lodge** (☎808-335-6061); see p. 417.

PARK NAME	PAGE
Kokee State Park	p. 417
Na Pali Coast State Park (3 campsites along the Kalalau Trail, 1 beyond it)	p. 395
Polihale State Park	p. 422

COUNTY PARKS

HONOLULU COUNTY. Permits are free and available from the Department of Parks and Recreation on the ground floor of the Honolulu Municipal Building, 650 S. King St., Honolulu 96813. (Open M-F 7:45am-4pm.) They can also be picked up at any one of 10 Satellite City Halls. A conveniently located satellite is in the Ala Moana Shopping Center (p. 103). Camping is allowed from 8am Friday to 8am Wednesday. Some campsites are open only on weekends and during certain months (see below). Permits must be obtained in person at least one week in advance but no more than two Fridays before your camping date. The permits are very popular, so you should count on showing up early in the morning two Fridays in advance, or have alternate lodging arrangements. One permit allows up to 10 people and two tents. Call ☎808-768-3440 or visit the county park website (www. co.honolulu.hi.us/parks/permits.htm).

PARK NAME	PAGE
Bellows Field Beach Park (50 campsites; weekends only)	p. 155
Hauula Beach Park (15 campsites)	p. 164
Kaiaka Beach Park (7 campsites)	p. 174
Kalaeloa Beach Park (13 campsites; weekends only)	p. 164
Kualoa "A" Regional Park (7 campsites; no camping June, July, Aug.; weekends only)	p. 164
Kualoa "B" Regional Park (30 campsites; extremely popular)	p. 164
Maili Beach Park (12 campsites; weekends only)	p. 185
Nanakuli Beach Park (12 campsites)	p. 185
Swanzy Beach Park (9 campsites; weekends only)	p. 164
Waimanalo Bay Recreation Area (10 campsites)	p. 155
Waimanalo Beach Park (22 campsites)	p. 155

MAUI COUNTY. Permits cost $3 per person per night ($0.50 per minor) and are available from the Department of Parks and Recreation. They are good for a maximum of three consecutive nights. For Maui parks, mail a money order to 700 Halia Nakoa St., Wailuku 96793. Pick up or apply for permits in person at the Permit Office in the War Memorial Gym next to Baldwin High School on Rte. 32 in Wailuku. (Open M-F 8am-4pm.) For more information call ☎808-270-7389. For Molokai parks (which are in Maui County and follow the same regulations), send a money order to 90 Aiona St., Kaunakakai 96748. Pick up or apply for permits in person at the same address. Open M-F 8am-4pm. For more information call ☎808-553-3204.

PARK NAME	PAGE
Kanaha Beach Park (on Maui, closed last T-Th of each month)	p. 278
One Alii Beach Park (on Molokai)	p. 330
Papalaua Wayside Park (on Maui; closed W-Th)	p. 265
Papohaku Beach (on Molokai)	p. 349

HAWAII COUNTY. Permits cost $5 per night, ages 13-17 $2, 12 and under $1; they can be purchased no more than one year in advance. You can camp at each site for a maximum of seven nights total in summer and 14 nights in winter. Permits can be purchased online (https://www.ehawaii.gov/Hawaii_County/camping/exe/campre.cgi) with a processing fee and a major credit card, or you can write to the Department of Parks and Recreation, 101 Pauahi St., Ste. 6, Hilo 96720. For more information call ☎808-961-8311 or visit http://co.hawaii.hi.us.

PARK NAME	PAGE
Hookena Beach Park (22 campsites)	p. 203
Isaac Hale Beach Park (22 campsites)	p. 224
Kapaa Beach Park (22 campsites)	p. 250
Kolekole Gulch Park	p. 233
Laupahoehoe Point Beach Park	p. 240
Milolii Beach Park (22 campsites)	p. 203
Punaluu Black Sand Beach (22 campsites)	p. 209

KAUAI COUNTY. Permits cost $3 per night and are free for minors if accompanied by an adult. Each permit is good for a maximum of six consecutive nights and no more than 60 nights in a year-long period. Permits can be obtained by mailing in the application (available at www.kauaigov.org) to 4444 Rice St., Ste. 330, Lihue 96766 and may be picked up at the same address M-F 8:15am-4pm. For more information, call ☎808-241-4460 or visit www.kauaigov.org.

PARK NAME	PAGE
Anini Beach Park (closed Tu)	p. 385
🏖 Haena Beach Park (closed M)	p. 393
Hanalei Blackpot Park (closed M-Th, Su)	p. 389
Hanamaulu Beach Park (closed M-W, Su)	p. 368
Lucy Wright Beach Park (closed M)	p. 414
🏖 Salt Pond Beach Park (closed Tu)	p. 413

OTHER PLACES TO CAMP

FORESTRY AND WILDLIFE. Some campsites are designated as State Forest Reserves and therefore require a permit, available from the Division of Forestry and Wildlife. Permits are available free of charge. On Oahu, call ☎808-587-0166. On the Big Island, call ☎808-974-4221. On Kauai, call ☎808-274-3433. On Molokai, you need to give one week advance notice. Call ☎808-984-8100.

OAHU	PAGE
Mokuleia Forest Reserve (max. 2 weeks)	p. 180
HAWAII	**PAGE**
Waimanu Valley/Maiwalu Trail (max. 6 nights)	p. 244
KAUAI	**PAGE**
Kaluahaulu Campground in Waimea Canyon (max. 4 nights)	p. 416
Kawaikoi (max. 3 nights)	p. 417
Sugi Grove (max. 3 nights)	p. 417
Lonomea Campground in Waimea Canyon (max. 4 nights)	p. 416
Wiliwili Campground in Waimea Canyon (max. 4 nights)	p. 416
MOLOKAI	**PAGE**
Waikolu Lookout (max. 2 nights)	p. 337

PRIVATE CAMPING. Many establishments will also allow you to pitch a tent.

OAHU	PAGE
Camp Mokuleia ($7 per person)	p. 179
Hoomaluhia Botanical Garden (F-Su only)	p. 166
YMCA Camp Erdman (cabins only)	p. 179
MAUI	**PAGE**
YMCA Camp Keanae ($15 per person)	p. 303
HAWAII	**PAGE**
Kalani Oceanside Retreat (campsite $20)	p. 223
Margo's Corner Bed and Breakfast ($35 per group)	p. 207
Arnott's Lodge ($10 per person)	p. 229
KAUAI	**PAGE**
YMCA Camp Naue ($10 per person)	p. 391
YMCA Camp Sloggett ($10 per person)	p. 418
MOLOKAI	**PAGE**
Waialua Pavilion and Campground ($10 per person)	p. 345

WILDERNESS SAFETY

Staying **warm, dry,** and **well-hydrated** is key to a happy and safe experience in Hawaii's wilderness. For any hike, prepare yourself for an emergency by packing a first-aid kit, a reflector, a whistle, high-energy food, and extra water. The sun can be brutal, so take a hat, sunscreen, and sunglasses on any trip.

Check **weather forecasts** often and pay attention to the sky when hiking, as weather patterns can change suddenly. Always notify someone—a friend, your hostel, a park ranger, or a local hiking organization—about your whereabouts. Know your limits and do not attempt a hike beyond your ability.

For beach outings, pay attention to all posted signs and notices; be aware of areas with frequent riptides and dangerous surf. As is the case with hiking, make sure someone knows you're going in the water before you dive in.

DANGEROUS WILDLIFE

BOX JELLYFISH. Transparent box jellyfish swarm to Hawaii's leeward shores a week or so after the full moon. A jellyfish can measure 1-3 in. with tentacles of up to 2 ft. long. Its painful sting can sometimes cause anaphylactic shock. If you are stung, apply vinegar to the sting and then pluck any tentacles out of the affected area using tweezers, a towel, or cloth (avoid using your bare hands). Make sure it is in fact a jellyfish sting, as using vinegar on Portuguese Man-of-War stings (see below) is potentially dangerous. Never rub the affected area or use freshwater, as the tentacles can release more venom even after detached from the jellyfish. Contrary to popular belief, there is little proof that urinating on your sting is helpful and will probably just leave you a little more messy. If you are at all concerned about the sting seek medical care.

PORTUGUESE MEN-OF-WAR. Not technically a jellyfish (though it resembles one), the Portuguese Man-of-War (also known as a bluebottle) packs an excruciatingly painful sting. Purplish-blue in color with tentacles up to 33 ft. long., the Portuguese Man-of-War's sting can cause anaphylactic shock, interference with heart and lung function, and even death. Do not, under any circumstances, apply vinegar to a sting from a Portuguese Man-of-War. Instead, rinse the sting with saltwater or freshwater and apply a cold or hot compress to the affected area. Do not rub the affected area. Be careful on the beach as well—Portuguese Men-of-War carcasses and detached tentacles can still sting. If pain persists or if breathing difficulty develops, consult a medical professional immediately.

 BETTER SAFE THAN SORRY. While we list the tried-and-true treatments for jellyfish and Portuguese Men-of-War stings, you should always seek medical care if you are at all worried about an injury.

SHARKS. About 40 species of sharks inhabit Hawaiian waters, ranging in size from the 8 in. pygmy shark to the up-to-50 ft. whale shark. There are eight species that are commonly sighted near shore, most of which pose little threat to humans. The **tiger shark,** recognizable by its blunt snout and the stripes on its sides, is the most dangerous species of shark found in Hawaiian waters and is known to attack humans. Though they will not seek out humans, tiger sharks usually reside near the shore and therefore do come into contact with humans. That said, shark attacks in Hawaii are actually quite rare—only two to three occur each year. Surfers and spear fishers are at greatest risk of attack, and swimmers are advised to stay out of the water at dawn and dusk, when sharks are most active. Never swim alone, avoid murky water, and get out of the ocean if you're bleeding; blood can attract sharks. Experts also advise against wearing high-contrast clothing or shiny jewelry and to avoid excessive splashing.

FOR MORE INFORMATION. Consult *All Stings Considered*, by Susan Scott and Craig Thomas, M.D. (University of Hawaii Press; $25), and *How to Stay Alive in the Woods*, by Bradford Angier (Macmillan Press; $20).

ENVIRONMENTAL HAZARDS

HEAT EXHAUSTION AND DEHYDRATION. Heat exhaustion leads to nausea, excessive thirst, headaches, and dizziness. Avoid this condition by drinking plenty of fluids, eating salty foods (e.g., crackers), abstaining from dehydrating beverages (e.g., alcohol and caffeinated drinks), and wearing sunscreen. Continuous heat stress can eventually lead to **heatstroke,** characterized by a rising temperature, severe headache, delirium, and the cessation of sweating. Victims should be cooled with wet towels and taken to a doctor.

SUNBURN. The sunshine of paradise comes at a price if you're not careful. It is extremely easy to get sunburnt in Hawaii, even on a cloudy day. Be sure to apply sunscreen of SPF 15 or higher before you go out for the day and after swimming. If you are spending many consecutive hours in the sun, you should reapply sunscreen often—the trouble you take will be well worth avoiding the pain and discomfort of a persistent sunburn. A higher SPF is advisable at the start of your trip until you develop a tan. If you do get sunburnt, drink more fluids than usual and apply aloe. Severe sunburns can lead to **sun poisoning,** a condition that affects the entire body, causing fever, chills, nausea, and vomiting. Sun poisoning should always be treated by a doctor.

HIGH ALTITUDE. Allow your body a few days to adjust to lower oxygen levels before exerting yourself. At high elevations, alcohol is more potent and UV rays are stronger. Pregnant women, young children, and people with respiratory and heart conditions should consult a doctor before traveling to high altitudes.

HYPOTHERMIA. Though it seems unlikely, hypothermia can occur in Hawaii if you're unprotected from rain or if you spend too much time in the water. A rapid drop in body temperature is the clearest sign of overexposure to cold. Victims may also shiver, have poor coordination or slurred speech, hallucinate, or suffer amnesia. Do not let victims fall asleep. To avoid hypothermia, keep dry, wear layers, and stay out of the wind.

SURFING AND SWIMMING PRECAUTIONS. Hawaiian waves make for some of the world's best surf, but they can also be deadly. High surf brings strong currents and riptides, and each year lives are lost when surfers and swimmers fail to heed precautions. More people drown in Hawaii each year than anywhere else in the country. Know your limits and use caution whenever you get into the water. The following are a few simple precautions:
Never swim alone.
Swim and surf only in lifeguarded areas.
Do not struggle against a riptide; swim parallel to the beach across it.
Use a leash for surf and bodyboards.
Familiarize yourself with beach and surf conditions before you head out.

INSECT-BORNE DISEASES

Many diseases in Hawaii are transmitted by insects, mainly **mosquitoes, fleas, and ticks.** Beware of insects in wet or forested areas, especially while hiking and camping. Wear long pants and long sleeves, and use a mosquito net. Use insect repellents with DEET and soak or spray your gear with permethrin (licensed in the US for use only on clothing). Mosquitoes are particularly prevalent in wet, wooded areas, such as those in east Maui, Kauai, and the Big Island.

DENGUE FEVER. An acute viral disease transmitted by day-biting mosquitoes, dengue fever has symptoms that include a high fever, severe headaches, swollen lymph nodes, and muscle aches. Many patients also suffer nausea, vomiting, and a pink rash. If you experience these symptoms, see a doctor immediately, drink plenty of liquids, and take acetaminophen (Tylenol®). Never take aspirin to treat dengue fever. An outbreak of dengue fever occurred in 2001 with 119 confirmed cases, predominantly on Maui. The last locally transmitted case in Hawaii was in February 2002. Always use insect repellent when outside.

FOOD- AND WATER-BORNE DISEASES

Travelers in Hawaii experience food- and water-related illness much less often than in most parts of the world, thanks to good water-treatment facilities and fairly well-maintained restaurant standards. Just watch out for food from markets or street vendors that may have been cooked in unhygienic conditions. Other culprits are raw shellfish, unpasteurized milk, and sauces containing raw eggs. The tap water in Hawaii is treated to be safe for drinking. However, a few campsites do require water treatment. Purify your water by bringing it to a rolling boil or treating it with **iodine tablets.** Note, that some parasites have exteriors that resist iodine treatment, so boiling is more reliable. Exercise caution around natural bodies of water, which can harbor dangerous bacteria.

GIARDIASIS. Transmitted through parasites and acquired by drinking untreated water from streams or lakes. Symptoms include diarrhea, cramps, bloating, fatigue, weight loss, and nausea. Giardiasis occurs worldwide.

LEPTOSPIROSIS. This bacterial disease is caused by exposure to freshwater contaminated by the urine of infected animals. Leptospirosis enters the body through skin cuts or the mouth, nose, or eyes. Known exposure sites and all state and county parks that have freshwater streams or ponds are regularly posted with leptospirosis warning signs; never swim in freshwater if you have cuts. Symptoms include high fever, chills, nausea, and vomiting. If not treated, it can lead to liver failure and meningitis. Consult a doctor for treatment.

TRAVELER'S DIARRHEA. Results from drinking fecally contaminated water or eating contaminated foods. Symptoms include nausea, bloating, and urgency. Try quick-energy, non-sugary foods with protein and carbohydrates. Over-the-counter anti-diarrheals (e.g., Imodium®) may counteract the problem. The most dangerous side effect is dehydration; drink 8 oz. of water with ½ tsp. of sugar or honey and a pinch of salt or eat salted crackers. If you develop a fever or your symptoms don't go away after 4-5 days, consult a doctor.

NATURAL DISASTERS

EARTHQUAKES. Seismic activity on Hawaii is frequent due to its active volcanoes. The vast majority of earthquakes are too small to be felt, but about once a decade a stronger quake can cause real damage. The last destructive earthquake was in 2006, with no fatalities but major property damage. In the event of an earthquake, stay away from windows, tall furniture, and ceiling fixtures. Drop to the ground, find cover under a door frame, and protect your head.

HURRICANES. Hurricanes rarely hit Hawaii, but the state is not immune to these high-wind-speed storms or attendant large waves. The last massive hurricane was Hurricane Iniki, in 1992, which caused almost $2 billion in damage, mostly in Kauai. In the event that a hurricane or tropical storm watch or warning is issued, listen closely to the radio or TV for further updates and instructions from civil defense authorities. You should also prepare to cover all windows and doors; stock up on food, water, prescription medicine, and batteries; have an available supply of cash; and be ready to evacuate.

TSUNAMIS. Tsunamis are caused by any displacement of a large mass of water—often an underwater earthquake—that creates a rapidly traveling wave that slows and gains height as it approaches the shoreline. The wave floods low-lying areas and can be incredibly destructive; tsunamis have killed more people in Hawaii than all other natural disasters combined. Thirteen significant tsunamis have struck Hawaii in the last century; the most destructive were in 1946 and 1960. If a tsunami warning is issued, follow the evacuation procedures broadcast. Maps and more detailed information are in the front pages of phone books. For more information visit the **National Weather Service's Pacific Tsunami Warning Center** website (www.prh.noaa.gov/ptwc.)

VOLCANOES. Hawaii's volcanoes are typically considered safe, given the relatively gentle, non-explosive outflow of lava that characterizes the eruptions. However, Kilauea erupted violently in 1790 and 1924 and will undoubtedly do so again. Mauna Loa erupted for three weeks in 1984, with lava flows coming within 4 mi. of Hilo. The volcanologists at Volcanoes National Park continually monitor volcanic activity—heed all warnings and instructions they give regarding an impending explosive eruption. Other more dangerous hazards are commonplace in the park; be careful and follow park ranger guidelines (p. 210).

OUTDOOR ACTIVITIES

Let's face it. While we may claim that there are a many reasons to come to Hawaii, only one stands out in your mind: the beaches. The glorious crescents of sand that see millions of sunbathers, snorkelers, surfers, bodyboarders, and swimmers each year are at the heart of any Hawaiian getaway. In this section, we'll give you a quick overview of where you can find your favorite activities. Beach is indicated by "B." and beach park by "B.P."

☑ SURFING

The best surfing is almost always in the winter, when the biggest waves roll in along the northern shores of the islands. The surfing spots we list here run the gamut from the easiest surf to breaks you'd have to train for years to tackle. Note that during the summer some of these beaches may be quite calm.

OAHU
Baby Queen's B. (p. 138), Diamond Head B. (p. 139), Haleiwa Alii B.P. (p. 176), Kawailoa B. (p. 177), Keawaula Bay (p. 186), Kuhio B. (p. 138), Makaha B.P. (p. 185), Makapuu B.P. (p. 153), Nanakuli B.P. (p. 185), Sandy B. (p. 152), Sunset B.P. to Ehukai B.P. (p. 170), Three Tables B. (p. 171), Waikiki B. (p. 137), Waimea B.P. (p. 168).

GREAT OUTDOORS

THE BIG ISLAND
Isaac Hale B.P. (p. 224, Honolii B.P. (p. 232), Kahaluu B.P. (p. 195), Kekaha Kai B. (p. 196), Lapakahi Marine Life Conservation District (p. 252), Mahaiula Break (p. 196), Milolii B.P. (p. 203), Pine Tree B. (p. 196), Waipio B. (p. 244), Wawaloli B. (p. 196).

MAUI
D.T. Fleming B.P. (p. 279), Hamoa B. (p. 311), Honolua Bay (p. 279), Hookipa B. (p. 305), Jaws (p. 306), Koki B. (p. 310), Launiupoko Wayside Park (p. 266), Maalaea Harbor (p. 288), Mokuleia Bay (p. 279).

MOLOKAI AND LANAI
Molokai: Rock Point (p. 346), Halawa Bay (p. 345), Make Horse B. (p. 349). Lanai: Lopa B. (p. 359), Polihua B. (p. 358).

KAUAI
Anini B.P. (p. 385), Black Pot B. (p. 389), Donkey B. (p. 380), Haena B.P. (p. 393), Hanamaulu B.P. (p. 368), Kalapaki B. (p. 367), Kalihiwai B. (p. 385), Kealia B. (p. 380), Kepuhi B. (p. 394), Lawai B. (p. 402), Pakala B. (p. 413), Poipu/Kiahuna B. (p. 403), Secret B. (p. 385), Shipwreck B. (p. 403), Waioli B.P. (p. 390).

⚡ SNORKELING AND SCUBA

Many of the snorkeling spots are also good places to dive.

OAHU
Hanauma Bay (p. 150), Keawaula Bay (p. 186), Makaha B.P. (p. 185), Nanakuli B.P. (p. 185), Pupukea B.P. (p. 172), Shark's Cove (p. 171), Swanzy B.P. (p. 164), Three Tables B. (p. 171), Waimanalo B.P. (p. 155), Waimea B.P. (p. 171).

THE BIG ISLAND
Anaehoomalu B. (p. 255), Kahaluu B.P. (p. 195), Kapoho Bay (p. 225), Kealakekua Marine Life Conservation District (p. 203), Kiholo B. (p. 196), Lapakahi State Hist. Park (p. 252), Mahaiula Break (p. 196), Makalawena B (p. 196), Mauna Kea B. (p. 256), Milolii B.P. (p. 203), Punaluu Black Sand B. (p. 209), Puuhonua O Honaunau Natl. Hist. Park (p. 205), Richardson Ocean Park (p. 231), Waialea Bay Marine Life Conservation District (p. 256), Waipio B.P. (p. 244).

MAUI
Ahihi Bay (p. 299), Black Rock (p. 276), Canoe B. (p. 276), Honolua Bay (p. 279), Kahekili B.P. (p. 268), Kaihalulu Red Sand B. (p. 310), Kamaole B.P.s (p. 294), Kapalua B. (p. 278), Keawakapu B. (p. 297), La Pérouse Bay (p. 299), Mokapu B. (p. 297), Makena Landing (p. 298), Mokuleia Bay (p. 279), Ulua B. (p. 297), Wailea B. (p. 297).

MOLOKAI AND LANAI
Molokai: Waialua B. (p. 345), Murphy's B. (p. 345). Lanai: Manele B. (p. 359).

KAUAI
Hideaways B. (p. 390), Kee B. (p. 394), Kepuhi B. (p. 394), Koloa Landing (p. 402), Lydgate State Park (p. 374), Pali Ke Kua B. (p. 390), PK's (p. 402), Poipu B.P. (p. 403), Queen's Bath (p. 390), Tunnels B. (p. 393).

⚡ BODYBOARDING

Many places listed as bodyboarding beaches may be great for **bodysurfing,** too.

OAHU
Kalama B. (p. 160), Keawaula Bay (p. 186), Kuhio B. (p. 138), Maili B.P. (p. 185), Makapuu B.P. (p. 153), Nunakali B.P. (p. 185), Sandy B. (p. 152), Queen's Surf (p. 138), Waimanalo Bay Rec. Area (p. 155).

THE BIG ISLAND
Hapuna B. (p. 256), Mahaiula Break (p. 196), Richardson Ocean Park (p. 231), White Sands B. (p. 188), Waipio B.P. (p. 244).

MAUI
D.T. Fleming B.P. (p. 279), Hamoa B. (p. 311), Kaanapali B. (p. 276), Koki B. (p. 310), Little B. (p. 298), Maalaea Harbor (p. 289), Oneloa B. (p. 279), Puamana B. (p. 267), Ulua B. (p. 297).

MOLOKAI AND LANAI
Molokai: Halawa (p. 345). Lanai: Hulopoe B.P. (p. 359).

KAUAI
Black Pot B. P. (p. 389), Hanalei Pavilion B.P. (p. 389), Hanamaulu B.P. (p. 368), Kalapaki B. (p. 367), Kalihiwai B. (p. 385), Kealia B. (p. 380), Lawai B. (p. 402), Poipu/Kiahuna B. (p. 403), Shipwreck B. (p. 403).

◙ STUNNING SUNSETS

OAHU
Ala Moana B.P. (p. 116), Makaha B.P. (p. 185), Sans Souci B. (p. 138).

THE BIG ISLAND
Hapuna B. (p. 256), Makalawena B. (p. 196), Papakolea Green Sands B. (p. 208), Waialea B. (p. 256).

MAUI
Dig Me B. (p. 276), Launiupoko Park (p. 267), Little B. (p. 298), Wailea B. (p. 297).

MOLOKAI AND LANAI
Molokai: Make Horse B. (p. 349), Halawa Bay (p. 345), Lauhue B. (p. 349). Lanai: Shipwreck B. (p. 358), Hulopoe B.P. (p. 359).

KAUAI
Black Pot B. (p. 389), Hanalei Bay (p. 389), Kee B. (p. 394), Lawai B. (p. 402), Lumahai B. (p. 393), Secret B. (p. 385), Tunnels B. (p. 393).

▓ EVERYTHING ELSE

ATV TOURS
Oahu: Kualoa Ranch (p. 167). **Maui:** Maui ATV (p. 315). **Lanai:** Adventure Lanai Ecocentre (p. 352).

DOLPHIN OR WHALE WATCHING
Oahu: Deep Ecology (p. 177). **Maui:** Pacific Whale Foundation (p. 289). **Molokai:** Molokai Action Adventures (p. 347). **The Big Island:** Dolphin Journeys (p. 197).

HORSEBACK RIDING
Oahu: Kualoa Ranch (p. 167). **Maui:** Thompson Ranch (p. 315). **Molokai:** Puu O Hoku Ranch (p. 346). **The**

**BEST ADVENTURES
ON LAND**

Any exploration of the varied terrain of Hawaii, from off-road trails to majestic peaks, will bring you face-to-face with nature's peerless, awesome beauty.

1. Oahu: Trek to the top of **Diamond Head** (p. 139) for an uninterrupted view of city and sky.
2. Oahu: Tiptoe along the water through lowland coastal dunes and pass tide pools in **Kaena Point State Park** (p. 186).
3. The Big Island: Muddy your shoes in the rugged, amazingly lush **Waipio Valley** (p. 243) on the way to Hiilawe Falls, Hawaii's longest single-drop waterfall.
4. The Big Island: Feel the heat from flowing lava at **Hawaii Volcanoes National Park** (p. 210).
5. Maui: Catch the sun cresting over the ocean at **Haleakala National Park** (p. 318).
6. Maui: Splash in the pools at **Oheo Gulch** (p. 312).
7. Molokai: Hike through the **Moomomi Preserve** (p. 341), home to half a dozen plants found nowhere else on the planet.
8. Lanai: Off-road on the **Munro Trail** (p. 357), and catch sight of the other islands.
9. Kauai: Scale down to the base of the **Waimea Canyon** (p. 416) or skirt its edge on its trail in **Kokee State Park** (p. 417).
10. Kauai: Take the multi-day **Kalalau Trail** (p. 396), winding through valleys and hugging plunging cliffs, to some of the world's most spectacular beaches.

Big Island: Waipio Naalapa Stables (p. 243), Waipio on Horseback (p. 243), Paniolo Riding Adventures (p. 248), Dahana Ranch (p. 248).

KAYAKING
    Oahu: Kailua B. (p. 160), Kualoa Regional Park (p. 167), Haleiwa B.P. (p. 177), Mokuleia B. (p. 180). **Maui:** Hana Bay (p. 312), Makena Landing (p. 295), Ahihu Bay (p. 295). **The Big Island:** Kealakekua Bay (p. 203), Flumin' da Ditch (p. 253). **Molokai:** North Shore Sea Cliffs (p. 347), Kaunakakai (p. 333). **Lanai:** Adventure Lanai Ecocentre (p. 352). **Kauai:** Huleia National Wildlife Refuge (p. 370), Wailua River (p. 374), Kapaa B. (p. 382), Na Pali Coast (p. 390), Haena B.P. (p. 393).

KITEBOARDING
    Oahu: Kailua B. (p. 160), Mokuleia (p. 180). **Maui:** Kanaha B. (p. 278). **Kauai:** Kapaa B.P. (p. 382), Waioli B.P. (p. 390), Kepuhi B. (p. 394), Gillins' B. (p. 403).

WINDSURFING
    Oahu: Diamond Head B. (p. 139), Kailua B. (p. 160). **Maui:** Kanaha B.P. (p. 285), North Kihei B. (p. 294), Hookipa B. (p. 305). **The Big Island:** Anuehoomalu B. (p. 255). **Kauai:** Anini B.P. (p. 385), Tunnels B. (p. 393).

USEFUL RESOURCES

A variety of publishing companies offer hiking guidebooks to meet the needs of novices or experts.

Hawaii Trail and Mountain Club. Oahu-based hiking club founded in 1910 to explore and enjoy Hawaii's unique natural heritage and environment. Guests are welcome on their hikes (see schedule online at www.htmclub.org). $2 suggested donation.

The Mountaineers Books, 1001 SW Klickitat Way, Ste. 201, Seattle, WA 98134 (☎206-223-6303; www.mountaineersbooks.org). Over 600 titles on hiking, biking, mountaineering, natural history, and conservation.

The Nature Conservancy of Hawaii, 923 Nuuanu Ave., Honolulu 96817 (☎808-537-4508; www.nature.org/wherewework/northamerica/states/hawaii).

Wilderness Press, 1200 5th St., Berkeley, CA 94710 (☎800-443-7227; www.wildernesspress.com). Carries over 100 hiking guides and maps for the western US.

ORGANIZED ADVENTURE TRIPS

Organized adventure tours offer another way of exploring the wild. Activities include hiking, biking, canoeing, kayaking, and sailing. Tourism bureaus often can suggest parks, trails, and outfitters. Organizations that specialize in camping and outdoor equipment, like **REI** and **EMS** (p. 83), are also good sources.

Hawaii Activities, Aloha Tower 5th fl., 1 Aloha Tower Dr., Honolulu 96813 (☎877-877-1222; www.hawaiiactivities.com). Service that books activities for tourists. Website with links to tour companies offering every kind of activity under the sun.

The Real Hawaii (☎877-597-7325; www.therealhawaii.com). Eco-cultural excursions led by Native Hawaiians.

Specialty Travel Index, P.O. Box 458, San Anselmo, CA 94979 (☎888-642-4030 or 415-455-1643; www.specialtytravel.com). Tours worldwide.

Wild Side Specialty Tours, 87-1286 Farrington Hwy., Waianae 96792 (☎808-306-7273; www.sailhawaii.com). Sailing and kayaking adventures on Oahu.

aliens in hawaii

Hawaii is famous for tropical plants: golden-sweet pineapple, aromatic guava, (chocolate-covered) macadamia nuts, Kona coffee, white plumeria, purple orchids, and bird of paradise are iconic of this island state. In fact, each of these plants was brought here by humans; none are "native" to Hawaii. A "native" species is one that arrived in an area without the intervention of humans, and Hawaii's native species are in trouble.

The Hawaiian Islands are the most isolated place on the planet, in the middle of the world's largest ocean. Not surprisingly then, a distinguishing feature of ancient Hawaii was the absence of any land mammals. (How could a cow or pig get there on its own?) Protection from mammal attack became unnecessary for the species present on the islands, and evolution favored members of these species that could focus their energies elsewhere. Native bees lost their stings, native mint lost its distasteful mint flavor, and native raspberries lacked threatening thorns. Instead, species focused their energies on increasing reproduction. The flower spikes of native mints are often 2-3 times the height of the rest of the plant; endemic raspberries grow so large that it's difficult to hold more than five in your palm. When Polynesians arrived sometime before AD 400, they found islands with no stinging insects, no harmful plants or animals. It was truly paradise.

It was with Western contact that the pace of alien species introduction in Hawaii grew exponentially. Western settlers transported their favorite organisms to Hawaii's paradise. Cows, sheep, goats, and deer selectively munch native Hawaiian plants because they lack thorns and distasteful toxins. These same mammals avoid the more-difficult-to-deal-with alien plants that came pre-adapted to mammal attack. Alien birds flourish too, immune to avian malaria, the disease responsible for exterminating 50% of native species. If alien snakes ever get to Hawaii, many of the last few native birds would suffer a similar fate.

State agencies and NGOs now work together to limit new alien species introductions (which now number several each month). Nurseries assess the threat to the environment of any plant import. The declaration form airplane passengers fill out is the first line of defense against unintentional species introductions. In spite of these safeguards, new organisms continue to get through: two species of noisy tree frogs were recently introduced from Puerto Rico.

By introducing new organisms and changing ecological rules, humans have permanently altered the evolutionary trajectories of species in Hawaii. Had this transformation been gradual, species might have had a chance to respond. However, most of this change happened within the last two centuries. This was simply not

"...humans have permanently altered the evolutionary trajectories of species in Hawaii."

enough time: nearly half of all native Hawaiian species are now extinct.

Yet hope remains. Several *amakihi*, a species of native Hawaiian birds, were recently found living in avian-malaria-ridden zones. It turns out that this species, widespread before the introduction of mosquitoes, had enough genetic diversity for some individuals to carry mutations that allowed them to survive an avian malaria infection. These individuals passed on the mutations while their susceptible compatriots died. Now the majority of these rare creatures is not prone to malaria. Evolution, pushed into overdrive by rapid ecological change, responded to produce populations of resistant birds, creating a pleasant exception to the invasion process so devastating to most of Hawaii's native species.

Michael Judge and Michael Bassford are both Harvard graduates teaching high school science in Honolulu.

OAHU

Oahu appropriately means "the gathering place"— not only is the island the seat of the state government and Hawaii's financial and business center, it is also the home of nearly three quarters of the state's total population. Over half its residents are concentrated in Honolulu, Hawaii's state capital and premier city. This bustling metropolis is the nexus of Oahu, with all the glamor of a major urban center and tourist mecca. Waikiki, a magical mile of beachfront hotels, shops, restaurants, and endless entertainment in the southeastern quarter of the city, is one of the most famous destinations in the world.

Oahu's urban nature makes it a less scenic island than the others, but the commercial tourism does have its benefits. Visitors need not look further than Waikiki to get their fill of tropical kitsch and frenzied nightlife, and downtown Honolulu offers myriad opportunities to explore Hawaii's historical and cultural past. However, with little effort, visitors can venture beyond the gift shops and guided tours and uncover the island's subtler treasures. On the Windward Coast, a pleasant drive passes by rickety fruit stands and acres of pineapple fields on the way to the fabled North Shore, home to some of the world's best surf breaks. Drive 10 mi. up the Leeward Coast and both the scenery and the mood change dramatically; you're in rural Hawaii, where inhabitants embrace a slower, more traditional way of life. The luxuriant Manoa Valley overflows with fragrant blossoms and tropical fruit, and hikers have their pick of countless trails that lead to pockets of unspoiled Hawaiian rainforest.

On Oahu, visitors can discover the multifaceted appeal of Hawaii. Oahu offers the Big Island's hippie culture on the sands of the North Shore, Maui's beauty and opulence in the Windward Coast's resorts, Kauai's natural splendor in the lush interior valleys, and Molokai's rustic charm in the streets of Waimanalo. Consider this your crash course in appreciation of these magnificent islands.

HIGHLIGHTS OF OAHU

PAY YOUR RESPECTS at the Pearl Harbor memorials (p. 144).

SNORKEL BESIDE TROPICAL FISH of all colors at Hanauma Bay (p. 150).

RELIVE THE GLORY of the Hawaiian monarchy at Iolani Palace (p. 116).

CATCH A WAVE at Waikiki Beach (p. 138), the perfect spot to learn to surf.

CLIFF JUMP into the crystalline waters of North Shore's Waimea Bay (p. 171).

✈ INTERISLAND TRANSPORTATION

Honolulu International Airport (HNL; ☎808-836-6413; www.honoluluairport.com) is off the Airport exit from H-1, 9 mi. west of Waikiki. The airport is also accessible via **Ala Moana Boulevard**. Take Ala Moana west until it becomes **Nimitz Highway** and continue west. Turn left into the airport after the Roger's Blvd. intersection underneath H-1. TheBus #8, 19, and 20 make three stops: the Interisland Terminal, Lobby 4, and Lobby 7. TheBus #20 is the Waikiki bus; travelers coming from other parts of the island will have to change at the Nimitz Hwy. stop.

The only **ATM** before security is in the American Airlines office in the main terminal next to the H-2 baggage carousel on the ground level. **Currency exchange**

Oahu

Kaiwi Channel

Kauai Channel

PACIFIC OCEAN

WINDWARD COAST

NORTH SHORE

LEEWARD COAST

Sunset Beach Park
Banzai Pipeline
Shark's Cove
Waimea Bay Beach Park

Malaekahana State Recreation Area

Kahuku

Kamehameha Hwy.

Waimea
Waimea Falls

KOOLAULOA

Laie
Polynesian Cultural Center
Sacred Falls

Hauula

Punaluu

Waimea
Kaawa

Kualoa Regional Park

Mokapu Peninsula

Kaneohe Bay

Kahekili Hwy.

Mokapu Rd.

KOOLAU MTNS.

WAIALUA

WAHIAWA

Wahiawa
Dole Plantation

KOOLAUPOKO

KOOLAU RANGE

HONOLULU

Kailua
Kailua Beach Park
Lanikai Beach

Waimanalo Bay State Recreation Area

Manana (Rabbit) Island

Makapuu Lighthouse

Moko Head

Hanauma Bay

Waimanalo Bay

Sea Life Park

Waimanalo

Maunawili

Nuuanu Pali State Park

Manoa Falls

Kaneohe

Likelike Hwy.

Pali Hwy.

Honolulu

Honolulu International Airport

Diamond Head
760'

Waikiki

Haleiwa

Waialua

Mokuleia Natural Area Reserve

WAIANAE MOUNTAINS

Waianae
Makaha

Maili

Nanakuli

Makaha Beach Park

Kaena Point State Park

Farrington Hwy.

Keaiwa Heiau State Park

Pearl City

Waipahu

Pearl Harbor

Mamala Bay

EWA

Makakilo

Barber's Point Harbor

Barber's Point

83
83
83
99
930
803
801
80
99
750
76
90
90
93
93
930
930
99
H2
H1
H1
H1
H2
H3
H3
78
61
63
72
72
72
92
83
836

5 miles
5 kilometers
0
0

services are available behind all international gates in the main terminal. Taxis and shuttles leave from the median strip outside the baggage claim. Taxis to Waikiki run around $25-30. A cheaper option is **Reliable Shuttle** (☎808-924-9292), which runs between the airport and hotels in Waikiki and Honolulu, as well as the *USS Arizona* Memorial, for about $10. Make reservations at least one day in advance. Shuttles run 24hr., most between 6am and 10pm. See **Interisland Transportation** at the start of each chapter for info on interisland flights.

FLIGHTS

Most of the incoming international, domestic, and interisland flights fly to or through Honolulu International Airport. See **Essentials,** p. 38, for more information. The following are a few major interisland carriers.

Aloha Airlines, 1001 Bishop St., Ste. 130 (☎808-484-1111 or 800-367-5250; www.alohaairlines.com), in downtown Honolulu. Also has ticket offices across Oahu. Service from Burbank, Oakland, Orange County, Las Vegas, Sacramento, and Vancouver, Canada. Also operates interisland flights from Honolulu to Hilo and Kona on the Big Island, Lihue on Kauai, and Kahului on Maui. Bishop St. office open M-F 8:30am-4:30pm.

Hawaiian Airlines (☎808-838-1555; www.hawaiianair.com) has an office at Ala Moana Center (p. 124). Service from: Las Vegas, Los Angeles, Phoenix, Portland, San Diego, Sacramento, San Francisco, and Seattle. Interisland service to Hilo and Kona on the Big Island, Maui, Kauai, Lanai, and Molokai. Ticket office open M-Sa 9:30am-5:45pm.

Island Air (☎808-484-2222; www.islandair.com) services many interisland flights in smaller turbo-prop planes. Usually more expensive than Hawaiian or Aloha Airlines.

HONOLULU

Hawaii's capital and largest city, Honolulu (pop. 377,379) is a commercial center, college town, and living landmark of Hawaiian history. Although downtown Honolulu is less of a tourist destination than Waikiki, its state buildings and civic center sights illuminate the complex history of Hawaii's modernization. Today's Hawaiians inherit a cosmopolitan city as their capital. On weekdays, downtown bustles with businesspeople as they walk through palm tree-lined, skyscraper-filled streets in their finest aloha shirts. Chinatown is crammed with daytime shoppers in search of a deal among its markets, gift shops, and restaurants. The mellow residential outskirts of Kaimuki and the University of Hawaii offset the fast pace of life in the city. Those who do live downtown kick back by slipping away to Manoa's tropical mountains, cruising Waikiki's gorgeous beaches, or barbecuing *ohana*-style at Ala Moana Beach Park.

⊟ LOCAL TRANSPORTATION

BY BUS. Oahu's public transit system, **TheBus** (☎808-848-5555; www.thebus.org) offers service across the island. Many people have expressed frustration that TheBus schedule is meaningless; indeed, the bus times we provide may not hold up, since buses are often stuck in traffic. Service is generally friendly, and if you are not sure of your bus route or stop, drivers are willing to help you find your way. Buses have the same number going in both directions, but the title of the bus changes. All buses are wheelchair-accessible and have A/C.

Fares: One-way fare $2; seniors, disabled, and ages 6-12 $1; under 6 free. Free transfers are good for 2hr. and available upon request from bus driver. **The Oahu Discovery Passport,** available at select ABC Stores, is good for 4 consecutive days of unlimited

Honolulu and Vicinity

OAHU

SEE HONOLULU MAUKA TRAILS MAP p. 129

SEE CHINATOWN MAP p. 112

SEE DOWNTOWN MAP p. 101

SEE ALA MOANA MAP p. 104

SEE WAIKIKI MAP p. 130

Honolulu Watershed Forest Reserve

Puu Konahuanui 3105'

Mt. Olympus 2486'

Manoa Falls

Lyon Arboretum

Mt. Tantalus 2013'

Tantalus Dr.

Round Top Dr.

Oahu Ave.

Kaholoa Dr.

Manoa Marketplace

Waahila Ridge State Recreation Area

10th Ave.

MANOA

MAKIKI

University of Hawaii Manoa

University Ave.

E. Manoa Rd.

Manoa Rd.

Kahala Ave.

Kealaolu Ave.

WAIALAE

Kilauea Ave.

Waialae Ave.

KAHALA

Kupikipikio Point

Diamond Head Rd.

Diamond Head 761'

Diamond Head Beach

Paiolo Ave.

KAIMUKI

KAPAHULU

Kapahulu Ave.

Honolulu Zoo

Monsarrat Ave.

Kapiolani Park

Waikiki Aquarium

MOILIILI

WAIKIKI

Waikiki Beach

Queen's Surf Beach

S. Beretania St.

S. King St.

Honolulu Academy of Arts

Punchbowl National Memorial Cemetery

Pali Hwy.

61

Liliha St.

DOWNTOWN

State Capitol

Palace

Iolani

CHINATOWN

N. King St.

Aloha Tower Marketplace

ALA MOANA

Ala Moana Blvd.

Ala Moana Beach

Mamala Bay

Maunalua Bay

WAILUPE

Wailupe Peninsula

WAIALAE

Kalanianaole Hwy.

TO KOKO HEAD (5m)

72

H1

Bishop Museum

Likelike Hwy.

63

Kalihi Ave.

Middle St.

Dillingham Blvd.

Nimitz Hwy.

KALIHI

Ft. Shafter Military Res.

Kamehameha IV Rd.

H1

78

64

Kapalama Mil. Res.

Sand Island

Keehi Lagoon

Lagoon Dr.

Nimitz Hwy.

Honolulu International Airport

Salt Lake

Moanalua Fwy.

Puuloa Rd.

Salt Lake Blvd.

Salt Lake Blvd.

Camp Catlin Naval Res.

Hickam Air Force Base

92

99 H1

TO PEARL HARBOR (0.5m)

1 mile

1 kilometer

N

travel ($20). **Monthly passes** available at 7-Eleven stores, Satellite City Halls, Times Supermarkets, Star Market Stores, and select ABC stores $40, youth $20, seniors and disabled $5. Monthly passes are valid only for the calendar month. All passes are available at TheBus Pass Office, 811 Middle St.

Routes: *Let's Go: Hawaii* lists TheBus stops near sights whenever applicable. Listed below are a few convenient routes from downtown. Consult a bus schedule or www.thebus.org for more information. Check p. 130 for another list of Waikiki-based buses.

Route A, the **CityExpress,** goes from **Kalihi** and **Waipahu** in the west, then down King and Beretania St. to University Ave. and **Manoa.**

Route B, the other **CityExpress,** runs from the **Kalihi Transit Ctr.** to **Waikiki.**

Route C, the **Country Express,** runs from Makaha to Ala Moana Ctr.

#1 runs from the Kalihi Transit Ctr. through Kalihi and downtown Honolulu on N. King St. It then switches to S. King St. through **Ala Moana, Manoa, Kaimuki,** and the **Kahala Mall.**

#6 runs from above **Punchbowl National Memorial Cemetery,** past the memorial, down Queen Emma St., bisecting downtown. Then it heads left on King St., through Ala Moana and Moiliili to the **University of Hawaii** and **Manoa Heights.**

#9 runs above Kaimuki, through Ala Moana, downtown, and Kalihi, all the way to the **airport.**

#11 starts at the **Alapai Transit Ctr.,** near the **Civic Center,** and runs through downtown onto **H1.** It runs to the **airport** and then heads north on Salt Lake Blvd. through **Foster Village** and **Aiea,** ending at the **Pearlridge Shopping Center.**

#52 starts at the **Ala Moana Center** and heads through downtown, near the **Civic Center,** onto **H1,** around **Pearl Harbor,** and eventually through **Waipio** and **Wahiawa** to the **North Shore.**

#55, 56 run from **Ala Moana Shopping Center,** up Alakea St. in downtown to Nuuanu Ave. where they meet Rte. 63 and continue to **Kaneohe** (#55) and **Kailua** (#56).

Information Lines: Call **TheBus Information Service** (☎808-848-5555) with your location, time of departure, and destination points, and they will find the best route. TheBus also publishes the **TheBus System Map,** available for free in very limited quantities at the Satellite City Hall in Ala Moana Ctr. and at TheBus Pass Office. TheBus website also has the System Map and an online search feature that will display individual routes.

THEBUS: PLUS OR BUST?

TheBus is thought to be one of the great success stories of American public transportation: it has the lowest cost per passenger mile of any system and it is widely used in one of the most expensive cities in the country. That said, the system's erratic schedules and lack of a comprehensive map are enough to driver any visitor nuts. Here are some tips for staying sane:

1. When riding TheBus, be sure to take a transfer from the driver even if you are planning on taking the bus later that day. Although transfers are only valid for two hours, drivers often do not enforce this rule.
2. Either look online or call TheBus route and schedule line for information. If the line's busy, don't fret. The friendly bus drivers are often your best bet for information. They can help you navigate the lack of signage and confusion between express and non-express buses.
3. Try to get yourself TheBus system map from Satellite City Hall. They are limited in number and often run out immediately after they are put out. Keep your eye out for any floating around the bus—finding one is like striking Hawaiian gold.
4. If you need a monthly pass, buy one at the beginning of the month for more bang for your buck. The passes are restricted to the calandar month.

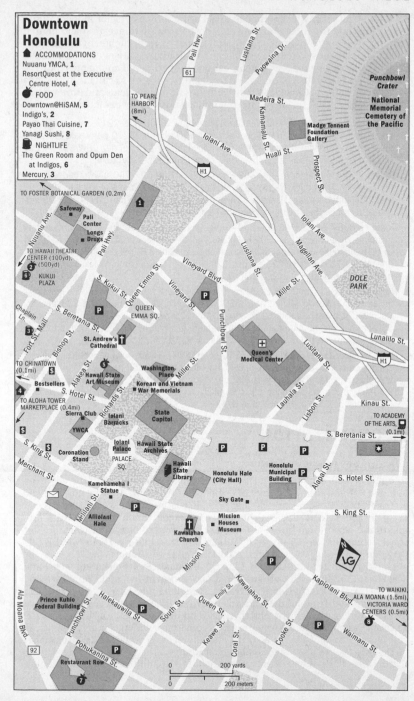

Downtown Honolulu

🏠 **ACCOMMODATIONS**
Nuuanu YMCA, **1**
ResortQuest at the Executive
Centre Hotel, **4**

🍴 **FOOD**
Downtown@HiSAM, **5**
Indigo's, **2**
Payao Thai Cuisine, **7**
Yanagi Sushi, **8**

🍸 **NIGHTLIFE**
The Green Room and Opum Den
at Indigos, **6**
Mercury, **3**

TO PEARL
HARBOR
(8mi)

Pali Hwy.

61

Lusitana St.

Puowaina Dr.

Madeira St.

Kamamalu St.

Iolani Ave.

Huali St.

Prospect St.

Punchbowl Crater

National Memorial Cemetery of the Pacific

Madge Tennent
Foundation
Gallery

Iolani Ave.

Magellan Ave.

H1

TO FOSTER BOTANICAL GARDEN (0.2mi)

Safeway

Pali
Center

Longs
Drugs

Nuuanu Ave.

TO HAWAII THEATRE
CENTER (100yd),
(500yd).

KUKUI
PLAZA

Pali Hwy.

S. Kukui St.

Queen Emma St.

Vineyard Blvd.

Vineyard St.

QUEEN
EMMA SQ.

P

Lusitana St.

Miller St.

DOLE PARK

Lunalilo St.

H1

Chaplain
Ln.

S. Beretania St.

Bishop St.

St. Andrew's
Cathedral

Alakea St.

Richards St.

Punchbowl St.

Miller St.

Lauhala St.

Lishon St.

Lusitana St.

✚
**Queen's
Medical Center**

Kinau St.

TO CHINATOWN
(0.1mi)

Bestsellers

TO ALOHA TOWER
MARKETPLACE (0.4mi)

Fort St. Mall

S. Hotel St.

Hawaii State
Art Museum

Washington
Place

Korean and Vietnam
War Memorials

Sierra Club

YWCA

Iolani
Barracks

State
Capitol

Hawaii State
Archives

TO ACADEMY
OF THE ARTS,
(0.1mi)

S. Beretania St.

✳

OAHU

S. King St.

Coronation
Stand

Iolani
Palace

PALACE
SQ.

Hawaii
State
Library

P

P

P

Merchant St.

Kamehameha I
Statue

Honolulu Hale
(City Hall)

Honolulu
Municipal
Building

P

Alapai St.

S. Hotel St.

Mililani St.

Aliiolani
Hale

P

Sky Gate

S. King St.

Mission
Houses
Museum

Kawaiahao
Church

Mission Ln.

Emily St.

Kawaiahao St.

N

Ala Moana Blvd.

Prince Kuhio
Federal Building

Punchbowl St.

Halekauwila St.

P

South St.

Queen St.

Coral St.

Cooke St.

Kapiolani Blvd.

TO WAIKIKI,
ALA MOANA (1.5mi),
VICTORIA WARD
CENTERS (0.5mi)

8

92

Pohukaina St.

Keawe St.

P

Waimanu St.

Restaurant Row

7

0   200 yards

0   200 meters

BY CAR. While many locals choose to get around by bicycle or moped, Honolulu is first and foremost a driving city, despite traffic congestion and limited parking. The major national car rental chains have branches by the airport and in Waikiki; most require a credit card. Honolulu's tourism capital, Waikiki, holds a number of excellent smaller car and moped rental companies (p. 132). Rental costs fluctuate by season and availability; be sure to call far in advance to reserve a vehicle. Check company websites for online deals and promotions. See **Essentials** (p. 38) for more information on traveling by car in Hawaii.

Enterprise Rent-a-Car, 677 Ala Moana Blvd. #101 (☎808-836-2213; www.enterprise. com), at the airport and in Waikiki. Cars from $30 per day, $210 per week. Unlimited mileage. 21+. Under-25 surcharge $10 per day. Liability $10 per day, CDW $17 per day. Check online for special rates. Open daily 6am-10pm. AmEx/D/MC/V.

Budget, 2424 Kalakaua Ave. (☎808-836-1700 or 800-527-7000; www.budget.com), at the airport and at the Hyatt Regency in Waikiki. Compacts from $34 per day, $210 per week. Unlimited mileage. Liability $14 per day, CDW $25 per day. 21+. Under-25 surcharge $75 per day. Open daily 4:30am-1am. Ask about special rates. AmEx/D/MC/V.

Dollar (☎808-831-2331 or 800-800-4000; www.dollar.com), at the airport and 3 other locations, including one at 2002 Kalakaua Ave., in Waikiki. Cars $30 per day, $210 per week, depending on season. Unlimited mileage. Liability $13 per day, CDW $18 per day. 21+. Under-25 surcharge $25 per day. $20 charge to return car to Waikiki branch. Open daily 4:30am-midnight. AmEx/D/MC/V.

Hertz (☎808-831-3500; www.hertz.com), at the airport and several locations in Waikiki, including the Waikiki Marriot at 2552 Kalakaua Ave. Cars from around $39 per day. Unlimited mileage. Liability $23 per day, CDW $25 per day. 21+. Under-25 surcharge $30 per day. Ask about returning car to another location during reservation; a fee may apply. Pickup and return service. Open 24hr. AmEx/D/MC/V.

National Car Rental (☎808-973-7200 or 800-227-7368; www.nationalcar.com), at the airport and at 1778 Ala Moana Blvd. Cars from around $40 per day, $175 per week. Unlimited mileage. Full coverage $22 per day. 21+. Under-25 surcharge $25 per day. Returns can be made at the other Honolulu locations (must specify at reservation). Open daily 5:30am-midnight. AmEx/D/MC/V.

✈ ORIENTATION

HIGHWAYS AND BYWAYS

Honolulu's main highway, H-1, runs east-west along the length of the city from Kaimuki to the southwest corner of Oahu, past the airport. Getting onto H-1 can be frustrating, as some streets only provide eastbound or westbound access. Freeway access is available via **Ala Moana Boulevard,** which stretches from Waikiki to the airport and turns into Nimitz Hwy. west of Nuuanu River, and **King Street,** which leaves H-1 north of Waikiki and splits into two one-way streets between University Ave. and the Aala Park edge of Chinatown. The one-way streets formed from the split of King St., **Beretania Street** (heading west) and **King Street** (heading east), are the backbone of downtown and Chinatown and bear the brunt of intra-Honolulu traffic. Beretania and King St. also run near many of greater Honolulu's sights and activities. **TheBus** has several routes that ply their way down King St. and then head up Beretania St. for the return trip. **Kapiolani Boulevard** is a major two-way thoroughfare, slicing a northwest-southeast passage from Wailae Ave. to H-1 and intersecting Waikiki's **Kalakaua Avenue** on the way over to its western endpoint at King St. and the Civic Center. Streets that intersect these east-west routes include Kapahulu Ave. (on the eastern edge of Waikiki), University Ave. (from Waikiki to Manoa), Piikoi (northbound one-way from Ala Moana Beach), Pensacola (southbound one-way from around Makiki), and Ward Ave. (along the western edge of the Ward Centers in Ala Moana).

THE LEI OF THE LAND

Honolulu is an abused place-name: it is often used to refer to whatever (or wherever) is presently under discussion. To many, Honolulu means the urban and suburban sprawl that stretches along the South Shore of Oahu, from Koko Head in the east to Kalihi and the airport in the west. Others consider Honolulu the small downtown area surrounded by the districts of **Chinatown** to the west, **Ala Moana** to the south, **Kaimuki** and the revitalized **Waialae** area to the east, and the **University of Hawaii** and **Manoa** valley neighborhoods to the north. Diamond Head Crater in the east provides some of the best views on Oahu while the Koolau Mountain Range forms a backdrop for the varying streetscapes.

HONOLULU NEIGHBORHOODS

Honolulu is a collection of small neighborhoods and Ala Moana, downtown, Chinatown, Manoa and the University Area, and Waikiki are the major districts that will be the focus in this guide. Waikiki is considered separately (p. 129).

ALA MOANA. Spanning Honolulu's waterfront along Ala Moana Blvd. from downtown to Waikiki, Ala Moana is a shopper's paradise. The area is dotted with a number of malls and complexes, including Aloha Tower Marketplace, Restaurant Row, the Victoria Ward Centers, and Ala Moana Shopping Center, which is also a major bus terminal. Many routes stop in front of the mall at Kona St. or behind it on Ala Moana Blvd. While Ala Moana Beach Park offers some opportunity for outdoor recreation, Ala Moana is one of the most commercialized parts of the island and mostly features popular American chain stores and restaurants.

DOWNTOWN. Downtown Honolulu is Hawaii's financial and legislative district. The centrally located Bishop Sq. is Oahu's business powerhouse, and the Senate and House of Representatives sit nearby in the State Capitol. During weekday hours, the streets are crowded with businesspeople, though at any other time of the week the area feels more like a ghost town. Downtown draws a small crowd with the historic sights of the Civic Center and the public art of the financial district for the public art. The downtown area, between Ala Moana and Chinatown, is bordered by the Fort St.

IN RECENT NEWS

RAILING AGAINST THE CITY

Honolulu seems to have it all: tropical beaches, luxurious hotels, and endless cultural sights. Despite its winning combination of fun and sun, this metropolis is plagued by the same problems as all major cities: pollution, crime, overcrowding, and homelessness are all important concerns. The major issue at the forefront of public debate is traffic. To cope with congestion, Honolulu has laid plans to build an above-ground public light rail system. The $4 billion, 10-year project has stirred up a heated public debate.

Proponents say it will relieve the city's traffic nightmare and improve the local economy. Opponents argue that the elevated rail would ruin the skyline and contribute to noise pollution. Either way, the project would be the largest in state history, funded by excise taxes. One group, Stop Rail Now, began a public campaign to collect signatures to place the rail issue on the ballot, insisting that the public has the right to vote on such a massive project.

The debate continues to intensify. Mayor Mufi Hanneman and other proponents in the Go Rail Go coalition have launched TV spots to convince the public. Meanwhile, Stop Rail Now is still gaining support, most recently collecting the John Hancock of Governor Lingle. However, the viability of both a special election ballot and a light rail system remains to be seen.

OAHU

Ala Moana and University Area

▲ ACCOMMODATIONS
Ala Moana Hotel, **11**
Central YMCA, **12**
Hostelling International, **15**
Manoa Valley Inn, **14**
Pagoda Hotel, **13**

● FOOD
California Beach Rock'n Sushi, **1**
Eastside Grill, **20**
Spices, 22
Yanagi Sushi, **3**

Kakaako Kitchen, **5**
Assaggio Ristorante Italiano, **9**
Auntie Pasto's, **7**
Bubbies, **19**
Tsukuneya, **16**
Maharani Cafe, **S**

■ SHOPPING
Ala Moana Shopping
Center, **8**
Victoria Ward
Centers, **4**

▲ NIGHTLIFE
Anna Bannana's, **17**
Brew Moon, **6**
Kimmie's
Cantina, **18**
Mai Tai Bar, **10**
Pipeline Cafe, **2**
The Varsity Bar, **21**

UNIVERSITY OF HAWAII AT MANOA

TO KAIMUKI (2mi)
Kaha Place Mini Park

Lower Campus Rd.

Campus Rd.

University Ave.

Hamell St.
Seaview Ave.
Hoonanea St.
Kaiulu St.
Metcalf St.
Oliver St.
Dole St.
Coyne St.
S. Beretania St.
S. King St.

Down to Earth

S. Beretania St.
Moiliili Park
Coolidge St.
Hausten St.
Isenberg St.

Old Stadium Park

Citron St.

Wilder Ave.
Slade Dr.
Chamberlain Dr.
Punahou St.
Dole St.
Lunalilo Fwy.

Wiliwili St.
McCully St.
Date St.
Fern St.
Lime St.

Kapiolani Women's and Children's Hospital

Shriners Hospital

Makiki St.
Mauu Pl.
Young St.
S. Beretania St.
S. King St.
Alapoko St.
Waiola St.
Citron St.
Hauoli St.
Malanai St.
Phillip St.
Kapiolani Blvd.

Kalakaua Ave.
Kaheka St.
Kanunu St.
Rycroft St.

Hawaii Convention Center

Atkinson Ave.

Ala Wai Blvd.
Kaumu St.
Niu St.
Ala Moana Blvd.

Ala Wai Canal
Ala Wai Blvd.

Kaioo

92

Holomoana St.

Ala Wai Boat Harbor

Keeaumoku St.
Kanaina St.
Makaloa St.
Sheridan St.
Birch St.
Eina St.
Cedar St.
Pensacola St.
Kinau St.
Piikoi St.
Alder St.
Kamanle St.

Hopaka St.
Kona St.
Kapiolani Blvd.
Piikoi St.

Ala Moana Shopping Center

Ala Moana Blvd.

Ala Moana Park Dr.

Ala Moana Regional Park

Aina Moana Recreation Area

500 yards
500 meters

Honolulu Academy of the Arts

THOMAS SQUARE

Neal S. Blaisdell Hall

Victoria St.
Young St.
Ward Ave.

S. Beretania St.
S. Hotel St.
S. King St.
Straub Hospital

TO DOWNTOWN AND CHINATOWN (0.5mi)

TO PUNCHBOWL NATIONAL MEMORIAL CEMETERY (1mi)

Kewalo St.

Waimanu St.
Kawaiahao St.
Kamakee St.
Queen St.
Auahi St.

Ala Moana Beach Park

Mamala Bay

TO 2 (0.2mi)

TO LYON ARBORETUM (3mi) (CONTEMPORARY MUSEUM) (2mi)

Pipers Pali

Kakela St.
Vancouver St.

N

LG

Mall in the west, South St. in the east, Honolulu Harbor in the south, and Vineyard Blvd. in the north. To avoid the headache of one-way streets and parking, take TheBus #1, 2, 13, or B CityExpress to Hotel St. and then explore on foot.

CHINATOWN. Chinatown assaults every sense with pungent fish markets, sizzling dishes, incense-shrouded shrines, and vocal street vendors. Honolulu is home to one of the nation's oldest Chinatowns, which dates back to 1860 and was originally the red light district for sailors. Now it's home to a diverse Asian population, including Chinese, Japanese, Korean, Thai, Vietnamese, and Filipino communities and is consequently a destination for tourists in search of a cultural experience, shopping bargains, and inexpensive food. Chinatown is a small grid of a few square blocks, bordered by downtown to the east and Aala Triangle Park to the west. You'll find Chinatown's shops lining River St., Maunakea St., Smith St., N. Hotel St., and Nuuanu Ave. between Nimitz Hwy. to the south and Kukui St. to the north. Start your exploration at the intersection of Hotel and River St.; from Waikiki take TheBus #2, 13, or B CityExpress.

MANOA AND THE UNIVERSITY AREA. The University of Hawaii (UH) hangs its mortarboard in the pleasant Manoa Valley district, north of the central Honolulu neighborhood of Moiliili. Manoa itself is a peaceful valley overflowing with greenery, lava rock walls, and mango trees. The streets become more tranquil and more hilly as you tread farther up into the valley, away from the city center and toward the Honolulu Watershed Forest Reserve. Two of Honolulu's main roads, University Ave. and Punahou St., become Oahu Ave. and Manoa Rd., respectively, once they hit Manoa. Past Punahou School, Manoa Rd. splits into E. Manoa Rd. and Manoa Rd. E. Manoa Rd. veers to the Manoa Marketplace; Manoa Rd. continues on to Lyon Arboretum and the Manoa Falls trailhead. Strip malls radiate out from the intersection of King St. and University Ave., in the more densely populated Moiliili. West of Manoa, between Punahou School and Punchbowl Crater north of H-1, is the high-rise-clogged neighborhood of Makiki. Excellent hiking and scenic drives are found at the extreme ends of Makiki Heights Dr., Round Top Dr., and Tantalus Dr.

TheBus #4 picks up on Kuhio Ave. in Waikiki and continues north on University Ave. The #5, 6, and 18 all pick up at Ala Moana Shopping Center and head to Manoa. On school days during 6-7:30am, the #80A is an express from Hawaii Kai to lower Manoa and downtown, going as far into Manoa as Dole St. and UH. In the afternoon, #80A runs from Punahou School back to Hawaii Kai.

KAIMUKI. Bordered on the west by Kapaluhu and on the north by Waialae, Kaimuki is an underappreciated neighborhood with inexpensive restaurants, bohemian coffee shops, and quiet residential neighborhoods. Far enough from Waikiki so as not to be touristy, Kaimuki deserves an afternoon of exploring, eating lunch, and browsing in the mom-and-pop stores that dot Waialae Ave. From Downtown take the #1, 3, or 9 bus.

▨ PRACTICAL INFORMATION

Many of Oahu's services are based in Honolulu, but most tourist services can also be found in Waikiki (see **Waikiki, Practical Information,** p. 133).

TOURIST AND FINANCIAL SERVICES

Tourist Information: Hawaii Visitors and Convention Bureau Information Office, 2270 Kalakaua Ave., Ste. 801 (☎808-923-1811 or 800-464-2924; www.gohawaii.com), at

Waikiki Business Plaza. A friendly office with a room full of free tourist magazines, such as *Islands of Aloha Official Vacation Planner.* Open M-F 8am-4:30pm.

Beyond Tourism (p. 67): The Clean Air Team (☎808-948-3299) volunteers lead a pleasant 2 mi., 3hr., stroll through Kapiolani Park and along the Diamond Head Coast, ending at the Diamond Head Lighthouse. Leaves from the Gandhi statue near the **Honolulu Zoo** entrance, 151 Kapahulu Ave. 1st Sa of the mo., 1-3:30pm. Under 18 must be accompanied by an adult. No reservations necessary; groups of 5 or more must call ahead. Parking available at the Waikiki Shell. Free. **The Program to Preserve Hawaiian Placenames,** at the **Liliha Public Library,** 1515 Liliha St. Take H-1 west to School St. and take N. School St. west to Liliha St. Catch the free "Introduction to Hawaiian Words" lecture, the easiest and fastest (1hr.) way to become acquainted with Hawaiian word structure. 1st W of every mo., 7pm. No late arrivals.

Banks and Currency Exchange: With the exception of the Philippine National Bank, all banks have ATMs throughout Honolulu.

Bank of Hawaii, 111 S. King St. (☎808-538-4171 or 888-643-3888; open M-Th 7:30am-3pm, F 7:30am-4:30pm), and in Ala Moana Ctr., 1441 Kapiolani Blvd. (☎942-6111; open M-Th 8:30am-4pm, F 8:30am-6pm, Sa 9am-1pm).

Central Pacific, 220 S. King St. (☎808-544-0500). Open M-Th 7:30am-3pm, F 7:30am-4:30pm.

First Hawaiian Bank, 999 Bishop St. (☎808-525-6340), and in Chinatown, 2 N. King St. (☎808-525-6888). 24hr. line ☎808-844-4444. Both open M-Th 8:30am-4pm, F 8:30am-6pm.

LOCAL SERVICES

Bookstores:

Bestsellers, 1001 Bishop St., #138 (☎808-528-2378, fax 808-528-2389), on the corner of Hotel St. Open M-F 7:30am-5:30pm, Sa 9am-3pm. AmEx/MC/V.

Libraries:

Hawaii State Library, 478 S. King St. (☎808-586-3500; www.librarieshawaii.org), east of Iolani Palace, in the Civic Center—look for the huge white pillars. Added to the State and National Register of Historical Places in 1975, the Hawaii State Library anchors the only state-wide library system in the United States, with a collection of over 3 million books and other materials. Temporary library passes can be purchased there or at any state public library for use at all branches. 3-month visitor's card $10, 5-year nonresident pass $25. Open Tu and F-Sa 9am-5pm, M and W 10am-5pm, Th 9am-8pm.

McCully-Moiliili Public Library, 2211 S. King St. (☎808-973-1099). Open Tu-W and F-Sa 10am-5pm, Th noon-7pm.

Manoa Library, 2716 Woodlawn Dr. (☎808-988-0459). Open Tu 1-8pm; M and W-Sa 10am-5pm.

Outdoor Services:

Department of Parks and Recreation, 1000 Uluohia St., Ste. 309 (☎808-768-3440), in Kapolei, Oahu. Camping permits available at the Main Permits Office, 650 S. King St. (☎808-768-3440). Both offices open M-F 7:45am-4pm.

Hawaii Nature Center, 2131 Makiki Heights Dr. (☎808-955-0100; www.hawaiinaturecenter.org), in Makiki Valley. Hands-on programs, community events, and guided hikes. Schedule available online. Open daily 8am-4:30pm.

Hawaiian Trail and Mountain Club (☎808-674-1459; www.htmclub.org) hikes a different trail every weekend; visitors are welcome. Quarterly hike schedules available online. All hikes meet at Iolani Palace at 8am on each Su and the second Sa of every month. Under 18 must be accompanied by adult. $2 suggested donation for nonmembers.

Sierra Club, 1040 Richards St. rm. 306 in the YWCA (☎808-538-6616). Hikes, outings, and service projects. Visitors and nonmembers welcome. Schedule available online. Unless otherwise noted, hikes leave at 8am from 2510 Bingham St., in Moiliili. Under 18 must be accompanied by adult. $5, Sierra Club members and under 14 $1.

EMERGENCY AND COMMUNICATIONS

Police: Honolulu Police Department, 801 S. Beretania St. (☎808-529-3111). **Downtown-Chinatown Substation,** 79 N. Hotel St. (☎808-529-3932), at the corner of Maunakea St. **Airport Sheriff** (☎808-836-6606).

Crisis Lines: Sex Abuse Center (☎808-524-7273). **Crisis Response Team** (☎808-832-3100). **Poison Center** (☎800-362-3585). **Missing Child Center** (☎808-586-1449).

Fire Department: ☎808-723-7139.

Red Cross: Hawaii Chapter ☎808-734-2101.

24hr. Pharmacies: Longs Drugs, 1330 Pali Hwy. (☎808-536-7302 or 808-536-5542), on the corner of Pali Hwy. and Vineyard Blvd. Both pharmacy and drugstore open 24hr. Another branch at 2220 S. King St. (☎808-949-4781, pharmacy 808-947-2651), across from Honolulu Stadium State Recreation Area. AmEx/D/MC/V.

Hospital: Queen's Medical Center, 1301 Punchbowl St. (☎808-538-9011). An **Emergency Services Department** (☎808-547-4311) provides pre-hospital emergency medical care. Their referral line (☎808-537-7117) can help visitors find a doctor.

Medical Assistance: Urgent Care Clinic of Waikiki, 2155 Kalakaua Ave., Ste. 308 (☎808-432-2000). **Straub Clinic and Hospital,** 888 S. King St. (☎808-522-4000). **Planned Parenthood of Hawaii,** Honolulu Clinic: ☎808-589-1149.

Internet Access: Non-Stop Cyber Cafe (☎808-955-9070) located just north of Rycroft St. on Sheridan St. in central Honolulu. Internet access $2 per 30min., $3 per hour. B/W printing $0.50 per page. Serves coffee, teas, hot noodles, and ice cream. Open 24hr. **Netstop,** 2615 S. King St. Ste. 100 (☎808-955-1020; www.netstopcafe.com), at the intersection of University Ave. in Moiliili. Internet access $0.10 per min. Members pay $2.50 per hour. B/W printing $0.20 per page, color printing $0.70 per page. Free scanning and CD-burning. Coffee $1. Open daily 7:30am-midnight. AmEx/D/MC/V.

Post Offices:

Airport, 3600 Aolele St. (☎808-423-6029), offers the only General Delivery service in Honolulu. Open M-F 7:30am-8pm, Sa 8am-4pm.

Ala Moana, 1450 Ala Moana Blvd., Ste. 1006 (☎808-532-1987). Open M-F 8:30am-5pm, Sa 8:30am-4:15pm.

Downtown Honolulu, 335 Merchant St. (☎808-532-1987). Open M-F 8am-4:30pm.

Postal Codes: 96819 (Airport); 96814 (Ala Moana); 96813 (downtown Honolulu); 96816 (Kaimuki); 96822 (Makiki); 96839 (Manoa); 96828 (Moiliili).

HONOLULU AND WAIKIKI INFORMATION LINES.
Oahu Surf Report: ☎808-973-4383.

US Weather Service Recording: ☎808-973-4380. Might as well be a broken record saying, "It's [82-86°F] and sunny."

Ocean Safety and Lifeguard Services: ☎808-922-3888. A daily message gives a safety report about current water hazards like box jellyfish or Portuguese Men-of-War and a surf and beach condition report.

Foreign Language Translation Service: ☎808-845-3918.

Honolulu Job Information: ☎808-768-8536.

Mayor's Office of Culture and the Arts (MOCA): ☎808-768-6622.

Parks and Recreation Department Information: ☎808-768-3440.

Camping Permits: ☎808-768-3440.

Fishing and hunting permits: ☎808-586-0300.

PUBLICATIONS

The Honolulu Advertiser (www.honoluluadvertiser.com) is Honolulu's most esteemed daily paper, covering national and international news, business, technology, entertainment, sports, and island life. It is available in grocery and convenience stores and street vending boxes (M-Sa $0.50, Su $1.75). **Honolulu Weekly** (www.honoluluweekly.com) is a free community paper with events listings, incisive articles, and reviews available on street corners throughout Honolulu. **This Week Oahu** and **Oahu Gold** are free weekly coupon- and ad-laden brochure magazines available throughout Oahu. Both publications include helpful maps of Waikiki and Oahu. Hawaii Pacific University puts out **Kalamalama,** its student newspaper, 12 times a year. Pick up the paper on magazine racks around campus and write (kalamalama@hpu.edu) if you're interested in writing about student or community issues. **TGIF,** in the Friday edition of the Honolulu Advertiser, is Hawaii's best source for island entertainment listings and editorials.

▐ ACCOMMODATIONS

You'll probably find the best deals in Waikiki, but options exist in other neighborhoods as well. These places usually cater to locals and businesspeople; in general expect a more homey atmosphere, unbeatable amenities, or both in the accommodations outside Waikiki.

BY PRICE

UNDER $25 (❶)		Pagoda Hotel and Terrace (108)	AM
Hostelling International Honolulu (110)	M	Waikiki Gateway Hotel (135)	W
Polynesian Beach Club Hostel (134)	W		
Seaside Hawaiian Hostel (134)	W	**$111-150 (❹)**	
		▨ Manoa Valley Inn (109)	M
$25-66 (❷)		▨ Waikiki Grand Hotel (135)	W
Hale Aloha Hostel (HI Waikiki) (135)	W	▨ Aqua Bamboo (135)	W
Central YMCA (109)	AM	Ala Moana Hotel (108)	AM
Nuuanu YMCA (109)	DC		
Waikiki Beachside Hostel (134)	W	**$151 AND UP (❺)**	
		ResortQuest at the Executive	DC
$66-110 (❸)		Centre Hotel (109)	
Pacific Marina Inn (110)	G		

AM Ala Moana **DC** Downtown and Chinatown **G** Greater Honolulu **M** Manoa **W** Waikiki

BY LOCATION

ALA MOANA

Ala Moana Hotel, 410 Atkinson Dr. (☎808-955-4811; www.alamoanahotel.com). A great location within walking distance of the shopping center, bus routes, and Waikiki, this colossal hotel has 36 floors and a sleek design, thanks to recent renovations. It tops all but the best of Waikiki's hotels, with a state-of-the-art fitness room, pool deck, 4 restaurants, and the popular Rumours nightclub. The enormous lobby features several shops and business center with Internet ($12 per hr.). 24hr. reception. Parking $15 per day. Check-in 3pm. Check-out noon. Doubles $150-190. AmEx/D/MC/V. ❹

Pagoda Hotel and Terrace, 1525 Rycroft St. (☎808-941-6611; www.pagodahotel.com). From Waikiki, take Kapiolani Blvd. west from McCully St. and turn right onto Kaheka St.; take second left onto Kanunu St. to the parking lot on the right. Outstanding rates and

OAHU

promotions make up for an inland location and dated decor. The Pagoda Hotel has standard 2-person doubles in the 12-floor tower and 1-2 bedroom suites and studios with kitchenettes in the terrace building. Terrace rooms can accommodate up to 6 people. All rooms have A/C, cable TV, Wi-Fi ($10 per day), and access to 2 pools. The Floating Pagoda restaurant is accessible by bridge over the koi pond. Parking $7 per day. 24hr. reception. Check-in 3pm. Check-out noon. Standard doubles and 2-bedroom terrace room with kitchenette start at $126 (weekday) and $148 (weekend). Check out "hot deal" promotional rates on their website. AmEx/D/MC/V. ❸

Central YMCA, 401 Atkinson Dr. (☎808-941-3344), across the street from the Ala Moana Hotel. Catering to budget tourists with a fantastic location outside Waikiki, 1 block from Ala Moana Beach Park. College-style dorms with a twin bed, desk, chair, and storage closet. Limited A/C available. Amenities include use of the pool, fitness room, and free access to exercise classes. Internet access in lobby ($1 per 10min.). Parking $5 extra per day. No reservations accepted. Check-out 10am. 18+ with photo ID. Single with shared bath (male only) $40, with private bath (male or female) $54; doubles $61. Building hours M-F 5am-10pm, Sa 5am-7pm, Su 7am-7pm. AmEx/MC/V. ❷

DOWNTOWN AND CHINATOWN

ResortQuest at the Executive Centre Hotel, 1088 Bishop St. (☎808-539-3000). From H-1 East, take Exit 21A and turn right onto Pali Hwy., which becomes Bishop St. As the only hotel in the financial district, the Executive Centre Hotel caters primarily to business travelers with same-day laundry and dry cleaning for a fee, free in-room Internet, and 24hr. business center. Rooms are neat, spacious, and comfortable but not luxurious. Outdoor whirlpool and sun deck with a 20m lap pool. Continental breakfast included. Check-in 3pm. Check-out noon. Business suites from $230. 1-bedroom executive suites with full kitchen and in-room washer/dryer from $290. AmEx/D/MC/V. ❺

Nuuanu YMCA, 1441 Pali Hwy. (☎808-536-3558; www.ymcahonolulu.org). From H-1 East, take exit 21A and turn right onto Pali Hwy. Make a U-turn at S. Vineyard Blvd. Simple rooms and well-maintained facilities. Guests have free access to a lap pool and cardio room. Hall phones with free outgoing local calls. No A/C. Key deposit $5. Reception 24hr. No reservations accepted. Check-in 3pm. Check-out noon. Single rooms $33. Weekly rooms $210. AmEx/MC/V. ❷

MANOA AND THE UNIVERSITY AREA

🏠 **Manoa Valley Inn,** 2001 Vancouver Dr. (☎808-947-6019; www.manoavalleyinn.com). Take Kapiolani

FROM THE ROAD

EUREKA, ALOHA!

Since my arrival on Oahu, I had heard a lot about the aloha spirit. I had yet to witness any extraordinary acts of this famous friendliness until about two weeks into my stay. I was assigned to explore some of the galleries in Chinatown and stumbled upon a gallery of pen-and-ink drawings. I knocked on the door and an older woman answered. Her name was Ramsay, the owner of the gallery. As I soon learned, Ramsay is an internationally recognized artist who has been instrumental in the preservation of historic Chinatown.

Ramsay took me around and told me the story behind each of her drawings. A piece replicating a cat's tongue while the animal was on PCP gave away that Ramsay was a bit... eccentric. As I prepared to move on, Ramsay noticed my substantial sunburn. "My husband is a dermatologist," she insisted. "I'll have him bring you some sunscreen."

Dr. Norm brought me sunscreen samples. Ten minutes later, both invited me out to dinner. After a four-course meal, they drove me home. They left me assured that they were my new adoptive parents and ordered me to call them if I ever needed anything. Each of the couple's acts of kindness was not only genuine, but impossible to refuse. Though Ramsay and Dr. Norm are singular people, I came to recognize their generosity as indicative of the openness of that elusive aloha spirit.

—Claire Saffitz

Blvd., S. King St., or H-1 to University Ave. and drive *mauka* (toward the mountains). Turn left onto Vancouver. Built in 1912, this cozy, Victorian-style inn is a perfect hideaway from the hurried pace of Honolulu; staying here is completely worth the 20min. drive to downtown. Complimentary continental breakfast is served each morning on the breezy veranda. Hot tub in the garden. Free parking for compact cars. 2-night min. Check-in 3pm. Check-out 11am. Make reservations at least 1 mo. in advance to reserve one of the inn's 8 rooms. Doubles with shared bath $140, private bath $170; cottage with A/C and fridge $145. Reduced rates in low season. MC/V. ❹

Hostelling International Honolulu, 2323A Seaview Ave. (☎808-946-0591; www.hiayh. org). Turn onto Seaview Ave. from University Ave.; the hostel is opposite the UH campus 4 blocks north of H-1. The best-kept hostel in Honolulu welcomes international travelers with tidy rooms in a mellow residential neighborhood. Free lockers (bring padlock). Linen $2. Communal bath, fully equipped and orderly kitchen, coin-op laundry, and comfortable cable TV lounge. 3-day max. for nonmembers, 7-day max. for members. Reception 8am-noon and 4pm-midnight. Reserve 2 weeks in advance. Single-sex 6- or 7-bed dorms $18 for members, nonmembers $21. AmEx/MC/V. ❶

GREATER HONOLULU

Pacific Marina Inn, 2628 Waiwai Loop (☎808-836-1131, fax 808-833-0851). Take the frontage road from Nimitz Hwy. outside the airport east to Lagoon Dr.; make a left onto Waiwai Loop. Just 5 min. from the airport, Pacific Marina Inn offers no-frills rooms at decent prices but is far removed from the activity of downtown and Waikiki. The closest beach is Ala Moana Beach Park, at least a 25-minute bus ride away. Pool, cable TV, and free Wi-Fi. Free 24hr. transportation to the airport. Limited free parking. 24hr. reception. Check-in 3pm. Check-out noon. Check online for "hot deal" promotions. Standard rooms (one queen or two twin beds) $128-140, 4-person room (2 double beds) $143-160, suites (1 queen and two twin beds; on request only) $170. AmEx/D/MC/V. ❸

🗲 FOOD

BY TYPE

ASIAN
🗾 Indigo's (111)	D ❹
🗾 Legends Seafood (113)	C ❷
🗾 Little Village (113)	C ❸
🗾 Mekong Thai Restaurant (115)	K ❷
🗾 Siam Palace Restaurant (115)	K ❶
California Beach Rock 'n Sushi (111)	AM ❸
Kit N Kitchen (115)	M ❸
Maharani Cafe (115)	M ❸
Matsugen (137)	W ❸
Payao Thai Cuisine (112)	D ❷
Pho To-Chau Vietnamese (113)	C ❶
Spices (114)	M ❸
Tsukuneya (114)	M ❸
Yanagi Sushi (112)	D ❸

AMERICAN
🗾 Andy's Sandwiches and Smoothies (114)	M ❶
Eastside Grill (114)	M ❷

ITALIAN
🗾 Petite Garlic (136)	W ❸
🗾 Auntie Pasto's (115)	K ❷
Arancino (136)	W ❸
Assaggio Ristorante Italiano (111)	AM ❸

CAFES AND BAKERIES
🗾 Bubbies (114)	M ❶
🗾 Coffee Talk (115)	K ❶
🗾 Leonard's Bakery (136)	W ❶
Covenant Books and Coffee (115)	K ❶

LOCAL
🗾 Ono Hawaiian Foods (136)	W ❷
Kakaako Kitchen (111)	AM ❷
South Shore Grill (136)	W ❶
Rainbow Drive-In (137)	W ❶

OTHER
🗾 Azteca Mexican Restaurant (115)	K ❷
🗾 Olive Tree (115)	K ❷

OAHU

The Pyramids (136)	W ❸	Maunakea Marketplace (113)	C
Ruffage Natural Foods (136)	W ❶	Food Pantry (135)	W
Brasserie du Vin (113)	C ❹	Manoa Marketplace (114)	M
Downtown @ the HISAM (112)	D ❸	Oahu Market (113)	C
GROCERY STORES AND MARKETS		People's Open Market Program (135)	W
Diamond Head Market and Grill (135)	W	Safeway (114)	M
Down to Earth (114)	M		

AM Ala Moana **C** Chinatown **D** Downtown **G** Greater Honolulu **K** Kaimuki **M** Manoa **W** Waikiki

BY LOCATION

ALA MOANA

California Beach Rock 'n Sushi, 404 Ward Ave. (☎808-597-8000). You pay for quality, not for ambience, in this restaurant which attracts a young clientele with its creative spin on traditional Japanese. The specialty rolls like Stuntman ($12) and Crunchy Roll ($12) are especially popular. 3-course early-bird special includes choice of salmon or chicken teriyaki, choice of sushi, sashimi, or california roll, and tempura (5-6:30pm; $13). Lunch specials $7-11. Small glass of sake $4-13. Happy hour sushi specials 5-6pm. Lunch M-F 11am-2pm. Dinner M-Th 5-10pm, F-Sa 5-11pm, Su 5-9pm. AmEx/D/MC/V. ❸

Kakaako Kitchen, 1200 Ala Moana Blvd. (☎808-596-7488), at the Ward Center. The flavorful cooking at Kakaako Kitchen is worth the wait in line: plates include *bubu arare* crusted fillet of wild salmon with lemon-ginger sauce and soy-*shichimi* aioli, $12. *Furikake* tempura catfish with *ponzu* sauce $9. Gourmet salads $9-12. Sandwiches $8-12. Special plates change daily. Takeout with outside seating available. Open M-F 8am-9pm, Sa-Su 8am-10pm. MC/V. ❷

Assaggio Ristorante Italiano, 1450 Ala Moana Blvd Ste. 1259 (☎808-955-9517), located inside Ala Moana Shopping Center. Assaggio is not your typical mall restaurant. The restaurant serves a variety of pastas ($14-18) and other Italian dishes in small or large portions at moderate prices. The elegant dining room and koi fountain help make up for the unsightly view of the Macy's parking lot. Reservations recommended. Lunch daily 11am-3pm; dinner M-Th, Su 4:30-9:30pm, F-Sa 4:30-10pm. AmEx/D/MC/V. ❸

DOWNTOWN

Restaurant Row, 500 Ala Moana Blvd., between Punchbowl and South St., houses an assortment of restaurants, nightclubs, gift stores, and theaters. The modern, geometrically designed, open-air structure appeals to a medley of tastes—visitors can choose between 11 restaurants that range from Italian to Thai and from casual to fine dining. From Waikiki, head west on Ala Moana Blvd., turn right onto South St., and park in the covered garage.

 SUNDAY MORNING. If you plan on exploring the downtown and Chinatown area on the weekend, do most of your sightseeing on Saturday. Many businesses and restaurants close their doors on Sunday.

Indigo's, 1121 Nuuanu Ave. (☎808-521-2900). Indigo's serves up a delicious fusion of European and Asian flavors with an emphasis on Hawaiian ingredients (miso marinated salmon filet $22; Indigo crab cakes with chipotle aioli $12). With island-chic decor, a relaxed atmosphere, and an open-air bar facing a garden, this place is a treat. Starters $8-14. Entrees $18-34. Lunch and dinner reservations recommended. Lunch Tu-F 11:30am-2pm. Dinner Tu-Sa 6-9:30pm. D/MC/V. ❹

OAHU

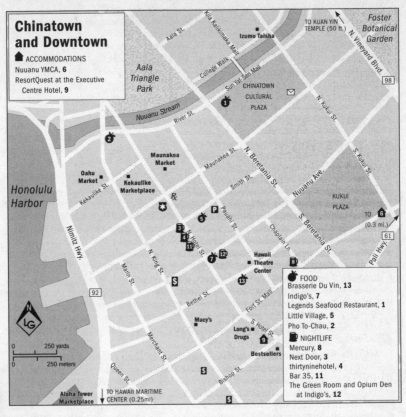

Chinatown and Downtown

⌂ ACCOMMODATIONS
Nuuanu YMCA, **6**
ResortQuest at the Executive
Centre Hotel, **9**

Aala Triangle Park

Honolulu Harbor

Izumo Taisha

TO KUAN YIN
TEMPLE (50 ft.)

Foster Botanical Garden

CHINATOWN
CULTURAL
PLAZA

Maunakea
Market

Oahu
Market

Kekaulike
Marketplace

KUKUI
PLAZA

Hawaii
Theatre
Center

Macy's

Long's
Drugs

Bestsellers

🍴 FOOD
Brasserie Du Vin, **13**
Indigo's, **7**
Legends Seafood Restaurant, **1**
Little Village, **5**
Pho To-Chau, **2**

🍸 NIGHTLIFE
Mercury, **8**
Next Door, **3**
thirtyninehotel, **4**
Bar 35, **11**
The Green Room and Opium Den
at Indigo's, **12**

Aloha Tower
Marketplace

TO HAWAII MARITIME
CENTER (0.25mi)

0   250 yards
0   250 meters

Yanagi Sushi, 762 Kapiolani Blvd. (☎808-597-1525; www.yanagisushi-hawaii.com). This 30-year-old sushi restaurant is a standout in a city with a slew of Japanese restaurants. A local favorite for hand-rolled sushi of the finest quality. Opt for a seat at the bar. The extensive menu includes several fine sakes and specialty rolls, like the volcano roll (reversed California roll, baked scallop, crab meat, cucumber, avocado, mayonnaise; $9.50). Sushi and sashimi $5-15. Late-night specials M-Sa 10:30pm-2am. Lunch daily 11am-2pm. Dinner M-Sa 5:30pm-2am, Su 5:30-10pm. MC/V. ❸

Downtown @ the HISAM, 250 Hotel St. (☎8808-536-5900) On the first floor of the Hawaii State Art Museum, this casual cafe offers diners gourmet lunch fare in a modern, light-filled setting. The menu emphasizes Mediterranean flavors with locally grown and organic ingredients. Try the seared *ahi* club sandwich with avocado, bacon, wasabi, and organic lettuce ($10.50). Soups $4-6, small plates $6-9, large plates $10-16. A take-out deli counter called **Downtown ASAP!** also serves salads, quiches, and panini at fair prices. Free Wi-Fi. Lunch M-Sa 11am-2pm. Plans to open for dinner soon. MC/V. ❸

Payao Thai Cuisine, 500 Ala Moana Blvd. #1E (☎808-521-3511), in Restaurant Row. You wouldn't know it from the sparsely decorated interior, but Payao has a devoted following of patrons who rave about its authentic approach to Thai food. Known as the "home of sticky rice," Payao serves the specialty extra-sticky in cute bamboo containers. Payao offers an assortment of affordable, appetizing selections (curries $8.50-10.50;

OAHU

pad thai ($8.50-10.50) as well as a varied vegetarian menu (all entrees $7.50). Try Payao's Evil Tofu. Lunch M-Sa 11am-2pm. Dinner daily 5-9pm. AmEx/D/MC/V. ❷

CHINATOWN

While this is the best place to get Chinese, the thrill of Chinatown is hunting through markets for other cheap and delicious ethnic specialties, such as giant bowls of Vietnamese *pho*, Filipino chicken *adobo*, and Korean *kimchee*. Dozens of flower shops also line the streets, selling leis strung right in front of you. Most markets are along N. King St. and Hotel St. and are bounded by River St. and Maunakea St. For fruits and vegetables, peruse the outdoor vendors along N. King St.; for fish and poultry, prepare yourself for unusual cuts of meat, including whole pigs' heads, hanging in the covered stalls of **Oahu Market,** at the corner of N King St. and Kekaulike St. (Most stalls are open 6am-4pm.) Connecting N King St. and Hotel St. is pedestrian-only Kekaulike Mall, where vendors sell fresh seafood and other produce. Hotel St. is also populated by fruit and vegetable stands and shops with extensive selections of sun-dried fruit. Inside Chinatown's primary shopping plaza, ▨**Maunakea Marketplace,** arranged around a sunny courtyard at Hotel St. and Maunakea St., you'll find fish and poultry vendors, a food court with Chinese, Vietnamese, Thai, Korean, and Filipino fast food (most entrees under $7), and small shops that sell everything from aloha-print T-shirts (starting at 2 for $5) to bubble tea, fake designer bags, and Thai movies. (Most stalls open around M-Sa 7am-6pm, Su 7am-3pm.) Keep in mind that these are not typical malls and most shops do not accept credit cards. Many vendors sell the same thing so look around for the best deal.

> **TIP** **CASH MONEY.** Be sure to bring cash if you plan on shopping in Chinatown. Most street vendors do not take credit cards.

▨ **Little Village Noodle House,** 1113 Smith St. (☎808-545-3008). Step into this spacious, bamboo-accented restaurant for exquisite, health-conscious Chinese food prepared with the freshest ingredients (no MSG). Signature dishes such as clams in black bean sauce ($14), sizzling scallops ($14), and eggplant with garlic sauce ($8) will renew your faith in Chinese restaurants. The tofu potstickers with chives ($4.50 for 4) are wildly popular. Free parking in the lot next to the restaurant. Open M-Th and Su 10:30am-10:30pm, F-Sa 10:30am-midnight. AmEx/D/MC/V. ❸

▨ **Legends Seafood Restaurant,** 100 N. Beretania St., Ste. 108 (☎808-532-1868), in the Chinatown Cultural Plaza. Legends is probably the nicest Chinese restaurant in Chinatown (read: linen tablecloths and napkins), and thankfully, that elegance does not inflate its price. Appetizing dim sum is served the traditional way: from a train of circling carts. The dumplings come in small ($2.15), medium ($3), and large ($4). There is also a regular menu with over 100 dishes, nearly a third of them seafood ($12-16) Open M-F 10:30am-2pm and 5:30-9pm, Sa-Su 8am-2pm and 5:30-9pm. MC/V. ❷

Pho To-Chau Vietnamese Restaurant, 1007 River St. (☎808-533-4549). Join the masses for the most unbelievable pho noodle soup you've ever had ($4-6). Get there early; sometimes a line forms by 9:45am. Open daily 8am-2:30pm. Cash only. ❶

Brasserie du Vin, 115 Bethel St. (☎808-545-1115). A romantic wine bar with dark wood interior, French-inspired decor, and an outdoor patio. The extensive wine menu is designed to be user-friendly, organized "by the region" and "by the grape." Bottles starting from $20 to over $100. The sommelier is more than happy to help you pair a wine with your meal and will pour a glass of any wine for 1/3 the bottle price. Try the escargot in herbed garlic butter ($10). Daily *prix-fixe* menu includes appetizer, entree, and des-

OAHU

sert $(25). Starters $4-14, entrees $16-25. Happy hour 4-6pm. Live music on W. Lunch 11:30am-4pm. Dinner M-Sa 4pm-late. AmEx/D/MC/V. ❹

MANOA AND THE UNIVERSITY AREA

To get to **Manoa Marketplace,** take University Ave. north from H-1 past the UH campus. Bear right to merge with Oahu Ave. and take a quick right onto E. Manoa Rd. The Manoa Marketplace parking lot is after Huapala St., the fourth street on the right. By bus, take Woodlawn Dr. #6 from Ala Moana Shopping Center. The marketplace is where Manoa residents run errands—a quiet area removed from the activity of downtown. The pink buildings are filled with small shops and inexpensive ethnic restaurants (choose among dim sum, sushi, plate lunch, and Korean barbecue). Most establishments don't take credit cards, but there is an ATM in Safeway and at the Bank of Hawaii. (Open M-Th 8:30am-4pm, F 8:30am-6pm, Sa 9am-1pm.)

Puck's Alley, at the intersection of University Ave. and King St., just south of H-1 in Moiliili, is a strip mall with a number of inexpensive restaurants and retail stores. A short walking distance from campus, Puck's Alley is also close to many popular college bars in the Moiliili area. The A CityExpress bus stops in front of Puck's; otherwise take TheBus #1, 4, 6, or 18.

For groceries, try ◙**Down to Earth,** 2525 S. King St., a reasonably priced health food store with a salad bar, sandwich and smoothie counter, and bakery full of good-for-you (or at least not-too-bad-for-you) goodies. There is also an upstairs area with seating for diners. (☎808-947-7678. Open daily 7:30am-10pm. AmEx/D/MC/V.) For basics, **Safeway** is next to Manoa Marketplace, 2855 E. Manoa Rd. (Open 24hr. AmEx/D/MC/V.)

◙ **Andy's Sandwiches and Smoothies,** 2904 E. Manoa Rd. (☎808-988-6161), across from Manoa Marketplace. This Manoa institution, family owned and operated for 30 years, is loved for big sandwiches on homemade bread (fresh-roasted turkey sandwich $4), vegetarian options (mushroom medley, $5), and fruit smoothies ($3.25-3.75). The Manoa Delite (avocado, mushroom, tomatoes, melted cheese, carrots, lettuce, sprouts, and papaya seed dressing; $6.85) is delicious. Open M-F 7am-5:30pm, Su 7am-2pm. Breakfast served M-F 7am-10:15am, Su 7am-noon. AmEx/MC/V. ❶

◙ **Bubbies,** 1010 University Ave. (☎808-949-8984), on Coyne St. Named for proprietor Keith Robbins's grandmother, Bubbies is recognized by the Hawaii State Senate as "one of the best things about Hawaii." The homey store offers 16 heavenly ice cream flavors (coconut delight, green tea, and rotating specials) and a long list of creative desserts. One of their specialties is mochi-wrapped ice cream ($1, chocolate-dipped $1.50). Full of students on weekends during the school year. For the best value, buy ice cream by weight. Open M-Th noon-midnight, F-Sa noon-1am, Su noon-11:30pm. Cash only. ❶

Spices, 2671 S. King St. (☎808-949-2679). Spices dishes up pan-Southeast Asian cuisine to regulars in a minimalist but warm atmosphere. Try the Buddha's Delight (a vegetarian stir-fry of baby vegetables; $14). Tapioca pudding with Okinawan sweet potato topping $4. Parking available behind restaurant. BYOB, $5 cork fee. Lunch Tu-F 11:30am-2pm. Dinner Tu-Sa 5:30-10pm, Su 5-9pm. MC/V. ❸

Eastside Grill, 1035 University Ave. (☎808-952-6555), in Puck's Alley. Popular with the UH crowd, Eastside Grill serves classic bar food like burgers, fried appetizers, and sandwiches. Their most popular dish is the sizzling steak, which diners can enjoy while watching sporting events on any of the numerous flatscreen TVs. In the evenings Eastside Grill becomes a bar scene with weekly live entertainment (2-drink minimum). *Pupu* $5-8. Entrees $8-10. Open daily 11am-1:30am. MC/V. ❷

Tsukuneya, 1442 University Ave. and Dole St. (☎808-943-0390), across from the UH campus. If you thought that Japanese cuisine was all about sushi, try Tsukuneya, which serves food from the region of Nagoya. Part of an upscale Hawaiian chain, Tsukuneya has a sleek interior with curved banquets and mood lighting. Their specialty is *tsukune*, a Japanese-style meatball made of chicken that is grilled on a skewer. Try the homemade tofu ($6.75). Skewers $2-10. Entrees $5-13. Open M and Su 5pm-midnight, W-Th 5pm-midnight, Sa 5pm-1am. AmEx/D/MC/V. ❸

Maharani Cafe, 2509 S. King St. (☎808-951-7447), next to Down to Earth. Indian cuisine in a casual atmosphere (an Indian film is usually on the TV). The *Shahi* chicken *korma* ($10.50), marinated in yogurt and cooked in a creamy spice sauce, is delicious. A range of vegetarian options includes eggplant tikka masala ($11) and mango *lassi* ($3). Open M-F 5-10pm. MC/V. ❸

Kit N Kitchen, 1010 University Ave. (☎808-942-7622). This offbeat, East-meets-West diner serves comfort food with a fusion of Italian and Asian flavors. The lengthy menu offers many types of spaghetti ($10), gratins ($11), pizzas ($5-10), and specialties for the adventurous (volcano chicken roasted with flaming spicy marinara sauce, $12; ox tail udon, $11). Lighter fare such as soups and salads are served at lunchtime. Open daily 11am-2:30pm and 5-10pm. MC/V. ❸

KAIMUKI

🍴 **Olive Tree,** 4614 Kilauea Ave. Ste. 107 (☎808-737-0303), in Kahala Korner. Located east of Kaimuki in Kahala, this hip and hidden Greek restaurant is worth the extra bus ride (take the #14 from Kaimuki). Don't leave without trying their mussel ceviche appetizer with ginger, lime, and herbs ($6) and the lamb souvlaki ($11) served with a Greek side salad. BYOB. Open nightly 5-10pm. Cash only. ❷

🍴 **Azteca Mexican Restaurant,** 3617 Waialae Ave. (☎808-735-2492) This neighborhood restaurant is a local favorite for classic Mexican food, like enchiladas ($9.50-12) and fajitas ($13). Light lunch plates ($6.50-7) served until 4pm. Margaritas $5-6.50. Open M-Th 11am-9:30pm, F-Sa 11am-10pm, Su 5pm-9:30pm. AmEx/D/MC/V. ❷

🍴 **Siam Palace Restaurant,** 3404 Waialae Ave. (☎808-732-7433). Siam Palace probably has the freshest and most flavorful Thai food in all of Oahu. Favorites include the calamari and spring roll appetizers ($6-8) and the *pad siew,* a chow-fun noodle with broccoli in a yellow bean sauce. BYOB. Open daily 5-10pm. AmEx/D/MC/V. ❶

🍴 **Mekong Thai Restaurant,** 1295 S. Beretania St. (☎808-591-8841). Long considered one of the best Thai restaurants in Honolulu, Mekong is unbeatable for three reasons: delicious Thai food, affordable prices, and friendly service. One of their signature dishes is the Evil Jungle Prince, which is less scary and more tasty than it sounds (sauteed beef, pork, chicken, or vegetables in a spicy coconut-milk curry sauce with chiles, lemongrass, and Thai basil; $10-11). Vegetarian entrees $10; green papaya salad $8; yellow, red, green, and Panang curries $12-14. Reservations recommended on weekends. Open M-F 11am-2pm and daily 5:30-9:30pm. AmEx/D/MC/V. ❷

🍴 **Auntie Pasto's,** 1099 S. Beretania St. (☎808-523-8855), on the corner of S. Beretania and Pensacola St. Auntie Pasto's serves inexpensive Italian American classics such as eggplant parmesan ($11) atop red-checkered tablecloths in a friendly atmosphere. The homemade gnocchi ($12) is a local favorite. Gourmet pizzas $11-13, pasta $8.50-13. Open M-Th 11am-10:30pm, F 11am-11pm, Sa 4-11pm, Su 4-10:30pm. MC/V. ❷

🍴 **Coffee Talk,** 3601 Waialae Ave. (☎808-737-7444). This colorful corner cafe serves coffee and espresso drinks ($2-4.50), sandwiches ($5.75-7), salads ($5-6.25), and delectable pastries and desserts (try the chocolate-chip bread pudding). The free Wi-Fi means you can sit in the sun-filled cafe for hours ($0.15 per minute). Also displays original art and photographs. Open M-F 5am-10pm, Sa-Su 6am-10pm. MC/V. ❶

Covenant Books and Coffee, 1142 12th Ave. (☎808-732-4600), If you don't mind eating your lunch surrounded by books about Christianity and theology, Covenant Books and Coffee is a holy choice. The cafe is known for its daily rotation of fresh, homemade soups, including creamy smoked salmon and asparagus, roasted garlic and potato, and crab bisque ($3.50). Soup with a half salad $6. Open M-Sa 7am-5pm. Breakfast served 7am-10am. AmEx/D/MC/V. ❶

🏖 BEACHES

As a rule, the closer you are to Waikiki, the more populated the sand will be. Ala Moana presents a peaceful, nearby option for avoiding the crowds.

ALA MOANA BEACH PARK. *(Open daily 4am-10pm. Lifeguards 9am-5:30pm.)* Ala Moana means "path to the sea," and the palm tree-dotted park leads the way. A popular jogging circuit runs around **Mamala Bay,** which is perfect for an easy swim. The circuit then veers onto **Magic Island (Aina Moana),** a peninsula that juts out on the east side of the bay, separating the beach from the Ala Wai Yacht Harbor. Magic Island may be the best spot in the city to watch the sun dissolve into the sea and sky, casting translucent beams of light through the looming clouds that frequently roll over the mountains. The beach is in front of Ala Moana Shopping Center, on Ala Moana Park Dr. Access driveways are at the western end of the park, just past Kamakee St. Alternatively, take TheBus #8, 19, 20, 42, or 58 to the Ala Moana Shopping Center. Public tennis courts are first-come first-served, with play limited to 45 minutes. Restrooms and outdoor showers are available. Alcohol, animals, ball-playing, frisbee, and camping are prohibited.

👁 SIGHTS

DOWNTOWN

THE HAWAII MARITIME CENTER. The family-friendly Maritime Center chronicles Hawaii's maritime history, from the outrigger ships of ancient Polynesian explorers to the present. The largest exhibit focuses on Hawaii's whaling industry in the 19th century and features a humpback whale skeleton on display—one of only a few in the world. Included in the price of admission is a rather dry 45-minute audio tour, access to a lookout tower with views of Honolulu harbor, and passage aboard the stationary Falls of Clyde, the last four-mast, fully-rigged ship in the world and the center's largest draw. *(On Pier 7 at Honolulu Harbor, across from Aloha Tower Marketplace, off Nimitz Hwy.* ☎ *808-536-6373. Open daily 8:30am-5pm. $8.50, seniors and students $5, ages 4-12 $5.50, under 4 free.)*

CIVIC CENTER

East of Honolulu's business district, skyscrapers give way to peaceful, open, grassy areas around the Civic Center's government buildings and historic sights. The center also includes the **Hawaii State Art Museum** (p. 121). Parking can be tight, though there are metered spots in front of the downtown Post Office at Richards and Merchant St., along King St., and on other side streets. Avoid the hassle by taking TheBus #1, 2, 13, or B CityExpress to S. Beretania and Punchbowl St., at the corner of the State Capitol's grounds.

🏛IOLANI PALACE. Hawaii's latter monarchs resided in the American-Florentine style Iolani Palace, situated amid lovely, coral-fenced grounds. Iolani Palace is an important symbol for some Hawaiian sovereigntists, who decry the overthrow of the Hawaiian kingdom for US business interests. The palace was originally built in 1883 for only $360,000 as a show of strength and independence. As the official residence of Hawaii's last royal family, King Kalakaua and Queen Liliuokalani, Iolani Palace is the only state residence of royalty on US soil. After falling into disrepair as the capitol of the subsequent Repub-

OAHU

lic, Territorial, and State governments, the palace has since been restored and maintained by the Friends of Iolani Palace. The building gleams as it did in the monarchy's early days; portraits of Hawaiian monarchs hang beside portraits of French, German, Russian, and British leaders. The palace contains one of Hawaii's first telephones, the royal crown jewels, and electric chandeliers, which Kalakaua had installed after meeting Thomas Edison. The preservation of this architectural marvel is ensured by strict regulations of guests and the clean booties all visitors are made to wear. An ancient temple once stood on the site and in 1825 the site was converted into a royal tomb that became the final resting place for Hawaiian monarchs before the palace was built. The **Royal Hawaiian Band** plays a free concert Fridays at noon.

The white-pillared building to the right of the palace is the **Hawaii State Library**, which holds the private book collections of several monarchs. *(Ticket office inside the Iolani Barracks, the white structure on the Richards St. side of the grounds. 364 S. King St. Tour reservations ☎ 808-522-0832; www.iolanipalace.org. Open Tu-Sa 9am-3pm. 1hr. grand tour $20, ages 5-12 $5; no children under 5. Tour leaves every 20min. 9am-11:15am. Self-guided audio tour of palace and basement $12, ages 5-12 $5, no children under 5. Self-guided basement tour $6, under 12 $3, under 5 must be accompanied by adult. Gallery open Tu-Sa 9am-4:30pm, last admission 3:30pm. No cell phones, photos, video cameras, or food. MC/V.)*

SAINT ANDREW'S CATHEDRAL. This beautiful early French-Gothic revival cathedral, built in stages between 1865 and 1958, sits serenely behind a fountain, in which a 10 ft. bronze statue of apostle (and fisherman) St. Andrew stands. The cathedral was named in honor of King Kamehameha IV, who died on St. Andrew's Day in November 1863 after inviting the Anglican Church to Hawaii and donating the land where the cathedral stands today. The magnificent stained-glass Great West Window, designed in 1950, depicts the life of Christ, the creation of the Anglican Church, and the story of the Church in Hawaii. The cathedral organist plays the enormous Aeolian-Skinner organ every Wednesday at 12:30pm. *(On the corner of Beretania and Alakea St., past the State Capitol in Queen Emma Sq. ☎ 808-524-2822; www.saintandrewscathedral.net. Mass Tu, Th, and F 7am; W-F noon; Su 7, 8, 10am. Evensong 7pm first Su of every mo. Office open M-F 9am-12:30pm, 1:30-5pm. Free historic tours are available after the Su 10am service. Call 1-2 wk. ahead to reserve. All are welcome to attend services in Parke Chapel daily at 7am.)*

HAWAII STATE CAPITOL. This unique building replaced Iolani Palace as Hawaii's capitol building in 1969 and is now the workplace of Hawaii's governor and legislators. The capitol's eccentric architecture is meant to reflect Hawaii's geography and culture. The structure's conical legislative chambers mimic the volcanoes that birthed the islands, the reflecting pool surrounding the building represents the Pacific Ocean, and the unique concrete pillars are meant to rise like coconut trees. The open-air design signifies the openness of Hawaii and its people, welcoming the winds that blow from the sea and over the mountains while the center lies open to sun, sky, and stars.

Across Beretania St., stately **Washington Place** was the home of Hawaii's last reigning monarch, Queen Liliuokalani, and for many years after was the home of Hawaii's governors. Current Governor Linda Lingle is the first governor not to live there, but she still hosts dignitaries and ceremonies in the house. Call the Washington Place Foundation (☎ 808-586-0240) at least 48 hours in advance for reservations. *(On the corner of S. Beretania and Punchbowl St. ☎ 808-586-0178; www.hawaii.gov/sfca. Building open M-F 8am-5pm. Grounds open 24hr. Free 1hr. tours M, W, F 1:30pm, meet in rm. 415. Groups of 10 or more must reserve 2 wk. ahead.)*

ALIIOLANI HALE. Built in 1874, Aliiolani Hale once housed both the legislature and the Supreme Court of the Hawaiian kingdom, and it is the current seat of

Hawaii's Supreme Court. Its name, Aliiolani ("Chief unto Heavens"), pays homage to King Kamehameha V, who initiated the planning and construction of the palace as a symbol of the stability and prosperity of an independent Hawaiian nation. The **Judiciary History Center** contains a 1913 courtroom, movie theater with educational programming, and exhibits that detail 200 years of Hawaiian legal history, with a special focus on the *kapu* (forbidden) law system and evolution of the complex Hawaiian land structure. Stop in even if you're not a legal history buff; the friendly program coordinators are more than happy to help or just chat. You can't miss the building—one of Hawaii's most recognizable and beautiful landmarks, the **King Kamehameha I Statue,** stands in front of it. The gleaming, golden-caped statue honors the man who established the Hawaiian kingdom and united the islands under one rule. *(417 S. King St. ☎ 808-539-4994. History center open for self-guided tours M-F 8am-4pm. Guided tours by reservation only. Free.)*

KAWAIAHAO CHURCH. Dubbed "The Westminster Abbey of Hawaii," Kawaiahao Church is the birthplace of Christianity on the islands and was the site where statehood was officially marked on August 21, 1959. Still a practicing Congregational Church today, the building was designed by Boston-based missionaries with no architectural background. Hawaiians dove 10-20 ft. under water to chisel out 1000 lb. slabs of coral, 14,000 of which were used as bricks in the foundation of the New England-style structure that was dedicated on July 21, 1842. The church gained its name from the sacred spring called *Kawaiahao* ("the water of Hao"), where Chieftess Hao bathed. The church is also home to over 20 portraits of various *alii* (royalty) and the tomb of King Lunalilo, the first democratically elected Hawaiian monarch. *(957 Punchbowl St., at the corner of S. King St. ☎ 808-522-1333. Open M-F 8am-5pm. Services Su 9 and 11am; all are welcome.)*

CHINATOWN

 FOSTER BOTANICAL GARDEN. Home to some of the oldest trees on Oahu and a world-class orchid collection, Foster Botanical Garden was first started in 1853 by Queen Kamala, wife of Kamehameha III. Twenty-four of Oahu's exceptional trees, chosen for their outstanding rarity, age, size, beauty, location, endemic status, or historical and cultural significance, grow in the garden, including the great Bo tree, which Hindus and Buddhists both consider sacred. Other notable attractions include the plants in the Prehistoric Glen and the Lyon Orchid Garden. *(50 N. Vineyard Blvd. Take H-1 W. to Vineyard Blvd. or Punchbowl St. north from Ala Moana Blvd. and take a left onto Vineyard Blvd. Turn right into the parking lot after the Kuan Yin Temple, the last drive on the right before the river and Aala St. You can also take TheBus #4 from University to Nuuanu Ave. and Vineyard Blvd. and walk up the block, toward the river. The entrance and visitor parking are on the right past the temple. ☎ Reservations 808-522-7066, info line 808-522-7060. Open daily 9am-4pm. 1hr. guided tours included. Tours given M-Sa 1pm or by phone request. Self-guided plant tour included. $5, ages 6-12 $1, under 5 free. MC/V.)*

☆TIP☆ | **EATEN ALIVE:** If going to a botanical garden or park, be sure to wear bug spray. The mosquitoes are vicious!

KUAN YIN TEMPLE. The intoxicating scent of incense pervades this beautiful, single-room temple dedicated to Kuan Yin Boddhisattva, a Buddhist goddess of mercy worshipped in China. The ornately carved red wood interior, green roof, inlaid carvings, and gold shrines make for a lovely respite on a tour of Chinatown though the linoleum floor looks a bit out of place. It is believed that Kuan Yin returned to this world after attaining enlightenment in order to help end the suffering of others. Offerings of fresh flowers, fruit, and other vegetarian foods are welcome at the altar. *(170 N. Vineyard Blvd., next to the Foster Botanical Gardens. Drive west on Vineyard from H-1 W. to Exit 22 and turn right at the entrance to Foster Botanical Garden before Aala St. ☎ 808-533-6361. Open 8:30am-2pm. Donations recommended.)*

MANOA AND THE UNIVERSITY AREA

LYON ARBORETUM. The University of Hawaii's 194 acre refuge in the Koolau Mountains holds thousands of tropical plants, some of which have become extinct in their native habitats. Today, in addition to being a beautiful locale and worthwhile visit, the facility is highly regarded by horticulturalists, conservation biologists, and botanists. The park is open to exploration on a self-guided tour or on weekly guided tours. A trail map and bird checklist are available at the Visitors Center. Be sure to wear appropriate footwear and bug repellent. *(3860 Manoa Rd. Leaving Waikiki on McCully St., take the 1st left after the Ala Wai Canal onto Kapiolani Blvd.; turn right onto Kalakaua Ave., then right on King St. Take the 1st left onto Puou St. After Punahou St., Puou becomes Manoa Rd. Go left at the fork in the road, just after Kamehameha Ave. Or, take TheBus #5 to the last stop and walk the remaining 1 mi. up Manoa Rd. ☎ 808-988-0456. All visitors must sign in at the Visitors Center. Open M-F 9am-4pm. 1hr. guided tours are available; call ☎ 808-988-0461 for schedule and reservations. Free. Suggested donation $5.)*

BEYOND TOURISM: The **Lyon Arboretum** offers many service opportunities for volunteers interested in gardening, educational programs, trail clearing, and other jobs. For more information, call ☎808-988-0461 or download a volunteer application at www.hawaii.edu/lyonarboretum.

GREATER HONOLULU

PUNCHBOWL NATIONAL MEMORIAL CEMETERY OF THE PACIFIC. Meaning "hill of sacrifice," the 116-acre Puowaina Crater was formed over 75,000 years ago and is now the location of the Punchbowl Memorial Cemetery of the Pacific. The site of secret *alii* (royal) burials, today it is the resting place of over 33,000 identified and unidentified soldiers from the Spanish-American War to the present. The monument includes a nonsectarian chapel, Courts of the Missing, battle scene tableaus, a dedication stone, and a 30-ft. sculpture of Lady Columbia, who symbolizes all grieving mothers. Over a million visitors pay their respects here each year. The path left of the memorial building leads to an overlook with a panoramic view of Honolulu. *(2177 Puowaina Dr. From Kuhio Ave. Take H-1 east and exit onto Lunalilo Freeway, then go north onto Pali Hwy. Immediately cross the interstate overpass, turn right, and proceed one block. Turn left after approx. 300 ft. then turn right onto Puowawina Dr. Alternatively, take TheBus #2, 13, or B CityExpress away from Diamond Head to Beretania and Alapai St., in front of the Honolulu police headquarters. Walk down Alapai St. toward the ocean a half block to the bus stop and transfer to the #15 Pacific Heights bus, which stops at the gate leading to the cemetery. 10-15min. walk to the memorial building. ☎ 808-532-3720. Open daily Oct.-Feb. 8am-5:30pm; Mar.-Sept. 8am-6:30pm. Free.)*

HAWAII NATURE CENTER. The Hawaii Nature Center has a changing schedule of weekly programs for families and adults. Knowledgeable guides lead hikes, answer questions, and distribute free maps of the trails. The center is also the trailhead of the popular **Makiki Valley Loop Trail** (p. 127). *(From Ala Moana Shopping Center take Keeaumoku St. beyond H-1 until Nehoa St., then turn right. Take the 1st left onto Makiki St. and bear left at the fork in the road onto Makiki Heights Dr. At the 1st hairpin turn, continue straight onto the narrow driveway where you see 5 mailboxes. Park along the side of the road, or take TheBus #15 to the intersection of Mott-Smith Dr. and Makiki Heights Dr. Walk down Makiki Heights Dr. (toward Diamond Head) 0.5 mi. Turn left up the driveway at the 5 mailboxes, walk past the*

THE BIG SPLURGE

SHANGRI LA

In 1935, 23-year-old tobacco heiress Doris Duke fell in love with Hawaii while circling the globe on her honeymoon. Although her marriage dissolved years later, Duke's love of Hawaii endured in the form of an extraordinary residence she built on the cliffs of Diamond Head, called **Shangri La.** Visitors can now tour the home, which houses Duke's world-class collection of Islamic art. Even at the steep admission price of $25, Shangri La is one sight that should not be missed while on Oahu.

Duke began collecting Islamic art while in India, and had Shangri La built around pieces she acquired from all over the Islamic world. Designed around a central courtyard, the house is unremarkable from the exterior but dazzles inside with Ottoman tiles, Moroccan screens, and Indian marble. It is a pastiche of styles, mixing 1930s modern with pieces dating back to the 13th century.

The most important piece in the collection is a stunning *mihrab,* an Islamic prayer niche, dating from 1265. Shangri La not only houses a rare collection of museum-quality artifacts, it paints an intimate portrait of a famous recluse and her personal relationship with art. ☎ *866-DUKE-TIX/385-3849. 90min. tours run W-Sa 8:30, 11am, and 1:30pm and leave from the Honolulu Academy of Arts. Visitors are shuttled 20min. to the property and received by knowledgeable guides. The price of admission also includes admission to the Academy.*

Makiki Forest Recreation Center and through a green gate, and continue for approximately 1/4 mi. ☎ *808-955-0100; www.hawaiinaturecenter.org. Open daily 8am-4:30pm. Free.)*

THE TENNENT FOUNDATION GALLERY. This charming gallery, a registered historic sites, is dedicated to the artist Madge Tennent. Born in England and considered a child prodigy, Tennent moved to Hawaii in 1923, where she lived until her death in 1972. She is considered one of Hawaii's greatest artists, and some of her pieces are on permanent loan to the National Museum of Women in Washington, DC. The large oils here show the influence of Gauguin, glorifying Hawaiian women as the embodiment of nature. *(203 Prospect St. Take Ward Ave. away from Ala Moana Blvd. to the base of Punchbowl Crater and turn left onto Prospect St.; bear right at the intersection, hugging the crater on the left between Huali and Madeira St. ☎ 808-531-1987. Open by appointment. Donations appreciated.)*

QUEEN EMMA'S SUMMER PALACE. This small palace, also known as *Hanaiakamalama* (foster child of the moon), was once the retreat of Kamehameha IV's cosmopolitan queen. The house frame was cut in Boston and shipped to Hawaii 1848, then sold to Emma's uncle in 1850 for $6,000, and bequeathed to the Queen in 1857. Today, the house holds many of the royal family's personal belongings, furnishings, and memorabilia. Emma outlived both her son and husband; after her death, the Hawaiian Monarchy purchased and leased the property. In the early 1900s, the Daughters of Hawaii averted plans to turn it into a baseball park and assumed management of the palace, turning it into a museum. Among the objects in the museum are a porcelain tub and *koa* stand (a gift from the Chinese Emperor), several *kahili* (feather standards), and a bracelet with a lock of Queen Victoria's hair. Ask the guides to point out the furniture woodwork made of native *koa, kou, milo,* and *kamani. (2913 Pali Hwy. ☎ 808-595-3167. Going north from Honolulu, 2 mi. down H-1. Open daily 9am-4pm. $6, seniors $4, children $1.)*

🏛 MUSEUMS

DOWNTOWN

🖼**HONOLULU ACADEMY OF ARTS.** Over 30 galleries display the permanent collection and visiting exhibits of the Academy's classic and contemporary artwork from local and international artists amid beautifully landscaped courtyards. Notable galleries include the James A. Michener Gallery of Japanese Ukiyo-e wood-block prints, the Kress

Collection of Italian Renaissance paintings, and the impressive John Dominis and Patches Damon Holt Hawaiian art gallery. The museum is also world famous for its collection of Asian art, including works from China, Japan, Korea, India, and Southeast Asia. Works by Picasso, Monet, Matisse, Van Gogh, Gauguin, and Cezanne are also on display in the European galleries, with paintings dating from the Italian Renaissance to the modern era. **The Doris Duke Theatre** (☎808-532-8768) screens experimental, contemporary, international, and revival films. Refuel at the **Pavilion Cafe ❷** on the patio, shaded by an ancient monkeypod tree with views of gardens and a waterfall. Reservations are recommended. **Free Wi-Fi** in the outdoor pavilion areas near the cafe. *(900 S. Beretania St., in front of Thomas Sq. From Waikiki, take TheBus #2 toward downtown. If driving or going to the theater, enter on Kinau St. ☎808-532-8700, cafe ☎808-532-8734; www.honoluluacademy.org. Parking $3 per 4hr. with validation. Museum open Tu-Sa 10am-4:30pm, Su 1-5pm. Cafe open Tu-Sa 11:30am-2pm. Guided tours Tu-Sa 10:15am, 11:30am, 1:30pm and Su 1:15pm, free with admission. Call ☎808-532-8726 for group tour information. $10; seniors, students, and military $6; children under 12 and members free; first W of every month free.)*

AFTERNOON TOUR AND TEA AT THE HONOLULU ACADEMY OF ART: Every Tuesday, Thursday, and Sunday from 2:30 to 4pm, docents at the Academy lead themed discussions in one of the 30 galleries with tea and refreshments to follow. Call ☎808-532-8700 to reserve a spot. The tour is free with museum admission.

HAWAII STATE ART MUSEUM. In November 2002, the Hawaii State Art Museum opened its doors as the jewel of the Art in Public Places program, which began in 1967. The Art in Public Places Collection comprises over 5000 works from more than 1400 artists and is displayed and rotated in state buildings all over Hawaii. The Hawaii State Art Museum houses a large selection of works from this collection and is devoted to the display of art by Hawaiian artists and the expression of Hawaii's multicultural artistic heritage. Much of the art combines a Western aesthetic with Hawaii's Asian roots and reflects the state's rich ethnic history. The unique focus of the museum and the beautiful setting in an old Spanish mission-style YMCA building make this a must-see for all those interested in Hawaiian culture, tradition, and art. *(No. 1 Capitol District Building, 250 S. Hotel St., 2nd fl., west of the State Capitol building. ☎808-586-0900. Open Tu-Sa 10am-4pm. Tours Tu-Sa 1pm. Call to arrange group tours. Free.)*

MISSION HOUSES MUSEUM. These three 19th-century buildings once formed the headquarters of the Sandwich Island Mission. Built over a 40 year period by Protestant missionaries, the buildings house various artifacts, including desks, four-post beds, and settees. The frame house is the oldest wooden structure on the islands and its frame was pre-cut in New England before being shipped to the islands. You'll also find a replica of the printing press where the written Hawaiian language was first developed in order to translate the English bible. Admission to the houses and to a rotating exhibit may be purchased from the Mission Houses Museum, whose historians lead informed tours of the mission. *(553 S. King St., past Kawaiahao Church. ☎808-531-0481; www.missionhouses.org. Open Tu-Sa 10am-4pm, 45min. tours of the mission Tu-Sa 11am and 2:45pm, Tu-F also 1pm. House tour s$10, seniors $8, students $6, under 5 free. Free printing press demonstration W 1pm. MC/V.)*

MANOA AND THE UNIVERSITY AREA

THE CONTEMPORARY MUSEUM. This modern, minimalist museum has a pleasant view of Honolulu from the base of Makiki Heights. Housed in a former residence, the museum's exhibits address contemporary visual, performance, and media art, with an educational bent. Here you can see a seasonally rotating exhibit and David Hockney's haunting *L'Enfant et les Sortileges*, a permanent audio-visual display inspired by Maurice Ravel's opera about a naughty child's dreamworld. A walk through the museum brings you across the beautiful 3-acre grounds which are interlaced with sloping lawns, outdoor sculptures, and secluded gardens cut into the hillside. The friendly staff and beautiful indoor/outdoor gallery make the museum a fantastic place for a picnic or just a break from downtown. *(2411 Makiki Heights Dr. Take Punahou St. past the YWCA at Vineyard toward Manoa Valley. Turn left on Nehoa St. and right on Mott Smith Dr. Drive until you see the signs for the museum's driveway. Or take TheBus #15 to Makiki Heights Dr. ☎ 808-526-1322; www.tcmhi.org. A branch of the museum, dedicated solely to Hawaiian art, is in the First Hawaiian Center, downtown at 999 Bishop St. Contemporary Museum open Tu-Sa 10am-4pm, Su noon-4pm. $5, seniors and students $3, 12 and under free. Guided tours Tu-Su 1:30pm. AmEx/D/MC/V.)*

GREATER HONOLULU

▧BISHOP MUSEUM. Founded in 1889, the Bishop Museum is the best place to learn about the history and culture of Hawaii. The hefty admission is justified by the spectacular collection of over 24 million works of art and artifacts of the Pacific, including publications, photographs, films, audio recordings, manuscripts, and millions of animal and plant species, many of which are extinct. The impressive Kahili Room, which showcases the world's largest collection of *kahili* (feather standards of Hawaiian royalty) and portraits of 19th-century Hawaiian monarchs, is a must-see. Hawaiian Hall, which houses treasured objects of Hawaiian culture given to the museum by Hawaiian royalty, is under construction until mid-2009 but should not be missed when it opens. A program of museum tours, garden tours, planetarium shows, and music, dance, and dramatic performances is included with admission; events take place every 30min. from 10am to 3:30pm. *(1525 Bernice St. From Kuhio Ave., heading away from Diamond Head, take the #2 School St./Middle St. bus to School St. and Kapalama Ave. Walk toward the ocean on Kapalama Ave. to Bernice St. ☎ 808-847-3511; www.bishopmuseum.org. Open daily 9am-5pm, last admission at 4:30. General admission $15, seniors and ages 4-12 $12, under 3 free.)*

⚏ ARTS AND ENTERTAINMENT

THEATER, MUSIC, AND DANCE

THE KENNEDY THEATRE. On the University of Hawaii at Manoa campus, the Kennedy Theatre is known internationally for its English-language presentations of Chinese, Japanese, and Southeast Asian theater and dance. Highlights include plays by local playwrights Lisa Matsumoto and Ed Sakamoto, Indonesian martial arts dance-drama, pidgin versions of Shakespeare's comedies, and the annual dance concert. *(1770 East-West Rd. Take H-1 to University Ave. From University Ave., turn right onto Dole St. and follow it to the corner of East-West Rd. Or take the #6 Woodlawn Dr. bus from Ala Moana Shopping Center. Box office ☎ 808-956-7655, fax 808-956-4234; www.hawaii.edu/kennedy. Box office open M-F 10am-1pm, closed in summer. MC/V.)*

HAWAII THEATRE CENTER. Built and opened by Consolidated Theaters in 1922, the Hawaii Theatre Center is now the spearhead of the Honolulu Culture and Arts District, serving as a venue for theatrical, musical, dance, and multimedia performances. Called "The Carnegie Hall of the Pacific," the theatre underwent major renovations in 1992. It has an excellent volunteer-run gift shop. *(1130 Bethel St. ☎ 808-528-0506; www.hawaiitheatre.com. 1hr. guided tours on the theater's history, art,* *and architecture Tu 11am, show schedule permitting. Tours $5, reservations recommended ☎808-528-0506. Open Tu-Sa 9am-5pm and 2hr. prior to performances. AmEx/D/MC/V.)*

HONOLULU SYMPHONY. Founded in 1900, the symphony is the oldest orchestra west of the Rocky Mountains. Performances are held at the Neil S. Blaisdell Hall and include performances of works by Tchaikovsky, Beethoven, Mozart, and more. *(At the corner of S. King St. and Ward Ave., in Ala Moana. ☎808-792-2000; www. honolulusymphony.com. Box office open M-F 9am-5pm and 2hr. prior to a performance, or use TicketMaster ☎888-750-4400. Performances Sept.-May. Box office located behind the Neal S. Blaisdell Hall on Blaisdell Arena Ward Ave. Event parking $6. $21-75. AmEx/MC/V.)*

FILM

MOVIE MUSEUM. The museum screens classic, contemporary, and foreign films as they should be seen: on the big screen in digital sound, from the comfort of one of the theater's 19 leather recliners. Bring your own concessions; alcohol is permitted but not encouraged. *(3566 Harding Ave. In Kaimuki, at the corner of Harding and 12th Ave. TheBus #1 or 3. ☎808-735-8771. Open M and Th-Su noon-8pm. One movie is screened 4 times daily. Reservations recommended. $5, members $4. MC/V.)*

WARD 16 THEATRE. First-run movies show in the highest quality movie theater in town at the **Ward Entertainment Center** (p. 124). It's everything you've come to expect from multiplexes, including great A/C, high schoolers, and the steep price. Get discounts at many of the Victoria Ward establishments with a movie ticket stub. *(1044 Auahi St. ☎808-594-7000; www.wardcenters.com/Movies. $9.50, matinee special before 4pm $7.75, seniors $6.75, military $7.25, ages 2-12 $7. AmEx/MC/V.)*

⬚ SHOPPING

PEOPLE'S OPEN MARKETS. These markets provide the chance to buy inexpensive produce from local farmers and fishermen. There are markets in Waikiki's Queen Kapiolani Park *(p. 135)*, Makiki District Park *(1527 Keeaumoku Ave., next to the Makiki Public Library 1 block north of H-1; take TheBus #17, 18, or 83; M 8:30-9:30am)*, City Hall Parking Lot Deck *(At Alapai and Beretania St.; M 11:45am-12:30pm)*, Manoa Valley District Park *(2721 Kaaipu Ave., 2 blocks down Lowrey Ave. from the 5-way intersection of Manoa Rd. and Oahu Ave.; M 6:45-7:45am)*, and Old Stadium Park *(2237 S. King St.; W 8:15-9:15am)*. The program is run by the City and County of Honolulu *(www. co.honolulu.hi.us/parks/programs/pom/sked.htm)*.

DOWNTOWN

Catherine's Closet, 2733 E. Manoa Rd. #204 (☎808-286-2746). This vintage boutique is on the 2nd fl. of the shopping center down the street from Manoa Marketplace. The friendly owner sells one-of-a-kind clothing, hats, jewelry, and purses from the 60s, 70s, and 80s. The small store is also cluttered with antiques and other vintage collectibles. Open W-Sa noon-5pm or by appointment.

Macy's Downtown, 1032 Fort St. Mall (☎808-521-5147). Dominated mostly by office buildings and the Civic Center, downtown has few noteworthy retail stores. The freestanding Macy's on Fort St. Mall is your best option for moderately-priced clothing or other necessities. There are other Macy's locations in Ala Moana and Waikiki, but the Fort St. location is the only department store in the downtown area. Open M-Sa 8:30am-6pm.

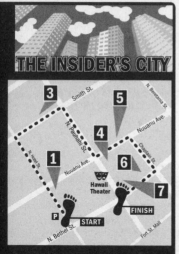

THE INSIDER'S CITY

CHINATOWN GALLERIES

On the first Friday evening of every month Chinatown transforms itself in the evening hours as local businesses, galleries, and restaurants open their doors for the First Fridays celebration. Many galleries offer wine and refreshments while local vendors and artisans open up street stalls to display their wares. This short walking tour takes you through a few of the area's best galleries, although there are many others scattered throughout the route. First Fridays run from 5-9pm, but this walking tour is also a great way to spend any afternoon.

1. Louis Pohl Gallery, 1111 Nuuanu Ave. (☎808-521-1812, www.louispohlgallery.com). This space displays original artwork by a wide variety of Hawaiian artists. Open Tu-Sa 11am-6pm.

2. thirtyninehotel, 39 N. Hotel St. (☎808-599-5009, www.thirtyninehotel.com.) This all-white lounge and bar offers modern and alternative exhibit space to local artists. Open Tu-Sa noon-6pm.

ALA MOANA

ALA MOANA SHOPPING CENTER. A tri-level temple of commerce with approx. 1.8 million sq. ft., Ala Moana is the world's largest open-air shopping center. Over 290 of the best-known retailers intersect with more than 56 million sophisticated shoppers each year. While all the stores are air-conditioned, the mall itself is open-air. Standard mall stores such as Gap and Abercrombie & Fitch stand alongside some of the glitziest names in fashion, including Burberry, Versace, Prada, and Chanel.

The **Honolulu Satellite City Hall,** Ste. 1286., on the first level, provides camping permits, motor vehicle permits and registration, and TheBus passes. (☎808-973-2600. Open M-Tu and Th-F 9am-5pm; W 9am-6:45pm; Sa 8am-4pm.) There's also a small **post office,** Ste. 1006., on the first level of the mall. (☎808-532-1987. Open M-F 8:30am-5pm, Sa 8:30am-4:15pm. Last collection M-F 2:30pm. **Postal Code:** 96814.) The Ala Moana Center also has plentiful dining options, with over 25 fine and casual dining restaurants, over 20 specialty food shops, and Makai Market Food Court with over 20 international and fast food restaurants. (*1450 Ala Moana Blvd., between Ala Moana Blvd., Kapiolani St., Atkinson Dr., and Piikoi St. From Waikiki, take the #8, 19, 20, 42, or 58. The center's private shuttle service, the Pink Line trolleys, runs every 8-10min. M-Sa 9:42am-9:39pm, Su 9:42am-7:29pm through 8 Waikiki stops; one-way $2. For shuttle info, call the Waikiki Trolley Hotline at ☎808-593-2822. The Customer Service Center, ☎808-955-9517, near Centerstage has maps, guides, and shopping center magazines, free wheelchairs, and Ala Moana Gift Certificates. Open M-Sa 9:30am-9pm, Su 10am-7pm. Department stores and restaurants may have different hours.*)

VICTORIA WARD CENTERS. This four-block complex mixes old-fashioned markets with modern shops, trying to sell visitors the true island experience in a setting that is decidedly less pretentious (and generally less pricey) than the Ala Moana Center. On the corner of Ward Ave. between Ala Moana Blvd. and Auahi St., **Ward Warehouse** is a bi-level, open-air mall that peddles Hawaiian souvenirs, clothes, and other items. **Ward Centre,** across Kamakee St. from Ward Warehouse, contains art galleries, specialty stores, bars, and restaurants. **Ward Farmers' Market,** across Auahi St. from Ward Warehouse, is a quaint row of indoor markets where savvy shoppers can buy fresh produce, seafood, groceries, and various Asian and Hawaiian delicacies. (Markets generally open M-Sa 7am-5pm, Su 7am-1pm.) **Ward Gateway Center,** next to the Farmers' Market along Ward Ave., houses several bargain stores across the street from the **Ward 404** restaurant complex. **Ward Entertainment Center,** on the corner of Auahi St. and Kamakee St., houses a 16-screen theater. (☎808-597-1243. Open W-Su noon-9pm.) **Ward Village Shops,** adjacent to the Entertainment Center, has stores like Pier One Imports and Nordstrom Rack. *(Between Queen St., Ward Ave., and Ala Moana Blvd., 1 block west of Ala Moana Shopping Center. Free parking lots and garages have entrances on Auahi St., Kamakee St., and Ward Ave. Take the Pink Line Trolley to Ala Moana Center. ☎ 808-593-2822, or TheBus #19, 20, or 42 from Kuhio Ave. in Waikiki, or the #6 from Manoa. www.wardcenters.com. Shopping hours M-Sa 10am-9pm, Su 10am-6pm; restaurants open later. Concierge Services in Ward 16 Theater Lobby, ☎ 808-597-1243.)*

▓ NIGHTLIFE

Honolulu has all the tried-and-true nightlife formulas: laid-back budget dives, sports bars, swanky lounges, and live music venues. Fickle Honolulu crowds—including surfer boys, socialites, and the ever-changing tourist hordes—ebb and flow from nightlife spots daily. To keep up with the constantly evolving scene, visit **http://quadmag.com** for event listings and message board posts, or pick up a copy of *Honolulu Weekly* for nightly live music and party listings, free on street corners and stores. *DaKine* magazine, "the voice of Hawaii's Out Community," (www.dakinemagazine.com) and *Odyssey* magazine (www.odysseyhawaii.com) frequently list gay-friendly events and nightlife. Both magazines are free and available in stores throughout Honolulu.

DOWNTOWN AND CHINATOWN

▓ **Bar35,** 35 N. Hotel St (☎808-537-3535), between Smith St. and Nuuanu Ave. Located on the edge of Chinatown, Bar35 offers more than 100 kinds of specialty beers, a dine-in menu featuring an oyster bar, and a sleek red and black interior. Bar35 overflows on First Fridays, the first F of every month. Happy hour M-F 4-8pm and Sa 6-8pm (select bottles, drafts, martinis, and mixed drinks $3). 21+. Open M-Sa 4pm-2am.

The Green Room and Opium Den at Indigo's, 1121 Nuuanu Ave. (☎808-521-2900). The party starts at Indigo's with ▓**Martini Madness** (Tu-F 4-7pm; $3.50 martinis and a free mini-buffet of *pupu*). Its 2 bars—the French-themed Green Room and the Chinese-inspired Opium Den—are popular nightspots. A slightly older crowd gathers in the open-air Opium Den for drinks and a late-night menu of *dim sum* and dessert. Sophisticated 20-somethings mingle in the smaller Green room for drinks and dancing. The drink menu

3. Ramsay Museum, 1128 Smith St. (☎808-537-2782). A long-time resident of Hawaii, Ramsay displays her truer-than-life pen-and-ink drawing in the upstairs museum and features local artists' work on the 1st-fl. gallery. Open M-F 10am-5pm, Sa 10am-4pm.

4. The ARTS at Mark's Garage, 1159 Nuuanu Ave. (☎808-521-2903, www.artsatmarks.com). The unofficial epicenter of First Fridays, the ARTS at Mark's Garage is a gallery and performance space that hosts workshops in theater, dance, sculpture, and painting. Open Tu-Sa 11am-6pm.

5. Studio of Roy Venters, 1160 Nuuanu Ave. (☎808-381-3445). This vanity gallery displays mixed media works by artist Roy Venters and others. On First Fridays, vendors of vintage jewelry and accessories take over the space. Open First Fridays and by appointment.

6. rRed Elephant, 1144 Bethel St. (☎808-545-2468, www.rredelephant.com). More a cafe than gallery, rRed Elephant serves delicious espresso to energize the rest of your afternoon or evening while doubling as an exhibit space and live music venue. Open M-Sa 7am-9pm, Su 9am-9pm.

7. Bethel St. Gallery, 1140 Bethel St. (☎808-546-8000, www.bethelstreetgallery.com). Hawaii's largest artist-owned and -operated gallery, Bethel St. Gallery features rotating art by local artists in a variety of media.

features 20 specialty martinis (try the popular lychee martini, $8) and 20 kinds of bottled beer ($4-6). Tu-Sa DJs and special events until 2am. Usually live bands on weekdays. Happy hour Tu-F 4-8pm. Lunch Tu-F 11:30am-2pm. Dinner Tu-Sa 6-9:30pm. Lounges open nightly 4pm-2am. AmEx/D/MC/V.

Next Door, 43 N. Hotel St. (☎808-548-6398). Occupying a former warehouse, Next Door offers club-goers an enormous dance floor with 30 ft. ceilings, exposed brick walls, and a stage for live music. Despite the open space, Next Door gets packed every W on Acid Wash 80s night and the dance floor steams up. Th-Sa DJs spin a mix of house, hip-hop, and techno. Cover free-$20 depending on day of the week. Happy hour F 5-9pm; $3 beers and $4 martinis. Open Tu-Sa 9pm-2am, F 5pm-2am. 21+. AmEx/D/MC/V.

thirtyninehotel, 39 N. Hotel St. (☎808-599-2552), between Smith St. and Nuuanu Ave. This stark, futuristic bar also functions as a multimedia gallery space and movie theater with weekly screenings. This hyper-trendy spot is a favorite among locals-in-the-know who can escape the noisy lounge to the adjoining breezy rooftop bar. Every 1st W at 8pm is open-mic night. 21+. Cover generally $5. Open Tu-Sa 2pm-2am.

Mercury, 1154 Fort St. Mall, Ste. 10 (☎808-228-2486). Enter on Chaplain Ln. This dimly lit, artsy bar brings in an eclectic crowd. Popular among students from Hawaii Pacific University and you'll find the same regulars at the bar on any given night. Drum and Bass Nights (1st F and 2nd Sa) are especially fun. Beer $3-4, mixed drinks $3-7. Try the Trinity, an original cocktail of three tropical rums, 7UP, and cranberry juice ($6). 21+. Open M-Sa 4:30pm-2am. MC/V.

MANOA AND THE UNIVERSITY AREA

◪ **Anna Bannana's,** 2440 S. Beretania St. (☎808-946-5190). This dim hole-in-the-wall is a love-worn Manoa and UH institution, having rocked live music since 1969. Excellent happy hour daily 2-7pm (drafts and bottles $2, mixed drinks $2.50). Band or DJ depending on the night. M open-mic night, 9pm, 18+. Su all-ages blues night. All other nights 21+. Cover generally $5. Open M-Th 2pm-2am, Sa-Su 11am-2am. MC/V.

The Varsity Bar, 1015 University Ave. (☎808-447-9244), is a favorite nighttime UH student hangout due to the $1-2 drafts at the open-air bar. The bar's neon walls, red stools, electric juke box, and young crowd give it a lively vibe. The Varsity also makes a mean pizza ($9.50-30), big enough to justify another pitcher ($7 and up). Th $2 wells starting at 7pm. F at 5pm is the "atacolypse" ($1 tacos, $2.50 Cuervo shots, and $2 margaritas). 21+ after 9pm. Open daily 11am-2am. AmEx/MC/V.

Kimmie's Cantina, 2535 Coyne St. Formerly the much-loved Red Lion University, Kimmie's Cantina is a sports bar with a Tex-Mex twist. This UH bar gets crowded on Freaky Fridays when they serve $2 pints of Miller and $1 Jello shots. Nightly drink specials. Taco Tuesdays feature $1 tacos 5-9pm. Kimmie's also serves classic Tex-Mex fare like nachos ($7.25) and fish tacos ($11.50), which can be enjoyed around any of the bar's flatscreen televisions, pool tables, or dart boards. Open daily 2pm-2am.

ALA MOANA

Pipeline Cafe, 805 Pohukaina St. (☎808-589-1999). The huge dance floor with a 500-person capacity fills up fast, especially on Ultimate Tu when Pipeline breaks out hip-hop and $1 drink specials. Arrive before midnight on Foreplay Fridaze for a $3 Sex on the Beach. Pool tables, dart boards, and a foosball table in the bar upstairs. Happy hour M-F 4-9pm (drinks and *pupu;* $2). Dress code for men Tu and F. M, W, and Th sports bar 10pm-4am, 21+; Tu, F and Sa club nights 10pm-4am, 18+. Cover $10, F and Sa $12; ages 18-20 Tu, F, and Sa $15. Open M-Sa 4pm-4am. AmEx/D/MC/V.

Mai Tai Bar, 1450 Ala Moana Blvd. (☎808-947-2900), in the Ala Moana Shopping Center. Mai Tai brings in droves of young, energetic bar-goers with a happy hour daily

8-11pm (pitchers $7-8, mixed drinks $3, and ▨ **Icy Lychee Mai Tais** $4). Live Hawaiian music daily 4-7pm and 9:30pm-12:30am. Tank and Grindz specials daily 4-7pm. 21+ after 5pm. Food served 11am-midnight. Open daily 11am-1am. AmEx/D/MC/V.

Brew Moon, 1200 Ala Moana Blvd. (☎808-593-0088), in the Ward Center. This restaurant and microbrewery (6 original beers on tap) hosts live entertainment during dinner on its breezy outdoor patio. Th comedy night. Try one of their beers during the Zero Gravity happy hour (daily 3-7pm; pints and wine $3, *pupu* $5-6). F and Sa dance party; 21+ after 10pm; cover $10. Open M-Th 11am-10pm, F-Sa 11am-2am. AmEx/MC/V.

▨ HIKING

The pedestrian-only trails of the **Honolulu Mauka Trail System** lead through a variety of climates within a small area, where many unique plants grow. The bugs can get aggravating; pack insect repellent, water, and sunscreen. Allow enough time to return with daylight to spare, never hike alone, and always **stay on the trail**—unmarked offshoots and access roads may be private and are not maintained. Be careful of hunters while hiking; always wear bright clothing. Drinking or bathing in freshwater streams is not advised, as some areas may have leptospirosis. Never leave valuables in your car, and respect the land by taking out everything you brought. If you get lost during a hike call the **Hawaii Nature Center** (☎808-955-0100; open daily 8am-4:30pm). For more information, go to **www.hawaiitrails.org** or **www.backyardoahu.com**.

MANOA FALLS TRAIL. *(0.8 mi. one-way. Elevation gain: 800 ft. Easy.)* This is one of Oahu's most popular trails, and for good reason. The well-marked path leads from the Manoa Falls parking area through eucalyptus and bamboo groves, over bubbling streams, and by old guava and mountain apple trees. Manoa Falls cascades down a stone face into a pool at the end of the trail. Small fissures in the rock wall contain stacks of rocks left by locals out of respect for the *mana* (spirit) of the area. *(Do not leave valuables in your car. The trailhead is in the same place as the Lyon Arboretum. See p. 119 for directions. $5 parking available in a private and guarded lot in Paradise Park at the base of the trail.)*

AIHUALAMA TRAIL. *(1½ mi. one-way. Elevation gain: 1200 ft. Moderate.)* This trail takes more experienced hikers on a trek that starts 50 ft. before the end of the Manoa Falls Trail and climbs the west ridge of Manoa Valley. Aihualama features bamboo forests and views of Honolulu, Diamond Head Crater, and the valley below. The trail also links the Manoa Valley hikes and the Tantalus area hikes. To get to the Tantalus trails, keep going 1 mi. after the lookout to **Pauoa Flats** and the **Puu Ohia Trail.** Otherwise, return the way you came. *(Follow the directions through the Manoa Falls Trail to the marker for Aihualama. Not suitable for novice hikers.)*

MAKIKI VALLEY LOOP. *(2½ mi. Elevation gain: 760 ft. Moderate.)* Combining three Tantalus area hikes—**Maunalaha, Kanealole,** and **Makiki Valley**—this loop takes hikers on an adventure. Hikers start the loop on the Maunalaha Trail, which is clearly marked behind the Hawaii Nature Center (see p. 119). After crossing a bridge the trail splits in two: the Maunalaha Trail continues to the right and the Kaneaole Trail begins to the left. Most people veer right and hike Maunalaha first, but to avoid a steeper uphill climb, head left and start with Kanealole. This path ascends for ¾ mi. and becomes the Makiki Valley Trail just before the Kaneaole Stream. After approximately 1 mi., the trail meets a four-way intersection after passing through a field of Job's Tears, a tall, thick grass that grows up to 5 ft. tall. To continue on the loop, take Maunalaha Trail, the rightmost path. The leftmost *mauka* (mountain) side trail is the **Moleka Trail** (see below) and the middle path (between Maunalaha Trail and a brief continuation

OAHU

of Maikiki Valley Trail) is **Ualakaa Trail**, an easy ½ mi. path under a canopy forest with a gorgeous view of Diamond Head. It ends at Round Top Dr., while Maunalaha Trail completes the Maiki Valley Loop from the four-way intersection back down the mountain through webs of difficult roots from immense Norfolk pines and eucalyptus trees. The steep ¾ mi. trail ends back above the Hawaii Nature Center. *(See directions to the Hawaii Nature Center, p. 119. Area closes at 6:30pm.)*

MANOA CLIFF TRAIL. *(2½ mi. one-way. Elevation gain: 500 ft. Easy.)* Known for its range of indigenous flora and amazing scenic points, this trail climbs gradually through a dense guava and swamp mahogany forest, emerging at an overlook with three waterfalls toward the back and a sweeping view of Manoa Valley. Near the end of the hike, the trail connects with Puu Ohia Trail and Pauoa Flats Trail (see below). If you stick with Manoa Cliff Trail, you'll find that it ends at a third junction, this time with **Kalawahine Trail** (formerly considered part of the Manoa Cliff Trail). Kalawahine Trail delivers you to Tantalus Dr. via a 1 mi. trek along the contours of Mt. Tantalus through a lush forest that has *koa*, guava, and banana trees, as well as scenic points looking out across Pauoa Valley.

Toward the end of Manoa Cliff Trail, the path intersects **Puu Ohia Trail** on the left. This simple path leads ¾ mi. to an overlook at the highest point of Tantalus Crater. Puu Ohia passes night-blooming jasmine, wild ginger, guava, avocado trees, and inspiring views of Honolulu. Past the Puu Ohia fork, Manoa Cliff Trail meets **Pauoa Flats Trail** on the right. Heading inland, the ¾ mi. Pauoa Flats Trail traverses through swamp mahogany trees before connecting with Nuuanu Trail (see below). *(Follow the directions to the Moleka trailhead. The parking lot for Manoa Cliff is the same as the one for the Moleka Trail. The trail starts across the street from the parking lot. To reach Kalawahine Trail from the road, head toward the mountains on Tantalus Dr. There will be a sign for the trailhead on the left, next to a private road about 1 mi. before the Manoa Cliff trailhead.)*

NUUANU TRAIL. *(1½ mi. one-way. Elevation gain: 600 ft. Moderate.)* This trail can be reached from **Kalawahine Trail**. Climbing up the west side of Pauoa Valley, Nuuanu Trail catches periodic views of Honolulu and intersects **Pauoa Flats Trail** on the valley side (see above) and the **Judd Trail** on the cliff side (see below). After peaking atop the ridge, the trail continues down to the Nuuanu Valley floor. *(From Honolulu take Pali Hwy. away from town and take a right on Nuuani Pali Dr. Continue approx. 1 mi. until you reach a concrete bridge. Immediately to your right is an open area in the ironwood trees. This is the trailhead for Judd Trail. You can park here, but be aware that it is a high-theft area. Hike Judd Trail in either direction 0.7 mi. until you reach the intersection with Nuuanu Trail. Alternatively, hike on Kalawahine trail until it intersects the Pauoa Flats Trail. Go left on Pauoa Flats Trail about 0.1 mi. to the Nuuanu Trailhead on the left. Nuuanu Trail will end at Judd Trail.)*

JUDD TRAIL. *(0.75 mi. one-way. Elevation gain: 200 ft. Easy.)* This trail connects Nuuanu Pali Dr. with the Nuuanu Trail and can be reached from either. If you start from the road, Judd Trail crosses a stream and becomes a loop that takes hikers through damp valley of bamboo, eucalyptus, and ironwood trees. The rocks can be slick, so be careful keeping your balance. Midway through the path, the trail connects with Nuuanu Trail. *(See above directions for the Nuuanu Trail.)*

KOLOWALU TRAIL. *(1 mi. one-way. Elevation gain: 1100 ft. Challenging.)* This, one of the area's most challenging hikes, is for experienced hikers only. The steep trail rises 1100 ft. through dense forest to Waahila Ridge and intersects Waahila Ridge Trail. *(The trailhead is on the right side of the Forestry and Wildlife picnic shelter near the Puu Pia Trailhead. You may also access this trail by hiking 2½ mi. along Waahila Ridge Trail, and then proceeding left at the junction.)*

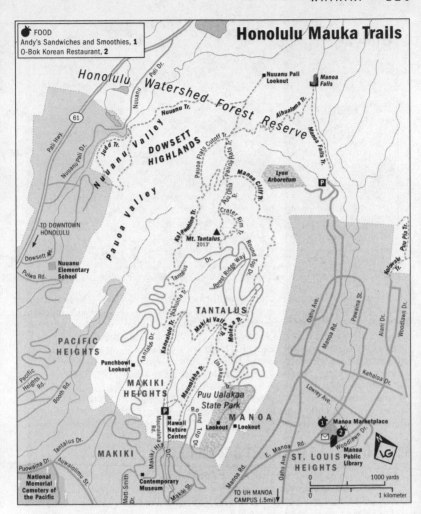

FOOD
Andy's Sandwiches and Smoothies, **1**
O-Bok Korean Restaurant, **2**

Honolulu Mauka Trails

OAHU

WAIKIKI

From surf swells to sushi to beachside Mai Tais and vibrant nightlife, there's always something going on in Waikiki. Start out on the main drag along Waikiki Beach, Kalakaua Ave., where designer shops, restaurants, and beachside bars provide spectacular people-watching. On your beach day, you can plan for bodyboarding and beach volleyball near Kapahulu Pier, surfing at Canoes break on Waikiki Beach, or a more relaxed lounge near the calmer Fort DeRussy and Duke Kahanamoku Beach. Waikiki offers something for every traveler: idyllic sunsets, gorgeous weather, and plenty to do.

In 1922, Waikiki's water was diverted into the Ala Wai Canal, turning the marshland into the beach it is today. The Waikiki wetlands, a former gathering

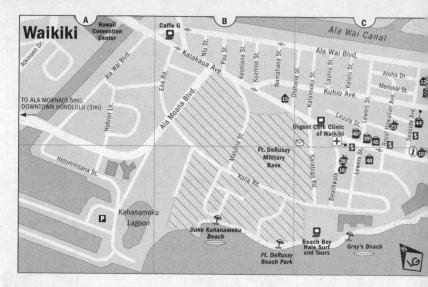

place for Native Hawaiians, were transformed into Waikiki Beach by importing sand. Upon the beach's completion tourism gained an early foothold. An international melange of travelers and tourists and a smaller contingent of locals consistently crowd the area's streets, shops, sights, sands, and dance floors.

The center of tourism in Hawaii's biggest city, Waikiki is less a site of local culture than a thoroughly commercial vacation destination, but the area has an allure nonetheless. If manufactured gimmicks do not fulfill your culture craving, take an afternoon stroll down the offbeat Kapahulu Ave. on the east end of town, where you can explore a street full of mom-and-pop shops, antique stores, and authentic local eateries. To put it simply, if Oahu is "the gathering place," Waikiki is where the party's at.

LOCAL TRANSPORTATION

Bus: For help on how to reach a specific destination, call ☎808-848-5555 5:30am-10pm. Listed below are a few convenient routes that leave from Waikiki. Consult a bus schedule or www.thebus.org for more information. Check p. 98 for another list of bus routes through downtown Honolulu.

#2 goes up Kuhio and Kalakaua Ave. through the heart of **downtown** and **Chinatown** and back through Waikiki to **Kapiolani Park.**

#4 goes up University Ave. by the **University of Hawaii in Manoa,** west through Makiki, and up Nuuanu Ave. into **Nuuanu Valley** via **downtown Honolulu.**

#8 begins its island voyage at Kalakaua and Monsarrat Ave., hugs the coastline on Kuhio Ave. through Waikiki, and finishes at the **Ala Moana Shopping Center.**

#13 goes from the intersection at Kapahulu and Campbell Ave. up Kuhio and Kalakaua Ave., through **downtown** via S. Beretania St., and up Liliha St.

#19 leaves Monsarrat and Kalakaua Ave. for Ala Moana Blvd, passing through Waikiki, **Ala Moana Shopping Center, downtown,** and finally the **airport** and **Hickam Air Force Base.**

#20 follows the route of #19 to the airport, then north heading to the **Pearl Harbor Historical Sites, Aloha Stadium,** and the **Pearlridge Shopping Center.**

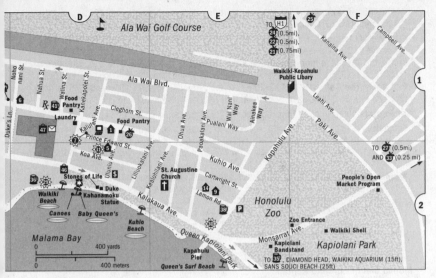

Waikiki

⌂ ACCOMMODATIONS
Aqua Bamboo,	**1**	*D1*
Hale Aloha Hostel (Waikiki HI),	**5**	*D2*
Hawaiian King,	**6**	*D1*
Polynesian Beach Club Hostel,	**9**	*E2*
Seaside Hawaiian Hostel,	**12**	*C1*
Waikiki Beachside Hostel,	**14**	*E2*
Waikiki Gateway Hotel,	**15**	*B1*

🍴 FOOD
Arancino,	**18**	*C2*
Diamond Head Market & Grill,	**A**	*F2*
Leonard's Bakery,	**21**	*E1*
Matsugen, (renumber)	**28**	*C2*
Ono Hawaiian Foods,	**22**	*E1*

Petite Garlic,	**23**	*C1*
The Pyramids,	**24**	*E1*
Rainbow Drive-In,	**25**	*F*
Ruffage Natural Foods,	**26**	*D1*
South Shore Grill,	**27**	*F2*
Top of Waikiki,	**A**	*C2*

☀ ACTIVITIES
Aloha Beach Services,	**29**	*D2*
Hans Hedemann Surf School,	**30**	*E2*
Koa Board Sports,	**31**	*D2*
Go Nuts Hawaii,	**D**	*D1*

🍸 NIGHTLIFE
Diamond Head Grill,	**35**	*E2*
Duke's Canoe Club,	**36**	*D2*

Fusion Waikiki,	**37**	*C1*
Hula's Bar and Lei Stand,	**38**	*E2*
Kelley O'Neil's,	**39**	*C1*
Moose McGillycuddy's Pub and Cafe,	**40**	*C1*
Nashville Waikiki,	**41**	*D1*
Zanzabar,	**44**	*C1*

🛍 SHOPPING
DFS Galleria,	**45**	*C1*
Hyatt Shops,	**46**	*D2*
The International Marketplace,	**47**	*D1*
Royal Hawaiian Shopping Center,	**48**	*C2*

#22, known as the **Beachbus,** starts at the northwest end of Waikiki at Pau St. and Ala Wai Blvd., then turns around at Niu St. onto Kalakaua Ave. and then Kuhio Ave. The Beachbus continues on to the intersection of Kapahulu and Paki Ave., up Diamond Head Rd. to **Diamond Head** and by **Kahala Mall.** It then jumps on to the Kalanianaole Hwy. to **Hanauma Bay, Sandy Beach, Maka-puu Beach,** and **Waimanalo** ending at **Sea Life Park.**

#23 leaves **Ala Moana,** goes through Waikiki east to **Hawaii Kai** and **Sea Life Park** more directly.

#42 leaves Waikiki via Ala Moana Blvd. and heads west through **Ala Moana, Kakaako,** and **down-town Honolulu** past the **airport, Pearl Harbor Historical Sites, Pearlridge Shopping Center,** and **Pearl City Shopping Center** to **Waipahu** and **Ewa.**

Trolley: Waikiki Trolley (☎808-593-2822; www.waikikitrolley.com) runs 4 lines: Red (Honolulu City Line), Blue (Ocean Coast Line), Yellow (Local Honolulu Shopping Shut-tle) and Pink (Ala Moana/Waikiki Shopping Shuttle Line). Red line runs every 40min., first trolley leaves from Waikiki Hilton Hawaiian Village starting at 9:10am, ends at Bishop Museum. Blue line runs every hr. from DFS Galleria Waikiki starting at 8:30am. Pink line runs every 10min. from DFS Galleria Waikiki starting 9:30am. Yellow line runs every 45min. from Ala Moana Center starting at 10am. 1-day tickets $27, ages 4-11 $13, seniors $20. Check online or call for up-to-date route schedules.

Taxis: Waikiki is small—a ride across the district is around $6. Taxis to the airport are expensive ($30-35); it is wise to arrange transportation through your hotel or hostel, or via the myriad airport shuttle services (around $7). **Charley's Taxi & Limousine** (☎808-531-1333) has 24hr. service to most of Oahu. Most locations have flat rates that apply. **The Cab** (☎808-422-2222) offers 24hr. island-wide service. $2.25 for the first 1/8 mi., $0.30 for each additional 1/8 mile or 40 seconds idle.

Car Rentals: Keep in mind that rates can differ significantly based on season.

Enterprise, 1888 Kalakaua Ave., #C107 (☎808-979-2600; www.enterprise.com), or 445 Seaside Ave., Ste. 3C facing Nohohani St. (☎808-922-0090). Cars from $30 per day, $210 per week. Unlimited mileage. Liability $10 per day, CDW $17 per day. 21+. Under-25 surcharge $10 per day. Check online for special rates. Open M-F 7am-6pm, Sa-Su 8am-5pm. AmEx/D/MC/V.

Paradise Rent-a-Car, 151 Uluniu Ave. (☎808-926-7777), and 1843 Ala Moana Blvd (☎808-946-7777). Standard daily rates: compacts from $29, mid-size from $40, Jeeps $70, Mustangs $80. 3-day min. Uluniu Ave. shops rent bikes ($15 per 24hr., $75 per week), mopeds ($35 per 24hr.), and motorcycles ($179 per 24hr.) as well. CDW $19 per day. Under-25s surcharge $10 per day; under-21 surcharge $20 per day. Open daily 8am-5pm. AmEx/D/MC/V.

VIP Car Rentals, 234 Beachwalk (☎808-922-4605). VIP rents older, less expensive cars. Standard daily rates: compacts from $30, mid-size from $34. 3-day rentals get $13 off the first day. CDW $14 per day. Under-25 surcharge. Open daily 7am-5pm. AmEx/MC/V.

Moped and Motorcycle Rentals:

Hawaiian Peddler, 2139 Kuhio Ave. (☎808-926-5099 or 808-382-9049 for reservations). Offers personal service and a wide selection of mopeds (8am-4:30pm $35, overnight $40) and Jeeps ($95 per day). Their pride and joy are their Harley-Davidsons (8am-4:30pm $140). They also rent bikes ($21 per 24hr.) and watersports equipment. Ask about promotions and special rates. Discounts for longer rentals. Open daily 8am-4:30pm. D/MC/V.

Moped Direct, 750A Kapahulu Ave. (☎808-732-3366), about 1 mi. outside of Waikiki past the Ala Wai Golf Course. Generally has the lowest rates and loans out helmets for free. Mopeds 9am-6pm $25, full day $37, 3 days $78, 5 days $109, 1 wk $129. 18+. Open M-F 9am-6pm, Sa-Su 9am-5pm. Credit card or driver's license required. AmEx/D/MC/V.

⊞ ORIENTATION

Waikiki's boundary is defined on the north and west by the **Ala Wai Canal,** on the south by its beaches, and on the east by Diamond Head Crater. Three main thoroughfares run Waikiki's two-mile length from east to west: **Ala Wai Boulevard** runs parallel to the canal with one-way traffic going west; **Kalakaua Avenue** runs by the ritziest hotels and beaches with one-way traffic going east; **Kuhio Avenue** splits off Kalakaua Ave. at the western end of Waikiki and bears the brunt of the two-way traffic all the way to **Kapahulu Avenue** on the east end of town. The three main east-west streets intersect numerous one-way side streets, which are confusing when on the road—drivers should carry a good map.

The Ala Wai Canal is a scenic area that is popular with joggers and walkers, but its distance from major tourist areas makes it the least safe part of Waikiki at night. The district on the whole is safe, and the Waikiki Police substation is located centrally near the **Duke Kahanamoku Statue** on Kalakaua Ave. The safest area is around the intersection of Kalakaua Ave. and Kuhio Ave., which is noisy with traffic during the day and the occasional moped pack at night. Kalakaua Ave. is more for show than transportation: it has no bus traffic, loads of pedestrians, and all manner of street performers and vendors.

To get to **H-1 West** from Kalakaua Ave. or Kuhio Ave., make a left onto Kapahulu Ave. Take Kapahulu past Kaimuki, under the H-1 overpass and left on Waialae Ave., following the signs to merge onto H-1. For **H-1 East** take Ala

Moana Blvd. over the canal, leaving Waikiki, and turn right on Atkinson Dr., then right again on Kapiolani Blvd. toward H-1.

⚑ PRACTICAL INFORMATION

TOURIST AND FINANCIAL SERVICES

Tourist Office: Hawaii Visitors and Convention Bureau Information Office, 2270 Kalakaua Ave., Ste. 801 (☎808-923-1811; www.gohawaii.com), in the Waikiki Business Plaza. A friendly office with free tourist magazines. Open M-F 8am-4:30pm.

Tours: See **Honolulu, Practical Information,** p. 105.

Banks:

American Savings Bank, 321 Seaside Ave. (☎808-923-1102), in the Waikiki Business Plaza. Currency exchange for bank customers only. Fee 1%. M-F 9am-6pm, Sa 9am-1pm.

Bank of Hawaii, 2228 Kalakaua Ave. (☎808-543-6900). Currency exchange fee $10 for nondepositors. Call ahead. Open M-Th 8:30am-4pm, F 8:30am-6pm.

First Hawaiian Bank, 2181 Kalakaua Ave. (☎808-943-4670). Currency exchange fee for noncustomers $3 for $300 or less, $5 for $300 or more. 24hr. ATMs outside. Open M-Th 8:30am-4pm, F 8:30am-6pm.

LOCAL SERVICES

Library: Waikiki-Kapahulu Public Library, 400 Kapahulu Ave. (☎808-733-8488), across from Leahi Ave., before the Ala Wai Golf Course. Internet access available with a 3-month visitor's card ($10). 3 Internet terminals available; call to reserve. Printing $0.10 per page; color $0.20 per page. Open Tu-W and F-Sa 10am-5pm, Th noon-7pm.

Laundromats: Waikiki Laundromats (☎808-926-2573) operates numerous self-serve, coin-operated laundromats in Waikiki that are on hotel premises but are open to the public. One is in the Ohana East, 150 Kaiulani Ave., on Kuhio between Waina and Kanekapolei. Wash $2; dry $2. Open daily 6:30am-11pm.

Weather/Surf Conditions: See **Honolulu and Waikiki Information Lines,** p. 107.

EMERGENCY AND COMMUNICATIONS

Police: Waikiki Substation, 2405 Kalakaua Ave. (☎808-529-3801), in the Duke Paoa Kahanamoku Building on Waikiki Beach opposite the Hyatt Regency. Officers are on foot patrol throughout Waikiki to offer information. Open 24hr.

Crisis Lines: Sex Abuse Treatment Center, 55 Merchant St., 22nd fl. (☎808-524-7273). 24hr. crisis hotline, medical and legal exams, counseling and education.

Red Cross: American Red Cross, Hawaii Chapter (☎808-734-2101).

Medical Services: Urgent Care Clinic of Waikiki, 2155 Kalakaua Ave., Ste. 308 (☎808-924-3399), at Beachwalk above Planet Hollywood. Accepts walk-ins. Free ride to clinic; call for information. Open daily 8:30am-7pm, last patient 6pm. **Straub Doctors on Call** at the Hyatt Regency Waikiki (☎808-971-8001).

Pharmacy: Prince Kuhio Pharmacy Waikiki, 2330 Kuhio Ave. (☎808-923-4466, fax 808-922-1104). Open daily 7am-10pm. Prescription pickup M-F 9am-5pm, Sa 9am-2:30pm. AmEx/D/MC/V.

Internet Access: Internet Cafe and Beach Boy Hale Surf and Tours, 2161 Kalia Rd., Ste. 110 (☎808-382-4524), on the Waikiki Shores beachfront next to the US Army Museum, offers Internet access. An Internet card must be purchased at the beach stand, which will provide a username and password. $6 per 30 min., $10 per hr. Open daily 9am-5pm. Cash only. **The US Post Office** at the **International Marketplace,** 2230

Kalakaua Ave., also has Internet access. $2 per 10min., $10 per hr., $20 per 3 hr., printing $1 per page for B&W, $2 per page for color. Open M-Su 8am-11pm.

Post Office: Waikiki Post Office, 330 Saratoga Rd. (☎808-973-7515). Open M-F 8am-4:30pm, Sa 9am-1pm. Last collection M-F 4:30pm, Sa 12:30pm. AmEx/D/MC/V. **Satellite Post Office** at the International Marketplace, 2230 Kalakaua Ave., 2nd floor., M-Su 8am-11pm. Last collection 3pm M-F. **Postal Code:** 96815.

ACCOMMODATIONS

As Oahu's center of tourism, Waikiki is not short of places to stay. Hotels dominate the skyline, and some have quite inspiring views 30 floors above Waikiki. Travelers should ask to see rooms before paying extra for any view, be it ocean, mountain, or "city" (which can range from a lit-up, panoramic Honolulu landscape to the slightly less exhilarating ABC Store across the street). In general, oceanfront accommodations are more expensive but tend to have overcrowded beaches. Many high quality hotels can be found for lower prices along Ala Wai Blvd. overlooking the canal. The prices listed below are standard rates, but be sure to ask about current deals and Internet prices, which can be substantially lower. Unless otherwise noted, all accommodations have A/C and 24hr. reception, check-in at 3pm, and check-out at noon.

HOSTELS

These establishments are "travelers only," so be prepared to show out-of-state identification and a departing ticket at check-in.

Polynesian Beach Club Hostel, 2584 Lemon Rd. (☎808-922-1340; http://hostelhawaii.com), near the Waikiki Beachside Hostel. Just 1 block from the beach, the Polynesian Beach Club welcomes guests with a friendly, low-key atmosphere. Outdoor common space on the ground level with cable TV and several hammocks strung from the ceiling. Complimentary group activities include barbecues, hikes to Diamond Head, surf lessons, cliff jumping, and catamaran rides. Guests have free use of bodyboards, snorkel gear, safety deposit boxes, and storage. Continental breakfast included. Coin-op laundry. Internet access $1 per 10min., $5 per hr. $10 key deposit. Check-out 10am. Quiet hr. after 10pm. 2-week max. 6-person dorms (all co-ed) $23-28, 4-person dorms (all co-ed) $25-30; semi-private single or double $45-65; private studio with double or single occupancy $67-82. Ask about short-term work. Special online rates. MC/V. ●

Waikiki Beachside Hostel, 2556 Lemon Rd. (☎808-923-9566; www.waikikibeachsidehostel.com). Follow Kalakaua Ave. east. Turn left on Kapahulu Ave. and take the 1st left onto Lemon Rd. Guests share animated, nighttime conversations on a parking lot-turned-courtyard (with a big-screen TV). The hostel also rents surfboards ($10), bodyboards ($7), and snorkel equipment ($7) for the day. Continental breakfast included. Lockers $3. Coin-op laundry. Internet cafe ($1 per 10min.). Free Wi-Fi. Parking $5 per night, $30 per week. 2-week advance reservations recommended. 30-day max. 18+. All rooms feature full kitchen. No A/C except in semi-private rooms. 8-bed co-ed or all-female dorm $26, 4-bed dorm $32, semi-private rooms $75. 7th consecutive night half-off in low season. Ask about long-term work. AmEx/D/MC/V. ❷

Seaside Hawaiian Hostel, 419 Seaside Ave. (☎808-924-3303; www.seasidehawaiianhostel.com). Turn left onto Seaside Ave. from Kalakaua Ave. Take Seaside past Kuhio Ave. and turn right down the alley just before Manukai St. Turn left at the end of the alley; Hawaiian Hostel is 50 ft. back. This hostel manages to survive among giants by offering cheap, clean accommodations to travelers. Cable TV in the courtyard, free Internet access, and use of bodyboards and snorkel equipment. Biweekly barbecues and nightly activities planned. Communal kitchen. Breakfast, linens, and towels included. Coin-op laundry. Reception daily 8am-noon and 4pm-10pm. Check-in after 4pm. Check-out 11am. 2-night min., 2-week max stay. Quiet hr. begins 10pm. Single-sex 6-bed dorm with full bath $23; co-ed $20; semi-private single $39; private double $54. MC/V. ❶

 BREAKING THE FAST. When hostels say Continental Breakfast, they typically mean just coffee, tea, and toast. These items don't last long, so rise early. Better yet, stock up on granola bars at a nearby store.

Hale Aloha Hostel (HI Waikiki), 2417 Prince Edward St. (☎808-926-8313). Head up Kaiulani Ave. from Kalakaua Ave. and turn right onto Prince Edward St. Hale Aloha offers quiet, standard accommodations. Guests share a large, comfortable common room with a kitchen and cable TV. Lockers in all rooms (provide your own padlock) and hotel quality bathrooms. Parking $5 per day. Towels not provided. Breakfast not included. Coin-op laundry. Internet access. Reception daily 7am-3am. Check-in after 1pm. 7-day max.; extended stay possible depending on availability. Non-member prices: 6-bed dorm $26; private studio $60. Member prices are slightly discounted. AmEx/MC/V. ❷

HOTELS

🏨 **Waikiki Grand Hotel,** 134 Kapahulu Ave. (☎808-923-1814; www.waikikigrand.com). The hotel rents out privately owned, luxury vacation units, most of which were recently renovated; amenities include a swimming pool, coin-op laundry, and parking (reserve in advance, $14 per night). Breakfast included. Reception daily 6am-10pm. Reservations recommended 1 month in advance. Rates are for 1-2 guests, add $15 per night per additional guest. Studios for 2 $120; $700 per week depending on view. Rates can drop to $85 during low season. Suites for 4 $169, $1078 per week. AmEx/D/MC/V. ❹

🏨 **Aqua Bamboo,** 2425 Kuhio Ave. (☎808-922-7777; www.aquabamboo.com). The units and hallways in this boutique hotel are accented with a cool beige and black decor and a bamboo motif. All rooms are newly renovated as of July 2008 and feature flatscreen televisions and high-quality linens. The small saltwater pool is surrounded by a beautiful garden area, spa, and sauna. Guests receive discounts at Waikiki restaurants. "Bamboozled!" cocktail reception held every Th from 5-6pm. Continental breakfast. Complimentary Wi-Fi in lobby. Parking $18 per day. Some rooms 2-night min. stay. 1-2 person room with *lanai* $120-140. Roll-away bed $25. Under 17 stay free without extra bed. See website for discounts. AmEx/D/MC/V. ❹

 AHHH, THE VIEWS. If you've opted for a hotel room without a view, ask at the front desk about an upgrade upon check-in. Hotels often have special promotions offering room upgrades for a small additional fee.

Waikiki Gateway Hotel, 2070 Kalakaua Ave. (☎808-955-3741; www.waikiki-gateway-hotel.com), on Kalakaua Ave. before Olohana St. just after the Kuhio Ave. split. The Waikiki Gateway offers standard hotel rooms close to Ft. DeRussy Park at reasonable prices. All rooms have cable TV, fridge, and private *lanai* (except rooms on the 17th fl.). Breakfast included. Parking $15 per day. Check-in 3pm. Check-out 11am. Singles and doubles $78-105, with kitchenette $130-160. Rates change frequently. Extra bed $28. Under 18 free without extra bed. Website discounts. AmEx/D/MC/V. ❸

◖ FOOD

With everything from tempting tourist traps to hidden local eateries, Waikiki is full of good places to dine. If you're on a tight budget, stocking up at a grocery store and cooking in hostel kitchens or hotel kitchenettes is an inexpensive way to keep fortified and beach-ready. Head to ◪**Diamond Head Market and Grill,** 3158 Monsarrat Ave., (☎808-732-0077) just five minutes from central Waikiki and worth the short trip for the market's gourmet deli, bakery, and prepared foods. The market also features a takeout window offering delicious plate lunches, sandwiches, and daily specials. (Market open 6:30am-9pm, grill open 7-10:30am and 11am-9pm. AmEx/D/MC/V.) **Food Pantry,** 2370 Kuhio Ave. (☎808-923-9831), has a much better selection and lower prices than the ubiquitous ABC stores. (Open daily 6am-1am. AmEx/D/MC/V.) Finally, the unique **People's Open Market Program** (☎808-522-7088), in Kapiolani Park at Monsarrat and Paki St., sells fresh produce from local farms. (Open W 10-11am. Cash only.)

RESTAURANTS

◪ **Ono Hawaiian Foods,** 726 Kapahulu Ave. (☎808-737-2275). For over 40 years, Ono has been serving the traditional Hawaiian food, from *pipikaula* (Hawaiian beef jerky) to *poi*. *Kalua* pig, *laulau*, or chicken rice plates come with *pipikaula*, *lomi* salmon, *haupia*, rice, and *poi* ($12.25). The combo plate includes both *kalua* pig and *laulau* ($16). Out-the-door lines are evidence that Ono serves the best Hawaiian cuisine on Oahu and lives up to its name—"delicious." BYOB. Open M-Sa 11am-8pm. Cash only. ❷

◪ **The Pyramids,** 758-B Kapahulu Ave. (☎808-737-2900). Be prepared for a bit of a trek from Waikiki; the restaurant is above the Ala Wai golf course. Take the #13 bus. While the Egyptian-inspired decor and server outfits can only be described as cheesy, the food is garlicky and delicious. Belly dancers perform nightly at 7:30 and 8:30pm. Huge bowl of hummus $6. Tabbouleh salad $5. *Shawarma* $14. All-you-can-eat lunch buffet ($13) daily 11am-2pm. Dinner reservations recommended F-Su. Free parking. Lunch daily 11am-2pm; dinner M-Sa 5:30-10pm, Su 5-9pm. AmEx/D/MC/V. ❸

◪ **Petite Garlic,** 2238 Lauula St., 2nd fl. (☎808-922-2221). This small cafe/kitchen/wine bar is at once sophisticated and laid-back, with a warm, intimate atmosphere. An experimental blend of Eurasian cuisine uses the freshest garlic and herbs. Entrees range from garlic rice ($12) to Kona lobster ($24). Salads $8-14. Wine $6.25-8. Tropical drinks $8.50. Dinner daily 6-11pm, late-night *pupu* 11pm-1am. AmEx/MC/V. ❸

◪ **Ruffage Natural Foods,** 2443 Kuhio Ave. (☎808-922-2042). This hole-in-the-wall sandwich shop serves fresh, local, and healthy goods at low prices. The veggie burrito ($8.50) and papaya smoothies ($5.45) are favorites, as is their popular tuna avocado sandwich ($7). With a health food store in the back, Ruffage also sells vitamins, herbs, and groceries. Open M-Sa 9am-6pm. After Ruffage closes, it becomes ◪**Morio's Sushi,** one of the best, and surprisingly unknown, sushi bars in Waikiki. There may be a wait, as seating is limited and rolls are painstakingly made to perfection by their single sushi chef. Try the Dragon Roll or the Spider Roll for $8. AmEx/MC/V. ❶

◪ **Leonard's Bakery,** 933 Kapahulu Ave. (☎808-737-5591). Locals have been coming to Leonard's since 1952 for tasty tarts ($1-1.25), delectable danishes ($0.67), and a host of other inexpensive treats. Mouth-watering *malasadas* (Portuguese doughnuts, $0.80) are worth the hike from Waikiki. Lines form in the morning, so get there early for the freshest selection. Open M-Th and Su 6am-9pm, F-Sa 6am-10pm. ❶

South Shore Grill, 3114 Monsarrat Ave. (☎808-734-0229), a half-mile stroll toward Diamond Head from Kapiolani Park. TheBus #13, 22, or 23. This casual eatery serves fresh and healthy dishes for a reasonable price without the cheesy gimmicks all too pervasive in Waikiki. The barbecue chicken plate ($7.25), cooked Korean-style, is generous enough for a day without breakfast. Other specialties are the grilled *mahi mahi* sandwich ($6.75) and the Caprese sandwich ($5). Open M-Sa 10:30am-9pm and Su 12:30pm-9pm; all orders after 8:30pm are takeout only. ❶

Arancino, 255 Beachwalk Ave. (☎808-923-5557). This small Italian restaurant has lines of people outside waiting for food bursting with bona-fide flavor. Candlelit tabletops and

Italian music create an intimate escape from the many tourist traps of Waikiki. Run by a Japanese proprietor, the menu is in both English and Japanese, but the dishes are all Italian-American. Spaghetti with meatballs $16. Pizzas $11-22. Homemade tiramisu $7. Open daily 11:30am-2:30pm and 5-10:30pm. AmEx/D/MC/V. ❸

Rainbow Drive-In, 3308 Kanaina Ave. (☎808-737-0177), a 15min. walk down Kapahulu Ave. until it intersects Kanaina Ave. Hard to miss with its faded rainbow roof and neon rainbow light, Rainbow Drive-In's packed parking lot is testament to its long-established reputation as an authentic provider of plate lunches. Try the Mix Plate (with steak, *mahi mahi*, and chicken accompanied by fries or rice and macaroni salad or slaw; $6.50). Sandwiches $1.80-3.25 Open daily 7am-9pm. Cash only. ❶

Matsugen, 255 Beachwalk Ave. (☎808-926-0255), next to Arancino. Don't be alarmed when greeted with loud slurping noises as you enter this authentic Japanese restaurant specializing in *soba* and *udon* noodles. Their *soba* are made fresh several times a day from freshly ground buckwheat flour and water, kneaded and cut with a special knife right in front of patrons. Noodles served hot or cold ($9-18). Open daily 11:30am-2pm (last call 1:40pm) and 5-10pm (last call 9:30pm). AmEx/MC/V. ❸

◪ BEACHES

Waikiki Beach is the name that refers to all of the beaches on the South Shore of Oahu. It begins on the Waikiki side of the Hilton Lagoon in the west and continues along the coastline of Waikiki's premier beach hotels all the way to the edge of Diamond Head Crater. Although the beach reaches moments of absolute saturation and can be overwhelming, the perpetual daytime crowds can also be enlivening—the throng of people creates an audible and infectious enthusiasm. The Waikiki beaches see a variety of watersports: surfers paddle between catamarans, canoers navigate around snorkelers, and swimmers try to keep their space close to shore. If you're the type who prefers long walks on the beach, the **Waikiki Historic Trail,** which stretches 2 mi. along the Waikiki sands and Kalakaua Ave. sidewalks, is studded with bronze statues and surfboard placards that inform the curious about such legendary figures as Duke Kahanamoku and the days when Waikiki was a marshland of taro root patches and fishponds. Quieter, more romantic moments occur on the bookends of the frenetic day, at dawn and sunset, when the crowds have dispersed, and the plumeria breeze soothes sunburnt skin.

DUKE KAHANAMOKU BEACH. *(Surfing. Open daily 24hr.)* At the edge of the Hilton Lagoon, Duke Kahanamoku is the westernmost Waikiki beach. The beach is open to the public but is populated primarily by guests of the Hilton Hawaiian Village. The beach is easily distinguished by the Hilton's "rainbow tower" mural, made of over 8,000 ceramic tiles. This is where legendary surfer Duke Kahanamoku grew up and learned to swim and surf; some say you can still feel his *mana* (spirit) in the area. To the right of the Hilton, on the other side of the rock wall (next to the marina), is a small stretch of beach with a rocky shoreline and a few good surfing spots—**Kaiser's** and **Ala Moana Bowls,** for example— preferred by locals. *(There is limited free 24hr. parking near the Hilton Lagoon. Take Ala Moana Blvd. west to Hobron Ln. and turn left after the Renaissance Ilikai Hotel. At the stop sign, turn left and follow the road past the yacht harbor to the parking lot on the left.)*

FORT DERUSSY BEACH PARK. *(Open daily 5am-10pm.)* Next to Duke Kahanamoku Beach, in front of Fort DeRussy, is this beach park, a stretch of white sand before a large grassy area. The sharp shells and coral near the shore make the beach less than ideal for wading or swimming, but the park has grills, picnic tables, and palm-shaded lawns for an afternoon picnic.

WAIKIKI BEACH (ROYAL MOANA BEACH). *(Surfing. Wind sports. Open daily 24hr. Life-guards on duty 8am-5:30pm.)* Tourists happily cram themselves into the beachfront between the Sheraton Waikiki and the Westin Moana Surfrider. This stretch of sand is often called Royal Moana Beach and there are almost as many tourists cavorting in the water as lounging on the soft shore. Swimmers, catamarans, bodyboards, canoes, and all manner of water toys dot the gently rolling Pacific all the way out to the surfers on the break. The Waikiki Historic Trail continues on this section of beach, with several important sites. The tall **Duke Kahanamoku Statue** of the Hawaiian hero, sheriff, Olympic champion, surfer, and movie star stands here, to the east of the police station. The frequently lei-adorned, bronze Duke faces away from the Pacific, his board between him and the water.

Between the statue and the substation are four large, fenced-off stones, which are said to be the living legacies of four Tahitian healers who once lived near the site and traveled the islands to dispense miraculous cures. Before leaving Hawaii, the healers gave their names and *mana* (spiritual power) to the boulders—known as the **Stones of Life**—which survive as a tangible reminder of their services to many Native Hawaiians.

Directly in front of the Duke Kahanamoku Building and police substation is a surf break favored by some locals as the safest spot to learn to surf. The area, known as **Baby Queen's,** is less dangerous and busy than other sites favored by professional instructors. To the right of that area is another surf break called **Canoes,** which is often full of outrigger canoes and novice surfers.

 PARK FOR CHEAP. A great spot to park near Waikiki Beach is the Hono-lulu Zoo's metered lot on Kapahulu Ave., near the intersection with Kalakaua Ave. It's a 2min. walk to the beach, and parking only costs $0.25 per hr. The 4hr. limit is strictly enforced by Waikiki Police.

KUHIO BEACH. *(Bodyboarding. Surfing. Open daily 24hr. Lifeguards on duty 9am-5:30pm.)* Kuhio Beach extends from the center of Waikiki Beach to just beyond the recently improved Kapahulu Pier, or as locals call it, the "Waikiki Wall." From the overlooking pier, beachgoers watch surfers and bodyboarders catch monstrous waves in waters that often conceal shallow coral. Swimming within the calm, shallow pools formed by the seawalls is enjoyable, but inexperienced and unfamiliar boarders should not test the waves on the other side (to the right of the Kapahulu Pier). They should also avoid the strong current and the slippery rock wall. **The Waikiki Marine Life Conservation Project** extends from the lookout at Kapahulu Ave. along Kuhio Beach to the end of the **Waikiki War Memorial Natatorium;** no fishing is allowed inside these boundaries to protect the reef. Concessions and restrooms available. **Queen's Surf Beach,** located left of the pier, lies roughly between the zoo and aquarium and is named after Queen Liluokalani, whose beach house used to stand there.

SANS SOUCI BEACH (KAIMANA BEACH). *(Open daily 9am-5:30pm. Lifeguards on duty 9am-5:30pm)* East of the Waikiki Aquarium (p. 140), on the beach, is the **Natatorium,** a WWI monument and former Olympic training pool. The Natatorium perpetually awaits further renovation before re-opening, despite a refurbishment that recently improved its appearance. Left of the Natatorium is Sans Souci Beach, commonly called Kaimana Beach by the locals who frequent the area. It's a favorite spot among families, because it's farther from the louder, more urban part of Waikiki but still close to the water and park recreation. Many tri-athletes come here to swim the channel that stretches beyond the reef. It's also an especially good place to watch for the "green flash," a quick, bright flash of green light that occurs on the horizon right as the sun goes down. Beyond Sans Souci is the **Outrigger Canoe Club Beach,** which extends all the way to the beaches at foot of Diamond Head. Fishing is permitted here but only on even-numbered years. Parking lot east of the natatorium off Kalakaua Ave.

🎐 ACTIVITIES

Most rental agencies on the beach are fairly expensive and don't take credit cards. Other rental stores can be found on Kapahulu and Kuhio Ave.

Aloha Beach Services, 2335 Kalakaua Ave. (Westin Moana Surfrider Hotel ☎808-922-3111, ext. 2341 for information). In the wooden hut on the left as you walk onto the beach from Duke's Canoe Club. For $30, you can get a 1hr. lesson with a surfboard and the guarantee that you'll be able to stand up. Semi-private lessons $50, private lessons $80. Go early to avoid the crowds. Surfboards $10 for 1hr., each additional hour $5. Bodyboards $5 per hr., all-day $15. Also offers outrigger canoe rides ($10 per person for 2 waves) and catamaran rides ($20 per person per hr., sunset ride $25). Open daily Sept.-May 7am-4pm; June-Aug. 7am-5pm. Cash only.

Hans Hedemann Surf School, 2586 Kalakaua Ave. (☎808-924-7778; www.hhsurf. com), at the Park Shore Hotel. Other locations at Sheraton Waikiki (booth on beach), Outrigger Reef (sign says HH Surf School), and the Otani Kaimana Beach Hotel. The premier surf school in Waikiki, founded by famous surfer Hans Hedemann. Sign up for a 2hr. group surfing lesson ($75 per person including the board). Semi-private lesson $125, private lesson $150. Lessons go out 3 times a day at 9am, noon, and 3pm. Surf-board rentals are $10-15 per hr., $25 per 4hr., $30 per day. Must provide a credit card for rentals. Bodyboards and bikes $8/15/20. Open daily 8am-5pm. AmEx/D/MC/V.

Koa Board Sports, 2420 Koa Ave., 2nd fl. (☎808-923-0189). Rents used longboards for $25 per day and $100 per week, shortboards $20/80, and bodyboards $10 per day. Must provide identification and credit card for rentals. Open daily 10am-6pm. MC/V.

🅖 SIGHTS

🅶DIAMOND HEAD. The 350-acre Diamond Head crater was created about 300,000 years ago during a single brief eruption that flung ash and fine particles into the air. These particles eventually cemented together into a rock called tuff, and geologists now consider Diamond Head one of the world's best examples of a tuff cone. Nicknamed *Leahi,* Diamond Head's 760 ft. summit resembles the *lae* (forehead) of an *ahi* (tuna) when seen from the west. The site finally earned the name "Diamond Head" when Western explorers mistook calcite crystals for diamonds in the late 1700s. In 1904, Diamond Head was purchased by the federal government for defense purposes.

At the park entrance, you'll find picnic tables, restrooms, a pay phone, and drinking water. The fairly easy hike takes about 1-1½hr. round-trip and is 0.8 mi. one-way, winding along rocky switchbacks, through a tunnel, and up steep stairs 560 ft. to the summit. Flashlights are unnecessary; lights have been added to the narrow 225ft. underground tunnel. If claustrophobia still holds you back, rest assured that the journey is worthwhile—the views are spectacular. (*By car, take Monsarrat Ave. to Diamond Head Rd. The park comes up quickly on the right. By bus, take the #22 or 23 from Waikiki. Walk against traffic in the tunnel to the park as there is no sidewalk. Open daily 6am-6pm. Last hike to summit 4:30pm. Go before 8am or after noon to beat the morning rush. Individual walk-in $1, private vehicle $5.*)

OAHU

NEED A BREAK FROM THE SUN?

Organizations across Hawaii are always looking for volunteers. For a comprehensive list of opportunities on any island, visit www.volunteerhawaii.org. If you're reading this on the beach, here are a few examples to get you started:

For animal lovers: Wild Bird Rehab Haven is dedicated to the rehabilitation and eventual release of orphaned and injured wild birds. They are always looking for volunteers willing to clean cages, answer telephones, and feed baby birds. For more information, call ☎808-447-9274 or go to www.wildbirdrehabhaven.org. **Eye of the Pacific Guide Dogs** provides guide dogs and related services to legally blind residents of Hawaii. They sometimes need volunteers to help exercise the dogs if their owners are unable to do so. For more information, call ☎808-941-1088 or go to www.eyeofthepacific.org.

For tree-huggers: The Hanauma Bay Education Program is a nonprofit organization dedicated to promoting education and awareness of Hawaii's marine wildlife. Volunteers are always welcome to staff the Visitors Center, lead informational tours, and provide clerical or maintenance support. Contact ☎808-394-1374 for more information or go to www.hawaii.edu/~hanauma. **KAHEA: The Hawaiian-Environmental Alliance** is a community-based organization

WAIKIKI AQUARIUM. Specializing in coral reef ecosystems, the aquarium is home to more than 2500 marine creatures including tropical fish, sea dragons, jelly fish, reef sharks, and endangered Hawaiian monk seals. The small exhibit space is located next to a living reef at the foot of Diamond Head. Hordes of school children mob the place on weekdays, communicating with the animals at a high-pitched (read: grating) frequency. *(2777 Kalakaua Ave. #2 bus stops directly in front every 10-20min. Limited free parking on the aquarium side of Kalakaua Ave. ☎808-923-9741. http://waquarium.org. Open daily 9am-5pm; last admission 4:30pm. $9; locals and military $6; students and seniors over 60 $6; people with disabilities and ages 13-17 $4; ages 5-12 $2; 4 and under free. Audio guide included.)*

HONOLULU ZOO. The Honolulu Zoo is conveniently located just minutes away from Waikiki Beach but lacks the more elaborate attractions of bigger zoos. The main exhibit showcases animals from the African Serengeti, but the aging lions don't put on much of a show. Also present are the many birds and reptiles of the Pacific Islands, including the endangered *nene* goose of Hawaii. Keeper talks are held inside the elephant exhibit daily at 11am and 1:30pm. The recently expanded Children's Zoo allows kids to get close to llamas, sheep, goats, and cows, and family programs explore the zoo in depth via the Saturday Twilight Tours or the monthly Snooze In The Zoo camping program. During summer, the zoo opens for free on Wednesday for the popular ▨**Wildest Show,** which features different live Hawaiian musical and dance performances. Bring a blanket, pack a picnic, and come early to claim dibs on lawn space. *(151 Kapahulu Ave., on the corner of Kapahulu and Kalakaua Ave. Parking lot entrance on Kapahulu Ave., $0.25 per hr. 4hr. limit. Free parking across the street at the Waikiki Shell on Monsarrat Ave. ☎808-971-7171; www.honoluluzoo.org. Zoo open daily 9am-4:30pm; Children's Zoo open daily 9am-4pm. Wildest Show 6-7pm, doors open at 4:35pm, suggested donation $2. Zoo admission $8; ages 6-12 with adult $1, under 5 free. Family Pass $25. Twilight Tours $12, ages 4-12 $8. Reservations recommended. Snooze In The Zoo $50 ages 4 and up; reservations required. MC/V.)*

ST. AUGUSTINE CHURCH BY-THE-SEA. In 1854, this church was built from coconut fronds and driftwood; three renovations later the church has been transformed from an old Hawaiian hut into today's grand church. Its beautiful stained-glass interior is a Waikiki rarity. *(130 Ohua Ave. ☎808-923-7024. Mass M-Sa 7am and 5pm, Su 6:30, 8, 10am, and 5pm.)*

🎵 ENTERTAINMENT

KUHIO BEACH TORCH LIGHTING AND HULA SHOW. In Waikiki, watching beautiful island girls shake their hips and surf-chiseled men flex in nothing but sarongs is not only socially acceptable; it's free. The Kuhio Beach Torch Lighting and Hula Show goes on at the Kuhio Beach Hula Mound, near the Duke Kahanamoku Statue across Kalakaua Ave. from Uluniu Ave. (☎808-843-8002. Tu-Su Feb.-Oct. 6:30-7:30pm, Nov.-Jan. 6-7pm. Free.)

ROYAL HAWAIIAN SHOWS AND LESSONS. The Royal Hawaiian Shopping Center hosts free lessons and entertainment, including Hawaiian quilting, 1hr. ukulele and hula lessons, and lei-making. (☎808-922-2299. Quilting Tu 9:30-11:30am on the 3rd level bridge, building A, near Chibo Okonomiyaki Restaurant; ukulele lessons Tu-F 10-11am on the ground level, building A, near Fendi, limited to 25; lei-making F 1-2pm ground level, building A, near Fendi; hula lessons Tu 11am-noon and Th 4:15-5:15pm in the Royal Grove; Twilight Entertainment featuring Hawaiian Music and Hula in the Royal Grove Tu 5-7pm, W-F 6:30-8:30pm.)

FREE OUTDOOR FILMS. On alternate weekends, The Kuhio Beach Torch Lighting and Hula Show (see above) is followed by 🌅**Sunset on the Beach.** The Mayor's Office sets up a movie screen on the beach for a double feature of family films. Before the show, area restaurants set up portable booths on the east side of Kapahulu Pier, selling over-priced concessions to the first-come, first-seated beach blanket crowd. (☎808-923-1094. Queen's Surf Beach. Most Sa-Su at sunset around 7pm. Check the Honolulu Events Calendar, listed above, for film dates.)

BLAISDELL CENTER AND WAIKIKI SHELL. The Blaisdell Center Complex hosts a wide array of attractions in its arena, exhibition hall, galleria, and concert hall. The Waikiki Shell is an outdoor amphitheater near the beach with a background view of Diamond Head. Both make excellent venues for evening concerts and shows; check the website for a current schedule of events. The Royal Hawaiian Band also performs weekly (Su 1-3pm) at the Kapiolani Bandstand, near the Waikiki Shell. (Blaisdell Center, 777 Ward Ave., between King St. and Kapiolani Blvd. King St. gate open M-Sa 5:30am-6pm, Su and holiday hours determined by events. Box office ☎808-591-2211; www.blaisdellcenter.com. Open M-Sa 9am-5pm. Waikiki Shell, 2805 Monsarrat Ave., at the Diamond Head end of Waikiki.)

HOTEL HULA SHOWS. Several hotels offer free hula performances, many of which are open to non-guests. Arrive early for a better view. The

that encourages public involvement and protection of public trust resources like the Northwestern Hawaiian Islands and the summit of Mauna Kea. Volunteers are often needed in the Outreach and Education divisions to develop educational materials and plan events. For more information, call ☎808-524-8220 or go to www.kahea.org.

For the keiki in you: The Boys and Girls Club of Hawaii often looks for coaches, referees, and scorekeepers for seasonal sports including flag football, basketball, volleyball and soccer. Games are usually held during the afternoons and on weekends. Contact the Director of Program Operations (☎808-792-5111), for more information or go to www.bgch. com. **The Christmas Wish Program** provides year-round support to homeless and abused children with food, clothing, toiletries, and other necessities. They are always looking for volunteers to work on projects, photograph fun events, and teach dance to children all over the state. For more information, call ☎808-982-8128.

For the activist: The Legal Aid Society of Hawaii is the largest and oldest nonprofit law firm in Hawaii. Volunteer opportunities range from clerical work to website maintenance to providing legal advice. There is a 3-month minimum commitment. For more information, call ☎800-499-4392 or go to www.legalaidhawaii.org.

Hilton Hawaiian Village's popular King's Jubilee hula show on Fridays at the hotel's super pool (☎808-949-4321, 7-8pm) is highlighted with a fireworks display. Seating is available for $20, which includes one drink. The Halekulani's House Without a Key restaurant has live Hawaiian music nightly on the outdoor patio from 5:30-8:30 with a hula dancer (☎808-923-2311, hula begins 6pm). The Renaissance Ilikai Waikiki's Paddles Bar (☎808-949-3811) features traditional sunset conch-blowing and brief torch-lighting ceremony daily around 6pm. Farther from the beach, the Sheraton Princess Kaiulani Hotel hosts live Hawaiian music and hula dancing outside the Pikake Terrace Restaurant. Dinner buffet is available at the restaurant ($36 M-Th and Su, $39 F-Sa) but the show may be enjoyed for free from the poolside bar (☎808-922-5811, daily 6:15-9:15pm).

▐ SHOPPING

If you're shopping in Waikiki you have two options: either the 4-for-$1 Hawaiiana at the International Market and Duke's Lane, or the chic high-end (and high-priced) designer items that dominate the Royal Hawaiian Shopping Center. For everything in between, you'd be better off elsewhere.

THE INTERNATIONAL MARKETPLACE. The market is a maze of kiosk stands that peddle the same wares as every other kitschy tourist capital in the world. It's the premier venue for cheap aloha wear and Hawaiian carvings, macadamia nut leis, puka wares, jade Buddha statues, and jewelry. **Duke's Lane,** which runs along the Waikiki Beachcomber Hotel on the same block as the International Marketplace, lays things out in much the same way and sells at similar prices. *(2330 Kalakaua Ave. between Duke's Lane and Kaiulani Ave. ☎808-922-2000. Open daily 8am-10pm. Most stores in Duke's Lane open 10am-10pm. Most take AmEx/D/MC/V. Live Hawaiian entertainment in the food court F-Sa 7-9pm; "Islands of Aloha" hula show M, W, Th 8:30-9:15pm.)*

ROYAL HAWAIIAN SHOPPING CENTER. This center holds court with the nobility of the fashion world, including names like Bulgari, Cartier, Fendi, and Hermes. The only people you'll see wearing formal black suits in all of Waikiki are the guards in the Royal Hawaiian's Salvatore Ferragamo. The 4-level, 310,000 sq. ft. shopping center hosts a range of free entertainment and lessons (p. 141) in the Asian-inspired interior. *(2201 Kalakaua., from Lewers St. to past Duke's Lane. Info booth ☎808-922-2299. Open daily 9am-10pm; shopping daily 10am-10pm.)*

DFS GALLERIA. DFS Galleria is at the crux of the lit-up, glitzy, all-for-show Kalakaua Ave., across from the Royal Hawaiian. The behemoth duty-free center, catering mostly to Japanese travelers, houses many of the same upscale stores as the Royal Hawaiian. There are gift shops on the first floor, upscale American boutiques on the second, and a free hula show on some evenings. The red, pink, and yellow trolley lines all stop at the DFS Galleria; schedule is posted at DFS Galleria. *(At Kalakaua and Royal Hawaiian Ave. ☎808-931-2655; www.dfsgalleria.com. You must show an international ticket or e-ticket to gain access to the duty-free brand boutiques on the 3rd fl. Free hula show W-F 5:30-7:30pm. Open daily 9am-11pm.)*

HYATT SHOPS. Two towers scrape the sky over the little Hyatt Shops. Check out everything from original Hawaiian art to the plethora of gift stores. *(2424 Kalakaua Ave. Most stores open daily 9am-11pm. Call the Hyatt ☎808-923-1234, for more info.)*

⚑ NIGHTLIFE

CLUBS

Diamond Head Grill, 2885 Kalakaua Ave. (☎808-922-3734), in the W Hotel. The most posh place to see and be seen, the Diamond Head Grill hosts one of Waikiki's best weekend parties. DJs spin hip hop and pack the dance floor tight. F night is most popular. Beer $5. Mixed drinks $7-8. W-Th Jazz in the Wonderlounge 5-10pm. Dress to impress: no slippers, shorts, hats, or tank tops (for men). Cover $10-20. Bar open 5:30pm-midnight. Wonderlounge open F-Sa 10pm-2am. AmEx/D/MC/V.

Zanzabar, 2255 Kuhio Ave. (☎808-924-3939), in Waikiki Trade Center. Despite the ostentatious exterior and hotter-than-thou vibe, clubbers get down on debaucherous theme nights. Live DJs nightly. No T-shirts, ripped jeans, tanks, sandals, or hats for men. Evening attire for ladies. Exclusive VIP room for $30. 21+ Tu and F-Sa, cover $10-15; 18+ M, W-Th, and Su. Parking $3. Open W-Su 9pm-4am, Tu 8pm-4am. AmEx/D/MC/V.

Fusion Waikiki, 2260 Kuhio Ave. (☎808-924-2422). Live DJs spinning house and techno keep the 2 dance floors pumping in this gay bar, starting M-Th and Su at 10pm, and F-Sa from midnight on. Beer $4-5.50. Nightly drink specials. M-Tu free karaoke 10pm-1:30am. F-Sa drag show 9:45pm. 21+. No cover M-Th and most Su. Cover F-Sa and event Su $5. Open M-Th and Su 10pm-4am, F-Sa 8pm-4am. Cash only.

BARS

Duke's Canoe Club, 2335 Kalakaua Ave. (☎808-922-2268), inside the Outrigger Waikiki, on the beach. A Waikiki institution, Duke's is the ultimate beachside bar. F-Su live contemporary Hawaiian music 4-6pm and 10pm-midnight. Su local legend Henry Kapono plays. Tropical drinks $6, beer $3.25-4.25, *pupu* $5-10. Duke's also has a busy seafood restaurant. Food served daily 7am-midnight. Lunch buffet $11. Bar open daily 4pm-1am. AmEx/D/MC/V.

Hula's Bar and Lei Stand, 134 Kapahulu Ave. (☎808-923-0669), in the Waikiki Grand. In this famous gay bar, crowds come to watch the sunset and stay for the fun, social atmosphere. Sophisticated interior with black lighting, pool table, and a view of the beach. Pitchers $5.50-6.50 daily 3pm-2am, W until 9pm $4.50. Wine and mixed drinks $2.50 daily 10am-3pm. F-Sa free *pupu* 5-9pm. Live DJ nightly. GoGo Boyz perform Th-Sa at 10:00pm and Su at 8pm. F Martini Sunset 3-9pm (martinis $3.75). M-F tropical drinks special 10am-3pm $3.50. Hula's Cafe open M and F-Su 5-9pm. Cover Th-Sa $3, on promotional nights $5. Open daily 10am-2am. AmEx/MC/V.

 FUN, AHOY! Hula's hosts a gay catamaran sail every Saturday at 2pm. Go early to ensure tickets are available; $30 per person.

Kelley O'Neil's, 311 Lewers St. (☎808-926-1777), across from Moose's. A laid-back, and surprisingly authentic, Irish bar where locals and tourists enjoy pints and live music in a comfortable atmosphere. Happy hour daily 11am-8pm (domestic beer $2.25, pints $3.25, mixed drinks $5.25). Live music M-Sa 9pm-1:30am, F-Sa 5pm-3:30am. Su Irish music 4-9pm. Fish and chips $9. Guinness Pie (beef marinated in Irish stout and baked into a pie) $7.50. Food served daily 11am-9pm, bar open until 4am. AmEx/D/MC/V.

Moose McGillycuddy's Pub and Cafe, 310 Lewers St. (☎808-923-0751; www.moose-waikiki.com). In the daytime, this laid-back sports bar is a great place to watch the game; after hours it gets a little scandalous. The bar proudly flaunts its mostly-college crowd in online photo albums; check out their website for a taste. Happy hour daily

4-8pm (half-priced drinks and *pupu* $4-6.50, Mai Tais $1.50, mixed drinks and domestic drafts $3). 21+ after 8pm. Cover F-Sa after 8pm $3, Tu after 8pm $5. Live music and dancing. Cafe open daily 7:30am-10pm, pub open daily 4pm-3:30am. AmEx/MC/V.

Nashville Waikiki, 2330 Kuhio Ave. (☎808-926-7911), in the basement of the Ohana West, between Walina St. and Nahua St. on Kuhio Ave. Despite being thousands of miles from the real deal, The Nashville Waikiki feels like authentic country. Line dancing and real cowboys on the scene. W line dancing lessons 7-9pm. Live entertainment 5 nights a week; pool table and dart boards. Happy hour daily 4-8pm (Mai Tais $2.50, domestic bottles $2.75, mixed drinks $2.70). M-Th and Su compete for gift certificates in their pool tournaments. 21+. No cover. Open daily 4pm-4am. MC/V.

CENTRAL OAHU

PEARL HARBOR

On December 7, 1941, 350 Japanese bombers flew 230 miles from carriers stationed in the Pacific Ocean to Pearl Harbor, Hawaii. They launched a devastating, 2-wave military attack on the US Pacific Fleet, wrenching the US out of steadfast neutrality and into the thick of WWII. The US suffered the deaths of over 2400 military personnel and civilians in addition to the destruction of 188 aircraft and 21 vessels. The US government moved swiftly into action, raising their fleet of battleships from the bottom of the Pacific in the greatest maritime salvage in history. While many ships were returned to service, the *USS Arizona* and *USS Utah* were total losses, and remain beneath the harbor. Located 40min. outside of Honolulu, the Pearl Harbor Historical Sites pay tribute to the massive loss from the Japanese attack and the US armed forces' triumphant response. For more information, see **History,** p. 14.

ARIZONA MEMORIAL. Solemn and graceful, the *USS Arizona* Memorial is a fitting tribute to the 1177 crewmen who died aboard the ship. The 184 ft. memorial spans the width of the sunken battleship's midsection, affording visitors a close, poignant view of the ship that still entombs over 900 men. Plans for the memorial began in 1946, but President Eisenhower didn't approve its creation until 1958. After his initial plan was rejected, architect Alfred Preis designed the final structure that was dedicated in 1962. The dip in the center of the memorial's unique, concave shape symbolizes America's defeat at Pearl Harbor while the raised sides represent the eventual American and Allied Forces' victory. The ship began to sink after just 11 minutes of attack and now rests in 40 ft. of water and 23 ft. of mud. Today an active reef, the Arizona is visible about 8 ft. below the monument depending on the tide. Visitors can still see spots of oil that continue to leak from the ship at a rate of 2 quarts per day; some say the oil represents the tears of those who perished aboard. The on-shore **Visitors Center** has a museum, gift shop, snack bar, and outdoor lawn that looks out at Battleship Row. The somber tour begins with a documentary film on shore and is followed by a 7min. boat ride to the memorial itself. The tour is free, but every visitor must pick up his or her ticket in person on a first come, first served basis. An announcement summons visitors every 15min. when it is time from their tour. Audio guides that begin in the museum and conclude at the memorial are $5 and come in 7 languages. Be prepared for an enlightening, reflective experience and overwhelming crowds. *(From Honolulu, take H-1 West to the Arizona Memorial/Stadium Exit 15a, which will put you on Kamehameha Hwy. Follow the signs to the Pearl Harbor Historical Sights. TheBus #20, 42, or CityExpress A will also get you there; the bus stop is across the street from the Battleship Missouri trolley pickup at Bowfin Park. ☎ 808-422-0561 or*

OAHU

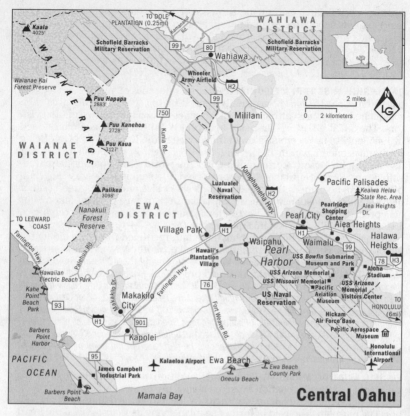

Central Oahu

(Map labels:)

Kaala 4025'

WAIANAE RANGE

TO DOLE PLANTATION (0.25mi)

WAHIAWA DISTRICT

Schofield Barracks Military Reservation

99 80

Wahiawa

Schofield Barracks Military Reservation

Wheeler Army Airfield

H2

99

Waianae Kai Forest Preserve

Puu Hapapa 2883'

750

Mililani

Puu Kanehoa 2728'

Puu Kaua 3127'

WAIANAE DISTRICT

Kunia Rd.

Kamehameha Hwy.

Palikea 3098'

Lualualei Naval Reservation

Pacific Palisades

Keaiwa Heiau State Rec. Area

Aiea Heights Dr.

EWA DISTRICT

Nanakuli Forest Reserve

TO LEEWARD COAST

Farrington Hwy.

Palehua Rd.

Village Park

H1

H2

Pearl City

Pearlridge Shopping Center

Aiea Heights

Waimalu

Halawa Heights

99

Waipahu

Pearl Harbor

USS Bowfin Submarine Museum and Park

Hawaii's Plantation Village

78 H3

Aloha Stadium

Hawaiian Electric Beach Park

Makakilo Dr.

Makakilo City

Fort Weaver Rd.

Farrington Hwy.

76

USS Arizona Memorial

USS Missouri Memorial

US Naval Reservation

Pacific Aviation Museum

USS Arizona Memorial Visitors Center

TO HONOLULU (6mi)

Kahe Point Beach Park

93

H1

901

Kapolei

Hickam Air Force Base

Pacific Aerospace Museum

Barbers Point Harbor

95

PACIFIC OCEAN

James Campbell Industrial Park

Kalaeloa Airport

Ewa Beach

Ewa Beach County Park

Honolulu International Airport

Barbers Point Beach

Mamala Bay

Oneula Beach

N LG

0   2 miles

0   2 kilometers

(end map)

808-422-2771. Open daily 7:30am-5pm. 1hr. tours every 15min. 7:45am-3pm. No bags, purses, or other items that allow concealment. Baggage storage available in the parking lot $3. Free.)

WAITING ROOM. If you plan on visiting the Arizona Memorial come early, as wait times can reach 2hr. On busy summer days most tickets are gone by noon. If you find yourself with more than a 90min. wait for the ride out to the ship, walk over and tour the *USS Bowfin* while you wait. Just hold on to your ticket and return to the *USS Arizona* 15min. before your tour begins.

BOWFIN PARK. One of 15 remaining WWII submarines, the *USS Bowfin* is the centerpiece of its own historical park. Called the "Pearl Harbor Avenger," the sub was set into action one year after the 1941 attack. In the course of nine war patrols, the *Bowfin* sank 44 enemy ships and suffered only one casualty. In 1981, it was pulled out of commission and given educational duty instead. Each year, over 250,000 visitors get a taste of what life was like for the 80 seamen who worked and lived on the *Bowfin*. The free audio guide takes visitors into the claustrophobic interior of the sub, through torpedo rooms, the galley, and the mess hall. Visitors can also explore several outdoor exhibits, including a waterfront memorial and various models of missiles and torpedoes (such as

Kaiten, a WWII Japanese suicide torpedo). The museum (included in admission) exhibits submarine-related paraphernalia, paintings, photographs, battle flags, and other models. *(Adjacent to the USS Arizona Visitors Center. See directions above.* ☎ *808-423-1341. The park grounds include a picnic area with food vendors. Open daily 8am-5pm, last tour 4:30pm. Submarine and museum admission $10; military, senior citizens, Hawaii residents $7; ages 4-12 $4. Museum only $5, ages 4-12 $2. AmEx/D/MC/V.)*

BATTLESHIP MISSOURI MEMORIAL. After four decades of military service, the battleship *USS Missouri* was finally retired in 1992. "Mighty Mo" was then relaunched as a tourist attraction and has since drawn in over two million visitors. The 887 ft. *Missouri* first saw action in WWII but was decommissioned in 1955, only to be recommissioned for service in the Korean War. After being recommissioned again in 1985, "Mighty Mo" fought in the Persian Gulf War and Operation Desert Storm, making her the world's last operational battleship. Marvelously refurbished and preserved, the ship is a 20-story labyrinth of rooms and corridors that awes with its sheer size and scale. Among other historic spots, guests can visit the **Signature Deck,** where General MacArthur accepted the Instrument of Surrender from the Japanese on September 2, 1945, ending WWII. The 90min. **Explorer's Tour** ($29, ages 4-12 $12) outfits visitors with hardhats and flashlights, taking them into restricted rooms including the engine rooms, gun control center, prison, and post office. Next to the entrance to the Missouri is the **USS Oklahoma Memorial,** honoring the 429 sailors who died aboard. The **USS Utah Memorial** is also on Ford Island. *(From Honolulu, take H-1 West to the Arizona Memorial/Stadium exit, which will deposit you on Kamehameha Hwy. Follow the signs to the Pearl Harbor Historical Sights, turning left after 1 mi. Take TheBus #20, 42, or CityExpress A. From the USS Bowfin, take the free trolley every 10min.* ☎ *808-455-1600; www.ussmissouri.com. Call for tour reservations within 24hr. of scheduled tour. Open daily 9am-5pm. Last ticket sold at the Bowfin 4pm. $16, ages 4-12 $8, under 4 free. 1hr. battleship guided tour $7. Audio tour $7. Flight simulator $5. Tickets for the Missouri should be purchased at the ticket office in front of Bowfin Park. Ask about combination tickets for both attractions. AmEx/D/MC/V.)*

PACIFIC AVIATION MUSEUM. The newest addition to the Pearl Harbor Historical Sights, the Pacific Aviation Museum stands on the site of the US's first aviation battlefield on Ford Island, strategically located in the middle of Pearl Harbor. The museum is housed in former seaplane hangars that survived the Pearl Harbor attack. These remained abandoned until the late 1990s when a group of concerned Hawaiian citizens developed plans to turn the former Navy complex into a museum. While a blanket of weeds now covers the former runways, the control tower and concrete hangars look as they did during the war, complete with bullet holes and bomb craters. Phase 1 of the museum opened on Dec. 7, 2006 in **Hangar 37,** a 42,000 sq. ft. structure that houses a collection of WWII planes and artifacts. One of the dioramas displays a rare **Niihau Zero,** the only remaining Zero wreckage from the attack on Pearl Harbor. This Zero was part of the second wave and was damaged by shell fire; it crash-landed on the island of Niihau (p. 24) and is displayed in the same condition as it's crash landing. The museum focuses in particular on the personal stories of the individual pilots who flew the planes. Phases 2 and 3, detailing the attack on Pearl Harbor and technological advances in aviation, respectively, will inhabit other hangars. Phase 2 is not expected to open until 2011. The **Lani Akea (Blue Heaven) Cafe** is located inside Hangar 37 and serves burgers and sandwiches ($9.50), grill items ($9.50-12), and salads ($7.50-9.50). *(Follow directions above to the USS Arizona Memorial and Bowfin Park. The Pacific Aviation Museum can be reached via the free trolley that leaves from outside Bowfin Park. Open daily 9am-5pm.* ☎ *808-441-1000; www.pacificaviationmuseum.org. Purchase tickets at the USS Bowfin ticket office. $14, ages 4-12 $7. Aviator's Tour $7. Ask about combination tickets for the Bowfin, Missouri, and Aviation Museum. AmEx/D/MC/V.)*

OAHU

FOOD

The food options in and around the Pearl Harbor Historical Sights are limited to the hot dog stand in front of the *USS Bowfin*, but there are several options just a few miles down the road on Kamehameha Hwy. toward Pearl City. **Pearlridge Shopping Center** is a large outdoor shopping complex located between Kamehameha Hwy. and Moanalua Rd. in Aiea. There is a ⬛**Down to Earth Natural Foods** in Pearlridge West, Ste. 306. (☎808-488-1375; open daily 8am-10pm, AmEx/D/MC/V), which has a salad bar, deli counter, and other healthy prepared foods in addition to groceries. The center also has plenty of fast food restaurants.

⬛ **Chun Wah Kam Noodle Factory,** 98-040 Kamehameha Hwy. (☎808-485-1107), in Waimalu Center. This busy takeout restaurant fills up around lunchtime with locals who covet Chun Wah Kam's delectable *manapuas* (fluffy bread filled with meat or other fillings and baked or steamed, $1.60 each). The extensive menu has a variety of noodle and stir fry dishes, *dim sum,* and plate lunches ($8). The generous portions, served cafeteria-style in a clean, bright space, are enough for 2 people to share. Open M-F 7:30am-6:30pm, Sa 8:30am-6:30pm, Su 8:30am-4pm. MC/V. ❷

Anna Millers, 98-115 Kaononi St. (☎808-487-2421), in Pearlridge Shopping Center. This 24hr. coffee shop and diner is famous for its fresh baked pies. Breakfast served all day. Try a slice of their seasonal strawberry pie ($3.69). Entrees $10-13, sandwiches $5-10. Open 24hr. AmEx/D/MC/V. ❷

ALOHA STADIUM

When not hosting a football game, Aloha Stadium is the site of the largest flea market on Oahu: the **Aloha Stadium Swap Meet.** Vendors sell everything from bathing suits and 8-for-$20 T-shirts to gadgets, ukuleles, and other Hawaiiana. It's the place to go for cheap jewelry, flavorful local treats, and any aloha print garb. Edibles include homemade fruit jams, ice-cold coconuts, home-baked breads, and fresh-smoked marlin. Many vendors sell identical merchandise, so shop around. Take note of your parking spot or you'll be walking in circles. *(TheBus: 1 stop past Pearl Harbor. By car, take H-1 West to the exit 1E/ Stadium exit. From Kamehameha Hwy, turn left on Salt Lake Blvd. Open W, Sa, and Su 6am-3pm. $1, under 12 free. Most vendors take MC/V. ATMs are available.)*

WAIPAHU

Located in suburban Waipahu (pop. 33,012), **Hawaii's Plantation Village** recaptures the lifestyle, struggles,

IN RECENT NEWS

MA-HAKA-RENA

What the haka is a haka dance? Most folks can't answer that question, but many sports fans were enlightened in 2007 when controversy sparked after the **University of Hawaii Warriors** were charged a 15 yard penalty for performing the dance. The haka is a form of traditional Maori dance, practiced in ancient New Zealand as a prewar ritual and more recently adopted by the All Blacks, the New Zealand national rugby team, as a pregame pump-up. Though the dance is certainly an ancestral homage, sports teams have learned to take advantage of its intimidation techniques—muscular athletes slapping their thighs, flashing their tongues, and chanting in angry unison surely doesn't instill warm and fuzzy feelings in observing opponents.

Perhaps this was the line of thinking of the referee who penalized the UH Warriors for doing the pregame dance. Considered a taunt by the NCAA, the routine was recognized by UH coaches as a Polynesian tradition, important to the people and players of Hawaii. The controversy sparked the creation of a new pregame warm-up for the Warriors. The full squad now performs a traditional Hawaiian war chant, quite reminiscent of the haka, prior to their games, and faces the stands, rather than the opposing team. The Warriors continue to incur the penalty for their new, fierce dancing, but who can blame them for gettin' jiggy wit' it.

and stories of workers on Hawaii's sugar plantations back when "sugar was king." The site is composed of 30 buildings modeled after the homes and workplaces of the plantation workers in the early 20th century. They are furnished with original items donated by descendants of plantation workers.

Between 1852 and 1946, plantations recruited over 400,000 workers from nearly a dozen nations after diseases had ravaged the local workforce. Many Chinese, Portuguese, Japanese, Puerto Ricans, Okinawans, Koreans, Filipinos, Caucasians, and indigenous Hawaiians came to work, seeking a better life. Laborers endured a strenuous 10hr. workday but managed to find time for recreation and religious practice. The managers segregated the workers by ethnicity in order to stymie collective wage bargaining. However, the workers began sharing food, joining in athletic competitions, and intermarrying, forming the roots of the diverse ethnic community of today's Hawaii.

A trained docent takes visitors through a range of village sites, including a 1930s barber shop, a public bathhouse, a turn-of-the-century RC Cola general store, and the last active shrine of the Inari, a minor sect of the Shinto religion often associated with the working class. Admission to the village is allowed only with one of the guided tours, which are scheduled every hour, but visitors should call ahead, as tours with insufficient demand are regularly cancelled. A small museum shows a rotating exhibit of plantation artifacts and presents a more detailed historical background. The village, tour, and museum will be of interest to any Hawaiian history buff but may be a bit slow for those uninterested in plantation life. *(94-695 Waipahu St. 40min. from Honolulu. By car, take H-1 west to Exit 7 and turn left at the stoplight onto Paiwa St. Continue until the 5th stoplight, Waipahu St. Turn right onto Waipahu St.; the entrance to the Plantation Village is on your left. Take the Express bus E or A from the Ala Moana Shopping Center to the Waipahu Transit Center. Transfer to the #43 bus which stops at Plantation Village. ☎808-677-0110. Open M-F 9am-3pm, Sa 10am-3pm. Tours run on the hr.; last tour at 3pm. $13, seniors $10, ages 4-11 $5, under 4 free.)*

KEAIWA HEIAU STATE RECREATION AREA

Located above Aiea Heights, a quiet, residential neighborhood north of Pearl Harbor, Keaiwa Heiau State Recreation Area is a peaceful place to camp that is far from Waikiki's throngs and yet close enough for an easy daytrip. Filled with tall Norfolk pines and pockets of eucalyptus, the park has an enveloping sense of serenity. You'll have a great view of Honolulu and Pearl Harbor while looking out over the 384 acres of lush vegetation.

While the area's natural beauty and tranquil atmosphere are its real attractions, the area's namesake *heiau* (temple) gives it spiritual and historical significance. In the late 15th century, *kahuna lapaau* (herbal healers) practiced their craft in the Keaiwa Heiau, a squat, stone structure, harnessing the natural energy of the site and medicinal properties of nearby plants. The site is considered sacred by the Hawaiian people. Today, all that remains of the *heiau* are waist-high lines of rocks where, archaeologists believe, walls once stood. It is disrespectful (and illegal) to move the stones, but you may leave offerings.

The park has four **campsites,** which can accommodate ten people each (though you'll rarely find more than five at any given site). All campsites have restrooms, shower facilities, and picnic tables. They are all recently renovated, spotless, and modern. The campsites are accessible via a 1 mi. road that circles the ridge beginning at the entrance to the park.

Try a bit of hiking on the **Aiea Loop Trail,** an easy 4½ mi. hike through the forest, that meanders between the first and second campsites. Trailheads are behind the restrooms at each site, about ¼ mi. and ½ mi. down the road, respectively. Superb views of the mountains and Pearl Harbor accompany the hundreds of indigenous plants along the trail. Near the end of the hike, wreckage of a 1943 C-47 cargo plane is visible through the trees. The trail takes 2-3hr. to complete, and athletic shoes or lightweight hiking boots are suggested. *(By car, take Hwy. 78 west from Honolulu to the Stadium/Aiea exit and continue onto Moanalua Rd. At the 2nd light, turn right onto Aiea Heights Dr., which winds into the park, about 3 mi. up. By bus, take TheBus #11 from Alapai Transit Center. TheBus leaves daily every hr. 7am-9:30pm, running every 30min. from 2:30pm-5pm, last return 8:10pm. Ask the driver to let you off at Kaamilo St. The park is a strenuous 30min. walk up Aiea Heights Dr. ☎808-587-0300. Open daily Apr.-Sept. 7am-7:45pm; Oct.-Mar. 7am-6:45pm. Camping M-W and F-Su. See **Camping in Hawaii, p. 82**. $5 per group.)*

WAHIAWA

Once strategically important for Hawaiian royalty, Wahiawa (pop. 16,151) is now an unremarkable town in Central Oahu. Frequent thunder claps were thought to be divine voices welcoming new royalty, though today the atmospheric booms greet the pawn shops, tattoo parlors, fast food joints, and bars that dominate the military town close to the Schofield Barracks. Wahiawa is interesting mostly for its nearby sights but the town itself is best seen from the inside of a car on the way to the North Shore.

About 3 mi. north of Wahiawa, the **Dole Plantation,** 64-1550 Kamehameha Hwy. (☎808-621-8408; www.dole-plantation.com), fulfills all pineapple cravings. The complex is becoming a major tourist attraction, with nearly one million visitors per year. Watch 20min. of staggering pineapple growth (one fruit develops in 15-18 months) on the Pineapple Express, a 2mi. narrated educational train ride. (Open daily 9am-5:30pm. Trains leave every 30min. Last train departs 5pm. $7.75, children $5.75.) From there, you can get lost in the **world's largest maze,** or meander through the Dole Plantation Gardens and gain an appreciation for the incredible life cycle of a *halakahiki* (pineapple). The garden tour is educational, offering an up-close look at the North Shore's crops, tropical flora, and the lives of plantations workers. (Maze and gardens open daily 9am-5:30pm. Maze $6, children $4; gardens $4/3.75. Garden tours every 30min. Last tour 4pm.) When you're done, hit up the gift shop for a well-deserved ☒**"Dole Whip,"** a pineapple-flavored soft-serve ($3.75), or some pineapples to send home.

The **Wahiawa Botanical Garden,** 1396 California Ave. (☎808-621-7321; www. hawaiibotanicalgardens.com), is a breath of fresh air in this humdrum town. Twenty-seven acres of water-loving plants thrive in the cool rainforest setting of this tranquil garden. A pleasant walk around the upper terrace takes visitors through an Australian forest, Okinawan garden, and bamboo grove, while the ravine floor offers a more adventurous hike. (Open daily 9am-4pm. Free.)

Hungry travelers should stop for local fare at ☒**Sunnyside ❶,** 1017 Kilani Ave., four blocks east of Kamehameha Hwy., in Wahiawa. Easy-to-miss, but a favorite of those in the know, Sunnyside serves cheap, super-good local food. The cheeseburger ($2.25) and the plate lunches ($6-7.25) are delicious, and people come from all over Oahu for the ☒**cream and fruit pies** ($8.50 each, $1.50 per slice), which tend to sell out by noon. Walk up to the window or sit down inside. (☎808-621-7188. Open M-F 6am-6pm, Sa 6am-4pm. Cash only.)

To reach Wahiawa by car from Honolulu, take H-1 West, then take H-2 North to Exit 8. Follow HI-99/Kamehameha Hwy. through the middle of town. Wahiawa is also on the #52 and 62 bus lines, just over 1hr. from the Ala Moana Shopping Center hub in Honolulu.

OAHU

SOUTHEAST OAHU

KOKO HEAD REGIONAL PARK AND ENVIRONS

The area east of Honolulu along **Highway 72 (Kalanianaole Highway)** from Koko Head to Sandy Beach is a county park that includes **Hanauma Bay,** the **Halona Blowhole and Cove,** and **Koko Crater.** These sites are easily accessible by car from the highway. **TheBus #22,** nicknamed the "Beach Bus," runs along the highway from Waikiki to Sea Life Park, and has stops at Hanauma Bay and Sandy Beach. (Departs Waikiki 8:15 and 9:15am, then every hr. at 5min. before the hr.; last departure M-F 4:25pm, Sa-Su 4:40pm; last return from Sea Life Park M-F 5:30pm, Sa-Su 5:45pm. Does not run on Tu.) **TheBus #23** leaves from the Ala Moana Shopping Center and serves a similar area, but goes through **Hawaii Kai,** serving the same destinations with the exception of Hanauma Bay and Sandy Beach. (Every 30min; M-F 7am-7:05pm, Sa-Su 7am-6pm.)

HANAUMA BAY MARINE LIFE CONSERVATION DISTRICT. *(Snorkeling. Lifeguards in summer M and W-Su 6am-7pm; in winter 6am-6pm.)* In the world of beach parks, Hanauma Bay is like Disneyland—fun, but the crowds can be maddening. Over 1000 people flock to this crater-cradled beach every day (over one million visitors annually), and while the snorkeling is among the best on the island, the legions of tourists and children detract from the experience. It's best to arrive before 10am, when throngs of tourists start to flood the water.

> **TIP SNORKELING FOR LESS.** Hanauma Bay offers free snorkeling instruction upon request. If you are a beginner or are with first-time snorkelers, stop by the Visitors Center at the beach and ask for a complimentary lesson.

Formed 32,000 years ago in a series of volcanic explosions, Hanauma Bay is a flooded crater. Named by Polynesian settlers, Hanauma means "curved bay." The wide, sandy beach is at the base of a ring of rock below **Koko Head,** and its waters bristle with hundreds of species of brightly colored fish. The area was once a favorite spot of Hawaiian royalty. Also once a local fishing spot, the bay has been a **Marine Life Conservation District** since 1967, protecting the area from fishing for the reproduction of aquatic life. Respect the bay (and the law) by not feeding the fish. Other reef etiquette is discussed in a 9min. video which visitors are required to watch. If you plan on visiting Hanauma Bay more than once during your visit, be sure to sign the return visitor's log. This will allow you to skip the video the second time around.

While it is a good family destination, Hanauma Bay has more serious injuries and deaths each year than any beach on the island. If you have health problems, are a weak swimmer, or are a first-time snorkeler, take precautions and heed red flags. Talk to the lifeguards to find out about surf conditions and the safe swimming areas, and stay within the bay. The largest open area, **Keyhole,** is in the center of the bay. It is quite shallow and calm, which makes it a good spot for novice snorkelers. Snorkeling is better outside the reef, but the current is strong, and a surprise wave can throw even an experienced swimmer against the rocks. There is also a strong rip current called the **Molokai Express** (few make it to Molokai). *Let's Go* does not recommend swimming beyond the reef.

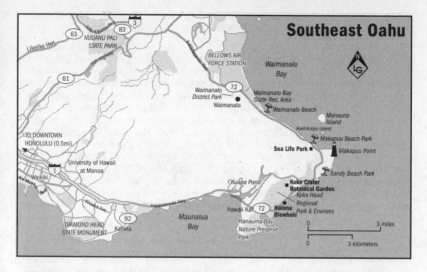

The park has showers, restroom facilities, changing rooms, pontoon wheelchairs, and a picnic area. There is also a snack bar at the top of the park near the entrance. Snorkeling equipment is available for rent at the park but it is cheaper in Waikiki. *(By car, take Kalanianaole Hwy. east from Honolulu. The entrance to the parking lot is on the right on top of the hill past the Foodland shopping center. Parking $1; the lot is usually full by midday. TheBus #22 runs between Waikiki and Sea Life Park and stops right in Hanauma Bay; leaves every hr. 8:15am-5:40pm. $5, under 13 free.)*

HALONA BLOWHOLE. About 1½ mi. past Hanauma Bay is the Halona Blowhole, a lava tube submerged in the ocean. Passing waves push through the tube and create a mesmerizing, geyser-like explosion of sea and sound. The quality of the spectacle depends on surf conditions: on some days the water barely bubbles out of the blowhole, while on others it shoots high into the sky. Do not climb over the fences to get a closer look; people have been killed by the fall.

To the right of the parking lot and down a set of steep rocks is the small, sparkling Halona Cove, a quiet, sheltered lovers' beach to swim or sunbathe away from crowds. Locals know the cove as **Eternity Beach,** since the award-winning flick *From Here to Eternity* was filmed here. The path was made from a natural lava flow, which created the smooth boulders. There is no easy path down, so be careful scrambling through the rocks. Look for sea turtles at the cove. *(The parking lot is located along Kalanianaole Hwy. and the #22 bus route.)*

KOKO CRATER. Formed just 7000 years ago, Koko Crater is the tallest, best-preserved cinder and ash cone on the islands and represents one of the latest volcanic events in Hawaii. Koko Crater encloses a 60-acre **Botanical Garden** and **Equestrian Center** that offers horseback-riding lessons ($40) and pony rides for kids ($26). A pleasant 2 mi. walking trail begins in a plumeria grove and goes through the garden's far-flung plant collection, which includes species from Madagascar and other African countries. The gardens are a worthwhile stop if you're in the area for the afternoon. *(Kokonani St. inside Koko Crater. By car, take Kalanianaole Hwy. east from Honolulu until you reach a stoplight just past Sandy Beach at Kealahou St. Turn left, and then left again after about 1 mi. onto Kokonani Blvd. TheBus #23 leaves from the Ala Moana Center and runs along Kealahou St., stopping near Kokonani. #23 runs every 30min. M-F 6:50am-6:05pm, Sa 7:10am-6:05pm, Su 8:10am-6:05pm. ☎808-522-7063. Stables open Tu-F 8am-7pm, Sa-Su 8am-8pm. Call ahead to schedule a lesson. ☎808-395-2628 1hr. horseback tour through the crater $40. Gardens open daily sunrise to sunset. Free.)*

▨ **SANDY BEACH PARK.** *(Bodyboarding. Surfing. Open daily 24hr. Lifeguards daily.)* With the best waves on Oahu's South Shore, Sandy Beach is the premier spot for experienced bodyboarders. The rocky shoreline along the east part of the beach also has two breaks—**Full Point** and **Half Point**—for advanced surfers. "Sandy's," as the beach is affectionately called, is great whether you're an advanced boarder, bodysurfer, or enthusiast. It is also among the most dangerous beaches on the island, seeing a lot of neck and back injuries. Full Point, the far left side of the beach, breaks over a deep reef bottom, while Half Point, where the wave breaks over a shallow bottom, is a bit more dangerous. The inexperienced should keep out of the water when the current is strong. Surfers and bodyboarders should be wary of a riptide when trade winds are strong. Check with the lifeguards at either station for surf information and keep an eye out for red flags, which indicate dangerous water conditions.

The beach itself is wide enough to accommodate sunbathers, and it has a reputation as a popular hangout for the island's youth come nighttime. The large grassy area to the left of the first park entrance is a popular kite-flying location and is sometimes used as a landing strip for hang-gliders. There are usually a few food stands around, and the park has restrooms and showers. *(Sandy Beach is on the #22 bus route on Kalanianaole Hwy., 1 mi. past the Halona Blowhole.)*

MAKAPUU POINT. The lighthouse marking the easternmost point of Oahu, atop the 647 ft. Makapuu Point, has been in operation for nearly 100 years. While it's fenced off, there's still an amazing view of Sandy Beach and Makapuu Beach from the lookout at the top of a mile-long paved hike. Both the lookout and the lighthouse have fantastic views of **Manana** and **Kaohikaipu** Islands. Manana, the larger of the two, means "rabbit," and the island bears the name because it both resembles and is inhabited by rabbits. Kaohikaipu, the smaller island, was declared a bird sanctuary in 1972. *(The start of the 1 mi. paved hike to the lighthouse is on the right, a quarter of the way up the hill past Sandy Beach. From the opposite direction, it's 1 mi. beyond Makapuu Beach. There's a new parking lot at the trailhead along Kalanianaole Hwy.)*

SEA LIFE PARK. A standard aquatic amusement park, and Oahu's largest, Sea Life Park is pricey and full of students on field trips and children dragging their parents from tank to tank. The park features a string of shows for families, including the Dolphin Cove Show and the Kolohe Kai Sea Lion Show. The park also has breeding programs for endangered animals like the giant sea turtle and Hawaiian monk seal, and capture-and-release programs for wounded birds and animals. The 300,000-gallon aquarium has thousands of species of fish, moray eels, stingrays, sharks, and other indigenous reef life. A spiral walkway around the tank provides views of the reef from different depths. Sea Life Park is home to the world's only wolphin, a false killer whale and dolphin hybrid, which gave birth to another wolphin in 1991. The park also has various programs for swimming with dolphins and the like for a hefty price of $150. *(41-202 Kalanianaole Hwy. By car, take Kalanianaole Hwy. east from Honolulu for approx. 35min. The park is on the left, across from Makapuu Beach. Both the #22 and 23 buses run from Waikiki to Sea Life Park; the ride is just under 1hr.; buses leave every 30min. The park also runs a shuttle service to major Waikiki hotels for those who purchase one of the extra adventures in advance. $14, ages 4-12 $8. ☎ 808 259-7933; www.sealifeparkhawaii.com. Park open daily 9:30am-5pm. $29, ages 4-12 $19.)*

MAKAPUU BEACH PARK. *(Bodyboarding. Surfing. Open daily sunrise to sunset. Lifeguards 9am-5:30pm.)* Preferred hangout of hang-gliders and surfers, Makapuu Beach Park has some of Oahu's best bodysurfing and bodyboarding. The beach, located at the bottom of a steep sandhill, is rather small and surrounded by dark, volcanic rocks that form a striking contrast with the white sand. Makapuu isn't only about charming vistas and scenery, however. Powerful winter waves (up to 12 ft.) retain some of their kick in the summer, too. Makapuu is almost as infamous as Sandy Beach for neck and back injuries, and has more drownings due to deeper water; be mindful of red flags, strong tides, and dangerous shore breaks. Pack a picnic lunch; the nearest food is overpriced at Sea Life Park. *(The parking lot is across the highway from Sea Life Park. Restrooms and showers.)*

WAIMANALO

Waimanalo (pop. 3644) is the quintessential Hawaiian small town—diverse, undisturbed, and relaxed. Residents go about their lives at a slow pace, unaffected by the touristy glitz and glam of Waikiki farther south. Whether they were born and raised here or relocated from the mainland, most people here plan to stay, resulting in a largely uncommercial town. The area does have rough neighborhoods though, so don't leave your valuables unattended. Waimanalo's main attraction is its stunning ⊠**beach,** the longest (and perhaps the best) on Oahu. Backed by the Koolau Mountains, Waimanalo Beach stretches nearly five miles in an arc of white sand against the green-azure waters of the Pacific.

◼✦🔋 ORIENTATION AND PRACTICAL INFORMATION

Waimanalo is located along **Highway 72 (Kalanianaole Highway),** about 50min. by car or 1hr. on the #57 bus (every hr. starting at 7:35am) from Honolulu. Kalanianaole Highway is also accessible from **Pali Highway** near Kailua. The town itself is spread thinly along the highway for about 2 mi. **Waimanalo Community-School Library,** 41-1320 Kalanianaole Hwy., has Internet access with a 3-month visitor's card ($10). (☎808-259-2610. Open M-Tu and Th-F 9am-5pm, W 1-8pm, Sa 10am-2pm.) **Waimanalo Laundry,** 41-1537 Kalanianaole Hwy., is in the Waimanalo Town Center. (☎808-259-5091. Wash $1.75, dry $0.25 per 5min. Drop-off service $10.50 for 0-10 pounds, each additional pound $1. Open daily 6am-10pm. Last wash 8:30pm, last dry 9pm.) **Waimanalo District Park,** 41-415 Hihimanu St., has free Internet access. (☎808-259-7436. M-F 3-7pm.) **Waimanalo Post Office,** 41-859 Kalanianaole Hwy., is next to Keneke's. (☎808-259-0106. Open M-F 9am-4:30pm, Sa 9-11am. Last collection M-F 5pm, Sa 4pm.) **Postal Code:** 96795.

▐ ACCOMMODATIONS

There aren't many budget options in Waimanalo. **Beach Houses Hawaii ❹,** at 41-866 Laumilo St., offers many beach house accommodation rentals. Their studio options include the Captain and the Ohana Studio in the Ocean View

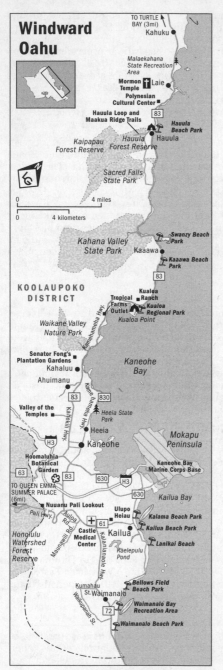

Windward Oahu

TO TURTLE
BAY (3mi)
Kahuku

Malaekahana
State Recreation
Area

Mormon
Temple · Laie
Polynesian
Cultural Center

Hauula Loop and
Maakua Ridge Trails · 83
Hauula
Beach Park
Kaipapau
Forest Reserve
Hauula
Forest Reserve · Hauula

Sacred Falls
State Park

0 ————— 4 miles
0 ————— 4 kilometers

Kahana Valley
State Park
Swanzy Beach
Park
Kaaawa
Kaaawa Beach
Park
83

KOOLAUPOKO
DISTRICT
Kualoa
Tropical · Ranch
Farms
Outlet · Kualoa
Regional Park
Kualoa Point
Waikane Valley
Nature Park

Senator Fong's
Plantation Gardens
Kahaluu ·
Ahuimanu ·

Kaneohe
Bay

83 · 830
Heeia State
Park

Valley of the
Temples ·
H3
Heeia
Kaneohe

Mokapu
Peninsula

Hoomaluhia
Botanical
Garden
63 · 83
630 · H3
Kaneohe Bay
Marine Corps Base

TO QUEEN EMMA
SUMMER PALACE
(6mi)
630
Nuuanu Pali Lookout
Pali Hwy.
Kailua Bay

Ulupo
Heiau
Kalama Beach Park
Castle
Medical
Center · Kailua
Kailua Beach Park

Honolulu
Watershed
Forest
Reserve
Kaelepulu
Pond
Lanikai Beach

Kumahau
St. Waimanalo
Bellows Field
Beach Park
72
Waimanalo Bay
Recreation Area
Waimanalo Beach Park

OAHU

Suites. Both studios include a king-size bed, kitchenette, couch, private bathroom, and sliding glass doors to the backyard patio and jacuzzi. (☎808-259-7792; www.beachhousehawaii.com. Reserve in advance. $120-250 per night. AmEx/D/MC/V.) Also try **Paradise Found Beachside Suite ❹**, 41-928 Laumilo St., in the back of the owner's home; it has one bedroom with a queen bed, a sun room with a fold-out bed, a kitchenette, and a bath. The room sleeps four and has open access to the house's large, well-kept yard. (☎808-255-4625; www.homeaway.com/vacation-rental/p120389. 3-night min. stay. $125-185. Additional guests $15. $75 cleaning fee. MC/V.) Other houses on this street may also have rooms. Several beaches also have **campsites** (see **Beaches**, p. 155).

🍴 FOOD

Shima's Supermarket, 41-1606 Kalanianaole Hwy., is a one-stop market with a wide selection of ready-to-eat *poke* and cheap produce. (☎808-259-9921. ATM inside. Open M-Sa 8am-8pm, Su 9am-6pm. MC/V.) **Bobby's,** 41-867 Kalanianaole Hwy., is a small, local grocery with cheap beer (12-pack, $10-15) and wine (bottles under $10). (☎808-259-5044. Open M-Sa 7am-8:45pm, Su 7am-7pm. MC/V.) **🌂Keneke's ❶**, 41-857 Kalanianaole Hwy., is an old-school plate lunch mecca. Mixed plates ($7) and mini plates ($4), as well as sandwiches ($4) and shave ice ($2.50), will satisfy barefoot beachgoers. (☎808-259-9811. Open daily 8:30am-5:30pm. MC/V.) Those looking for something other than plate lunch will have to be satisfied with **Ken's ❶**, 41-1537 Kalanianaole Hwy., which offers breakfast all day. Big Boy Breakfast ($4.25) includes two eggs, rice, toast, and choice of meat. (☎808-259-8900. Open M-F 6am-9pm. AmEx/D/MC/V.)

BEACHES

WAIMANALO BEACH PARK. *(Bodyboarding. Snorkeling. Open 24hr. Lifeguards 9am-5pm.)* Waimanalo Beach is one of the most beautiful beaches on the island, with scintillating turquoise water, a long shoreline with incredibly soft sand, and gentle surf ideal for novice ocean swimmers or beginning bodyboarders. The first beach on the right heading north from Makapuu Point to Kailua is Waimanalo Beach Park, identifiable by the city of tents along the highway. Manana Island peeks around the southern portion of the beach, and the tall ironwood trees complement the vast Koolau Mountains on the inland side of the highway. Camping (20 sites) requires a county permit available from any satellite City Hall. The permits are free (see **Camping in Hawaii,** p. 82, for more information). The snorkeling is decent, though the area is not quite as beautiful as other parts of the beach. There are bathrooms and outdoor shower facilities.

WAIMANALO BAY RECREATION AREA. *(Bodyboarding. Open daily 6am-7:45pm. Lifeguards 9am-5pm.)* One mile farther down the highway toward Waimanalo, the gorgeous Waimanalo Bay Recreation Area, locally referred to as "Sherwood Forest," has a wider beach and the striking view of the bay's electric-blue waters. In the summer, the water is the bunny hill of bodyboarding, but the surf picks up in winter, so be careful. Be wary of jellyfish, sharp coral, rocks, and red flags indicating dangerous conditions. There are bathrooms and showers. Camping (10 sites) requires a **county permit** (p. 85). Do not leave valuables in your car.

BELLOWS FIELD BEACH PARK. *(Open Sa-Su 7am-8pm.)* This beach park in the Bellows Air Force Base sits next to Waimanalo Bay Recreation Area. Surfing is not allowed at the beach though the water is relatively safe for swimming all year. Enter at the first base entrance. Camping (50 sites) is free but requires a **county permit** (p. 85). Picnic, restroom, and shower facilities are spartan but neat. Park along the concrete platforms next to the beach.

WINDWARD COAST

An exuberant wind blows across the Kamehameha Highway and along the Windward Coast of Oahu. The roads that run around the misty Koolau Mountains and up the rural eastern edge of the island are chaotic, but they promise a scenic cruise from Honolulu to the North Shore. You'll pass through a wide range of sights, from small towns like Lanikai and Laie, to roadside rooster fights, hidden hiking trails, and miles of unspoiled beaches. Kailua, the major tourist destination of the Windward Coast, lures visitors with a pristine white sand beach, brilliant turquoise bay, first-class windsurfing, and fine cuisine, all within shouting distance of Honolulu. Kaneohe is the starting point for sightseeing tours along the coast and North Shore. The smaller settlements along Kamehameha Hwy. add distinctive beauty, and the terrain varies from rugged mountain to barren oceanscape, rainy valley to sunlit beach.

KAILUA

Kailua (pop. 36,513) is the downtown suburb of the Windward Coast, where visitors will find cozy lodgings, exceptional food, and gorgeous beaches. Spend some extra time here before heading up the relatively scarce coast.

OAHU

 **ORIENTATION**

Kailua, which lies south of **Kaneohe** and east of Kailua Bay, is the southernmost town on the Windward Coast. Three highways zip over the Koolau Mountain Range which separates the Windward Coast from the South Shore. They are **H-3, Highway 63** (**Likelike Highway,** pronounced "lee-kay lee-kay"), and **Highway 61 (Pali Highway).** Pali Hwy. is the most direct route from Waikiki.

To reach Kailua from **Honolulu Airport,** take H-1 West to Exit 1D, H-3 East/ Kaneohe. Exit at Mokapu Blvd. and make the third right onto Oneawa St., which becomes Kailua Rd. after the Kailua town center. From **H-1 East,** take Exit 21A, Pali Hwy., and turn left. Continue straight ahead on Hwy. 61, which is called **Kailua Road** after the junction with Hwy. 72. A complex intersection marks the center of Kailua town—if you turn left you will be on **Oneawa Street,** and if you drive straight you will be on **Kuulei Road.** To stay on Kailua Rd., you must turn right at the Kailua town center intersection (following signs for Visitors Information) and then left half a mile later at the **Wanaao Road** intersection and blinking yellow traffic light. From this second left, Kailua Rd. heads straight for the western end of **Kailua Beach Park.**

TRANSPORTATION AND PRACTICAL INFORMATION

TRANSPORTATION

Bus: From Ala Moana Shopping Center in Honolulu, TheBus #56 and 57 run to Kailua. $2; seniors, disabled persons, and students $1.

Car Rental: Enterprise Kailua, 345 Hahani St. (☎808-261-4282; fax 808-261-0037; www.enterprise.com). Compact $30-35 per day. 21+. Collision damage waiver $17 per day, personal accident insurance $3 per day, liability $10 per day. $30 fee to return car at the airport. Open M-F 8am-6pm, Sa 9am-noon. AmEx/D/MC/V.

TOURIST AND FINANCIAL SERVICES

Tourist Information: Kailua Information Center, 600 Kailua Rd. (☎808-261-2727), in the Kailua Shopping Center. A friendly and reliable volunteer staff provides maps, bus schedules, phone numbers, and directions. Open M-F 10am-4pm, Sa 10am-2pm.

City Hall: Kailua Satellite, 1090 Keolu Dr. (☎808-261-8575). Open M-F 8am-4pm.

Banks: First Hawaiian Bank, 705 Kailua Rd. (☎808-261-3371). Open M-Th 8:30am-4pm, F 8:30am-6pm, Sa 9am-1pm. Drive-up closed Sa. **Bank of Hawaii,** 636 Kailua Rd. (☎808-266-4600). Open M-Th 8:30am-4pm, F 8:30am-6pm. Drive-up hours M-F 8:30am-2:30pm. **24hr. ATMs** outside both.

LOCAL SERVICES

Library: Kailua Public Library, 239 Kuulei Rd. (☎808-266-9911) Internet access available with a 3-month visitor's card ($10). Open M, W, F-Sa 10am-5pm; Tu, Th 1-8pm.

Laundromat: U-Wash-N-Dry, (☎808-235-1238), on the corner of Hoolai St. and Kailua Rd. Listen to local tunes while doing your laundry in this open-air, oddly relaxing washerette. Parking available. Wash $2.50, dry $0.25 per 5min. Open 24hr.

EMERGENCY AND COMMUNICATIONS

Police: Kailua Substation, 219 Kuulei Rd. (☎808-262-6555).

Medical Services: Braun Urgent Care, 130 Kailua Rd., Ste. 111 (☎808-261-4411), in the Kailua Beach Center. Walk-ins welcome. Open daily 8am-8pm. **Castle Medical**

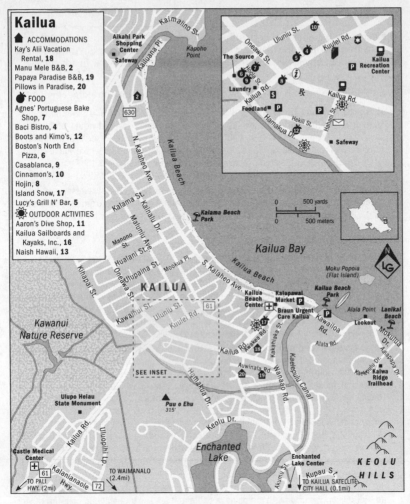

Kailua

🏠 ACCOMMODATIONS
Kay's Alii Vacation
  Rental, **18**
Manu Mele B&B, **2**
Papaya Paradise B&B, **19**
Pillows in Paradise, **20**

🍎 FOOD
Agnes' Portuguese Bake
  Shop, **7**
Baci Bistro, **4**
Boots and Kimo's, **12**
Boston's North End
  Pizza, **6**
Casablanca, **9**
Cinnamon's, **10**
Hojin, **8**
Island Snow, **17**
Lucy's Grill N' Bar, **5**

☀ OUTDOOR ACTIVITIES
Aaron's Dive Shop, **11**
Kailua Sailboards and
  Kayaks, Inc., **16**
Naish Hawaii, **13**

Center, 640 Ulukahiki St. (☎808-263-5500, emergency services 808-263-5164), at the junction of Hwy. 61 and 72, 1 mi. south of Kailua.

Fax Services: Island Printing Centers, 25 Maluniu Ave. (☎808-261-8515; fax 808-261-9958). 1st fax page to mainland $2, subsequent pages $1.25. Copies $0.08, color $0.95. Open M-F 7:30am-7pm, Sa 9am-5pm. AmEx/D/MC/V.

Internet Access: Kailua Recreation Center, 21 S. Kainalu Dr. (☎808-266-7652), around the corner from the Kailua Public Library. Free with registration. Internet available when staffed; call for open hours. **Morning Brew,** 600 Kailua Rd. Ste. 119 (☎808-262-7770), in Kailua Shopping Center. $3 per 30min. Wi-Fi available. Open daily 6am-8pm. **Island Printing Center** also has Internet access. $2 per 15min. (see above).

Post Office: Kailua Main Office, 335 Hahani St. (☎808-266-3996). Last collection M-F 5pm, Sa 4pm. Open M-F 8:30am-5pm, Sa 9am-4pm. **Postal Code:** 96734.

ACCOMMODATIONS

The beautiful beaches and crystalline water that surround Kailua beckon vacationers from around the world. Cozy B&Bs supplant impersonal hotels, but they tend to fill up weeks, months, and sometimes even a year in advance.

BOOKING SERVICES

Many B&Bs can be found on the Windward Coast through booking agencies.

All Islands Bed and Breakfast (☎808-263-2342 or 800-542-0344; www.all-islands. com) matches travelers with available B&B clients based on individual preferences. Their list of clients numbers over 1000 from across the islands. Reserve 2-3 months in advance with a 20% deposit. The balance must be paid to the B&B where you're staying. While All Islands accepts credit cards, note that the individual B&Bs they book may not. Reserve online or by phone. Office hours M-F 8am-5pm. AmEx/D/MC/V.

Bed and Breakfast Association of Oahu, Inc., (☎808-262-8286; www.stayoahu.com). A network of area bed and breakfasts; send an email in with approximate dates, price range, and location. If they can offer you a place, they'll respond with availability.

BED AND BREAKFASTS

Manu Mele Bed and Breakfast, 153 Kailuana Pl. (☎808-262-0016). Hawaiian for "birdsong," Manu Mele was named for the birds that sing by the pool. All 3 units are immaculate and self-sufficient, with mini-fridge, microwave, coffee maker, cable, and A/C. Fruit and baked goods for breakfast. This B&B's beach is popular with locals; ask to borrow beach gear from the common guest closet. Pristine outdoor pool and extremely private *lanai*. 2-night min. No children. Refundable $100 deposit. Check-in afternoon. Check-out 11am. $100 for queen-size bed, $120 for king. Cash only. ❸

Papaya Paradise Bed and Breakfast, 395 Auwinala Rd. (☎808-261-0316; www.kailuaoahuhawaii.com). From Kailua Rd. continue straight onto Wanaao Rd. Turn right onto Awakea Rd. and make a quick left onto Auwinala Rd. Lovely units furnished in tropical rattan and wicker, each with a private entrance, bath, A/C, cable TV, and telephone. Guests share a kitchenette with refrigerator and microwave as well as a poolside *lanai* with an amazing view of the mountains. Breakfast of bagels, cereal, fruit, and coffee. Bodyboards, snorkels, masks, and beach gear available to guests free of charge. 3-night min. Check-in 3pm. Check-out 11am. Doubles $100, each additional person $15. $100 deposit for 3-day stay, $200 for a longer stay. Cash or travelers checks only. ❸

Kay's Alii Vacation Rental, 232 and 237 Awakea Rd. (☎808-262-9545; www.kaysvacations.com). Heading to town on Kailua Rd., continue onto Wanaao Rd., then turn left onto Awakea St. Kay's properties are across the street from each other, before Aumoe Rd. Rooming options vary. All rooms have cable and access to a grill and coin-op washer and dryer. 3-night min. Check-in 4pm (call ahead). Check-out 11am. Rates range from $55 for shared bath units to $255 for 4-bedroom house that sleeps up to 10; additional adults $15, kids $10. Cleaning fee $25-150. AmEx. ❸

FOOD

While the beach is Kailua's most obvious gem, unique restaurants make the town's food scene almost as enticing. Kailua also has the outstanding ◨**Kalapawai Market,** 306 S. Kalaheo Ave., which sells beer, wine, specialty coffee, and prepared foods. This independent market has been around since 1932 and has an outstanding deli counter with sandwiches ($6.79-8.49) and a gourmet coffee bar. (☎808-262-4359. Open daily 6am-9pm; deli open 7am-8pm. MC/V.) There's also a **Foodland,** 108 Hekili St., for basic groceries, (☎808-261-3211; open 24hr.

AmEx/D/MC/V.), and **The Source,** 32 Kainehe St., for all your natural food needs. (☎808-262-5604. Open M-F 9am-7pm, Sa 9am-6pm, Su 10am-5pm. D/MC/V.)

RESTAURANTS

▨ **Cinnamon's,** 315 Uluniu St. (☎808-261-8724). This charming neighborhood restaurant serves some of the best breakfast on the island, pleasing residents and tourists alike with their famous guava chiffon pancakes (stack of 4, $9). It seems like the entire town of Kailua shows up on Su for brunch, but the outside in the sunny courtyard is worth the wait. Open daily for lunch 7am-2pm, dinner Th-Sa 5:30-8:30pm. D/MC/V. ❸

▨ **Boots & Kimo's Homestyle Kitchen,** 131 Kehiki St., Ste. 102 (☎808-263-7929). This "home of the original macadamia nut pancake sauce" vies with Cinnamon's for the best pancakes on Oahu and consistently draws lines out the door for breakfast and lunch. Breakfast-lovers pack themselves into this tiny eatery for omelets ($9.25), eggs benedict ($10), and Hawaiian-style *pulehu* ribs ($12). Open Tu-F 7am-2pm, lunch starting at 11am; Sa-Su 6:30am-2:30pm, lunch starting at noon. Cash only. ❷

▨ **Lucy's Grill N' Bar,** 33 Aulike St. (☎808-230-8188), off of Kuulei Rd. Lucy's serves gourmet *pupu,* inexpensive pizzas ($9-12), and grill favorites, such as *kiawe* broiled baby back ribs ($16). The specialty is the Ahi Tower appetizer, a stacked dish of rice, avocado, and fresh *ahi* fish ($13). W wine night (½-price bottles with a $15 entree). Dinner daily 5-10pm. F-Sa bar open until 11pm. Reservations recommended. MC/V. ❸

▨ **Agnes' Portuguese Bake Shop,** 46 Hoolai St. (☎808-262-5367), across the street from Boston's North End Pizza. Agnes' is popular for its homemade soups (cup $4.75), coffee (small $1.65), and above all, for the specialty baked goods and desserts. Call 15min. ahead for hot, fresh *malasadas*—divine, Portuguese-style doughnuts ($0.80, $7.70 per dozen). Customers can eat in a clean, sunny cafe or take their treats to go. The full-line bakery also makes specialty breads ($3-8) and delectable pastries ($1-2). Internet access $2.50 per 15min. Open Tu-Sa 6am-6pm, Su 6am-2pm. D/MC/V. ❶

Casablanca, 19 Hoolai St. (☎808-262-8196), heading into Kailua from Pali Hwy., Hoolai St. is the last left before the town center. Well worth the splurge, Casablanca serves an exclusive 5-course *prix-fixe* menu, with a choice of an entree ($33) or the house special ($39). The restaurant offers a truly authentic Moroccan dining experience—patrons sit on floor cushions and eat with their hands in a luxuriously decorated interior. A shower of orange blossoms follows each meal. Belly dancers may be reserved. BYOB. Open Tu-Sa 6-8:30pm. Reservations recommended. MC/V. ❺

Baci Bistro, 30 Aulike St. (☎808-262-7555). Emphasizing old world know-how, Baci Bistro has earned a reputation as Kailua's best Italian restaurant. The restaurant serves a range of hot and cold antipasti (bruschetta $7), salads ($4-8), and entrees (*gnocchi con gorgonzola* $15). Lunch sandwiches $7-10. Lunch M-F 11:30am-2pm. Dinner daily 5:30-10pm. Weekend reservations recommended. AmEx/MC/V. ❸

Island Snow, 130 Kailua Rd. Ste. 103, (☎808-263-6339), in the Kailua Beach Center. The #1 destination for beachgoers straight off the sand. Their excellent shave ices are the perfect antidote to a sunburn and feature unusual flavors like passion fruit, lychee, coffee, and guava orange. A regular ($2.50) comes with a choice of 3 flavors. Try the snowcap (a scoop of ice cream on top) for $0.50 extra. Island Snow also doubles as a retail store selling surfer apparel. Open daily 10am-7pm. AmEx/D/MC/V. ❶

Hojin, 609 Kalua Road, Ste. 111 (☎808-263-6636). This Mongolian barbecue and sushi restaurant offers fresh and healthy dishes without sacrificing taste. Try the Mongolian BBQ plate ($8), bento meals ($7-9), and sushi (maki) rolls ($4-8). Open M-Sa 10:30am-8:30pm, Su 10:30am-8pm. MC/V. ❶

Boston's North End Pizza, 29 Hoolai St. (☎808-263-8055), Hoolai St. is the last left on Kailua-bound Kailua Rd. A 19 in. cheese pizza pie ($20) weighs in at 3 lb. Enormous quarter-pie slices start at $5. Open M-Th and Su 9am-8pm, F-Sa 9am-9pm. MC/V. ❶

OAHU

BEACHES

KAILUA BEACH. *(Bodyboarding. Wind sports. Open daily 24hr. Lifeguards on duty 9am-5:30pm.)* Though proclaiming the nation's most beautiful beach is difficult, the delicately curving neck of white sand around Kailua Bay's splendid, turquoise waters pleads a strong case. The fickle trade winds, which blow from nearly every direction, make the bay the best wind sports area on Oahu. Particularly during the winter, spectators gather to gape at the expert windsurfers and kiteboarders who careen over the whipped-up waves. Paddlers and windsurfers launch from the north end of the beach and are not allowed inside the buoyed area, making swimming along the shore a safe activity. In addition, kayakers frequently cross to the Bird Sanctuaries on the Flat and Mokulua Islands. A popular scenic bike path winds through the edge of the park and is crowded with cyclists, runners, and dog-walkers on the weekends. There are parking lots (which fill up early on weekends), bathrooms, showers, a small craft storage building, and a boat ramp in Kailua Beach Park. Park facilities close from 10pm-6am; parking lots closed 10pm-5am. *(Take the Lanikai-bound bus #70 from Kailua town center. By car, turn right off Kailua Rd. onto S. Kalaheo Ave. The 1st parking lot is on the left as S. Kalaheo Ave. becomes Kawailoa Rd. before crossing the drainage canal.)*

KALAMA BEACH. *(Bodyboarding. Open daily 7am-6pm.)* The secluded northern half of Kailua Beach is the grassy Kalama Beach Park. The virgin sand here has fewer visitors than Kailua Beach Park, and the calmer waters are free from the congestion of watersport traffic farther south. Kalama is a good learning spot for novice bodyboarders and bodysurfers. Beach facilities include a restroom, showers, and picnic tables. The small parking lot at 248 N. Kalaheo Ave. fills up before noon, so arrive early or walk from the town center. *(Turn left on N. Kalaheo Ave. from Kuulei Rd.; the parking lot is on the right at the intersection with Hauoli St.)*

LANIKAI BEACH. *(Snorkeling. Open daily 24hr.)* Hawaiian for "heavenly sea," Lanikai lives up to its name. Sugar-like sand is Lanikai's calling card; even the most flattering postcards don't do justice to this utterly romantic destination. Tradewinds from the Windward Coast glide over the Koolau Mountains and lap up on Lanikai, creating an unusually soft and smooth shoreline. The offshore coral reef provides a light surf, and the tide's gentle waves are inviting to sunbathers, newlyweds, and artists alike. Lanikai Beach is situated along a secluded residential neighborhood; narrow public access walkways are located along Mokulua Dr. There is no parking lot. *(Driving east on Kawailoa Rd. past Kailua Beach Park, make a left at the stop sign onto Alala Rd. Follow Aalapapa Dr. as it loops around Lanikai and becomes Mokulua Dr. TheBus #70 also makes a loop around Lanikai.)*

ACTIVITIES

Kailua Sailboards and Kayaks Inc., 130 Kailua Rd. (☎808-262-2555; www.kailuasailboards.com), in Kailua Beach Center. Paddle out to Popoia and Mokulua islands, sail with sea turtles, or see the Mokulua Island Bird Sanctuary up close in one of Kailua Sailboards' tours. Guided kayak tour $89-249 depending on time and skill-level; self-guided tour $69 (lunch included). Windsurfing lessons (2hr. group lesson $89), and surfing lessons (private 1hr. lesson $109, 90min. group lesson $89). Rent kayaks (from $49 per day), surfboards ($25), sailboards ($59+), kiteboards ($45), and bicycles ($25). Weekly and half-day rates available. A Funpak allows you to use any of their water toys for 7 days ($299 per person). Open daily 8:30am-5pm. AmEx/D/MC/V.

Naish Hawaii, 155 Hamakua Dr. (☎808-262-6068; www.naish.com). Rick Naish, father of 1976 world champion windsurfer Robby Naish, no longer sells custom-built boards from his garage, but his family still runs this premier windsurfing rental and instruction center. Beginner boards $25+ for 2hr.; intermediate to advanced boards $40+ for half day, $45+ for full day. Beginner group lessons $45, semi-private lessons $100; intermediate and advanced private lessons $65 per hr. Kiteboarding lessons $150. Call 1 week in advance. Open daily 9am-5:30pm. AmEx/D/MC/V.

Aaron's Dive Shop, 307 Hahani St. (☎808-262-2333; www.hawaii-scuba.com), from Kailua Rd., turn right at the town center and then right onto Hahani St. Rent scuba gear for around $50 per day, or join the ranks of Tom Selleck, Jerry Garcia, and David Hasselhoff and go on one of the daily dive trips (4-5hr.; 2-tank dive includes equipment, lunch, and transportation; $125). Also offers dolphin excursions starting at $90. Reserve 3-4 months in advance. Open M-F 7am-7pm, Sa 7am-6pm, Su 7am-5pm. AmEx/D/MC/V.

◉ SIGHTS

ULUPO HEIAU. This sacred *heiau* (temple) is set on a peaceful plateau of lava rocks beside a shady grove with benches and a few placards. *Heiau* were traditionally built at the orders of *kahuna* (priests) to ensure success in war and agricultural fertility. The temple is said to have been built by the mythical Menehune people in a single night. From the top of the temple platform, the *alii* (royalty) could survey the lands all the way to the ocean. Farmers grew taro along the waterways next to the temple, as well as sweet potatoes and bananas on the slopes following the abolition of the native religion in 1819. Chinese buyers converted the same land into a rice paddy in the late 1800s, but it was abandoned as marshland by 1920. For non-history buffs, the state monument still provides a nice walk through well-kept flower gardens. *(Near Kailua. Heading to Kailua from Pali Hwy., turn left onto Uluoa St., at the corner of First Baptist Church Windward, and take the 1st right onto Manu Aloha. Go to the end of the block and take a right towards the YMCA. Park behind the Windward YMCA's lot and walk around it to the heiau.)*

◪ HIKING

KAIWA RIDGE TRAIL. *(2 mi. 1hr. Moderate.)* This hike climbs up the ridge behind Lanikai beach to WWII army bunkers, or "pillboxes," overlooking the beach. From the top, 600 ft. up, you can see Molokai, Lanai, and, on a superbly clear day, Maui. Despite its popularity, the trail receives minimal maintenance, and hikers are advised to use caution and not to climb the bunkers. Kaiwa Ridge is dusty, lacking the moisture and vegetation common to most of Oahu's other trails. You may either return the way you came up, or continue along the trail to loop back around to Mokolea Dr. *(Take Aalapapa Dr. into Lanikai and then turn right on Kaelepulu Dr. At the Mid-Pacific Country Club, park in the turnout on the right side of the street. The trailhead is unmarked, across the street at the bend in the private uphill road.)*

MAUNAWILI DITCH TRAIL. *(2¾ mi. 1-2 hr. Easy.)* This equestrian, bike, and hiking red-dirt trail rises an easy 200 ft. and ends at the Waimanalo side of the **Maunawili Trail.** *(Drive 3 mi. toward Waimanalo from Castle Junction on Kalanianaole Hwy., and turn right on Kumuhau St. At the end of Kumuhau St., turn right onto Waikupanaha St. and drive less than mi. down the street, past Mahiku Pl. Park in the pullout at the right side of the road. The narrow, unfenced trailhead is in front of this pullout.)*

MAUNAWILI TRAIL. *(10 mi. 4-6hr. Elevation gain: 500 ft. Moderate.)* The terrain of the Maunawili ("twisted mountain") Trail varies from wet, overgrown gulches to open forest canopies as it traverses the Windward base of the Koolau Mountain Range. The voyage among *koa, lobelia, ohia,* and other vegetation ends with transcendent views of Olomana, the Koolaupoko watershed, and Waimanalo. Bikers are also allowed on this trail, but must yield to pedestrians. The fresh-

OAHU

water streams and mud may contain leptospirosis. *(On Pali Hwy. from Honolulu to Kailua, drive out of the tunnels for approx. 1 mi. before turning right into the parking area marked "Scenic Point," along the turn to the left. There are yellow blinking lights and arrows pointing left. The trailhead is located at the entrance to this parking area.)*

 INSIDE THE OUTDOORS. For an insider's look at Oahu's natural side, check out **www.backyardoahu.com.** The site offers trail listings, descriptions, and discussion forums for backpackers and hikers and FAQs for newbies.

KANEOHE AND THE WINDWARD COAST

At the base of northbound Kamehameha Hwy., Kaneohe (pop. 34,970) is where the Windward road trip starts. Stock up here before hitting the road; farther up the coast, B&Bs are replaced by campsites and restaurants become sparse.

ORIENTATION AND PRACTICAL INFORMATION

To get to Kaneohe from Honolulu, take **H-1** to **Route 63 (Likelike Highway)** or **Route 61 (Pali Highway)** and head northeast. Turn left onto **Route 83 (Kamehameha Highway),** which intersects both after the mountains and continues northwest to Kaneohe. From the northern part of Kailua, take North Kalaheo Ave. farther northwest and out of town as it becomes **Route 630 (Kaneohe Bay Drive).** It travels through the southern part of Kaneohe and later becomes Rte. 63/Likelike Hwy. as it heads toward Honolulu. Kaneohe's main artery, Rte. 83/Kamehameha Hwy., runs north-south through Kaneohe and up the Windward Coast.

Bus: TheBus #55 Circle Island and #65 Kahaluu go to **Kaneohe.** The Circle Island route runs up the Windward Coast's Kamehameha Hwy. and returns to Ala Moana as the #52 via Wahiawa and central Oahu. The #65 goes up Pali Hwy. and stops at Windward Mall. $2; seniors, disabled persons, and students $1.

Car Rental: Enterprise, 46-003 Alaloa St. (☎808-247-2909). Take Rte. 83 northbound and turn right on Kahuhipa St., then left onto Alaloa St. Compact $28-33 per day. Collision damage waiver $20 per day; full coverage $33 per day. Major credit or debit card required. Refundable deposit at least $100. Free pickup and dropoff service within Kaneohe. 21+. Open M-F 8am-6pm, Sa 9am-noon. AmEx/D/MC/V.

City Hall: Kaneohe Satellite, 46-056 Kamehameha Hwy. (☎808-235-4571), in the Windward Mall, 2nd fl. next to Sears. Camping permits available here. Open M-Tu and Th-F 9am-5pm, W 9am-6:45pm, Sa 8am-4pm.

Bank: Bank of Hawaii, 45-1001 Kamehameha Hwy. (☎808-233-4670). Turn on William Henry Rd. to parking lot. Open M-Th 8:30am-4pm, F 8:30am-6pm, Sa 9am-1pm.

Library: Kaneohe Public Library, 45-829 Kamehameha Hwy. (☎808-233-5676). Turn right on Waikalua Rd. and make another quick right into the library's driveway, which runs alongside the police station. Open Tu, Th, and Su 10am-5pm; M and W 10am-8pm; F 1-5pm. **Internet access** with a 3-month visitor's card ($10). Copies $0.20 per page.

Laundromat: Kaneohe Washerette (☎808-235-1238), next to the post office on Kamehameha Hwy., in the same shopping center as Pah Ke's. Wash $2.50, dry $0.25 per 4min. Soap $0.75. Open 24hr.

Police: Kaneohe Substation, 45-270 Waikalua Rd. (☎808-247-2166). **Kahuku Substation,** 56-470 Kamehameha Hwy. (☎808-293-8565).

Pharmacy: Longs Drugs, 46-047 Kamehameha Hwy. (☎808-235-4511). All-purpose drug store with pharmacy and 1hr. photo lab. Open daily 7am-midnight. Pharmacy open M-F 7am-10pm, Sa 7am-9pm, Su 7am-7pm.

Medical Services: Straub Kaneohe Family Health Center, 46-056 Kamehameha Hwy. (☎808-233-6200), 2nd fl. inside the Windward Mall. Appointment only. M-F 8am-5pm, Sa 8am-noon; extended hours M-Sa noon-7:30pm, Su 10am-4:30pm.

Fax Office: Kinko's (with FedEx), 46-047 Kamehameha Hwy. (☎808-234-5500). Open M-Th 7am-10pm, F 7am-9pm, Sa 9am-9pm, Su 9am-5pm.

Internet Access: In addition to the library, **Kaneohe District Park,** 45-660 Keaahala Rd. (☎808-233-7308). Free Internet access on 6 terminals M, W, and F 5-7pm.

Post Offices: Kaneohe Main Office, 46-036 Kamehameha Hwy. (☎808-235-1055). Open M-F 8:30am-5pm, Sa 8:30am-2pm. Last collection M-F 5pm, Sa 4:30pm. **Kaaawa Main Office,** 51-480 Kamehameha Hwy. (☎808-237-8372). Open M-F 8am-noon and 1-3:45pm, Sa 9:30-11:30am. Last collection M-F 4pm, Sa noon. **Laie Main Office,** 55-510 Kamehameha Hwy., Ste. 20 (☎808-293-0337). Open M-F 9am-3:30pm, Sa 9:30-11:30am.

Postal Codes: 96744 (Kaneohe); 96730 (Kaaawa); 96762 (Laie).

ACCOMMODATIONS AND CAMPING

BED AND BREAKFASTS

Alii Bluffs Windward Bed and Breakfast, 46-251 Ikiiki St. (☎808-235-1124 or 800-235-1151; www.hawaiiscene.com/aliibluffs). Take Kamehameha Hwy., turn right onto Ipuka St. after S.W. King School, then take an immediate left onto Ikiiki St. This charming, antique-filled home has 2 themed rooms (Victorian and circus) each with a private bath. Very private and quiet with lovely owners. No children. Continental breakfast served by the pool. Laundry and parking available. Private outdoor pool with a beautiful view of Kaneohe Bay. No A/C. Victorian room $80, circus room $70. MC/V. ❸

Schrader's Windward Country Inn, 47-039 Lihikai Dr. (☎808-239-5711; www.schradersinn.com), on a small peninsula in Kaneohe Bay just north of town. Close proximity to the water makes up for modest rooms. Schrader's also offers free kayaking and snorkeling, a free Sa sandbar cruise, complimentary W dinner, and a free F happy hour. Rooms range from studios to 1,- 2-, and 3-bedroom suites. Breakfast included. Check-in 3pm. Check-out noon. Ask about weekly, group, and low-season rates. Studios $100-$150, 2-bedroom suites $200-225. AmEx/D/MC/V. ❸

DID YOU KNOW? In the late 1980s, Oahu banned the establishment of new Bed and Breakfasts. Today, many accommodations call themselves "Bed and Breakfasts" but are actually vacation rentals that often don't include breakfast and provide separate entrances for guests. If you want a true B&B experience (i.e. you want to stay in a person's actual home and have breakfast prepared each morning) your options are limited. Alii Bluffs Windward Bed and Breakfast in Kaneohe is a wonderful example of a traditional B&B.

CAMPING

Permits for the state parks along the Windward Coast are free and available at the **Division of State Parks,** 1151 Punchbowl St. Rm. 310, Honolulu (☎808-587-0300; www.hawaiistateparks.org). The **Department of Parks and Recreation** in the Honolulu Municipal Building, 650 South King St. (☎808-523-4525) and any Satellite City Hall in the area can issue permits for City and County Parks. See **Camping in Hawaii, p. 82,** for more information.

Malaekahana Campgrounds, 1 mi. north of Laie on Kamehamena Hwy. These grounds are privately owned by the Friends of Malaekahana (☎808-293-1736; www.malaekahana.net) and are available 7 days a week. Popular and somewhat secluded camping area has campsites, yurts, and cabins. Outdoor shower facilities, 24hr. security, and a swimming beach on Laie Bay. Gates locked 7pm-7am. Alcohol-free premises. Check-in 3pm. Check-out noon. Most units require 2-day min. stay. 30 campsites. $8.50 per person per night (under 3 free); 6-person yurt with bath $150; beach cabins with bath (sleeps 4) $60-130. "Lil' Grass Shacks" thatched cabins (sleep 2) $40. MC/V. ●

Kualoa Regional Park "B," 49-479 Kamehameha Hwy., on Kaneohe Bay, about 1 mi. past Tropical Farms. Families frequent this campsite for its scenic surroundings and safe swimming. Lifeguard on duty daily in summer. To reserve a space, go to a Satellite City Hall 2 Fridays before you intend to camp. Get there soon after it opens, as permits are usually gone by 9am. 30 sites. Restrooms, showers, and parking. Kualoa Regional Park "A" is connected to Kualoa Park "B" and has 7 campsites (weekend only, closed in the summer). Camping at Kualoa "B" daily. Park closed to public daily 8pm-7am. Free. ●

Swanzy Beach Park, 51-369 Kamehameha Hwy., about 3 mi. north of Kualoa Regional Park, beyond Kaaawa Point. Swanzy Beach, while rocky and not great for swimming, is suitable for fishing and some snorkeling. The park, also popular with families, is protected by a concrete wall with stairs leading down to the water. Basketball court, restrooms, and showers on premises. Not gated. 9 sites. Weekends only. Make reservations 2 Fridays in advance at the Satellite City Hall (Kaneohe) or the Department of Parks and Recreation in Honolulu. Camping F-Su. Free. ●

Hauula Beach Park, 54-135 Kamehameha Hwy., north of Kaneohe, beyond Kahana Bay on Kamehameha Hwy. The beach is a bit littered and rocky, but Hauula's calm waves allow good swimming when waters are calm. The park has restrooms, picnic tables, and volleyball nets. Not gated. 15 undesignated sites. Camping M-Tu and F-Su. Free. ●

◗ FOOD

Travelers should check out Kaneohe's restaurants, especially before heading up the Windward Coast. Farther north, dining options are sparse. To stock up on groceries, there's a **Foodland,** 45-480 Kamehameha Hwy., in the Windward City Shopping Center. (☎808-247-3357. Open daily 6am-midnight. AmEx/D/MC/V.) **Room Service in Paradise** is also worth a try; they deliver from many restaurants in the area. Check website for participating businesses. (☎808-261-3463 for Kailua; www.941dine.com. Open daily 8:30am-9pm. AmEx/D/MC/V.)

▨ **Pah Ke's,** 46-018 Kamehameha Hwy. (☎808-235-4505). Many locals consider Pah Ke's the best Chinese restaurant on the island (a big statement considering the competition in Chinatown), though most items on the extensive menu are under $10. The fresh food is cooked in a health-conscious manner, with mostly local ingredients and no MSG. The lunch plate ($6.25) includes sweet and sour pork spareribs, *kau yuk,* pork chop suey, steamed rice, and 2 crispy wontons. Entrees include black pepper steak sizzling platter ($11), braised black mushrooms with vegetables ($7.50), and Hong Kong-style fried chicken ($6.50). BYOB; corkage fee $5. Open daily 10:30am-9pm. AmEx/MC/V. ●

▨ **Kaneohe Bakery,** 45-1026 Kamehameha Hwy. (☎808-247-0474). The doughnuts ($1), danishes ($1), cakes ($10-15), and cream pies ($11) are only matched in sweetness by the service. Open M-Th and Su 4am-11pm, F-Sa 4am-midnight. MC/V. ●

Zia's Caffé, 45-620 Kamehameha Hwy. (☎808-235-9427). Zia's greets locals as well as weary Windward travelers with hearty, traditional Italian-American fare and an inviting atmosphere. The lunch menu offers a selection of pasta or sandwich combos ($8-9). The real specialties, such as the Tuscan chicken penne ($16), emerge at dinner. Entrees $10-23. Eat on the patio, or take it to go. Open daily 11am-10pm. MC/V. ●

Masa and Joyce, 45-582 Kamehameha Hwy. (☎808-235-6129), in Kaneohe. Locals consistently crowd this bastion of Hawaiian and Japanese dishes, known for its excellent *poke.* Breakfasts (special includes 2 eggs, choice of meat, 2 scoops rice, and toast;

$5), plate lunches (*kalua* pig and cabbage $6.50), *bentos* ($6-8), *pupu,* and *poke.* Call ahead for breakfast (served all day) and plate lunches. The generous Hawaiian plate (*lau lau, poi* or rice, *kalua* pork, chicken, long rice, *lomi lomi* salmon, and *shoyu poke;* $10) is a great value. Open W-F 9am-6pm, Sa 9am-4pm, Su 9am-2pm. MC/V. ❶

Chao Phya Thai Restaurant, 45-480 Kaneohe Bay Dr. #A1F (☎808-235-3555), in Kaneohe. Many restaurants claim to serve authentic Thai food, but Chao Phya Thai actually delivers that promise. Don't be fooled by its location in the Windward Shopping Center; Chao Phya Thai serves a variety of delicious salads ($7.50-8.50), soups ($8) and vegetarian, beef, chicken, and seafood entrees ($7.50-10) at extremely reasonable prices. Lunch M-Sa 11am-2pm. Dinner M-Su 5-9pm. MC/V. ❷

Uncle Bobo's Smoked BBQ, 51-480 Kamehameha Hwy. (☎808-237-1000) in Kaaawa across from Swanzy Beach Park. This casual joint serves slow-smoked backyard barbecue favorites like beef brisket (plate $10.50, sandwich $8) and pork ribs ($12.50) as well as burgers (Bobo burger $5). Drop in for an entire meal or just a shave ice ($3). Open Tu-Su 10:30am-7:30pm. D/MC/V. ❷

🕑 SIGHTS

🏛 **VALLEY OF THE TEMPLES.** A Christian chapel and Buddhist temple honor followers of all religions, races, and creeds who are buried in this beautiful, unconventional cemetery. Byodo-In, the Buddhist temple of equality, is a perfect replica of the 900-year-old temple in Uji, Japan, built around an enormous statue of Buddha. The temple was begun in 1966 and dedicated on June 7, 1968, nearly 100 years to the day after the first Japanese immigrants arrived in Hawaii. Built entirely without the use of nails, the temple represents the mythical figure of the phoenix, a bird of good omen who rises from symbolic ashes. The ring of the temple's three-ton brass bell (said to bring good fortune to the ringers) echoes over the koi-filled pools and tranquil groves, which are inhabited by wild black swans and peacocks. *(47-200 Kahekili Hwy. ☎808-239-8811. Driving north on Kamehameha Hwy. toward Kaneohe, turn left onto Likelike Hwy. and then right onto Kahekili Hwy. To enter The Valley of the Temples, turn left onto Hui Iwa St. Open daily 8am-5:30pm. Temple open 9am-5pm. Entrance to Byodo-in Temple $2, children and seniors $1.)*

ART DEMOS. Every Tu from 11am-2pm, the Byodo-In temple holds a demonstration by local artists, including the art of cast paper sculpture. Free with admission to the temple. Call ☎808-239-9844 for more information.

🏛 **SENATOR FONG'S PLANTATION AND GARDENS.** This breathtaking 725-acre garden and plantation was the private estate of Senator Hiram Leong Fong, the first Asian American to serve in the US Senate. Originally a banana plantation, the property was purchased by Fong in 1950 and he transformed it into a series of five gardens, each named for a president he served alongside during his 17 years in the Senate: the Eisenhower Plateau, Johnson Plateau, Kennedy Valley, Nixon Valley, and Ford Plateau. Nestled at the base of the Koolau Mountains, the serene gardens are devoted to the preservation of Hawaiian flora, and much of the land remains untouched in its natural state. Enjoy a stroll through the gardens amidst over 80 species of palms, 7 lily ponds, endless varieties of tropical flowers, and a meadow of lychee-bearing trees. *(47-285 Pulama Rd. ☎808 239-6775; www.fonggarden.com, in Kaneohe. Turn left on Pulama Rd. from northbound Kamehameha Hwy. and follow signs to the entrance of the garden, about 1 mi. Open 10am-1pm daily. 1hr. guided walking tours depart 10:30am and 1pm. Visitors must be with a guide to tour the grounds. $14.50, seniors $13, ages 5-12 $9, under 5 free. Cash only.)*

OAHU

TIP **MAKE A LEI.** Daily sessions cost $6.50 at Senator Fong's Garden and teach guests the art of sewing leis by hand. Flowers are grown on-site at the garden. Over 60,000 lei flowers such as bouganvillias, jade flowers, *pikakes*, and *puakenekenes* are used each week. Classes held at the Visitors Center.

HOOMALUHIA BOTANICAL GARDEN. Hoomaluhia can be translated as "a place of peace and serenity," and this beautiful, 400-acre botanical garden is steeped in tranquility. Originally built to provide flood protection for Kaneohe, the site is home to plants, trees, and flowers from major tropical climates around the world. Driving and biking are permitted along designated paths. Visitors can participate in a free "catch and release" fishing program Saturday and Sunday 10am-2pm; equipment is available to borrow. Call the garden to see when they will be hosting a new art exhibit in their popular gallery. Opening nights, featuring the works of local artists, offer drinks and *pupu* at a public reception. Camping, with a permit available from the Visitors Center, is allowed from 9am Friday to 4pm Monday. Restrooms, showers, fire pits, picnic tables, and parking lots are spread throughout the park. Campers should expect wet conditions in the rainforest-like setting—don't forget the bug repellent. *(45-680 Luluku Rd. ☎ 808-233-7323. Driving north on Kamehameha Hwy., turn left onto Luluku Rd. at the Aloha Gas Station. Alternatively, take TheBus #55 to this junction. The garden is 1 mi. from Kamehameha Hwy. The Visitors Center is 1 mi. beyond the entrance. Open daily 9am-4pm. Guided tours Sa 10am and Su 1pm. After 4pm all cars staying in the park must be registered. Free.)*

NUUANU PALI LOOKOUT. This is the site of the Battle of the Nuuanu Pali's dramatic finish, where Oahu warriors were driven up and over the 980 ft. *palis* (cliffs) by King Kamehameha who was fighting to unite the Hawaiian Islands. Oahu was under the control of Maui's Chief Kalanikupule when King Kamehameha arrived at Waikiki in 1795. After several battles, Chief Kalanikupule was driven up Nuaanu Valley to this location, where the final battle took place. Legend claims the wind is strong enough to knock a man from the cliffs and then blow him right back up; local kids sometimes take advantage of the raging wind, holding sheets and getting blown into the air. Two million years ago a massive landslide sank half of the Koolau volcano into the Pacific; the Pali lookout is the edge of what remains. When standing at this point, visitors are surrounded by miles of 2000 ft. cliffs and an amazing panoramic view of the Hoomaluhia Botanical Garden, Kaneohe, Mokolii Island, Mokapu Peninsula, and the infinite horizon. The lookout is positioned along an abandoned stretch of the Old Pali Road. Visitors can hike down the road and enjoy the incredible vistas up close. *(The lookout can be accessed via Pali Hwy. northbound and southbound about ½ mi. south of the tunnels. Look for signs for the turnoff and follow the road to the parking lot in front of the lookout. Call the Office of Forestry and Wildlife, ☎ 808-587-0166, for more information. The Pali Lookout has informative placards and plenty of parking. North of Honolulu on the Pali Hwy. Open daily 9am-4pm. Don't leave valuables in your car.)*

THE POLYNESIAN CULTURAL CENTER. Equal parts cultural exhibit and amusement park, this 45-year-old, 42-acre mammoth tourist attraction employs an army of native and Polynesian performers, artisans, cooks, and cultural conservators to display the rich traditions of Polynesian cultures. Six separate villages, each devoted to a different Polynesian Island nation, allow visitors to throw Tongan spears, play Fijian bamboo drums, learn how Samoans start a fire with sticks, and hear the blowing of a Hawaiian conch shell. The spectacular **"Rainbows of Paradise"** canoe pageant at 2:30pm gives a sampling of the music and dance from all of the islands. There's an IMAX screen, a nighttime luau buffet and show, and much more, depending on the variety of ticket purchased. The center is a nonprofit institution run by the Church of Jesus Christ of Latter-Day Saints. The organization runs a scholarship program for its employees, providing their tuition at Brigham Young University Hawaii in exchange for work at the center. *(55-370 Kamehameha Hwy. ☎ 808-293-3333 or 800-367-7060; www. polynesia.com. In Laie; you can't miss the 10 ft. wooden Tiki statues that frown over the roadside and in front of the parking lot. Call for transportation reservations; a motorcoach bus departs from eight different locations in Waikiki starting at 10am. Round trip $19; curbside or hotel pickup $27. Parking $5 for individual vehicles. Open M-Sa noon-9:30pm. All-day packages starting at $58 (ages 3-11 $43), evening packages starting at $48 (ages 3-11 $29). Visitors may return within three days free of charge with the purchase of an all-day ticket. No alcohol. AmEx/D/MC/V.)*

KUALOA RANCH AND REGIONAL PARK. This privately owned 4000-acre cattle ranch-turned-tourist attraction stretches over five miles of coast. The land was originally owned by Kamehameha III before he sold it in 1850 to his advisor Dr. Gerrit P. Judd. Visitors can go horseback riding or off-roading on an ATV (both $59 per hr.). Other activities include a 1hr. Movie Set Tour ($19), with sites from *Jurassic Park* and TV series *Lost*; a Jeep Jungle Expedition in a six-wheel Swiss Army off-road Jeep ($19); and a voyage through Kanoehe Bay aboard a 49-passenger catamaran ($19). Ask about the self-guided tour of Secret Island which includes kayaks, snorkel gear, volleyball nets, and hammocks ($30 half day, $40 full day). Visitors can dine inside at **Aunty Pat's Paniolo Cafe ❷,** which offers Hawaiian specials (all under $12). Nearby Kualoa Regional Park, on the coastal side of the highway south of the ranch entrance, is the closest point to Mokolii Island, commonly referred to as Chinaman's Hat, a Windward landmark nicknamed for its resemblance to the hats Chinese laborers wore when they came to Hawaii. *(49-560 Kamehameha Hwy. Main entrance to the ranch is on the mountain side of Kamehameha Hwy., north of Kualoa Regional Park. ☎ 808-237-8515, reservations 808-237-7321; www.kualoaranch.com. Open daily 7am-4:30pm. See Camping, p. 82. MC/V.)*

TROPICAL FARMS OUTLET. Set in the midst of Kualoa Ranch, about 1 mi. south of Kualoa Park, Tropical Farms Outlet sells nuts from the only working macadamia nut farm on Oahu. The extensive gift shop offers free samples of freshly harvested nuts, Kona-macadamia coffee, and locally produced items such as macadamia nut brittle, cooking oil, and sea salt. Visitors can explore the surrounding Kualoa Tropical Gardens by bus and the 800-year-old "Secret Island" fish pond by canoe on the ◧**Alii Tour,** which also includes an educational presentation and a fire display. *(49-227A Kamehameha Hwy. ☎ 808-237-1960 or 877-505-6887. Open 9:30am-5pm daily. For information about the Alii Tour call ☎ 808-781-2474. $15, under 10 free. Tour leaves every hr. Alii tour cash only. Gift shop D/MC/V.)*

 HIKING

HAUULA LOOP AND MAAKUA RIDGE TRAILS. *(2 mi. each. 1-1½hr. Easy.)* The trailhead for both trails is Hauula Homestead Rd., across from **Hauula Beach Park** (p. 167). The initial paved trail comes to a fork close to the start; to hike the **Hauula Loop Trail** take the right fork, which climbs up the ridge to cross Waipilopilo Gulch. The path then turns back toward the ocean, overlooks Kipapau Valley, and passes several waterfalls before it loops back to the beginning of the trail. Although uphill on the way out, the initial trail is fairly easy and well-suited for families. The **Maakua Ridge Trail** is slightly more rugged than the Hauula Loop and has steeper switchbacks. It begins in a *hau* forest on the left side of the access road, 50 yards beyond the Hauula Loop Trailhead. After a stream crossing, there is a switchback to a ridge-top shelter with benches overlooking seaside Hauula. The loop begins here and you may proceed in either direction, up

800 ft., in moderate-to-difficult terrain. Wear blaze-orange clothing; this area is also a hunting ground. *(From Kamehameha Hwy. northbound, turn left at the 2nd entrance to Hauula Homestead Rd., at the corner with a 7-11. Where the road curves sharply to the left, continue straight onto Maakua Rd. Park roadside before the cable gate.)*

NORTH SHORE

There are only a few words to describe the break on Oahu's North Shore: gnarly, mean, and real. Surf isn't a sub-culture here; it's the consciousness of an entire tight-knit community. For Oahu, this stretch of coastline is a place to kick back and relax. It's tranquil, low-key, and downright empty in certain parts. In the winter, however, the North Shore nearly explodes, as monstrous waves bring the world's best surfers in search of the perfect ride. From the rural surroundings of Turtle Bay to Sunset Beach and Waimea, one spectacular beach follows another, and some are astonishingly empty. Past Waimea, Haleiwa (p. 172) is the center of life on the North Shore, with first-rate restaurants, shops, galleries, and plenty of places to stock up on surf gear or Brazilian bikinis. West of Haleiwa, Wailua, once the North Shore's sugarcane powerhouse, has seen better days, but the old sugar mill has been revamped and houses a handful of attractive local businesses. Farther west, the small town of Mokuleia beckons thrill-seekers with myriad skydiving and mountain-biking adventures.

To reach the North Shore by car, take H-1 from Honolulu to the end of H-2, then follow Rte. 803 or Hwy. 99. Hwy. 83 (Kamehameha Hwy.) is the main road that runs along the coast from Haleiwa to Kahuku and down the Windward Coast. The North Shore is also served by TheBus #52, which runs from Honolulu to Haleiwa, and then up the coast on Kamehameha Hwy. to Turtle Bay. TheBus #76 runs between Haleiwa and Waialua along Farrington Hwy.

WAIMEA AND SUNSET BEACH

Kamehameha Hwy. continues along the northeastern coast of Oahu and through Waimea and Sunset Beach. Though there are no real town centers, both have clusters of roadside food stands, surf shacks, hostels, and miles of beach. This is the place to stay if you're serious about winter surfing, but it's also worthwhile during the calmer summer months, when in addition to the surfable "bumps," there is great snorkeling, swimming, and hiking. Rollerbladers, bikers, and strollers enjoy the bike path that stretches between Sunset Beach and Waimea; separated by thick trees from the highway, the path provides a scenic, secluded view of the North Shore.

ORIENTATION AND PRACTICAL INFORMATION

Kamehameha Highway is the main road through Waimea and Sunset Beach. There is an **ATM** inside **Foodland**, at the intersection of the highway and Pupukea Rd. (Open daily 6am-11pm.) The nearest post offices are the **Haleiwa Post Office** (p. 173) and the **Kahuku Post Office**, 56-565 Kamehameha Hwy. (☎808-293-0485. Open M-F 8:30am-3:30pm, Sa 8:30am-11:30am.) **Postal Code:** 96731 (Kahuku).

ACCOMMODATIONS

There are many vacation rentals available near Waimea; call the real estate agents listed in **Haleiwa** (p. 172) for more information. Try **www.hawaiibeachfronts. com** for larger groups; they've got good prices and amazing views.

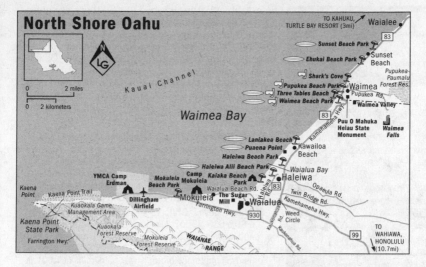

North Shore Oahu

TO KAHUKU,
TURTLE BAY RESORT (3mi)

Waialee

83

Sunset Beach Park

Ehukai Beach Park

Sunset
Beach

Shark's Cove

Pupukea-
Paumalu
Forest Res.

Pupukea Beach Park
Three Tables Beach
Waimea Beach Park

Waimea

Pupukea Rd.

Waimea Valley

Kauai Channel

Waimea Bay

83

Puu O Mahuka
Heiau State
Monument

Waimea
Falls

Laniakea Beach
Puaena Point
Haleiwa Beach Park

Kawailoa
Beach

Haleiwa Alii Beach Park

Waialua Bay

YMCA Camp
Erdman

Mokuleia
Beach Park

Camp
Mokuleia

Kaiaka Beach
Park

Haleiwa

Opaeula Rd.

Kaena
Point

Kaena Point Trail

Waialua Beach Rd.

83

Twin Bridge Rd.

Kuaokala Game
Management Area

Dillingham
Airfield

Mokuleia

The Sugar
Mill

Farrington Hwy.

Waialua

Kamehameha Hwy.

Kaena Point
State Park

Kuaokala
Forest Reserve

930

Weed
Circle

Farrington Hwy.

Mokuleia
Forest Reserve

*WAIANAE
RANGE*

99

TO
WAHIAWA,
HONOLULU
(10.7mi)

0   2 miles
0   2 kilometers

Shark's Cove Rentals, 59-672 Kamehameha Hwy. (☎808-638-7980; www.sharkscov-erentals.com), across the Shark's Cove and Log Cabins breaks, look for 2 American flags just east of the old gas station next to Foodland. Each of the 4 houses has its own living room with cable TV, kitchen, and full bath. All rooms have bunk beds, and some also have a full-size bottom bunk. Grill, pay phone, soda machine, and coin-op laundry in the central courtyard. Free snorkel equipment for guests. Refundable security deposit $20. 3-day min. Room $75-185. AmEx/D/MC/V. ❸

Backpackers, 59-788 Kamemeha Hwy. (☎808-638-7838; http://backpackers-hawaii.com), low-key and relaxed, right across from Three Tables beach, has 50 beds for surfers, backpackers, and anyone else looking for the cheapest digs in town. A variety of set-ups, from 2- to 6-bed dorms to private beachfront cottages. Perks include free daily airport shuttle (with reservations), inexpensive nightly meals, free snorkel equipment and bodyboards, discounts on activities, Internet access ($6 per hr.), and storage. Ask about short-term work exchange. Reception 8am-7pm. Check-in after 10am. Check-out 10am. Reservations recommended. 10% discount for 7-day stay or more. No A/C. Dorms $22-25; private rooms $58-67; apartments/cottages $112-250. MC/V. ❶

Ke Iki Beach Bungalows, 59-579 Ke Iki Rd., (☎808 638-8229; www.keikibeach.com), between Shark's Cove and Ehukai Beach. The beach bungalows have an unbeatable location directly on a long, sandy, and almost always empty beach. The studio and 1- and 2-bedroom bungalows are newly renovated and landscaped, with patios and hammocks lining the beach. Bungalows feature either beachfront or garden views. Surfboards are usually available to borrow. Reservations recommended. Cleaning fee $45-100. Streetside bungalows during high season $145-185; low season $120-175. Beachside $180-210/195-230. Discounts for stays 1 week or more. MC/V. ❹

🏠 FOOD

Restaurants are scarce in the Sunset Beach area; if a lunch wagon doesn't satisfy your culinary cravings, head west a few miles to Haleiwa (p. 172). **Foodland,** 59-720 Kamehameha Hwy., at the intersection of Kamehameha Hwy. and Pupukea Rd., in Waimea, has the largest selection of groceries on the North Shore as well as a sushi bar, bakery, and deli. (☎808-638-8081. Open daily

AN AMATEUR'S GUIDE TO THE NORTH SHORE

After staying in the Honolulu area for close to 5 weeks, I was eagerly anticipating my visit to the North Shore. The clear water and soft beaches did not disappoint, but it was soon apparent that the North Shore ethos remains somewhat of a mystery to the uninitiated visitor. Here is my list of the top 5 things to do on the North Shore if you are seeking some surfer cool.

1. Shark's Cove: Rent some equipment and take a dip at Shark's Cove—a perfect place for novice snorkelers (p. 171).

2. Matsumoto's Shave Ice: Even if you are not a card-carrying member of the surf scene, you can still eat shave ice like an insider—and there's no better place than Matsumoto's (p. 176).

3. Giovanni's: This graffiti-covered lunch spot is easily the most famous North Shore Shrimp Truck. It prepares fresh shrimp simply and deliciously. Usually parked in the lot on the left just past Cafe Haleiwa (p. 176).

4. Beach Sunset: My favorite time to visit the beach is in the early evening, when the crowds have thinned and the sun sits a bit lower in the sky. Pack a picnic and watch the sun go down at Sunset Beach Park (p. 170).

5. Work up a Sweat: Make the easy hike through the scenic Waimea Valley to the cool, clear, pool below historic **Waihi Falls** (p. 171). Jump right in!

–Claire Saffitz

6am-11pm.) Within the two towns, there are quite a few roadside food stands and takeout establishments that have earned solid reputations. Be sure to stop by the **North Shore Country Market,** 59-530 Kamehameha Hwy., across from Ehukai Beach Park, at Sunset Beach Elementary School. Local farmers gather at this community event to sell fresh organic produce. The market is a great opportunity for travelers to catch a glimpse of the local community. (☎808-638-7172. Open Sa 8am-2pm.)

Ted's Bakery, 59-024 Kamehameha Hwy. (☎808-638-5974), has been a North Shore favorite for 20 years. The *malasadas* and doughnuts here would tempt a vegan. Some show up later for plate lunches ($7-10), but the wise prey on the chocolate-haupia cream pie. Open M-Tu 7am-6pm, W-Su 7am-8pm. D/MC/V. ❶

Shark's Cove Grill, 59-712 Kamehameha Hwy. (☎808-638-8300). A roadside shack with a shaded patio, the grill is popular for breakfast and mid-afternoon smoothies. "Dawn patrol" breakfast of oatmeal, raisins, cinnamon, brown sugar, and milk ($4.50) is a popular post-surf meal. For lunch, try the fresh *ahi* sandwich ($7) and the popular banana-protein shake ($4). Breakfast served until 11am. Free Wi-Fi. Open daily 8:30am-8:30pm. MC/V. ❶

🇨 BEACHES

Welcome to surfing heaven. Between Sunset Beach and Ehukai Beach there are 12 named breaks, and to Waimea Bay, there are another 10. However, if riding isn't your thing, the endless stretch of sand is equally pleasant for sun-bathing and water-splashing. These are organized north to south.

SUNSET BEACH PARK. *(Surfing. Open daily sunrise to sunset. Lifeguards 9am-5:30pm.)* Sunset Beach entices visitors year-round. In the summer, sunbathers flock to its 2 mi. of extra-wide, white sandy beach and calm, crystal clear water. Summer swells are also not unheard of here, and they often attract a flock of longboard surfers to the point break. In the winter, powerful waves bring professional surfers and enthusiastic spectators to the site of several international surfing competitions. In winter, this beach is strictly for experts; waves reach 25 ft. and there is a notorious riptide—lifeguards have saved many overly-ambitious surfers here from certain death. The park has restrooms and parking.

EHUKAI BEACH PARK. *(Surfing. Open daily sunrise to sunset. Lifeguards 9am-5:30pm.)* Between Kalalua Point and the beach park is a long stretch of sandy beach that is almost always empty. In December, surfers and fans from all over the world flock to this beach to watch the Pipeline Masters (one of the three Triple Crown surfing events) as they barrel down intense waves over the most famous shallow reef break on the North Shore, the **Banzai Pipeline. Log Cabins** is farther south, and equally gnarly. Swimming is safe over the sandbar in summer months, though the rip current can still be strong. Shoreline access is marked along the path between Kamehameha Hwy. and the beachfront homes; park at Ehukai Beach Park or the pullouts on the path. Restrooms and showers are on the premises.

SHARK'S COVE. *(Snorkeling. Surfing. Open daily 24hr.)* Between the Foodland in Waimea and Kalalua Point, Shark's Cove, part of a Marine Life Conservation District, offers some of the best summer snorkeling and scuba diving on Oahu. It has caves, coral, and colorful reef fish, as well as sea turtles and an occasional white-tipped reef shark. The cove also has tide pools that are well-suited for children who wish to snorkel. A bit south of Shark's Cove, across from Foodland is **Pupukea Beach Park** (not to be confused with Pupukea, a surf spot north of Ehukai Beach Park), another good place to snorkel. The northern part of the beach park is **Three Tables Beach,** named for the plateaus of reef that emerge at low tide and make for great snorkeling in summer. In winter the waves overtake these calm waters. Snorkeling equipment can be rented at several kiosks across the street. Shark's Cove has restrooms and showers.

WAIMEA BAY BEACH PARK. *(Snorkeling. Surfing. Open daily sunrise to sunset. Lifeguards 9am-5:30pm.)* Heading north after Kawailoa Beach, you'll come to a bend in the road, overlooking an amazing, deep crescent of sea that is Waimea Bay. Summer mornings bring some of the clearest and calmest waters on the island, perfect for swimming and snorkeling. In the golden afternoon sunlight, visitors test their cliff-jumping luck, scurrying up and off a giant rock into the bay. In the winter, sailboats and sunbathers make way as this bay comes alive, releasing an awe-inspiring energy in ⬛**big waves** that reach as high as 30 ft. The entrance to the beach is across the street from the Waimea Valley. Get there early, as the parking lot fills up quickly and you may be ticketed if you park on the road above. The beach has restrooms, showers, and picnic tables.

⬛ ⬛ HIKING AND SIGHTS

WAIMEA VALLEY. Formerly known as Waimea Falls Park, the biggest tourist attraction in the area emphasizes the natural and cultural preservation of the valley over entertainment and features a pleasant ¾ mi. (one-way) paved "nature walk" that passes beautiful botanical gardens, cultural and historical sites, and a variety of endangered indigenous species while heading to the final waterfall. For the slightly more adventurous, the old waterfall trail to the left offers an unpaved hiking experience. Swimming in Waihi Falls at the end of the walk is a cool break. Although the pool is probably more heavily infested with tourists than any deadly parasites, be sure to check in with the lifeguards about leptospirosis. The valley is also a bird sanctuary and affords visitors a rare opportunity to catch a glimpse of the **endangered Hawaiian moorhen.** Guided activities such as lei making, hula lessons, and Hawaiian games are offered daily at 10, 11am, 1, and 2pm. Activities are free with admission; inquire at the entrance booth about the schedule. ⬛**North Shore Yoga,** a nomadic crew of yogis led by Paul, can be reached at Cholo's in Haleiwa (☎808-637-3059) and makes stops at the Waimea Valley Center on Tuesday, Thursday, and Saturday mornings for a 7:30-8:45am class. The suggested donation of $2 is well worth the price of this energizing gathering. *(59-864 Kamehameha Hwy., across the street from the Waimea Bay Beach Park. Follow the driveway ¾ mi. until you reach the parking lot. ☎808-638-7766. Open daily 9am-5pm. $10, seniors $5, ages 4-12 $5. AmEx/D/MC/V.)*

RUNNIN' DRY. The Waimea Valley waterfall stops flowing periodically during the summer months. Call beforehand to see if swimming is possible.

PUPUKEA. Hiking the trails at Pupukea affords a more direct communion with nature. Trails begin at the end of Pupukea Rd. next to Foodland; follow the steep and winding Pupukea Rd. about 3 mi. up the hill until you see Camp Pupukea, the Aloha Council Boy Scouts of America Camp, on your left. From camp, you can take the **Kaunala Loop** (5 mi.). When it rains, negotiating the muddy conditions can prove quite difficult. Rain gear, sturdy hiking boots, and mosquito repellent are strongly recommended.

KAUNALA LOOP TRAIL. *(5 mi. 2hr. Moderate.)* The loop trail winds through several gulches full of ti plants, sandalwood, and *koa* trees, as well as the occasional wild orchid. To reach the trailhead, follow the dirt road past the camp and around the locked gate; sign in at the hunters/hikers mailbox and take a peek at the trail map next to the mailbox to get an idea of where you're going. Continue down the road, keeping to the left; there's a marked trailhead on the left side when you reach the first major fork, about 1 mi. down the road. Follow the yellow hiker's arrows on the signs whenever there's an intersection or ambiguous fork. The trail connects with a dirt road; turn right onto it and follow the ridge along several ups and downs. On clear days, there are views of the shore along this leg. The road eventually loops back to the original dirt road you started on (turn right at the intersection and continue down the hill about 1 mi. to return to the parking area). On the weekends, public hunting presents another dangerous risk—wear blaze-orange to distinguish yourself from the wild prey.

PUU O MAHUKA HEIAU STATE MONUMENT. Stop by the Puu o Mahuka Heiau for a cultural reality check amongst the largely *haole* (Caucasian) surf culture below. Off Pupukea Rd., about a mile from Kamehameha Hwy., look for a sign on your right. Follow the winding, speed-bump-covered road to the remains of an ancient Hawaiian *luakini heiau*, a temple honoring the god of war, whose construction involved human sacrifice. Today, only the rock walls and stone floor are left at the national historic landmark, but 250 years ago a major temple stood on the site. High priest Kaopulupulu presided over the temple in the 1770s, and Kamehameha I's *kahuna* (priest) Hewahawa oversaw it until 1819, when the Hawaiian religion was abolished. The monument offers a commanding view of the shoreline and the channel between Oahu and Kauai, where fires used to provide visual communication between the islands. A visit to this sacred site can be a spiritual retreat from the frenzy of North Shore surfing.

HALEIWA

Haleiwa (pop. 2225) is the undisputed center of life on the North Shore. Characterized by a distinctive surfer culture, Haleiwa moves at a slower pace than the rest of the island; it's the refuge of choice for Oahu's residents. An entire day could be spent perusing the local craft galleries or slurping down shave ice; be aware that store hours often depend on customer interest or the size of the surf. Haleiwa is the gateway to the world-famous beaches along the North Shore, earning the town its title, the "Surfing Capital of the World."

◼ ORIENTATION

Haleiwa center is located along **Route 83 (Kamehameha Highway),** north of the traffic circle where **Highway 99** meets Rte. 83. **Haleiwa Road** runs along the harbor

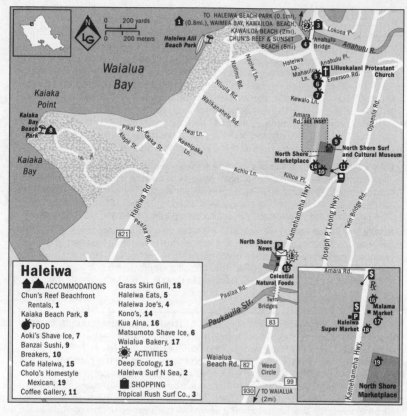

Haleiwa

ACCOMMODATIONS
Chun's Reef Beachfront
Rentals, **1**
Kaiaka Beach Park, **8**

FOOD
Aoki's Shave Ice, **7**
Banzai Sushi, **9**
Breakers, **10**
Cafe Haleiwa, **15**
Cholo's Homestyle
Mexican, **19**
Coffee Gallery, **11**

Grass Skirt Grill, **18**
Haleiwa Eats, **5**
Haleiwa Joe's, **4**
Kono's, **14**
Kua Aina, **16**
Matsumoto Shave Ice, **6**
Waialua Bakery, **17**

ACTIVITIES
Deep Ecology, **13**
Haleiwa Surf N Sea, **2**

SHOPPING
Tropical Rush Surf Co., **3**

toward Waialua, intersecting Kamehameha Hwy. by the **Anahulu Bridge.** Haleiwa
is served by TheBus #52 Wahiawa/Circle Isle and #76, which shuttles between
Haleiwa and Waialua. The trip from Honolulu to Haleiwa takes about 1½ hr.

▣ PRACTICAL INFORMATION

Banks: Bank of Hawaii, in the Haleiwa Shopping Center, and **First Hawaiian Bank,**
between Haleiwa Super Market and Aoki's Shave Ice, on Kamehameha Hwy., have **24hr.
ATMs** outside. (Both open M-Th 8:30am-4pm, F 8:30am-6pm.)

Pharmacy: Haleiwa Pharmacy, 66-150 Kamehameha Hwy. (☎808-537-9393). Open
M-F 9am-1pm and 1:30-5:30pm, Sa 9am-1pm. AmEx/D/MC/V.

Copy and Fax Services: North Shore News, 66-437 Kamehameha Hwy., Ste. 210
(☎808-637-3138, fax 808-637-8862), on the 2nd fl., behind the post office. Copies
$0.10 per pg. Fax to mainland $3 per pg, local $1. Open M-F 9am-5pm. AmEx/MC/V.

Internet Access: Coffee Gallery (☎808-637-5355), in North Shore Marketplace, has 1
terminal. $4 per 30min. Free Wi-Fi with your own laptop. Open daily 6:30am-8pm.

Post Office: Haleiwa Post Office, 66-437 Kamehameha Hwy. Ste. 102 (☎808-637-
1711), in the building complex on the southeast edge of town. Open M-F 8am-4pm, Sa
9am-noon. Last collection M-F 5pm, Sa 4:15pm. AmEx/D/MC/V. **Postal Code:** 96712.

ACCOMMODATIONS

Numerous properties ranging from surfer shacks to luxurious homes line the beaches of Haleiwa. Vacation rentals are a more economical option for those traveling in groups; rates for multi-bedroom homes work out to be quite reasonable (houses that sleep 4-5 start around $100 per night). **Sterman Realty** (☎808-637-6200; www.sterman.com; open M-F 8am-5pm) and **Team Real Estate, Inc.** (☎808-637-3507; www.teamrealestate.com; open M-F 8am-4:30pm), both with offices in the North Shore Marketplace, handle vacation rentals. Both companies require a refundable security deposit (usually $300-500) and charge a one-time cleaning fee (around $60-150). Reserve three months in advance for a winter trip, but be on the lookout for last minute discounts.

Chun's Reef Beachfront Rentals, 61-529 Kamehameha Hwy. (☎808-637-6417; www.hawaiibeachfronts.com). Part of a larger group of beachfront rentals, this one is in the middle of all the action. Ranging $150-450 per night, Chun's offers 3 set-ups; the smaller studio with private bath and queen-size bed in the back ($150) is the best deal. The beachfront rooms are more "deluxe," but so are their prices. AmEx/D/MC/V. ❹

Kaiaka Bay Beach Park, 1 mi. west of town across from the fire department on Haleiwa Rd. The beach park allows free camping with a county permit. The scenery is unbeatable—the park sits directly on the beach. Kaiaka has 7 sites, with restrooms, showers, and picnic tables. Swimming is not safe. Camping prohibited from W 8am to F 8am. Gates lock daily 6:45pm-7am. See **Camping in Hawaii,** p. 82, for more info. ❶

FOOD

From a variety of ethnic tastes to plenty of fresh fish, Kamehameha Hwy. is littered with seemingly endless dining opportunities. Shave ice is not in want, either. Vegetarians will have no problem finding their fare here.

Celestial Natural Foods, 66-445 Kamehameha Hwy., next to the post office, has been supplying the North Shore with healthy, organic, and natural food since 1974. It has a large selection of produce, packaged foods, vitamins, and health care products. (☎808-637-6729. Open M-F 9am-6pm, Su 10am-6pm. MC/V.) **Malama Market,** 66-190 Kamehameha Hwy., in the center of town, sells basic staples and produce. There's a deli, bakery, and ATM inside. (☎808-637-4520. Open daily 7am-9pm. AmEx/D/MC/V.) Across the street, **Haleiwa Super Market,** 66-197 Kamehameha Hwy., has similar offerings. (☎808-637-5004. Open M-Sa 8am-8pm, Su 8:30am-5:30pm. AmEx/D/MC/V.) Many opt to do their shopping at the **Foodland** in Waimea (p. 168), which has a bigger selection.

RESTAURANTS

Banzai Sushi, 66-246 Kamehameha Hwy. (☎808-637-4404), in the North Shore Marketplace. This dinner-only sushi bar is the local favorite for wrapping up a hard day's work. Most of the seating is on the breezy deck, where an international-surfer-bohemian crowd kicks back on the padded floor seating in front of a projection screen playing surfing footage. Maki rolls $8-14, sashimi dinners $21-35. Open daily 5-9:30pm; W and Su nights go much later with local live music and $3 Red Stripe specials. MC/V. ❸

Haleiwa Joe's, 66-011 Kamehameha Hwy. (☎808-637-8005). Though you could probably dine undisturbed in board shorts and flip-flops, this is one of Haleiwa's most upscale dining options. *Pupu* (*ahi* spring rolls $10, Thai fried calamari $8.50) are a popular barstool stop, and the fresh fish entrees are well-prepared, with plenty of rice and veggies on the side. Wine selection is excellent and reasonably priced (glasses $5-7). M-F aloha hour 4:30-6:30pm (discounted fish, drinks, and *pupu*). Lunch daily

11:30am-4:15pm. Dinner M-Th 5:30-9:30pm, F-Sa 5:30-10:30pm, Su 5-9:30pm. F features live music (21+; $10 cover). AmEx/MC/V. ❹

Haleiwa Eats, 66-079 Kamehameha Hwy. (☎808-637-4247). Considering Haleiwa is about 30 years behind Honolulu, the cool quotient of this small Thai restaurant is surprisingly high. The colorful tiled interior and red lotus flower light fixtures create a relaxed ambience in which to enjoy inexpensive curries, noodle dishes, and sautees (all $12). Sit in the indoor or outdoor seating area, take yours to go, or simply grab a sweet Thai iced tea ($4). Open daily noon-9:30pm. AmEx/MC/V. ❷

Kono's, 66-250 Kamehameha Hwy. (☎808-637-9211), in the North Shore Marketplace. Go to Kono's for their jam-packed breakfast burritos filled with scrambled eggs, potatoes, sour cream, avocado, and your choice of Portuguese sausage, bacon, or roasted vegetables ($5.59). Kono's bottomless Kona coffee is a perfect pick-me-up and, at $2, an awesome deal. Their *kalua* pig is also a specialty ($9). Open daily 8am-3:30pm. Breakfast served 8am-1pm. Cash only. ❶

Grass Skirt Grill, 66-214 Kamehameha Hwy. (☎808-637-4852), right next to Strong Current Surf Shop. This may be the best place in town to taste the day's fresh catch. Usually *ahi, hebi, mahi mahi,* or *ono*; have it grilled then topped with their signature sauce ($13). Open daily 11am-6pm. Cash only. ❷

KuaAina, 66-160 Kamehameha Hwy. (☎808-637-6067). Seats are often hard to come by at this jam-packed sandwich and burger joint. Kua Aina makes a case for their claim of the "world's best hamburgers" by adding a Hawaiian twist; try yours with avocado or pineapple ($6.50-8). Crispy fries ($3) are a perfect compliment. Open daily 11am-8pm. Cash only. ❶

Cholo's Homestyle Mexican, 66-250 Kamehameha Hwy. (☎808-637-3059), in the North Shore Marketplace. Fun, festive, and always packed. Try the *tamale* plate ($13) which contends with the ever-popular grilled *ahi* fish tacos ($13) as the local favorite. Head to the bar for one of Cholo's famous margaritas (specialty Cadillac margarita $8.50). Open daily 11am-9:30pm. Bar open F-Sa until 10:30pm. AmEx/MC/V. ❸

Breakers, 66-250 Kamehameha Hwy. (☎808-637-9898), in the North Shore Marketplace. This lively bar and grill is a frequent hangout for surfers, surf enthusiasts, and surf-loving tourists alike. The breezy space is marked by surfboards on the ceiling and surfing footage on the TVs. One of the few places on the North Shore open past 11pm, Breakers is probably best enjoyed from a seat at the bar. Try the *ahi poke* in a ginger glaze ($8). Most entrees under $20. 2 happy hours daily 4-6pm and 9-11pm. Mixed drinks $7.50. Su Jazz 6-9pm. Open daily 11am-11pm. AmEx/D/MC/V. ❸

ON THE MENU

AÇAÍ BOWLS

Every winter, the huge North Shore waves attract a host of hopeful surfers from every corner of the world. More than any other nation, the smiling Brazilian nationals have left their mark, as well as some of their countrymen. The tastiest vestige of this influence has recently become a North Shore staple at breakfast, lunch, snack, or even dinner: açaí.

This frozen concoction is unparalleled in scrumptious goodness, and it also happens to be one of the healthiest drinks around. For $5-7, it'll keep your wallet in good shape as well.

Açaí is a dark purple berry that grows atop Amazonian palm trees. The caffeinated berry contains 10-30 times the antioxidants of red wine and over two times that of blueberries. Once the pulp is harvested, it must be processed and frozen within 24hr. in order to preserve its nutritional benefits.

The pulp is then thrown into a blender along with other berries and guarana juice. For the authentic experience, order an açaí bowl. More of a meal than a snack, the bowl is filled with sliced bananas, granola, and honey.

While there are a number of açaí sources along the North Shore, the best is **Kava Roots** (☎808-638-5282), inside Devocean, a boutique across the street from Foodland on Pupukea Rd. Açaí bowl $6.75. Open 8:30am-6:30pm.

BAKERIES AND CAFES

🔲 **Coffee Gallery,** 66-250 Kamehameha Hwy. (☎808-637- 5355), in the North Shore Marketplace. Everyone in Haleiwa might well come here for their daily caffeine fix. Though the menu offers a variety of wraps ($5) and smoothies ($3.75), patrons are drawn to the good conversation, great atmosphere, and top-quality beans, roasted fresh on-site daily. Small cups of 100% Hawaiian java will only set you back $1.50. Coffee Gallery also ships their unique roasts and blends all over the country. Free Wi-Fi. Internet terminal ($4 per 30min.) and ATM. Open daily 6:30am-8pm. AmEx/D/MC/V. ❶

Waialua Bakery, 66-200 Kamehameha Hwy. (☎808- 637-9079). One of Haleiwa's highlights, known for its excellent baked goods (cookies $1-1.50) and juice bar (smoothies, $4-5). The fresh loaves of bread (honey white $2.75, wheat $3, cheese and herb $4) are soft and make great sandwiches ($5-7.50). Try the Hungry Hawaiian ($6.50) and look for special breads like pineapple banana. Open M-Sa 9am-4pm. Cash only. ❶

Cafe Haleiwa, 66-460 Kamehameha Hwy. (☎808-637- 5516). Surf paintings, posters, and pictures line the walls of this diner where you can try their popular fruit bowl ($6.25) or their daily specials like banana-nut bread ($3.50). For breakfast, try "Breakfast in a Barrel" (egg and potato burrito with salsa and cheese, $8) or "Dawn Patrol" (2 buttermilk pancakes with 2 eggs any style, $4.50). For your caffeine fix, there is hot java from the espresso bar in back. Lunch around $10. Open daily 7am-2pm. Breakfast M-Sa until 12:30pm; lunch M-Sa 11am-2pm. No lunch on Su. AmEx/MC/V. ❶

SHAVE ICE

Shave ice is to Haleiwa what gelato is to Venice—you're doing yourself a disservice if you pass up these cheap, colorful, and tasty treats.

🔲 **Matsumoto Shave Ice,** 66-087 Kamehameha Hwy. (☎808-637-4827). By far the most famous shave ice place—tour buses stop right outside, and the line is always long. There is strict protocol for ordering: state how many small or large cones you want, whether you want ice cream and/or sweet azuki beans, and your flavors, but only when asked. Flavors include *li hing mui* (dried plum), *lilikoi* (passionfruit), and pineapple, to name a few. Small $1.75, with ice cream and beans $2.50. Large $2/2.75. Spoonful of condensed milk on top ($0.50). Open daily 9am-6pm. Cash only. ❶

🔲 **Aoki's Shave Ice,** 66-117 Kamehameha Hwy. (☎808-637-7017), next to Matsumoto and just as good. Aoki's has fewer flavors and a shorter line. The same ordering rules as above apply. Small $1.75, with ice cream and beans $2.50. Large $2/2.75. Open daily "Hawaiian Time," usually 11am-6:30pm "almost everyday." ❶

DO YOU SCREAM FOR ICE CREAM? Try your shave ice with a scoop of ice cream. Really. While it sounds dubious, the scoop of vanilla in the bottom of the paper cone will greatly enhance your shave ice experience. The azuki beans are more of an acquired taste. *-Claire Saffitz*

🔲 BEACHES

Although the beaches in town do not compare with the picture-perfect Waimea and Sunset Beaches (p. 170), Haleiwa has a few popular breaks. The beaches east of Haleiwa off Waialua Beach Rd. are frequented by sharks, but there is excellent kiteboarding farther west in Mokuleia.

HALEIWA ALII BEACH PARK. (*Surfing. Open daily 6am-10pm. Lifeguards 9am-5:30pm.*) Though placid during the summer, the winter brings three good surf breaks offshore to the left. The one farthest left is known as **Walls,** to the right of Walls is **Avalanche,** and **Haleiwa** is directly out from the beach park. The last break is a good place for beginners when the waves are small. The small protected bay on the south end of the beach is better-suited for swimmers. The beach, at 66-167 Haleiwa Rd., has restrooms, showers, and picnic tables.

HALEIWA BEACH PARK. *(Surfing. Open daily 5am-10pm.)* In winter, there are two surf breaks off the point on the right side of Haleiwa Beach Park: **Puaena** and expert-only **Puaena Point.** Neither surfing nor swimming is great here due to a shallow and rocky bottom. However, this beach is popular with kayakers and does host a number of summer activities. In late July, this park is also host to the **Haleiwa Arts Festival,** a gathering of local artists that takes over the North Shore for a weekend. For at least one Sunday during the summer, the area becomes the site of an island tradition when locals compete in **outrigger canoe races.** Past Anahulu Bridge on the left when heading to Waimea Bay, it has restrooms, showers, basketball courts, and picnic tables.

KAWAILOA BEACH. *(Surfing. Open daily sunrise to sunset.)* Kawailoa Beach is the catch-all name for the stretch of sandy and rocky coastline between Puaena Point and Waimea. Surfers head to several generally unmarked spots along this stretch to try to catch a wave. The most local of these breaks is **Lani's,** the nickname of Laniakea Beach. Lani's is also called "Turtle Beach," for the green sea turtles that swim to and from shore to bask in the sun. People who get in the way of a turtle's path or touch the creatures will incur a $1000 fine. *(1 mi. northeast of Haleiwa Beach Park. After passing a large horse pasture on the right and driving over a short bridge, park your car on the dry side of the road before the intersection of Pohaku Lao Way and Kamehameha Hwy. Cross the street to the surf break.)*

TIP
> **TURTLE TURTLE.** If you are anxious to see the sea turtles at Laniakea Beach, the best time to go is usually late afternoon. Although the turtles are around all day, the camera-toting crowds have usually cleared out by 5pm.

ACTIVITIES

If it happens in the water, you can do it in Haleiwa, which is home to a good number of outfits that provide equipment rental, surf lessons, dive trips, and (in the winter) whale-watching tours.

Deep Ecology, 66-456 Kamehameha Hwy. (☎808-637-7946; www.deepecologyhawaii. com), next to Cafe Haleiwa, offers snorkel tours (Jun.-Aug. $99), scuba certification, year-round diving (boat dive $139, gear included), and coordinates 3hr. whale and dolphin tours (Jan.-Apr. $99). Open water classes are held 3 days a week (F-Su) and start at $350 for 3 or more people. Open daily 8am-6pm. AmEx/D/MC/V.

Haleiwa Surf N Sea, 62-595 Kamehameha Hwy. (☎808-637-9887; www.surfnsea. com). This place has it all: scuba dives, scuba lessons (non-certified $95), surf lessons (2hr. beginner lesson $75), shark tours, snorkel tours (2hr. $45), windsurfing lessons (2hr. beginner lesson $75), whale-watching tours (Dec.-May $58, ages 2-12 $40), and fishing charters ($300-500). Surfboard rentals 1st hr. $5; $3.50 per each additional hr.; 24hr. $24. Kayaks $15/10/75. Open daily 9am-7pm. AmEx/D/MC/V.

SIGHTS

While Haleiwa's major draws are its unique businesses and world-famous surf breaks, the town also has a few cultural sights worth a quick visit.

NORTH SHORE SURF MUSEUM. "No shirt? No shoes? No problem!" If you couldn't tell from this sign hanging on the front door, we'll let you know: North

THE HIDDEN DEAL

PRODUCE AND PRAWNS ON-THE-CHEAP

While the Dole Plantation beckons visitors as the only major (read: corporate) tourist attraction on the North Shore, you don't have to spend the time or money going there if what you're after is great fresh produce. Just stop at one of the many roadside fruit stands east of Haleiwa on Kamehameha Hwy. You're sure to find some of the best mango, papaya, lychees, and coconut you've ever tasted—and for only a few dollars.

All of the fruit is grown locally, and many varieties are so plentiful during the growing season that squashing them under your feet is unavoidable as you hike. It'll make you cringe to see that $5 mango in the grocery store back home.

Fruit is not the only food you can find for cheap. The North Shore shrimp trucks are legendary on Oahu for their garlicky prawns, dragged out of ponds daily in Kahuku and served fresh. For about $12, you can get a dozen shrimp, cooked to your order with two scoops of rice. The meal is restaurant-quality but half the price. While **Giovanni's** in Haleiwa is the most famous shrimp truck, **Romy's** and **Fumi's** are tough competitors about 7 mi. down Kamehameha Hwy. in Kahuku. The trucks move around and the hours depend on the shrimp supply. Giovanni's is usually parked in the lot just past **Cafe Haleiwa** (p. 176), along with several other high-quality and inexpensive lunch wagons.

Shore Surf is quite possibly the planet's most laid-back museum. Former museum curator Stephen Gould's collection of surf memorabilia includes posters, album covers, monochrome photos by legendary surf photographer LeRoy Grannis, vintage surfboards, and a cool 1936 hollow-bodied "kook box" surfboard—so named because only 'kooks' surfed with it. Browse their selection of jewelry and bottles collected from the ocean floor; all watches are "guaranteed not to work." Chat with current curator "Hurricane Bob" Brown or catch a surfing film in the backroom theater. Most items are for sale. *(66-250 Kamehameha Hwy., in the North Shore Marketplace.* ☎ *808-637-8888. Usually open M and Th-Su 11am-6pm, W 10:30am-5pm. Donations appreciated.)*

LILIUOKALANI PROTESTANT CHURCH. Founded by Protestant missionaries in 1832, the church takes its name from Queen Liliuokalani, who spent her summers in Haleiwa and attended services here (the current building dates to 1961). Services were conducted entirely in Hawaiian until the early 1940s. The numerals on the face of the seven-dial clock are replaced with the letters of the queen's 12-letter name. *(66-090 Kamehameha Hwy., across from Matsumoto Shave Ice.* ☎ *808 637-9364. Service Su 10am.)*

🛒 SHOPPING

In addition to surf boutiques, tourist haunts, and Quiksilver stores, Haleiwa has a number of unique shops and galleries worth perusing.

- 🏄 **Haleiwa Surf N Sea,** 62-595 Kamehameha Hwy. (☎808-637-9887; www.surfnsea.com), just past the Anahulu Bridge on the left when driving away from Haleiwa. Of the town's several surf shops, Haleiwa Surf N Sea is the best known and has the best selection of merchandise. Since 1965, they've supplied the North Shore surf community with affordable boards, accessories, and clothing. Open daily 9am-7pm. AmEx/D/MC/V.

  Tropical Rush Surf Company, 62-620A Kamehameha Hwy. (☎808-637-8886; www.tropicalrushhawaii.com). When Haleiwa Surf N Sea is too busy, head across the street to this pristinely-maintained surf shop. The shop, which shares a building with the Haleiwa General store, offers a variety of gear, from clothing to surf and skim boards (and a free shave ice with purchase!). They also rent equipment; inquire inside (surfboards $20 per day, $100 per week). Open daily 9am-7pm. MC/V.

WAIALUA AND MOKULEIA

At the base of the Waianae Range on the western stretch of the North Shore, Waialua (pop. 3761) was originally a port for the sandalwood trade and, until recently, a prime producer of sugarcane. The town has lacked stable agricultural production since its sugar mill closed in 1996, and the "Home of the World's Best Sugar" is now in the grips of a serious insulin low. Much of the old mill has been converted into a handful of local small businesses, peddling everything from soap to surfboards. The rest of this town is unremarkable and mostly residential. The respectable waves and unpopulated beaches of Mokuleia (pop. 1839) to the west, however, draw adventurous travelers and are ideal for camping and water sports.

⚜ 🔁 ORIENTATION AND PRACTICAL INFORMATION

The small commercial center of Waialua sits where **Goodale Avenue** meets **Kealohanui Street.** To reach Mokuleia from Waialua, drive *mauka* (toward the mountains) on Goodale Ave. and turn right on **Farrington Highway,** which cuts through the center of town and ends 2 mi. before **Kaena Point,** the northwest corner of Oahu. TheBus #76 connects Haleiwa and Waialua.

The **Waialua Public Library,** 67-068 Kealohanui St., has schedules for TheBus and self-serve photocopying ($0.20 per pg.). A 3-month visitor's card ($10) grants the use of four relatively new computers with quick Internet access. (☎808-637-8286. 15min. max. when busy. Open Tu-Th 9am-6pm, F 9am-5pm, Sa 9am-2pm.) Wash your duds at **M and C Washerette.** (☎808 258-8954. Wash $2.50, dry $0.25 per 5 min. Open daily 5:30am-9:45pm.) **ATMs** are located at the **Waialua Federal Credit Union,** the **Aloha Gas station,** and **The Brown Bottle** convenience store (see below). If you've slept through the North Shore Yoga's 7:30am Waimea Valley class (p. 171), there's still time to make the 8:30am class (M-F) at **Bikram's Yoga College of India,** 67-208 Goodale Ave. (☎808-637-5700), in the Waialua Shopping Center behind the library, which offers daily drop-in classes (1hr., $15). The **Waialua Post Office,** 67-079 Nauahi St. (☎800-275-8777; open M-F 8:30am-4pm), is conveniently located. **Postal Code:** 96791.

🏠 🛏 ACCOMMODATIONS AND CAMPING

There are no hotels in Waialua, so travelers must move on to Mokuleia where there are places (though limited) to camp or lodge.

Camp Mokuleia, 68-729 Farrington Hwy. (☎808-637-6241; www.campmokuleia.org), is a serene, palm-tree lined "quiet interval from the world" often booked by conference groups. Its small, windswept beach is frequented by brave swimmers and thrill-seeking kiteboarders. The tent area, in a wooded grove near the beach, has hot-water showers and toilets. Cabins A & B sleep 14, cabins C-F sleep 22, with 2 shared baths in each. 10 double rooms with private bath and 8 double rooms with shared bath. Ropes course, basketball court, volleyball court, swimming pool, and archery. Dining hall offers a substantial lunch ($7.50) and a hefty dinner ($9). Kayaks ($15 per hr.). Reception M-F 8am-5pm, Sa-Su 11am-5pm. Check-in 4pm. Check-out 1pm. Reservations required. Camping fees $15-160 per site per night (sites sleep 2 to 30 people). No alcohol. W no camping. Lodge rooms $80-90; 14-person cabin $190; 22-person cabin $273; 6-person beach house $200; 2-person cottage $90. Parking $5. AmEx/D/MC/V. ❶

YMCA Camp Erdman, 69-385 Farrington Hwy. (☎808-637-4615; www.camperdman.net), about 2 mi. before Camp Mokuleia, on another beautiful, secluded beach. The friendly staff and quiet hours will make you feel like you're back at summer camp. Six 8-person cabins (2 cabins have kitchens), or 15 16-person cabins. Facilities include ropes course, swimming pool, climbing wall, and tennis courts. Meal plans for individuals staying in some cabins for an additional price. Frequently rented to large groups, especially during the summer and weekends; call for availability. Reservations required. Cabins $185. Inquire about possible work exchanges. AmEx/D/MC/V. ❶

SURFING 101

When the words "surf" and "North Shore" fall serendipitously into the same sentence, one hardly expects to find the word "school" tagging alongside. **Surf Hawaii 4 U,** a locally-based surf school with a lot of personality, looks to change this conception.

In the summer months, when the water is clear and the waves calm, the North Shore actually lends itself to the adventurous beginner. Edison de Paula, a world-class big wave rider, heads up the school. When he's not recklessly flying down the face of a 60 ft. wall of rushing water, Edison's focus is teaching novices to surf. Edison is an expert instructor, certified in basically every type of water rescue that exists. His enthusiasm lends itself generously to the business of beginners, and the only screams coming from the water are "yahoos!" What's more, he has an astronomical success rate; even the clumsiest tourists end up standing on a wave.

Surfing is one of the fastest growing sports on the planet, and it's no wonder—the exhilaration of taking off on a thrusting North Shore wave is tough to beat. Edison's surf school opens the door into this world, and his lesson is a foothold you should not miss. His most popular, and most useful, 3hr. introductory course is $150.

Surf Hawaii 4 U, ☎808-295-1241; www.surfhawaii4u.com. MC/V.

🄲 FOOD

Between the library and the Aloha Gas Station is the **Waialua Shopping Center,** 67-208 Goodale Ave., which offers a few dining options. For basic needs, visit the **Waialua General Store,** 67-272 Goodale Ave. (☎808-637-3131. Open daily 9am-7pm.) **The Brown Bottle** sells groceries, beer, wine, and liquor. (Open daily 7am-10:30pm.) Be sure to stock up if you plan on heading west for the night, as there are no convenience stores in Mokuleia. **Waialua Chop Suey ❶,** 67-292 Goodale Ave., in the Waialua Shopping Center, serves local favorites to go. Get the sweet and sour spare ribs ($5.25) for a quick lunch. (☎808-637-1688. Open M-Tu and Th-Sa 10am-7pm, W 10am-3pm, Su 11am-7pm.) **Kaala Cafe ❶,** 66-216 Farrington Hwy., is the last food stop before Mokuleia. If that's not enough to make you pull over, their delicious all-natural açaí bowls ($6), sandwiches ($7) and smoothies ($5-6.50) might change your mind. Try the avocado wrap with papaya seed dressing and sweet chili sauce on a whole wheat tortilla for $7. (☎808-637-7600, in the same building as North Shore Workout.)

🄲 🄺 BEACHES AND HIKING

The beaches and hiking around Mokuleia extend from the touristy Haleiwa coast to the rugged and local Kaena Point. Visitors should use caution; rented vehicles are easy targets for thieves. The safest parking is in the Dillingham Airfield lot, accessible through the northwest entrance.

MOKULEIA BEACH PARK. *(Wind sports. Open daily 7am-7pm.)* Perfect winds sweep gracefully over a shallow clear blue ocean making for kiteboarders' paradise. The sharp reef, visible from shore and not too far beneath the surface of the water limits its swimming and surfing. More sandy sections of the beach are on either side of the park, opposite the Dillingham Airfield. Other popular activities include fishing and beachcombing. The park has porta-potties and showers. Camping is allowed in the park by permit between 8am on Friday and 8am on Wednesday. See **Camping in Hawaii,** p. 82.

KAENA POINT. *(2½ mi. 1-3hr. one-way. Easy.)* Hike or mountain bike from the end of Farrington Hwy. along the path of the former sugarcane railroad leading to Kaena Point (p. 186), a *wahi pana* (celebrated place) for the Hawaiian people. Legend says that Kaena Point, the northwestern tip of Oahu, is a "leaping place of souls," where the spirits of the dead can reunite with their ancestors. The area, designated a Natural Area Reserve since 1983, is a precious part of Hawaiian heritage as one of the islands' last dune ecosystems. Many species here are not found anywhere else in the world. If you opt to take the trek, park your car in the lot overlooking Molukeia's beaches 1 mi. past Camp Erdman.

🎿 ACTIVITIES

Thrilling aerial experiences are available at Dillingham Airfield, on Farrington Hwy., where several adventure sports companies operate. Go to **Glider Port,** the 2nd entrance to Dillingham Airfield, for plane and glider flights. Skydivers should turn in the first entrance while driving west.

Pacific International Skydiving Center, 68-760 Farrington Hwy. (☎808-637-7472; www.pacific-skydiving.com). While 2 companies offer essentially the same package on paper (safe, tandem diving with licensed instructors), locals agree that Pacific, with a perfect safety record, higher dives, and bigger planes, is the superior company. Allot 2hr. to complete the skydive, allowing time to sign a safety waiver and watch an instructional video. $298 plus tax for tandem rates. Open M-F 8am-2pm, Sa-Su 8am-sunset.

Soar Hawaii Sailplanes, (☎808-637-3147; www.soarhawaii.com) offers flying lessons and scenic and aerobatic flights. Call for free hotel pickup from Waikiki. Rides start at $39 for 10min. and go up, though significant discounts are available if you buy your tickets through their website. Open daily 10am-5:30pm.

The Original Glider Rides (☎808-637-0207; www.honolulusoaring.com). 10min.-1hr. glider and sailplane rides. Flights leave every 20min. Flight lessons and "Wild or Mild" aerobatic rides also available. 10min. scenic flight (1-2 passengers) $49-59 per person, 15min. aerobatic flight $149. Open daily 10am-5:30pm.

LEEWARD COAST

The Leeward Coast has been called the Wild West of Oahu. Driving from Honolulu to the Leeward side of the island is like entering New Mexico—arid brown mountains replace lush green ones, and thick tangles of dry undergrowth supplant the canopy of tall trees. This sunnier, drier side of the island has a striking, stark beauty, complemented by some of the least-spoiled and most beautiful beaches on the island, due to a lack of development and tourism; this is also the reason for worse socioeconomic conditions on this part of the island. On calm days, the Pacific resembles a rippling mirror, and in winter, the surf can surge up to 20 ft. in height. Depending on the waves, the Leeward Coast has great conditions for snorkeling, scuba diving, swimming, canoeing, bodyboarding, and surfing. Anyone is bound to get a rush while admiring some of the most liberating swaths of land and sea Oahu has to offer.

The Leeward Coast is home to a large population of Native Hawaiians; despite some foreign development in the area, many locals are possessive of their land and way of life. While there are plentiful campgrounds, if you plan to camp, it's a smart idea to bring some friends along. Don't get caught in the Leeward area alone at night; it's among the more dangerous areas of the island.

▟ TRANSPORTATION

By Bus: TheBus Country Express C, #93 Waianae Coast Express, and Rte. #40 all run up the Leeward Coast as far as **Makaha.** The Country Express C starts at the Ala Moana Shopping Center (1hr., every 30min. 5:09am-8:35pm, last bus leaves Makaha Beach Park 10:18pm) and runs frequently with the fewest stops; the #93 brings commuters from

OAHU'S HOMELESS

As you drive along Oahu's Leeward beaches on Farrington Hwy., you might be surprised at the number of camps along the shore. Hundreds of tents and makeshift shelters line the coast. Not all are used for recreational camping—they are home to much of Oahu's homeless population. It would be wrong, however, to assume that all of these people are jobless or destitute. Many of them are families who simply cannot afford the high cost of living on Oahu.

Honolulu is one of the most expensive cities in the country. The median home price in Honolulu rose to $625,000 in the first quarter of 2006, up 18% over the same period last year. Even on less expensive Leeward Coast, the cost of living is well above the national average. Many of the homeless have jobs, but they simply cannot afford a place to live. Local laws prohibit residences on the beach, so each morning the camps are dismantled and packed into cars, which adults drive to work.

The problem of homelessness has long been a source of embarrassment for Hawaiian lawmakers and the droves of tourists they welcome each year. The state has made recent efforts to build shelters for the homeless, but have not addressed the problem of low-cost permanent housing. The hundreds of tents lining the Leeward Coast on Farrington Hwy. are a testament to the fact the problem isn't going away any time soon.

downtown in the evenings, and runs from the Leeward side to **downtown** in the morning. $2; seniors, ages 17 and under, and disabled persons $1.

By Car: Driving is by far the easiest way to get around the Leeward Coast. Car rentals are available at the airport (p. 102) and Waikiki (p. 132). Waianae is 1hr. from Waikiki. Do not leave valuables in your car, as there is a high incidence of theft in the area.

✳ ORIENTATION

The Leeward Coast encompasses the land west of the Waianae Mountains. To get there, take **H-1 West** from Honolulu for 40min.; H-1 will end at **Highway 93 (Farrington Highway).** From here, the highway goes directly up the coast, past the rural communities of **Nanakuli, Maili, Waianae,** and **Makaha,** and peters out before **Kaena Point.** The paved road ends before Kaena Point State Park, and it is nearly impossible to drive around the western tip of the island.

🛈 PRACTICAL INFORMATION

City Hall: Waianae Satellite, 85-670 Farrington Hwy. (☎808-696-6371), at the Neighborhood Community Center, north of where the Kaupuni Channel meets Pokai Bay. Bus schedules, bus passes, and camping permits available. Open M-F 8am-4pm.

Banks: Bank of Hawaii, 86-120 Farrington Hwy. (☎808-696-4227), in the Waianae Mall Shopping Center. Open M-Th 8:30am-4pm, F 8:30am-6pm. **First Hawaiian Bank,** 86-020 Farrington Hwy. (☎808-696-7041). Open M-Th 8:30am-4pm, F 8:30am-6pm.

Library: Waianae Public Library, 85-625 Farrington Hwy. (☎808-697-7868). **Internet access** with 3-month visitor's card ($10). Open M-Tu and Th-Sa 9am-5pm, W 1-8pm.

Equipment Rental: Hale Nalu Surf and Bike, 85-876 Farrington Hwy. (☎808-696-5897; www.halenalu. com), on the right side of the highway heading north. Snorkeling gear ($8 per 24hr., $24 per week), bodyboards ($12/38), shortboards ($19/70), longboards ($22/80), fins ($5/15), and bicycles ($22/80). Open daily 10am-7pm. AmEx/D/MC/V.

Internet: Cyberwest Internet Cafe, (☎808-695-9200). $6 per hr. ($4.75 with student ID), $4 per 30min. Open M-F 9am-8pm, Sa-Su 10am-7pm.

Police: Waianae Station, 85-939 Farrington Hwy. (☎808-696-4221). **Kapolei Station,** 1100 Kamokila Blvd. (☎808 692-4262).

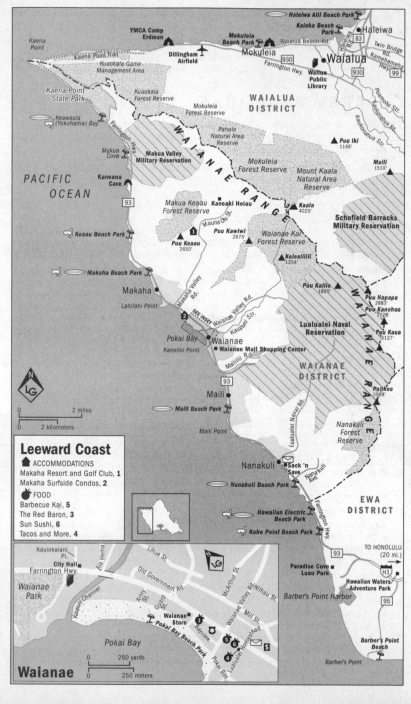

Leeward Coast

ACCOMMODATIONS
Makaha Resort and Golf Club, **1**
Makaha Surfside Condos, **2**

FOOD
Barbecue Kai, **5**
The Red Baron, **3**
Sun Sushi, **6**
Tacos and More, **4**

Waianae

OAHU

Medical Services: Waianae Coast Comprehensive Health Center, 86-260 Farrington Hwy. (☎808-696-7081), turn right onto Mailiilii Rd. 24hr. emergency care.

Post Offices: Nanakuli Post Office, 87-2070 Farrington Hwy., next to Sack 'n Save. Open M-F noon-4pm. **Waianae Main Office,** 86-014 Farrington Hwy. (☎808-696-0161). Open M-F 8am-4:15pm, Sa 9am-noon. **Postal Code:** 96792 (Waianae).

☎ ACCOMMODATIONS

There are few accommodations on the Leeward side of Oahu. Camping at a county beach park is allowed with a permit, but it may be unsafe. **Let's Go does not recommend camping at Leeward beaches.**

Makaha Resort and Golf Club, 84-626 Makaha Valley Rd. (☎808-695-9544; www.makaharesort.net). From Farrington Hwy., turn right on Makaha Valley Rd. and follow the signs. All of the spacious, comfortable rooms have 2 doubles or 1 king-size bed, with bath, cable TV, A/C, mini-fridge, and *lanai* with patio seating. Amenities include a restaurant and bar, large pool, and golf course nestled in the striking Makaha Valley. Free parking. A friendly staff is always available to shuttle guests around the sprawling grounds on one of the resort's many golf carts. Reception 24hr. Check-in 3pm. Check-out noon. Rooms $109-500. Call or go online for special rates. AmEx/D/MC/V. ❹

Makaha Surfside Condos, 85-175 Farrington Hwy. (☎808-696-6991; www.rmmanagementllc.com), 1 mi. south of Makaha Beach Park. This 4-story cinder block condominium sits on the beach and owners rent 1 bed, 1 bath units independently to visitors; conditions and rates vary. Pool, hot tub, and coin-op laundry. A bulletin board inside the complex lists owners who rent out rooms. Most units are rented on a monthly basis and average about $900. Office open M-F 8-5pm, Sa 8am-noon. ❷

◖ FOOD

Most of the dining options on the Leeward side are in Waianae, and many are fast-food joints. **The Waianae Store,** 85-863 Farrington Hwy., sells inexpensive groceries. (☎808-696-3131. Open M-F 7am-9pm, Sa-Su 7am-8pm. D/MC/V.) A wider selection can be found in **Sack 'n Save,** 87-2070 Farrington Hwy., in Nanakuli. (☎808-668-1277. Open daily 5am-11pm. AmEx/D/MC/V.)

ROADFOOD. If you get hungry driving up Farrington Hwy., stop at one of the unnamed plate lunch stands on the side of the road. They grill fresh steak and chicken, served Hawaiian-style with rice and macaroni salad ($6-8).

Tacos and More, 85-993 Farrington Hwy. (☎808-697-8800). The Leeward Coast is possibly the last place you'd expect to find great Mexican food on Oahu, but Tacos & More is the real deal. Mexican favorites such as *flautas, carne asada, chile relleno,* and tacos are homemade. All menu items under $15, most under $10. Margaritas $7. Dine in their newly expanded space or take it to go. Open M-Sa 11am-8pm. AmEx/MC/V. ❷

The Red Baron, 85-915 Farrington Hwy. (☎808-697-1383), is a cozy restaurant that mixes local flavor and Italian fare, with dishes like the spaghetti plate lunch (served until 5pm; $8). The specialty pizzas ($9-14 for a small) are popular. "Pezzoli's Passion" is a water glass of chianti, served "only to those of robust temperament" for $1.75. Beer $2.75-3.25. Open M-Th 11am-9pm, F-Sa 11am-10pm. AmEx/MC/V. ❷

Sun Sushi, 85-979A Farrington Hwy. (☎808-696-5518). Sun Sushi serves fresh sushi rolls and large bentos at low prices (8 piece maki $3.50-6, 15 piece lunch bento $6). Open daily 10am-8pm. Closed 1st and 3rd M of the month. Cash only. ❶

Barbecue Kai, 85-973 Farrington Hwy. (☎808-696-7122), at Waianae Valley Rd. Their Barbecue Mix Plate comes with chicken, teriyaki steak, and barbecue short ribs ($7). Open M-Tu and Th-Su 8am-11pm, W 8am-10pm. Cash only. ❶

🅖 BEACHES

Beautiful beaches with uncrowded sand, clear water, and excellent conditions are the biggest draw of the Leeward Coast. Always check with lifeguards for current surf conditions. Be wary of broken glass in parking lots. The following beaches are listed from south to north.

NANAKULI BEACH PARK. *(Bodyboarding. Open daily 5am-9pm. Lifeguards daily.)* This popular local beach is in the Native Hawaiian stronghold of Nanakuli. A lifeguard mans the south end of this steep, rolling, gold sand shoreline whose calmer waters are usually gentle enough for swimming. The beach, referred to locally as "Subland," also sees traffic from canoers, fishermen, and local bodyboarders. In the middle of the beach is a camping area referred to as "The Flats," with 14 sites that are primarily populated by locals. *(Nanakuli is north of Hawaiian Electric Beach Park. Turn left into the parking lot at Nanakuli Ave.. The park has restroom and shower facilities, basketball courts, a baseball diamond, and a playground.)*

MAILI BEACH PARK. *(Bodyboarding. Surfing. Open daily 5am-9pm. Lifeguards daily.)* Named for the numerous *iliili* (pebbles) found along its shoreline, Maili's long, wide stretch of sand is especially popular among Leeward locals. There are two well-known surf spots: "Tumbleland," at the center of the beach, and "Green Lanterns," at the northernmost edge, but they are for experienced surfers only. The best spot to swim is near the lifeguard stands. Swimmers should watch for boat traffic from the nearby jetty. There are picnic tables, restrooms, and showers. *(At the south end of the town of Maili.)*

MAKAHA BEACH PARK. *(Snorkeling. Surfing. Open daily 5am-9pm. Lifeguards daily.)* Makaha is famous for its ferocious winter surf (averaging 5-8 ft., with the occasional 15-footer), several surfing competitions, and amazing sunsets. The beach is also popular on waveless days, when the calm water makes swimming safe and superior scuba diving possible in "Makaha Caverns," the coral and lava caves 150 yd. offshore, where dolphins, eels, manta rays, turtles, and white-tipped reef sharks frequently roam. Makaha also has some of the best snorkeling on the Leeward Coast along the reef on the north end of the beach. The beach has picnic

LOCAL LEGEND

SHARK-MAN ATTACKS

A number of captivating legends revolve around the Leeward Coast and its graphic mythology. The **Kaneana Cave,** legendary for its ritualism and magic, is steeped with stories about its history. Best known is the story of **Kamohoalii,** the shark god known today as "Makua Charley," who sired a son with a Hawaiian woman. His son—a half-man, half-shark—was called **Nanaue** and lived in what is now Kaneana Cave. When Nanaue was born, he was just like any other boy except that he had a shark mouth on his back, which he concealed by wearing a cape made of tree bark. As he grew up, his grandfather fed him animal meat in hopes that he would become a brave, strong warrior. However, Nanaue developed a strong taste for meat that could only be sated by human flesh, and he began devouring humans. If a swimmer was alone in the water, Nanaue would dive in, transform into a shark, and eat the unsuspecting victim to satisfy his craving.

Kaena Point is another area that features prominently in Hawaiian mythology. As the westernmost point on the island, and the closest to the setting sun, it was thought to be the jumping point, or *leina kauhane*, into Po, the Hawaiian spiritual underworld, or "sea of eternity." The souls of the dead were tested before they could jump off; those who had led an honest life could continue to Po, but those who did not were doomed to wander the island.

tables, restrooms, showers, and lifeguard towers. *(North of Makaha Valley Rd., off Farrington Hwy. Park on the ocean side of the road.)*

KEAWAULA BAY (YOKOHAMA BAY). *(Bodyboarding. Snorkeling. Surfing. Open daily 5am-9pm. Lifeguards daily.)* On the tip of the island, Keawaula Bay is the gem of the Leeward Coast. Nicknamed "Yokohama Bay," and affectionately called "Yoko's," the wide stretch of secluded white sand curves along a vast expanse of crystal-clear water. Watching the powerful waves break is a liberating experience, but only expert surfers, bodyboarders, and bodysurfers should try to tackle them. The beach catches the north, south, and west swells year-round, creating waves as large as 8 ft. in summer and 20 ft. in winter. Snorkeling and scuba diving are popular in gentle water, and local fishermen crowd the point at the end of the beach. There are restrooms and showers. *(Keawaula Bay is at the end of Farrington Hwy., in Kaena State Park, p. 186.)*

SIGHTS AND HIKES

KAENA POINT STATE PARK. Kaena translates to "the heat," appropriate as the point is one of the hottest and driest spots on the island. The park is almost completely undeveloped and untouched, and is home to the beautiful **Keawaula Bay** (p. 186). In 1983, Kaena Point Natural Area Reserve, which encompasses Kaena Point and its surroundings, was created to protect the region's rare coastal lowland dune ecosystem. Laysan albatross, Hawaiian monk seals, green sea turtles, and dolphins are among the animals that frequent the point. Excellent conditions for surfing, snorkeling, and scuba diving make for a nature-lover's paradise. *(At the end of Farrington Hwy.)*

KANEAKI HEIAU. This 17th-century site is Oahu's most authentically restored *heiau*. Visitors observe ancient Hawaii reincarnated with traditional prayer towers and altars. Plentiful taro root patches have led archaeologists to believe the *heiau* was originally dedicated to Kane, the god of agriculture. It was remodeled three times, each by a different chief whose purpose was to renew and strengthen the people's relationship with the gods. The temple was restored to the sacrificial arrangement it was left in; it is very likely that human sacrifice took place here in the past. Today, it is a site of spiritual ceremonies for Native Hawaiians. *(Take Farrington Hwy. to Makaha Valley Rd. and turn right. Pass the Makaha Golf Resort and make a right onto Mauna Olu St. Check in with the guard at the security gate and follow the signs to the heiau, which sits inside a private residential community. Open Tu-Su 10am-2pm. Visitors can only enter by car. Free.)*

MAKUA COVE. A blue emergency call box marks this sandy beach, located on one of the most secluded and undeveloped parts of Oahu (translation: no lifeguards or facilities). Dolphins frequently swim near shore each morning. Remember that it is illegal to get within 50 ft. of them. *(1 mi. north of Kaneana Cave near the beginning of Kaena State Park. An unpaved parking lot is next to a gate that is closed during the week, but visitors can still reach the beach.)*

OAHU

THE BIG ISLAND

Let's come clean about the Big Island: it's not exactly the destination of choice for resort-hopping high rollers. While many Hawaiian tourists are willing to settle for no more than a crowded Waikiki sunset, Big Island visitors watch the sun go down from empty cliffs, overlooking the Kohala Mountain Range; or at the end of an unmarked trail, near a 1200 ft. waterfall; or at the summit of Mauna Kea, huddled around a warm Jeep, 1000 ft. above the clouds. Vacationers do not come here for the nightlife; they're here to explore a vastly untouched natural enigma. In this island alone, 11 out of the world's 13 climate regions are represented. From the subarctic tundra conditions of the Mauna Loa summit to the lush rainforests of the Hamakua coast to the dry and barren lava-covered Kau desert, a day of hiking can take visitors through a natural display more diverse than a roadtrip across the continental US. Yet a vacationer's paradise can still be found here; when you're done flirting with the rawest forces of nature, some of the state's most beautiful beaches are waiting, with Mai Tais on tap.

The Big Island has an unmistakable spiritual force. A legacy of the historical *mana* (spiritual power) remains on this most sacred island, the birthplace of Hawaii's most powerful king, Kamehameha I. In addition to the tangible energy that still emanates from the ancient *heiau* (temples) and historic villages dotted about the island, the volcanic rumble from below creates an exciting atmosphere. While development rapidly encroaches on the Kohala Coast and Kailua-Kona, the quintessence of the island is still preserved in the unadulterated landscape of the rest of the island. By foot, bike, horse, surfboard, or kayak, the island is an adventure-seeker's paradise.

HIGHLIGHTS OF THE BIG ISLAND

SNORKEL among a rainbow of fish in Kealakekua Bay (p. 203).

CLIMB DOWN to the floor of Waipio Valley (p. 243) to a secluded, mile-long beach.

TRAVERSE the Kilauea Iki Crater, only 40 years ago a lake of lava (p. 214).

FEEL YOUR JAW DROP at the stunning 400 ft. Akaka Falls (p. 239).

STARGAZE from the summit of Mauna Kea (p. 235).

✈ INTERISLAND TRANSPORTATION

The Big Island has two major airports. **Keahole-Kona International Airport,** Keahole Airport Rd. (☎808-329-3423), 8 mi. north of downtown Kailua-Kona off Rte. 19, is closest to South Kohala's crescent of resorts and sees the majority of international traffic. It is also served by interisland carriers. Flights from the Big Island to neighboring islands start at around $90 each way. **Hawaiian Airlines** (☎800-367-5320; www.hawaiianair.com) flies from Kona to: Honolulu, Oahu; Kahului, Maui; and Lihue, Kauai (via Honolulu). **go! airlines** (☎888-435-9462; www.iflygo.com) offers some of the cheapest rates between Kona and: Honolulu, Oahu; Kahului, Maui; Hoolehua, Molokai; Lihue, Kauai (via Honolulu); and Lanai City, Lanai (via Kahului). Surfers beware: both Hawaiian and go! charge a fee for surfboards (and go! only takes surfboards under 6 ft.).

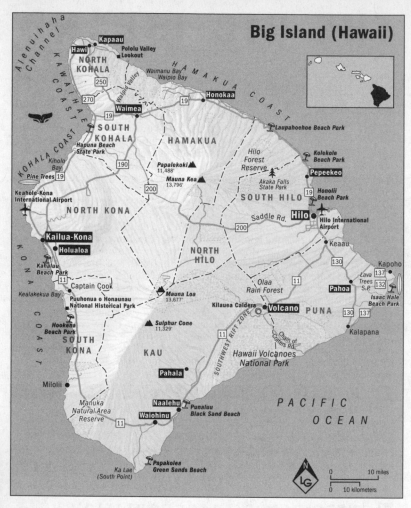

Big Island (Hawaii)

A half mile south of the intersection of Rte. 11 and Rte. 19, **Hilo International Airport,** Airport Access Rd. (☎808-934-5840), sees mostly interisland flights, but it is also served by **United Airlines** (☎800-241-6522). Both **go!** and **Hawaiian** fly from Hilo to Honolulu, Oahu, and connect to the neighboring islands through Honolulu. An $8-10 taxi is the only transportation from the airport to Hilo.

⌸ TRANSPORTATION

Based in Hilo, the **Hele-On Bus** (☎808-961-8744; www.co.hawaii.hi.us/mass_transit/heleonbus.html) is the Big Island's only island-wide system of public transport. Buses are clean, modern, comfortable, and ⌸**free!** Luggage, backpacks, and bicycles are $1 per piece. Unfortunately, catching a bus from anywhere other than downtown Hilo can be a challenge. This can be problematic because most inexpensive flights (especially those via Honolulu) now arrive in Kona, where the only bus out of town departs daily at 6:50 am.

Renting a **car** is the best and most convenient way to see the Big Island. Many beaches, volcanoes, and waterfalls are otherwise inaccessible. Although 4WD is not necessary, it does make getting to more remote locations possible. Such vehicles may be hard to come by because most rental companies only allow their cars on paved roads and assume that visitors who abide by contract shouldn't need 4WD. Only a handful—including **Alamo, Dollar,** and **Harper**—guarantee 4WD upon reservation. **AAA** (☎800-736-2886) provides roadside assistance to cardholders throughout the Big Island, but excludes coverage of the Kona half of Saddle Rd. Call ahead for complete coverage information. For intercity and local transportation, see the **Transportation** section of each town.

⌂ ACCOMMODATIONS

Budget travelers do best on the Hilo side, where a handful of **hostels** offer beds for $20 per night and public transportation to Volcanoes National Park and the Waipio Valley area is feasible. **B&Bs** have been popping up all over the Big Island (especially in South Kona and along the Hamakua Coast), offering the best mid-range accommodations. The **Hawaii Island B&B Association, Inc.** is a collection of over 50 B&B owners. Their website, www.stayhawaii.com, lists accommodations by region. **B&Bs Online** (www.bbonline.com/hi/region4.html) is another good resource, with links to B&B websites throughout the Big Island. For a longer stay, **vacation rentals** are another affordable alternative. In addition to the booking agencies listed in the accommodations section for Kailua-Kona (p. 189), **West Hawaii Property Services,** 78-6831 Alii Dr., Ste. 234A (☎808-322-6696; www.konarentals.com), is another excellent option. Hotels ($50-200) are ubiquitous in downtown Hilo and Kona, and mega-resorts ($250-the moon) line the beaches of South Kohala. Low season (April 15-December 15) can offer discounts of up to 40% at even the swankiest establishments. If you plan to stay for more than a week, **www.craigslist.org** makes finding a room to rent quite easy, especially in Kona, Pahoa, and Hilo.

KAILUA-KONA

Most people will arrive in the city of Kona (pop. 9870) and wonder where the heck the city is. Is this just a local surfer town? The answer is a resounding "yes." While some remember the town as a tourist trap in earlier years, the only tourist destinations are quickly being run out of town. The quaint city of Kona is home to many proud residents, some of whom have just moved here from the mainland and some of whom have been here since birth. Though Kona is not full of bumpin' clubs and swank bars, there is still plenty to entertain the adventurous traveler. Cafes, bistros, and surfer shops pepper the waterfront and 4WD paths lead to some of the most pristine beaches around.

⊟ TRANSPORTATION

Flights: Keahole-Kona International Airport, Keahole Airport Rd. (☎808-329-2484), is 7 mi. north of downtown Kona, off Rte. 19. Keahole is served by international and interisland carriers: **Hawaiian Airlines** (☎800-882-8811; www.hawaiianair.com); **Island Air** (☎800-323-3345; www.islandair.com); and **go!** (☎888-435-9462; www.iflygo.com).

Buses: Public transportation is minimal. The **Hele-On Bus** (☎808-961-8744; www.co.hawaii.hi.us/mass_transit/heleonbus.html), the only option on the Big Island, is based in Hilo. Catching a bus anywhere else can be quite a feat. Check the website for schedules. A free bus departs M-Sa at 6:50am from the Matsuyama Store at 73-4354 Mamalahoa Hwy. and passes through **Waimea** (1hr.) on its way to **Hilo** (3hr.).

Taxis: Aloha Taxi (☎808-329-7779). Call 24hr. in advance for their 6-person van. Other options include **C&C Taxi** (☎808-329-0008), **Dakine Taxi** (☎808-329-4446), and **Mel's Taxi** (☎808-329-1977), which have island-wide service. Taxis usually run 6am-9pm. Charge $3 for first mi. and $2.40 per additional mi. Airport to town $25.

Car Rentals:

In the airport: **Alamo** (☎808-329-8896 or 800-462-5266). 21+. Under-25 surcharge $25 per day. Open daily 5:30am-9pm. **Avis** (☎808-327-3000 or 800-331-1212). 25+. Open daily 5am-9pm. **Budget** (☎808-329-8511 or 800-527-7000). 25+. Open 5am-9:30pm. **Dollar** (☎800-342-7398). 21+. Under-25 surcharge $20 per day. Open daily 5am-9pm. **Thrifty** (☎800-367-2277). 21+. Under-25 surcharge $20 per day. Open daily 5:30am-10pm.

Beyond the airport: ▨**Enterprise,** 74-5583 Luhia St. (☎808-331-2509). Operates out of a hard-to-find office in the industrial center on Luhia St., off Kaiwi St., 8 mi. from the airport. Although it'll cost you a taxi ride to get to the office from the airport, the excellent service and basement prices make this one of the best car rental companies on the island. Get a ride from the airport with **Mel's Taxi** (see above) for a special Enterprise discounted rate ($20).

✦ ORIENTATION

Kailua-Kona lies on the western, leeward coast of the Big Island, sheltered by cloud-covered Halualai (still considered active by volcanologists). From Keahole-Kona Airport, **Route 19** runs south toward Kona, becoming **Route 11** after crossing **Palani Road.** Take note that Rte. 11 is also referred to as **Hawaii Belt Road** or **Mamalahoa Highway,** and Rte. 19 is also called **Queen Kaahumanu Highway.** North of Palani Rd., Rte. 19 cuts through the lava fields of South Kohala, whose banks hide excellent beaches and a resort-lined coast. Heading south, Rte. 11 leads to the slow-paced coffee towns **Holualoa** and **Captain Cook,** and the dramatic Kealakekua Bay. Uphill from Rte. 11, Palani Rd. ascends inland to become **Route 190,** the way to Waimea and **Saddle Road.** Descending into town, it crosses **Kuakini Highway** and becomes **Alii Drive,** Kona's seawall-hugging main street.

▧ PRACTICAL INFORMATION

There are two **Visitor Information Centers** (☎808-329-3423) at the Kona Airport, but it is often difficult to catch an employee. Free maps and pamphlets are available even if no one's there to answer questions. Costco members with a car save almost $0.30 per gallon by using the **Costco gas station,** 73-5600 Maiau Street (☎808-331-4800). From the airport, take Rte. 19 south and turn left on Hina Lani St. Turn right on Kanalani St. and left onto Maiau St.

TOURIST AND FINANCIAL SERVICES

Bank: Bank of Hawaii, 75-5595 Palani Rd. (☎808-326-3900), next to the Lanihau Center, exchanges currency. 24hr. ATM. Open M-Th 8:30am-4pm, F 8:30am-6pm.

Equipment Rental: If you're planning to snorkel for more than a week, consider purchasing your own flippers at **Walmart,** on Henry St., above Hwy. 11. Full snorkel set: adult $35, junior $15. Otherwise, check out the listings below.

Honu Sports, 75-5744 Alii Dr., #108 (☎808-327-3483; www.honusports.com), in the Kona Inn Shopping Center. This place is put-together and professional. Guests meet dive crews in the Honokohau Marina for an array of dives. The Manta Ray Night Dive ($79) is the most popular. Gear available at the shop. Open daily 9am-9pm. AmEx/MC/V.

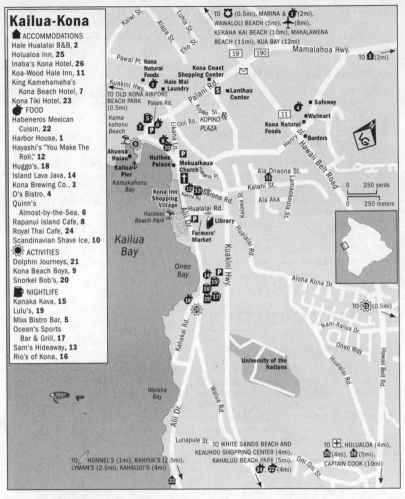

Kailua-Kona

ACCOMMODATIONS
Hale Hualalai B&B, **2**
Holualoa Inn, **25**
Inaba's Kona Hotel, **26**
Koa-Wood Hale Inn, **11**
King Kamehameha's
   Kona Beach Hotel, **7**
Kona Tiki Hotel, **23**
FOOD
Habeneros Mexican
   Cuisin, **22**
Harbor House, **1**
Hayashi's "You Make The
   Roll," **12**
Huggo's, **18**
Island Lava Java, **14**
Kona Brewing Co., **3**
O's Bistro, **4**
Quinn's
   Almost-by-the-Sea, **6**
Rapanui Island Cafe, **8**
Royal Thai Cafe, **24**
Scandinavian Shave Ice, **10**
ACTIVITIES
Dolphin Journeys, **21**
Kona Beach Boys, **9**
Snorkel Bob's, **20**
NIGHTLIFE
Kanaka Kava, **15**
Lulu's, **19**
Mixx Bistro Bar, **5**
Ocean's Sports
   Bar & Grill, **17**
Sam's Hideaway, **13**
Rio's of Kona, **16**

Snorkel Bob's, 75-5831 Kahakai St. (☎808 329 0770) or 73-4976 Kamanu Street #101 (☎808-329-0771) in Hale Kui Plaza, near the airport (www.snorkelbob.com). Snorkel rental $2.50-8 per day, $9-32 per week. Open daily 8am-5pm. AmEx/D/MC/V.

LOCAL SERVICES

Library: Kailua-Kona Public Library, 75-138 Hualalai Rd. (☎808-327-4327), on Hualalai Rd., connecting Kuakini Hwy. to Alii Dr. **Internet access** with a 3-month visitor's card ($10). Appointment needed for 1 of the 3 1hr. terminals, limit 1hr. per week. 15min. walk-in terminal available. Open Tu 11am-7pm, W-Th and Sa 9am-5pm, F 11am-5pm.

Outdoor Supplies: Hawaii Forest and Trail, 74-5035B Queen Kaahumanu Hwy. (☎808-331-8505), next to GasPro. Sells USGS topography and trail maps, water filters, and solar shower contraptions. Open M-F 7am-5:30pm, Sa-Su 7am-4:30pm.

Laundromat: Hele Mai Laundromat, 75-5629 Kuakini Hwy. (☎808-329-3494), in the building next to the Kona Brewing Co. Wash $2.50, dry $0.25 per 8 min. Drop-off service $0.75 per lb., 10 lb. min. Open daily 6am-10pm. Last load 8:45pm.

Weather Conditions: ☎808-961-5582.

EMERGENCY AND COMMUNICATIONS

Police: Kealakehe Station (☎808-326-4646), on Queen Kaahumanu Hwy., about 1 mi. north of town, next to the Kealakehe Transfer Station.

Sexual Assault Crisis Line: ☎808-935-0677.

Pharmacy: Longs Drugs, 75-5595 Palani Rd. (☎808-329-1632), intersection of Hwy. 11 and Palani Rd. in Lanihau Shopping Center. Open M-Sa 8am-9pm, Su 8am-6pm.

Hospital: Kona Community Hospital, 79-1019 Haukapila St. (☎808-322-9311), 15 mi. south of Kona, in Kealakekua. 24hr. emergency room.

Internet Access: In addition to the Kona Public Library, **Island Lava Java,** 75-5799 Alii Dr. (☎808-327-2161), in Alii Sunset Plaza, offers free Wi-Fi for customers. They also have 2 terminals to rent at $3 per 15min., or $10 per hr. Open daily 6am-10pm. For something cooler than coffee, **Scandinavian Shave Ice,** 75-5699 Alii Dr. (☎808-331-1626), in a blue building by the boat harbor on the northern end of Alii Dr., provides 6 terminals for users. $8 per hr. Open M-Sa 10am-9:30pm, Su noon-9pm.

Post Office: Kailua-Kona Post Office, 74-5577 Palani Rd. (☎808-331-8307 or 800-275-8777), next to Lanihau Center. Open M-F 8:30am-4:30pm, Sa 9:30am-1:30pm. **Postal Code:** 96740.

✚ ACCOMMODATIONS

HOTELS, RESORTS, AND B&BS

▨ **Kona Tiki Hotel,** 75-5968 Alii Dr. (☎808-329-1425). Kona Tiki maintains a 50s tropical paradise feel and guests gather around the pool each evening to chat. The hotel is built on a seawall right on the water, and the low-key husband-wife managing pair exude aloha spirit. Although the ground floor can be humid, the 2nd and 3rd floors are breezy and sunlit. Breakfast included. Reception 7am-7pm. Check-in 3pm. Check-out 11am. Reservations essential. Doubles with queen bed $69, queen and twin $82, with kitchenette $92; each additional guest $9, ages 2-12 $6. Cash only. ❸

▨ **Holualoa Inn,** Mamalahoa Hwy. (☎800-392-1812; www.holualoainn.com), 5 mi. from downtown Kona in Holualoa Village. Turn *mauka* (toward the mountains) from Palani Rd. or Kuakini Hwy. onto Halualai Rd. Turn left onto Mamalahoa and look for the inn's sign on the left. Surrounded by Holualoa's quaint art galleries, the secluded 6 rooms in the eucalyptus-floored cedar house are an exceptional retreat. Authentic Kona coffee served at breakfast (daily 7:30-9am). Pool-side day rooms equipped with bath, shower, and luggage storage for guests with late flights. Ages 13+. Doubles $260-290; $30 per additional person. 10% off for 7 or more nights. MC/V. ❺

Inaba's Kona Hotel, 76-5908 Mamalahoa Hwy. (☎808-324-1155), in Holualoa Village, 5 mi. from Kona. Turn left on Mamalahoa Hwy. from Halualai Rd.; the hotel is 1 mi. into town. You can't miss the building—it's all pink! Arrive with respect: the Inaba's old-fashioned residence has been a local fixture since 1926. Back rooms #10 (double and twin) and #11 (double) are steals. High ceilings, wood floors, and sweeping ocean views. Check-in 3pm. Check-out 11am. Reservations essential. 2-night min. Owners will rent any room as a single ($30), double ($40), or triple ($50). Cash only. ❷

Koa-Wood Hale Inn (Patey's Place), 75-184 Ala Ona Ona St. (☎808-329-9663). Heading downhill on Palani Rd., turn left onto Kalani St., then left onto Alahou St., and right onto Ala Onaona St. Essentially a small apartment complex converted into hostel-like accommodations, Koa-Wood nurtures a social, relaxed environment. Dorms are single-sex, with 4 beds per room. Private rooms on the 2nd fl. share a balcony and common room. Kitchen, TV room, coin-op washing machines ($1 per load). Reception daily 8am-noon and 4:30-10pm. Check-in 4:30pm. Check-out 10am. Dorms $25; private rooms $55; one side of the apartment (sleeps 4 people comfortably) $130. MC/V. ❶

Hale Hualalai Bed & Breakfast, 74-4968 Mamalahoa Hwy. (☎808-326-2909; www.hale-hualalai.com). Take Palani Rd. toward the mountain and turn right onto Mamalahoa Hwy. (Hwy. 180). After 1 mi., turn right at the sign. Hale Hualalai is a small, quiet retreat with splendid ocean views. The suites are large, with individual balconies, kitchens, and king-size beds. The owner (and professional chef) lives right on the premises, and cooks up a mean breakfast. Call for reservations. Suites $135 per night. ❹

King Kamehameha's Kona Beach Hotel, 75-5660 Palani Rd (☎866-435-0565; www.konabeachhotel.com), behind Kamakahonu Beach, where Palani Rd. meets Alii Dr. Tucked away in a top-notch location, this spot is away from it all and at the same time right in the mix, as the land where King Kamehameha once resided. Doubles $105-130, check online for discounts. Check-in 3pm. Check-out 11am. AmEx/MC/V. ❹

CONDOS

Visitors who plan to stay for more than a few days can often find better deals with condos than with the line of beach hotels lining Alii Dr.

Hawaii Resort Management, 75-5776 Kuakini Hwy. (☎808-329-3333 or 800-244-4752; www.konahawaii.com), has some amazing deals ranging from $67-113 per day (or around $700 per week) during the low season (Apr. 15-Dec. 14). Magic Sands, Banyan Tree, Billfisher, and many other condo-complexes along Alii Dr. are advertised. ❸

Knutson and Associates, 75-6082 Alii Dr. (☎808-329-6311 or 800-800-6202; www.konahawaiirentals.com), in Casa de Emdeko mall. Upscale options, including the Kona Riviera and Casa de Emdeko. 4-night min. Winter $90-210; summer $70-180. ❸

CAMPING

The closest camping in the area is at ◪**Hookena Beach Park,** p. 201.

◪ FOOD

Groceries are extremely expensive in Kona. Sushi is often more cost-effective than a supermarket run. Do-it-yourselfers can still try **Kona Natural Foods,** 75-1027 Henry St. (☎808-329-2296; open M-Sa 9am-9pm, Su 9am-7pm), in Crossroads Shopping Center, or the 24hr. **Safeway** (☎808-329-2207) next door. For a camping trip stock-up, consider a trip to **Costco Wholesalers.** Home to charter boats that venture off the coast for deep sea fishing, **Honokohau Marina,** 3 mi. north of town off Queen Kaahumanu Hwy., is the best spot to buy fresh ahi steak, charbroiled right on the dock. At the end of each day (3:30-5pm), fishermen display their catches on **Kailua Pier.** For fresh fruit and vegetables, try the **farmers' market,** on Hualalai Rd. next to the library. The avocados are larger than softballs and under $2 (☎808-895-7970. Open W-Su 8am-5pm.)

RESTAURANTS

◪ **Kona Brewing Co.,** 75-5629 Kuakini Hwy. (☎808-334-2739). A happening restaurant and microbrewery with a patio perfect for enjoying one of their award-winning beers such as the Lavaman Red Ale or Lilikoi Passion Fruit Ale (pints $4). You can also try the sampler (four 6 oz. beers, $6.50). Killer pizzas made with the spent grain they used for beer $8-23. Happy hour M-F 3-5pm. Free brewery tours with tasting M-F 10:30am and 3pm. Open M-Th 11am-10pm, F-Sa 11am-11pm. AmEx/D/MC/V. ❸

Habaneros Mexican Cuisine (☎808-324-4688), in the Keauhou Shopping Center on Kamehameha III Rd. right next door to Royal Thai Cafe. Habaneros is rightly recommended by locals as the best Mexican food in town. Basic burritos, quesadillas, and enchiladas $7. Breakfast ($5) until 11:30am. Open M-Sa 9am-9pm. Cash only. ❶

O's Bistro, 75-1027 Henry St., Store 102 (☎808-327-6565; www.osbistro.com), this upscale spot is located in Crossroads Shopping Center, but sacrificing one night of an ocean view for this exceptional food is well worth the loss. Locals rave about the noodle bowls ($10-18), and the Grilled Eggplant Stack ($12) is out of this world. Try the ▨**tuna noodle casserole** with seared ahi tuna ($18). Breakfast $8-12. Dinner $24-32. Open daily 10am-9pm. MC/V. ❹

Quinn's Almost-by-the-Sea, 75-5655A Palani Rd. (☎808-329-3822), next to the Kona Seaside Hotel, just before Palani Rd. becomes Alii Dr. This local favorite earns its keep with a friendly fisherman vibe and exceedingly fresh fare. Sit at the bar for fish and chips ($10) or have a pint. Dinner entrees $18-25. Open daily 11am-10:30pm. MC/V. ❹

Royal Thai Cafe (☎808-322-8424), in the Keauhou Shopping Center. Follow Alii Dr. until it becomes Alii Hwy.; the shopping center is at the corner of Alii and Kamehameha. All the Buddhas in this refined restaurant are smiling for good reason: Royal Thai keeps prices low and food quality high. Curries $9-14. Veggie dishes $8-10. Open M-F 11am-2:30pm and 4:30-9:30pm, Sa 2:30-9:30pm. AmEx/D/MC/V. ❷

Harbor House (☎808-326-4166), in the marina off Hwy. 19, between mi. markers 97 and 98. Packed during happy hour, when an older, local crowd comes to unwind with a ice-cold 18 oz. schooner ($2.75-4.25). The food, primarily fish and chips ($8-9), is decent. It's know as the Kona "Cheers," where everyone's family. Happy hour M-Sa 4-6pm, Su 4-5:30pm. Open M-Sa 11am-7pm, Su 11am-5:30pm. AmEx/MC/V. ❷

Huggo's, 75-5828 Kahakai Rd. (☎808-329-1493), at the south end of Alii Dr., across from the seawall. A great place for a fancy date, this place serves up excellent food but high prices, due in part to its stellar location. Live music nightly. Lunchtime sandwiches $12. For dinner, try Huggo's popular *lilikoi miso ahi* ($35). The vegetarian wild mushroom pasta with ginger ($21) is awesome. Lunch M-F 11:30am-4:30pm, dinner daily 5:30-10pm; bar open daily 5:30pm-12:30am. AmEx/D/MC/V. ❺

CAFES AND TAKE OUT

Island Lava Java, 75-5799 Alii Dr. (☎808-327-2161), diagonally across from Waterfront Row. Look for the red umbrellas. Genial surfer-types serve Kona coffee and fresh-baked goods to an easygoing morning crowd. The chef uses only locally grown produce and fresh greens as his ingredients, making the dishes here some of the best in Kona. People have been known to drive for hours just to get their hands on a huge cinnamon bun ($4.25), but arrive before 9am, when they tend to run out. Oat-berry muffins ($3), brewed iced mochas ($4.55), and hearty sandwiches ($6-8). Dinner specials $16-18. Wi-Fi available to customers only. Open daily 6am-10pm. MC/V. ❷

Hayashi's 'You Make the Roll,' (☎808-326-1322), behind the Sarona Dr. Kona Marketplace Plaza. Mr. Hayashi dishes out sizable sushi rolls to go for unbelievable prices. Fill out a notecard to concoct a personal roll. There's no space inside, but ample outdoor seating includes umbrella-shaded patio furniture. Try the ninja star roll (ahi tuna, shrimp tempura, and avocado). Rolls $2-5. Platters ($23-25) available with 2hr. advance notice. Open M-F 11am-7pm, Sa 11am-4pm. MC/V. ❶

Rapanui Island Cafe, 75 Alii Dr. (☎808-329-0511). A local hotspot with Pacific-rim fusion cuisine, started by a family of New Zealanders. Rapanui has some of the best local cuisine that the Big Island has to offer. Fresh seafood pastas are served up for lunch ($6-16) and for dinner ($10-22). Free parking. Open M-Sa 11:30am-3pm and 5-9pm; Su 5-9pm.

Scandinavian Shave Ice, 75-5699 Alii Dr. (☎808-331-1626). Shave ice is packed into neon blossom cups, then doused with Crayola-colored syrups (small $2.50). The whirring cast-iron ice shavers, swirling colors, and blaring rock music create an entertaining cacophony. Internet access available. Open M-Sa 10am-9pm, Su noon-9pm. MC/V. ❶

◪ BEACHES

The best beaches in Kona are usually accessible only on foot or via unmarked roads left in disrepair to deter an avalanche of visitors. The following beaches are listed in south-to-north order.

KAHALUU BEACH PARK. *(Snorkeling. Surfing. Bodyboarding. Open 6am-11pm. Lifeguards 9am-5pm.)* Once an ancient Hawaiian fishing harbor, Kahaluu is protected by a crumbling seawall that provides calm waters for the giant sea turtles to hang out. They are the compelling reason to visit this beach (certainly not the crude sand or lackluster view). Kahaluu is touted by the locals as the best snorkel spot on the island. All swimmers must keep a distance of 10 ft. from wildlife. Surfers, there's a right/left break beyond the sea wall, but beware; the bay creates strong rip currents. *(5 mi. south of downtown Kona on Alii Dr., near the Keauhou Beach Resort. The park is clearly marked and has plenty of parking.)*

WHITE SANDS BEACH. *(Bodyboarding. Open daily 7am-8pm. Lifeguards 9am-5pm.)* Also called Magic Sands, this beach is the area's most accessible. The promise of white, magic sand draws a large crowd, and the beach is full of bodyboarders and swimmers. *(4 mi. south of downtown Kona on Alii Dr., just past Jameson's.)*

KAMAKAHONU BEACH. *(Open daily until 7pm.)* "King Kam" is a calm inlet amid the busy Alii Dr. The water is gentle, predictable, and usually swarming with kids. A closer view of Ahuena Heiau (p. 197) is attainable by swimming a few yards out. *(In downtown Kona near the intersection of Alii Dr. and Palani Rd.)*

OLD KONA AIRPORT PARK BEACH. *(Open daily 7am-8pm.)* When Kona's first airport closed in 1970, the runway was converted into parking for this state park, perfect for running, walking, and rollerblading. The tranquil mile of beach is close to town, but relatively unused. Old Kona's rocky, dangerous shoreline means swimming is only passable and better watersports can be found elsewhere. *(Follow Kuakini Hwy. north until it ends at a parking lot.)*

WAWALOLI BEACH. *(Surfing. Open daily until 8pm.)* Wawaloli is well known for its warm, protected tide pools, which are great for exploring and deep enough for splashing about. Bathrooms and showers available. A mile to the right, if you face the ocean, is Pine Trees, the most-talked-about surf spot near Kona, with three breaks and a range of surfing levels. Those with 4WD should be able to access it. *(5 mi. north of Kona on Rte. 19, between mi. markers 95 and 94, accessible via the paved entrance to the Natural Energy Lab.)*

KEKAHA KAI BEACH. *(Surfing. Open M-Tu and Th-Su 9am-7pm.)* The bumpy and twisted drive down to the beach entrance is well worth the trouble: a peaceful swath of white sand awaits the adventurous. Save the distant surf break, Mahaiula's, this beach is calm and quiet. Don't forget a water bottle with your towel and sunscreen. *(10 mi. north of Kona, down a rugged road between mi. markers 90 and 91.)*

■ **MAKALAWENA BEACH.** *(Open daily 24hr.)* Isolated and unknown, Makalawena is a 20-30min. walk or a bumpy 4WD ride across baking lava fields. For those seeking exquisite sand and pure blue water and sky, look no further. Just don't forget shoes; the lava rock is incredibly sharp. Fine sand cradles sunbathers, and tide pools provide makeshift bathtubs. No drinking water or facilities. *(The beach is north of Kona on Rte. 19, between mi. markers 89 and 90. Following the dirt path, head left whenever it forks, and then follow the shoreline until you reach white sands.)*

KIHOLO BAY. *(Snorkeling; open 7am-7pm).* Kiholo Bay is better described as a region than as a beach. This stunning bay was once home to a giant fish pond built by Kamehameha the Great in the early 1800's. Snorkeling, swimming, and lava tube exploring are among the many activities Kiholo's sandy land have to offer. Camping is illegal on the beach. *Let's Go* does not recommend camping on this beach. *(Follow a gravel road between mi. markers 82 and 83 on Hwy. 19. If you pass the scenic point coming from Kona, you've gone too far.)*

▓ ACTIVITIES

SNORKELING. Although the island's best snorkeling is south of Kona in Captain Cook (p. 199), a number of companies sail snorkel cruises from the bay. Be sure to bring extra water, sunglasses, and plenty of sunscreen. For a do-it-yourself snorkel experience, head to **Snorkel Bob's** (p. 191) or **Walmart**.

SCUBA DIVING. Even those who aren't certified can have an underwater adventure on an introductory dive for around $125. Open-water certification courses run between 3-4 days ($425). Almost every rental place, including **Kona Beach Boys** (see below), books scuba dives as well. An appealing excursion for experienced divers is ▓**Manta Ray's Night Dive.** Lights attract plankton, which in turn attract manta rays to the dive site; as you sit underwater, the mammoth manta rays will zoom around you in an underwater acrobatic act. Those hesitant to dive deep can try "snuba," a shallower version of scuba diving, also available through **Kona Beach Boys** (see p. 196).

BODYBOARDING. Bodyboard and surfboard rentals are not the easiest finds in town, although certain shops on Alii Dr. carry them. Try **Kahaluu Surf Rentals** at Kahaluu beach. Again, buying a bodyboard at **Walmart** ($40) may be most cost-effective for multiple days of boarding.

CANOEING. Come down to Kamakahonu Beach where the ▓**Kona Boys** (☎808-326-7686; www.konaboys.com) are just hangin' loose in their humble hut. More than just a paddle around the bay, their outrigger trips are adventures into Hawaii's past. Guides explain the significance of the area, focusing on Ahuena Heiau and the past importance of the outrigger canoe as a mode of transport. *(79-7539 Mamalahoa Hwy. Also on the shore at Kamakahonu. Canoe trips $38. 2hr. surf lesson includes rental, $119. Fins and goggles, $10. Open daily 8am- 5pm.)*

DOLPHIN DIVING. For the curious traveler looking for a break from the busy Kona tourist industry, the dolphin tours at **Dolphin Journeys** are unforgettable. Dolphin Journeys offers whale-watching and volcano tours. *(☎808-329-3030; www.dolphinjourneys.com. Meals included. Half-day tours $100-175.)* Remember, too, that dolphins often swim just offshore of some the beaches listed above.

◎ SIGHTS

HULIHEE PALACE. The Daughters of Hawaii, with their impressive collection of Hawaiian artifacts, maintain this historical Kona site, a modest but exciting piece of Hawaiian history. Hula dances and musical performances liven up the palace, built by one-time governor of Hawaii John Adams Kuakini in 1838. A former favorite royal retreat, the grounds and oceanfront location eclipse the actual building, which only has six rooms. King Kalakua, the "Merrie Monarch," was famous for being quite the socialite, and he filled the abode with countless parties. The palace lay abandoned in the early 20th century, serving as a playground for neighborhood children and an impromptu parlor for an enthusiastic group of card players. It has since been restored and contains numerous Hawaiian artifacts, including the javelins and spears of Kamehameha the Great. *(75-5718 Alii Dr. ☎808-329-1877; www.huliheepalace.org. Open M-F 9am-4pm, Sa-Su 10am-4pm. Guided tour available. $6, seniors $4, ages 18 and under $1.)*

MOKUAIKAUA CHURCH. Built in 1837 out of lava rock and coral lime mortar, this is the oldest church in the state. It's also the tallest structure in town; for years fishermen used the 112 ft. steeple for navigation. There is a small exhibit explaining the building's history at the entrance and beautiful stained glass over the altar. A model of the Brig Thaddeus, the boat that carried missionaries to the Big Island during a 164-day voyage, sits in the back of the church. *(At the northern end of Alii Dr. ☎808-329-1589. Open daily sunrise to sunset. Free.)*

AHUENA HEIAU. Ahuena Heiau was the centerpiece of Kamehameha the Great's government from 1813-1819. Kamehameha, the only man to unite the Hawaiian islands under one ruler, was born on the Kohala coast in the 16th century. After consolidating his power over the other islands, he returned to Kona to rule (see **History**, p. 14). He built the *heiau* and dedicated it to Lono, the god of agriculture and prosperity. At the top of the hut is a golden plover, a slight bird thought to have led the first Polynesian settlers to the Hawaiian islands. *(At the northern end of Kailua Bay, adjacent to King Kamehameha's Kona Beach Hotel. The heiau sits on hotel property, but can be seen from the pier or water of Kamakahonu Beach.)*

▣ NIGHTLIFE

A normal night out in Kona ends at 11pm, after the ephemeral green flash of the sunset, and a few Mai Tais. Those who want more do have a few options, but as Alii Dr. fills with a diverse crowd, the savvy traveler may want to turn in for the night. The scene has been known to get a little dangerous after dark, and fights are not uncommon in the area's bars.

KAVA 'NOTHER?

In Hawaii they have a saying about kava: one shell is good. Two is better. Three—it's where you want to be. Kava (*'awa* in Hawaiian) is as intoxicant formed from kava plant roots known for its anti-anxiety, anti-depressant, and stress relieving effects. Native only to the South Pacific, kava is consumed primarily to relax without disrupting mental clarity. To prepare kava properly, the maker will dry the root, grind it into a powder, and put the substance under water in a mesh fiber cloth. After about half an hour, the drink is ready. Kava is thought by many to taste horrible so current preparation of the beverage may include fruit juice. Other establishments sell it in a extract form, having their participants swig "shots" of kava, rather than endure the sips from the traditional coconut shell.

Kava is a legal intoxicant in the US, though driving after consumption can lead to DUI charges. Kava's active ingredients are kavalactones which produce psychoactive (typically euphoric) effects, though the potency varies from plant to plant. After drinking your first shell, it is recommended to sit and wait 15-20 minutes before consuming your next. Effects can last anywhere from 2 to 8 hours so plan your "trip" accordingly.

Travelers can find great kava and knowledgeable kava bartenders at both Kanaka Kava (p. 198) in Kona, Kava Kafe (p. 252), in Kohala, and Kava Roots (p. 175) on Oahu's North Shore.

BARS

Kanaka Kava, 75-5803 Alii Dr. (☎808-327-1660), down the alley next to the Sunset Plaza. The first thing you'll notice about this hut is a large bowl filled with what appears to be mud water. That's kava, an ancient Pacific herbal beverage nicknamed "the peace drink" for its mellowing (read: numbing) effects. After a shell of kava ($5) try the Hawaiian food—the best in Kona. For first-timers, a mix of kava, coconut milk, and pineapple juice is only $5. For all kava questions see our **feature article** (p. 198). Plates $8-14. Open M-W and Su 10am-10pm, Th-Sa 11am-11pm. Cash only.

Ocean's Sports Bar and Grill, 75-5819 Alii Dr. (☎808-327-9494), just behind Lulu's and Jake's. This bar has music (live or by DJ) almost every night. Dozens of beers available ($4-6). **Taco Tu** serves up tacos ($2.50) and brews ($2.50). Open daily 11am-2am, *pupu* until midnight. MC/V.

Huggo's on the Rocks, 75-5828 Kahakai Rd. (☎808-329-1493), at the southern end of Kailua Bay, next to the Royal Kona Resort. With Hawaiian music, a hula dancer, and a sunset backdrop, Huggo's embodies the *sine qua non* of a tropical paradise. It's a tourist spot, but one of the more fun places to hang out. The only downside are the steep prices (beer $4-7; frozen mixed drinks $6-8). Open M-Th and Su 11am-11pm, F-Sa 11am-midnight. AmEx/D/MC/V.

Sam's Hideaway (☎808-326-7267), behind the Kona Marketplace, on Kakina Rd. This hole-in-the-wall is as local a place as you're likely to find. Drinks are cheap, the lighting is dim, and come midnight, everyone's drunk and singing karaoke. Beer $2-3.50; mixed drinks $2.50. 21+. Open daily 10am-2pm. AmEx/MC/V.

Rio's Seafood Grill and Bar, 75-5805 Alii Dr. (☎808-329-8200), in the Coconut Grove Marketplace, right upstairs from the volleyball court on Alii Drive. Rio's is a favorite local hangout. Try the crab cake sandwich ($13) and have a Kona long board lager ($4). Don't miss Tu live lobster night ($18). Open M 5-10pm, Tu-F 11:30am-3pm and 5-10pm, Sa-Su 5-10pm. MC/V.

Mixx Bistro Bar, 75-5626 Kuakini Highway (☎808-329-7334). Next to the King Kamehameha Hotel stands Mixx Bistro Bar, entertaining with live music every night. A full bar lit up with white lights and palm trees adds to the lively ambiance of the place. For those on the move, check out W salsa dancing. Big patio serving drinks ($4-7). Open noon-late.

Lulu's, 75-819 Alii Dr. (☎808-331-2633). While Lulu's may seem like the place to party in Kona, the bar can be dangerous—fights regularly break out. Pool tables, TVs, chili lights, and a vast upstairs *lanai* make it the closest thing to a nightclub you'll find on the Big Island.

M open-mic night, Tu salsa night, W college night (18+). 21+ all other nights, Cover F-Sa $5. Open daily 11am-2am. AmEx/D/MC/V.

LUAUS

Island Breeze Luau, (☎808-326-4969 or 808-329-8111), at King Kamehameha's Kona Beach Hotel, on the beach adjacent to Kamalahonu and Ahuena. Shows Tu-F and Su nights. Reservations advised. $65, ages 5-12 $29, under 5 free.

Luau at Kona Village Resort, 14 mi. north of Kona, takes the experience to another level. The W and F night luaus have been a tradition for over 30 years. It's the oldest running luau on the Big Island, featuring traditional Hawaiian food and dancing. Reservations are essential. Luau starts at 5:30pm. $98, ages 6-12 $67, ages 2-5 $40.

HOLUALOA

Holualoa (pop. 6170) is a century away from nearby Kailua-Kona. One of Kona's coffee-growing centers, the face of the town's main street has been remade by an influx of artists and craftspeople, who have converted old pool halls and saloons into art galleries, yoga centers, and eclectic shops. One exemplary gallery, the **Ipu Hale Gallery,** 75-5893 Mamalahoa Hwy. (☎808-322-9069), features fantastically old French engravings of the Sandwich Isles. The store also specializes in ancient Hawaiian gourd decoration, a unique artistic technique from Niihau, rediscovered in the late 20th century.

Visitors who ascend to the hillside greenery of Holualoa tend to return often. Stay awhile at ◪**The Holualoa Inn ❺**, or at hyacinth-pink **Inaba's Kona Hotel ❷** just up the street. For more information on either lodging, see **Accommodations,** p. 192. To reach Hulualoa, head *mauka* (toward the mountains) on Palani Rd. until the highway on the right, then head down Mamalahoa for about 5 mi.

SOUTH KONA

On the Big Island, a few miles can make a world of difference. **Kealakekua, Captain Cook,** and **Honaunau** blithely maintain their sleepy coffee-town existence, unaware of the hustle and bustle in nearby Kailua-Kona. Lining the Mamalahoa Hwy. (Rte. 11), this series of towns has a funky vibe all its own, along one of the most culturally and ecologically rich stretches of coastline on the island. Puuhonua o Honaunau preserves artifacts of Hawaiian history, while Kealakekua Bay's water provides fantastic snorkeling. The towns keep to an organic farming lifestyle and a few turnoffs along the highway lead to untouched beaches.

South Kona

⌂ ACCOMMODATIONS
Affordable Hawaii Pomaikai "Lucky" Farm B&B, **6**
Cedar House B&B, **4**
Da Third House, **1**
Hotel Manago, **5**
Pineapple Park B&B, **2**
Rainbow Plantations, **3**

THE BIG ISLAND

▐ TRANSPORTATION

Driving is the easiest way to get around South Kona. Some travelers hitchhike, but *Let's Go* does not recommend it. **Taxis** service the area, though they're expensive. **D&E Taxi** (☎808-329-4279; from 6am-10pm) and **Paradise Taxi and Tours** (☎808-329-1234; 24hr.) are two options. All taxis charge $2 initially and then $2 per mi. The free **Hele-On Bus** (☎808-961-8744) runs from Honaunau north to Kailua-Kona and west to Hilo. Buses run from Honaunau Elementary School to Kailua-Kona (50min.; M-Sa 5:55am) via Yano Hall in Captain Cook, Konawaena Schools in Kealakekua, and Ben Franklin in Kainaliu, and from Captain Cook to Kailua-Kona (M-Sa 10:45am, 2:15pm). See http://co.hawaii.hi.us/mass_transit/heleonbus.html for the most up-to-date fares and schedules.

✦ ORIENTATION

Route 11 (also known as the **Hawaii Belt Road** or **Mamalahoa Highway**) runs through South Kona, and most places of interest can be found along this road. A number of smaller roads branch off Rte. 11 and wind down to the coast and west up the mountain. The more significant ones are **Napoopoo Road,** which runs into **Middle Keei Road** and drops to the southern end of Kealakekua Bay, and **Route 160,** which accesses Puuhonua o Honaunau and also leads to the Bay.

▐ PRACTICAL INFORMATION

Banks: Bank of Hawaii (☎808-322-9377), on Mamalahoa Hwy. in downtown Kealakekua. Open M-Th 8:30am-4pm, F 8:30am-6pm. **24hr. ATM.**

Bookstore: Island Books, 79-7430 Mamalahoa Hwy. (☎808-322-2006), in the Kainaliu Center. Shelves an impressive collection of used and new titles, as well as used CDs and DVDs. Open daily 10am-8pm.

Library: Kealakekua Public Library (☎808-323-7585), on Mamalahoa Hwy. in Kealakekua. **Internet access** with a 3-month visitor's card ($10). Open M-Tu noon-6pm, W 1-7pm, F 11am-5pm, Sa 10am-4pm.

Laundromat: Hale Holoi Laundromat, mi. past Napoopoo Rd., next to Cap's Drive-In, north of downtown Captain Cook. Wash $2, dry $1.75. Open daily 6am-9pm.

Weather: ☎808-961-5582.

Police: A substation on Mamalahoa Hwy. in the center of Captain Cook is sporadically manned. The nearest **district station** (☎808-935-3311), north of Kona, fields calls.

Pharmacy: Oshima Drugs, 79-7400 Mamalahoa Hwy. (☎808-322-3313), south of mi. marker 113. Open M-F 9am-6pm, Sa 9am-5pm.

Hospital: Kona Community Hospital (☎808-322-9311), on Haukapila St. in Kealakekua. Follow the signs from Rte. 11 around mi. marker 112. 24hr. emergency room.

Internet Access: At the Kealakekua Public Library and **The Funkyard,** 81-6394 Mamalahoa Hwy. (☎808-345-7421), in downtown Kealakekua near mi. marker 111. In addition to hip T-shirts and psychedelic art, it has 4 Internet terminals. $2 per 15min., $6 per hr. Open Tu-Sa 9am-5pm and occasionally M and Su.

Post Office: Kealakekua Post Office, Mamalahoa Hwy. (☎800-275-8777), in Central Kona Center. Open M-F 9am-4:30pm, Sa 9:30am-12:30pm. **Captain Cook Post Office,** Mamalahoa Hwy., just past mi. marker 110. Open M-F 8am-4pm, Sa 9am-noon.

Postal Codes: 96750 (Kealakekua); 96704 (Captain Cook).

⚑ ⚑ ACCOMMODATIONS AND CAMPING

▨ **Hookena Beach Park** (☎808-961-8311; www.hawaii-county.com). Heading south on Hwy. 11, turn right between mi. markers 101 and 102 and go almost 3 mi. You will find this immaculate black sand beach, brimming with palm trees and stretching up to massive cliffs. Offers the only legal camping in the area and can get quite crowded. Pitch your tent under palms right on the beach—just watch for falling coconuts. Warm showers, flushing toilets, firepits, picnic tables, and a small concession stand. Check out the dolphins that come out in the bay in the morning and provide a show full of flips and barrel rolls. Permits required, see **Camping in Hawaii**, p. 82. June-Aug. 7-day max. stay; Sept.-May 14-day max. stay. $5, teens $2, under 13 $1. ❶

▨ **Cedar House B&B and Coffee Farm,** 82-6119 Bamboo Rd. (☎808-328-8829). From downtown Captain Cook, turn uphill onto Kiloa Rd. at mi. marker 110. Kiloa becomes a single lane; turn right at the T-junction onto Kinue Rd. Take the next left onto Greenwell Mountain Rd., then left again onto Bamboo Rd. In the midst of a coffee farm high above Kealakekua Bay, rooms have gorgeous views of the South Kona Coast. The Hibiscus Suite is quite large, with a private kitchenette, perfect for families. Full breakfast included. Make reservations far in advance. Rooms from $110, cottage (sleeps up to 3) $125. Hibiscus Suite $135, $810 per week. Additional guests $20. MC/V. ❸

Affordable Hawaii at Pomaikai "Lucky" Farm B&B, 83-5465 Mamalahoa Hwy. (☎808-328-2112; www.luckyfarm.com), south of Captain Cook between mi. markers 107 and 106, down a steep driveway. The innkeeper Nita also works a macadamia nut and coffee farm, providing a 100% pure Kona taste of Big Island ecotourism. With a green tin roof, bare plank construction, and high ceilings, 2 spacious "greenhouse" rooms (sleep up to 4) and a 1-bed "farmhouse" double off the living room. The cook prepares killer breakfasts in the morning, fresh from the farm. $80-95; $5 off a night for 4+ nights in a row. Additional guests ages 5 and up $10 per night. MC/V. ❸

Rainbow Plantation (☎808-323-2393 or 800-494-2829; www.rainbowplantation. com), on Rte. 11 between Pineapple Park and the Chevron Station, just north of the turn-off for Kealakekua Bay. The "Crow's Nest" is set in a former coffee shack, and the "Jungle Queen" refers to a suite within a restored fishing boat moored permanently in the backyard. Outdoor kitchen pavilion has midnight snacks. Continental breakfast included. 2-night min. stay. Doubles $80-100; additional guests $15. MC/V. ❸

Hotel Manago (☎808-323-2642; www.managohotel.com), on Mamalahoa Hwy. Look for the neon sign between mi. markers 109 and 110 in Captain Cook. One of the cheapest places to stay in South Kona. Attached to the hotel is the **Manago Hotel Restaurant ❷**. The rich and famous have been known to fly in for the pork chops ($8.75); don't forget to ask for gravy and onions. Check-in, check-out noon. Singles with shared bath $33, private bath $56-59; doubles $59-78. Restaurant hours 7am-7:30pm. MC/V. ❷

Pineapple Park B&B, 81-6363 Mamalahoa Hwy. (☎877-806-3800 or 877-865-2266; www.pineapple-park.com), north of downtown Captain Cook between mi. markers 110 and 111. More of a hostel than a B&B. The 4 private rooms upstairs are spacious. 2 street-side bunk rooms also available. Full kitchen, grill, Internet access ($10 per hr.), and kayaks for rent ($40-60). The landlady can often arrange some form of short-term work. Check-in afternoon. Check-out 10am. Free Wi-Fi. Dorm bunks $25; private rooms with shared bath $65, with private bath $85. MC/V. ❶

▣ FOOD

Most restaurants in South Kona serve organic, homegrown food, and while the dishes have a refreshing earthy quality, expect a large bill to support the farmers who supplied the ingredients. The food is good, but nothing to write home about; the coffee, on the other hand, is something to ship home by the pound. Kona coffee, grown in this humble part of the Big Island, is world-famous.

Kona Pacific Farmers Cooperative, 82-5810 Napoopoo Rd. (☎808-328-2411; www. kpfc.com), hosts a farmers' market every Friday from 8am to 4pm behind the old cooperative mill on Napoopoo Rd. and Middle Keei Rd., uphill from Kealakekua Bay. From Captain Cook, continue south on Rte. 11 to mi. marker 111. Turn right down Napoopoo Rd., and follow the signs for Kealakekua Bay. Keep right on Napoopoo Rd. at the intersection with Middle Keei Rd.; the coop will be a half-mile down. Follow the pink donkeys to the market out back.

The Coffee Shack, 83-5799 Mamalahoa Hwy. (☎808-328-9555), south of Captain Cook, before mi. marker 108. Perched over the coastline that's hundreds of feet below, the Coffee Shack makes breakfast (eggs benedict $11), deli sandwiches, pizzas ($9-12), desserts ($2.50-5), and freshly brewed coffee ($3-4.50) that are as amazing as the view. Open daily 7:30am-3pm. D/MC/V. ❷

Keei Cafe (☎808-322-9992), south of mi. marker 113 on Mamalahoa Hwy. Large portions of fresh fish draw a steady stream of customers to the *lanai* for fish tacos and other specialties. Try the spicy chicken fajitas that come with black bean chili and avocado, or the mango martini, made with fresh mango juice—yum. Lunch $10-13. Dinner $15-30. Lunch M-F 10:30am-2pm; dinner Tu-Sa 5-9pm. Cash only. ❸

South Kona Fruit Stand, 84-4770 Mamalahoa Hwy. (☎808-328-8547), in Captain Cook, between mi. markers 103 and 104, on the *mauka* (mountain) side. This fruit and vegetable farm and store is exotic and definitely worth the stop. Try a spiky chayote, a gnarly-looking dragon fruit, or a guanabana, all from their 6-acre organic farm which uses hundreds of geckos as pesticides. Open M-Sa 9am-6pm. AmEx/MC/V. ❶

Evie's Natural Food, 79-7460 Mamalahoa Hwy. (☎808-322-0739), next to Subway in Mango Court, south of Kainaliu. 100% organic, Evie's has all-fruit smoothies ($4), creative sandwiches (Maui Taro Burger $7), dinner combos ($8-15), and vegan options. Evie's also posts a list of short-term work opportunities, including farm jobs that trade room and board for labor. Open M-F 9am-7pm, Sa-Su 9am-5pm. AmEx/D/MC/V. ❶

Aloha Angel Cafe, 79-7384 Mamalahoa Hwy. (☎808-322-3383; www.alohatheater. com). This hip cafe envelops the artsy Aloha Theater (p. 204). Its outside seating lines a long descending *lanai* that gives refreshing views of the wild coast below. The menu offers french toasts, mango bread ($2), sandwiches, and breakfast until 1:30pm. Lunch $9-12; dinner $12-24. Open daily 8am-2:30pm and 5pm-9pm. MC/V. ❹

Teshima (☎808-322-9140), across from Aloha Kayaks. This place is always bustling with people seeking its unique fusion of Japanese and Hawaiian food and fantastic tempura. $10 lunch special 11am-1:45pm. Chicken Teriyaki $9. Kona Fried Rice Platter $9. Dinner meat and seafood $15-18. Open daily 6:30am-1:45pm and 5-9pm. Cash only. ❸

Adriana's Mexican-Salvadoran Food, 82-6066 Mamalahoa Hwy. (☎808-217-7405 or 808-936-8553), just across the highway from the old Kona Theater. This place is raved about in town, and it'll only cost you between $2-9. The menu is small but incredibly tasty. Open M-F 10am-5pm. Cash only. ❶

SPIN THE BOTTLE-NOSE. Kealakekua Bay is one of the best spots in Hawaii to see spinner dolphins, who make this crescent of water their personal playground. They are slender dolphins, generally 7 ft. long or less, that have dark gray backs and white stomachs. Seemingly natural performers, they leap out of the water to incredible heights before spinning and splashing down. While there's no schedule for this show, your best bet of catching a glimpse is in the early morning.

THE BIG ISLAND

⚑ BEACHES

❄ KEALAKEKUA BAY. *(Snorkeling. Surfing. Open 24hr.)* The steep-cliff crescent of Kealakekua Bay was formed when many acres of land plunged into the sea, and the bay and its spectacular coral reef haven't changed much since. What visitors see today is much like what Captain Cook saw upon his arrival over 200 years ago. The area is a Marine Life Conservation District, which makes this a truly fantastic place to snorkel. In addition to a launching site, the park has restrooms, picnic tables, some big surf, and Hikiau Heiau State Monument, a significant Hawaiian temple. *(To reach the park from Rte. 11, take Napoopoo Rd. between mi. markers 110 and 111. The road winds down the mountainside for a few miles before joining Middle Keei Rd. and continuing on to the bay. The only part of the bay accessible to automobiles is the southeastern end of the bay at the end of Napoopoo Rd.)*

HOOKENA BEACH PARK. *(Open 24hr.)* Another of the island's black sand beaches, Hookena doesn't stand out save its camping, but it's worth a visit, especially for those traveling with children; the beach is protected by a natural barrier, which means calm waters. Full facilities make it easy to spend a day here. *(For directions, see Accommodations, p. 201.)*

MILOLII BEACH PARK. *(Surfing. Open 24hr.)* In the no-man's-land of lava fields and forest between the Kona coast and the pastures of Kau is Milolii, one of the Big Island's last true fishing villages and a vestige from another era. The serpentine drive down to the town provides panoramic views of the titanic lava flow that devastated the area in 1926, and there is still so little vegetation that the lava seems freshly cooled. At the end of the road is Milolii Beach Park, a popular surf spot. The park offers restrooms, a sheltered picnic area, and camping. *(5 mi. below Rte. 11, just after mi. marker 89.)*

⚒ ACTIVITIES

Almost all of the activities in South Kona focus on the natural beauty of Kealakekua Bay and the diversity of its underwater inhabitants.

KAYAKING. Kealakekua Bay also offers some of the best kayaking in the Kona area, perhaps in all of Hawaii. Kayak-rental companies line Mamalahoa Hwy., but for superior service and the best orientation, try ❄**Kona Boys** (p. 196). Their guides are excellent, and their private tour consistently ranks among the best in the state. *(☎808-328-1234. Lunch,*

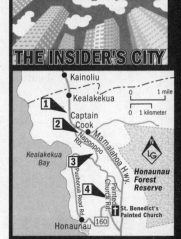

THE INSIDER'S CITY

Kainoliu
Kealakekua
Captain Cook
Kealakekua Bay
Honaunau Forest Reserve
Puuhonua Road Rd.
Painted Church Rd.
Mamalahoa Hwy.
Napoopoo Rd.
St. Benedict's Painted Church
Honaunau 160

0 — 1 mile
0 — 1 kilometer

ESPRESSO WAY

South Kona is the Napa Valley of coffee; its perfect climate, rich volcanic soil, and plentiful sunshine grow the finest coffee in the world. What's better, most of its 40+ farms offer free tasting sessions and tours. We found these to be the best of the bunch:

1. Rancho Aloha Coffee (☎808-322-1740). Certified organic (no pesticides, herbicides, or harmful fertilizers). One fantastic, clean cup of coffee.

2. Greenwell Coffee, 81-6581 Rte. 11 (☎808-323-2275). Free tours and tastings. Known especially for its plantation reserve coffee (made from the cherries of their 100 year old trees). Open M-F 8am-5pm, Sa 8am-4pm.

3. Kona Joe Coffee, on Rte. 11 between mi. marker 113 and 114. Home of the award winning "Trellis Grown" Coffee. Try it for yourself on their tour. Open M-F 7am-5pm and Sa-Su 9am-5pm.

4. Bay View Farms, 83-5249 Painted Church Rd. Known for their macadamia nut creme coffee. Open 9am-5pm daily for tours.

paddles, life vests, dry bag, cooler, and car rack included. Private tour $225 per person; group rate $159. Kayaks $47-67 per day, $27-37 per ½ day. Open daily 7:30am-5pm.)

SNORKELING. Kealakekua Bay boasts the best snorkeling on the Big Island. The ideal location is the bay's far side, where a white obelisk marks the British monument to Captain Cook. Dolphins and sea turtles frolic nearby, but laws mandate that snorkelers keep 50 ft. and 10 ft. away from these animals, respectively. Turtles, dolphins, eels, and countless fish dart in and out of a coral reef that drops off suddenly 40 ft. from shore, creating a dynamic underwater landscape. Almost all the kayak outfits rent snorkels as well, usually for $6-10.

BAY TOURS. Many companies in the area offer snorkel or kayak excursions to the Kealakekua reef. Of all the adventure companies, **Fair Wind**, 78-7130 Kaleiopapa St. (☎808-322-2788), is the only one with a permit to moor its catamaran in Kealakekua Bay. It has a range of tours, including the AM Deluxe Tour (daily 9am-1:30pm; $119, ages 4-12 $75, under 4 $29) and the PM Snack Cruise (Tu, Th, and Sa 2-5:30pm; $75, ages 4-12 $45, under 4 free). Fair Wind sells out up to three days in advance; reservations should be made early.

◎ 🎞 SIGHTS AND ENTERTAINMENT

▨ ALOHA THEATER. The theater, next to Aloha Angel Cafe (p. 202), hosts screenings of mostly foreign or independent films in its single auditorium. Brought to life in 1932, the theater began as a silent movie house. After a fire in 1948, renovation allowed for movies with sound and the theatre became a gathering place for the mountain community. Now, the theater serves as a performing arts center featuring live plays, music, dance, and film. *(79-7384 Mamalahoa Hwy. ☎808-322-2323; www.alohatheatre.com. Showings W-Su 6:30pm. $7, students and seniors $6, ½-price with dinner at Aloha Angel Cafe. Tickets for live shows around $15.)*

CAPTAIN COOK TRAIL AND MONUMENT. The Captain Cook Monument looms at the northwestern end of Kealakekua Bay, a 27 ft. pillar erected in Cook's honor by fellow Brits in 1874. The monument stands near the site where Cook was killed and has sparked much controversy because some Hawaiians see it as a tribute to cultural domination. (See **History**, p. 14, for more on Cook's landing.) A number of ships recreating Cook's voyage have since anchored in the bay and left plaques commemorating his "discovery." A good deal more interesting to explore are the ruins of the village, Kaawaloa, which was founded when Britain was still an uncivilized hinterland of the Roman Empire.

To reach the monument, head to the **Captain Cook Monument Trail** *(4 mi., 2hr., moderate).* The trail is on the downhill side of Napoopoo Rd., the first unmarked dirt road 200 yd. from the intersection with Rte. 11. The hike descends the slope to Kaawaloa Cove, passing overgrown sugarcane, exposed lava fields, and dense foliage along the shoreline. The trail follows a road for the first 100 yd. before branching off through fields of tall grass and wild brush. The terrain opens up to *aa* lava fields, approaching the coast with views of the countryside.

If you'd rather ride on horseback down the trail, **King's Trail Rides**, on Mamalahoa Hwy. between Kealakekua and Captain Cook, runs 4hr. excursions that include lunch, snorkeling gear, and 2hr. of riding. *(81-6420 Mamalahoa Hwy. ☎808-323-2388; www.konacowboy.com. Ages 7+. M-F $135, Sa-Su $150. $75 advance deposit required by credit card or money order to King's Trail Rides.)*

AMY GREENWELL ETHNOBOTANICAL GARDEN. The garden gives a sense of the close relationship the Hawaiians had with the land before Cook's arrival. Home to native Hawaiian species and those brought by Polynesian settlers, this 15-acre garden provides a representative look at the plants and cultivation techniques perfected by the islanders before the arrival of Europeans. *(On Mamalahoa Hwy, look for mi. marker 110 and turn left into the next driveway. ☎ 808-323-3318. Open M-F 8:30am-5pm. Tours W and F 1pm; $5.)*

SAINT BENEDICT'S PAINTED CHURCH. John Berchman Velge, a Belgian Catholic priest, built Saint Benedict's between 1899 and 1904. With ordinary house paints and divine inspiration, he created the closest thing to a Gothic cathedral on the Big Island. The vibrant colors of the interior blend the islands with the Old World, from the faux marble columns blossoming into palm trees to the vaulted ceiling masquerading as a tropical sky. Be sure to look back through the doors from the aisle—the church opens to an astounding view of the ocean hundreds of feet below. *(84-5140 Painted Church Rd. Just up the hill from Puuhonua o Honaunau. Take Rte. 160 north onto Painted Church Rd., just west of mi. marker 1; or take Napoopoo Rd. and turn onto Middle Keei Rd., then right onto the road. ☎ 808-328-2227.)*

PUUHONUA O HONAUNAU NATIONAL HISTORICAL PARK. Once the home of Kona's royal chiefs, the reconstructed thatched buildings and lava rock walls of this place still evoke the spirit of ancient Hawaii. The area, along with the canoe landing, was historically open only to *alii* (royalty) and their attendants. All others were prohibited by *kapu* (sacred laws) from entering the grounds or marring the *mana* (spiritual power) held by the *alii*.

There are actually two parts to Puuhonua o Honaunau: the **Royal Grounds** and the *puuhonua*, or **Place of Refuge.** They are separated by a massive stone wall, built in 1550. The walking tour of the Royal Grounds and Place of Refuge covers the points of interest. Kiilae Village, 1 mi. from the Visitors Center along the 1871 trail, explores the daily life of early Hawaiians. You can pick up a guide at the Visitors Center. *(Left off Rte. 160, 4 mi. from where Rte. 160 leaves Rte. 11, between mi. markers 103 and 104. The park can also be reached via Puuhonua Rd., a 4 mi., one-way road that runs from Napoopoo Beach. ☎ 808-328-2288 or 808-328-2326; www.nps.gov/puho. Visitors Center open daily 7:30am-5:30pm. Park open M-Th 8am-8pm, F-Su 8-11am. $5 per car.)*

KAU AND KA LAE

Tucked away in the southwest corner of the island, the Kau district (pop. 5827) is a striking blend of landscapes, people, and ideas. The history of the region is bleak. In the northwest corner of Kau lies Hawaiian Ocean View Estates, a real estate development that was laid out but never finished. One of Hawaii's former sugar plantations lies to the south; when the sugar industry dried up, the region had to fend off government attempts to use the area as a rocket launch site. Today, sugar plantations have been replaced by coffee and macadamia nut farms, and the rocket debate left a land divided by political ideologies. The green and black beaches, however, are still havens of peace.

▐ TRANSPORTATION

The only transportation to and from Kau is the free **Hele-On Bus** (☎808-961-8744; www.hawaii-county.com), which runs from Ocean View Center to Hilo (2¾ hr.; M-F 6:40am) via the Waiohinu/Naalehu gas station (7am) and Pahala Shopping Center, adjacent to the bank (7:30am). Farthest from Hilo, the stop at Ocean View Center is serviced by request only. Travelers are required to phone in their request by 3pm of the afternoon prior to travel.

✈ ORIENTATION

Route 11, also known as the **Hawaii Belt Road** or **Mamalahoa Highway,** is Kau's main thoroughfare. Ocean View, Waiohinu, Naalehu, and Pahala are all close to the route, the district's only link to the outside world. The only other major roads in the area are **South Point Road,** which runs between Rte. 11 and Ka Lae, and **Kamani Street,** which forks from Rte. 11 and runs through downtown Pahala.

▨ PRACTICAL INFORMATION

TOURIST AND FINANCIAL SERVICES

Tourist Information: Punaluu Bake Shop (☎808-929-7343), Hawaii Belt Rd., in downtown Naalehu, is the closest thing to a tourist office in Kau. The good-natured staff offers more sweet bread samples than ready answers, but they will provide a few useful brochures with directions to the green and black sand beaches. Open daily 9am-5pm.

Banks: Kau Federal Credit Union (☎808-929-7334), across from the Naalehu Theatre on Rte. 11, has an ATM and is open M-Sa 9am-4pm. **Bank of Hawaii** (☎808-928-8356), in the Pahala Shopping Center at the corner of Kamani and Pikake St. in Pahala, has a **24hr. ATM.** Lobby open M-F 8:30am-noon and 1-3pm.

LOCAL SERVICES

Library: Naalehu Public Library, 95-5669 Hawaii Belt Rd. (☎808-939-2442), provides **Internet access** with a 3-month visitor's card ($10). Call early to reserve a time on the 2 computers. Open M, W, and F noon-5pm; Tu and Th 1-6pm.

Laundromat: The Wash (☎808-929- 7072) sits adjacent to Desert Rose Cafe (p. 207), making laundry a potentially delicious experience. Wash $2, dry $0.25 per 5min. Drop-off service $1.50 per lb. Open M-Sa 6am-8pm, Su 7am-8pm.

Weather: ☎808-961-5582.

EMERGENCY AND COMMUNICATIONS

Police: Kau District Police Station (☎808-939-2520, non-emergency 808-935-3311) is southeast of Naalehu at mi. marker 62. Open M-F 7:45am-4:30pm.

Hospital: Kau Hospital, 1 Kamani St. (☎808-928-8331), on Rte. 11 in Pahala, provides basic medical services and a 24hr. emergency room. Clinic open M-F 8am-4:30pm.

Pharmacy: The on-site community health clinic at Kau Hospital in Pahala doubles as the region's only pharmacy, **Kau Community Pharmacy** (☎808-928-6252). Open M, W, and F 8am-noon and 1-5pm; Tu 8am-noon and 1-3pm.

Internet Access: Internet Cafe (☎808-929-8332), on Naalehu Shopping Center's Main St. $3 per hr. Hours vary, call ahead. There's also Wi-Fi ($4 per hr.) and a computer ($6 per hr.) at the Naalehu Theatre's cafe, **Simple Good Food** (☎808-929-9133). Open M-Sa, 8am-4pm and during evening showtimes.

Post Office: Naalehu Post Office, 95-5663 Mamalahoa Hwy. (☎800-275-8777). Open M-F 7:45am-1pm and 2-4:15pm, Sa 10:15-11:15am. **Pahala Post Office,** next to the Bank of Hawaii in the Pahala Shopping Center, is open M-F 8am-12:15pm and 12:45-4pm, Sa 8:30-11am.

Postal Codes: 96772 (Naalehu/Waiohinu); 96737 (Ocean View); 96777 (Pahala).

⚐ ⚐ ACCOMMODATIONS AND CAMPING

There aren't many places to stay in Kau, so be sure to make reservations early. Good directions are also essential; the highway and backstreets are not lit at night. Comfortable accommodations can be had at the ⚐**Nechung Dorje Drayang Ling ❷,** a non-sectarian Buddhist temple, which lets rooms at prices that will calm the weariest traveler (p. 209). For campers, **Punaluu Black Sand Beach ❶** (p. 209) allows camping by permit and has full facilities.

⚐ **Kalaekilohana Bed and Breakfast,** 94-2152 South Point Rd. (☎808-939-8052; www. kau-hawaii.com). The goal in building this B&B was to cultivate a "better-educated visitor," but between lei-making classes and traditional hat-weaving workshops, the hosts certainly did not skimp on the luxuries of a fine vacation retreat. Breakfast, often a delicious sausage, egg, rice, and mango plate, is a splendid start to a Kau day. 4 spacious rooms with rain showers and private *lanai.* Doubles $189; additional guests $25. Daily workshops start at $45. Group rates available. AmEx/D/MC/V. ❺

Macadamia Meadows, 94-6263 Kamaoa Rd. (☎808-929-8097; www.macadamiameadows.com). Turn onto Kamaoa Rd. next to Wong Yuen Store and head up the hill. An 8-acre working macadamia nut farm with rooms that are spacious yet cozy; amenities include a tennis court, swimming pool, and grill. Ask about potential work-exchange. 4 of the 5 rooms include refrigerators and microwaves. All have cable TV. Breakfast included. Check-in 3pm. Check-out 11:30am. Rooms $89-129. AmEx/MC/V. ❸

Margo's Corner (☎808-929-9614; www.margoscorner.com), Wakea Ave. From Kona, turn down South Point Rd. (mi. markers 69-70), and after a couple miles turn left on Kamaoa Rd. Turn right on Wakea, and look for the rainbow flag and the star window. 2 beautifully crafted suites pamper guests with a sauna and home-cooked breakfast. Guests on a budget may also set up a tent in the front garden. Work-exchange possible after staying as a paying guest. 2-night min. stay. Camping $30 per person; suites $90-130; additional guests after 2 $30. Wi-Fi. Cash only. Camping ❶/rooms ❸

Shirakawa Motel (☎808-929-7462; www.shirakawamotel.com), Mamalahoa Hwy., across from Wong Yuen Store. The basic yet surprisingly spacious rooms are not a bad place to stay for the night. Check in 12-5pm, check-out 11am. Singles and doubles $50; with kitchenette $60; with full kitchen $70; roll-away beds $10. Cash only. ❷

⚐ FOOD

⚐ **Hana Hou,** 95-1148 Naalehu Spur Rd. (☎808-929-9717), off Mamalahoa Hwy., across from Naalehu Town Center. One of Naalehu's new restaurants, Hana Hou strives to use only local ingredients in its American/Hawaiian-style dishes. Try the roast pork ($7) or the fresh fish burgers ($12). Pastries $1.50-3. Open M-Th 7am-3pm, F 7am-8pm, Sa 8:30am-8pm, Su 8:30am-3pm. MC/V. ❶

⚐ **The Desert Rose Cafe** (☎808-939-7673), on Hawaii Belt Rd., in Pohue Plaza in Ocean View. This roadside cafe charms the weary driver with its toothsome American, Italian, and Filipino treats. Famous for its greasy burgers ($7-9), fish burgers ($12), and differ-

THE LOCAL STORY

SEVENTH HEAVEN

Our favorite Big Island sunsets:

1. Mauna Kea (p. 235). Because the air at the summit is so clear, the sunsets are world-class. The summit has the added benefit of being above the clouds, making for a grand perspective. Stay late for some stargazing.

2. Makalawena Beach (p. 196). Makalawena Beach has all the elements for a picture-perfect beach sunset. The seemingly endless horizon may be your best chance to see the elusive "green flash." Be sure to pack a flashlight so you can find your way back.

3. Pololu Lookout (p. 253). A Feet up from the ocean crashing below, this jagged stretch of coastline bursts with sunset pastels in the evening. Maui looms just to the left if you're facing the ocean.

4. Waipio Lookout (p. 243). Waipio is picturesque anytime, but when the setting sun strikes the valley, the viewing conditions are golden in more ways than one.

5. Hawaii Volcanoes National Park, end of Chain of Craters Rd. (p. 214). This area of the park is best known for the after-dark views of lava hitting the ocean, but come an hour earlier to watch day fade to night.

6. South Point (p. 209). The roar of the ocean here provides the perfect soundtrack for the dropping sun.

7. Huggo's on the Rocks (p. 194). Not all the best sunsets are remote. Huggo's sets the stage for tropical paradise photo-ops with a sunset from the window.

ent vegetarian options. Desserts ($1.50-3), including Hawaiian sweet yam bites and fresh banana walnut bread, are heavenly. Open daily 7am-8pm. MC/V. ❷

Simple Good Food (☎929-9133), in the old concession stand of the Naalehu Theatre and Museum. Simple Good Food is just that: no pretensions here. Serving breakfast (eggs and coffee $5) and lunch (wraps and sandwiches $7.50), Eric and Shannon stay open during evening screenings and events at the theater to serve a no-frills dinner. Open daily 8am-4pm, or until the last show is over. MC/V. ❶

Keoki's Cafe, 95-5587 Mamalahoa Hwy. (☎808-929-9437), next to the 76 Gas Station in Naalehu. A local cafe that serves up town-famous smoothies ($3.75), burgers ($5), and fresh *ahi* sandwiches ($7.50). Open daily 6:30am-6:30pm. AmEx/D/MC/V. ❶

Shaka Restaurant, 95-5763 Mamalahoa Hwy. (☎808-929-7404), in Naalehu, near the post office. Shaka is the southernmost restaurant and bar in the US and is quite proud of it. Serves hearty island fare. Cheeseburgers $7.50; baby-back ribs $20. Open daily 10am-9pm; bar open until 10pm. MC/V. ❷

Punaluu Bake Shop (☎808-929-7343), on Mamalahoa Hwy., in Naalehu Town Center. Its famous sweet bread is a Hawaiian modification of the traditional Portuguese treat. Everything is baked on-site and is shipped around the island. It also serves plate lunches ($8) and offers an array of dry goods in its small general store. Open daily 9am-5pm. AmEx/D/MC/V. ❶

◪ BEACHES

The 12 mi. road that goes from the Hawaii Belt Rd. (between mi. markers 69 and 70) to South Point is like a runway to another world. Lush green valleys give way to the **Kamaoa Wind Farm** and to brown pastures full of cattle. Most rental companies don't permit their cars on this road, but 2WD cars can make it to the entrances of all areas of interest without any problems. Near the coast, the road enters the 710-acre **Ka Lae District** and eventually forks. The right fork heads to a parking lot and the 30 ft. cliffs of South Point. The left fork leads to a set of abandoned buildings and a parking lot convenient to **Green Sand Beach.**

PAPAKOLEA GREEN SAND BEACH. *(Open daily 24hr.)* From the parking lot (see above), Papakolea is a 3 mi. trek along the coast, often over craggy lava rocks and torn-up, off-road paths. This beach is for the adventurer, not the sun-bather. The unusually beautiful sand is caused by a geological phenomenon; the olavine (a greenish mineral that crystallizes from magma) from aged lava is eventually eroded by the sea, forming a green-ish slope that falls into turbulent water. The vista from up top is unique, but the climb down and dip in the ocean can be dangerous because of steep sharp pathways and rough windy seas. Also, be mindful of the surroundings—some locals do not appreciate guests.

KA LAE BEACH/SOUTH POINT. *(Open daily 24hr.)* A 5min. walk from the end of the right hand fork after the Ka Lae Historic Landmark District sign, Ka Lae is a spectacular spot—the convergence of currents from the windward and leeward sides of the beach creates intense surf. Although swimmers may leap into the rip current below, the ladders that used to support these thrill seekers are no longer there. Try not to get tangled in the dozens of fishing lines stretching out to sea. "The Point" itself is beyond the parking lot at the extremity of the island. It is thought to be the spot of the Polynesians' first landing in the Hawaiian Islands and has been important throughout Hawaiian history because of the **Kalalea Heiau,** a temple which still stands today.

PUNALUU BLACK SAND BEACH. *(Open daily 24hr.)* Eight miles northeast of Naalehu and 5 mi. south of Pahala along Rte. 11 between mi. markers 56 and 57, is Punaluu Beach, the island's largest black sand beach. The dazzling volcanic sand is home to a large population of hawksbill turtles and an even larger contingent of tourists; getting there by 9am will get you a parking spot. Punaluu has some wicked surf that makes for messy boarding at best. Swimming usually affords a close look at turtles, whose primary feeding ground is around the lava rocks near the shore. Just south of the beach are county park facilities, including protected picnic areas, restrooms, showers, and campsites. A permit is required to camp; see **Camping in Hawaii,** (p. 82) for more information.

👁 🎞 SIGHTS AND ACTIVITIES

NECHUNG DORJE DRAYANG LING. Once a Japanese mission, this Buddhist temple was established by Nechung Rinpoche in 1973 as a non-sectarian center for Buddhist teachings and is worth even a short visit. The entire complex is painted in the traditional Tibetan style and beautifully maintained. The Dalai Lama visited in 1980 and again in 1994. The immaculate grounds, home to peacocks and shaded by bamboo and palm trees, add to the tranquility. Rooms are available for those wishing to prolong their stay. *(From Rte. 11 take Kamani Rd. when it forks off the highway to Pahala. Take the 3rd right onto Pikake St. and follow the paved road 5 mi. The temple will be on the right. ☎808-928-8539; www.nechung.org. 2-night min. stay. Dorms $50; singles $50; doubles $70. Suggested donation for viewing the temple $5.)*

KULA KAI CAVERNS. Over 1000 years old, the Kula Kai Caverns are some of the island's most spectacular lava tubes. Trips range from an easy walking tour to an all-out spelunking extravaganza in Maelstrom Cave. *(In the town of Ocean View, on Hwy. 11, 40min. south of Kona. ☎808-929-9725; www.kulakaicaverns.com. Tours daily by appointment only. 30min. walking tour $12. 3-4hr. Maelstrom Cave tour $65. Call for details.)*

MANUKA STATE NATURAL AREA RESERVE. Cast off the chains of resort packages in favor of the natural calm of Manuka State Natural Area Reserve. The 2 mi. Manuka Loop Trail runs through eight acres of land that were set aside in the 1930s for 48 species of native Hawaiian flora. The trail is rocky in some places and bug-filled in all places, so wear proper hiking shoes and bring insect repellent. The park, which has bathrooms and shaded picnic tables, is a quiet locale for a lunch or rest stop. *(Between mi. markers 81 and 82 on the Hawaii Belt Rd.)*

HAWAII VOLCANOES NATIONAL PARK

Home to the world's most active oceanic hot spot and the only two active volcanoes on the Hawaiian Islands (Mauna Loa and Kilauea), Hawaii Volcanoes National Park is constantly changing. Along the park's southeastern coast, 2000°F lava flows enter the Pacific Ocean, redefining the island's coastline. Between 1983 and 2005 the continuing eruption from Kilauea's Puu Oo vent added 525 acres of new land to the state. Both Mauna Loa and Kilauea are shield volcanoes with gentle slopes that rise gradually over many miles. Although they aren't characterized by the dramatic steep-angle peaks, continuous activity makes them much more accessible for scientific study and general viewing. The Kilauea Caldera is often jokingly referred to by rangers as "the drive-in volcano." On most days, visitors can witness lava flows oozing from the East Rift Zone near the end of Chain of Craters Rd. One of the most unforgettable experiences in the park is the night hike (see **Going with the Flow,** p. 216) that many visitors take to watch lava flows light the sky.

AT A GLANCE: HAWAII VOLCANOES NATIONAL PARK

AREA: 333,000 acres.

FEATURES: Kilauea, Mauna Loa, Kau Desert, Puna Coast, Puu Loa Petroglyphs.

HIGHLIGHTS: Hiking over lava rocks, steam vents, cinder cones, craters, ancient petroglyphs, and active lava flows.

QUICK FACT: Astronauts have trained in the Kau Desert and Kilauea Iki Crater because of their moon-like surface.

GATEWAY TOWNS: Volcano, 1 mi. (p. 219). Hilo, 30 mi. (p. 226).

CAMPING: Camping is free (p. 211). Stays limited to 7 days per month and no more than 30 days per year. Registration required for backcountry camping.

FEES: $10 per vehicle; $5 per pedestrian, bicyclist, or motorcyclist.

FOR MORE INFO: ☎808-985-6000.

▣ TRANSPORTATION

Volcano (p. 219) is the nearest gateway town and can satisfy all visitors' basic needs. A **car** is indispensable (unless participating on a guided tour); however, if renting a car is impossible, the Kau/Hilo **Hele-On Bus** runs between the park's Visitors Center and the Mooheau Bus Terminal in Hilo. (☎808-961-8744; www.co.hawaii.hi.us. Leaves Volcanoes National Park M-F 8:10am, arrives in Hilo 9:20am; leaves Hilo 2:40pm, arrives in Volcanoes National Park 3:45pm. Free.)

✸ ORIENTATION

The only entrance to the park is from **Route 11 (Hawaii Belt Road),** 30 mi. southwest of Hilo and 96 mi. southeast of Kona. There was another entrance from Hwy. 130 (Kalapana Rd.) in the southeast, but this route has been closed since 1989, when lava took out more than 8 mi. of highway. Within the park there are two main roads: the 11 mi. **Crater Rim Drive,** which circles Kilauea Caldera, and the 20 mi. **Chain of Craters Road,** which descends along the east side of Kilauea toward the coast and ends abruptly where it meets an active flow. This area serves as the trailhead for the night hike to see the lava flow. **Hilina Pali Road** accesses the remote western portion of the park, and **Mauna Loa Road** ascends Mauna Loa and ends at the trailhead to the summit.

THE BIG ISLAND

☑ PRACTICAL INFORMATION

Much of the park is **wheelchair accessible,** including the Visitors Center, Jaggar Museum, Volcano House Hotel, Volcano Art Center, Devastation Trail, and the pathways to the Steam Vents, Keanakakoi, Pauahi Crater, and Muliwai a Pele.

Tourist Information: Hawaii Volcanoes National Park, P.O. Box 52, Hawaii National Park, 96718-0052 (☎808-985-6000; www.nps.gov/havo).

Hours: Open 24hr. Ranger hours vary by location: at the Visitors Center 7:45am-5pm; at the end of Chain of Craters Rd. 7:45am-midnight. Hours subject to change.

Fees, Permits, and Regulations: $10 per car or $5 per pedestrian, bicyclist, or motorcyclist; good for 7 days. Year-long Hawaii Volcanoes Pass $20.

Guided Hikes and Events: The Visitors Center shows a 25min. introductory film about the park daily 9am-4pm on the hr. Ranger-led lectures and walks also offer a good introduction to the natural history and geology of the region. Daily schedule for lectures and walks varies; consult the Ranger Activity bulletin board at the Visitors Center. Check the website, www.nps.gov/havo, for a schedule of events and a list of hikes.

CLIMATE HOPPING. In his *Letters from Hawaii*, Mark Twain writes in awe of the volcano landscape; one "could see all the climes of the world at a single glance of the eye, and that glance would only pass over a distance of 4 or 5 miles as the bird flies." Twain wasn't too far off; visitors should come prepared for extremes of hot and cold, as well as wet and dry, often within the same day. Covering elevations from sea level to 13,677 ft., the range of ecosystems in such a small space is nothing short of extraordinary.

Camping Equipment: Hilo Surplus Store, 148 Mamo St. (☎808-935-6398), in Hilo, sells tents, backpacks, and other equipment at discount prices. **True Value Hardware,** in Volcano, also sells supplies, including iodine tablets for water purification (p. 220).

Facilities: Kilauea Visitors Center (☎808-985-6000) and **Park Headquarters,** a couple hundred yards beyond the entrance station along the northern arc of Crater Rim Dr., has maps and eruption updates. Visitors Center open daily 7:45am-5pm. **Showers** are available at Namakani Paio Campground, 3 mi. west of the park entrance along Rte. 11. Shower keys ($3) are available from Volcano House (p. 212). **Drinking water** is available at the Visitors Center, Jaggar Museum, Thurston Lava Tube, and Namakani Paio Campground. However, drinking water is scarce, so it's a good idea to store up.

Gas: The archaic pumps of the **Volcano Store** (☎808-967-7210), next to the Volcano Post Office, still function daily 5am-7pm. There is also an **Aloha Gas Station,** 19-3972 Old Volcano Rd. (☎808-967-7555). Open daily 6:30am-7:15pm.

Weather: ☎808-985-6000. The park also broadcasts on AM 530.

Medical Services: The nearest major medical facility is the **Hilo Medical Center,** 1190 Waianuenue Ave. (☎808-974-4700). 24hr. emergency room.

Banks: There is a **24hr. ATM** in the Volcano House Hotel, across the street from the Visitors Center. The nearest banks are in Hilo: **Bank of Hawaii,** 120 Pauahi St. (☎808-935-9701), and **First Hawaiian Bank,** 1205 Kilauea Ave. (☎808-969-2211). Both open M-Th 8:30am-4:30pm, F 8:30am-6pm.

⛰ ⛰ ACCOMMODATIONS AND CAMPING

The park is completely accessible for day and night hikes from Volcano Village, where comfortable accommodations are readily available. On the other hand, anyone with the urge to really explore Volcano Park should plan to camp. Many of the best hikes require a solid day of walking, and camping greatly expands options. **Backcountry camping** is allowed at designated cabins, shelters, and campgrounds by permit only. Permits are free and can be easily obtained at the Visitors Center on a first-come, first-served basis no earlier than one day before. Stays limited to seven days per month and no more than 30 days per year. Tent sites, a small shelter, pit toilets, and water catchments are available on the coast at **Kaaha, Halape,** and **Keauhou Shelters. Apua Point** has tent sites but no shelter or water. The **Pepeiao Cabin,** in the Kau desert, has three bunks and water catchment. **Napau Crater** has only tent sites and pit toilets. There are two rustic cabins en route to the summit of Mauna Loa, one at Red Hill (7½ mi. from the trailhead) and the second at the summit caldera (11½ mi. from Red Hill). Both have bunks and mattresses. Stays are limited to three nights per site and to groups of no more than 12. Be aware that the water catchments at all of these sites must be treated before drinking. Backcountry campers are encouraged to follow "leave no trace" ethics. No fires are allowed; ask the ranger about camp stoves when you pick up your permit. Camping is strictly prohibited anywhere other than the sites listed above.

▓ **Namakani Paio Campground** (☎808-985-6000), 3 mi. west of the park entrance on Rte. 11. Sheltered in a grove of giant eucalyptus and *koa* trees, Namakani provides a tranquil escape from a day of volcano exploring. Campsites are free and available on a first-come, first-served basis. The 2 large fields and pavilion are often crowded, but campers usually find enough room to set up a tent, and maybe even some friends to help. Restrooms and fire pits. Shower keys ($3 per 24hr.) can be obtained from the Volcano House reception desk. 7-night max stay. A 1 mi. path directly across from the entrance on leads to the Jaggar Museum, useful for people without cars. Free. ❶

Namakani Paio Cabins (☎808-967-7321), in the Namakani Paio Campground. All cabins have 1 full bed, 1 bunk bed, linens, a sheltered picnic bench, and fire pit. Extra blankets are recommended. There are lights in the cabins but no electrical outlets. Check-in 3pm. Check-out noon. Reservations required well in advance through the Volcano House reception desk. Singles and doubles $50; additional guests (up to 2) $8. ❷

Volcano House Hotel (☎808-967-7321; www.volcanohousehotel.com), along Crater Rim Dr., across from the Visitors Center. Perched on a ledge overlooking the Kilauea Caldera, Volcano House was built in 1877 to lodge everyone who flocked to the great lava lake that filled the Halemaumau Crater. Unfortunately, the boiling fire drained away along with much of the charm. Simple rooms are comfortable, but with crater views starting at $200, you might expect more. Restaurant serves buffet-style breakfast ($11.50, ages 2-12 $7.25) and lunch ($14/$9), as well as sit-down dinners ($18-25). Reception 24hr. Check-in 3pm. Check-out noon. Reservations required. Singles and doubles $95-225; additional guests (up to 2) $15. AmEx/D/MC/V. ❸

Kulanaokuaiki Campground (☎808-985-6000), off Hilina Pali Rd., 4 mi. southwest of Chain of Craters Rd. In the middle of the Kau Desert, the seclusion might give a sense of the backcountry without the trek. There's no shade or water, and you'll be sleeping on lava, but there's probably not another person for miles (perhaps for good reason). 8 sites with more on the way. Pit toilets and fireplaces but no drinking water. Free. ❶

◎ SIGHTS

Almost all of the major attractions are accessible by car along **Crater Rim Drive, Chain of Craters Road,** and **Mauna Loa Road.** Below, the sights are divided up by the roads they're on (the first three are by the park entrance). Crater Rim Dr., which circles Kilauea Caldera and Halemaumau and Kilauea Iki, is the busiest.

In the evening, Chain of Craters Rd. sees a decent amount of traffic as park visitors head to the end of the road for the night hike. Mauna Loa Rd., off Hwy. 11, is part of the park, though it is not past the park's entrance (meaning you don't have to pay to see the sights off Mauna Loa Rd.).

GALLERIES AND EVENTS

VOLCANO ART CENTER GALLERY. Adjacent to the Visitors Center, the Volcano Art Center Gallery holds a large collection of works by over 200 local artists, all inspired by the volcanoes. Built in 1877 as the original Volcano house, the gallery houses exceptional woodwork (handmade *koa*, *ohia*, and *milo* crafts) and drawing. The photography, by G. Brad Lewis, apparently the only photographer to witness the last major eruption, is worth a glance. Also, check out the sweet glasswork and paintings. *(☎808-967-7565. Open daily 9am-5pm. AmEx/D/MC/V.)*

AFTER DARK IN THE PARK. On most Tuesday evenings, guest speakers give lectures and slide presentations on topics ranging from water catchment to vent creation. *(In the Kilauea Visitors Center Auditorium. Tu 7pm. Free.)*

KILAUEA CULTURAL FESTIVAL AND OTHER EVENTS. In mid-July, the park hosts Hawaiian artists and musicians from across the islands during the Kilauea Cultural Festival. Hawaiian music and hula, instruction in Native Hawaiian crafts and games, and demonstrations of island traditions are all part of the festivities. A hula performance is in late May or early June, and a procession to Halemaumau Crater is at the end of August. The free food is delectable. *(At the Kilauea Military Camp, 1 mi. west of the Visitors Center on Crater Rim Dr. Admission included in the park entrance fee. Check the park information desk or www.nps.gov/havo for more information.)*

CRATER RIM DRIVE

Beginning at the Visitors Center, Crater Rim Dr. is an 11 mi. loop that circles the Kilauea Caldera and passes through various recent and past lava landscapes. There is a lot that you can miss from the car, so if you have time, consider walking at least part of the 11 mi. trail. The sights from the Jaggar Museum to the Kilauea Iki Overlook are especially groovy on foot. Overlooks and points of interest are marked by road signs and clearly labeled on park maps. Traveling counterclockwise from the Visitors Center, you will pass sulfur banks, steam vents (or Pele's Saunas), crater pits, cinder cones, lava tubes, and fissures along the southwest rift zone. Placards explain the geology, history, and legends of each sight. The following are a few highlights of Crater Rim Dr.

KILAUEA CALDERA. Don't be fooled—the barren summit crater that you will be circling for the next 11 mi. is one of the most active volcanoes in the world. From the 1800s until 1954, the caldera was the site of Kilauea's most dramatic eruptions, including fountains of lava up to 2000 ft. high and a boiling lava lake. However, after 1955, most of the action has shifted to Kilauea's Southwest and East Rift Zones. Nonetheless, evidence of volcanic activity, past and present, is still visible around the caldera.

 PASSED GAS. Kilauea and Halemaumau emit strong sulfur fumes—children, pregnant women, and people with heart or respiratory problems should avoid the crater. Sometimes the emissions get so intense that the park closes a number of its roads and trails. Call ahead for current conditions.

JAGGAR MUSEUM AND HAWAIIAN VOLCANO OBSERVATORY. This museum, while a bit dated, is a fascinating introduction to the science behind the park.

THE BIG ISLAND

Stop in pre- or post-hike for a better understanding of both the current geologic research at the park and the ancient Hawaiian legends that surround the volcanoes. Pele's hairs and tears, for example, are explained in scientific detail, as well as in the context of their mythical conceptions. The observatory, right next door, is closed to the public, but the Jaggar Museum sometimes explains part of their current research. *(On Crater Rim Dr. ☎808-985-6049. Open daily 8:30am-5pm. Admission included in park entrance fee.)*

HALEMAUMAU CRATER. Until 1924, Halemaumau was the site of a lake of lava which captivated the world. The crater visible today was formed in 1924 when the lava suddenly drained and the ground dropped several hundred feet. According to legend, the fire goddess Pele settled in Halemaumau after fleeing her sister, Namakaokahai, the goddess of the sea. The legend insists that she still resides there. Although Pele's home is visible from Crater Rim Dr., it is seen best from the Jaggar Museum (p. 213) or the Steaming Bluff Lookout.

KILAUEA IKI CRATER AND PUU PUAI CINDER CONE. In November 1959, the cliff walls of Kilauea Iki ("Kilauea the Little") burst open, flooding the crater with liquid fire 400 ft. deep. Lava soon started blasting vertically in fountains nearly 2000 ft. high—the highest ever recorded on Kilauéa. When it was over, a massive crater remained; it measures 1 mi. long, 3000 ft. across, and 380 ft. deep. During the eruption, lava splatter from the fountain oxidized, forming the red-brown Puu Puai cinder cone. The cinder cone formed on the southwest side of the crater because the splatter and ash were carried by the prevailing trade winds. For a closer look at Kilauea Iki, hike the **Kilauea Iki Trail** (p. 216).

DEVASTATION TRAIL. *(1 mi. Easy.)* This self-guided plank trail stretches through a portion of rainforest buried in pumice cinders during the 1959 eruption of Kilauea Iki. The rain of volcanic debris left only a skeleton of what was once a densely forested area—hence the name.

⬛ THURSTON LAVA TUBE. *(30min. Easy.)* Lava tubes are formed when a river of lava's edges cool enough to harden while the molten interior continues to move, leaving a tunnel behind. In 1913, Lorrin Thurston, a local newspaperman, was the first non-native to discover the tube, and it has been a popular attraction ever since. The first portion of the tube is lit up, and you can walk down and investigate. Although stairs lead back to the surface after a couple hundred yards, the tube extends another 300 ft. Damp and dark, this extra stretch is far more exciting than the short, guided part. You will absolutely need a flashlight. Much of the tube is overrun with a living canopy of roots that have penetrated the rock, revealing the density of *ohia* and fern rainforest above.

CHAIN OF CRATERS ROAD

From the lava flowing over the cliffs to the shades of gray and orange coloring the landscape, this is unlike any other drive you'll ever take. The drive along Chain of Craters Rd. is about 40 mi. round-trip, and there is neither gas nor water available below the Visitors Center, so make the necessary preparations before leaving. Chain of Craters is also the road most likely to be closed due to lava flow or fires; check with the Visitors Center about current conditions.

HILINA PALI ROAD. This road intersects with Chain of Craters Rd. after about 2 mi. Heading into the heart of the Kau Desert, the 9 mi. Halina Pali Rd. is an escape into barren solitude, one missed by most visitors. It ends at the **Hilina Pali Overlook,** where a vast horizon of ocean and sky meets the edge of the 2280 ft. Halina Cliff. Notwithstanding numerous scenic overlooks, perhaps the coolest part is where the road ends, cut short by the massive Puu Oo lava flow.

PUU LOA PETROGLYPHS. One of the most striking features of Volcanoes National Park is its juxtaposition of old and new. The petroglyphs lining the slopes of Puu Loa, the largest collection in Hawaii (over 15,000 carvings), are the perfect place to find such a contrast. From the parking lot along Chain of Craters Rd., a 2 mi. round-trip trail leads to a boardwalk that allows a close look at the symbols and figures tattooing the rock.

HOLEI SEA ARCH. Although sea arches are common on the coasts of Hawaii, where large waves provide the raw power for erosion, the Holei Arch is exceptional. Standing more than 90 ft. tall, this is the site where Hawaiian legend says a great battle took place between Pele and her sister Namakaokahai, goddess of the sea. It is also an unusual example of a sea arch formed by the creation of new land (by oozing lava), not by the usual erosion. Find the arch just before mi. marker 19. The walk to it takes less than a minute.

END OF CHAIN OF CRATERS ROAD. Since Puu Oo first blew her top on January 3, 1983, the Puu Oo-Kupaianaha rift zone has been erupting continuously, though things have calmed down since the dynamic early years, when lava fountains blasted 1500 ft. high. Today, the eruption is characterized by gentler *pahoehoe* flows and lava tubes. With tubes insulating the lava from heat loss, these flows are able to travel across the long *palis* (cliffs) all the way to the ocean, where they continue to add substantial landmass to Hawaii's youngest island in a display almost as spectacular as the fountains were two decades ago. In total, more than 8 mi. of highway have been swallowed and the entire town of Kalapana was destroyed. The volcano's power is viscerally apparent; if you hike northeast along the coastal lava rocks from the end of the road, you'll come upon a series of road signs buried by lava that make for ironic pictures.

 WHAT THE HELL IS A CALDERA? A "caldera" and a "crater" look suspiciously similar, but don't be fooled: the terms are not interchangeable. A caldera (from the Portuguese *caldeira*) is a volcanic crater with a large diameter that is formed by collapse of the central part of a volcano or by explosions of extraordinary violence.

MAUNA LOA ROAD

This scenic drive starts 2 mi. west of the park entrance off Rte. 11. The road climbs 3000 ft. through rainforest to the ◪**Mauna Loa Lookout** (13 mi. from Rte. 11), a secluded spot perfect for a quiet moment of reflection. This trailhead also happens to be one of the best bird-watching spots on the island, with a diverse range of native and non-native species cruising overhead.

Mauna Loa is the world's tallest mountain if measured from the ocean floor. Climbing 18,000 ft. to the surface of the Pacific and then another 13,677 ft. above sea level, Mauna Loa dwarfs even Mt. Everest. In sheer bulk, it's 100 times the size of Mt. Rainier. If the enormity of what rests beneath your feet doesn't overwhelm you, watching the sunset might.

Near the beginning of the road there is a turnoff to see the lava trees. These phantoms of the old forest were formed when *pahoehoe* lava flows engulfed a tree that carried a lot of water (usually *ohia*) and hardened around it before the tree burned away. Just over 1 mi. on Mauna Loa Rd. after the turnoff from Hwy. 11 is Kipuka Puaulu, an enclave of native forest that has managed to avoid the torrents of lava. This oasis of upland forest is full of *koa* and *ohia* trees, as well as many other native plants, insects, and birds that have been

THE BIG ISLAND

partially sheltered from invasive foreign species by the surrounding fields of lava. An easy 1 mi. trail offers a good view of this treasure.

HIKING

The hiking in Hawaii Volcanoes National Park is some of the best on the island, and with over 150 mi. of well-maintained trails, there's certainly a lot of it. A list of suggested hikes at the Visitors Center includes routes for all abilities and endurance. Whatever the adventure, sunscreen, a hat, lots of water, sturdy close-toed shoes, rain gear, a flashlight, long pants, and all-purpose gloves are highly suggested. Most of the hikes offer little shade and cover hot black lava rock fields; drinking water and replenishing electrolytes (found in sports drinks) is a must if you plan on avoiding heat stroke and dehydration. Trails over lava flows are loosely marked by piles of neatly arranged rocks known as *ahu* or lighted beacons. Strong winds can knock down even the best *ahu*, though most trails are fairly well trafficked, making it possible to guess the direction of the next *ahu* while keeping the last *ahu* in sight. Don't spend all your time at the Visitors Center (which features an informational film given "two thumbs up" by park rangers) or the Jaggar Museum—many of the park's highlights are accessible only by hiking.

> **GOING WITH THE FLOW.** Exploring lava flows past the end of Chain of Craters Rd. requires vigilance and care; the newly formed land is unstable and lava flows are unpredictable. The hike, which changes every day with the movement of the flow, is easier in the daytime but much more rewarding around sunset. As the sky darkens, "skylights" through the upper crust of a lava tube often appear. Before you set out, be aware of the dangers of lava. Whether the flow is 3hr. or 30min. from the end of the road, it pays to heed warnings. Consult the ranger station or national park service for eruption updates and safety information, watch the safety video at the Visitors Center (every hr. on the hr. daily 9am-4pm), and be prepared with gear (sunscreen, hat, sturdy shoes, water, a flashlight, pants, and all-purpose gloves.) Perhaps most importantly, stay on Pele's good side; what you actually see at the end of the road will depend wholly on her temperament at the time of your visit. It's always possible that conditions may be too dangerous to allow hikers onto the flow or that there is no visible lava. Precautions to keep in mind:
> **Stay off "benches"** created by lava flowing into the sea, and don't go near the water! Benches are extremely unstable and inevitably crash into the ocean below. The water itself is dangerous because splashing waves can carry molten lava into curious crowds.
> **Watch for fires!** Lava can easily set grasslands on fire. With a bit of wind, this can be very dangerous. Also, burning organic material causes the buildup of methane gas underground, which can ignite in powerful methane explosions.

KILAUEA IKI TRAIL. *(4 mi., 2-3hr. Moderate.)* The trail starts from the lava tube parking lot along Crater Rim Dr. If you only have time for one hike in the park, this may be it. Just over 40 years ago, the surface of the crater was a boiling lake of molten lava. Today, hikers revel in the experience of walking on what might be called hell frozen over. The hike itself is not very long, but give yourself plenty of time to enjoy the view from the crater floor. The first part of the hike descends 400 ft. through *ohia* and *hamuu* (tree fern) rainforest. Once in the crater, the desolate, moon-like landscape provides a rare opportunity to witness the first stages of ecological development following an eruption. Just 40 years after the lava drained from Kilauea Iki, signs of life are everywhere: fern fiddles have broken through and *ohia* trees have planted their first roots.

HALEMAUMAU TRAIL. *(3 mi. one-way, but many trail combinations possible. Moderate.)* This trail leaves from the Volcano House Hotel and traverses the smooth *pahoehoe* lava on the Kilauea Caldera floor to the Halemaumau Crater. The trail is perhaps the best way to experience the massive scale of the caldera, because it takes you directly through the center. The ground is often so hot that thermal updrafts create their own system of wind currents—if you're lucky, you may spot the *io*, a small red-brown hawk native to Hawaii, on a late afternoon glide. The Halemaumau trail connects to many other trails, and the best connections are with the **Kilauea Iki Trail** and the **Byron Ledge.** This trail traverses heavy sulfur emissions from the caldera; persons with respiratory problems or heart difficulties, pregnant women, infants, and young children should avoid this area.

PUU HULUHULU TRAIL. *(3 mi. Moderate.)* This short hike leaves from the Mauna Ulu Overlook and takes you to the summit of Puu Huluhulu ("shaggy hill"), a 150 ft. cinder cone formed by buildup from the eruption of Mauna Ulu in 1974. From here, you can see just about everything on a clear day: Mauna Loa, Mauna Ulu, Puu Oo's steaming vent and Kilauea's east rift zone, the beach, and the dramatic course of the 1969 and 1974 lava flows as they seared across the forest, leaving *kipukas* (islands of untouched forest) in their wake. Hiking beyond this point requires a permit from the Visitors Center, so most visitors turn back. To go farther into the heart of the current eruption, see below.

☒ NAPAU TRAIL. *(14 mi., 6-9hr. Challenging.)* Taking up where the Puu Huluhulu trail leaves off, the Napau trail is the only dayhike that requires hikers to register at the Visitors Center, due to Puu Oo's unpredictability, remote location, and risk. Napau is also the only trail that brings you as close as legally possible to the heart of the current eruption at the Puu Oo vent. If you were able to walk to the rim of Puu Oo and peer in, you'd see a giant, bubbling lava lake. Unfortunately, the land around Puu Oo is too unstable, so you can only go as far as Napau Crater to watch the billowing clouds of volcanic gas. On a clear day, the sight humbles even the bravest hikers. The surrounding rainforest houses an array of interesting birds; bring your binoculars. Also, be prepared to hike over long stretches of *aa* and *pahoehoe* flows, and bring a lot of water; the trail is hotter than asphalt in August and there are no facilities.

KEAUHOU AND PUNA COAST TRAILS. *(16 mi. through Keauhou or 19 mi. through Halape. Challenging.)* The hike leaves from Mau Loa o Mauna Ulu on Chain of Craters Rd., and descends the Hilina and Puueu cliffs through an ever-changing landscape of black lava, *ohia* forest, and grasslands. Interspersed throughout the hike are thin slivers of golden lava rock, known as Pele's hair, and small drops of shiny black lava rock, Pele's tears. At the end of trail (5 mi.) you can head straight to the tide pools of **Keauhou Shelter** (2 mi.) or continue to **☒Halape Shelter** (3 mi.).

If you have time, don't skip Halape. After hours of hiking, it appears on the horizon—a palm tree oasis in the desert. The white sand beaches here are a popular nesting site for endangered hawks bill and green sea turtles. Halape is only accessible by hiking 19 mi., and many travelers camp at the backcountry campsite. For those interested in exploring, there are two spots at Halape not to miss. The first is **Kumu Niu,** popularly called Halape Iki ("Halape the little"), a cove of white sand and palm trees that's great for snorkeling. To reach it, hike southwest along the coast for about 20min.; you can't miss it. The second is a **freshwater swimming hole.** To get there, stand with your back to the ocean, facing the pit toilet at Halape. You will notice a cliff that drops off into a ravine. Head toward the cliff and follow the ravine to your left until you see the pool.

Although not quite as magical as Halape, Keauhou is a great place to camp in the area. Beware of high surf and dangerous rip currents at all sites, and check weather forecasts before leaving. As for the facilities, expect pit toilets and bring water-purification tablets as the sites only offer non-potable water.

KAU DESERT AND HILINA PALI TRAIL. *(1-21 mi. Easy to challenging.)* The adventure starts at the **Kau Desert Trailhead,** along Rte. 11, 10 mi. west of the main park entrance, and can last as long as you want it to. In total, there are more than 21 mi. of trail between Crater Rim Dr. and Hilina Pali Overlook, but hiking any portion gives a taste of the desert and the intense heat and solitude that characterize this region. From the trailhead, it's an easy 1 mi. walk to the **Footprints Trail,** left in the desert rock after the 1790 eruption of Kilauea. A band of warriors was traveling across the desert back to Kau when the volcano spewed clouds of gas and ash that suffocated the men and immortalized their path.

 DESERT RAINS. A quick trip around Kilauea Caldera reveals a strange anomaly: within minutes the barren landscape of the Kau Desert in the southwest suddenly becomes a region of lush rainforest. The transition is so abrupt it seems impossible. The fact is, the Kau Desert is not technically a desert—it receives about as much rainfall as a tropical rainforest. The catch is that this rain, contaminated by sulfur dioxide gas, is as acidic as vinegar, with a pH level of about 3.4 during eruptions. Trade winds guide the acid rain over the Kau Desert, creating a stark contrast with the lush rainforest to the northeast. For more information, contact the **US Geological Survey, Hawaii Volcano Observatory** (☎808-967-7328; http://volcanoes.usgs.gov).

MAUNA LOA TRAIL. *(36 mi., 3-4 days. Challenging.)* The trailhead is the Mauna Loa Strip Rd. This steep 7000 ft. route climbs an average of 388 ft. per mile. The ascent to the summit of Mauna Loa passes through a moon-like expanse of barren *aa* and *pahoehoe.* Most hikers spend a night in the cabin at Red Hill (7 mi. from the lookout) in order to pace themselves and acclimate before trekking to Mauna Loa Cabin, at 13,250 ft. (For an intense day hike, just hike to Red Hill and back.) The immensity of the Mokuaweoweo Caldera may blow you away— that or the year-round flash snowstorms, which occur at this high altitude. The ascent is only for experienced and well-equipped backpackers. Altitude sickness is a frequent problem even among the extremely fit, causing dizziness, headaches, nausea, and fatigue. Prospective hikers should consult the rangers at the Visitors Center. Mauna Loa can also be reached by a less rigorous trail starting at the Mauna Loa Weather Observatory (p. 238).

PUNA

Cloaked in a canopy of lush green leaves and veiled in an edgy, alternative aura, Puna is perhaps the Big Island's best-hidden secret. Perched along the northern slopes of Hawaii's only two active volcanoes, Kilauea and Mauna Loa, Puna's risky nature evades the tourist and development craze that has destroyed much of the island's natural beauty. Although almost 80% of the rainforest here has been hacked away in recent decades, Puna is still a fertile haven for yogis, hippies, and generally open-minded travelers. The black sand beaches, natural lava pools, and volcano access welcome an amazing array of adventurers.

SHOULD-A, WOULD-A, PUNA. Though most of Puna's residents are welcoming, be certain to lock your car and park it in a safe, lighted area. If you are camping, park your ride as close to your campsite as possible to lower the risk of theft from or of your vehicle.

VOLCANO

Nestled in the thick of an ancient *hamuu* (tree fern) and *ohia* rainforest, Volcano Village (pop. 2231) sits at an elevation of nearly 4000 ft. During the 19th century, the fertile volcanic soil of the village attracted workers from around the world to labor in local sugarcane plantations. Drawn from across continents, these immigrants brought fragments of life from their native homes. Today, the native rainforest is interlaced with bamboo, wild orchid, ginger, Portuguese fire trees, and the purple *lasiandra*—a visual display of the patchwork in Volcano's history. Just over a mile northeast of Volcanoes National Park, Volcano Village has two historic general stores and beautiful B&Bs that accommodate the heavy traffic without losing a distinctive sense of community. Unless you plan on camping, stay here for the best volcano experience.

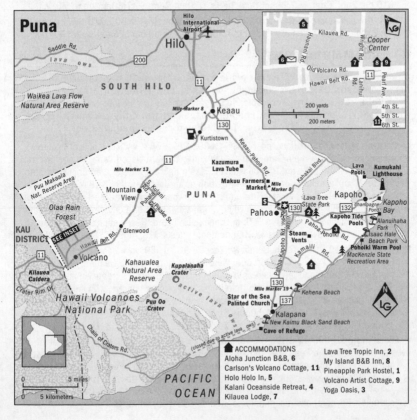

ACCOMMODATIONS
Aloha Junction B&B, **6**
Carlson's Volcano Cottage, **11**
Holo Holo In, **5**
Kalani Oceanside Retreat, **4**
Kilauea Lodge, **7**

Lava Tree Tropic Inn, **2**
My Island B&B Inn, **8**
Pineapple Park Hostel, **1**
Volcano Artist Cottage, **9**
Yoga Oasis, **3**

THE BIG ISLAND

⊕ ⚡ ORIENTATION AND PRACTICAL INFORMATION

Life in Volcano centers on **Old Volcano Highway (Old Volcano Road)**, which forks off **Route 11** and runs parallel to it for slightly over 1 mi. before stopping in a dead end at the northeast end of the village. **Haunani Road** and **Wright Road,** perpendicular to Volcano Rd., connect the village to Rte. 11. A car is the best option for getting to and from Volcano. Alternatively, the **Hele-On Bus** runs from the Mooheau Station in Hilo to the Visitors Center in Volcanoes National Park (p. 210), 1 mi. away, and might detour upon request.

Tourist Information: Volcano Visitor Center, 19-4084 Volcano Rd. (☎808-967-8662), in Volcano Village. Usually unmanned but full of brochures. Open daily 9am-5pm.

Laundromat: Volcano Wash and Dry, in Volcano Village, behind Volcano True Value. Wash $2.75, dry $2.00. Open daily 8am-7pm. Last wash 7pm.

Supplies: Volcano True Value (☎808-967-7969) carries batteries, flashlights, and water-purifying iodine tablets. Open daily 7:30am-5pm. AmEx/D/MC/V.

Police Station: The nearest **police station** (☎808-966-5835) is on Old Volcano Rd. in Keaau, just outside of Hilo.

Internet Access: Lava Rock Cafe (☎808-967-8526), on Old Volcano Rd. $4 per 20min., $10 per 24hr. Open M 7:30am-5pm, Tu-Sa 7:30am-9pm, Su 7:30am-4pm. MC/V.

Post Office: Volcano Post Office, 19-4030 Old Volcano Hwy. (☎800-275-8777), next to the Volcano Store. Open M-F 7:30am-3:30pm, Sa 11am-noon. **Postal Code:** 96785.

⚡ ACCOMMODATIONS

Since many visitors to Volcano decide to spend the night last minute, a lot of places have surcharges for one-night stays, and it's a good idea to book reservations before taking a trip here. **Volcano Lodging** (☎808-967-8617 or 800-908-9764), the **Volcano Village website** (www.volcanovillage.com), and the **Volcano Visitor Center** (see above) are good resources for finding local accommodations.

▨ **Carson's Volcano Cottages,** on 6th St. (☎808-967-7683; www.carsonscottage.com). Detached from the main strip, Old Volcano Rd., Carson's is off Jade St., before mi. marker 26 heading toward Hilo on Rte. 11. Take a right on Jade and another right onto 6th St. If you're aching for a pampering, look no further than this B&B located in the heart of the rainforest. Most of the large, ornate rooms and cottages feature luxuries like wood-burning stoves, goose-down comforters, cable TV, and private hot tubs. Breakfast buffet included. Check-in 3-5pm. Check-out 11am. Reservations recommended. Doubles $115; private cabins $130; additional guests $15. AmEx/D/MC/V. ❸

▨ **Holo Holo In,** 19-4036 Kalani Honua Rd. (☎808-967-7950; www.enable.org/holoholo). From Volcanoes Park, make a left onto Volcano Rd.; turn left onto Haunani Rd. just past the Volcano Store, and left again onto Kalani Honua Rd. Built to create an inviting spot for international travelers, the Holo Holo In is a backpacker's dream, with laundry, showers, a spacious kitchen, free Internet access, and an eclectic (mostly Japanese) library collection. Linens $1. Wash $1.50, dry $0.25 per 7min. Check-in 4:30-9pm. Check-out 11am. Quiet hours 10pm-6am. Dorms $18; doubles $45. Cash only. ❶

My Island B&B Inn, 19-3896 Old Volcano Rd. (☎808-967-7216; www.myislandinnhawaii.com), between Pearl Ave. and Wright Rd. The owner of this family-run B&B, Gordon Morse, has written several guides to the Hawaiian Islands, all of which are available to guests. The house was originally built by the Lyman family (the Big Island's first missionaries) in 1886, and all of the rooms—though on the small side—are quaint and charming. Reservations recommended. Rooms $65-150. MC/V. ❷

Volcano Artist Cottage, 19-3436 Old Volcano Rd. (☎808-985-8979; www.volcanoartistcottage.com). Drawn away behind the Volcano Garden Arts gallery and natural foods cafe, this cottage is a quiet little getaway for 2. The room is simple but elegant with 1 queen-size bed and a remarkably indulgent granite walk-in shower. Contemplative gardens and greenhouse behind. $129, 10% discount for 3 or more nights. MC/V. ❸

Aloha Junction B&B, 19-4037 Post Office Ln. (☎808-967-7289; www.bnbvolcano.com), off Old Volcano Hwy., behind a gate. Extremely well-maintained and equipped with a state-of-the-art entertainment room, Aloha Junction is furnished with big comfy beds, Internet, equipment for guest use, and a hot tub to recuperate after a long day of *pahoehoe* hikes. Full kitchen. Breakfast of delicious fruit included. Check-in 3-6pm. Check-out 10am. Rooms with private bath $125-165; additional guests $15. MC/V. ❸

Kilauea Lodge, Old Volcano Rd. (☎808-967-7366; www.kilauealodge.com), between Haunani and Wright Rd. The community spirit is still evident around the 1938 Fireplace of Friendship at this old YMCA summer camp, but with a ski chalet vibe and plenty of inviting reading nooks, the rooms are nothing like the average camp. Hot tub. Check-in 3pm. Check-out noon. Reservations recommended. Rooms $160-280; additional guests $20. AAA discount 10%. AmEx/MC/V. ❹

▐ FOOD

Volcano is a great place for park daytrippers to stock up on food and supplies. **The Volcano Store,** 19-4005 Haunani Rd., at the corner of Old Volcano Hwy. and Haunani Rd., has groceries and general supplies. (☎808-967-7210. Open daily 5am-7pm. AmEx/D/MC/V.) **Kilauea General Store,** 19-3972 Old Volcano Hwy., between Haunani and Wright Rd., serves a soup of the day ($3.75) and pizza by the slice ($2.25), and stocks general supplies. (☎808-967-7555. Open M-Sa 7am-7:30pm, Su 7am-7pm. AmEx/D/MC/V.) The **Volcano farmers' market** sets up shop on Sundays (7am until the merchandise runs out—usually before 8am) at the Cooper Center, near the corner of Old Volcano Rd. and Wright Rd.

Volcano's Lava Rock Cafe, Old Volcano Rd. (☎808-967-8526), behind Kilauea General Store. A little obsessed with the volcano theme, this cafe offers "seismic sandwiches," "lava tube plates," and "tsunami salads." At around $8 for every item, it's a steal. Favorites include sweetbread french toast ($7) and grilled *mahi mahi* ($8). Free Wi-Fi for customers. Open M 7:30am-5pm, Tu-Sa 7:30am-9pm, Su 7:30am-4pm. MC/V. ❷

Volcano Golf and Country Club, Pii Mauna Dr. (☎808-967-8228), head left out of Volcanoes National Park on Hwy. 11, turn right on Pii Mauna Dr. This restaurant in the clubhouse is the perfect place to fuel up for breakfast ($5-10) before heading into the park (try the "choose 3" omelettes), or to refuel after hiking around the lava flows at lunchtime ($8-15). Open M-F 8am-3pm, Sa-Su 7:30am-4pm. ❷

Thai Thai Restaurant, 19-4084 Old Volcano Rd. (☎808-967-7969). Classic Thai cuisine adds another dimension to Volcano's fiery mix. Massaman curry $11, with shrimp $16. Thai basil stir-fry $10. Dinner $12-30. Open daily 5-9pm. AmEx/D/MC/V. ❸

Kiawe Kitchen (☎808-967-7711), next to the Old Volcano Store, off Old Volcano Rd. After a day of hiking in the park, Kiawe's 10 in. pizzas ($13 and up) hit the spot. Sandwiches, like the wood-fired roasted chicken ($10), are tasty but a little pricey. Specials change daily. Open M-Tu and Th-Su noon-2:30pm and 5:30-9:30pm. MC/V. ❸

PAHOA

The hippie center in Puna, Pahoa (pop. 962) is perhaps best known for its beach gatherings and cultural retreat facilities, where visitors come to rejuvenate their spirits with yoga, dance, and meditation in an unspoiled region.

Set on striking lava flows, the area around Pahoa offers a diverse natural environment that is best captured as a roadtrip from Rte. 130 to Rte. 132, to the historic coastal Rte. 137, and back to Rte. 130. On weekends, pass through one of Pahoa's popular farmers' markets and assemble a fresh picnic lunch before hitting the long stretch of black sand and lava cliff beaches on Rte. 137.

ORIENTATION AND PRACTICAL INFORMATION

From Volcano, **Route 11** heads northeast, where it intersects **Route 130 (Pahoa-Kapoho Road).** Pahoa is located to the south, off Rte. 130 near its intersection with **Route 132,** slightly less than 20 mi. south of Hilo. Heading *makai* (toward the ocean), take a right at the sign for Pahoa Village onto **Pahoa Village Road** (also called **Old Pahoa Road** or **Government Main Road**); most of Pahoa's attractions can be found along this 1 mi. stretch through town, although accommodations and activities are down the hill. Most of the whole area's sights are in the triangle formed by Rte. 130, Rte. 132, and **Route 137** (a scenic ocean highway that is cut off by an old lava flow). These highways are often labeled by the towns they connect; for instance, part of Rte. 130 is known as **Pahoa-Kapoho Road,** and Rte. 137 is often referred to as the **Red Road,** because it used to be a red clay road.

Banks: First Hawaiian Bank (☎808-965-8621), on Government Main Rd., has a **24hr. ATM.** Open M-Th 8:30am-4pm, F 8:30am-6pm.

Libraries: Pahoa Public Library, 15-3070 Pahoa-Kalapana Rd. (☎808-965-2171), adjacent to the school at the intersection of Hwy. 132 and Hwy. 130. From town, turn right just before the stoplight. **Internet access** is available with a 3-month visitor's card ($10). 3 terminals available on the hr. Open M 1-8pm, Tu-F 9am-5pm.

Laundromat: Suds 'N Duds (☎808-965-2621), off Old Pahoa Rd. in Pahoa Village Center. Wash $1.50-2.50, dry $0.25 per 5min. Open daily 7:30am-7:30pm.

Swimming Pool: There is a free public swimming pool behind Pahoa Cash & Carry. Open M-F 9am-6pm, Sa-Su 9am-5pm.

Internet access: Enjoy a cup of joe or a fresh smoothie while surfing the web at **Aloha Outpost Cafe** (☎808-965-8333), in the Pahoa Village Marketplace just off Rte. 130. $7 per hr., rates are cheaper during the middle of the day; F $4 per hr. all day. Open M-F 8am-6pm, Sa-Su 8am-5pm. AmEx/D/MC/V.

Police: Police Satellite (☎808-935-3311), on Government Main Rd., across from Pahoa Hardware. Phone outside the station connects to dispatcher.

Pharmacy: Pahoa Rx Pharmacy (☎808-965-7535), in the Pahoa Village Center. Open M-F 9am-12:30pm and 1:30-5pm, Sa 9am-noon.

Post Office: Pahoa Post Office, 15-2859 Puna Rd. (☎800-275-8777). Open M-F 8:30am-4pm, Sa 11am-2pm. **Postal Code:** 96778.

ACCOMMODATIONS

In addition to the places below, it is possible to camp in Mackenzie State Recreation Area (p. 225), which offers some of the best camping along the coast. There is also roadside camping in Isaac Hale Beach Park (p. 224).

Pineapple Park Hostel, 7927 Pikake St. (☎877-800-3800; www.pineapple-park.com). In Mountain View, heading west on Rte. 11, turn left onto South Kalani Rd. after mi. marker 13. At the T-junction, turn right onto Pohala St., follow it to the end of the pavement, and turn left onto Pikake St. Although a bit out of the way, Pineapple Park sees a lot of student traffic and has a large kitchen with complimentary snacks, a grill, laundry facilities (wash $1, dry $2), Internet access, and a nice backyard with a gazebo. Ask about getting a bed for a few hr. of housekeeping per week. Quiet hours after 10pm. Bunks $30; private rooms $80; VIP suite $100. MC/V. ❷

🏚 **Yoga Oasis,** 13-1776 Pohoiki Rd. (☎808-965-8460; www.yogaoasis.org), about 2 mi. from Rte. 137. The colorfully flagged driveway marks a rollicking route towards relaxation and rejuvenation at this place which "attempts to stretch more than your body!" Most guests stay in cabins painted with invigorating colors and adorned with soft linens and inviting tubs. Others stay in the main house, while bargain hunters camp on the lawn. All stays include morning yoga class and a fresh fruit breakfast spread. Classes ($10) open to non-guests each day at 8am. Call for reservations. Camping $35; singles $75-175; doubles $100-145; cabins $120-145. MC/V. Camping ❷/Rooms ❸

🏚 **Kalani Oceanside Retreat,** RR2 Box 4500, on Rte. 137 (☎808-965-7828; www.kalani. com), between mi. markers 17 and 18. This New Age oasis of creativity is a unique experience. Spectacular oceanfront setting, sumptuous vegetarian and vegan options ($11-22), a tight-knit community of volunteers, and a variety of classes including yoga, ecstatic dance, waterdance, salsa, and hip hop during the week (prices vary from donations to $12). Free Internet access in the cafe 7-10pm. The 1- or 3-month volunteer program provides a unique short-term work alternative. Quiet hours after 10pm. Check-out 11am. Reservations recommended. Campsites $30; dorms $60; rooms with shared bath $105-140, with private bath $150-270. AmEx/D/MC/V. Camping ❷/Rooms ❸

Lava Tree Tropic Inn, 14-3555 Puna Rd. (☎808-965-7441; www.lavatreetropicinn.com), next to Lava Tree State Park; follow the sign about 500 yd. past the park entrance and turn right up the driveway. This house sits in a patch of sunlight among a dark green forest. The iron gate at the bottom of the driveway is unlocked—just slide it across yourself and drive in. The rooms are neat, spacious, and recently renovated. Breakfast included. Check-in 3pm. Check-out noon. $80-130, $10 extra for 1-night stays. MC/V. ❸

🍴 FOOD

Weekends in Pahoa offer endless options to explore local farmers' markets and craft villages. The largest two are the **Makuu Farmers Association Cultural and Craft Village** on Sundays from 8am to mid-afternoon (located on Hwy. 130, just over 2 mi. north of Pahoa near mi. marker 8; look for the "slow down" signs), known for its signature **Cane Juice Stand** offering juices, sorbet, and hemp seed and cane ice cream ($2-3); and the 🏚**Pahoa farmers' market** (☎808-965-9990), weekends from 6am to 3pm, on Pahoa Village Rd. at the intersection with Kauhale St., which has great fresh fruit and produce. **Raisin' Cane,** 15-2958 Pahoa Village Rd. (☎808-965-5486), hidden in a clothing store just in front of Yoga Shala, has some of the best homemade sorbet on the island. The free "Discovery Tour of the Dipper Freezer" is well worth the hunt. One scoop $2; smoothies $6. For an indoor option try **Island Natural Groceries,** 15-1403 Pahoa Village Rd. (☎808-965-6263), next to the Pahoa Natural Emporium. The organic and all-natural products here are a tad pricey, but have attracted a cult following. Hot lunch and sandwiches are sold for reasonable prices.

🏚 **Luquin's Mexican Restaurant,** 15-2942 Pahoa Village Rd. (☎808-965-9990). For breakfast, lunch, or dinner, Luquin's is a Tex-Mex lover's heaven. The famous *huevos rancheros* ($7.25) come with a healthy portion of beans, eggs, tortillas, and their own secret sauce. During happy hour (4-6pm), double shot margaritas are sure to please the tequila lover (only $5!). One of the few places to find both breakfast and nightlife in Pahoa; stop here to get your party fix with the locals. Open daily 7am-2am. Breakfast served 7-11am. Lunch and dinner served 11am-9pm. ❶

🏚 **Kaleo's,** 15-2969 Pahoa Village Rd. (☎808-965-5600). Touted as the best new restaurant in town, Kaleo's offers a huge variety of fantastic food at fair prices. The turkey, avocado, and Swiss wrap ($8) makes a great lunch. For dinner, try the delicious *Kalbi* ribs (korean short ribs $12). Kaleo's also offers live music nightly. Get there M-F 5-5:30pm and get ½ off your entree. Open Tu-F for lunch 11am-3pm; daily for dinner 4-10pm. ❷

▨ **Ning's Thai Cuisine,** 15-2955 Pahoa Village Rd. (☎808-965-7611), is a popular Pahoa destination known for its reasonable prices and luscious spices. The coconut soup ($5) has reached celebrity status in town. Try the yellow curry (with chicken, beef, pork, fish, or tofu; $8-12). Entrees $8-12. Open M-Sa noon-9pm, Su 5-9pm. AmEx/D/MC/V. ❷

Paolo's Bistro, 15-2951 Pahoa Village Rd. (☎808-965-7033). This quaint, cozy restaurant feels like home—if home had an award-winning Italian chef in the kitchen, that is. Follow your nose past the kitchen and onto the flowery garden gazebo seating area for a breath of fresh air over dinner. Entrees like the pasta primavera ($15) run between $11-17. Open daily 5:30-9pm. MC/V. ❸

Baraka Foods Cafe, 15-2945 Pahoa Village Rd. (☎808-965-0305). Here, organic food, teas, and smoothies are the names of the game. Sandwiches, like the Mediterranean avocado pesto sandwich, go for $9. Smoothies $6.75. Open W-Su 5-9pm. MC/V. ❷

Pahoa Fresh Fish, (☎808-965-8248), in Pahoa Village Marketplace. The ideal stop before a BBQ or fishing outing; besides fresh fish, they sell tackle and supplies. Buy a rod and get a free, if premature, fish sandwich. Whole *ahi* $2.50 per lb.; *mahi mahi* $12 per lb.; fish and chips $8. Open M-F 8am-7pm and Sa-Su 9am-7pm. MC/V. ❷

▷ BEACHES

▨ **KEHENA BEACH.** *(Open daily 24hr.)* One of the few undiscovered places left on the island, this secluded black sand beach is private and quiet during the week. Weekends are busy, especially on Sunday afternoons, when the Kalani ecstatic dance crowd meanders down for a drum circle that lasts until sunset. Nudity may be illegal on Hawaiian beaches, but bikinis and board shorts are regularly used here as makeshift pillows. *(Roadside parking is somewhat questionable, so be sure to lock up before trekking down. Located at mi. marker 19 on Hwy. 137. The path is marked by the "Government Property" sign to the left of the parking area when you're facing the ocean.)*

ALANUIHAHA PARK. *(Open daily 7am-7pm. Lifeguards 9:30am-4:45pm.)* Alanuihaha Park is an ocean- and spring-fed pool warmed by volcanic steam vents and protected from strong tides by a man-made wall. The site is one of the few places on the southeast coast where swimming is safe and bath-water warm year round, making it a popular weekend attraction for local families. Toilets and shelters are available. *(½ mi. past mi. marker 10 on Hwy. 137.)*

ISAAC HALE BEACH PARK. *(Surfing. Open daily 24hr.)* One of the few surfing spots on the Big Island, Isaac Hale is fun for both surfers and spectators, as the bay allows those on the beach to get close to the action. It's also a popular launching spot for local fishermen and a favorite place for roadside camping, with toilets and picnic shelters. For the surfers, this beach goes by the moniker Pohoiki. There are four breaks here, from south to north: 1st Bay, 2nd Bay, Shacks, and Bowls. Be respectful; many locals are hesitant to share the waves. *(Take Hwy. 137; the beach is near mi. marker 11, less than 1 mi. south of Alanuihaha.)*

◐ SIGHTS

The triangle defined by Rte. 130, 132, and 137 makes an exceptional daytrip, and the drive itself, especially along the coastal highway (Hwy. 137), is as enjoyable as any of the sights. The scenery alternates between old forests, lava fields, and ocean views. But be careful if thinking of swimming: the surf can be dangerous. The calmest water is at Champagne Pond and Alanuihaha.

LAVA TREE STATE PARK. As you head east on Hwy. 132, giant *albizia* trees arch over the road where an eruption from Kilauea's East Rift Zone in 1790 drowned the surrounding rainforest in *pahoehoe* lava. Formed as lava cooled around water-holding *ohia*, the trees eventually burned away, leaving a hardened forest of lava shells behind. The park allows visitors a closer look at the lava trees (though they can be seen easily from the road) as well as restrooms and picnic shelters.

KUMUKAHI LIGHTHOUSE. The old lighthouse has been replaced by a new and unremarkable steel structure that is useful mostly as a landmark for the popular Champagne Pond and the great-for-snorkeling tide pools of **Kapoho Bay**. Champagne Pond (often bubbling, hence the name) is one of the island's most-talked-about swimming havens, protected from the turbulent surrounding surf by the bay and heated by volcanic activity below. *(Coming east on Hwy. 132, don't turn onto Hwy. 137, but continue straight on the dirt road toward the ocean. From the lighthouse, the road to the ponds is only accessible with 4WD, but the 1½ mi. walk isn't too bad. The tide pools of Kapoho Bay are more easily reached by Kapoho-Kai Rd. off Hwy. 137.)*

LAVA POOLS. Wade through this natural pool as the waves crash continuously against a craggy wall of *aa* lava. The pools are somewhat difficult to find, but well worth the chase. *(3 mi. north on Rte. 137 after the intersection with Rte. 132, turn down a well-covered dirt driveway beneath a low ceiling of trees. Continue for about 1500 yd. until you reach the ocean, then turn left and walk for another 100 yd. Those without 4WD should walk.)*

MACKENZIE STATE RECREATION AREA. Set on elegant cliffs overlooking the Pacific under the shade of an old Ironwood grove, this area is quiet, secluded, and the best place to camp along the coast. Permits are required for camping. To get to the entrance, face the ocean and walk left for approximately 100 yd. See **Camping in Hawaii**, p. 82, for permit information. *(Off Hwy. 137 between mi. markers 13 and 14. Note: The stretch of road between Isaac Hale and Mackenzie often floods during high tide. 4WD in the park is a good idea to ensure that you don't get stuck.)*

KALAPANA. Although Kalapana was once home to a thriving Hawaiian fishing village and world-renowned black sand beaches, Pele's merciless lava flows covered this town between 1989-1991. **Kalapana Cafe**, 12-5032 Pahoa Kalapana Rd. (☎808-965-0121), still stands. Sandwiches $8-10, burgers $9. This fast-food drive-in now has an

ON THE MENU

THE COLOR PURPLE

Most visitors, upon first look, would pooh-pooh *poi*, a purple Hawaiian paste made from the boiled tuber of a taro plant. The dish—with its slightly sour taste, gray-purplish color and gluey consistency—strikes many as unpalatable; indeed, hotels make sure to throw cream and sugar into the mix when serving it to tourists. Locals, however, relish it sans sweetener. They can only pity those who are missing out on the delicate flavors of a staple that is chock-full of fiber, vitamin C, magnesium, potassium, and other minerals.

For the Polynesians who colonized Hawaii and much of the South Pacific islands, taro was one of the few sources of starch in their diet. Its importance as a food source spilled over into various myths and customs. For one thing, taro was believed to be an ancestor of the Hawaiian people. Only men were allowed to cultivate taro, and an initiation during childhood was making one's first batch of *poi*. Additionally, when a bowl of *poi* was unveiled during mealtime, all family strife had to cease.

Today *poi* still has a lead role in Hawaiian cuisine, making regular appearances on plate lunches, supermarket shelves, and family BBQs. While most of the country's taro crop is turned into *poi*, an increasingly large percentage of it is fried, salted, and eaten as chips. Visitors are advised, however, that chips can be eaten anywhere on the mainland, but nothing is as quintessentially Hawaiian as *poi*.

excuse to be as pricey as it wants, and when that *pahoehoe* starts heating up, the $4.55 milkshakes are worth every penny.

HILO

Kona and Hilo (pop. 40,759) may be the only two cities on the Big Island, but they are worlds apart. Kona is a tourist magnet, and Hilo is the opposite pole: a laid-back town that sees comparatively little outside traffic. Due to driving ocean winds, Hilo's beaches pale in comparison with those on the leeward coast. However, Hilo offers endless road and mountain biking trails, good summer surfing, and easy access to Saddle Road. The streets of Hilo's old-fashioned downtown also offer a glimpse into the city's tragic past. Devastated by tsunamis in 1946 and 1960, the city remembers the natural disasters through park memorials and the Pacific Tsunami Museum. Clear from the tourism that clogs up the Kona side of the island, Hilo's residents are usually less friendly to tourists. Indeed, the city itself may seem a bit run-down. However, with great food and easy access to adventure, Hilo may be a worthwhile stop.

◪ TRANSPORTATION

INTERCITY TRANSPORTATION

Bus: Hilo is the hub of the **Hele-On Bus** (☎808-961-8744; www.co.hawaii.hi.us); it is easier to get around the island from here than from anywhere else. Buses depart from the green-roofed **Mooheau Bus Terminal,** at the corner of Mamo St. and Kamehameha Ave. Open M-F 8:30am-4:30pm. The office, which employs a very helpful staff, is a light in the dark of an utterly confusing bus system. Every Hele-On bus is free (though drivers might charge you $5 for baggage), but the schedules are hard to follow. Still, going from Hilo to the major sights is entirely feasible and economical with the Hele-On. It runs to: **Kailua-Kona** (3hr., M-Sa 1:10pm) via **Honokaa** (1hr.); **Waimea** (2hr.); **Kau** (2hr.) via **Hawaii Volcanoes National Park** (1hr., 2:40pm); **Pahala** (1hr.); **Naalehu/Waiohinu** (2hr.); **Ocean View** (2hr.); **Pahoa** (1hr., M-F 5 times a day). See **Interisland Transportation,** p. 187, for more information on transportation and the Hilo International Airport.

LOCAL TRANSPORTATION

Bus: Hele-On (☎808-961-8744) also runs an intra-Hilo bus system that makes stops throughout town, including Banyan Dr., Prince Kuhio Plaza, Hilo Library, and Hilo Medical Center via Mooheau Bus Terminal. The bus is free to ride, but there is a $5 dollar charge per bag for travelers. (M-F 7:05am-4:30pm).

Taxis: All taxis charge $3 initially, the $2.40 per additional mi.

A-1 Bob's Taxi (☎808-959-4800) serves Hilo, Puna, and Hamakua. Operates 5am-10pm.

Hilo Harry's (☎808-935-7091), based in Hilo, covers most of the island. Operates 5am-10pm.

Shaka Taxi (☎808-987-1111) has 24hr. service and 6-person vans.

Car Rental: All national chains have offices at the airport (☎808-934-5840), on Airport Access Rd., off Rte. 11 about 1 mi. south of the intersection of Rte. 11 and Rte. 19.

▨ Enterprise (☎808-331-2509) in Kona (p. 190) has low rates; call before reserving elsewhere.

Alamo (☎808-961-3343). 21+. Under-25 fee $25 per day. Open daily 6am-8:30pm.

Budget (☎808-935-6878, ext. 25). 21+. Under-25 fee $25 per day. Open daily 6am-8:30pm.

Harper Car and Truck Rentals of Hawaii, 456 Kalanianaole Ave. (☎808 969-1478), rents 4WD and economy cars. Few travel restrictions. 25+. Open M-Th 6:30am-5pm, F-Su 6:30am-6pm.

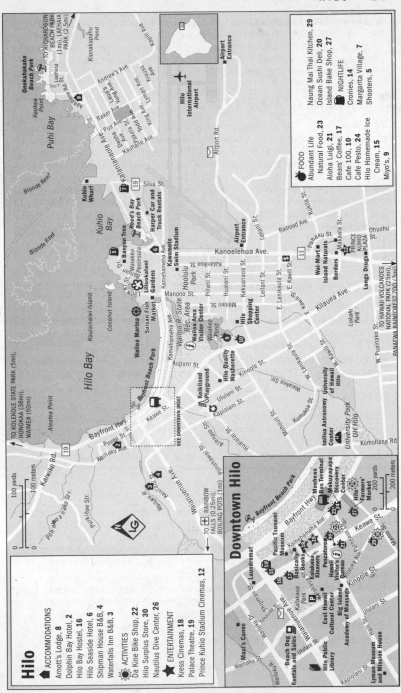

THE BIG ISLAND

Hilo

▲ ACCOMMODATIONS
Arnott's Lodge, **8**
Dolphin Bay Hotel, **2**
Hilo Bay Hostel, **16**
Hilo Seaside Hotel, **6**
Shipman House B&B, **4**
Waterfalls Inn B&B, **3**

☀ ACTIVITIES
Da Kine Bike Shop, **22**
Hilo Surplus Store, **30**
Nautilus Dive Center, **26**

★ ENTERTAINMENT
Kress Cinemas, **18**
Palace Theatre, **19**
Prince Kuhio Stadium Cinemas, **12**

♨ FOOD
Abundant Life
  Natural Food, **23**
Aloha Luigi, **21**
Bears' Coffee, **17**
Cafe 100, **10**
Cafe Pesto, **24**
Hilo Homemade Ice
  Cream, **15**
Miyo's, **9**
Naung Mai Thai Kitchen, **29**
Ocean Sushi Deli, **20**
Island Bake Shop, **27**

NIGHTLIFE
Cronies, **14**
Margarita Village, **7**
Shooters, **5**

Downtown Hilo

Bike Rental: ◼**Da Kine Bike Shop,** 12 Furneaux Ln. (☎808-934-9861). Run by a group of cycling enthusiasts, Da Kine is at the center of the island's cycling scene. The community of riders is very welcoming; newcomers may find themselves invited on biking excursions around the island. Although they don't technically rent bikes, their "sell and buy back" program ends up around $10-15 per day. Open M-Sa noon-6pm. D/MC/V.

✈ ORIENTATION

Hilo lies' on the Big Island's east coast, at the intersection of **Route 19 (Bayfront Highway),** from the Hamakua Coast and Waimea, and **Route 11,** from Hawaii Volcanoes National Park. Kailua-Kona is 87 mi. away, across Saddle Rd. Rte. 19 and **Kamehameha Avenue** run parallel to each other next to Hilo Bay, and Kamehameha serves as downtown's de facto Main St. Farther back from the water, **Kilauea Avenue** (which turns into downtown's Keawe St.) and **Kinoole Avenue** are the main arteries that run parallel to the bay. **Waianuenue Avenue** is the major cross street and becomes Kaumana Drive, and then Saddle Rd. Rte. 11 **(Kanoelehua Avenue),** southeast of downtown, goes from the water to the airport.

⚡ PRACTICAL INFORMATION

TOURIST AND FINANCIAL SERVICES

Tourist Information: The Hawaii Visitor's Bureau, 250 Keawe St. (☎808-961-5797 or 800-648-2441; www.bigisland.org), at the corner of Keawe and Haili St., is primarily a marketing agency for the island but provides a decent map and helpful directions. Open M-F 8am-4:30pm. **Mooheau Bus Terminal** (p. 226) also serves as a Visitors Center.

Banks: Visitors should have no problem finding a bank in Hilo. **Bank of Hawaii** and **First Hawaiian Bank** have multiple locations, most with **24hr. ATMs.**

LOCAL SERVICES

Bookstores: Otherwise known as "The Map Shop," **Basically Books,** 160 Kamehameha Ave. (☎808-961-0144), on the waterfront, stocks the reliable Nell's Maps and shelves of Hawaiiana (Hawaiian literature). Open M-Sa 9am-5pm, Su 10am-4pm.

Library: ◼**Hilo Public Library,** 300 Waianuenue Ave. (☎808-933-8888), is blessed with a dynamic and welcoming staff. Centered around a grassy courtyard, half of this library is open-air. Internet access available on 6 computers with a 3-month visitor's card ($10). Open Tu-W 11am-7pm, Th and Sa 9am-5pm, F 10am-5pm.

Laundromats: Hole-in-the-wall and unnamed, Hilo's cheapest laundromat is around the corner from Hilo Bay Hostel, at the intersection of Keawe and Shipman St. Wash $1.50, magma-temperature dry $0.25 per 5min. Open daily 4am-11pm. Last wash 10pm. **Hilo Quality Washerette,** 210 Hoku St. (☎808-961-6490), near the corner of Kinoole. Wash $1.50-4, dry $0.25 per 5min. Open daily 6am-10pm. Last wash 8:45pm.

Swimming Pool: 799 Piilani St. (☎808-961-8698), in Hoolulu Sports Complex. Facing the waterfront in downtown Hilo, take Kamehameha Ave. south toward Volcano-bound Rte. 11 and turn right on the street before Kanoelehua St. Olympic-sized pool open to the public daily, but hours are subject to lifeguard availability. 3 designated public swim sessions daily: 9-10:45am, 1:30-3:45pm, and 6-7:10pm.

Equipment Rental: Hilo Surplus Store, 148 Mamo St. (☎808-935-6398). Much of the equipment here is military surplus, and another large portion is secondhand. Open M-Sa 8am-5pm. AmEx/D/MC/V. Scuba divers should drop by **Nautilus Dive Center,**

382 Kamehameha Ave. (☎808-966-8773), across from the bus terminal, next to the farmers' market. Instruction, certification, and rentals. Open M-Sa 9am-4pm.

Weather Conditions: ☎808-935-8555. The Internet-connected touch screen outside of Mokupapapa Discovery Center, on Kamehameha Ave. near the farmers' market, next to **Cafe Pesto** (p. 231), also provides detailed weather and surf conditions. 24hr.

EMERGENCY AND COMMUNICATIONS

Police: Hilo Police Station, 349 Kapiolani St. (☎808-935-3311), at the corner of Kapiolani Ave. and Hualalai St.

Rape Crisis Hotline: ☎808-935-0677. 24hr.

Pharmacy: 111 E. Puainako St. (☎808-959-5881), in Prince Kuhio Plaza, next to Safeway. Open M-F 8am-10pm, Sa-Su 8am-9pm.

Medical Services: Hilo Medical Center, 1190 Waianuenue Ave. (☎808-974-4700). 24hr. emergency room.

Internet Access: When the library is closed, try **Beach Dog Computer Services,** 62 Kinoole St. (☎808-961-5207), at the corner of Kinoole and Waianuenue. $2.50 for 1st 20min., $0.13 per min. thereafter; $8 per hr. **Hilo Bay Hostel** (☎808-933-2771) also has 4 Internet terminals for $5 per hr.

Post Offices: Hilo Main Post Office, 1299 Kekuanaoa St. (☎800-275-8777), on the road to the airport. Open M-F 8am-4:30pm, Sa 8:30am-12:30pm. **Downtown Hilo,** 154 Waianuenue Ave. Open M-F 8am-4pm, Sa 12:30-2pm.

Postal Code: 96720 (Main Post Office); 96721 (Downtown Hilo).

ACCOMMODATIONS

▨ **Hilo Bay Hostel,** 101 Waianuenue Ave. (☎808-933-2771; www.hawaiihostel.net), on the corner by Keawe St. This is a clean, airy, well-run hostel in a perfect downtown location. Crisp cotton linens provided. Well-kept kitchen available until 9:45pm. Internet access $3 per 30min., $5 per hr. Refundable $10 key deposit. Check-out 11am. Quiet hours after 10pm. Dorms $25; 2 double beds (up to 4) with bath $65. Hilo Bay Hostel also owns an offsite property called "The Garden" which rents campsites ($15 per night); there are, however, better places to camp around Hilo. MC/V. ❶

▨ **Dolphin Bay Hotel,** 333 Iliahi St. (☎877-935-1466; www.dolphinbayhotel.com). Take Keawe St. over the Wailuku River north of town and make the 2nd left onto Iliahi. A short walk from downtown, this meticulously maintained hotel is one of the best values in Hilo. All 18 large rooms have a full kitchen and cable TV; some have their own *lanai*. Local coffee, fresh papaya, and bananas are available in the lobby, along with warm cinnamon rolls shipped from a local bakery. Free Wi-Fi in the lobby, BBQ pits for guest use, and coin-op laundry. Check-out 11am. Reservations recommended. Doubles for 4 $79-89; suites for 6 $109-129; additional guests $10. MC/V. ❸

NEED INTERNET NOW? If you're desperate, almost all hotels have business centers with Internet access for public use. This convenience does come at a cost: be prepared to pay around $0.50-0.75 per min.

Arnott's Lodge, 98 Apapane Rd. (☎808-969-7097; www.arnottslodge.com). From the end of Rte. 11, turn right onto Kalanianaole St. and continue for over 1 mi. Turn left on Apapane Rd. This well-run hostel has plenty of camping space, dorm beds, and private rooms. Common area has cable TV and hundreds of DVDs. Internet access, full laundry, and kitchen facilities. Also rents bikes and snorkeling equipment, and runs tours to

Volcanoes National Park, Mauna Kea, and Hamakua Coast (guests $50-60, non-guests $75-90). Info on short-term work available in the area. Sa free pizza and beer parties. Check-out 10am. Camping $10 per person; bunks $25; singles $60; doubles $57, with bath $70; 2-bedroom suite for 6 with kitchen $130. AmEx/D/MC/V. ❶

Hilo Seaside Hotel, 126 Banyan Dr. (☎808-935-0821; www.hiloseasidehotel.com), near the Kalanianaole Ave. Overlooking a quiet sliver of Hilo Bay, this low-key hotel is a no-frills place for a night. Clean and simple rooms with A/C, ceiling fans, fridges, *lanai*, and cable TV. Rooms near the swimming pool are secluded from the noisy street. An attached (but unaffiliated) restaurant, Coconut Grill, serves up seafood and steak dinners. Check-in 3pm. Check-out noon. Rooms $82-110. AmEx/D/MC/V. ❸

Shipman House Bed and Breakfast, 131 Kaiulani St. (☎808-934-8002; www.hilo-hawaii.com). From Rte. 19, take Waianuenue Ave. 5 blocks, turn right on Kaiulani St., and cross over the rumbling bridge. Family owned since 1901, a Victorian-style house with spacious rooms, porches, lofty ceilings, and classy ambience. All with private bath: 1 with claw-foot tub and 1 with magnificent ocean view. Robes and kimonos provided. Continental breakfast included. Check-in 3-6pm. Check-out 10am. Reservations recommended. Doubles $219-249; each additional guest $35. AmEx/MC/V. ❺

Waterfalls Inn, 240 Kaiulani St., (☎808-969-3407; www.waterfallsinn.com). Head out of town on Saddle Rd., and make a right on Kaiulani St. The Inn is ½ mi. up on the right. In the same spirit of the Shipman House down the road, this wonderful old house, built at the end of the Victorian period, fits well within its tropical surroundings, with windows that reach from the floor to the roof, and a breakfast nook with a 270° view of the lush outdoors. 2-person whirlpool tub. Rooms $140-160. AmEx/D/MC/V. ❹

◘ FOOD

Hilo is full of fantastic food joints. To do it yourself, the colorful **Hilo farmers' market,** on Mamo St. between Kamehameha and Kilauea, runs all day, every day. **Island Naturals,** 303 Makaala St., in the Waiakea Center, is Hilo's best natural food store. Their gourmet takeout buffet has a ◙vegetarian lasagna that rivals any Italian grandmother's. (☎808-935-5533. Hot dish and salad buffet with vegan options. $7 per lb. Open M-Sa 8am-8pm, Su 9am-7pm. AmEx/D/MC/V.) **Suisan Retail Market,** 85 Lihiwai St., has fresh fish at market prices. (☎808-935-9349. Bidding starts M-F 7:30am. Store open M-F 8am-5pm, Sa 8am-4pm. D/MC/V.)

◙ **Miyo's,** 400 Hualani St. (☎808-935-2273), in Waiakea Village. A peaceful view over the Waiakea Pond gives this homestyle Japanese restaurant an unparalleled ambience. The food is equally exquisite, plentiful, and surprisingly affordable. Sesame chicken and sashimi served over a bed of rice and garden greens with a bowl of miso $9.50. *Donburi* and noodles $5-9. W live music. Open M-Sa 11am-2pm and 5:30-8:30pm. MC/V. ❶

◙ **Bears' Coffee,** 106 Keawe St. (☎808-935-0708), between Waianuenue and Kalakaua, just around the corner from Hilo Bay Hostel. Despite the flurry of changing owners, locals convene daily for early morning conversation over Big Island coffee ($1.50-3) and sizable breakfasts at low prices. Waffles $3.50. Eggs $3-4. Granola, fruit, and yogurt $5. Sandwiches $4.25-5. Open M-Sa 7am-5pm, Su 8am-noon. Cash only. ❶

Cafe 100, 969 Kilauea Ave. (☎808-935-8683), near the corner of Kekuanaoa St. and Kilauea. Birthplace of the *loco moco*, this is fast food, Hawaiian-style. Most meals, like the Kilauea Loco (homestyle chili, sausage, Spam, 2 eggs, rice, and potato salad), are right around $5; all items under $7. Open M-Th and Sa 6:45am-8:30pm, F 6:45am-9pm; phone order 10:30am-2pm. Cash only. ❶

Aloha Luigi, 264 Keawe St. (☎808-934-9112), a 2-story, unmistakable pastel joint. Luigi insists it's an Italian specialty restaurant, but the Mexican fare is the star of the menu. The *huevos rancheros*—featuring Luigi's handmade corn tortillas—are only $7.

Slices $2.50. Open Tu 9am-3pm; W, Th, and Sa 9am-7pm; F 9am-7:30pm. MC/V. ❶

Ocean Sushi Deli, 239 Keawe St. (☎808-961-6625). A bustling business that rolls up lunch for most of downtown Hilo. The staff is happy to help novices navigate the selection. Nigiri $2.50-4. *Hosomaki* and *temaki* $1.40-4.50. Specialty rolls $5-7. BYOB. Open M-Sa 10am-2pm and 5-9pm. AmEx/MC/V. ❶

Naung Mai Thai Kitchen, 86 Kilauea Ave. (☎808-934-7540), near the corner of Kilauea and Mamo St., behind Garden Exchange. Everything at this authentic Thai restaurant is done with unassuming grace, from the exquisite food to the flowered table arrangement. Spring rolls $7-8. Curries $10-12. BYOB; corkage fee $1 per glass. Lunch M-F 11am-2pm. Dinner M-Th 5-8:30pm, F-Sa 5-9pm. MC/V. ❸

Abundant Life Natural Foods and Cafe, 292 Kamehameha Ave. (☎808-935-7411). This bayfront market and cafe makes both a great morning coffee spot and a lunch sandwich stop. Mixed plate combos $6-8, salads and sandwiches $4-7, bagels $3, smoothies $4. Check out the market for alternative food shopping. Open M-Tu and Th 8:30am-7pm; W and Sa 7am-7pm; Su 10am-5pm; cafe closes at 5:30pm. MC/V. ❶

Island Bake Shop, (☎808-934-8227) Mamo St., beyond the farmers' market. Get good coffee ($1) and delicious baked goods, like their famous bran muffins ($1). Open M-Sa 5am-7pm. Cash only. ❶

Cafe Pesto, 308 Kamehameha Ave. (☎808-969-6640), near the corner of Kamehameha Ave. and Mamo St. Enormous bayfront windows, checkerboard floor, high ceilings, and candlelight create a unique ambience. The designer thin-crust pizzas ($9-18) are top-notch. Lunch sandwiches $9-11. Organic salads $5-11. Dinner pasta $11-12. Open M-Th and Su 11am-9pm, F-Sa 11am-10pm. AmEx/D/MC/V. ❸

Hilo Homemade Ice Cream, 41 Wainuenue St. (☎808-933-1520), in a nook downhill from the Hilo Bay Hostel. In addition to traditional flavors, they scoop ginger, banana macadamia nut fudge, and *poi* and cream. Single scoop $2; double $3.25. Open M-F 10:30am-7:30pm, Sa noon-6pm, Su noon-4pm. Cash only. ❶

◪ BEACHES

Hilo is not known for its beaches, in part because it's dominated by rocky coastline. The best places to go are east of downtown Hilo along Kalanianaole Ave. **Onekahakaha Beach Park,** a little less than 2 mi. northeast of the intersection of Rte. 11 and Kalanianaole Ave., has a sandy-floored swimming pool and a lawn for the perfect picnic, with

NO WORK, ALL PLAY

IN THE MARKET FOR A GOOD TIME?

Though the small cities of the Big Island often seem to have their eyelids half closed when the surf is down, there are exceptions on Wednesdays and Saturdays: the farmers' markets. These gatherings, sprayed throughout the Big Island (most notably in Kona, Hilo, and Waimea), offer invigorating experiences with a wide array of people searching for deals. You'll find hippies, townies, surfers, farmers, tourists, and resort bigwigs all within 10 ft. of each other browsing the fruit stands.

The farmers' markets were originally showcases for the sugar plantations that dotted the eastern coast. Today, in Hilo alone, over 100 local farmers and craftspeople have set up shop to cater cheap fruits, kitsch, and clothing to locals and tourists alike. Here baked goods have taken over the western end, while to the south, clothing and crafts have sunk their roots. Fruits, vegetables, and summer wraps (spring rolls, not fried) are ubiquitous throughout.

The locals love the markets because of the unbeatable prices, the tourists for their authentic goods. Trying to beat the middle men (read: gift shops) is the common goal. The markets have become such social epicenters that some residents go just to have a half-hour of inevitable gab with fellow shoppers. They're double shots of espresso for otherwise drowsy towns—a real trip.

basic facilities. A bit of black sand masquerading as beach, **Richardson Ocean Park,** at the end of Kalanianaole Ave., about 4 mi. east of Hilo, has picnic tables, restrooms, showers, and lifeguards on duty 8am-4:30pm. The protected cove's calm water sees plenty of snorkelers, and the dozens of natural pools make for a scenic sunset. To hit what little surf there is, head to **Honolii Beach,** north of Hilo, just before the Honolii Bridge. Surfers pack in here before and after work, but the water is somewhat cold and murky. Families sometimes head to Reed's Bay, where the water is calm and perfect for small swimmers.

◎ SIGHTS

▨ MERRIE MONARCH FESTIVAL. When **King David Kalakaua** ascended the throne in 1883 following half a century of missionary influence, he took great measures to reassert Hawaiian culture. Kalakaua (also known as the **Merrie Monarch** for his support of dance and music) brought hula back into the public sphere by including it in his coronation ceremony. Hilo celebrates the reign of this last Hawaiian king each year during the week after Easter. The celebration, which includes a giant parade and other festivities, culminates in a hula competition among dancers from all the islands of the Pacific. Take a look at any of the photo books by Kim Taylor Reece; nearly half of his shots are from Hilo's Merrie Monarch Festival. Tickets go on sale on New Year's Day and sell out quickly. *(For tickets, call the Hawaii Naniloa Resort at ☎808-935-9168.)*

IMILOA ASTRONOMY CENTER OF HAWAII. This recent addition to the Hilo museum community prides itself on bridging the gap between Hawaiian history and state-of-the-art astronomical technology. The mind-blowing planetarium screens three times a day (11am, 1, and 2:30pm), while the rest of the building houses a comprehensive tour through the origins, navigation, and celestial underpinnings of ancient Hawaiian culture. This veritable journey through time is child-friendly and bilingual (Hawaiian and English). Don't miss the "Sky Tonight" show ($5) on the last Saturday of every month. *(600 Imiloa Pl. at the UH Hilo Science and Technology Park. On the corner of Komohana and Puainako St., at the back of the UH Campus. ☎808-969-9700; www.imiloahawaii.org. $14.50, ages 4-12 $7.50.)*

LYMAN MUSEUM AND MISSION HOUSE. The Lyman Mission House, built in 1839 and the oldest frame building on the Big Island, has been restored to represent the lifestyle of early missionaries to Hawaii. A guided tour takes you through the home, which includes many original furnishings, tools, and household items. Next door is the Lyman Museum, itself a fascinating inquiry into Hawaiian history. The Earth Heritage exhibit explores topics like the formation of the islands and the astronomical observations of Mauna Kea, while the Hawaiian culture exhibit focuses on migration to Hawaii. The Lyman Museum also features rotating exhibits of modern Hawaiian art. *(276 Haili St. ☎808-935-5021; www.lymanhouse.org. 30min. guided tours of Mission House every hr. 10am-3pm on the hr. Open M-Sa 9:30am-4:30pm. $10, seniors $8, students $3, families $21.)*

PACIFIC TSUNAMI MUSEUM. In the old First Hawaiian Bank, the museum's diagrams explaining tsunamis become all the more profound alongside chronicles of Hilo's history, a city ravaged twice by tsunamis, once in 1946 and again in 1960. Knowledgeable tour guides provide insightful introductions, and exhibits shed light on tsunamis recorded around the world. One of the most compelling sections of the museum is a video entitled "Raging Sea." *(130 Kamehameha Ave., at the corner of Kalakaua St. ☎808-935-0926; www.tsunami.org. Open M-Sa 9am-4pm. $7.)*

PANAEWA RAINFOREST ZOO. Panaewa is the only tropical rainforest zoo in the US. Over 75 animal species are kept here, including a white Bengal tiger, water buffalo, Aldabra tortoise, and pygmy hippo. Families can find plenty of shade (and nice picnic spots) under the many palm trees. The petting zoo (Sa 1:30-2:30pm) will certainly delight young children. *(A few mi. south of Hilo on Mamaki St., off Rte. 11. From Hilo, turn right onto Mamaki St., between mi. markers 4 and 5. The zoo is about 1 mi. down. ☎ 808-959-7224; www.hilozoo.com. Open daily 9am-4pm. Free.)*

KALAKAUA PARK. A statue of Hawaii's Merrie Monarch, David Kalakaua, sits beneath the park's immense Banyan tree with a hula drum and taro root leaf in hand. The park, a splendid bit of green in the midst of sidewalks and streets, makes a good resting place on a tour of Hilo. In the summer, the **Hilo Community Players** produce their annual Shakespeare in the Park rendition here. *(In downtown Hilo at the corner of Kinoole St. and Waianuenue Ave.)*

RAINBOW FALLS. When it's been rainy for a while, head to this relaxing spot for a break from the city. This powerful (when rainy) waterfall drops over a rock ledge to the river below. A calm swimming hole behind the falls contrasts starkly with the thunderous crashing water. Restrooms available. *(Take the left-hand trail through the trees, passing to the right of the enormous Banyan tree. From downtown, follow Waianuenue Ave. 2 mi. uphill; turn right onto Rainbow Dr. Look for the green sign.)*

BOILING POTS. Broken waterfalls cascade down a rocky ledge at Boiling Pots, a scene so tropical you should stop just for the photo-op. Near Rainbow Falls, this is a lesser-known but equally worthwhile sight and it, too, is most enjoyable after a few rainy days when the water flows powerfully. Restrooms are available. *(From downtown, follow Waianuenue Ave. past the turnoff for Rainbow Falls; turn right onto Peepee Falls Dr. Look for the green sign. Park open daily 7am-6:30pm.)*

KAUMANA CAVES. Right off Saddle Rd., **Kaumana Caves County Park** is a quick subterranean diversion. Created by a 1881 Mauna Loa lava flow, the park contains a series of caves with fascinating rock formations and hanging tree roots. Unlike any other lava tubes and caves on the Big Island (due to Hilo's uniquely heavy rainfall), Kaumana is surely worth the stop. Restrooms and pavilions at the rest stop. Appropriate footwear and a flashlight needed for exploration. *(When coming from Hilo, between mi. markers 4 and 5 on the right-hand side of Saddle Rd.)*

KOLEKOLE STATE PARK. At Kolekole you'll find an outdoor lover's playground. A jungle river and adjacent waterfall runs into the ocean and cools afternoon swimmers. A rope swing hung from a weary palm tree entertains the brave, and caves and trails occupy the adventurous. Kolekole is a favorite of locals, who come to BBQ and hang out for the day. Camping is available (permit $10); see **Camping in Hawaii** (p. 82). *(Near mi. marker 14, off Hwy. 19 heading north out of Hilo.)*

🎭 🎵 NIGHTLIFE AND ENTERTAINMENT

Despite being the largest city on the island and a college town, Hilo's nightlife is fairly unremarkable. There are, however, plenty of movie showings, from artsy and foreign shows to $1 Hollywood flicks. If you're up for a different sort of nightlife, take Saddle Rd. (p. 234) to Mauna Kea for nightly stargazing.

BARS

Cronies, 11 Waianuenue Ave. (☎808-935-5158), on the corner of Kamehameha St. and Waianuenue Ave., lures the youngest and liveliest crowd in Hilo. 2 fluorescent-lit pool tables attract the most attention in this large bar, which also has electronic dart boards and a big-screen TV. Cronies is known for the best crab cakes ($8) and sashimi ($9) in town and also has a nice selection of beers ($3.50-4.50). M-W and F-Sa karaoke 10:30pm-1:30am. Food served M-Sa 11am-11pm; bar open until 2am. AmEx/MC/V.

Shooters, 121 Banyan Dr. (☎808-969-7069). A boisterous crowd of all ages packs the tiny dance floor while a DJ spins (W-Sa after 10pm). Happy hour daily 3-7pm (domestic drafts $2.25, imports $3.25). W and Sa $1 beers. Variety of drink specials, themes vary by weeknight. 21+; Th 18+. Open M-W 3pm-2am, Th-Sa 3pm-3am.

Margarita Village, 11 Silva St. (☎808-961-3290), just east of downtown Hilo. Your average hole-in-the-wall bar with a bit of Tex-Mex flair. Drafts $2.50-3.50 and dozens of margaritas ($6). Open Tu-W and Su 11am-1:30am, M and Th-Sa 3pm-1:30am. MC/V.

MOVIES

Kress Cinemas, 174 Kamehameha Ave. (☎808-935-6777), on the corner of Kamehameha and Kalakaua St. New Hollywood films for back-in-the-day prices. Reels arrive a few weeks after mainland release. Shows $1. Matinees before 6pm $0.50. Tu $0.50.

Palace Theatre, 38 Haili St. (☎808-934-7010, box office 808-934-7777), between Kamehameha Ave. and Keawe St. A relic from Hilo's glory days, the theater plays a single art-house (often foreign) film each week, hosts local and visiting musicians, and puts on live theater performances. Most film showings M-Tu and F-Sa 7:30pm, Su 2:30pm; sometimes Th 7:30pm. $6; children, students, and seniors $5. Palace also shows children's films F-Sa mornings 9-11am, $2. Check for seasonal specials.

Prince Kuhio Stadium Cinemas, 111 E. Puainako St. (☎808-959-4595; www.wallacetheaters.com), in Prince Kuhio Plaza. 1st-run Hollywood films. $8.25, seniors and ages 3-11 $5.25. Matinees M-F before 6pm, Sa-Su before 3:30pm $5.50.

SADDLE ROAD

Saddle Rd. (Rte. 200) climbs up and down a topographic cross-section of Hawaii. The only major route through the middle of the Big Island, Saddle Rd. starts on the Kona coast and rolls across the grasslands of Parker Ranch before cutting between the two highest points on the Big Island—Mauna Kea to the north and Mauna Loa to the south. As the road comes down from the mountains and into Hilo, the foliage becomes more dense and luxuriantly green from the moisture in the air on the windward side.

ORIENTATION

On the Kona side, **Saddle Road** leaves Rte. 190 about 6 mi. south of Waimea and 33 mi. northeast of Kailua-Kona. On the Hilo side, **Waianuenue Avenue** splits just above downtown Hilo, and one fork, **Kaumana Drive,** becomes Saddle Rd. in the foothills outside of town. Saddle Rd. runs 54 mi. from end to end.

From Hilo, the road climbs between Mauna Loa and Mauna Kea in a series of twists and turns that is made more difficult to navigate by the fog; it can get so thick that it's hard to see the road in front of you. Mi. marker 28 indicates an unmarked turnoff to the road up **Mauna Loa,** where you will find a weather observatory and sparse parking. Another unmarked road, the **Mauna Kea Access Road (John A. Burns Way),** near mi. marker 28, leads up **Mauna Kea** to the **Onizuka Center for International Astronomy.** A graded track continues from there onto the mountain's summit. Seven miles farther down Saddle Rd. is the **Mauna Kea State Recreation Area,** about 19 mi. from the intersection of Rte. 190 and Saddle Rd. From here the road descends into the Kona Coast.

POTHOLES AND PITFALLS. From Kona to Hilo, saddle up and keep your eyes open, because Saddle Rd. is as wild as it is captivating. On the Kona side, the road is decrepit and crumbling; not only does it see heavy action from military vehicles making the trip between Pohakuloa Military Training Area and Kawaihae Harbor, but the Kona side hasn't been repaved in years. As you head toward Hilo, however, the road improves drastically; a recent lava flow across the road made a repaving essential. Almost all rental car companies, except for local **Harper Car and Truck Rentals** (p. 226), forbid you from driving on Saddle Rd. In reality, the road is fine between Hilo and the Mauna Kea Access Rd., around mi. marker 28. After this point, only the center lane is well-maintained and, as a result, cars tend to drive (sometimes speeding) down the middle. Stay alert over blind hills and sightless turns on the Kona side of the road—it's seen its fair share of head-on collisions. Except for the Mauna Kea Observatory Visitors Center, there are no places to stop for food, gas, or warmth along this road.

MAUNA KEA

Though it towers 13,796 ft. above sea level, Mauna Kea, or "White Mountain," is notable less for its size than its world-class astronomical viewing conditions. The summit's stable air and extremely dark sky have led scientists from 11 countries to set up telescopes on the mountain and have drawn innumerable travelers to gaze and gape at the night sky.

 WATCH FOR INVISIBLE COWS. Free-roaming cattle are a hazard taken quite seriously on Mauna Kea Access Rd. Dark cattle hide so well under the cover of the nightfall that they're very difficult to see. Signs warn drivers to "Watch For The Invisible Cows." Be careful. Those cows are out there.

The Onizuka Center for International Astronomy, 6 mi. up Mauna Kea Access Rd., from mi. marker 28 of Saddle Rd., teaches visitors about the advanced telescopes on the summit. The access road's nearly 3000 ft. ascent up Mauna Kea leads to more than just stargazing; it also has vistas of the saddle between Mauna Loa and Mauna Kea's cinder cones.

◉ SIGHTS

MAUNA KEA STATE RECREATION AREA. Near mi. marker 35, 7 mi. west of the Mauna Kea summit road, this simple park is a base for an exploration of Saddle Rd. The park has less-than-nice restrooms, picnic tables, a pay phone, and a short hike with good views of Mauna Kea, Hulalai, and Mauna Loa. There are also eight 8-person **cabins** for rent with kitchens, non-drinking water, linens, toilets, and a warm shower. *(To reserve a cabin, call the Department of Land and Natural Resources, State Parks Division, 75 Apuni St. ☎ 808-974-6200. $35 per night.)*

▩ **ONIZUKA CENTER FOR INTERNATIONAL ASTRONOMY.** Perched on the slope of Mauna Kea at 9200 ft., the center for the summit telescopes is an invaluable resource. Named after Ellison Onizuka, an astronaut from the Big Island who died in the 1986 Challenger explosion, the center's exhibits detail the form and function of the 13 summit telescopes, used by 11 countries. The powerful **Keck**

THE BIG ISLAND

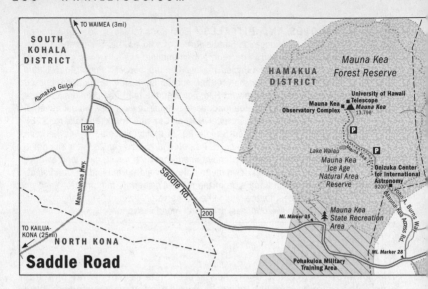

and Subaru Telescopes on the summit boast enormous dual 10 and 8m mirror diameters, respectively, and the Onizuka Center offers a 4 in. refractor and a pair of 14 in. and 16 in. reflective amateur telescopes for free public viewing.

The center also observes the sky in nightly **☆stargazing sessions.** The program begins with an orientation video, followed by a discussion of Mauna Kea and astronomy in general. Visitors are able to see a variety of stellar phenomena, including stars in their many stages of life (from red giants to white dwarfs), globular clusters, binary stars, planets, constellations, and, perhaps most fascinatingly, entire distant galaxies. It is essential to dress warmly; temperatures drop to 40-50°F during the summer and 25-50°F during the winter.

If you have your own 4WD vehicle, consider going on one of the weekend **summit tours.** The 4hr. tour includes an video, acclimatization period, caravan to the summit, overview of the telescopes, and a guided visit to one or two of them. *(From Saddle Rd., turn onto the Mauna Kea Access Rd. at mi. marker 28. The center is 6 mi. up the road. ☎808-961-2180; www.ifa.hawaii.edu. Open daily 9am-10pm. Stargazing daily 6-10pm. Free. Summit tours Sa-Su 1-5pm. Free. Under 16 and pregnant women not allowed on tours due to high-altitude health hazards. Scuba divers should be careful: going to the summit can produce the same effects as flying immediately after diving. Free.)*

DRIVING TO THE SUMMIT. If you have 4WD, you can also drive to the top yourself. Visitors are allowed on the summit only from sunrise to 30min. after sunset, as car headlights interfere with observations after dark. The road to the observatories is well-maintained but unpaved until the last few miles, and its extremely steep grade makes 4WD a necessity. The drive from the Onizuka Center to the summit (8 mi.) should take about 30min. Once there, both the University of Hawaii telescope and the W.M. Keck Observatory have Visitors Centers. While the telescope's technological sophistication makes for an unrivaled view of space, the clear night sky is spellbinding even to the naked eye.

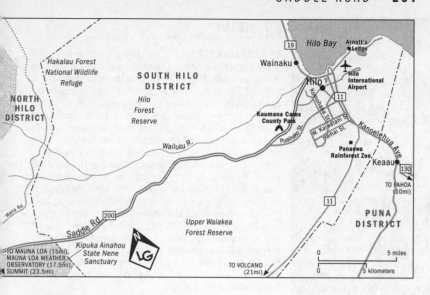

ACTIVITIES

Arnott's Lodge, 98 Apapane Rd. (☎808-969-7097; www.arnottslodge.com), in Hilo. Trips from Hilo to Mauna Kea for sunsets and stargazing several times a week. Parkas and a stop at a grocery store provided. M, W, and F departure time seasonally adjusted; trips usually from 3-9 or 10pm. $60, nonguests $90.

Paradise Safaris (☎808-322-2366) leads nightly tours to the summit to watch the sunset and stargaze. The 7hr. trip includes pickups at various spots along the Kona and Kohala Coasts, hooded parkas, and a light supper. $185.

HIKING

MAUNA KEA TRAIL. *(6 mi. one-way. Elevation gain: 2250 ft. Challenging.)* The trail climbs from the Onizuka Center to the summit and takes around 4-5hr. to complete round-trip. The path is marked by posts and *ahu* (rock piles) and essentially runs parallel to the summit road. Given the altitude and elevation gain, this is an extremely difficult (though worthwhile) hike. Among the unique sights are the eerie landscapes of the Mauna Kea Ice Age Natural Area Reserve. The trail leads straight to the magical Lake Waiau, the third-highest lake in the US, set amid Mauna Kea's lava fields at 13,020 ft. The lake is considered to be the physical manifestation of the goddess Waiau and is therefore very sacred.

MAUNA LOA

East of the Mauna Kea turnoff, a serpentine road climbs the volcano to the Mauna Loa Observatory, 11,000 ft. above sea level. The drive takes about 45min. and though the road is slowly crumbling, it is passable in any car. The observatory is purely scientific and there is no Visitors Center.

GIVING BACK

W.M. KECK TELESCOPES

Atop Mauna Kea, the naked eye has the ability to see millions of stars that are invisible when down below in surrounding areas. Thankfully, the W.M. Keck Telescopes, a two-telescope array near the summit of Mauna Kea, allow scientists to see much further than the naked eye will allow.

University of California astronomer Dr. Jerry Nelson was the innovative scientist who dreamed up this seemingly impossible idea. Instead of using one single piece of reflective glass, Nelson used 36 different mirrors to act as one giant one. Amazingly, these 36 hexagonal shaped mirrors are deployed in a perfect hyperbolic shaped adjusted in one-millionth-of-an-inch increments, twice a second, to counteract the movement of the telescope and the wind. If this technological marvel weren't enough, in recent years, adaptive optics adjustment mirrors have been installed on both Keck telescopes, that have the ability to change the mirrors' shape 670 times per second, adjusting for atmospheric distortions of incoming starlight and sharpening resolution by a factor of 10 to 20. Additionally, instead of creating just one of these technological wonders, the W.M. Keck Foundation funded the construction of a pair, two 10m telescopes spaced 85m apart, effectively creating a reflective telescope with a primary mirror diameter of 85m.

HIKING

OBSERVATORY TRAIL. *(6 mi. one-way. Elevation gain: 1250 ft. Challenging.)* The paved road ends at the Mauna Loa Weather Observatory, which is the trailhead for a hike to the summit of Mauna Loa or the cabin on the opposite rim of Mokuaweoweo Caldera. There is nothing easy about this hike; a good portion of your time will surely be spent scrambling across the precariously loose rubble of *aa* lava fields in temperatures that consistently drop below freezing on the summit. Inclement weather is common here. While it is easy enough to follow the *ahu* (rock piles) up the mountain, this hike should not be done without a partner. Proper hiking gear and plenty of water are also essential; dehydration is a deadly process at high altitudes. However, for all the obstacles of the trail, the gaping expanse of the Mauna Loa summit is a reward well worth the hardship suffered on the way up. For more information about hiking Mauna Loa, see **Hawaii Volcanoes National Park,** p. 210.

HAMAKUA COAST

The drive along Rte. 19 (Hawaii Belt Rd.) between Hilo and Waimea features some of the most spectacular scenery on the Big Island. Waterfalls peek around each bend and brilliant blossoms dot the mountainside. Although Hamakua was once the sugarcane gold mine of the Big Island, not a single plantation remains. Attempting to fill the void left by sugar's decline, the area has become engaged in historical preservation—the coast's official name is the Hilo-Hamakua Heritage Coast. From Hilo's historic downtown to botanical gardens and Honokaa's early-1900s facades, a drive down the coast is a journey into the Hawaii of yesteryear.

PEPEEKEO SCENIC DRIVE

The well-marked **Pepeekeo Scenic Drive** (also known as **Papaiko Road**) starts about 5 mi. north of Hilo. Watch for the blue scenic route sign leading right off Rte. 19. Before connecting up again with Rte. 19, the 4 mi. winding road stretches across one-lane bridges, curls through lush rainforest, and negotiates twists over the crashing surf below.

About 1 mi. in, the road leads to the **Hawaii Tropical Botanical Garden,** 27-717 Old Mamalahoa Hwy., overlooking Onomea Bay. Home to over 2500 species of tropical plant life from around the globe, the botanical gardens started as one couple's desire to cull the world's rarest plant species, often endangered, and allow them a space to grow in Hawaii. The garden slopes downhill from the old highway to the sea; a 1 mi. trail meanders through scenery rich with bromeliads, orchids, and different types of ginger under Banyan and palm trees. The solar-powered aviary is an impressive addition. The only drawbacks are the mosquitoes. (☎808 964-5233; www.hawaiigarden.com. Open daily 9am-4pm. $15, ages 6-16 $5, under 5 free.)

Before returning to the highway, the drive passes 🌊What's Shakin' ❶, a stand that blends superior smoothies ($5.75). Their concoctions, with names like Papaya Paradise and Peanut Bruddah, use only fresh juice, milk, and PB. (☎808-964-3080. Open daily 10am-5pm. MC/V. Credit card min. $15.)

(NOT) GOING CUCKOO IN AKAKA. If you stare halfway up the falls for 20 seconds and then look directly to the right, where the moss grows on the rock, your eyes might mislead you! (Spoiler alert: the rock to the side of the waterfall will look like it's growing.)

AKAKA FALLS STATE PARK

The lofty and delicate **Kahuna Falls** (400 ft.) and **Akaka Falls** (442 ft.) make Akaka Falls State Park a highlight of the Hamakua Coast. The tiny park is packed with delights, including the awe-inspiring falls and a well-kept walking path. The ½ mi. paved loop begins at the parking lot and travels between the two falls, and then turns back for a short trek through a vibrant rainforest filled with orchids, redhead ginger, mossy Banyan trees, gigantic ferns, and bamboo groves. While the trail never gets close enough to Kahuna for more than a glimpse of the long free-falling water, at Akaka Falls visitors can look down a couple hundred feet to where the water splashes into a pool. The park is 15 mi. north of Hilo, about 4 mi. up the side of Mauna Kea. From Rte. 19, a marked turnoff between mi. markers 13 and 14 leads to Rte. 220; the falls are about 3 mi. up the road. Restrooms and picnic tables are next to the parking lot.

World Botanical Gardens & Umauma Falls, off Hwy. 19, at the 16 mi. marker, is plotted on 200 acres of land, right next to the dramatic Umauma Falls—a triple-tiered stream of crashing water. **Rainbow Gardens**, located next to the reception area, is home to hundreds of exotic plant species from around the world. Gift and snack shop. Open daily 9am-5:30pm. $13, ages 13-19 $6, under 13 $3.

Even more breathtaking than watching the dome open and shift along its altitude-azimuth track as the sun sets over Mauna Kea are the intensely precise measurements behind such movement. Although the weight of each piece of glass is 14.4 tons, it requires just 10 lb. of pressure to rotate the mirror; each one sits on a bed of oil lubricant a mere 50 nanometers thick. As for the structure as a whole, each telescope weighs in at a stunning 270 tons, frozen in the daytime with high-powered air conditioners which reduce the stress of gravity over time and increase the lifespan of these super seeing structures.

Ultimately, these elaborate sets of measurements, precise ion polishing processes, and long trails of fiber optics cables combine to answer fundamental questions for all of humanity: what is out there? Where did it come from? And where is it going?

For more information about how you can get involved with this exciting research, contact the Institute for Astronomy. ☎808-961-6516, www.ifa.hawaii.edu. Additionally, the University of Hawaii at Manoa has one of the country's top-ranked graduate programs in astronomy. See their website, www.uhm.hawaii.edu, for information on applying to the program.

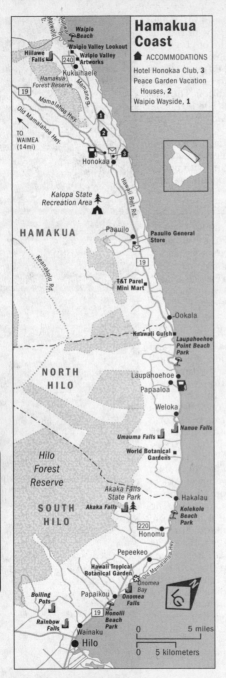

Hamakua Coast

⌂ ACCOMMODATIONS

Hotel Honokaa Club, **3**
Peace Garden Vacation
Houses, **2**
Waipio Wayside, **1**

LAUPAHOEHOE

Laupahoehoe ("leaf of smooth lava") was once a bustling and active sea village. Much like Kalapana, which was rubbed off the map by merciless lava flows in 1989, Laupahoehoe also fell victim to the violent whim of Mother Nature. The deadly 1946 tsunami devastated the entire developed town and surrounding neighborhood, and it swept over 20 unfortunate students and four teachers into the sea. Today, the point is home to the well-maintained **Laupahoehoe Point Beach Park** with a monument dedicated to those lost in the tragedy. Facilities include volleyball courts, restrooms, showers, picnic tables, campsites, and a large lawn as well as panoramic views of the sonorous crashing waves. The park is halfway between Hilo and Honokaa, 1 mi. off Hwy. 19 near mi. marker 27, and is open daily 6am-11pm. Camping with permit only; see **Camping in Hawaii**, p. 82, for more information.

In the sleepy town of Laupahoehoe itself, the **Laupahoehoe Train Museum,** located right on Hwy. 19, is housed in a railroad worker's old abode. An introductory video informs visitors of Laupahoehoe's storied past; artifacts and photos supplement the video as reminders of a long-gone era of trains and sugarcane. The staff is gracious, knowledgeable, and eager to share what they know with visitors. (☎808-962-6300. Open M-F 9am-4:30pm, Sa-Su 10am-2pm. Adults $3, students and seniors $2.)

HONOKAA

For much of the 19th and 20th centuries, Honokaa (pop. 2233) occupied a lofty position in the Big Island's sugarcane production. However, the industry waned, and Honokaa's last mill closed in the 1990s. Since then, Honokaa has rallied, forging a future on its own terms. The 1920s-era storefronts of the town's main street still house a hardware store and a five-and-dime, but recently, funky art galleries, antique shops, and restaurants have filled the spaces around them. The range of establishments mirrors the diversity of Honokaa's residents—a tightly-knit group passionate about everything that's going on in this small town, from family to the feisty local concerts at the Honokaa Club.

▌▐ ORIENTATION AND PRACTICAL INFORMATION

Honokaa sits along **Route 240,** off Rte. 19, about 40 mi. northwest of Hilo and 15 mi. east of Waimea. **Waipio Valley** is 9 mi. northwest of town, at the end of Rte. 240. Life in Honokaa centers on **Mamane Street (Rte. 240),** which is home to almost all of the town's businesses; a handful more lie along Rte. 19 up the hill. From Waimea, **Plumeria Street** leaves Rte. 19 and drops down through Honokaa, meeting Mamane St. in the center of town.

Honokaa is on the main route between Hilo and Kona and receives more **Hele-On Bus** traffic than any other small town. Buses run from the high school to Hilo (1hr.; M-Sa 5:50, 8:30am, 3:15, 5:10, 5:25pm) and Kona (1hr., daily 2:40pm) via Waimea (40min.) from the Dairy Queen on Rte. 19.

Tourist Information: Honokaa Visitor Center (☎808-775-0598 or 808-966-5416; www.hawaii-culture.com), is the gift shop of Tex Drive-in along Rte. 19. It offers a few brochures and some basic maps, as well as restrooms. Open daily 9am-5pm.

Banks: Bank of Hawaii, 45-574 Mamane St. (☎808-775-7218) has a 24hr. ATM. Open M-Th 8:30am-4pm, F 8:30am-6pm.

Library: Honokaa Public Library, 45-3380 Mamane St. (☎808-775-8881), offers Internet access on 1 of 3 terminals with a 3-month visitor's card ($10). Open M and Th 11am-7pm, Tu-W 9am-5pm, F 9am-3pm.

Laundromat: PJ Suds Washerette, 45-493 Kika St. (☎808-987-7731), on Kika St., near the corner of Kika and Mamane St., turnoff next to First Hawaiian Bank. Wash $3.50, dry $0.25 per 4min. Open daily 6am-9pm. Last wash 8:30pm.

Swimming Pool: Honokaa Swimming Pool (☎808-775-0650), on Mamane St., next to the high school; turn away from the ocean onto Pakalana St. Open M-F 8am-4:30pm, 10-11:30am for adult lap swim; Sa-Su 9am-3:30pm. Hours vary during school year.

Weather: ☎808-961-5582.

Police and Fire Department: Honokaa Station (☎808-775-7533), on Mamane St., near mi. marker 1.

Pharmacy: Hamakua Family Pharmacy, 45-3551A Mamane St. (☎808-775-0496), located across from the Bank of Hawaii. Open M-F 8:30am-6pm, Sa 9am-1:30pm.

Post Office: Honokaa Post Office, 45-490 Lehua St. (☎800-275-8777), on the corner of Lehua and Mamane St. Open M-F 9am-4pm, Sa 8:15-9:45am.

Postal Code: 96727.

▛ ▜ ACCOMMODATIONS AND CAMPING

Hotel Honokaa Club, 45-3480 Mamane St. (☎808-775-0678; www.hotelhonokaa. com), just past Maile St. across from the sign for Honokaa Park. You can't miss this rambling establishment, built in 1908 as a club for plantation managers. When the sugar industry died, it was remade into a hotel; the eccentrically decorated rooms are reminiscent of an earlier era. Basic continental breakfast included. Linens not included in dorms. Reception 8am-1pm and 4-8pm. Check-in 4pm. Check-out 11am. Private dorms $30; hotel rooms with bath and full, queen, or king bed $62-80; family suite with bath and room for 4 $120-130. Ask about seasonal specials. MC/V. ❷

Waipio Wayside, 42-4226 Waipio Rd (☎800-833-8849; www.waipiowayside.com), on the way toward Waipio Valley, west of downtown Honokaa near mi. marker 4, recognizable by a small white sign on the front lawn. Formerly a plantation house, this secluded inn offers an incredible view of the Pacific. The gazebo and decks are the best places to enjoy the atmosphere. Breakfast included. Check-in 3-6pm. Check-out 10:30am. Rooms $99-180; $10 surcharge for 1-night stays. Additional guests $25. MC/V. ❸

Peace Garden Vacation Houses, 45-4623 Waipio Rd. (☎808-775-1505; www.hawaii-peacegardenvacationhouses.com.). This luxurious facility is the perfect spot for relaxation, rejuvenation, and self-reflection. It offers a spa with sauna, hot tub, showers, hammocks with a view, yoga spaces, and a focus on privacy and indulgence. Fresh mango and coconut in the morning. 2 different houses offer accommodations to either groups, couples, or individuals. 3-night min. $75-150, $20 extra for 3rd-6th guests. MC/V. ❸

Kalopa State Recreation Area, Kalopa Rd. off Rte. 19, 2 mi. south of the intersection of Rte. 19 and Rte. 240. Excellent, grassy tent sites under an *ohia* and eucalyptus canopy at a cool 2500 ft. Tent sites available on a first come, first served basis. It rains here regularly, so look to the adjacent cabins for a drier stay. Reserve cabins by calling ☎808-974-6200, or speak to the caretaker at the park entrance. Bedding provided. Check-in 2pm. Check-out 10am. 5-day max. Camping $5; cabins $55-175. Rates rise with the number of guests. See **Camping in Hawaii**, p. 82, for more information. ❶

◻ FOOD

▣ **Cafe Il Mondo,** 45-3626A Mamane St. (☎808-775-7711). The folks behind the counter love what they're doing, and the fresh aroma of baking dough and homemade sauce makes us love them. Pizza (available by the slice before 5pm) $12-15. Appetizers $4-11, dinner $11-13. Open M-Sa 11am-8pm. Cash only. ❶

Simply Natural (☎808-775-0119), on Mamane St. Opened 10 years ago by an 18 yr. old girl, Simply Natural has flourished into the staple food stop in Honokaa. Breakfast is the highlight with taro-banana pancakes ($6), but a variety of deli and veggie sandwiches (spicy tuna melt $9) can satisfy any appetite. The decor is cute, with rainbow ceiling fans and a colorful menu. Free Internet access on house computer with food purchase. Last F of every month open-mic night. Open M-Sa 9am-3:30pm. Cash only. ❶

Tex Drive-In, 45-690 Pakalana St. (☎808-775-0598), off Rte. 19 above downtown Honokaa. Owner Ada makes *malasadas* (Portuguese doughnuts) famous throughout the Big Island ($1). The beef for her excellent burgers ($3-6) comes from right up the street. Heaping fish salads $9. Open daily 6am-9pm. MC/V. ❶

Jolene's Kau Kau Korner Restaurant (☎808-775-9498), on the corner of Mamane and Plumeria St., across from True Value. A friendly local joint serves Hawaiian favorites for dine in and takeout, including *mahi mahi* and teriyaki anything. Plate lunches $6.50-8. Dinners $8-17. Open M, W, and F 10am-8pm, Tu and Th 10am-3pm. Cash only. ❶

◉ ♫ SIGHTS AND ENTERTAINMENT

While much of the surrounding land has been destroyed by sugarcane production, the 615-acre Kalopa State Recreation Area has been protected since 1903. This reserve encompasses 100 acres of virgin Hawaiian rainforest at 2000 to 2500 ft. above sea level and receives approx. 100 in. of precipitation a year. A quick 1 mi. loop, the **Native Forest Nature Trail** passes through the heart of the *ohia* forest. In addition, the **Gulch Rim Trail,** which skirts Kalopa Gulch and Hanaipoe Gulch, is in the greater forest reserve area. Group cabins, a campground, and a picnic area (see **Camping in Hawaii,** p. 82) are available to the public. The park is off Rte. 19, about a mile south of the intersection of Rte. 19 and Rte. 240. Watch for the green sign marking the turnoff south of Honokaa.

Back in town, the **Honokaa People's Theater,** on Mamane St. (☎808-775-0000), has been meticulously restored and shows a wide range of movies, from art-house films (Tu-W) to Hollywood blockbusters (F-Su). Adjacent **People's Cafe** functions as the concessions stand. (Shows 7pm. $6, seniors $4, under 12 $3.)

WAIPIO VALLEY

Walled in by 2000 ft. *palis* (cliffs), the mile-wide Waipio Valley is a world unto itself. The wide, twisting Waipio Stream channels freshwater from the Kohala Mountains to the sea. This natural irrigation nourishes a wealth of fruit trees, ripe for the picking. Lush taro root patches dot the landscape and trees bend under the weight of avocados, coconuts, mango, guava, and passion fruit. With a stunning gray sand beach, striking waterfalls, myriad vistas, and canopied rainforest, the valley is, in a word, paradise.

Before the arrival of Captain Cook in 1778, between 4000 and 10,000 Native Hawaiians had established a private Eden in the crevices of Waipio Valley, which once served as the cultural center of the Big Island. Until the 1946 tsu-nami, a diverse people and developed land characterized this valley, estab-lished solely on the economic prosperity of 16th-century taro root fields. Today, no more than 100 residents call the valley home, and much of the cultivated land has been reclaimed by the rainforest. The valley's days as the center of Big Island agriculture are over, but the beauty of this fertile land remains.

◼ ORIENTATION

Route 240 ends here; it dead ends at the parking lot for the **Waipio Valley Lookout.** From here, an extraordinarily steep paved road winds down 900 ft. to the val-ley floor. With grades of 20-35% and sharp hairpin turns, it is passable only with a hearty **4WD** in first gear. Descending vehicles must yield to ascending traffic. An eerie graveyard of rusting truck spines at the bottom of the ravine stands testament to this road's treacherous conditions. Visitors with 2WD can park at the lookout and hike 1 mi. to the valley floor.

◼ ACTIVITIES

If you've been to the valley floor already and want to see things from a new perspective, there are several companies that run tours along the Waipio rim.

ON HORSEBACK

Waipio Naalapa Stables (☎808-775-0419; www.naalapastables.com), offers 2hr. adventures in the valley. Trips begin at Waipio Valley Artworks in Kukuihaele. M-Sa 9:30am and 1pm. Reservations required. Ages 8 and up. $90. MC/V.

Waipio on Horseback and ATV (☎808-775-7291). Leisurely excursions highlight the waterfalls and one of the largest taro root farms. Meet at the Last Chance Store in Kuku-ihaele for a drive to the valley. M-Sa 9:30am and 1:30pm. Reserve 24hr. in advance. $85. The same outfit offers guided tours on ATV through the valley. Sa-Su 9:30am and 1:30pm. 2hr. tour with snack $100; 3hr. tour with picnic $150. Ages 16 and up. MC/V.

BY WHEEL OR SPOKE

Waipio Valley Shuttle (☎808-775-7121) leaves from Waipio Valley Artworks. The 2hr. tour features views of Hiilawe Falls and taro root patches, and is led by knowledgeable guides who narrate Hawaiian history and legends. M-Sa 9, 11am, 1, 3pm. Reservations recommended. $45, ages 11-17 $35, 10 and under $20.

Waipio Valley Wagon Tours (☎808-775-9518; www.waipiovalleywagontours.com) departs from the WOH Ranch, Hwy. 240, ½mi. past the 7 mi. marker on the left side of the street. Explore the taro root fields, tropical vegetation, and waterfalls of the valley in a 1hr. tour from the seat of a mule-drawn covered wagon. M-Sa 10:30am, 12:30, 2:30pm. Reservations required. $57, over 60 $50, ages 4-12 $28, under 4 free.

HIKING

While you can get a great look from the Waipio Valley Lookout at the top of the eastern cliff, it is far more rewarding to hike through the valley. Below are some of the available hikes; stay on the trails and avoid trespassing. For a guided adventure, **Hawaiian Walkways** (☎808-775-0372 or 800-457-7759; www.hawaiianwalkways.com), on Mamane St. in downtown Honokaa, leads 5hr., fully equipped hikes into the valley. Other trips hike in Volcanoes Park or along Saddle Rd. (Open M-F 8am-5pm. $95-135 per person.)

HIILAWE FALLS. *(2-2½hr. one-way. Challenging.)* At the end of the descent into the valley where the beach trail forks right, take the left path back into the interior of the valley, revealing views of the shimmering Hiilawe Falls (waterfall is 1400 ft. tall, and the water plunges down 1200 ft.), Hawaii's highest single-drop waterfall. From here, it's about a 2hr. bushwhacking and stream-crossing session until reaching the falls. Continue on the road and turn left just before the river into the dense forest. The faint path to the falls zigzags under at least two barbed-wire fences and across the river numerous times. The rocks are slippery, and getting soaked is unavoidable; come prepared with appropriate footwear, water, and insect repellent. Hikers with open cuts may want to avoid this trek; stream-walking exposes swimmers to leptospirosis.

WAIPIO VALLEY BEACH TRAIL. *(40min. one-way. Challenging.)* From the lookout, a steep (but relatively short) paved road plunges to the valley's floor. Hikers and motorists share the road, so be alert. All rented vehicles are prohibited below the valley rim, so strap on a pair of sturdy shoes and start trekking.

Turning right at the fork takes you on a muddy 10min. walk to Waipio Beach, known for its dynamic currents and gnarly shore break. Spectacular cliffs and tumbling cascades border the sandy expanse, which is splashed with a shallow shore break. A tight-knit group of surfers call this beach home; these guys start up early and are *pau* (finished) when the trade winds perk up at around 8:30am. Surfers brave the mighty riptides, but be aware of a deceptively powerful current. Waipio Stream splits the beach on its way to the ocean; if you plan to visit the western end, the easiest avenue is a wade through the stream.

KALAUAHINE FALLS. *(45min. one-way. Moderate.)* From Waipio Beach, you can see Kalauahine Falls sparkling in the east. There's a rough trail along loose lava rock that runs from the intersection of the cliffs and the ocean to the falls.

MAIWALU TRAIL. *(7 mi. one-way. Challenging.)* At the western end of Waipio Beach, opposite the stream from the lookout, a switchback trail leads up the cliffs and over to Waimanu Valley. The switchback panoramas surpass even the astounding views from the lookout. This trail reveals unique and unparalleled waterfall and valley views. However, during rainfall, this trail can be quite treacherous, with narrow and slippery cliff-side passes and unclear paths. Most hikers plan on spending three days on the excursion; don't forget to pack enough water, food, rain gear, and insect repellent. While you can't camp in Waipio, it is possible to get a free backcountry camping permit from the Division of Forestry and Wildlife, 19 E. Kawili (☎808-974-4221), in Hilo, to camp in Waimanu Valley.

WAIMEA

A history of Waimea (pop. 7028) is a history of Parker Ranch. This is cattle country, a cross between the American Rockies and Scotland. Though only 10 mi. from balmy Kohala beaches, the air is crisp and cool. The Parker story began in 1793, when George Vancouver gave a herd of cattle to King Kamehameha. Kamehameha then bade them "go forth and multiply" and declared hunting them to be *kapu* (forbidden). This ban lasted for 10 years, during which time the cattle became a ferocious lot, notorious for rampaging and even chasing Hawaiians from their homes. By the early 19th century, Kamehameha had hired Massachusetts-born marksman John Palmer Parker to round up the cows, shoot those which were wild, and tame the rest. Parker did as ordered and garnered royal favor, so much, in fact, that he was granted a small plot of land on the slopes of Mauna Kea, beginning a collection of land that would reach 225,000 acres and become the vast Parker Ranch.

More than a decade after the death of Samuel Smart, the ranch's last heir, the board of the multimillion-dollar Parker Corporation still runs this town and 44% of the Big Island's real estate. In addition to financing several public service trusts, the copious Parker cash flow funds Waimea's private prep school and public hospital. The presence of the Parker millions has dramatically altered Waimea's trajectory as a small Hawaiian town.

The drive around Waimea is one of the most beautiful drives on the island. The well-paved road makes for an easy trip, and the numerous views try to steal your eyes from the road. Horses hang out around the fences and create a landscape similar to a country western movie. At sunset, the sun rays glisten through the trees and give the mountain sides a sublime glow.

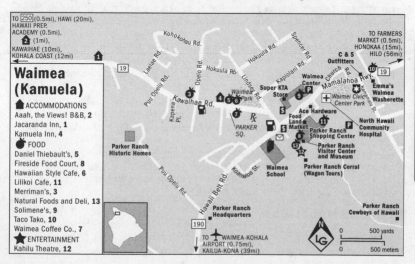

THE BIG ISLAND

▛ TRANSPORTATION

Flights: Waimea-Kohala Airport is 1 mi. south of Waimea Center, off Rte. 190, heading toward Kona. Pacific Wings Airlines (☎888-575-4546; www.pacificwings.com) runs daily flights to **Honolulu** (1hr.; 12:15pm) and **Kahului** (45min.; 8:25am). All express service flights are $87, while flights operating out of the bigger airports are subject to much higher fares. Open F-Su 8am-noon and 5-6pm.

Bus: The free **Hele-On Bus** (☎808-961-8744; www.hawaii-county.com/mass_transit/heleonbus) passes through Waimea with some consistency. Trips to **Hilo** from Foodland (1hr.; 7 per day 8:25am-11:55pm) and the Parker Ranch Center (1hr., M-Sa 8:05am). To **Kailua-Kona** from the Parker Ranch Center (1hr., M-F 8:15am).

Taxis: Alpha Star Taxi (☎808-885-4771), 10 mi. away, is the only taxi company in the Waimea area. Does not serve the airport. $3 initial charge; $2.40 per additional mi.

▟ ORIENTATION

Forty miles northeast of Kona and 54 mi. northwest of Hilo, Waimea is set in the Kohala hills in the northern part of the Big Island, at the intersection of **Route 190 (Mamalahoa Highway)** and **Route 19 (Hawaii Belt Road)**. From the Parker Ranch Plaza, the eastern half of Rte. 19 runs 15 mi. to Honokaa and the Hamakua coast. The other half of Rte. 19 heads toward Kawaihae, while **Route 250 (Kohala Mountain Road)** splits off toward Hawi.

▟ PRACTICAL INFORMATION

Banks: Bank of Hawaii, 67-1191 Mamalahoa Hwy. (☎808-885-7995). Open M-Th 8:30am-4pm, F 8:30am-6pm. **First Hawaiian Bank** (☎808-885-7991), in front of the Parker Ranch Center at Mamalahoa Hwy. and Kawaihae Rd. Open M-Th 8:30am-4pm, F 8:30am-6pm, Sa 9am-1pm. Both have 24hr. ATMs.

Library: Thelma Parker Memorial Library, 67-1209 Mamalahoa Hwy. (☎808-887-6067), behind the middle school gym, offers Internet access with a 3-month visitor's card ($10). Open M-Tu and Th 9am-4:30pm, W 12:30-7pm, F-Sa 9:30am-1:30pm.

Laundromat: Emma's Waimea Washerette is the yellow building on Mamalahoa Hwy., north of the intersection with Rte. 19. Wash $2.25, dry $1.75. Open M-Th and Su 5:45am-9pm, F-Sa 5:45am-11pm.

Swimming Pool: Hawaii Preparatory Academy, 65-1692 Kohala Mt. Rd. (☎808-881-4028), off Rte. 250 just past Rte. 19. Showers. Open M-F noon-1pm, Su 1-4pm. $3.

Police: Waimea Police Station (☎808-935-3311), at the corner of Kamamalu St. and Mamalahoa Hwy. Open daily 24hr. Emergency phone outside.

Pharmacy: Village Pharmacy, 65-1267 Kawaihae Rd. (☎808-885-4824), in the Hale Ola Pono Health Center. Open M-F 8:30am-5:30pm, Sa 8:30am-2pm.

Hospital: North Hawaii Community Hospital, 67-1125 Mamalahoa Hwy. (☎808-885-4444)., next to Ace Hardware.

Post Office: Kamuela Post Office, 67-1197 Mamalahoa Hwy. (☎800-275-8777), off Hwy. 190, across from the Parker Ranch Shopping Center. As there are 2 other Waimeas, on Kauai and Oahu, be sure to address mail to Kamuela, not Waimea. Open M-F 8am-4:30pm, Sa 9am-noon. **Postal Code:** 96743.

▛ ACCOMMODATIONS

Jacaranda Inn, 65-1444 Kawaihae Rd. (☎808-885-8813; www.jacarandainn.com). From the intersection of Rte. 19 and Rte. 190 in Waimea Center, continue west down

Rte. 19 (Kawaihae Rd.) toward Kawaihae; Jacaranda is just past mi. marker 58. With rich interiors and quaintly decadent architecture, Jacaranda offers luxury at a fraction of the resort price. The understated plantation feel is complemented by 4-poster beds, hot tubs, hardwood floors, chandeliers, and a wood-paneled library. Each room is unique. Breakfast included. Check-in 3-6pm. Check-out 11am. Reservations recommended. Rooms $159-225; 3-bedroom cottage $450. MC/V. ❺

Kamuela Inn, 65-1300 Kawaihae Rd. (☎808-885-4243; www.hawaii-bnb.com/kamuela), west of Waimea Center along Rte. 19 (Kawaihae Rd.) and past the ball field. More of a stylish motel than an inn, Kamuela is Waimea's best mid-range value. Spacious, clean rooms exhibit an upcountry motif. Breakfast included. Check-in 2-8pm. Check-out noon. Doubles $59-185, depending on number of people. AmEx/D/MC/V. ❷

Waimea Country Lodge, 65-1210 Lindsey Rd. (☎808-885-4100; www.castleresorts.com/wcl), off Kawaihae Rd. west of Waimea Center, before the Parker school. The lodge's central location, optional kitchenettes, and smiling staff make this a value for longer stays. Reception 7am-11pm. Check-in 3-11pm. Check-out noon. Reservations recommended. Rooms $120, with kitchenette $140. AmEx/D/MC/V. ❹

"Aaah, The Views!" Bed and Breakfast, 66-1773 Alaneo St. (☎808-885-3455; www.aaahtheviews.com). Take Kawaihae Rd. about 1 mi. past the Rte. 250 turnoff from Waimea, take a left on Akulani St., then a right on Alaneo. A comfortable, friendly, and low-key B&B, with some pretty decent mountain scenery. With a few lofted rooms and famous "chocolate breakfast," it's great for the whole family. $175-225. MC/V. ❺

▣ FOOD

Some of the best gourmet restaurants on the island are in Waimea. You can also pick up fresh produce and bouquets at the **Homestead farmers' market** (Sa 7am-noon), in the parking lot of the State of Hawaii Department of Home Lands, 2 mi. east of Waimea Center at mi. marker 55 on Rte. 19. However, if you're looking for something quick and cheap, check out the food court in Waimea Center, on Rte. 19, open daily 9am-9pm and serving pizza, Mexican, Japanese, Chinese, and ice cream. Dinner prices range from $7-20.

▣ **Hawaiian Style Cafe** (☎808-885-4295), on the right side of Kawaihae Rd. coming from town, 1 mi. from the intersection of Rte. 19 and Rte. 190. Some of the best breakfast on the island is made here, and they don't short you on the order. Try finishing a whole breakfast order—we dare you. Steak and chicken $7-9. Specials, like the smoked pork omelet, go for $7.25. Open M-Sa 7am-1:30pm, Su 7am-noon. Cash only. ❷

▣ **Merriman's** (☎808-885-6822), on Kawaihae Rd. at Opelo Rd. Specializing in cutting-edge Hawaiian cuisine, Merriman's is consistently ranked the best restaurant on the Big Island. Inventive dishes, like the wok-charred ahi and sesame-crusted fresh catch, will measure up to the high praise. Lunch $10-14. For dinner, the *ponzu*-marinated *mahi mahi* ($35) or prime cuts ($40), are worth the high prices. Reservations recommended. Lunch M-F 11:30am-1:30pm. Dinner nightly 5:30-9pm. AmEx/MC/V. ❺

▣ **Lilikoi Cafe,** 67-1185 Mamalahoa Hwy., Ste. 143 (☎808-887-1400), in the Parker Ranch Shopping Center. This cafe is a winner; their creative dishes are succulent, healthy, and made with fresh fruit and a smile. Rotating salads like chicken papaya and avocado mango $5. Sandwiches and hot entrees ($5.50-11) are equally delicious. Open M-Sa 7:30am-4pm. MC/V. ❶

▣ **Waimea Coffee Co,** 65-1280 Kawaihae Rd. (☎808-885-4472), in Parker Ranch Sq. This local stop has great coffee, tasty sandwiches, sweet pastries, and free Wi-Fi. Turkey and avocado wrap $8. Open M-F 7am-5pm, Sa 8am-5pm, Su 9am-3pm. MC/V. ❶

Solimene's, 65-1158 Mamalahoa Hwy. (☎808-887-1313), in the Waimea Shopping Center. This pizza, pasta, and panini place is a quick dinner spot. The father-son staff is friendly and possesses an uncanny knack for remembering your favorite dish. Try the Napa pizza, with artichoke hearts, olives, roasted peppers, onion, mozzarella, and fresh herbs. Pizza $17-24, pastas $9-13. Open Tu-Su 11am-3pm and 5-9pm. MC/V. ❷

Tako Taco, 64-1066 Mamalahoa Hwy. (☎808-887-1717), across from the Parker Ranch Center. This tin-roof joint is the place to go for cheap Mexican food. Burritos $6.25-8.50. Tacos $3.50-8.50. Salads $6.50-8.50. Open daily 11am-8pm. AmEx/MC/V. ❶

Daniel Thiebaut's, 65-1259 Kawaihae Rd. (☎808-887-2200). Housed in what was a general store in 1900, Daniel Thiebaut's gourmet restaurant caters unabashedly to the Kohala resorts down the hill. The crab-crusted *mahi mahi* ($37) receives accolades. Lunch $7.50-11.50. Dinner $20-35. Rack of lamb $35. Nice attire encouraged, especially for dinner. Excellent selection of wines. Lunch M-F 11:30am-2pm. Dinner daily 5:30-9pm. Reservations recommended. AmEx/D/MC/V. ❺

🦂 ACTIVITIES

Welcome to *paniolo* (cowboy) country: tighten your spurs, dig out your jeans, and jump on a horse. The misty, rolling chartreuse of the Kohala Mountains are a landscape best explored in the saddle. A number of quality outfits operate horseback tours both in Waimea and a few miles north near North Kohala; advance reservations should be made. Prepare for winds, rain, and fog.

Dahana Ranch (☎808-885-0057; www.dahanaranch.com), take Rte. 19 5 mi. toward Hilo, then bear right onto Mamalahoa Hwy. Continue 2 mi. and turn right at Dahana sign. Dahana's open range rides are outside Parker estate, and even farther outside the conventions of guided horseback tours. At Dahana, you're encouraged to lead the horse off the trail. Guides still navigate the rolling pasture, and invite tourists to help on ⚔ **weekly cattle drives**—an unparalleled experience ($130). Reservation required. 1hr. rides at 9, 11am, 1, 3pm; $70. 2hr. privately booked advanced ride $100. AmEx/D/MC/V.

Paniolo Riding Adventures (☎808-889-5354; www.panioloadventures.com), 14 mi. north of Waimea Ct. on Rte. 250, just past mi. marker 13 in Kohala. Guides lead riders across the open expanses of a working ranch, all the more exciting during calving season. Bring long pants and closed-toed shoes. 1hr. sunset ride $89; 2hr. *paniolo* ride $96; 3hr. picnic ride $124; 4hr. wrangler ride $159.

Parker Ranch Wagon Tours (☎808 885-7655; www.parkerranch.com/wagonrides.php), in Parker Ranch Corral, next to the Parker Ranch Visitor Center. A tame 45min. spin around a small section of Parker Ranch in a covered *paniolo* wagon. Every hr. Tu-Sa 10am-2pm. $15, seniors and ages 12 and under $12.

👁 🎵 SIGHTS AND ENTERTAINMENT

PARKER RANCH HISTORIC HOMES. These exquisitely maintained homes illustrate two different eras in the history of Parker Ranch. **Mana Hale,** "house of the spirit," is the New England-style wooden saltbox that served as John Palmer Parker's home during his first years as a rancher. Parker actually hauled the lumber from Mauna Kea to the house's site 12 mi. away. **Puuopelu,** or "meeting place," was built in 1862 and was home to Richard Smart, a 6th-generation Parker, until his death in 1992. The home is an excellent showcase for his French Impressionist and Chinese art collection. (*Off Rte. 190, 1 mi. south of town; the turnoff is on the right heading from Waimea to Kona. ☎808-885-5433. Open M-Sa 10am-5pm, last admission 4pm. $9, discounts for seniors and children available.*)

PARKER RANCH VISITORS CENTER AND MUSEUM. A small exhibit explores a bit of Hawaiian history before focusing on the owners of one of the oldest and largest ranches in the US, from John Palmer Parker in the early 1800s to the

6th-generation Parker, who died in 1992. A 25min. video details the ranch's history and may only be interesting to the Hawaiian history buff. *(67-1185 Mamala-hoa Hwy., in the Parker Ranch Center. ☎ 808-885-7655; www.parkerranch.com. Open M-Sa 9am-5pm. Last admission 4pm. $6.50, seniors $5.50, children $5.)*

KAHILU THEATER. This is where the Big Island comes for big-name performances. 2007 brought the Shanghai Quartet and Jake Shimabukuro, among many other internationally acclaimed acts. The theater starts its season in September and continues until May. It also hosts local performers and screens independent and blockbuster films throughout the year. *(67-1186 Lindsey Rd., behind the Parker Ranch Center. ☎ 808-885-6868; www.kahilutheatre.org. Box office open M-F 9am-3pm and 1-4pm. Tickets for major events $28-45. Movies $6, under 13 $4.)*

NORTH KOHALA INCLUDING HAWI AND KAPAAU

North Kohala is an example of living history. On this northern perch, the unforgiving winds and racing ocean currents have sculpted the island's oldest volcanic mountain range into one of the state's most striking vistas. Hawi (pop. 938) and Kapaau (pop. 1159) used to be powerful fixtures in Hawaii's sugarcane industry and royal power structure; King Kamehameha rose to power and united the entire island chain from this windy range. Today, a row of stores (and empty storefronts) lines the sides of Akoni Pule Hwy. in a jungle of wild sugarcane. These once-booming towns and the surrounding hills are the perfect place to get a glimpse into Hawaii's past; the slopes of the Kohala Mountains are lined with ancient *heiau* (temples) and reminders of the not-too-distant caning past. Hike up, kayak down, or just tear right on through—the alluring charm of North Kohala is everywhere.

✦ ORIENTATION

Hawi is at the intersection of **Route 250 (Hawi Road)** and **Route 270,** 19 mi. north of Kawaihae and 20 mi. northwest of Waimea. This stretch of Rte. 270, also known as **Akoni Pule Highway,** is the town's main road. It continues east from Hawi, through Kapaau, and ends 7 mi. later at the **Pololu Valley Lookout** (p. 253).

North Kohala is the one district not linked via the Hawaii Belt Rd, The free **Hele-On Bus** (☎808-961-8744) leaves daily from downtown Kapaau (6:20am) and makes a 1hr. loop to Hawi and the six resorts in South Kohala; it returns from the last of those resorts, the Hilton Waikoloa, at 4:15pm.

▮ PRACTICAL INFORMATION

Banks: Bank of Hawaii, 54-388 Akoni Pule Hwy. (☎808-889-1073), in downtown Kapaau. 24hr. ATM. Open M-Th 8:30am-4pm, F 8:30am-6pm. Another ATM can be found in Hawi at **Kohala Mailbox,** 55-3419 Akoni Pule Hwy., #28 (☎808-889-0498). Open M-F 8:30am-4pm, Sa 9am-2pm.

Gas: Hawi Shell Station, 55-503 Hawi Rd. (☎808-889-5211), on the corner of Hawi Rd. and Akoni Pule Hwy. Open M-F 5:30am-6:30pm, Sa 6am-6:30pm, Su 8am-4pm.

Bookstore: ▨**Kohala Book Shop,** 54-3885 Akoni Pule Hwy. (☎808-889-6400), in downtown Kapaau. The largest used bookstore on the island also has an extensive collection of Hawaiiana. Open M-Sa 11am-5pm. Closed in Sept. MC/V.

Library: Bond Memorial Public Library, 54-3903 Akoni Pule Hwy. (☎808-889-6655), in downtown Kapaau, offers Internet access with a visitor's card ($10). Open M noon-8pm, Tu-Th 9am-5pm, F 9am-1pm.

Police: North Kohala District Police Station, 54-3900 Akoni Pule Hwy. (☎808-889-6540; Hilo dispatch 808-935-3311), in Kapaau, behind the Kamehameha statue and Civic Center. Office open daily 8am-4pm.

Pharmacy: Kamehameha Pharmacy, 54-3877 Akoni Pule Hwy. (☎808-889-6161), in downtown Kapaau. Open M-Tu and Th-F 9am-12:30pm and 1:30-5pm, W 9am-1pm.

Hospital: Kohala Hospital, 54-383 Hospital Rd. (☎808-889-6211), on the *makai* (ocean) side of downtown Kapaau, off Hwy. 270.

Internet Access: In addition to the **library** (see above), **Kohala Computer Center,** 55-3407 Akoni Pule Hwy. (☎808-889-1002), in downtown Hawi, provides superior tech support and Internet access. $3 per 15min., $10 per hr. Open M-F 8am-4:30pm. **Kohala Mailbox,** 54-3419 Akoni Pule Hwy. (☎808-889-0498) charges $3.50 per 15min. Fax $5.25 per page; copies for $0.16 per page.

Post Offices: Hawi Post Office, 55-515 Hawi Rd. (☎808-275-8777), near the corner of Rte. 250 and 270. Open M-F 8:30am-noon and 12:30-4pm, Sa 9-10am. **Kapaau Post Office,** 54-396 Union Mill Rd. (☎808-889-6766). Open M-F 7:30am-4pm, Sa 9-10:30am. **Postal Code:** 96719 (Hawi); 96755 (Kapaau).

ACCOMMODATIONS AND CAMPING

Kohola Village Inn, 55-514 Hawi Rd. (☎808-889-0404), in Hawi, at the corner of Rte. 250 and 270. The rooms here are nicer and cheaper than in most places in Kohala. TV and continental breakfast. Be sure to check out their Bar & Tiki Lounge blasting live music daily, or the salsa dancing on Sa night. Check-in 3-8:30pm. Check-out 11am. Quiet hours after 9pm. Singles $65; doubles $75. 2-room suites $100-120. MC/V. ❷

Kohala's Guest House, 52-277 Keokea Park Rd. (☎808-889-5606; www.kohalaguest-house.com), about 3 mi. east of Kapaau. Turn *makai* (toward the ocean) from Hwy. 270 onto the road that leads to Keokea Beach. The white Guest House is less than 1 mi. down on your right; look for a labeled mailbox. A bright, sunny, and tidy place to stay. Check-in 2pm. Check-out 11am. Single room $59; 1-bedroom with use of kitchen and common area $79; either side of a fully furnished duplex house equipped with full kitchen, 3 bedrooms, TV, and washer/dryer $140; $800 per wk. ❷

Kohala Country Adventures Guest House, 54-529 Kapau Rd. (☎808-889-5663; www. kcadventures.com), 1 mi. above Kapaau. Turn away off Hwy. 270 onto the road between the Bank of Hawaii and the Kamehameha statue; the guest house is on the left by the aloha sign. "Cozy" is an understatement; here, you're at home. Rooms vary in size, though all have refrigerator and kitchen access. Check-in 3pm. Reservations recommended. Doubles $85-175; additional guest $15. 3 night min. AmEx/D/MC/V. ❸

Kapaa Beach Park, turn toward the ocean from Hwy. 270 between mi. markers 15 and 16. This small rocky beach has water calm enough for swimming. Restrooms and picnic tables surround a covered structure that is often converted into a makeshift camper's luau spot. Permits required; see **Camping in Hawaii,** p. 82, for information. ❶

Mahukona Beach Park, less than 1 mi. north of Lapakahi Historical Park on Hwy. 270, before mi. marker 15. Although the campsites have little shade and are a bit scummy, many locals come to snorkel in this unique industrial underwater area. The snorkeling reveals an underwater treasure trove with all kinds of fish and sights, including yellow tang and boat debris. The ambitious diver can follow an anchor chain from the port to the remains of a sunken steamboat that rests largely intact under 20 ft. of water. The campground has showers, a pavilion with electricity, and toilets, but bring your own water. Permits required; see **Camping in Hawaii,** p. 82, for information. ❶

☐ FOOD

Despite being in the Big Island's backcountry, North Kohala has some surprisingly good places to eat. From Mexican to sushi, the hungry hiker will find plenty of satiating options. Plan on eating in Hawi—the food options in Kapaau are quite limited. **Nakahara Grocery Store** (☎808-889-6359), on Hawi Rd., is Hawi's local grocer, with the bonus of an informal **farmers' market** that congregates on the grass outside. (Open M-Sa 8am-7pm, Su 8am-3pm.)

■ **Sushi Rock,** 55-3435 Akoni Pule Hwy. (☎808-889-5900), in Hawi, just east of the intersection with Hwy. 250. This upscale sushi studio rolls out creative lunches and dinners ($3-7). Also try their irresistible salads, like the baked macadamia nut chèvre with caramelized onions ($7). Fish and chicken dishes $11-15. Open M-Tu, Th, and Su noon-3pm and 5:30-8pm; F-Sa noon-3pm and 5:30pm-9pm. AmEx/D/MC/V. ❷

■ **Kohala Coffee Mill** (☎808-889- 5577), across from Bamboo, on Akoni Pule Hwy. in Hawi. Heaping scoops of Tropical Dreams Hawaiian Ice Cream ($2-4), fruit smoothies ($4), and a wide selection of tea and coffee ($1.75-4). Burgers $4.50. Ice cream flavors rotate daily and include white chocolate ginger, banana-mango, jamocha-macadamia nut, and white pineapple sorbet. Lunch specials, like the angel hair pasta with *mahi mahi,* around $7. Open M-F 6:30am-6pm, Sa-Su 7am-5:30pm. MC/V. ❶

Bamboo, 55-3415 Akoni Pule Hwy. (☎808-889-5555), in downtown Hawi. Quality Hawaiian-style local plates have become the reason many people come to Hawi. Favorites include *kalua* pork and cabbage ($14), *Puaa A Opai* (pork tenderloin and black tiger shrimp on papaya salad), and their ■**original passion fruit margarita.** Try a bit of everything Hawaiian on the sampler plate ($13). F-Sa live Hawaiian music. Open Tu-Sa 11:30am-2:30pm and 6-9pm, Su 11am-2pm. MC/V. ❸

Short N Sweet Bakery and Cafe, 55-3419 Akoni Pule Hwy. (☎808-889-1444), in Hawi. This bakery turns dessert into fine art, with delicate cookies and stunning sugar flowers. They've also got delicious panini served on homemade focaccia (mozzarella and Italian ham, $9). Salads $4-8. Baked treats $2-5. MC/V. ❷

Hula La's Mexican Kitchen, 54-3419 Akoni Pule Hwy. (☎808-889-5668), in the Kohala Trade Center in Hawi. A basic taqueria with satisfying burritos ($6-7.50). Try the chicken or beer enchiladas, a local favorite ($9). 4 varieties of salsa are so

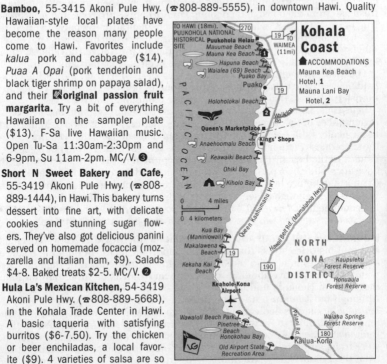

Kohala Coast

🏠 ACCOMMODATIONS
Mauna Kea Beach Hotel, **1**
Mauna Lani Bay Hotel, **2**

THE BIG ISLAND

popular they sell by the pound ($10) or the more reasonably sized bowl ($1.50). Open daily M-F 11am-8pm, Sa-Su 11am-4pm. MC/V. ❶

Kava Kafe, 54-3419 Akoni Pule Hwy. (☎808-896-6073), in the Kohala Trade Center. The local kava hole, and a great place to unwind after a long day's hike. Shells of kava $4, kava brownies $3. Open ◼ M-F 4:21pm-8:59pm, call for Sa-Su hours. Cash only. ❶

Pico's Bistro, 54-3866 Akoni Pule Hwy. (☎808-884-5555), in Kapaau. This new family run, Greek/grilling bistro resides in a small lime- green building directly in front of Kenji's House Gallery Museum. The 6 tables provide a very fine outdoor dining experience with friendly service. Try the open-faced lamb sandwich ($9). Salads, wraps, and burgers $5-11. Open daily 11am-7pm. ❷

Rainbow Cafe, 54-3897 Akoni Pule Hwy. (☎808-889-0099), in Kapaau. One of the few eating options in Kapaau, people come here for the friendly ambience. Try the Hawaiian Bleu (grilled chicken, ham, and pineapple topped with a *lilikoi* dressing; $9). Salads and wraps $7.50. Sandwiches $8. Burgers $10. Open M-F 10am-5pm. MC/V. ❷

◉ 🏛 SIGHTS AND ACTIVITIES

LAPAKAHI STATE HISTORICAL PARK. When Polynesian sailors arrived at the sheltered coves of Lapakahi nearly 600 years ago, they agreed upon its security and built a village. Soon thereafter, many of the villagers hiked into the wetter Kohala Mountains, where extensive farming was more feasible. For nearly 500 years, a trade arrangement between the upland farmers and *ahupuaa* (their coastal counterparts) united these Kohala natives. Their exchanges included fresh fish from the coast and coconut, *kamani* nuts, taro root, and *ulu* (breadfruit) crops. In 1918, when struggling sugar plantation owners diverted the seven streams that fed Lapakahi, lush fields quickly dried into a red sand desert. The fate of Lapakahi became a common tragedy for Native Hawaiians. Today, Lapakahi is the only native village that has been at least partially restored.

The **Visitors Center** at Lapakahi has maps of a 1 mi. trail, indicating canoe landings, salt pans, fish shrines, burial grounds, and the fragments of the taro-for-fish trade road that once connected the mountains and the coast.

In its time, Lapakahi was considered a sacred healing ground because of the high number of medicinal roots and plants that grew on its coast. Many traditional healers still frequent the site for ceremonies and ask that visitors respect the sacredness of their historic home. Signs request that visitors not bring their picnics to the beach. The **snorkeling** is exceptional but is permitted only in the cove accessible by a path directly *makai* (toward the ocean) from the Visitors Center. Ask before leaving to be sure you are swimming in the right spot. The water is clear enough to see a rainbow of fish from the rocks without any snorkel equipment. *(Off Hwy. 270; turn toward the ocean near mi. marker 14. ☎808-889-5566. Bring your own water and sunscreen. Open daily 8am-4pm, gate closes 3:30pm. Free.)*

MOOKINI LUAKINI HEIAU AND KAMEHAMEHA'S BIRTHPLACE. Hawaiian chants and oral histories stress that the most important factor in building a sacred *heiau* (temple) is not the building's design, but the choice of the site. On a windy green cliff overlooking the Pacific and Haleakala Mountain on Maui, the Mookini Heiau is undoubtedly a site of great *mana*, or spiritual power. Although most *heiau* tend to be dedicated to Lono, the god of harvest, the *heiau* at Mookini is dedicated to Ku, the god of war. Known as *luakini heiau*, temples dedicated to Ku were the only spiritual sites to offer human sacrifices. Built in 480 BC, the Mookini Heiau has 30 ft. walls which, according to legend, were transported by a 9 mi. long human chain that extracted volcanic stones from the Pololu Valley. Traditionally restricted to *alii* (royalty) and *kahuna* (priests), Mookini Luakini Heiau was designated the first National Historic Landmark in Hawaii and opened to the public in 1963.

A few hundred yards down the coast from the *heiau* there is a large enclosure reputed to be the site of Kamehameha's birth. The exact date is disputed, but according to oral tradition, Kamehameha was born on a stormy night following an unusual celestial light that was seen rising in the east. Towering at a peak of 5480 ft., the North Kohala mountains would provide Kamehameha with a commanding view of Maui, allowing him strategic vision in his advance to unify the islands. *(Both of these sacred sites are almost unmarked. To reach the heiau, turn toward the ocean at the sign for Upolu Airport at mi. marker 20 on Rte. 270. Follow the road for 2 mi. At the airport, turn left on the dirt road that runs parallel to the coast. This road is often swamped with mud pools, making it impassable for cars with 2WD. After about 1 mi. you will see a signpost indicating the direction of each historic site; the heiau is on the hill to the left. Kamehameha's birthplace is another mi. down the right-hand fork, just up from the coast. For more information call ☎ 808-591-1170 or 808-591-1142.)*

KAMEHAMEHA STATUE. On the *mauka* side of the highway through Kapaau, this "true-to-scale" 8 ft. tall statue of King Kamehameha asserts the legendary status of Hawaii's uniting king. It's a heavily touristed sight and not really worth the stop.

⧫ POLOLU VALLEY LOOKOUT. This is a fantastic place for a stop; the view is spectacular and would probably halt traffic even if the road continued forward. The parking lot at the end of the highway looks out over rocky cliffs and waves crashing against a black sand beach. Behind this, the start of the seven valleys (from Pololu to Waipio) stretches out in sharp green arcs. Thousands of years of Pacific erosion carved these lush valleys from the Kohala Mountains: a miracle of time, water, and circumstance found nowhere else on the island. Waipio is the only other valley accessible by car from the east. If the view ensnares you, several trails into the valley start from the parking lot. For more information, see **Hiking,** p. 254. *(7 mi. past Kapaau on Rte. 270, at the end of the road.)*

FLUMIN' DA DITCH. A unique option for seeing the North Kohala countryside, Flumin' Da Ditch coordinates wet and bizarre group kayak adventures that explore the area's undeveloped rainforests and remnants of the long-gone era of sugar plantations. Kids who grew up on these plantations were known to grab anything that floated and go flumin' in the ditches, tunnels, and flumes of Kohala's irrigation

IN RECENT NEWS

THE BIG GREEN ISLAND

In 2000, Hawaii became the eighth state to pass a bill allowing the possession of marijuana for medical purposes. The US's 50th state was the first to pass the bill without using ballot measures, using legislation to decriminalize the use of the drug instead. The law allows medical marijuana patients to possess up to one ounce of marijuana and grow up to three mature marijuana plants as long as the patient meets the law's requirements. These regulations include being diagnosed with cancer, glaucoma, HIV, AIDS, severe pain, severe nausea, seizures, or severe muscle spasms.

To get a blue card, a patient must first fill out a five-page application. After paying a $25 fee, the patient's application is sent to the Department of Public Safety's Narcotics Enforcement Team. Within four to six weeks the successful applicant will receive a blue medical marijuana card.

Of all the seven major Hawaiian Islands, the Big Island has been the one to take advantage of this chronic opportunity. The islands have 4200 medical marijuana patients combined, and 2640 of them live on the Big Island. This means that the Big Island, which only accounts for 13% of the state's population, accounts for over 60% of Hawaii's bud-smoking community. With so many blue cards on the Big Island, Hawaii is as green as ever.

system. Over the course of the trip, guides explain the design, construction, and history of the Kohala Ditch Project and the 600 Japanese laborers who made it possible. The ride is very cool: little paddling is involved, and the guides are as entertaining as the scenery. Flumin' also runs 3hr. HMV Tours, a drier venture into the same rainforests and past the same waterfalls. Unfortunately, an earthquake in October 2006 damaged the ditch, causing Flumin' Da Ditch to cancel their tours for a few years. Tour operators have been working on repairing the ditch and plan to reopen in October 2008. Check their website for updates. *(55-519 Hawi Rd. above the intersection of Hwy. 250 and 270 in Hawi.* ☎*808-889-6922; www.flumindaditch.com. Both trips daily 8:15am and 12:15pm. $89, ages 5-18 $68. AmEx/D/MC/V.)*

ATV OUTFITTERS. This is a rumbling, bumpy, muddy, and spectacular way to see the North Kohala mountains and waterfalls. These guides, all of whom are 4th-, 5th-, and 6th-generation Kohala natives, lead groups along the King Kamehameha and Kohala sugar plantation trails. They offer ATV trips on the Historical Ocean Cliff Trail (1.5hr., $109, ages 7-15 $75), 15 mi. Waterfall Adventure (2hr., $169, ages 7-15 $125), and 22 mi. Deluxe Adventure (3hr., $249, ages 7-15 $125). Reservations required. *(Just off Rte. 270 in Kapaau; turn toward the ocean at the sign.* ☎*888-288-7288; www.atvoutfittershawaii.com. Open M-Sa 7am-4pm. Ages 16+ to drive, 7+ to ride with a guide. AmEx/D/MC/V.)*

⚑ HIKING

The landscape of the northwest corner of the Big Island is often mistakenly overlooked. However, the valleys, beaches, and rainforest yield some of the most adventuresome and scenic hikes on the island. Bring water and sturdy shoes, and, for stream hikes, be prepared for extensive wading and aggressive mosquitoes. Rock-hopping is much easier in a pair of waterproof shoes, such as Tevas, Chacos, Crocs, or Tabis.

◪ **POLOLU VALLEY TRAIL.** *(15-20min. one-way. Easy.)* The Pololu Valley Trail leaves the Pololu Valley Overlook at the end of Rte. 270 and quickly drops down the slope to the valley's gray sand beach. This short and easy (though steep) jaunt wraps around the cliff, allowing views of the tip of at least four valleys, the thick vegetation of Maui, and the boundless Pacific. The trail leads to a few rope swings into the water; use caution in both the ocean and the streams.

◪ **HONOKANENUI VALLEY TRAIL.** *(3-4hr. round-trip. Moderate to challenging.)* Honokanenui trail is an energizing hike from Pololu Valley Beach to the Honokanenui lookout: bring water, good hiking shoes, bug spray, and sunblock. The trail is well maintained but not always well-marked, and, at least once, the trail crosses into private property. The Honokanenui Trail begins on the other side of the stream from the end of the Pololu Valley Trail (see above). Following the beach initially, the trail eventually climbs to a ridge with an arresting view. Unfortunately, the trail is closed from here on out; it is not advised to continue on this trail. Returning from Honokanenui, a trail (trail markers are any stack of stones three or higher) just before the stream leads to a boulder beach. With wonderful cliff views and crashing waves, this is the place to break for lunch.

KAPU. Signs that read *"kapu"* (forbidden) are common throughout the Kohala range. This sign is not just a decoration—it marks private property. Always be respectful when hiking, and consult tourist offices for the most up-to-date information on the following trails. Let's Go recommends asking landowners for permission before venturing into *kapu* territory.

WAIKAMA FALLS HIKE. *(0.5mi., 20min. one-way. Challenging.)* The trailhead is on the mountain side of Rte. 270 about 1 mi. from the Pololu Valley Overlook (p. 253). Look for a plain, white post; the trailhead is otherwise unmarked, just follow the stream. Strap on a pair of waterproof shoes and prepare for a very slippery, muddy, and bug-filled adventure. Note that stream hiking with open cuts can result in leptospirosis infections. At the end of the trail, you'll stand wet in a murky rainforest pool as a stunning waterfall tumbles over large boulders.

SOUTH KOHALA

The most luxurious resorts of South Kohala are islands within an island; there are no true towns, only resort endeavors backed by multi-million dollar budgets. The South Kohala coast enjoys a near-perfect 363 days of sun annually. The resorts take meticulous care of the beaches, combing the sand smooth and providing beach chairs, cool showers, and hammocks along some stretches. Because the entire Hawaiian shoreline is publicly accessible by law, even travelers on a shoestring can live it up on these beaches—just don't forget your bag lunch. Hwy. 19 carves through these desolate lava flows on its way toward the Kohala mountain range; it is along this formidable route that men and women run the grueling marathon leg of the annual Ironman Triathlon.

⛰ ACCOMMODATIONS

In South Kohala, the overwhelming majority of the accommodations are pricey resorts. Vacation rentals in nearby Waikaloa and Puako are sometimes available online. Try **www.sunquest-hawaii.com** for condo rentals in Waikaloa. **Vacation Rentals** (☎808-882-7000; www.vacationbigisland.com) offers reasonably priced condos and cottages in Puako. For those interested in the full South Kohala experience, resort and all, you can save a bunch by giving up the ocean view.

▨ **Mauna Kea Beach Hotel,** 62-100 Mauna Kea Beach Dr. (☎808-882-7222; www.maunakeabeachhotel.com), 32 mi. north of Kona on Hwy. 19. Far and away the best of South Kohala, the opulence of the Mauna Kea is intoxicating. Breeze-swept buildings overlook a stunning crescent of sand. 40 years later, the entire complex is as swank— and ridiculously expensive—as ever. Tu night luau starts at sunset ($82, ages 5-12 $40). Reservations recommended. Check website for special rates. Check-in 3pm. Check-out noon. Rooms $390-660; suites $975-1650. AmEx/D/MC/V. ⑤

Mauna Lani Bay Hotel, 68-1400 Mauna Lani Dr. (☎808-885-6622; www.maunalani. com). In one of the most intimate of the South Kohala resorts, guests in search of tranquility are rewarded. Rooms are thoughtfully designed, with marble-floored baths and balconies. Ask about the ancient fishponds, settlement remains, and the extensive petroglyph collection. Standard room $430, with ocean view $670; bungalow $5200-5900. Cash only... just kidding. AmEx/D/MC/V. ⑤

🏖 BEACHES

Kohala's got sunshine on a rainy day; when it's gray to the north or south, the sky is usually blue over the South Kohala coast. Some of the island's best white sand beaches, listed here from south to north, are only a paved resort driveway away. Just don't forget the sunblock.

ANAEHOOMALU BEACH. *(Snorkeling and wind sports. Open daily 6am-8pm.)* Waikoloa Beach Resort sits on a white sand beach that stretches south toward Kona

GIVING BACK

HUMPBACK HEAD COUNT

Every summer, nearly two thirds of the entire North Pacific population of humpback whales make the 3500 mi. journey from their feeding grounds in the arctic waters of Alaska to their reproduction grounds along Hawaii's tropical shores. While most of the whales honeymoon off the coast of Maui, humpbacks can be spotted from the shores of every island.

The **Hawaiian Islands Humpback Whale National Marine Sanctuary** is devoted to the protection and study of these endangered creatures and offers numerous volunteer activities. The most popular volunteer event is the yearly **Sanctuary Ocean Count**, held on the last Saturdays in January, February, and March. Hundreds of volunteers show up at over sixty selected sites on Oahu, Kauai, and the Big Island to record the number of whales they spot in a four-hour period.

Counting whales helps the sanctuary to learn more about the distribution and behavioral trends of the humpback whale population throughout the seasons in Hawaii. While the majority of volunteers are local residents, visitors are encouraged to participate.

☎808-587-0106. *Registration begins in Nov. No prior experience is necessary. Event runs 8am-noon but volunteers are asked to arrive early to receive instructions from site leaders.*

along a picturesque bay. Known to locals as "A-Beach," or "A-Bay," its consistently calm waters and sandy bottom make it one of the most popular swimming, snorkeling, and windsurfing spots around. The beach has showers, toilets, and drinking water at its southern end.

At the northern end of A-Beach, **Ocean Sports,** the beach hut on the sand, arranges aquatic activities in the area—from snorkeling ($6 per hr., $50 per wk.) to sunset cruises to scuba diving and windsurfing. (☎808-886-6666. Open daily 8am-5pm. Cruises M, W, F-Sa 4:30pm. $73, ages 3-12 $53; windsurfing lessons $60 per hr.; rental $30 per hr.; snacks and drinks $1-3.) Past Ocean Sports to the north, at the Marriott, non-guests are free to enjoy a volleyball net, a running/circuit training loop, and beach chairs. To reach the beach, make the turn for the Waikoloa Beach Resort between mi. markers 76 and 77, 8 mi. south of Kawaihae and 25 mi. north of Kailua-Kona. The parking lot is the first left turn on the road across from the Kings' Shops.

WAIALEA BEACH (69 BEACH). *(Snorkeling. Open daily 24hr.)* Curl up in your favorite position on this little-known stretch of white sand, given its scandalous moniker because of the seclusion it once offered. It's much busier these days, but it's still a good find. A white tree twists out over the beach, providing visitors with shade and a place to spend a day without worrying about sunburn. Full facilities. *(Turn toward the ocean onto Puako Rd. from Hwy. 19 between mi. markers 70 and 71. Take your first right at the dump gate onto a single-lane road and drive until telephone pole #71, indicated by small gold numbers about 10 ft. up. A dirt path leads to a parking lot and the beach.)*

🐋 **HAPUNA BEACH.** *(Bodyboarding and snorkeling. Open daily 7am-8pm. Lifeguards 9am-4pm.)* One of America's best beaches, this 1 mi. stretch of sand is exactly what you picture when you think of Hawaii. It's not a secret either: expect crowds, as tourists and locals plant themselves firmly on the sand from the early morning until the fabled green flash of the sunset. Swimming is excellent in the calm seas, and when the surf kicks up, the beach becomes a body-boarder's heaven. **Paradise Grill,** on the northern end of the grassy walk down to the sand, offers a full menu of beach food (fish tacos $8) and a healthy inventory of beach rentals ($10 each; open daily 9am-4pm). *(Off Rte. 19 between mi. markers 69 and 70.)*

🐋 **MAUNA KEA BEACH.** *(Surfing. Open daily sunrise to sunset. Lifeguards 8am-sunset.)* At the end of the luxury resort, yet another flawless crescent of sand awaits. Check with the hotel lifeguards on the surf conditions—in the winter this beach sees some impressive swells. Full facilities. *(Thirty-two miles north of downtown Kona on Rte. 19 between mi. markers 68 and 69, there is access the beach through the road to Mauna Kea Hotel. Those not staying at the hotel have to stop at the gate and get a beach parking pass, valid from sunrise to sunset. Parking is limited to 30 cars, so be sure to be there by 10am.)*

MAUUMAE BEACH. *(Open daily 8am-5pm.)* Although at the same resort as Mauna Kea, Mauu Mae couldn't be more different. Smaller, shady, and murky, Mauu Mae rarely hosts any resort guests, though it does offer a great spot to park it beneath a tree and get out of the sun. Like Mauna Kea, this beach is accessed through the Mauna Kea Beach Hotel Rd. (see directions above). The hotel provides free parking passes and directions. Those who fear the scantily-clad beware: this beach is known to be frequented by nudists. *(The beach is the third right inside the resort; follow the road as it crosses two bridges and park just before the road turns to dirt. Follow the trail and go left at the sign post.)*

 PUBLIC SHORELINE ACCESS. Look for small white rectangular signs peppered along any coast road reading Public Shoreline Access for entrance to another beach on Hawaii's coastline. Some of Hawaii's most charming beaches are nestled away along the trail from one of these signs.

◎ SIGHTS

PUUKOHOLA HEIAU NATIONAL HISTORICAL SITE. According to legend, Puukohola played a key role in Kamehameha's unification of the islands. Today, while stripped of some of its natural splendor by development, it still retains its historic and cultural significance and commanding position on the coastline. The park's Visitors Center gives out pamphlets for a self-guided tour of three *heiau* (temples). Don't miss the 3 minute video. The first site along the walking path is the sprawling Puukohola Heiau, built by Kamehameha in the late 18th century. Farther down the hillside is Mailekini Heiau, an older structure thought to have been built for war or agricultural purposes. The final *heiau*, Hale o Kapuni Heiau, submerged offshore, was dedicated to the shark gods. Although initially built above the high-water mark, it has been underwater since the 1950s. King Kamehameha is believed to have labored on this *heiau* alongside his men. *(10 mi. west of Waimea and 34 mi. north of Kona along Rte. 270, near the intersection of Hwy. 19 and 270. ☎808-882-7218; www.nps.gov/puhe. Open daily 7:30am-4pm. Free.)*

 NUTS FOR NUTS? Looking for a cheap way to spend an afternoon? Check out the **Hamakua Macadamia Nut Company's** new factory in Kawaihae for free tours and samples. See Big Island macadamia nuts and other delicacies from 8am to 5pm daily. Call ☎808-882-1690.

MAUI

Although it is the second-oldest, second-largest, and second most-developed island in the Hawaiian chain, Maui is far from second-best. Not as commercial as Oahu, but with more attractions than the Big Island and Kauai and much of the same natural beauty, Maui stakes a solid claim that *Maui no ka oi!* (Maui is the best!) Its 727 sq. mi. have a little something for every taste: rugged trails, historic towns, a flourishing art scene, and cuisine that runs the gamut of healthful, gourmet, and greasy. Families delight in beachside activities while honeymooning couples swoon on secluded coasts and waterfall hikes.

Most visitors first become familiar with the dry leeward side of West Maui, where resorts have turned *kiawe* tree deserts into golf courses. The less-developed, dense rainforest of the windward side of the West Maui mountains grows acres of fruit trees and ferns. In eastern Maui, at the high altitudes of the Haleakala Crater, rainforest gives way to miles of towering pines, redwoods, and eucalyptus. The central valley, located in the narrow isthmus between Haleakala and the West Maui mountains, is carpeted from one end to the other with sugarcane, the heart of agriculture on the "Valley Isle." Maui is the only Hawaiian island that retains a significant sugarcane crop (43,000 acres), staving off residential and commercial development in the valley.

The island's surrounding waters bristle with marine life, including hundreds of species found only in Maui's reef. Winter is high season, when the largest group of humpback whales (about 3000 of them) gather off the south coast. Big-wave surfing on the North Shore coincides with whale watching and attracts its own onlookers. Surfing, bodyboarding, and windsurfing are popular year-round and are the center of both tourism and island life. Countless young people move to Maui to work, surf, and generally embrace the aloha spirit. Still, as popular as Maui has become, the identity of the Hawaiian community remains strong. Grassroots movements have sprung up to reclaim sacred lands, educate visitors about Hawaiian culture, and deal with community issues. There is a growing number of opportunities for visitors to learn from locals about native traditions. Maui's rich local culture is the essence of what makes the island so special—a fusion of ethnic groups whose love of the island is contagious.

HIGHLIGHTS OF MAUI

BE THE FIRST TO SEE DAY BREAK from the summit of **Haleakala** (p. 318).

DRIVE THERE AND BACK AGAIN along the **Hana Highway** (p. 300), stopping to enjoy the waterfalls along the road and the **Pools of Oheo** past Hana.

SHED YOUR INHIBITIONS at **Little Beach** (p. 298) in Makena.

ADMIRE the majestic grace of hundreds of **humpback whales** (p. 289) as they swim off the coast of Maui from December to April.

SNORKEL IN THE AQUARIUM, a hidden cove in **Ahihi-Kinau Natural Area** (p. 299).

✈ INTERISLAND TRANSPORTATION

Flights from the neighboring islands start around $120 round-trip, although some cost as much as $200, and prices vary depending on the season. Maui's

Maui

PACIFIC OCEAN

Alenuihaha Channel

Waianapanapa State Park
Hana Bay
Kaihalulu Bay
Red Sand Beach
Hana Airport
Hamoa Beach
Koki Beach
Hana
Wailiumalu Falls
Kanahualii Falls
HANA DISTRICT
WAIHOI VALLEY
KIPAHULU VALLEY
360
Waimoku Falls
Kipahulu
Ohéo Gulch

Nahiku
Hana Hwy.
Keanae
Wailua
360
Honomanu Bay
Hanawi Natural Area Reserve
Kaupo Tr.
Kaupo Gap
Kaupo
Haleakala National Park
Sliding Sands Tr.
Puu Ulaula Summit 10,023'
Piilani Hwy.
31

Huelo
Hana Hwy.
Twin Falls
Puohokamoa Falls
Uaoa Bay
Ulumalu Rd.
Kaupakalua Rd.
Makawao
Makawao Forest Reserve
Piiholo Rd.
Olinda Rd.
MAKAWAO DISTRICT
Haiku
36
365
398
Kokomo
R.d.
390
Baldwin Ave.
Makawao Ave.
Haleakala Hwy.
377
378
Crater Rd.
Haleakala Hwy.
Hookipa Beach
Paia
37
Pukalani
Omaopio Rd.
Puleia Rd.
Puunene
Waipoli Rd.
Kula Hwy.
Kula Hwy.
Boundary Tr.
Kula
Polipoli State Park
37
Kanaio Natural Area Reserve
Hoapili Tr.
Ulupalakua Ranch
Makena Rd.
31
Upper Kihei Rd.
Mokulele Hwy.
Kahului Airport
Kahului Harbor
Kaahumanu Ave.
Kuihelani Hwy.
Wailuku
Kahului
Mokulele Hwy.
311
N. Kihei Rd.
310
S. Kihei Rd.
Piilani Hwy.
Kihei
Maalaea Bay
Wailea
Keokea
Makena
Ahihi-Kinau Natural Area Reserve
La Perouse Bay
Molokini
Alalakeiki Channel

Kahakuloa
WAILUKU DISTRICT
Kahekili Hwy.
Iao Valley Rd.
Iao Valley
WEST MAUI MOUNTAINS
30
380
30
Maalaea
Honoapiilani Hwy.
30
Olowalu

Nakalele Point
Honokohau Bay
340
Honokahua Bay
D.T. Fleming Beach Park
Kapalua
Honoapiilani Hwy.
Napili
Kahana
West Maui Airport
LAHAINA DISTRICT
Kaanapali
Honokowai
30
Lahaina

Honolua Bay
Pailolo Channel
Auau Channel

Kahoolawe

MAUI

5 miles
5 kilometers
0
0

major airport is **Kahului International Airport (OGG)**, in Kahului in Central Maui. International and interisland carriers fly to Kahului, and their flight schedules change constantly. **Hawaiian Airlines** (☎800-367-5320; www.hawaiianair.com) flies to Hilo, the Big Island; Honolulu, Oahu; Hoolehua, Molokai; Kona, the Big Island; Lanai City, Lanai; and Lihue, Kauai. **Pacific Wings** (☎808-873-0877 or 888-575-4546; www.pacificwings.com) offers daily service to Hana, Maui; Honolulu, Oahu; Hoolehua, Molokai; Kamuela, the Big Island; Kona, the Big Island; the Kalaupapa Peninsula, Molokai; and Lanai City, Lanai. There are two other airports on Maui: **Hana Airport (HNM)**, on Maui's east coast, which sees a lot of commuter flights and unscheduled air traffic; and **Kapalua Airport (JHM)**, which handles only prop planes and commuter flights.

The **Hawaii Superferry** (☎877-443-3779; www.hawaiisuperferry.com) has daily service from Kahului, Maui to Honolulu, Oahu (3hr.; daily 11am, M, W, F, Sa 8pm; prices vary depending on fuel surcharge and season). The **Molokai Princess** (☎808-667-6165 or 800-275-6969; www.molokaiferry.com) makes daily trips between Maui and Molokai. It leaves from Lahaina Harbor (90min.; daily 6pm, M-Sa 7:15am; one-way $40, ages 4-12 $20). **Expeditions** (☎808-661-3756 or 800-695-2624) runs ferries from Lahaina Harbor to Lanai (45min.; 5 per day 6:45am-5:45pm; one-way $25, children $20).

The most convenient way to get around Maui is by renting a **car**. However, the new **Maui Bus** (☎808-871-4838; www.mauicounty.gov/bus) has begun service on the island. The Maui Bus service has nine routes funded by the county of Maui; these routes provide service in and between Central, West, South, and Upcountry Maui communities. The Kahului and Wailuku loops are free while the other routes cost $1 each time you board. For intercity and local transportation, consult the **Transportation** section for each town.

￼ ACCOMMODATIONS

In Maui, travelers can stay in budget hostels in Wailuku, Paia, or Lahaina for about $25 per night; in condominiums in Kihei from $70 per night; in B&Bs anywhere from $75 per night; in vacation rentals from $45 per night (check www.vrbo.com for an extensive listing); in hotels from $125 per night. For long-term accommodations, check the *Maui News*, in print or online at www.mauinews.com. Studios start around $500 per month.

Whatever you decide, make reservations as soon as you know the dates of your trip. High season runs from December 15 to April 15, and rates are highest during December and January. During high season, accommodations are booked three to four months in advance (even longer for popular B&Bs). Summer is a another peak season. Fall and spring are the least popular times to visit, and so you might have the best chances for a less expensive bed then.

WEST MAUI

West Maui's mountains are older than Haleakala and have been scarred over the years with deep rifts from stream erosion. Their hulking mass rises out of the cane fields in velvety folds before disappearing into the cloud cover. Unlike the valleys northwest of Wailuku, which get almost 400 in. of rainfall per year, the *pali* (cliffs) on the leeward side are extremely arid. Despite the lack of rainfall, West Maui has continued to grow, and resorts now stretch 10 mi. north of Lahaina from Kaanapali to Kapalua. The popularity of real estate in the area is understandable; the western coast is lined with gorgeous beaches, and few sunbathers would trade the dry heat for the windward side's rain showers.

There is only one road in and out of West Maui: Hwy. 30, or Honoapiilani Hwy., which becomes Rte. 340 (Kahekili Hwy.) past Honokohau. Hwy. 30 is a two-lane road that hugs the coastline from Maalaea north. Near Maalaea, Hwy. 30 intersects with Rte. 380 (Dairy Rd.), which goes northeast to Kahului, and Rte. 310/31, which heads southeast to Kihei. Although the northern route (Rte. 340) may be the quickest between Kapalua and Wailuku, it can be dangerous. The road narrows down to one lane, which in many places is scarcely the width of a car, and hugs the cliffs with no guardrail protection. This route can be done as a scenic drive at a leisurely pace, but for everyday travel, stick to Hwy. 30. When accidents close Hwy. 30, Rte. 340 might also get shut down so that people won't be tempted to take the back route. If this happens, be prepared to wait for a few hours, or just turn around and go to the beach!

LAHAINA

Lahaina means "land of the cruel sun," and as visitors soon realize, it is an apt title—in any season, Lahaina (pop. 9118) sizzles. Once the prize of Hawaiian royalty, due to its abundance of freshwater, Lahaina's natural harbor and convenient location made it the island's most bustling port. From the 1820s to the 1840s, King Kamehameha III resided here, turning it into the capital and center of the emerging Hawaiian democracy. Remnants of Lahaina's history are still visible in the restored buildings and sites of the downtown historic district, though they are overwhelmed in many places now by T-shirt shops, activity booths, and themed restaurants. Lahaina has become a tourist trap, but that doesn't keep people from enjoying it. Perching on the seawall on Front St. provides endless people-watching as well as front row seats to a dazzling sunset.

TRANSPORTATION

Bus: MauiBus Service is available between **Central, South, West,** and **Upcountry Maui.** On West Maui, buses make the following stops: Maalaea Harbor, Wharf Cinema Center, Papalaua St., Lahaina Cannery Mall, Whalers Village in Kaanapali, Kahana, Napili, and Kapalua. In Lahaina take the **Kaanapali Islander** from Lahaina Cannery Mall to Whalers Village where you can then pick up the **Napili Islander** to go all the way north to Kahana, Napili, and Kapalua. All routes are $1 one-way and run once an hour. Call the **Maui Transit Office** (☎808-270-7511) or check www.mauicounty.gov/bus.

Ferry: An easy and inexpensive way to reach Maui's neighboring islands is by ferry out of Lahaina Harbor. The **Molokai Princess** (☎808-667-6165 or 866-307-6524; www.molokaiferry.com) makes daily trips to **Molokai.** For more information, see p. 328. The **Expeditions Ferry** (☎808-661-3756 or 800-695-2624; www.go-lanai.com.) sails to **Manele Harbor** on **Lanai** (45min.; 5 per day 6:45am-5:45pm; one-way $25, children $20) and back (5 per day 8am-6:45pm).

Taxis: Although the town of Lahaina is pedestrian-friendly, cabs might come in handy for travelers staying slightly north or south of town. Call in advance to get a cab; they rarely search for passengers. Several taxi companies operate out of Lahaina, including **Island Taxi** (☎808-667-5656) until midnight, **Paradise Taxi** (☎808-661-4455), **La-Taxi** (☎808-661-4545), and **AB Taxi** (☎808-667-7575) all 24hr.

Car Rental: Most national chains operate out of Kahului, near the airport (see p. 281), but some, like **Enterprise,** have branches near Lahaina or the Kapalua Airport.

Mopeds: Cruising around Lahaina on a moped is an efficient and fun way to reach some of the best beaches in West Maui. **Island Riders,** 126 Hinau St. (☎808-661-9966), rents mopeds in addition to sports cars and Jeeps. $45 8am-5pm, $59 per 24hr.

MAUI

Bikes: Lahaina is more than manageable on 2 wheels. **West Maui Cycles** (☎808-661-9005) rents beach cruisers ($15 per day, $60 per week) and road bikes ($50/$200).

✈ ORIENTATION

Lahaina sits on the ocean, halfway up Maui's western coast. **Highway 30 (Honoapiilani Highway)** runs through the city and all the way north past Kaanapali and Napili. In light traffic, it takes about 25min. to drive the 10 mi. from Lahaina north to Kapalua. Lahaina's main road, **Front Street,** parallels the highway along the waterfront and is connected to it by six cross streets (from south to north: Shaw St., Prison St., Dickenson St., Lahainaluna Rd., Papalaua St., and Kenui St.). Drivers cannot make left turns onto the highway from Prison and Kenui. **Wainee Street** runs the length of Lahaina, between the highway and Front St.

⁊ PRACTICAL INFORMATION

TOURIST AND FINANCIAL SERVICES

Tourist Office: Lahaina Visitor Center, 648 Wharf St. (☎808-667-9193; www.visitlahaina.com), in the Old Lahaina Courthouse. Gift shop, museum, and restrooms. Arranges 10 annual events and festivals. Open daily 9am-5pm. ATM on-site.

Banks: American Savings Bank, 154 Papalaua St. (☎808-667-9561; open M-F 9am-6pm, Sa 9am-1pm), and **Bank of Hawaii,** 132 Papalaua St. (☎808-661-3762; open M-Th 8:30am-4pm, F 8:30am-6pm), are in the Old Lahaina Center and have **24hr. ATMs. First Hawaiian Bank,** 215 Papalaua St. (☎808-661-3655; open M-Th 8:30am-4pm, F 8:30am-6pm), is at the corner of Wainee St.

LOCAL SERVICES

Library: Lahaina Public Library, 680 Wharf St. (☎808-662-3950). Copies $0.20. Internet access with a 3-month visitor's card ($10), limited to 1hr. session each day. Open Tu noon-8pm, W-Th 9am-5pm, F-Sa 10:30am-4:30pm.

Laundromat: 24 Hour Laundry, 1036 Limahana Pl. Turn right on Hinau St. off Honopiilani Hwy. and take another right on Limahana Pl. Coin-op laundry. Wash $2, dry $0.25 per 5min. Open 24hr., appropriately.

EMERGENCY AND COMMUNICATIONS

Police: Lahaina Police, 1850 Honoapiilani Hwy. (☎808-661-4441), located north of Lahaina above the Civic Center; follow the road that curves behind the post office.

Pharmacies: Longs Drugs (☎808-667-4384), in Lahaina Cannery Mall. Open daily 7am-midnight; pharmacy open 8am-5pm. **Lahaina Pharmacy** (☎808-661-3119), in Old Lahaina Center. Open M-F 9am-5:30pm, Sa 9am-2pm.

Medical Services: Kaiser Permanente Clinic, 910 Wainee St. (☎808-662-6900, after-hours 808-243-6000). Open M-F 8am-5pm, Sa 8am-noon. **Maui Medical Group,** 130 Prison St. (☎808-661-0051), is at the south end of town and usually more crowded. Open M-F 8am-9pm. Both operate their own pharmacies.

Internet Access: Travelers go online at the **Lahaina Public Library** (see above). They might also try **Buns of Maui,** 878 Front St., Ste. 810, in the Old Lahaina Shopping Center. With 6 stations and A/C, this is the cheapest place to check your email. $0.08 per min. Printing $0.30 per page ($0.60 for color). A variety of sweets and gooey cinnamon rolls ($3.80) tempt hurried typists. (☎808-661-5407. Open daily 7:30am-6pm; closed last Su of the month. AmEx/D/MC/V.) **Maui Swiss Cafe,** 640 Front St., has 10 comput-

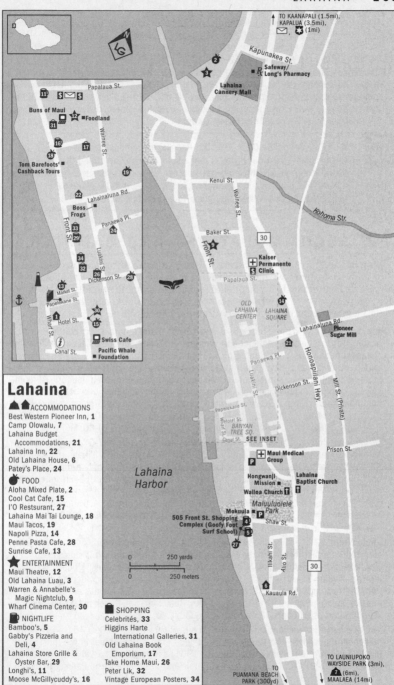

TO KAANAPALI (1.5mi),
KAPALUA (3.5mi),
✉ ✚ (1mi)

Kapunakea St.

Safeway/
Ṝ Long's Pharmacy

Lahaina
Cannery Mall

Papalaua St.

Buns of Maui
Foodland

Wainee St.

Tom Barefoots'
Cashback Tours

Kenui St.

Wainee St.

Kohoma Str.

Lahainaluna Rd.

Boss
Frogs

Panaewa Pl.

Baker St.

Front St.

30

Luakini St.

Kaiser
Permanente
Clinic

Dickenson St.

Papalaua St.

OLD
LAHAINA
CENTER

LAHAINA
SQUARE

Market St.

Papelekane St.

Lahainaluna Rd.
Pioneer
Sugar Mill

Hotel St.

Honoapiilani Hwy.

Mill St. (Private)

Swiss Cafe
Pacific Whale
Foundation

Canal St.

Panaewa Pl.

Dickenson St.

Luakini St.

Papelekane St.

BANYAN
TREE SQ.

SEE INSET

Prison St.

Maui Medical
Group

Lahaina
Harbor

Hongwanji
Mission

Lahaina
Baptist Church

Wainee St.

Hotel St.

Canal St.

Wailoa Church

Mokuula

Maluuluolele
Park

505 Front St. Shopping
Complex (Goofy Foot
Surf School)

Shaw St.

Ilikahi St.

Alio St.

30

Kauaula Rd.

0   250 yards

0   250 meters

TO
PUAMANA BEACH
PARK (300yd)

TO LAUNIUPOKO
WAYSIDE PARK (3mi),
ⓘ (6mi),
MAALAEA (14mi)

Lahaina

ACCOMMODATIONS
Best Western Pioneer Inn, **1**
Camp Olowalu, **7**
Lahaina Budget
  Accommodations, **21**
Lahaina Inn, **22**
Old Lahaina House, **6**
Patey's Place, **24**

FOOD
Aloha Mixed Plate, **2**
Cool Cat Cafe, **15**
I'O Restsurant, **27**
Lahaina Mai Tai Lounge, **18**
Maui Tacos, **19**
Napoli Pizza, **14**
Penne Pasta Cafe, **28**
Sunrise Cafe, **13**

ENTERTAINMENT
Maui Theatre, **12**
Old Lahaina Luau, **3**
Warren & Annabelle's
  Magic Nightclub, **9**
Wharf Cinema Center, **30**

NIGHTLIFE
Bamboo's, **5**
Gabby's Pizzeria and
  Deli, **4**
Lahaina Store Grille &
  Oyster Bar, **29**
Longhi's, **11**
Moose McGillycuddy's, **16**

SHOPPING
Celebrités, **33**
Higgins Harte
  International Galleries, **31**
Old Lahaina Book
  Emporium, **17**
Take Home Maui, **26**
Peter Lik, **32**
Vintage European Posters, **34**

MAUI

ers and Roselani's Hawaiian ice cream, and offers DVD-burning ($5) and handy post-card print-outs of your digital vacation photos ($1 each, 20 for $15). Internet is $0.15 per min. or $6 per hr. B&W and color printing, $0.50 per page. Wi-Fi $0.10 per min. (☎808-661-6776; www.maui-swisscafe.com. Open daily 9am-6pm. AmEx/D/MC/V.)

Post Offices: The downtown **Lahaina Post Office,** 132 Papalaua St. (☎808-661-0904), in the Old Lahaina Center, tends to have long lines. Open M-F 8:15am-4:15pm. The **main branch,** at 1760 Honoapiilani Hwy. (☎808-661-0904), 1 mi. north of town at the intersection of Leialii Pkwy., offers more flexible hours and general delivery pickup. Open M-F 8:30am-5pm, Sa 9am-1pm. **Postal Code:** 96761.

 METER MAIDS GET PAID. Parking in Lahaina can be difficult. If you're coming from out of town, make sure to arrive by 10am; the few free spots fill up quickly. Although pay lots can be expensive, several offer free parking with proof of purchase from specific stores. If you're planning on buying something anyway, consider going to a validating store.

ACCOMMODATIONS AND CAMPING

Staying in Lahaina is possible on any budget, and the affordable accommodations in the old town have more character than the chain hotels and condos in the resorts farther north. If you plan to partake in Lahaina's nightlife, it's a good idea to stay in town to avoid a drive home. Remember also that air-conditioning might be more important here than other areas of Maui.

Patey's Place, 761 Wainee St. (☎808-667-0999). There's no sign on the door of this hostel; look for the street number and wooden fence with surfboards. Patey's offers the cheapest beds in West Maui and a prime location just 2 blocks from Front St. However, long-term guests and daytrippers agree that the lodgings could greatly benefit from more frequent upkeep and a more disciplined staff. Shared kitchen, laundry, TV room, coin-op laundry, and back porch. 2 of the private rooms have their own bath. The hostel has quiet hours 10pm-8:30am; common areas are off-limits and guests either sleep or head to the beach or bars. Reception 8:30am-noon and 5-10pm. Check-in 5pm. Check-out 10am. 4-bed dorms $25; singles $40-65; doubles $70-80. MC/V. ❶

Old Lahaina House, 407 Ilikahi St. (☎808-667-4663 or 800-847-0761; www.accommodationsmaui.com), 1 block south of Shaw St. on the corner of Ilikahi and Kauaula Rd. Nestled in the residential end of Lahaina, this pink house is only a minute from a pretty beach. Gracious owner sees that rooms are equipped with beach towels and picnic cooler. Rooms have A/C, TV, phone, microwave, fridge, coffee maker, and private bath. Guests can enjoy the pool in the house's tropical courtyard. Activities booked for no extra fee. 3-night min. Reserve with 50% deposit. Rooms Dec.-Apr. $119-159; May-Nov. $99-149; cottage $250-280. AmEx/MC/V. ❸

Lahaina Inn, 127 Lahainaluna Rd. (☎808-661-0577 or 800-669-3444; www.lahainainn.com). Perfect for a romantic stay, the Inn offers 10 rooms and 2 suites decorated with turn-of-the-century furnishings and stocked with *yukata* robes. Modern comforts include in-room classical music, A/C, and a phone. Guests enjoy watching passersby from the rocking chairs on the *lanai.* Tea, coffee, and hot chocolate are served each morning in the living room. Parking $7 per day. Check-in 1pm. Check-out 11am. Reserve with 50% deposit. Rooms $150-205. AmEx/MC/V. ❹

Best Western Pioneer Inn, 658 Wharf St. (☎808-661-3636 or 800-457-5457; www.pioneerinnmaui.com), next to Banyan Tree Park. Certainly the bearer of the most idyllic location in town, the Pioneer Inn, built in 1901, sits regally atop Lahaina Harbor. All rooms come with A/C, cable TV, private *lanai,* and Internet access. Parking available.

Check-in 3pm. Check-out noon. Rooms $145-185; deluxe $185-205. Rates slightly higher at Halloween and Christmas. AmEx/D/MC/V. ❹

Lahaina Budget Accommodations, 252 Lahainaluna Rd. (☎808-661-6655), at the corner with Honoapiilani Hwy. Run by the same owner as Old Lahaina House; rooms come with A/C, fridge, and microwave. 5 rooms share a bath. Private double has its own bath and a separate entrance. Check-in 3pm. Check-out 11am. Rooms $49-79; double $89. $10 cleaning fee for 3 nights or less. AmEx/D/MC/V. ❷

Camp Olowalu, 800 Olowalu Village Rd. (☎808-661-4303), 6 mi. from Lahaina, between mi. markers 14 and 15. Off Honoapiilani Hwy. down a easy-to-miss gravel road. Look for a small white sign about 1 mi. south of the Olowalu General Store. The camp's secluded sites are right on the water and offer a nice, quiet place to spend the night. Shower, sink, porta-potty, clothesline, tables, coin-op laundry, payphone, and simple cooking sites available. Quiet hours 10pm-6am. No reservations. 2 week max stay. Check-in 9am-5pm. Camping $10 per person; ages 6-12 $5. ❶

Papalaua Beach Wayside Park, between mi. markers 11 and 12, just north of the tunnel on Honoapiilani Hwy. This beachfront county-maintained campsite can be noisy since it's close to the road and frequently crowded. Closed Tu. Permits required. See **Camping in Hawaii,** p. 82. Permits $5, $0.50 per child. ❶

▣ FOOD

Nearly every restaurant in Lahaina caters exclusively to tourists; however, inflated prices do purchase a larger selection of options. With a few exceptions, Lahaina restaurants stop serving by 9pm, so plan accordingly. For groceries, there's a **24hr. Safeway,** 1221 Honoapiilani Hwy. (☎808-667-4392), in the Lahaina Cannery Mall and a **Foodland** in the Old Lahaina Center (☎808-661-0975).

RESTAURANTS

Lahaina Mai Tai Lounge, 839 Front St. (☎808-661-5288). This restaurant sits right on the water and proudly boasts the best sunset in Lahaina. Along with tantalizing Mai Tais and scorpion bowls, the Lounge offers fresh fish, burgers, tacos, and island favorites. For a real treat, try Kealoha's baby back ribs (half rack $20, full rack $26). Happy hour 3-6pm and 9-11pm (drafts $2; mixed drinks $3.50). Open M-Th and Su 11am-10pm, F-Sa 11am-midnight. AmEx/D/MC/V. ❸

I'O Restaurant, 505 Front St. (☎808-661-8422; www.iomaui.com). Recipient of a governor's commendation for the best farm-to-table restaurant, this stylish venue serves up imaginative dishes that look as sensational as they taste. Start with the Mad Hatter (sauteed scallops, mushrooms, and chilis in a lobster coconut curry sauce and puff pastry; $12), linger over the Road to Hana (grilled catch with seasonal fruit, jasmine rice, passion fruit tarragon dressing, and basil yogurt; $32), and finish up with some guava-glazed coconut cheesecake ($10). Salads ($9-13), entrees ($30-39). Ask about occasional live music. Open daily 5:30-10pm. AmEx/D/MC/V. ❹

Thai Chef (☎808-667-2814; www.thaichefmaui.com), in the Old Lahaina Shopping Center. This cozy Thai restaurant has an extensive menu of curries ($11-13), seafood dishes ($11-13), and vegetarian and vegan options ($7-10.25). The spicy mussel chili ($12) and ginger coconut tofu soup ($9.50) are well-loved by hungry Lahaina surfer dudes. BYOB. Lunch M-F 11am-2pm; dinner nightly 5-9pm. D/MC/V. ❸

CAFES AND TAKEOUT

▨ **Aloha Mixed Plate,** 1285 Front St. (☎808-661-3322; www.alohamixedplate.com), right on the harbor next to the Old Lahaina Luau. A great way to sample Hawaiian food:

BEFORE SUNRISE

While promises of pancakes in paradise lure you into Front St.'s thriving establishments, you're likely to miss a shrubbery-covered sign announcing "Complete Breakfast! $5.95." However, if the corner of your eye knows what it's doing, then you may find yourself at the family-run Sunrise Cafe, enjoying a big wallet, a big breakfast, and a private patio meal.

Carefully tucked into a petite side street, this literal hole-in-the-wall offers pineapple boats, Belgian waffles, and picnic lunches at prices that won't deter from your souvenir collection. For less than $6, the cafe serves up a variety of breakfast specials, including French toast with scrambled eggs or eggs benedict. Once seated under the shade, you can drizzle your pancakes with some old-fashioned maple syrup, or douse them in Sunrise's unique offering of coconut, macadamia nut, and chocolate mint varieties.

No matter what meal it is, food is expensive in Lahaina, and given that you'll need plenty of nourishment in order to hit the hot pavement and sand, breakfast at Sunrise—served until 3pm—is a welcome reprieve and, perhaps, just the ticket to paradise.

The Sunrise Cafe is located 693 Front St. (☎808-661-8558). Open daily 6am-6pm. Cash only.

kalua pig and other meats are served plate lunch style. The ocean view is 1st class, and drumbeats emanating from the luau next door accompany dinner. Plate lunches $5.50-13, mini-plates $4-6. Mixed drinks $6. Outdoor seating only. Happy hour 2-6pm (Mai Tais $3, beer $1.75). Open daily 10:30am-10pm. MC/V. ❶

🌮 **Penne Pasta Cafe,** 180 Dickenson St. (☎808-661-6633). Sizeable portions of pasta drizzled in homemade sauce (bolognese fettuccine $10) are served in an understated, urbane atmosphere slightly removed from bustling Front St. Eat your olive appetizer inside under the sleek fans and flatscreen TV, or fill up on pizzas ($7-9.50), focaccia ($3), and sandwiches ($8-9) at one of the outdoor cafe tables. Dessert includes tiramisu ($7). Lactose and dairy-free mozzarella available. Open M-F 11am-9:30pm, Sa 5-9:30pm, Su 5-9pm. Delivery M-F 11am-2pm. AmEx/D/MC/V. ❷

Cool Cat Cafe, 658 Front St. (☎808-667-0908) in the Wharf Cinema Center. The burgers here have consistently been voted the best on Maui, and a bite of the Marilyn (topped with Jack cheese, mild green Ortega chili, mayo, lettuce, tomatoes, pickles, sweet Maui onions, and 1000-island dressing; $11) makes it easy as pie to see why. Sit inside and listen to doo-wop grooves, or take some shade on the patio overlooking busy Front St. Either way, it's the only joint in town where you can get a Betty Boop BLT ($8). Root beer float $4. Happy hour 3-6pm ($3 drink specials). Live music nightly at 7:30pm. Open daily 10am-10pm. AmEx/MC/V. ❷

Napoli Pizza, 840 Wainee St. (☎808-661-6773), in the back row of shops in Lahaina Sq. A super place to grab a quick slice of pizza, Napoli's offers slices for $2.50 and a special lunch deal (2 slices and a soft drink, $5.20). Specialty pies ($22-24) include the three meat combo, all veggie, and Da Kine (pineapple, ham, and onions). Delivery available. Open M-Sa 11am-9pm, Su noon-10pm. AmEx/D/MC/V. ❶

Maui Tacos, 840 Wainee St. (☎808-661-8883), in Lahaina Sq. Sells cheap, filling, tacos and burritos with 5 kinds of homemade salsa. Open for breakfast (egg burrito $4, *huevos rancheros* $6.25), but locals flood the place at lunch. Takeout or eat outside. Open M-Sa 9am-9pm, Su 9am-8pm. Delivery available 11am-2pm. AmEx/D/MC/V. ❶

◪ BEACHES

Lahaina itself is not the place for sunbathing and swimming. The few sandy beaches have somewhat murky water and are best put to use watching the sunset. There is a sandy beach behind the **Lahaina Shores Resort** with a good surf break a block south of the hotel and public access a few blocks farther south. At the north edge of town, **Baby Beach,** accessed via Ala Moana St. or Puunoa Pl., is popular because its shallow waters are good for children and beginning snorkelers. Just north of that is **Wahikuli Beach,** which offers picnic tables, restrooms, and decent snorkeling. (Open daily 7am-8pm.)

Still, the beaches north and south of town are much better. **Puamana Beach Park,** the first beach south of Lahaina, is peachy-keen for a beachside picnic. (Open daily 7am-8pm.) **Launiupoko Wayside Park,** a mile farther south at mi. marker 18, has restrooms, showers, and a surf break popular with beginners. (Open daily 7am-8pm.) **Ukumehame Beach Park,** 1 mi. after mi. marker 13, also has picnic tables and is usually a little less crowded. (Open daily 7am-8pm.) All three parks have small surf and are often filled with families and a mix of locals and young visitors. However, these beaches are unimpressive compared to those north of Lahaina in **Kaanapali** (p. 274), **Napili** (p. 276), and **Kapalua** (p. 278). For lifeguards, head to **D. T. Fleming Beach Park** or **Kapalua Beach** in the Kapalua area, or to **Kaanapali Beach** or **Hanakaoo Beach** in the Kaanapali area.

 LOOK LOCAL. Theft from parked cars at beaches is not uncommon. To protect your valuables, always lock your car, and try putting a Hawaiian flag on your dashboard or tying a lei on your rearview mirror to look more like a local (and less like a target).

ACTIVITIES

The activity booths that line Front St. offer an exciting number of choices, and it's easy for the budget traveler to become overwhelmed by glossy flyers and smooth-talking agents. There are also activities (bodyboarding, snorkeling, or hiking) that cost little or nothing and don't require a middleman. If you do opt to go with an activity booker, Let's Go recommends ◾**Best Hawaii Activities,** , (☎808-661-6655), a red-roofed house at the corner of Honoapiilani Hwy. across from the 76 gas station. **Tom Barefoot's Cashback Tours** (☎808-661-1246 or 888-222-3601; www.tombarefoot.com), in Kahului, offers a wide selection of well-organized activities at a discount. **Boss Frogs,** 150 Lahainaluna Rd. (☎808-661-3333) is a cheap place to rent snorkel gear ($1.50-8 per day; $9-30 per week), bodyboards ($5 per day; $15 per week), or surfboards ($20 per day; $75 per week). Customers can return equipment at any of six shops. Open daily 8am-5pm. AmEx/D/MC/V.

SNORKELING. Before you splurge on a boat excursion, keep in mind that there is excellent snorkeling at beaches all along the West Maui coast. A self-guided adventure will cost you only a few bucks for the mask and fins. Many companies in Lahaina rent snorkel equipment for $2-10 per day. **Maui Dive Shop** (☎808-661-6166; www.mauidiveshop.com) is courteous and professional, with several locations, including one at the Lahaina Gateway Mall, 315 Keawe St. The best West Maui snorkel spots are north of Lahaina in **Honolua Bay** (p. 279), **Kapalua Beach** (p. 278), **Kahekili Beach Park** (p. 276), and **Black Rock** or **Kaanapali Beach** (p. 276). Other good snorkel spots can be found near mi. marker 14 by the small town of Olowalu, and at **Slaughterhouse Beach** (p. 279). Kahekili has free parking, and if you walk 15min. down to the end of the beach toward the Sheraton, Black Rock offers some of the best snorkeling around. If you want to take a boat excursion, head to the submerged crater of **Molokini.** On a good day, visibility at Molokini is over 150 ft. Plan on spending anywhere from $60 to $95; excursions typically take a few hours, and include equipment, drinks, and lunch. Conditions vary, and many snorkelers set on Molokini have ended up at

Turtle Town or Coral Gardens, less glamorous spots that have decent snorkeling, but are not appreciably better than what you can see from the beach.

> **SWIMMING WITH THE FISHES.** Snorkeling is a great way to explore the deep blue waters of the Pacific, and an upgrade in snorkeling gear is definitely worth the money. Deluxe masks and snorkels with one-way valves run only about $8, and the splurge is well worth it. Better equipment will keep contact lenses dry and lungs saltwater-free.

SCUBA DIVING. The most popular places for offshore dives near Lahaina are the neighboring island of **Lanai** and the back wall of **Molokini.** There are multiple companies competing for boat dive business in Lahaina. **Extended Horizons** (☎808-667-0611 or 888-DIVE-MAUI/3483-6284; www.extendedhorizons. com) is known for good service on boat dives, and beginner dives are offered twice daily for $109. **Maui Dive Shop** (☎808-661-6166; www.mauidiveshop.com) is larger and less personal, though still reliable. For shore dives, **Kahekili Beach Park** is a good place for beginners (most certification classes start here). **Black Rock,** below the Kaanapali Sheraton, and the right side of Honolua Bay in summer are also popular West Maui dive spots. **Pacific Dive** (☎808-667-5331; www. pacificdive.com) is also reputable and reasonably priced with intro shore dives for $89. Numerous companies give introductory classes, starting around $90; 2-day full certification classes run $325 and higher.

SURFING. Driving into Lahaina from the south, you'll see surfers from the road. **Olowalu** and **Launiupoko** usually have reliable breaks, though conditions change daily. There is a surf spot about a block south of the Lahaina Shores Beach Resort that is usually uncrowded and good for beginners, but watch out for waves breaking in the shallow water over the coral. Honolua Bay is famous for its winter surf, but beginners should stick to watching from the sand. Board rentals start at about $20 per day with discounts for weekly rentals. Expect to pay about $65 for a 2hr. group lesson and twice that for a private lesson. For mid-priced, reliable surf lessons, contact **Goofy Foot Surf School,** in the 505 Front St. Shopping Center. Teaching surfers of all ages, from the young to the young at heart, beginners are guaranteed to stand and ride at least one wave in their first lesson, or it's free. Intermediate lessons also available *(☎808-244-9283; www. goofyfootsurfschool.com. Group lesson $65, private $150. Intermediate level lesson $250 for 2 people, $300 for 3 people. 6hr. surf camp $300.)* The **Nancy Emerson School of Surfing,** also at 505 Front St., is the oldest surf school on the island. Nancy was winning international surf contests by the age of 14 and says she'll have you standing up in one lesson. *(Group lesson $78, private $165. 5hr. group lesson with lunch $250. Also offers 3-day ($245-465), 5-day ($400-740), and 7-day ($950) surf clinics.)*

BODYBOARDING. Catching waves on a bodyboard is a lot easier than surfing, at least when you start. Driving toward Lahaina from the south, just look for places with good conditions and other boarders, pull over, and jump in. **Puamana Beach** (p. 266), just south of Lahaina, is usually good, but slightly rocky. Some of the beaches in Kaanapali are also excellent, especially the blissfully deserted █**Oneloa Beach** (p. 279) and the south end of **Kaanapali Beach..** Many recommend **D. T. Fleming Beach** (p. 279), which is sandy-bottomed and lifeguarded. All Lahaina surf shops also rent bodyboards ($5-8 per day; $20 per week). For a great deal, hit up **West Maui Sports,** 1287 Front St., which rents for $2.50 per day or $15 per week. (☎808-661-6252. Open daily 8am-6pm. AmEx/D/MC/V.)

SAILING. Lahaina looks even better from offshore than on land. Many companies have sunset and daytime sailing trips (some include dinner, others just snacks and drinks) on schooners or catamarans. **Trilogy,** 180 Lahainaluna Rd., is by far the biggest operator (and the only one Oprah-approved). In addition to its beautiful boats, another boon is Trilogy's excursion to Lanai; it is the only company that owns property on the island, enabling it to land and fix a nice barbecue lunch or dinner. (☎808-874-5649; www.sailtrilogy.com. Whale-watching expeditions start at $39, while an all-day Lanai excursion is $199.)

PARASAILING. Parasailing looks scarier than it is; the ride is a gentle, quiet glide that lasts about 10min. Companies only operate from May to December in order to avoid whale breeding season. **UFO Parasail,** 12 Ulupono St., offers a simulated free fall if you buy the 800 ft. ride. (☎808-661-7836; www.ufoparasailing.com. $60-75, depending on length of ride and time of day.) **West Maui Parasail** also offers singles ($65-75), tandems ($130-150), and early bird specials. (☎808-661-4060 or 808-669-6555; www.westmauiparasail.com.)

TRAIN. The **Lahaina Kaanapali Railroad** runs up and down Maui's northwest coast and is an entertaining way to get from Lahaina to the Puukolii Station in Kaanapali. The historic steam engine replicates the way islanders traveled during Maui's booming sugarcane era. A guide sits at the front of the red and yellow cars, explaining the more interesting historical facts, and every so often, the conductor blows off some extra steam. Panoramic views of the island make the ride a fun— though bumpy—afternoon diversion. All aboard! *(975 Limahana Pl. Turn right on Hinau St. off Honopiilani Hwy. and take another right on Limahana Pl. ☎808-667-6851; www.sugarcanetrain.com. Daily departures from Lahaina 11:05am, 1, 2:30, and 4pm. A one-way train also departs at 5:30pm. $22, ages 3-12 $15. Free parking available.)*

HELICOPTERS. Beautiful from the ground, West Maui and Molokai are spectacular from the air. Most companies tour both locations during a 1hr. trip, peeking at the waterfalls hidden in the West Maui mountains, zipping across to circle the sea cliffs of Molokai, and returning to Iao Valley on Maui. This ride generally runs around $225 per person, but **Tom's** (p. 267) sells trips at about $125 per person for 30min.; the trip is almost guaranteed to be cheaper if booked through an activity vendor. Almost all trips leave from Kahului. Of all the companies, **AlexAir** (☎808-871-0792; www.helitour.com) is the only one that has two-way headsets so you can talk to the pilots. **Blue Hawaiian** (☎808-871-8844; www.bluehawaiian.com) also has an excellent reputation.

WHALE WATCHING. From mid-December to mid-April, hundreds of humpback whales come to Maui to breed before continuing to Alaska. All along the southern and western coast, the whales put on quite a show, and you don't need to leave shore to see them breaching and spouting. If you do want a closer look, contact the **Pacific Whale Foundation,** 612 Front St., a non-profit organization that contributes to whale conservation. *(☎808-667-7447 or 808-249-8811 for reservations; www.pacificwhale.org. 2hr. whalewatch is $32, ages 7-12 $17. Runs Dec. 1-May 15.)*

🔄 SIGHTS

The **Lahaina Restoration Foundation,** a non-profit agency, maintains many of Lahaina's historic sites and publishes a brochure entitled *Lahaina: A Walking Tour of Historic and Cultural Sites*, available for free at **The Village Gift and Fine Arts,** 120 Dickenson St. (☎808-661-5199), the **Old Lahaina Courthouse Museum,** and the **public library.** The walking tour describes many sites in Lahaina's historic district, recounting the town's history through its whaling and missionary days and detailing the churches and cultural centers of Lahaina's various immigrant

Time: 45min.-1½hr.
Season: Any

The best way to acquaint yourself with Lahaina is on foot. Although the sun can be intense, a walking tour is an easy—and heart-healthy—way to peruse both the town's historical sights and more trivial pursuits (read: shopping). You can start your journey at any place along the route, but a picnic underneath the Banyan Tree is a fantastic way to end or start the trip. Bring some cold water and a camera to capture your favorite finds. Slather on sunscreen and march!

1. BANYAN TREE PARK. Now over 60 ft. high, ye olde Banyan tree was planted on April 24, 1873 to honor the 50th anniversary of the Protestants' first work in Lahaina. Today, its branches spread over almost an acre, providing refreshing shade to overheated tourists and locals alike.

2. HOLY INNOCENTS CHURCH. Although the present building was constructed in 1927, the island's Episcopal church dates back to 1862. It is best known for its native religious artwork, in particular the altar depicting a Hawaiian Madonna.

3. HALE PIULA, or "iron-roof house," was commissioned as a palace for Kamehameha III in the late 1830s. However, it was left incomplete, as the king preferred sleeping in a small grass hut nearby. For a while, it functioned as a courthouse, but after an 1858 storm, its stones were put to use in the construction of the newer one (see 21 below), in Banyan Tree Park.

4. & 5. MALUULUOLELE PARK & MOKUULA. Beneath the ballpark lays one of the most remarkable spots of pre-Western Hawaii. Where the bases now stand, there was once Loko O Mokuhinia (the pond of Mokuhinia), home of the powerful water spirit and lizard goddess Kilhawahine. Due to mosquitoes, it was filled with coral rubble in 1918, and the island in the middle, Mokuula, was leveled. The long-time home of Maui's chiefs, Kamehameha III received visitors at this royal mausoleum, and Queen Mother Keopuolani spent the last months of her life there. Nowadays, the County of Maui has discontinued use of the playing field, in the hopes of restoring the site to its former splendor.

6. WAIOLA CHURCH AND GRAVEYARD. Here, both commoners and chiefs lie beside one another. Among the departed are Queen Mother Keopuolani, missionary William Richards, and Governor Hoapili. The church itself was built between 1828 and 1832, originally called Wainee (flowing water). It was renamed Waiola (waters of life) in 1953, after thrice being demolished. During the fierce Kauaula Wind of 1858, a bell fell from the tower but landed undamaged.

7. HONGWANJI MISSION. A small school and Buddhist temple was originally built here in 1910. The current version dates back to 1927, and to this day it remains the site of the annual O-Bon Dance, when ancestors return to dance with their families.

8. HALE PAAHAO. This Lahaina jail of the 1850s—literally "stuck-in-irons-house"—was constructed from the remains of the waterfront fort (see 20 below). It had shackles for the most undisciplined of the lot, and inmates were generally there for minor offenses like drunkenness, dangerous horseback riding, or working on the Sabbath.

9. HALE ALOHA. The "House of Love" was built to commemorate Lahaina's escape from a smallpox epidemic that devastated Oahu in 1853. It was used for some time as a Protestant church and school before being rescued from disrepair by the County of Maui in 1974.

10. & 11. LUAKINI STREET. When Princess Nahienaena died at the age of twenty-one, her funeral processed down this quaint one-way street. Torn between the Western world and ancient ways, the princess worshipped a Christian god while also clinging to her birthright, eventually marrying brother Kamehameha III. On the way to her burial place in December 1837, this path was made through the groves of breadfruit and koa trees, and as you walk along it today, you can still see some dotting the road. Following Luakini to Dickenson, you'll pass the Buddhist Church (see 12 below) of the Shingon sect, a perfect example of many plantation-era churches.

12. & 13. WAINEE ST. DETOUR. At the corner of Luakini and Dickenson, you can segue way back up to Wainee St. to see the Maria Lanakila Church (12), built in 1928 to commemorate

LAHAINA

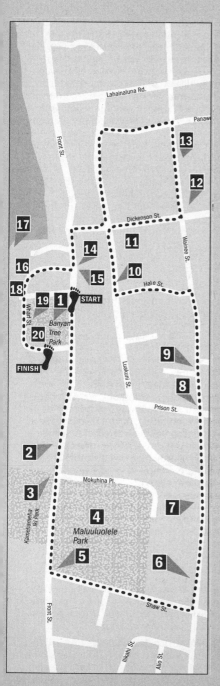

where the first Roman Catholic mass was held on Maui in 1841. Just beyond that is the Seamen's Cemetery (13).

14. BALDWIN HOME. Dr. Dwight Baldwin, a Protestant medical missionary, and his family lived in this two-story home from the mid-1830s to 1868. The grounds were restored to the present-day museum in the 1960s. Open daily 10am-4pm.

15. RICHARDS HOUSE. Rev. William Richards was Lahaina's first missionary and the premiere owner of a coral stone house in the islands. He ceased his missionary efforts in the mid-1830s in order to work directly for Kamehameha III. Richards not only helped draft Hawaii's first constitution, but he also served as the Minister of Education.

16. & 17. WHARF ST. Crossing Front St., you'll see a taro patch where Kamehameha III often labored, in the hopes of proving the dignity of manual work to his subjects. Beside it is the remains of the islands' first western-style brick building—the "brick palace" (16)—constructed by two ex-cons from Australia. Also nearby is the Hauola Stone (17), which is believed to have been used by Hawaiians for healing rituals.

18. LAHAINA LIGHTHOUSE. Commissioned in 1840, the lighthouse began as a 9 ft. wooden tower. In 1866, it grew to a height of 26 ft., and the caretaker's salary reached a whopping $20 annually. Today's concrete version was dedicated by the US Coast Guard in 1916. Its shining light, originally provided by a whale oil lamp, was the first on the US Pacific Coast.

19. COURTHOUSE. Built with stones from Hale Piula (see 3 above), it was the center of anti-smuggling activity during the whaling era. In August 1898, it was here that the American flag was first raised, formally acknowledging the annexation of the islands.

20. THE FORT. It was raised in the early 1830s, after some whalers fired a cannon at the Richards missionary house (an argument had transpired about the morality of native women visiting their ships). Serving mainly as a prison, it was torn down in the 1850s to the delight of all, as it had been seen as a sign of show rather than force.

groups who were brought to the island to work the sugar plantations. For those interested in Hawaiian history but lacking the budget or inclination to take the guided tour, this is a better option. That said, the most fulfilling way to explore Lahaina is to spend $37 on a guided tour with ☒**Maui Nei,** an award-winning grassroots organization devoted to relating the history of Lahaina from a Native Hawaiian perspective. Local guides, working from oral histories, traditional chants, and archival research, lead small groups along a 2hr. tour of Lahaina's harbor and backstreets. (☎808-661-9494; www.mauinei.com. Tours are conducted M-Sa 9:30-11:30am only a few times each month, depending on interest. Call for more information.)

Those looking for a more archaeological experience can venture south of Lahaina to the **Olowalu Petroglyphs.** The soft lava found here has many well-preserved ancient drawings, starting at ground level and continuing to a height of 60ft. The human figures with large bodies are *alii* (chiefs), and the stick figures are thought to represent commoners. On Honoapiilani Hwy., look for the Olowalu General Store by mi. marker 15. Directly behind the store and to the left is a water tower. Take the dirt road on the north side of the tower. Park by the gate, and then walk a quarter mile. The petroglyphs will be on your right.

⚑ HIKING

LAHAINA PALI TRAIL. *(5mi. 2-3hr. Elevation gain: 800 ft. Challenging.)* Built for horseback and foot travel between Wailuku and Lahaina in missionary times, the Lahaina Pali trail is still dotted with remnants of resting stops from long ago. This trail is most rewarding during whale season (Dec.-Apr.), when the view from the top of the ridge can include hundreds of whales cavorting in the channel—bring binoculars. This hike works best if you can be dropped off at mi. marker 5 and picked up at mi. marker 11. Starting from the eastern trailhead allows you to get the tough part over with before finishing at the beach. The path begins with a steep climb up to Kealaloloa Ridge; once there, hikers are treated to a view of the central valley and Haleakala, and Kahoolawe, Molokini, and Lanai offshore. The trail will meet up with a service road; at this junction stay left and don't go up the hill towards the windmills. Stay on the road for a short stretch until the trail picks back up. The trail will then cross over a gravel construction road and descend gradually from the ridge. *Kiawe* trees provide modest shade along the way. The hike ends across the highway from the beach. This hike gets incredibly hot; hikers should be equipped with sturdy hiking boots, plenty of water, and sunscreen. Trail guides with information on the cultural history of the trail are available at many retail outlets, but also at the **Division of Forestry and Wildlife,** 54 S. High St., in Wailuku. *(The eastern trailhead is on the mountain side of Hwy. 30 at mi. marker 5, just south of the jct. with Rte. 380. Parking is available for a 2nd car at mi. marker 11 on the mountain side of Hwy. 30, just north of the tunnel.)*

⚑ ENTERTAINMENT

HULA. To get a free dose of hula, head to the **Center Stage** at the Lahaina Cannery Mall; see **Polynesian Hula** Tuesdays and Thursdays at 7pm, and come back on the weekends at 1pm for your fix of **Keiki** (children's) **Hula.** There are also *keiki* shows at Lahaina Center Wednesdays at 2:30pm and Fridays at 3:30pm.

LUAU. If your visit to Maui won't be complete without a luau, Lahaina is definitely the best place to attend one. Many of the hotels offer their own versions of this traditional Hawaiian feast, but the most authentic is the **Old Lahaina Luau,**

1251 Front St., held nightly on the waterfront near Mala Wharf, across from the Cannery Mall. Guests are greeted with fresh orchid leis and a Mai Tai from the open bar. Along the water, craftspeople demonstrate lei-making and display their wares. Just before sunset, the *kalua* pig is unearthed from the *imu* (underground oven) in an intimate ceremony, and the feast begins. An exciting hula performance narrates the Polynesians' arrival in Hawaii and continues through the missionary and plantation periods to modern times. There are also two morning shows on Wednesdays and Fridays, which feature breakfast, a history of the islands, and a short hula show. Although not as authentic as the nightly luau, the morning shows are cheaper, and a fun cultural excursion. (☎ 808-667-1998 or 800-248-5828; www.oldlahainaluau.com. Reserve 2-4 weeks in advance, but last-minute cancellations may accommodate those without reservations. Show Apr.-Sept. 5:45pm; Oct.-Mar. 5:15pm. $92, 12 and under $62.)

SHOWS. Ulalena, 878 Front St., in the Old Lahaina Center, offers a modern interpretation of ancient Hawaiian myths and Hawaiian history, communicated through dance, song, text, images, and remarkable aerial acrobatics. A live percussion group provides a pounding rhythm. (☎ 877-688-4800 or 808-661-9913; www.ulalena.com. Limited parking. Tu-Sa 7:30pm, additional M show Jan.-Aug. $60-80, ages 3-15 $40-70. AmEx/MC/V.) Another fantastic, though not quite Hawaiian, show is **Warren & Annabelle's Magic Nightclub,** 900 Front St. Annabelle, an invisible ghost, opens the show with her ethereal piano-playing, then Warren amazes guests with his up-close magic. (☎ 808-667-6244; www.warrenandannabelles.com. 21+. M-Sa 5pm; occasional second show at 7:30pm. Show $56; drinks, appetizers, and dessert extra.)

▓ NIGHTLIFE

When the young families and newlyweds turn in early after eating ice cream and checking out the shops, a younger late-night crowd emerges to hit up the various bars. Special $1 draft nights and happy hours make for some good bar hopping with live music on certain nights. Pick up a copy of *Maui Time Weekly,* a publication free at many restaurants and stores, to learn more.

▓ **Lahaina Store Grille & Oyster Bar,** 744 Front St. (☎ 808-661-9090; www.lahainastore-grille.net). Maui's only rooftop restaurant has stellar drinks, a jaw-dropping view, and a raw oyster bar that is open until midnight. Even if you miss its incredible sunset, worry not—you've come to the right place to drown such sweet sorrow. Th-Sa DJs. Su live music 9pm. Happy hour 11am-5pm ($7 martinis, $2 domestic drafts). Call for evening events. Open daily 11am-10pm. AmEx/D/MC/V.

Moose McGillycuddy's, 844 Front St. (☎ 808-667-7758), is lively, especially on Tu, when drinks are $1. Tourists and locals dance to a DJ at 9pm nightly, but if dancing isn't your thing, you can watch sports on one of the 40 TVs. F-Sa live classic rock and blues during dinner. $5 cover Tu only. Happy hour 4-7pm ($3 you-call-it). Food served until 10pm. Open daily 7:30am-2am. ATM on-site. AmEx/D/MC/V.

Longhi's, 888 Front St. (☎ 808-667-2288; www.longhis.com). The smart, contemporary art that dangles on Longhi's walls makes it a chic venue for mixed drinks and dancing, with live music every F. Complimentary valet parking nightly 5-11pm. F night 21+ after 11pm. Open daily 7:30am-10pm. AmEx/D/MC/V.

Gaby's Pizzeria & Deli, 505 Front St. (☎ 808-661-8112). Locals head to Gaby's for the award-winning food and nightly happy hour specials, though billiards, a fortune-telling machine, and a jukebox add an extra-special touch. From noon-3pm and 9-11pm domestic drafts $2; pizza slices $3. Open daily 11am-midnight. MC/V.

☐ SHOPPING

Lahaina is a shopper's delight—countless small stores and boutiques line Front St., and there are a number of large shopping centers in the area. At the north edge of town is the **Lahaina Cannery Mall**. For light beach reading, head to the **Old Lahaina Book Emporium**, at 834 Front St., on the right side of a small alley. Selling new and used books, the Emporium has an extensive collection of Hawaiiana, fiction, mysteries, poetry, and more. In fact, there are even a few shelves on bullfighting. (☎808-661-1399. Open daily 10am-7pm. MC/V.) Less than a block off Front St. is **Take Home Maui, Inc.,** 121 Dickenson St., where you can break out the markers, decorate a coconut husk, and mail it home for $25. They also ship pineapples, papayas, and macadamia nuts, which make great, though expensive, gifts. Their small deli is known for its fresh smoothies ($4) and sandwiches ($4-7). (☎800-545-6284 or 808-661-8067; www.takehomemaui.com. Open daily 7:30am-6:30pm, deli closes at 4:30pm. AmEx/D/MC/V.)

☐ GALLERIES

To get some relief from the searing Lahaina sun, duck into any one of Front St.'s air-conditioned art galleries. A step inside will not only do your brow good, but also perhaps inspire some work of your own. Although they provide a great escape during the day, the most exciting time to mosey around the galleries is Friday night, when the **Lahaina Town Action Committee** hosts **art night** from 7-10pm. Every week, there are appearances by local and internationally recognized artists, as well as entertainment and refreshments in the galleries.

Celebrités, 764 Front St. (☎808-667-0727 or 800-428-3338). Boasting a "gallery of celebrity fine art" and featuring work by John Lennon and Miles Davis among others, this is where sex, drugs, and rock and roll converge on Front St. The radical work of pop culture's elite fetches anywhere from $250-100,000, but small prints of treasured icons are only $14. Original T-shirts $55-100. Open daily 10:15am-10pm. AmEx/D/MC/V.

Higgins Harte International Gallery, 844 Front St. (☎808-661-4439; www.higginshartegalleries.com), showcases rare works by the masters (including Picasso, Chagall, and Degas), while also displaying the works of more contemporary artists, like Anthony Quinn, Red Skelton, and Sir Anthony Hopkins. Open daily 10am-10pm. AmEx/D/MC/V.

Peter Lik, 712 Front St. (☎808-661-6623; www.peterlik.com). You'll likely recognize some of the Australian shutterbug's work from posters and calendars, but nothing beats a real-life look at the wonderfully vivid photos. Open daily 9am-10pm. AmEx/D/MC/V.

Vintage European Posters, 744 Front St. (☎808-662-8688; www.europeanposters.com). Carefully thumb through Alan Dickar's collection of vintage lithographs, one of the largest in the Western US, and marvel over art deco advertisements and antique circus posters. Most of his finds are expensive, but you can pocket some smaller prints for only $20. Also at Whaler's Village in Kaanapali. Open daily 10am-10pm. AmEx/D/MC/V.

KAANAPALI

Kaanapali (pop. 1375) has long been a resort community. Hawaiian chiefs once prized its beaches for surfing; now tourists use them for every beach activity imaginable. All the major hotel chains own property on Kaanapali Beach, a 3 mi. stretch of golden sand punctuated by the volcanic Black Rock, which makes for spectacular snorkeling, scuba diving, and cliff jumping. This is one of the most prized places to stay in all of Maui; hotel rooms run at least $200 per night. Travelers on a budget may have more luck staying in Lahaina or renting a condo north of Kaana-pali in Napili (p. 276).

■ ORIENTATION. Kaanapali is located on **Highway 30 (Honoapiilani Highway)**, just north of Lahaina. All the pristine beaches can be accessed from this road, which is punctuated by expensive resorts.

⌐ ACCOMMODATIONS. The best deal on the beach is the **Kaana-pali Beach Hotel ❺**, 2525 Kaana-pali Pkwy., more subdued and relatively cheaper than its posh neighbors. (☎800-262-8450; www. kbhmaui.com. Rooms $199-355 depending on the view.) Of the major hotels on Kaanapali Beach, the **Hyatt Regency Maui ❻**, 200 Nohea Kai Dr., is the most luxurious, with an incredible tropical lobby, lush garden with flamingos, and a set of ornate swimming pools. (☎800-233-1234; www.maui.hyatt. com. Rooms $475-755. Prices *slightly* lower if booked online.) A paved path runs between the Hyatt and the Sheraton; even if you're not staying at the resorts, a stroll along this path is pleasant, especially at sunset and during hotel live music concerts.

▢ FOOD. Many of Kaanapali's restaurants are located in its hotels and are expensive (entrees $25-40). However, there are affordable options available. **Jonny's Burger Joint ❶**, 2291 Kaanapali Pkwy, is where locals congregate in Kaanapali. A hole-in-the-wall that serves juicy burgers ($6-13) and cheap drafts ($4), it has a pool table, jukebox, and plenty of camaraderie inside. (☎808-661-4500. Parking available. Open daily 11:30am-2am; food served until midnight. ATM on-site. AmEx/D/MC/V.) To dine on the shore, check out **Hula Grill and Barefoot Bar ❹**, 2435 Kaanapali Pkwy., in Whalers Village. One of the shorefront's more reason-able dining options, serving salads

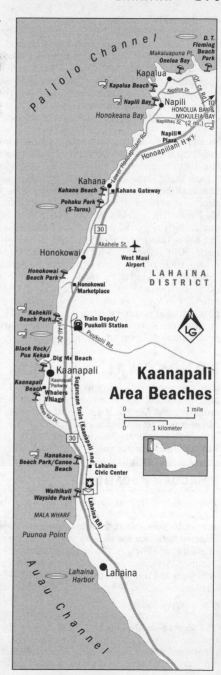

Kaanapali Area Beaches

($7-13), sandwiches ($9-13), and pizzas ($10.50) for lunch, and seafood ($18-34) for dinner. (☎808-667-6636. Happy hour 3-5pm. Live Hawaiian music daily. Hula show 8:30pm. Open daily 11am-11pm; dinner 5-9:30pm. AmEx/D/MC/V.) For family-stile dining and cheap happy hour drinks, **Rusty Harpoon Restaurant and Tavern ❸**, 2435 Kaanapali Pkwy. (☎808-661-3123), in Whalers Village, is your best bet. The "Daiquiri Capital of the World" serves the frosty concoction in 10 flavors for $3.50 (happy hour 2-6pm). Vacationers can enjoy the sun alight on passing sailboats or watch a variety of sporting events on the huge big screen TVs. (Early-bird dinner special 5-6pm $17. Open daily 8am-2am; food served until 10pm. AmEx/D/MC/V.)

🏖 BEACHES. Kaanapali's southernmost beach, **Hanakaoo,** or **Canoe Beach,** is the launch site for canoe races, jet skiing, and other activities. Canoe Beach has decent snorkeling, full facilities, and lifeguards on duty daily 8:30am-4pm. (Open daily 7am-8pm.) It is technically part of the same stretch of sand as **Kaanapali Beach,** a popular beach lined by the major hotels. The section of shoreline between the Kaanapali Beach Hotel and The Whaler is known as **Dig Me Beach.** The sunsets (if not the people) are particularly beautiful, although parking is pricey ($2 per 20min., $20 per day). Kaanapali Beach is marked by **Puu Kekaa (Black Rock),** an ideal place for snorkeling, but beware of strong currents. King Kahekili's warriors used to demonstrate their bravery by jumping off the rock; those with a penchant for danger still attempt it today.

For free parking and a lovely beach, drive to **Kahekili Beach Park,** on Kai Ala Dr. off Honoapiilani Hwy., on the north end of Kaanapali. Although close to a few hotels, this long, narrow beach is surprisingly quiet and uncrowded; its grassy park, shaded picnic tables, grills, restrooms, and showers make it a desirable destination. Kahekili's clear, calm waters are frequently used for introductory scuba classes. Open daily 3am-7pm.

HONOKOWAI, KAHANA, AND NAPILI

One condominium development after another lines Lower Honoapiilani Rd., and it's difficult to distinguish where each of the three dreamy "towns" ends and the next begins. Honokowai, the first development north of Kaanapali, offers a few good restaurants. Kahana, the next town, has 1970s-style condos and some fancier residences along its rocky beaches. Finally, wedged between Kahana and Kapalua, the Napili ("luck will cling") condos surround the sandy crescent of Napili Bay, a popular family beach.

📷 ACCOMMODATIONS

The condos in this area are generally more moderately priced than the hotels in Kaanapali and the resorts in Kapalua. It's a good vacation home base, with easy access to West Maui beaches and activities. *Let's Go: Hawaii* recommends **📷Accommodations Hawaii,** a vacation rental company based in Lahaina that handles 30 properties and over 200 units in Kaanapali, Honokowai, Kahana, and Napili. All units are privately owned. Pictures, rates, and details of the properties are on the website. (☎808-661-6655; www.accommodationsmaui.com. Rentals range $95-545 per night. Weekly and monthly rates available.)

🍴 FOOD

The **Honokowai Marketplace,** 3350 Lower Honoapiilani Rd., immediately after the turnoff to the highway, hosts several takeout places and a **Star Market.** (☎808-667-9590. Open 24hr.) The **Napili Market** grocery store, 5095 Napilihau Rd., has an ATM and a copy machine. (☎808-669-1600. Copies $0.20 per page.

MAUI

Open daily 6:30am-11pm. AmEx/D/MC/V.) The **Maui Farmers' Market & Deli**, 3636 Lower Honoapiilani Hwy., directly across from Honokawai Beach Park, has organic produce, vitamins, and full salad and soup bars. On Monday, Wednesday, and Friday, it hosts several stands offering fresh local produce from 7 to 11am. (Open daily 7am-7pm; deli closes at 6pm. AmEx/D/MC/V.)

Soup Nutz & Java Jazz (☎808-667-0787), in Honokowai Marketplace. This quirky sandwich shop by day and artsy bistro by night is a pleasant reprieve from standard strip-mall ambience. Its subtle lighting, walls of Polaroids, and background jazz makes it a great place to escape the heat and enjoy some great food. Live music nightly 7pm. Sandwiches $8-10. Entrees $18-26. Wine $8-10 per glass. Open M-Sa 6am-9pm, Su 6am-5pm. D/MC/V. Lunch ❷/Dinner ❺

Honokowai Okazuya and Deli, 3600D Lower Honoapiilani Rd. (☎808-665-0512), in the AAAAA Rent-A-Space Retail Center. Okazuya's quality takeout is a West Maui staple. Something for everyone, from sandwiches ($10-12) and pasta ($10.50) to spicy Szechuan eggplant ($10) and *mahi mahi* ($15-16). A stool-lined counter and some outdoor tables provide seating for the famished, but most of the food is taken to go. Open M-Sa 10am-2:30pm and 4:30-9pm. Cash only. ❷

China Boat, 4474 Lower Honoapiilani Rd. (☎808-669-5089; www.chinaboatandbowlmaui.com.), in Kahana. Quietly tucked inside one of the highways's winding curves, this local favorite whips up some of the island's best Chinese cuisine (the Szechuan chicken for $12 is out of this world) at many of its yummiest prices. Entrees are generally under $15; while seafood specialties, like the China Boat special (sauteed lobster meat, scallops, shrimp, chicken, and vegetables in a spicy brown sauce; $24), are somewhat pricier. Open M-Sa 11:30am-2pm, daily 5-10pm. AmEx/D/MC/V. ❸

Dollie's Pub & Cafe, 4310 Lower Honoapiilani Rd. (☎808-669-0266; www.dolliespubandcafe.com), in Kahana Manor. Residents line the bar at this dimly lit sports pub and sing praises of its pizzas ($20-27, individual $9), pastas ($13-16), and sandwiches ($9-11). Although Dollie's has a variety of vegetarian offerings, meat-lovers will delight in the "shombay malombay" pizza ($23). Happy hour daily 3-6pm and 10pm-midnight (pizza $2.50, Bud $3.50, Hefeweizen $4.50). Power hour daily 5-6pm (shots $3.50-4). ATM on-site. Open daily 11am-midnight. AmEx/D/MC/V. ❷

The Coffee Store, 5095 Napilihau St. (☎808-669-4170; www.mauicoffee.com). Blissful A/C and soothing music, delicious roasts (try the Vanilla Macadamia Nut), and Internet access ($0.20 per min., $2

ON THE MENU

THE PINT OF NO RETURN

Forget Rome. When in Hawaii, do as the Hawaiians do. However, before you flee towards mouthfuls of Spam and mac salad, take a swig of one of the ales at Maui Brewing Co. "Brewed with aloha," these award-winning local beers are fast becoming the mecca of happy hours everywhere.

From fans of the Bikini Blonde lager to Coconut Porter devotees, the company's Kahana brewpub—Maui's only microbrewery and restaurant—has its hands full keeping up with the ever-growing demand. Island-wide, pubs report that other Hawaiian beers have suffered in sales as Maui Brewing has developed a regular customer base. Pushing toward a capacity of 10,000 barrels a year, its business will soon near that of Kona Brewing Co., the Big Island's entry in the imaginary contest for best Hawaiian beer.

However head-spinning its spirits are, Maui Brewing Co. is also to be commended for its eco-friendly streak. All of its machines run on vegetable oil, and products are packaged in cans with quirky phrases, rather than breakable glass bottles. Now if that's not the aloha spirit, what is?

The Bikini Blonde Lager and more can be sipped, swirled, and swallowed at the **Maui Brewing Co. Brewpub,** *4405 Honoapiilani Hwy. (☎808-669-FISH; www.mauibrewingco.com), at the Kahana Gateway Center.*

min. with cash and $5 min. with card). A great place to pick up some coffee as a gift. Open daily 6am-6pm. AmEx/D/MC/V. ❶

Mama's Ribs 'N Rotisserie, 5095 Napilihau St. (☎808-665-6262), cooks up the most finger-licking barbecue on the island. Regulars and newcomers drop in to purchase baby back ribs (half-rack $12.50, full-rack $23) and whole chickens ($16), deliciously marinated in the secret family recipe. The meaty menu also includes plate meals ($8-13), chili ($3-6), and spinach lasagna ($9). Open M-Sa 11am-8pm. Cash only. ❷

 NAPILI EVER AFTER. Still looking for that perfect Hawaiian trinket? Maui Family Support Services sponsors a craft fair 9am-4pm on M, W, and Sa at Napili Plaza.

🏖 BEACHES

NAPILI BAY. *(Bodyboarding. Snorkeling. Open 24hr.)* The best beach in this area is a crowded crescent of sand—many families come here to swim and snorkel. You can also expect seasonal surf good for bodyboarding. Parking is difficult as the condos along the beach do not allow visitors in their lots. *(Access to the shore is on Hui Dr. and Napili Pl., both off Lower Honoapiilani Rd., where a few cars manage to park.)*

KAHANA BEACH. *(Open 24hr.)* A pleasant little cove in front of Kahana Beach Resort Condos, this beach has a sandy bottom but a lot of seaweed. Access to the beach is a bit difficult since the condos are private, and the public access puts you at a rocky cove a bit south of the actual beach. The nearest parking lot is for **Pohaku Beach** or **S-Turns Park,** which has a small strip of sand, portapotties, grills, an outdoor shower, and a few picnic tables. A great place to park to watch the sunset because you can pull up close to the ocean.

KAPALUA AND BEYOND

Tall Cook pines line the planned roads of Kapalua (pop. 467), the most exclusive resort area in Maui. The elegance of the **Ritz Carlton Kapalua** ❺ (☎808-669-6200) is a departure from the glitz of Wailea. Aside from the gloriously free beaches, there is little in Kapalua ("arms embracing the sea") for a budget traveler.

🍴 FOOD

Most vacationers in Kapalua either utilize their kitchens or eat at the resorts. **The Honolua Store,** 502 Office Rd., near the Ritz-Carlton, is a Kapalua standby with a full service grocery, coffee bar, and takeout counter. Their hybrid pineapples are satisfyingly sweet, and surfers and golfers alike flock here for an inexpensive breakfast or lunch, which can be enjoyed on the wooden patio or taken to go. (☎808-665-9105. Open daily 6am-9pm. AmEx/D/MC/V.) **The Pineapple Grill** ❹, 200 Kapalua Dr., at the Kapulua Resort, serves up acclaimed dishes alongside the neatly clipped beauty of its golf course. (☎808-669-9600. Sandwiches $9-16, dinner entrees $10-45. Open daily 11am-10pm. AmEx/D/MC/V.)

🏖 BEACHES

KAPALUA BEACH. *(Snorkeling. Open 24hr.)* A lovely, white sand spot with clear, calm waters, Kapalua Beach is great for swimming, lounging, diving, or snorkeling. Rare Hawaiian monk seals also enjoy sunning here. Kapalua is very popular with families and condominium renters in the area. The beach can get crowded, and the small parking lot fills up quickly. *(From Lower Honoapiilani Rd., look for a blue shoreline access sign immediately north of Napili Kai Beach Resort.)*

TALK STORY AT THE RITZ. In Hawaii, the phrase "talk story" means a long rambling conversation about anything. Its origins stem from the fact that Hawaii's history was recorded in chants, songs, and storytelling long before anything was written down. For a memorable tale, head to the Ritz-Carlton in Kapalua, where once a month on a Friday evening around the full moon, Hawaiian cultural advisor Clifford Naeole can be heard talking story as part of a program called **Moonlight Moolelo.** Appetizers and music quiet the onlookers as they sit on the lawn overlooking D.T. Fleming Beach and listen to Naeole and other local experts muse about Hawaii's indigenous people.

ONELOA BEACH (IRONWOODS). *(Bodyboarding. Open 24hr.)* Farther up the coast, Oneloa is usually nearly empty and perfect for secluded sunbathing. It's better suited for bodyboarding than swimming, though, as the sand gives way to reef and the waves are rather large. Also, though the beach is generally peaceful, the winds here can stir up a sandstorm from time to time. There's an outdoor shower. *(To reach public parking and beach access, take Office Rd., the main road leading from the highway into Kapalua, turn left at the end, and then right on Ironwood Ln. Parking is before the gate, and the small blue sign points to an access path opposite the parking lot.)*

D. T. FLEMING BEACH PARK. *(Bodyboarding. Surfing. Open daily 7am-8pm. Lifeguards 8am-4:30pm.)* Ranked America's best beach in 2006, Fleming Beach Park has full facilities, lifeguards on duty, a large parking area (although it's often full), shade, and a mighty riptide. In winter the waves can be great for bodyboarding and surfing. *(Turn left off the highway after mi. marker 31; the beach is at the end of the road.)*

MOKULEIA AND HONOLUA BAYS. *(Snorkeling. Surfing. Open 24hr.)* Between mi. markers 32 and 33, these bays offer some of the best snorkeling on the island when the water is calm. Mokuleia Bay, also known as Slaughterhouse Beach, has a sandy entrance to the water; just follow the concrete steps down through the cove. A small parking area is at the top of the steps. Visitors to Honolua park on the side of the road a quarter-mile past this parking area and walk down a dirt path and past a gate. Farther down the dirt path, and through a gorgeous jungled forest, the rocky Honolua Bay emerges. Snorkelers enter the water via an old boat ramp in the center of the bay. Be careful: huge swells roll into Honolua in winter, and only experienced surfers should take them on.

SIGHTS

One of the most beautiful and heart-pounding drives on Maui, **Route 340 (Kahekili Highway)** winds along the coast for 20 mi. between Kapalua and Wailuku. Although it's not always as lush as its eastern counterpart, Hana Hwy., the drive is full of red mesa rock formations and conifers that astound with their sparse grandeur. In some places, the one-lane road narrows to the width of a car, with a cliff on one side, no guardrail, and the ocean 100 ft. below. The road is paved, so 4WD is not necessary, just alertness and resignation to the 10 mph speed limit. You'll be glad for the slow speed if you encounter a car coming from the other direction and have to back up around hairpin turns. If you drive from Lahaina, you're less likely to encounter people coming the other way, as many find it more comfortable pulling off to the mountain side of the road to make room for oncoming traffic. Allow at least 90min. for the drive.

MAUI

CLICK IT OR TICKET. As with driving anywhere, in Hawaii it's best to adhere to the speed limit. On coastal highways, the limit changes frequently, and cops love to pull over motorists who aren't heeding the signs. Be sure to buckle up, since fines for driving without a seat belt run around $100.

DRAGON'S TEETH. Although lava formations are ubiquitous in Hawaii, the Makaluapuna Point's **Dragon's Teeth** formation in Kapalua is particularly distinctive. Years of ocean spray have bleached the lava a cool gray and even eroded holes in between spikes, creating a striking resemblance to one particular reptile's pearly whites. Only a 5min. walk from the parking lot, this is one sight for the scrapbook that all your friends will sink their incisors into. *(From Honoapiilani Hwy., make a left on Office Rd. After ½ mi., turn right and drive past the chapel parking lot. Park at the 2nd lot and continue on to the golf course. There will be a plaque announcing the "Honokahua Burial Site." Do not enter these sacred grounds. Keep the burial site on your right and the green on your left. Continue on past the trees, and you will see the lava formation.)*

NAKALELE BLOWHOLE. The blowhole is at the second major turnout, about half a mile past mi. marker 38. The water comes crashing up into the rocky cliffs, creating a misty mix of blue, white, and black. At high tide, the blowhole is visible just paces from the pullout, but there is also a dirt trail (30min. one-way.) leading down that allows for a closer look. There are two long ladders extending down a steep cliff toward the water. Do not use these ladders; they are old and unsafe. Use extreme caution: visitors have been killed when they venture too close and the spray catches them with surprising force.

KAHAKULOA. This remote village of less than 100 people is tucked into a valley as the highway dips between the two ridges. There are a few stands selling shave ice and banana bread to refresh drivers. After the short detour of Kahakuloa, a rock formation known as **Kahakuloa Head** towers 636 ft. above the water. Together with Kahulianapa behind it, the hills form a distinctive silhouette identifiable from beaches on the North Shore. There's not much between Kahakuloa and Wailuku save some shops, sculpture gardens, and galleries.

CENTRAL MAUI

Central Maui refers to the valley that stretches between the West Maui Mountains and the Haleakala Volcano. The valley receives a fair amount of rain, and the clouds and strong winds make it cooler than the west side. The 40-acre Kanaha Pond, a major bird sanctuary near the airport, is the only natural body of water on Maui. However, aside from the county seat of Wailuku and the commercial center of Kahului, there isn't much here except vast fields of sugarcane. Kaahumanu Ave. and Rte. 32 (Main St.) run along the northern part of the area, all the way to the spectacular Iao Valley (p. 286). Rte. 36 and 37 connect Central Maui with the North Shore (p. 299) and upcountry towns in the east (p. 313), Rte. 350/311 (Puunene Ave./Mokulele Hwy.) leads South Maui (p. 288), and Rte. 30 (Honoapiilani Hwy.) goes to Lahaina (p. 261).

KAHULUI AND WAILUKU

On the northern coast of the Central Maui Valley, these two uncharming towns offer several options for budget travelers. Kahului (pop. 20,146), "athletic contest" in Hawaiian, is a sprawl of shopping centers and is the site of Maui's main airport. Wailuku (pop. 12,296), west of Kahului, is more cohesive. Clusters of mom-and-pop stores and restaurants give it more character than its larger neighbor, though there's still not much draw. In Hawaiian, Wailuku means "waters of destruction," a reference to the area's history of battles and floods.

▌ TRANSPORTATION

Flights: Kahului International Airport (OGG), on the northern coast of Central Maui. Kahului is the main airport for Maui, served by international carriers as well as **Hawaiian Airlines** (☎800-367-5320; www.hawaiianair.com), **Pacific Wings** (☎808-873-0877 or 888-575-4546; www.pacificwings.com), and **go!** (☎888-435-9462; www.iflygo.com).

Bus and Van Services: Robert's (☎808-871-4838) runs **MauiBus** buses daily for $1 from Kahului to **Lahaina** via **Maalaea** (every hr. 5:30am-9:30pm), and Kahului to **Wailea** via **Kihei** (every hr. 5:30am-9:30pm). Also runs free buses on the **Kahului** and **Wailuku loops** (every hr. 7:30am-10pm). Check www.co.maui.hi.us/bus for schedules.

Car Rental: National car rental chains operate out of the airport; see **Essentials,** p. 38. **Maui Cruisers Car Rental** (☎808-249-2319; www.mauicruisers.net) rents cars for $30 per day and $133 per week in the summer; winter prices are higher. Car insurance required. 21+. MC/V. **Aloha Rent-a-Car** (☎808-877-4477; www.aloharentacar.com). Compacts for $27 per day and $159 per week. 3-day min. AmEx/D/MC/V.

◢▐ ORIENTATION AND PRACTICAL INFORMATION

Most of the stores in Kahului sprawl along the main road, **Kaahumanu Avenue,** and along **Dairy Road,** on the east side of town. Wailuku is centered around **West Main Street,** the continuation of Kaahumanu Ave.

Tourist Information: Maui Visitors Bureau, 1727 Wili Pa Loop (☎808-244-3530; www. visitmaui.com), off Imi Kala St., across from the Wailuku post office. Maps and brochures available to those who make the trek. Open M-F 8am-4:30pm.

Banks: Major banks line Kahului's highways. **24hr. ATMs** are located at all of the banks and in most shopping centers and malls. In Wailuku:
Bank of Hawaii, 2105 W. Main St. (☎888-643-3888). Open M-Th 8:30am-4pm, F 8:30am-6pm.
First Hawaiian Bank, 27 N. Market St. (☎808-877-2377). Open M-Th 8:30am-4pm, F 9am-6pm.
American Savings Bank, 69 N. Market St. (☎808-244-9148). Open M-Th 8am-5pm, F 8am-6pm.

Libraries: Kahului Public Library, 90 School St. (☎808-873-3097), off Kamehameha Ave. Open Tu noon-8pm, W-Sa 9am-5pm. **Wailuku Public Library,** 251 High St. (☎808-243-5766). Open M-W and F 9am-5pm, Th 1-8pm. Internet access at both is unlimited with a 3-month visitor's card ($10). Both offer copies at $0.20 per page.

Laundromats: There are several laundry centers scattered throughout Kahului, including **W & F Washerette,** 125 S. Wakea Ave. (☎808-877-0353). Wash $2-2.50, dry $0.25 per 3min. Snack bar and video arcade with horoscope reader. Open daily 6am-9:45pm. In Wailuku, **Happy Valley Laundry,** 340 N. Market St. (☎808-244-4677), is a few doors down from the Banana Bungalow and has a soda machine. Wash $1.75 (double load $2.50), dry $0.25 per 5min. Open daily 6am-8pm. Both have coin machines.

Pharmacies: In Kahului, head to **Longs Drugs** (☎808-877-0041), in the Maui Mall. Open daily 7am-midnight; pharmacy open M-Sa 8am-9pm, Su 8am-7pm. In Wailuku, **Longs Pharmacy,** 1900 Main St. (☎808-244-9099), is open M-F 9am-1pm and 1:45-5:30pm, Sa 9am-1pm.

Medical Services: Maui Memorial Medical Center, 221 Mahalani St. (☎808-244-9056), in Wailuku, serves both areas. In Wailuku, **Maui Medical Group,** 2180 Main St. (☎808-242-6464), has a night clinic. Open M-F 8am-9pm, Sa-Su 8am-noon.

MAUI

Copy and Fax Services: In Kahului, go to **Kinko's,** 395 Dairy Rd. (☎808-871-2000), in the Dairy Center in Kahului. Open M-F 7am-10pm, Sa 9am-9pm, Su 9am-6pm. In Wailuku, **Copy Services,** 1975 Vineyard St. (☎808-242-7651), is just south of Market St. $0.10 per page, color $1. Open M-F 9am-5pm.

Internet Access: Kinko's (see above), $0.20 per min. Also see libraries above.

Post Offices: Kahului Post Office, 138 S. Puunene Ave. (☎808-871-2487), next to the Shell station. Open M-F 8am-4:30pm, Sa 9am-noon. **Wailuku Post Office,** 250 Imi Kala St. (☎808-244-1653), off Mill St. Open M-F 8am-4:30pm, Sa 9am-noon.

Postal Codes: 96732 (Kahului); 96793 (Wailuku).

ACCOMMODATIONS AND CAMPING

Accommodations in Kahului and Wailuku are relatively budget. Wailuku's hostels attract backpackers, windsurfers, and hangabouts, while Kahului's functional hotels draw travelers looking for a bed near the airport. These towns provide a convenient base for exploring the natural beauty of the Iao Valley, and many visitors actually stay here and take daytrips to the rest of the island.

Banana Bungalow, 310 N. Market St. (☎808-244-5090; www.mauihostel.com), a few blocks from central Wailuku. The free tours to Haleakala, Hana, and other popular destinations are the reason to stay at this humble hostel. A lively, mostly international crowd congregates in the large kitchen, TV lounge with foosball table and billiards, hot tub, and other common areas. Numerous bathrooms and showers are a plus, though single-sex dorms aren't guaranteed. Luggage storage and safe available. Coin-op laundry. Free Internet access and Wi-Fi. Reception 8am-11pm. Check-out 10am. Quiet hours after 10pm. Reservations strongly recommended. 4- and 6-bed dorms $25; singles $60; doubles $71; triples $81.50. Call about short-term work. MC/V. ❶

Northshore Hostel, 2080 W. Vineyard St. (☎808-986-8095; www.northshorehostel. com). The entrance is down an alley between Market and Church St. in downtown Wailuku. This spacious hostel full of easygoing surfers will make you feel right at home. A comfortable common area merges with a fully furnished kitchen and often sees amiable guests watching surfing movies or TV. Free airport pickup depending on driver availability. Breakfast included. Luggage storage available. Laundry $1.75. Free Internet access and local phone calls. Reception 8am-1pm and 5-11pm. Check-out 10am. Dorms $25; singles $50; doubles $60; triples $80. Inquire about short-term work. MC/V. ❶

Happy Valley Hale, 332 N. Market St. (☎808-870-9100; www.nonalanicottages.com/ hvhale.htm), a few blocks from central Wailuku. Despite its less-than-stellar surroundings, guests enjoy the cleanliness of this simple hostel-like abode. Common kitchen. 2 shared bathrooms. Coin-op laundry. Check-in 2pm. Check-out 11am. 3-night min. Beds $33; singles and doubles $65; triples $99. $100 cancellation fee; all funds forfeited if cancelled in less than 30 days. ❷

Old Wailuku Inn at Ulupono, 2199 Kahookele St. (☎808-244-5897; www.mauiinn. com). Follow Main St. (Rte. 32W) through Wailuku and turn left on High St.; the 3rd left is Kahookele. In homage to Don Blanding, Hawaii's poet laureate of the 1920s and 30s, each of the rooms is dedicated to one of the flowers in his "Old Hawaiian Garden." Breakfast daily 8am. All rooms with private bathrooms. Fridge and microwave available in common area. 2-night min. Reception 9am-5pm. Check-in 2pm. Check-out 11:30am. Reserve 60 days in advance with $50 deposit. Doubles $150-190; rates slightly higher in Dec. Each additional person $20. AAA and seniors 10% discount. D/MC/V. ❹

Kanaha Beach Park, off Amala Pl. From central Kahului, make a left on Hobron Ave. off Kaahumanu Ave. The 1st right is Amala Pl.; follow this road past the factories and look for the park entrance on your left. Centrally located with the convenience of outdoor showers, restrooms, and picnic tables. Pitch your tent in the shaded park grounds or right on the

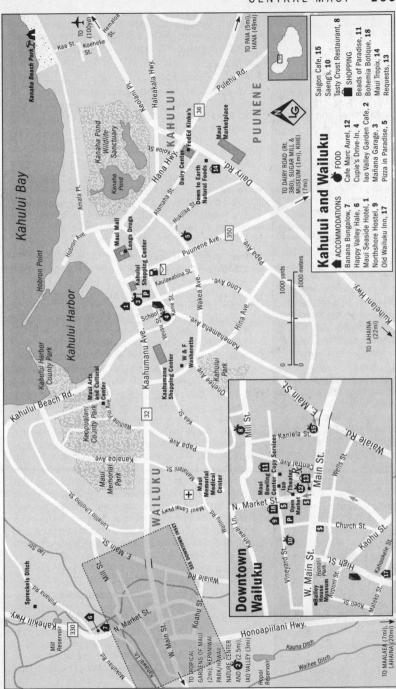

Kahului Bay

Kanaha Beach Park

TO (100yd)

Kaa St.

Koeheke St.

Hemaloa St.

Kahului Harbor

Hobron Point

Hobron Ave.

Amala Pl.

Kanaha Pond Wildlife Sanctuary

Kanaha Pond

Keolani Pl.

Haleakala Hwy.

Koloa St.

KAHULUI

Hana Hwy.

Atamana St.

Hukilike St.

FedEx Kinko's

Dairy Center

Down to Earth Natural Foods

Maui Mall

Longs Drugs

Kahului Shopping Center

36

Maui Marketplace

PUUNENE

Pulehu Rd.

Dairy Rd.

Puunene Ave.

350

Papa Ave.

Lono Ave.

Hina Ave.

Kamehameha Ave.

Kaulawahina St.

Wakea Ave.

Kane St.

Vevau St.

School St.

Kaahumanu Ave.

Onehee Ave.

Kahului Park

W & F Washerette

Kaahumanu Shopping Center

Kahului Harbor County Park

Kahului Beach Rd.

Maui Arts and Cultural Center

Keopualani County Park

Wahine Pio Ave.

Kanaloa Ave.

Maui Memorial Park

32

Papa Ave.

Kea St.

Mahalani St.

Maui Memorial Medical Center

Maui Lani Pkwy.

WAILUKU

Wailuku Rd.

Lumalilo Liholiho St.

Spreckels Ditch

Iao St.

Kahekili Hwy.

330

Mill Reservoir

E. Main St.

Kaohu St.

W. Main St.

N. Market St.

Mokuhau Rd.

Kaniwai Ln.

SEE DOWNTOWN INSET

Honoapiilani Hwy.

Kauna Ditch

Waihee Ditch

Iao Valley Rd.

Hepoi Reservoir

TO MAALAEA (7mi); LAHANA (20mi)

TO TROPICAL GARDENS OF MAUI (2mi); KEPANIWAI PARK/HAWAII NATURE CENTER AND 2 (2.5mi); IAO VALLEY (3mi)

Downtown Wailuku

Mill St.

E. Main St.

Kaniela St.

8

Central Ave.

Maui Bowling Center

Copy Services

11

Iao Theater

12 13

16

Open Market

9

18

5

P

10

N. Market St.

Waiale Rd.

Main St.

Wells St.

Church St.

Kaohu St.

Kahoolele St.

Vineyard St.

W. Main St.

Bailey House Museum

High St.

Honolii Park

Aupuni St.

Koeli St.

Malako St.

N

LG

MAUI

TO DAIRY ROAD (Rt. 380), SUGAR MILL & MUSEUM (1mi), KIHEI (7mi)

Kuihelani Hwy.

TO LAHAINA (22mi)

TO PAIA (5mi); HANA (49mi)

1000 yards

1000 meters

0

Kahului and Wailuku

▲ ACCOMMODATIONS
Banana Bungalow, **7**
Happy Valley Hale, **6**
Maui Seaside Hotel, **1**
Northshore Hostel, **9**
Old Wailuku Inn, **17**

● FOOD
Cafe Marc Aurel, **12**
Cupie's Drive-In, **4**
Iao Valley Garden Cafe, **2**
Mañana Garage, **3**
Pizza in Paradise, **5**
Saigon Cafe, **15**
Saeng's, **10**
Tasty Crust Restaurant, **8**

■ SHOPPING
Beads of Paradise, **11**
Bohemia Botique, **18**
Maui Tropix, **14**
Requests, **13**

beach. Campground closed Tu-W for maintenance. Permits $3 per person. Call ☎808-270-7389 or see **Camping in Hawaii**, p. 82, for permit information. ❶

🍴 FOOD

In Kahului, restaurants and supermarkets are located in the shopping centers along Kaahumanu Ave. **Down to Earth Natural Foods,** 305 Dairy Rd., in Kahului, has an impressive (and expensive) variety of organic produce, packaged foods, and a popular salad bar and hot buffet. (☎808-877-2661. Open M-Sa 7am-9pm, Su 8am-8pm. AmEx/D/MC/V.) There's also an **outdoor market** that sells fresh local produce and homemade baked goods right on Market St. (☎808-276-4966. Open M and Th 7am-6pm.) For a small town, Wailuku offers an impressive selection of international cuisine along Vineyard St., W. Main St., and N. Market St.

🍴 **Tasty Crust Restaurant,** 1770 Mill St. (☎808-244-0845), off N. Market St. in Wailuku. Tasty Crust is as local and cheap as they come; if you eat here twice in the same week, the gracious staff will remember your order. Locals crowd the 50-year-old Wailuku staple in the early morning for big, fluffy hotcakes ($1.85 each, banana hotcake $2.35) and cups of freshly brewed joe ($1). Lunch and dinner are good but less popular (sesame chicken with steamed rice and macaroni salad, $7.15). Open M 6am-3pm, Tu-Th and Su 6am-10pm, F-Sa 6am-11pm. Cash only. ❶

🍴 **A Saigon Cafe,** 1792 Main St. (☎808-243-9560). In Wailuku, take Central Ave. to Nani St. and then turn right onto Kaniela St. The restaurant is on your left, though there's no sign. This unassuming Vietnamese restaurant is constantly filled with locals and hungry tourists. The service is quick and affable, and the portions are generous. The house specialty *banh hoi* (vegetables, meat, and noodles that you roll in rice paper; $12-14) is especially popular, as is the *nhung dam* fondue ($16-24). Crispy noodles (served hot with shrimp, calamari, chicken, or beef with vegetables in a garlic sauce; $11-12) are also an excellent choice, and many dishes are available for under $10. Open M-Sa 10am-9:30pm, Su 10am-8:30pm. MC/V. ❷

Mañana Garage, 33 Lono Ave. (☎808-873-0220), off Kaahumanu Ave. Stuck between car dealerships and gas stations, Mañana Garage is a pleasant surprise. Bright purple walls and funky car parts create an inviting atmosphere that complements the Latin American cuisine. The dinner entrees are a bit pricey (chipotle-soy glazed salmon $21, fajitas $20-26), but they're 🍴 **buy 1, get the 2nd ½-price** 5-6pm daily. Lunch is more wallet-friendly, with sandwiches ($7-10), pastas

($10-12), and a business lunch ($16). Tempting desserts (chocolate toffee mousse cake, $7) and mixed drinks ($6-8) round out the flavorful menu. Margaritas $3.50 all day Th. Happy hour M-Sa 3-6pm. Open M-Th 11am-9pm, F-Sa 11am-9:30pm, Su 5-9pm. AmEx/D/MC/V. Lunch ❸/dinner ❺

Cafe Marc Aurel, 28 N. Market St. (☎808-244-0852; www.cafemarcaurel.com.), in Wailuku center. At Wailuku's resident bohemian stop post, rich roasts, gypsy teas, light fare (quiches, muffins, and scones), and Häagen-Dazs go down well with the soothing background music. If you brought an appetite, try one of the sophisticated salads or sandwiches ($7.50-8.50). Happy hour 4-6pm ($1 off beer, liquor, and wine). Coffee $1.50-4.50. Single espresso drinks $2-4. M open talent night; last M of the month is a radio broadcast. Th is an evening of jazz, and Sa brings art shows and a DJ. Open M-Sa 7-10am and 4pm-midnight. AmEx/D/MC/V. ❶

---

 2 FLAVORS, 1 CUP. The small portions of gelato at **Ono Gelato,** 115 Hana Hwy., in Paia, are as over-priced as they are delicious. However, at $0.99, the ▨ **iced coffee** is a refreshing deal that can't be beat.

Saeng's, 2119 Vineyard St. (☎808-244-1567), at N. Church St. in downtown Wailuku. Saeng's stands out for its elegant, dimly-lit dining room and handsome, open-air garden *lanai*. The extensive Thai menu features green, red, and yellow curries (pineapple red shrimp curry, $11) and highlights local seafood (ginger *mahi mahi*, $13). Saeng's also offers a large selection of creative vegetarian options (evil prince tofu, $8.50). Lunch served M-F 11am-2:30pm, dinner daily 5-9:30pm. MC/V. ❸

Iao Valley Garden Cafe, Iao Valley Rd. (☎808-269-2940), at the Hawaii Nature Center. The sister spot of the Makawao Garden Cafe, this counter-top has the same delicious menu and serves as the perfect stop for lunch en route to the Iao Valley. Sandwiches (brie and bacon, $8.50) are filling, and smoothies ($5) and honey lemonade ($2) are undeniably yummy. Open daily 10:30am-3pm. Cash only. ❷

Cupie's Drive-In, 134 W. Kamehameha (☎808-877-3055), in Kahului, is one of Maui's oldest and most popular plate lunch eateries. The lunch counter, originally a drive-in, offers cheeseburgers ($3), *chow fun* ($3.70), omelets ($7), and fried chicken (8-piece bucket $22), in addition to a full range of hardcore lunch plates ($7.50) and covered picnic tables. Open M 9am-4pm, T-Th and Sa 9am-8pm, F 9am-9pm. MC/V. ❶

Pizza in Paradise, 60 E. Wakea Ave. (☎808-871-8188), in Kahului. If paradise can't be complete without pizza, then swing by and enjoy a quick slice or grab some friends to split a huge pie. Diners chow on incredible upper-crust pizzas ($10.50-28), oven-baked subs ($7.50), calzones ($5.50), and filling pasta dishes ($7-10). Dessert pizza (apple, cinnamon, or blueberry; $7) is also on the menu. Pizza by the slice $1.50. Open M-Th 11am-9pm, F-Sa 11am-10pm. MC/V. ❷

◢ BEACHES

KANAHA BEACH. *(Wind sports. Open daily 6:30am-8pm.)* Kanaha Beach is the place windsurfers and kiteboarders go to play, and spectators go to enjoy watching them. Some say the swimming isn't too bad as long as you turn off the road before the beach park, but the murky water and choppy waves may make you think otherwise. After 11am, when windsurfers and kiteboarders are allowed in the water, it's a great place to watch colored sails jump through sea and sky as adventurous boarders catch air. **Action Sports** offers kiteboarding lessons and will deliver the equipment to the beach. (☎808-871-5857. 3hr. private lesson $240.) Kanaha Beach Park has large grassy areas, grills, picnic tables, and a

MAUI

few volleyball courts, making it nice for a barbecue. *(Parking spaces are abundant; remember to take your valuables with you. The beach is located off Amala Pl., behind the airport.)*

👁 SIGHTS

🏛 **IAO VALLEY STATE PARK AND THE IAO NEEDLE.** The result of 1.5 million years of water pressure eroding volcanic rock, the Iao (cloud supreme) Needle rises 2250 ft. above Iao Valley. The beauty of the mountains and needle is inspiring, and, also inspired, Hawaiians affectionately call the structure Kukaemoku, after the phallus of the sea god Kanaloa. The valley is considered a sacred space—*alii* (chiefs) were buried here, and it's also the site of many important battles. In 1790, Kamehameha I won a bloody victory here over the rival chief of Oahu, which ultimately led to his coronation as the first Hawaiian king. Exactly 133 stone steps lead to a lookout with a more intimate view. The paved path meanders down to the fast-moving Iao Stream, where local kids are unconcerned by the "no swimming" signs and frolic in the water that once irrigated taro crops on the lush valley floor. The valley can be windy and chilly even when it's sunny in downtown Wailuku, so bring along a light jacket. Restrooms are available at the beginning of the park. *(Take Main St. through Wailuku and continue for 3 mi. The road ends at Iao Valley Park. There is no off-trail hiking in Iao Valley. Allow 35min. to see the entire park via the paved paths and steps. Open daily 7am-7pm. Free.)*

HALEKII AND PIHANAKALANI HEIAU. Two of Maui's most accessible archeological sites, these ancient temples were originally built in 1240. According to tradition, **Halekii** (house of images) and **Pihanakalani** (gathering place of supernatural beings) were built with stones from the nearby Iao Stream. Kahekili, chief of Maui, lived and worshipped at Halekii during the 1760s, and the Pihanakalani Heiau is thought to be the last site where Kamehameha I performed human sacrifices to the war god Ku. The *heiau* were dismantled in 1819, when the traditional Hawaiian religion was abolished. In 1958, they were reconstructed and placed on the National and State Registry of Historic Places. The site itself may only require a quick visit, but it's worth the time for both its deep history and the panoramic views of Central Maui. The walk around the *heiau* is half a mile and takes about 15 min. Remember that this is a historical, religious site; do not remove any stones, climb on any structures, or cause any damage. *(From Waiehu/Kahului Beach Rd., turn on Kuhio Pl., away from the harbor. Make a left on Hea Pl. A large sign marks the entrance. No fees are required.)*

TROPICAL GARDENS OF MAUI. This magnificent four-acre garden showcases tropical trees and flowers from all over the world, including many rare native Hawaiian plants. If you're on the way to Iao Valley, you might consider stopping for a picnic and a leisurely stroll (30-45min.). Orchids, hibiscus, and the rare *nanu* (Hawaiian gardenia) are just some of the blossoms that grow along the garden paths that wind across a small bridge, around a small pond, and past a lovely gazebo. In the adjacent greenhouse, exotic plants are for sale, all of which come with a certificate stamping them airline-approved (though a shipping service is available for purchasers from the mainland, Puerto Rico, and Guam). *(200 Iao Valley Rd. ☎808-244-3085; www.tropicalgardensofmaui.com. Open M-Sa 9am-5pm; last entrance 3:15pm. $5, under 8 free.)*

KAHUNA PROFILE. Half a mile past Kepaniwai Park and the Hawaii Nature Center, a sign on the right side of the road indicates the viewing point for a profile of the rock formations of Pali Eleele gorge. Hawaiians claim the profile is of a powerful ancient *kahuna* (priest), but many visitors see the face of President John F. Kennedy. Then again, there are also those who see, well, rock.

♫ ENTERTAINMENT

In Wailuku, there's a **free block party** on N. Market St. on the first Friday of every month, when discounts abound and live music filters through the street from 5-7:30pm. The **Iao Theater,** 68 N. Market St. (☎808-244-8680; www.mauionstage. com), in Wailuku, and the **Maui Arts and Cultural Center (MACC),** 1 Cameron Way (☎808-242-2787; www.mauiarts.org), off Kahului Beach Rd., both host live performances. The latter attracts international stars as well as local artists.

 APPLAUSE APPLAUSE. If it's a Monday evening in Wailuku and you hear laughter filtering out of the historic Iao Theater, don't worry—it's not the voices in your head. Rather, you've stumbled across one of Maui's best-kept secrets: **Bare Essential Theater (B.E.T.).** Presented by **Maui OnStage (MOS)** on the second Monday evening of each month, B.E.T. sees some of the island's best actors performing on the bare stage, scripts in hand and ready to bare their souls. The community event is free and open to the public.

The two movie theaters in Kahului are both off Kaahumanu Ave.: the **Maui Mall Megaplex Cinemas,** 70 E. Kaahumanu Ave. (☎808-871-6684; $9.50, seniors and children $6.50, matinee $7), in the Maui Mall, and the **Kaahumanu 6 Theaters,** 275 W. Kaahumanu Ave. (☎808-873-3137; $9.50, children $6.25, seniors $6, matinee $6.75), in the Queen Kaahumanu Center. The **⬛Maui Film Festival** screens art films at the **Castle Theater** at the MACC, with live music and food before and after the first screening, and also at the **McCoy Theater.** Showtimes vary; call for an updated schedule. (☎808-572-3456; www.mauifilmfestival.com. Screenings 5 and 7:30pm. $12.) Sometimes there is free entertainment at the **Queen Kaahumanu Center;** call ☎808-877-4325 for details. Wailuku is home to the **Maui Bowling Center,** 1976 Vineyard St., just south of Market St. Get your roll on for $2.50 a game. (☎808-244-4596. Shoe rental $1. Open bowling M-F noon-4:30pm.)

▢ SHOPPING

Almost every major shopping chain has a store in Kahului. The town's highways are more like strip malls, and within a few miles' radius, shoppers can locate practically anything they forgot to bring from home. The **Maui Swap Meet,** on Puunene Ave. next to the Kahului post office, is Maui's biggest flea market and the place to buy amazing local produce and Hawaiian clothing and jewelry or to simply peruse the giant junk sale. (☎808-877-3100. Open Sa 7am-noon. Admission $0.50.) For over 25 years, **Maui Tropix,** North Main Street and Market Street in Wailuku are lined with antique stores, galleries, hair salons, pawn shops, and bookstores.

▨ Requests, 10 N. Market St. (☎808-244-9315), at the corner of Market and Main St., can easily fill a rainy afternoon for music lovers. This secondhand music store has an impressive selection of new and used DVDs and CDs ($8 and up, 3 for $20, 4 for $25), from hard-to-find indie labels to rows of reggae. There are tons of $2 vinyls in the frenzied basement. Open daily 10am-6pm. AmEx/MC/V.

Bohemia Boutique, 105 N. Market St. (☎808-244-9994), at the corner of Market and Vineyard St. This vintage couture and contemporary consignment shop offers fantastic prices on clothes, shoes, bathing suits, and accessories. All items are organized by color, and you can find everything from red cocktail dresses ($60) to lavender jeans ($9). Open M-F 10am-5pm, Sa 11am-4pm.

Beads of Paradise, 1930 Vineyard St.(☎808-242-8317), offers beads of every color, size, and shape and on-site jewelry-making. Open M-F 10am-5pm, Sa 10am-4pm.

Maui Tropix, 261 Dairy Rd. (☎808-871-8726) has provided the island with quality surf gear and the exclusive Maui Built brand (whose logo graces local truck bumpers). Surfboards, stickers ($1-20), T-shirts ($15-20), and sunglasses ($50 and up) are available. Open M-Sa 9am-8pm, Su 9am-6pm. AmEx/MC/V.)

SOUTH MAUI

Stretching from Maalaea to Kihei, Wailea, and Makena on the southwest slope of Haleakala Volcano, South Maui encompasses a varied region. Maalaea, the most depopulated, offers a state-of-the-art aquarium, while Kihei has expanded rapidly into a lively 6 mi. strip of condos and touristy restaurants. Past Kihei, the ritzy resorts of Wailea occupy the best beachfront property. Farther down in Makena, you'll find the most impressive beaches, with dramatic cliffs, sandy shores, and views of Kahoolawe and Molokini across the water. Beyond Makena, the paved road morphs into an ancient path, winding past lava fields and coves swimming with fish. Despite a steady breeze, South Maui is hotter than the rest of the island—to escape the heat, visit between December and April. In addition to the more pleasant weather, it's also whale-watching season, when hundreds of humpback whales migrate to Hawaii's coastal waters to breed.

MAALAEA

This unassuming seaport is a swell place for any fan of life under the sea to spend the afternoon. Famed for the legendary Maalaea Pipeline and its winter population of visiting whales, the majority of Maalaea (pop. 475) is concentrated in Maalaea Harbor Village, a complex off Rte. 30 between Lahaina and Kihei. Maui's **Coast Guard Station,** 233 Maalaea Rd. (☎808-986-0023 for business; ☎808-244-5256 for emergencies) stands watch over the bay's rocky waters.

🚺 FOOD

A recent bout of construction has brought several new dining options to Maalaea locals and visitors, permitting the Maalaea Harbor Village to expand its bragging rights beyond the generic clothing shops, candle factory, and whaler's general store that otherwise mark the area

🍪 **Hula Homemade Cookies and Ice Cream** (☎808- 243-2271; www.hulacookies.com), at Maalaea Harbor Village. Serving gourmet ice cream since 1932. Contemporary patrons can satisfy their sweet tooth here with shave ice ($4), smoothies ($5), milkshakes ($6), and impossibly scrumptious-looking ice-cream sandwiches ($5). Buy 3 cookies in store ($1.25 each), and get one free. Try Hula's Delight (morsels of mango and pineapple with ground coconut and macadamia nuts), or take home a tub of Hula Dough To Go ($11). Open M-Sa 10am-6pm, Su 10am-5pm. AmEx/MC/V. ❶

🍴 **Buzz's Wharf Restaurant** (☎808-244-3426; www.buzzswharf.com), at the Maalaea Harbor. Handed down the family tree since its doors opened in 1967, Buzz's delivers American cuisine with island flavor. An abundance of windows offers a pristine harbor view and the locale's homegrown style permeates every detail. The house specialty is beer-battered fish and/or shrimp and chips ($14), but try the macadamia chicken sandwich ($16) for an earthbound treat. Draft pints $6. Live local entertainment Th-Sa. Open 11am-9pm daily. AmEx/D/MC/V. ❸

Aloha Cafe and Deli (☎808-249-2708), at Maalaea Harbor Village. This petite, animated enterprise offers everything from chili ($3.60) to subs ($7) and salads ($6), but passersby mostly stop in for the freshly made smoothies and juicy Chicago-style hot dogs (both $5-6). Breakfast is served all day, and a 16 oz. order of iced coffee is only $1.89. ATM and Internet access available. Open daily 6am-6pm. MC/V. ➊

🌊 BEACHES

The narrow sands of **Sugar Beach** line Rte. 30, running from Haycraft Park (open daily 7am-7pm) to South Kihei. However, the current here is quite rough, and better swimming can be found farther south. When the surf is up, experienced surfers and bodyboarders rip the swells that roll unobstructed into **Maalaea Harbor;** you can watch them from behind the Harbor Village.

🏄 ACTIVITIES

In the port behind the Harbor Village, there are a number of boats that run **snorkel** trips to Molokini, as well as **sunset cruises, fishing expeditions,** and seasonal **dolphin- and whale-watching trips.** Several different companies run boats, all of which are represented in the activity kiosk in Maalaea Harbor Village. Prices vary based on the number of passengers, the length of trip, and the food and drink served. Open bar boats can adopt a frat-party feel; if you don't intend to drink, your money might be better spent elsewhere.

🐋 **Pacific Whale Foundation** (☎808-249-8811; www. pacificwhale.org), at Maalaea Harbor Village. Known for their eco-friendly and educational tours, this nonprofit organization, dedicated to marine research and conservation, runs several year-round trips led by certified naturalists. Includes toothed whale and wild dolphin tours. In addition, they organize stargazing and full moon cruises, a fireworks boat ride on July 4th ($78), and an adopt-a-whale program ($35). As well as the location in the Maalaea Harbor Village, the foundation has several other branches throughout Maui. Pacific Whale also offers volunteer programs; for more information, see **Beyond Tourism,** p. 67. AmEx/D/MC/V.

🐋 **Maui Ocean Center,** 192 Maalaea Rd. (☎808-270-0000; www.mauioceancenter.com). This indoor/outdoor aquarium showcases the bewildering diversity of Hawaii's marine life. Although the admission price is a bit steep, the fish don't disappoint. In fact, many of the beautiful and bizarre species displayed can only be found in local waters. The Shark Dive program allows certified scuba divers to actually dive in the 750,000-gallon tank and enjoy the fish, sharks, and stingrays first hand. Interactive displays, like the Touch Pool and the Marine Mammal Center, entertain small children, while the placards beside them aim to edu-

THE ENDEMIC EPIDEMIC

The main attraction in quiet Maalaea is the **Maui Ocean Center** (p. 289), where visitors can experience an aquarium with a very Hawaiian twist. Eye-popping exhibits in cool cobalt rooms entertain, and explain not only *'iliholoikauaua, nai'a,* and *kohala* (monk seals, dolphins, and humpback whales), but also detail historic Hawaiian aquaculture.

While displays on torch fishing, *kapu,* and netweaving elucidate how ancestral Hawaiians were sustained by the sea, the most fascinating phenomenon discussed is Hawaii's endemic explosion. Worldwide, 18% of algae species, 20% of sea stars, and 40% of snapping shrimp are found only in Hawaiian waters. These creatures, known as endemic species, combine with other marine life to make the 50th state's coastlines more endemic than any other tropical marine area.

How did this happen exactly? The region's strong currents and abundant sunlight easily support the growth of *limu* (seaweed), a crucial food source for many of the pioneer fishes that floated here off of ocean currents from the western Pacific. Many of Hawaii's endemic fishes are similar to their western cousins, but as mutations occur more quickly within these smaller populations, they are different enough to be considered separate species.

cate all visitors. Open daily Sept.-June 9am-5pm; July-Aug. 9am-6pm. $24, seniors $21, ages 3-12 $17. ATM on-site. AmEx/D/MC/V.

KIHEI

Cruising the busy Kihei strip, it's hard to believe that 50 years ago Kihei (pop. 18,981) was just a small town on an unpaved road. In the last decade, Kihei ranked among the fastest-growing towns in America. While some consider Kihei, with its traffic and noise, the least attractive of Maui's cities, others enjoy a vacation made affordable by the town's condos, takeout tacos, and cheap drink deals. If you do choose to stay in Kihei, reserve a place in advance. Make sure you find time to leave, too—the best beaches lie to the south.

▰ ▇ ORIENTATION AND PRACTICAL INFORMATION

Kihei sprawls along the southwest shore of the Haleakala volcano, which gradually rises above the condos and hotels on the *mauka* (mountain) side. **South Kihei Road** travels along the coast, studded with traffic lights, craft fairs, and shopping centers. Since cars move slowly here most of the day, the inland **Route 31 (Piilani Highway),** which runs all the way to Makena, is a smart alternative.

TOURIST AND FINANCIAL SERVICES

Tourist Information: Maui Information and Visitors Center (☎808-874-4919) offers a personal concierge service, making reservations for car rental, accommodations, activities, etc. free of charge. The very friendly center takes calls daily 8am-8pm.

Banks: Banks and **24hr. ATMs** dot both S. Kihei Rd. and Piilani Hwy. **American Savings Bank,** 1215 S. Kihei Rd. (☎808-879-1977), in Longs Shopping Center. Open M-F 9am-6pm, Sa 9am-1pm. **Bank of Hawaii** (☎888-643-3888), in Azeka Mauka. Open M-Th 8:30am-4pm, F 8:30am-6pm. **First Hawaiian Bank** (☎808-875-0055; www.fhb.com), in the Lipoa Center. Open M-Th 8:30am-4pm, F 8:30am-6pm, Sa 9am-1pm.

LOCAL SERVICES

Library: Kihei Public Library, 35 Waimahaihai St. (☎808-875-6833), across from Kukui Mall, behind the fire station. Unlimited **Internet access** with the purchase of a 3-month visitor's card ($10). Open Tu noon-8pm, W-Sa 10am-5pm. Copies $0.20 per page.

Laundromat: Lipoa Laundry Center, 41 E. Lipoa St. (☎808-875-9266), in Lipoa Center. Wash $2, dry $0.25 per 5min. Change machine. Open M-Sa 8am-9pm (last wash 8pm), Su 8am-5pm (last wash 4pm).

Surf Conditions: High Tech Surf Report (☎808-877-3611).

EMERGENCY AND COMMUNICATIONS

Police: (Non-emergency ☎808-244-6400.) Next to Foodland in the Kihei Town Center. Office open M-F 7:45am-4:30pm.

Pharmacy: Longs Drugs, 1215 S. Kihei Rd. (☎808-879-2259), in Longs Shopping Center. Open daily 7am-midnight, pharmacy open M 8am-7pm, Tu-F 8am-6pm, Sa-Su 8am-5pm. There is also a standalone **Longs Pharmacy** (☎808-879-8499) in Lipoa Center. Open M-F 8am-1pm and 1:45-6:30pm, Sa 8am-1pm.

Medical Services: Kihei-Wailea Medical Center, 221 Piikea Ave. (☎808-874-8100), in the Piilani Village Shopping Center. Open M-F 8am-8pm, Sa-Su 8am-5pm.

Copy and Fax Services: Mail Boxes Etc., 1215 S. Kihei Rd. (☎808-874-5556), in Longs Shopping Center. M-F 8:30am-5:30pm, Sa 9am-3pm. AmEx/D/MC/V.

Internet Access: The Coffee Store, 1279 S. Kihei Rd. (☎808-875-4244), in Azeka Mauka. $0.20 per min. Min. $2 (cash) or $5 (credit card). Open M-Sa 6:30am-6pm, Su 6:30am-5pm. AmEx/MC/V. There's also **Hale Imua Internet Stop,** 2463 S. Kihei Rd. (☎808-891-9219; www.haleimua. com), in Kamaole Shopping Center. $0.10 per min. Min. 10min. Wi-Fi access available for computers within 300 ft. of shop for $10 per day. Also offers computer repair. Open daily 8am-9pm. AmEx/MC/V.

Post Office: 1254 S. Kihei Rd. (☎808-879-1987), next to Azeka Makai. Open M-F 8:30am-4:30pm, Sa 9am-1pm. **Postal Code:** 96753.

ACCOMMODATIONS

Without any hostels or campsites, accommodations in Kihei are in the higher price ranges—garden-variety condominiums abound. However, many places do have price breaks for stays of a week or more. A stay at a B&B is a good alternative to the condo scene, although advance reservations are essential.

BED AND BREAKFASTS

B&Bs are typically located in residential neighborhoods close to the Kihei restaurants and beaches, but a world away from the clamor. Linda Little, of **Affordable Accommodations** (☎808-879-7865 or 888-333-9747), books cottages, B&Bs, condos, and vacation homes for no fee.

Kai's Bed & Breakfast, 80 E. Welaka-hao Rd. (☎808-874-6431; www.mauibb.com), off the *mauka* (mountain) side of S. Kihei Rd. Each of the 3 suites and 2-bedroom garden cottage have cable TV, microwave, and refrigerator making for a comfortable home away from home. Breakfast included. Beach chairs, bodyboards, snorkel gear, bicycles, garden hot tub, and washer/dryer are available. No children. Check-in 2pm. Check-out 10am. 4- to 7-night min. Reserve with 50% deposit at least 2 months

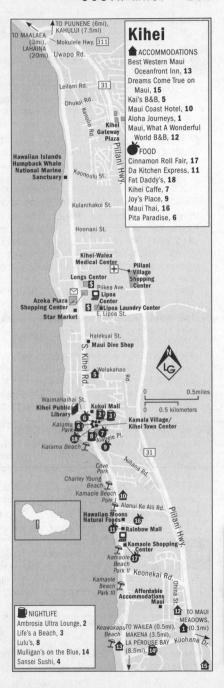

Kihei

ACCOMMODATIONS
Best Western Maui Oceanfront Inn, **13**
Dreams Come True on Maui, **15**
Kai's B&B, **5**
Maui Coast Hotel, **10**
Aloha Journeys, **1**
Maui, What A Wonderful World B&B, **12**

FOOD
Cinnamon Roll Fair, **17**
Da Kitchen Express, **11**
Fat Daddy's, **18**
Kihei Caffe, **7**
Joy's Place, **9**
Maui Thai, **16**
Pita Paradise, **6**

TO PUUNENE (6mi), KAHULUI (7.5mi)
TO MAALAEA (3mi), LAHAINA (20mi)

Mokulele Hwy. 311
Uwapo Rd.
Leilani Rd. 31
Ohukai Rd.
Kenolio Rd.
Kihei Gateway Plaza
Piilani Hwy.
Hawaiian Islands Humpback Whale National Marine Sanctuary
Kaonoulu St.
Kulanihakoi St.
Hoonani St.
Kihei-Walea Medical Center
Piilani Village Shopping Center
Longs Center
Piikea Ave.
Lipoa Center
Azeka Plaza Shopping Center
Lipoa Laundry Center
E. Lipoa St.
Star Market
Halekuai St.
Maui Dive Shop
S. Kihei Rd.
Welakahao
Welakahao Rd.
N
LG
0   0.5miles
0   0.5 kilometers
Waimahaihai St.
Kihei Public Library
Kukui Mall
Kamala Park
Kalama Beach
Alanele Pl.
Kamala Village/ Kihei Town Center
Cove Park
Charley Young Beach
Kamaole Beach Park I
Auhana Rd.
31
Alanui Ke Alii Rd.
Hawaiian Moons Natural Foods
Rainbow Mall
Kamaole Shopping Center
Kamaole Beach Park II
Keonekai Rd.
Kamaole Beach Park III
Affordable Accommodations Maui
Ohina St.
Kilohana Dr.
TO MAUI MEADOWS, (0.1mi)
Keawakapu Beach
TO WAILEA (0.5mi), MAKENA (3.5mi), LA PEROUSE BAY (8.5mi)

ahead in low season, earlier for high season; balance due 30 days before arrival. Rooms $85-125; $575-850 per week. AmEx/MC/V. ❸

NO PLACE LIKE HOME. Many Maui homeowners will rent rooms; check local newspapers for listings. These unofficial B&Bs are a fine last resort if everything else is booked. Still, despite the popularity of these unregistered B&Bs, they are not always safe and you should be especially careful in choosing one of these establishments.

Aloha Journeys (☎808-875-4840; www.alohajourneys.com), in Maui Meadows. A 3-bedroom Polynesian style home overlooking lava pools, waterfalls, and a garden of tropical fruit trees. All rooms have TV/VCR, stereo, and bathroom. Guests can borrow snorkel or beach gear and have access to kitchen, laundry, outdoor grill, and hot tubs. $200 cleaning fee. You learn the address upon reservation. Check-in 3pm. Check-out 10am. 7-night min. 50% deposit. Rooms $350-420. MC/V. ❺

Dreams Come True on Maui, 3259 Akala Dr. (☎808-879-7099; www.dreamscometrueonmaui.com), from Piilani Hwy., turn left on Mapu Pl., and then right on Akala Dr. 2 suites with kitchenettes, *lanai*, and breakfast included. A cottage has full kitchen, private carport, computer, TV/VCR, and washer/dryer. An 8ft. movie screen dominates the common room, where an additional computer is available to all guests. Beach and snorkel gear for loan. No children under 12. Suites 3-night min.; cottage 6-night min. Check-in 3pm. Check-out 11am. $200 deposit, balance due 40 days before arrival. Suites $90-110; cottage $170 in high season, $135 in low season. MC/V. ❸

Maui, What a Wonderful World Bed and Breakfast, 2828 Umalu Pl. (☎800-973-5804; www.amauibedandbreakfast.com), from Piilani Hwy., turn left on Keonekai Rd. and then left on Ohina St. Turn left on Alaume St., and the lodgings will be on the right-hand corner of Umalu Pl. The 4 suites in this friendly B&B all have their own entrance, bathroom, cable TV, and A/C; 2 have a kitchenette and 1 a full kitchen. Continental breakfast served in the common area or on the breezy *lanai*. Free laundry, Wi-Fi, and access to beach equipment. Check-in 4pm. Check-out noon. Reserve 2-3 months ahead with 50% deposit. 1-bedroom $89-110; suites $110-150. MC/V. ❸

CONDO RESERVATION SERVICES

If staying in Kihei for more than a few days, condos are your best bet. However, in addition to the price of a room, be prepared to pay the 11.42% tax on accommodations and the fee or commission charged by the booking service.

AA Oceanfront Condo Rentals, 1279 S. Kihei Rd. Ste. 107 (☎800-488-6004; www.aaoceanfront.com). From $90 per night. Reservation fee $30.

Affordable Accommodations Maui, 2825 Kauhale St. (☎888-333-9747 or 808-879-7865; www.affordablemaui.com). From $90 per night. No fee.

FILL 'ER UP. Still haven't found an affordable place to stay in South Maui? Check the listings at **www.vrbo.com** for last-minute specials. Condo life in Kihei can be expensive, but many condo owners offer "filler rentals" in between longer bookings. These gap-closers free you from minimum-stay requirements and will often eliminate the cleaning fee as well.

HOTELS

There are few hotels in Kihei, but they offer an alternative to the minimum stay and cleaning fees that condominiums usually require.

■ **Best Western Maui Oceanfront Inn,** 2980 S. Kihei Rd. (☎808-879-7744; www.maui-oceanfrontinn.com). With the best beach location in Kihei and reasonable prices, the Maui Oceanfront is a great choice. Each unit has a queen-size bed, A/C, TV, coffee maker, and fridge. Check-in 3pm. Check-out 11am. Reserve with credit card; 3-day cancellation policy. Standard rates start at $199, but walk-in specials can bring prices down to $99-139. Suites $275. AmEx/D/MC/V. ❺

Maui Coast Hotel, 2259 S. Kihei Rd. (☎808-874-6284; www.mauicoasthotel.com), across the street from Kamaole Park I. Fitness center, pool, tennis courts, 2 outdoor hot tubs, and activity desk. The 265 rooms all have A/C, *lanai,* cable TV, mini-fridge, and coffee maker. Live pool-side entertainment nightly and free shuttle for guests. Check-in 3pm. Check-out noon. Dec. 21-Mar. 31 reserve with 2-night deposit; 7-day cancellation policy. Apr. 1-Dec. 20, reserve with 1-night deposit; 3-day cancellation policy. Double $165-175; suites $190-225. Credit card required. AmEx/D/MC/V. ❺

◪ FOOD

Kihei restaurants run the gamut from fast food to fine cuisine, though it can be hard to find a good value. There are several supermarkets in the shopping centers on S. Kihei Rd., including a 24hr. **Foodland,** (☎808-879-9350) in the Kihei Town Center; a 24hr. **Safeway,** (☎808-891-9120) in the Piilani Village Center; and a 24hr. **StarMarket,** at Lipoa St. The hot bar at **Hawaiian Moons Natural Foods,** 2411 S. Kihei Rd., has healthy takeout meals and organic salads that you can enjoy at the beach across the street. (☎808-875-4356. Open M-Sa 8am-9pm, Su 8am-7pm. AmEx/D/MC/V.) **Aloha Discount Liquors,** 2439 S. Kihei Rd., in the Rainbow Mall, is your best bet for cheap beer, wine, and liquor. (☎808-874-8882. Open daily 10am-10:50pm. AmEx/MC/V.)

■ **Kihei Caffe,** 1945 S. Kihei Rd. (☎808-879-2230), across from Kalama Park. Serves fresh Kona coffee and breakfast classics for $10 or less, including French toast, 2 eggs with bacon, home fries, and the Papaya Delight (papaya filled with yogurt, granola, and raisins; $5). Quick service eggs for $1, and teddy bear and whale-shaped pancakes make this the busiest breakfast place in Kihei. Lunch salads, sandwiches, and burgers around $7. Open daily 5am-2pm. Cash only. ❶

Cinnamon Roll Fair, 2463 S. Kihei Rd. (☎808-879-5177), in the Kamaole Shopping Ctr. If only to get a waft of its incredible aroma, make sure to drop by this Kihei bakery. It's takeout for the most part (there are some scattered outdoor tables), but the smoothies ($4) and the gooey homemade cinnamon rolls ($4) are not to be missed. Buy 5 rolls, get 1 free. Open M-F 6am-7pm, Sa-Su 6am-5pm. Cash only. ❶

Pita Paradise, 1913 S. Kihei Rd. (☎808-875-7679), in the Kihei Kalama Village. Gyros, kabobs, wraps, salads, and pitas ($9-16) are staples at this relaxing Mediterranean-style cafe. Greek salad (large $7.50), veggie plates (includes salad, hummus, grilled pita, two falafels, and roasted red potatoes; $14), and homemade baklava ice cream cake ($6). Takeout available. Open 11am-9:30pm. MC/V. ❸

Maui Thai, 2439 S. Kihei Rd. (☎808-874-5605; www.mauithai.com). This simple Thai joint may be slightly out-of-the-way, but its savory, cheap dishes are worth the hunt. Serving nontraditional as well as truly Thai fare, its local following is easily understood once you sample the green papaya salad ($8) or the evil prince chicken ($11). Vegetarian options surpass the normal offerings, putting the tofu substitutions of other establishments to shame. Open M-F 11am-2:30pm, daily 5-9:30pm. ❷

Fat Daddy's, 1913 S. Kihei Rd. (☎808-879-8711; www.fatdaddysmaui.com), in the Kihei Kalama Village. After hitting the surf or working on your tan, stop in this small, stylish smokehouse and chow down on a heaping plate of ribs (with two sides $10), brisket ($12), smoked brats ($12), or chili with "the works" ($7.50). On your way out, cleanse your palate with a slushie ($3) or a slice of the tart homemade key lime pie

LOCAL LEGEND

OFF WITH HER HEAD

Once you set foot on Maui, activity centers will barrage you with glossy brochures promising dazzling snorkeling excursions to Molokini Crater, a small crescent-shaped island halfway between Maui and Kahoolawe. Most, however, neglect to tell you the star-crossed history of Little Miss Molokini herself.

Of the many legends surrounding the island, the most famous paints her as the romantic rival of Pele, goddess of fire. So filled with jealousy of her foe was she that Pele cut Molokini in half and turned her to stone. Locals claim that her head was transformed into Puu Olai, the cinder cone between Big and Little Beach. Her torso then became the island guarding the brimming bay that so many tourists now explore.

Even today, the marks of Pele's voodoo stand true. As she is a government-protected bird sanctuary, no one may ever touch Molokini again. So, as you jump in the gently flapping waters of her crater basin—snorkel in hand, fins afoot, face-to-face with enormous turtles, gorgeous humpback whales, vibrant fish, and coral reef—make sure to treat her with respect.

Several activity centers book snorkel trips to Molokini: Maui Dive Shop runs trips from Kihei Boat Harbor (☎808-879-3388; $60) and the Pacific Whale Foundation runs out of Maalaea Harbor (☎808-249-8811; $80, reserve 4-5 days in advance).

($4). *Keiki* (kids) sandwiches are only $5.50. Open M-Sa 11:30am-9pm, Su 4-9pm. MC/V. ❷

Da Kitchen Express, 2439 S. Kihei Rd. (☎808-875-7782), in the Rainbow Mall. This no-frills restaurant sells cheap, freshly prepared food. Try the Hawaiian Plate smorgasbord (pork *lau lau, kalua* pork, chicken long rice, and *lomi* salmon; $12), or the classic *loco moco* ($10), both served with rice and mac salad. Breakfast omelets ($7-10) and sweetbread french toast ($7). Open daily 9am-9pm. AmEx/D/MC/V. ❷

Joy's Place, 1993 S. Kihei Rd. (☎808-879-9258), in the Island Surf Shops Building. Tan, fit women and crunchy, granola types flock to Joy's, where organic, wholesome eating is a way of life. Plenty of vegan options include organic sandwiches, salads, and wraps ($8-11). Mostly takeout, but a glossy white counter space is available. If you like what you eat, speak to the owner, as cooking classes are offered. Open M-Sa 10am-3pm. ❷

🏖 BEACHES

The sandy expanse between Maalaea and Makena is one long beach broken up by lava formations. The North Kihei beaches are popular for windsurfing and sailing; beaches farther south are better suited for swimming. **Kalama Beach Park** is popular with skaters and has tennis courts and sports fields. Volleyball courts, picnic tables, and restrooms are scattered throughout the long park, while the southern edge is the best place to swim. South of Kalama, **Charley Young Beach** is a large stretch of sand around volcanic rock, usually filled with sunbathers and fishing poles. All the **Kamaole Beach Parks (I, II, and III)** have showers, lifeguards, and beautiful golden sand; Kam. II and III are set farther from the road than Kam. I and have some shaded areas. All have small parking lots and some parking on the streets. **Keawakapu Beach,** past Kam. III, is usually uncrowded and may be worth the walk, although there are no facilities (parking is past the Maui Oceanfront Inn, in a lot on the right). More beaches can be found farther south, in **Wailea** (p. 297) and **Makena** (p. 298).

🎿 ACTIVITIES

SNORKELING. With over 450 different fish, 25% of which are found only in Hawaii (and 20% of those only in Molokini!), Maui is a can't-miss snorkeling experience. Nearly every beach has lava rocks that jut into the sea where fish gather. **Kamaole Beach Parks (I, II, and III)** are great for novices. In Wailea, **Ulua Beach** (p. 297) has a rocky point and a reef that extends farther out. **Ahihi Bay** (p. 299) is a marine life preserve where fishing is prohibited, making it spectacular for snorkeling. Two miles past Ahihi Bay, the fish preserve at **La Pérouse Bay** (p. 299) is best suited for advanced snorkelers. If you get there early (around 5:30am) you may see a pod of dolphins, though by law you must keep 50 ft. away. Several companies run snorkel trips to Molokini and Turtle Arches, including the eco-friendly 🐋**Pacific Whale Foundation** (p. 289) and the **Maui Dive Shop** (p. 295), both of which include gear. Kihei has plenty of purveyors of snorkel gear, the most ubiquitous being **Boss Frog's,** 2395 S. Kihei Rd. (☎808-875-4477. $8 per day. Rx mask $10. $20-30 per week.)

 THE EARLY BIRD CATCHES THE FISH. When booking or setting out on a snorkeling expedition, keep in mind that earlier is better. Afternoon trips are often plagued by rocky waters. Four out of seven days, tours experience rough water as noon approaches, and you may find yourself sailing out to that special fin-filled spot only to have to turn around upon arrival.

SCUBA DIVING. Sea conditions change daily and, as a result, so do the best diving spots. Several dive shops on Kihei Rd. are more than willing to give advice; most shops that offer excursions plan their itineraries on a daily basis. Many companies also rent gear and offer certification classes. 🐋**Maui Dive Shop,** in the Kamaole Shopping Center and at 1455 S. Kihei Rd., offers basic certification ($350-400), 2-tank dives ($140-150), advanced classes, combination packages for gear and charters, and other activities (helicopter trips, Haleakala bike rides, etc.) with a smile. (☎808-879-3388; www.mauidiveshop.com. **Dive and Sea Maui,** runs 2-tank dives every day and charter tours. (☎808-874-1952. Dives include equipment, lunch, and drinks; trips leave around 7:30am and return around 12:30pm. $130 if certified, $140 with gear. AmEx/MC/V.)

SURFING AND BODYBOARDING. Summer is the season for South Shore surfing, but even then the big waves don't come every day—ask a local surfer or call the **High Tech Surf Report** (☎808-877-3611). Many places along Kihei rent surfboards (approx. $20 per day) and bodyboards (approx. $15 per wk.), although most surf schools operate out of Lahaina (p. 268). Beginner lessons are sometimes taught at **Cove Park,** the best spot in Kihei to dip your feet in the water and watch both *keikis* (kids) and the older crowd tackle the break. To get there, turn down Iliili Rd. on the *makai* (ocean) side of S. Kihei Rd. Open 7am-8pm.

KAYAKING. The Ahihi Bay fish preserve, between Makena and La Pérouse Bay, is a popular kayak and snorkel destination. Many companies also head to Makena Landing, but locations change depending on wind conditions. **Maui Eco-Adventures** (☎808-891-2223; www.mauiecotours.com) gives 3 and 4hr. guided tours starting at $74 (lunch and gear included). **South Pacific Kayaks and Outfitters** (☎808-875-4848) leads 2 and 4 mi. tours starting at $65 per person and rents kayaks (singles $40 per day, doubles $60). Reserve rental kayaks—previous experience required—a day in advance. Pickup is at 7am at Makena Landing and the rental lasts until noon. MC/V accepted for tours, cash only for rentals.

HORSEBACK RIDING. Forgo the crowded beaches and tourist traps of Kihei, and enjoy South Maui's beauty via horseback. **Makena Stables** (☎808-879-0244; www.makenastables.com) offers both an early morning and a sunset ride. Experienced local guides take you through the slopes of Ulupalakua Ranch to Kalua O Lapa, providing incredible views of La Pérouse Bay and the expansive lava flows. Rides are around 3hr., and groups are limited to six. Ages 13+. Morning rides leave around 8am, and sunset rides start around 3:45pm. Morning rides are $145, and sunset rides are $170. Private tours are available. The stables are located at the end of Makena Alanui Rd., which goes through Makena State Park and the Ahihi-Kinau Reserve. MC/V.

WHALE WATCHING. In South Maui, from December to April, you can see whales wherever you can see the ocean, and you can hear them anywhere you stick your head underwater. The **Maui Ocean Center** (p. 289) in Maalaea, the **Whale Observatory** near Kaleolepo Park off S. Kihei Rd., and any of the hotels in Wailea make especially good whale-watching sites. Whale-watching cruises are a fun and educational means of getting closer to these marine marvels (try ⊠**Pacific Whale Foundation,** p. 289, our eco-friendly favorite).

To learn more about these creatures, stop by the **Hawaiian Islands Humpback Whale National Marine Sanctuary,** 726 S. Kihei Rd. (☎808-879-2818; www.hihwnms.nos.noaa.gov), just south of Kaonoulu St. on the *makai* (ocean) side of the road. This free educational center is managed through a partnership between the State of Hawaii and the **National Oceanic Atmospheric Administration (NOAA)** to educate the public about humpback whales and their habitat around the islands. At the sanctuary, you'll find friendly volunteers, colorful displays about whales, and free brochures. Open M-F 10am-3pm. Free.

WELL ALE BE. If you have a tendency to get seasick and are planning to engage in activities that may instigate such a predisposition, make certain to avoid any Vitamin C-laden foods and beverages, like OJ. Instead, reach for some **ginger**—be it in pill, ale, or root form. You will feel refreshed instantly.

NIGHTLIFE

While Maui lacks the wilder nightlife of Oahu, it does have several nightlife bright spots, with Kihei arguably being the brightest. Throughout the week, vacationers will find a bustle in Kihei Kalama Village, a small but happening area with several bars. Pick up a free copy of Thursday's *Maui Time Weekly;* its nightly entertainment listings will point fun-seekers in the right direction.

 Lulu's, 1945 S. Kihei Rd. (☎808-879-9944; www.lulusmaui.com) in Kihei Kalama Village. Lulu's is Kihei's most dynamic nightlife venue: the elviki-tiki decor is vivid, the bartenders are outgoing, and the drinks flowing. An open patio fronts the large 2nd-story space, with couches and a pool table in back. Several TVs show various sports. Priding itself on "red carpet service at shag rug prices," Lulu's offers food, live music, and creations like the Big Lush ($4), Big Sweaty's BBQ Pit ($20), and the Dick Butkus burger (with peanut butter, $10). Happy hour 3-6pm (drafts, Mai Tais, and mixed drinks $3). Power hour 11pm-2am. Food served until 11pm. Open daily 11am-2am. D/MC/V.

Mulligan's on the Blue, 100 Kaukahi St. (☎808-874-1131), at the Wailea Golf Club Blue Course. This sleek hilltop retreat is the only Irish pub in Maui: the perfect place to savor a Guinness and a gorgeous view of the ocean. Drafts $6. Su night brings the Celtic Tigers, a toe-tapping Irish fiddle band. Happy hour 4-6pm and 10pm-midnight ($1 off drinks, *pupu* (appetizers) $2-3). Open daily 8am-1:30am. D/MC/V.

Life's A Beach, 1913 S. Kihei Rd. (☎808-891-8010), in Kihei Kalama Village. Home of the $1 Mai Tai, this drinking den fills up with an eclectic mix of hardcore bikers and surfers. Features karaoke, free Wi-Fi, and sought-after burritos. Kitchen open until midnight. Happy hour with live music 3-7pm. 21+ after 10pm. Open 11am-2am. MC/V.

Sansei Sushi, 1881 S. Kihei Rd. (☎808-879-0004; www.dkrestaurants.com), in the Kihei Town Center. Sansei's popularity is well deserved—the sushi is exceptional! The *maki* rolls are creatively assembled into caterpillars, 69s, and pink Cadillacs ($8), and the cooked noodles and entrees ($16-24) infuse local produce with Japanese flavor. An informative sake and wine list will help you pair your meal with the perfect beverage. More importantly, the elegant setting and *ono* (delicious) food comes cheapest late at night (Th-Sa 10pm-2am), with ◪**50% off** sushi and *pupu* (appetizers), $1 off drafts, and free 21+ karaoke. Open M and Su 5-10pm, Tu-W 5:30-10pm, Th-Sa 5:30pm-2am. 25% off Tu-Sa 5:30-6pm; early-bird special M and Su 5-6pm. AmEx/MC/V.

WAILEA

"Affordable paradise" is not the first thing that comes to mind driving along the impeccably landscaped Wailea Alanui Dr. However, while world-class golf courses line one side of the road and five-star resorts the other, everyone can take advantage of the beautiful beaches of Wailea ("ocean star" in Hawaiian), even if they can't afford the $200+ price tag. Our advice: check out the beaches but keep the food and accommodation spending to Kihei. Wailea is also home to the annual ◪**Maui Film Festival**, a weekend-long event in June with outdoor screenings on the lush grass of the area's many golf resorts. The festival organization (☎808-579-9244; www.mauifilmfestival.com) holds events throughout the year across Maui and also provides volunteer opportunities.

▐ FOOD

If you want to splurge on a gourmet beach picnic, head to **Caffe Ciao ❷**, behind the adult pool in the Fairmont Kea Lani hotel. This boutique grocer sells sandwiches ($9.50), high-end wine, cheese, pastries, and delicious desserts. They also make custom picnic baskets great for roadtrips to other parts of the island. (☎808-875-2225. Open 6:30am-10pm. AmEx/MC/V.) There are also a number of fine dining options within the **Shops at Wailea**, 3750 Wailea Alanui Dr. (☎808-891-6770; www.shopsatwailea.com), a collection of expensive specialty shops and restaurants in the middle of Wailea's resorts.

▐ BEACHES

There are five main beaches in Wailea, each occupying a crescent of soft sand bordered by outcroppings of volcanic rock.

KEAWAKAPU BEACH. *(Open daily 7am-7pm.)* The mile-long strand of Keawakapu stretches between Kihei and Wailea and will bring you to the lighted Wailea beach walk. Less of a scene than the Kihei beach parks, Keawakapu offers great swimming and snorkeling on an artificial reef 400 yd. offshore. Parking is available in the lot at the entrance to Wailea, on the *makai* (ocean) side of S. Kihei Rd. To enter the parking lot, make sure to follow S. Kihei Rd. to its end; don't veer left onto Okolani Dr. There is a shower at the south entrance.

MOKAPU AND ULUA BEACHES. *(Open daily 7am-7pm.)* Mokapu and Ulua are both pleasant but generally crowded with resort guests from the Renaissance Wailea Hotel. The rocky point between the beaches also provides excellent snorkeling, and a turtle cleaning station (an area where turtles congregate to get their shells cleaned by various algae-eating fish) near the reef is easily accessible by scuba diving. The entrance is south of the entrance to the Renaissance Hotel, on Halealii Pl.; parking is down the hill. Showers and restrooms available.

WAILEA BEACH. *(Open daily 7am-8pm.)* Sandwiched between the Grand Wailea Resort and the Four Seasons, Wailea Beach is the widest beach in Wailea and the most touristy. An access road between the hotels ends in a parking lot. The beach has great swimming and snorkeling along both the right and left sides. Public restrooms, picnic benches, and showers are available.

MAKENA AND BEYOND

Until very recently, Makena (pop. 5671) was entirely undeveloped. There is still only one hotel in Makena, the Maui Prince Resort, but the golf courses on the *mauka* (mountain) side of Makena Alanui (the only road) stretch ever farther south. After the Maui Prince and the last golf course, the *kiawe* tree desert resumes, and dirt roads on the *makai* (ocean) side lead to the best beaches in Maui. Past the last sandy beach, a number of mansions have sprung up, but even fancier dwellings don't detract from the area's natural rugged beauty.

🌀 BEACHES

POOLENALENA BEACH. *(Open daily 7am-7pm.)* Also known as Chang's or Paipu Beach, this is the least crowded of Makena's beaches, has ample parking space, and is a find at any time of day. Even with the windswept reddish sand and frequently strong current, the beach is a favorite among locals. You can see the Maui Prince down at the far southern end, but otherwise, the view touches on completely undeveloped land. There are showers and picnic tables but no life-guards or restrooms. Camping is not legal, and fires are also prohibited unless within the confinement of a grill or hibachi. *(After the Fairmont Kea Lani, but before the Maui Prince, 1½ mi. south of the Shops at Wailea, there is a small sign for Poolenalena Beach.)*

MAKENA LANDING (FIVE CAVES OR FIVE GRAVES). *(Open daily 7am-8pm.)* Heading south from Poolenalena, the next cove is Makena Landing. Once Maui's busiest port, its cloudy water has since rendered it a placid, though well-attended, beach. Kayaking companies often take advantage of the sheltered waters here. The Beach Park at Makena Landing has showers, restrooms, a boat-launching ramp, and good snorkeling on the south side. *(To get there, head south on Makena Alanui Rd., and then turn right on Makena Rd. for the beach, which is marked by a wooden sign.)* If you continue further down Makena Rd., you will reach the beautiful **Keawalai Church** (built in 1832 from offshore reef coral), which still holds Hawaiian-Anglo church services on Sundays at 7:30 and 10am. All are welcome.

BIG BEACH (ONELOA BEACH). *(Open daily 5:45am-7pm.)* Big Beach is part of Makena State Park. There are toilets, picnic tables, and (usually) a Jawz taco truck by the northernmost entrance. The last sandy beach for miles, Big Beach may look tempting, but its clear waters are mighty deceptive. Powerful waves break right on the shore, sweeping swimmers and bodyboarders off their feet and onto the sand at forces strong enough to break necks and backs. Swimming and bodysurfing should be exercised with caution. Camping is prohibited.

 I LIKE BIG BUTTS. Smoking at the beach? If you're under the impression that your bad habit will decompose quickly, you are sorely mistaken. Cigarette butts last 10 to 15 years and unleash toxins into the ocean. Bring a portable ashtray if you're going to light up. They're available at many local stores, or get one for free from the Pacific Whale Foundation (p. 289).

LITTLE BEACH (PUU OLAI BEACH). *(Open daily 5:45am-7pm.)* At the north end of Big Beach, beneath Puu Olai, volcanic rocks hide the short, steep trail that leads to Little Beach. A lingering hippie hangout, Little Beach is unofficially "clothing optional," though nudity is illegal on Hawaii's beaches. Beachgoers watch (and cheer) the surfers riding the break and make the beach a generally exciting place to be, whether or not you participate in the *sans*-clothing tradition. Sunday afternoons until sunset, the hippie contingent holds a drum and fire-dance circle that can be quite a spectacle for the uninitiated observer. The woods behind the northern end of the beach are commonly referred to as Naughty Pines, due to the romantic encounters of all flavors that occasionally take place in its shade. The surf at Little Beach may look choppier than at Big Beach, but it's generally safer since the waves break farther out. Nevertheless, the riptide and currents are incredibly strong—make sure someone is watching you, and signal if you feel yourself being pulled out. Camping is prohibited.

SECRET COVE (PAAKO BEACH). *(Open 24hr.)* Maui's most popular spot for beachside weddings, this photogenic cove was christened a "secret" because it's tucked away at the south end of Makena. You have to walk through a rock wall to enter; and if you can manage to get here with only a few other people on it, you've might want to consider playing the lottery. The ocean can be entered in two spots and has some fantastic snorkeling. There are no facilities and little parking; sometimes as many as four couples will be getting maui'ed at once.

ACTIVITIES

AHIHI-KINAU NATURAL AREA RESERVE. Past the last entrance to Big Beach, the road narrows to one lane and winds through the 2000-acre Ahihi-Kinau Natural Area Reserve. Since fishing is prohibited in the reserve, any calm spot along the coast makes for excellent snorkeling. As you enter the reserve, several protected coves of Ahihi Bay are visible from the road, including Ahihi Cove, which has good snorkeling but is often crowded with families. Past Ahihi Cove, the road winds inland through a lava field—the path of the flow during the last eruption of Haleakala around 1790. The area formed by the lava path is Cape Kinau, and the water around it is part of a protected reserve.

About 7 mi. from the Wailea Ike/Wailea Alanui intersection and a few hundred yards before the end of the road, a sign on the *makai* (ocean) side of the road begins the trail to the **Aquarium** (also known as "the Dumps"), where many diverse fish swim in a large, protected cove. No longer a secret but still an adventure, the trail is marked by two yellow poles and ventures through an alcove of trees until it reaches the lava formations. There is a large dirt lot where you can park, but don't leave valuables in your car. Walk about 100 yd. up to the trail. It's easy to lose the rugged path, but don't worry, local surfers abound by the Dumps area and are sure to direct any lost souls back to the right track. Make sure to turn left when the trail splits about 5min. in, and wear sturdy shoes. Since there's no sand—just rough, volcanic rock—water shoes or the equivalent will make entrance less painful. Enter the Aquarium from the southern edge to prevent damage to the reefs. Many of the inlets on the way to the Aquarium also offer good snorkeling. At the end of the road is **La Pérouse Bay**, or Keoneoio, a spot that European explorer La Pérouse "discovered" in 1786. Here visitors will find a black sand beach and a splendid ocean view.

NORTH SHORE

When the British first arrived in 1778, the lands of Hana, Kipahulu, and Kaupo were the most densely populated in Hawaii. Though hardly as bustling today, the North Shore definitely deserves a visit on a trip to Maui. Hana Hwy. begins right outside Kahului, but most travelers feel the road to Hana really begins in Paia, a town that epitomizes the laid-back surfing lifestyle on Maui. Past

MAUI

Time: 2-4hr.
Distance: 45 mi.
Season: Any

The 45 mi. trip from Paia to Hana is one of the world's most impressive coastal drives. With more than 600 turns and over 50 single-lane bridges, the "Road to Heaven" offers incredible views of Maui's rainforests and waterfalls, most of which are visible from the driver's seat. While it takes about 2hr. to make the journey itself, the experience is much more rewarding if you stop along the way. Highlights of the drive are outlined below; however, there's always more to explore. If you only have a day for the road to Hana and back, then consider skipping some of these sites to leave time for the Pools of Oheo and the hikes near Hana. Fill up on gas in Paia (there are no gas stations along the way), pack a cooler with snacks and aqua, and go!

1. TWIN FALLS. If you want to make this a worthwhile excursion, go at 7am. If you beat the crowds, you will enjoy a lovely private swim beneath the falls—just you and the mosquitoes. Otherwise, you're taking your chances—by 8:15am, the parking lot is full and the narrow trail to the falls is swarming with tourists. This is the first waterfall stop along Hana Rd., but by no means the most impressive—Twin Falls can be easily bypassed. To get to the falls, pull over and park when you see the fruit stand past mi. marker 2. Pass through the gate onto the dirt road; after 2min., a few small trails branch off to the left to a rope swing and small pool. After 10min. and a crossing of the Hoolawanui Stream, the trail forks at a small rock bearing a hand-painted arrow. The path to the left leads to the most popular waterfall, a lovely pool, and another rope swing. There's a little hurdle before getting there in the form of a concrete aqueduct; though you should plan on getting wet, it's easy to overcome. The path to the right includes a makeshift bridge over an irrigation canal and continues to a concrete step where the path splits. Going uphill to the left leads you through a forest where you can find the 150 ft. top of the falls on the left. Stay right at the concrete block to continue through a cove that will bring you to a less populated, but nonetheless rewarding, waterfall and pool. Porta-potties are available at the entrance to the trail. Small driveways to private residences dapple the hike to the falls; always be courteous.

2. WAIKAMOI NATURE TRAIL. On the *mauka* (mountain) side, between mi. markers 9 and 10, there is an excellent short hike among native ferns, bamboo, eucalyptus, mango, and strawberry guava. Just above the parking area, the pathway, one of few public trails on Maui, forks into 2 nested loop trails. To take the longer one (about 1 mi. total), bear left and then left again past the second bench. The trail climbs a bit past strawberry guava trees before leveling out and making a switchback to another bench. The right fork continues through a stand of bamboo and paper bark trunks. It ends under mango trees in a quiet, grassy clearing, with a picnic shelter overlooking the ocean. To loop back down to the parking lot, either backtrack down the trail or walk down the old road, bearing right when it splits. The ride from here to the next stop offers some of the most gorgeous views of the coast as the road winds in and out in large curves.

3. PUOHOKAMOA STREAM. A trail right next to the bridge at mi. marker 11 leads through the forest and down to a pool at the base of a 20 ft. waterfall. A sheltered picnic ground stands beside the oft-rainy area; and about 10min. upstream, the main fall (Lower Puohokamoa Falls) drops dramatically over a 200 ft. cliff. However, the trail up to this waterfall is slippery and unstable; the falls can be just as well viewed from the nearby Puohokamoa Falls Lookout.

4. KEANAE ARBORETUM. Right after the YMCA Camp Keanae, about 0.2 mi. past mi. marker 16, the Keanae Arboretum offers another chance to stretch your legs. A corridor of flowers and trees leads to the main park, a garden of labeled timber and native flowers that include taro, breadfruit, and sugarcane. The 6 acre park is pleasant, but extremely damp in the wet season, and the mosquitoes can be worse here than in other areas. Don't park in front of the aluminum gate and be careful—flash-flooding occurs spontaneously. Open 7am-7pm daily.

5. KEANAE PENINSULA. The taro farming village of **Keanae** lies on a wave-thrashed coast, a left turn off Hana Hwy. shortly after the arboretum. Here you'll find a peaceful Hawaiian town, centered on the **Keanae Congregational Church,** built in 1860. Before you reach the church,

Hana Highway Scenic Drive

you'll see a snack shop on the right that sells Aunt Sandy's delicious banana bread as well as fruit and smoothies. At the end of the road is a ball park with restrooms. Picnic tables overlook the rocky beach, where waves crash against the shoreline.

6. WAILUA. Just past mi. marker 19, the **Wailua Lookout** offers views of the tiny village of Wailua. The prides of the town are the **Our Lady of Fatima Shrine,** built in 1860, and the bougainvillea gardens maintained by its residents. For a more secluded picnic spot, head to the Wailua Valley State Wayside, just before mi. marker 19. There, a set of stone steps to the right will take you up to a grassy perch.

7. PUAA KAA. Between mi. markers 22 and 23 are the freshwater pools of **Puaa Kaa State Park.** The 2 swimmable pools connected by a small waterfall make for a refreshing dip; but since they are less than a 2min. walk from the car, they are frequently crowded. The park also has shaded picnic tables and restrooms (the last you'll find until you reach Hana). Parking is available on the makai side of the highway.

8. NAHIKU. Between mi. markers 25 and 26, a road leads seaward to **Nahiku,** a small village that is home to a Christian church, built in 1867. Nahiku is East Maui's wettest town, getting more than 300 in. of rain per year. The real draw here is the road—about 2½ mi. one way—it winds through lush rainforest growth and is particularly beautiful in the wet season. After the church, it becomes a private road, which leads to a spectacular ocean view.

9. VENUS POOL. Waikoa Pond, or, more amorously, Venus Pool, is one of the largest freshwater pools on the island; although it may be less famous than the Oheo pools, it is not any less replenishing or exquisite. Lava formations offer plenty of places to climb and to jump into the water, and a tidal wall creates a natural barrier to the salty ocean swells. The trail to the pool is easily missed by the crowds rushing to Kipahulu. Park at mi. marker 48, just before the bridge. On the other side of the fence, follow the footpath, and turn right toward the stream.

North Shore and Upcountry Maui

Map labels:

PACIFIC OCEAN

Maliko Bay · Kuiaha Bay · Uaoa Bay

Hookipa Beach · Pauwela · Peahi Rd.

H. A. Baldwin Beach Park · Kuau Bay · Holomua Rd. · Haiku Rd. · W. Kuiaha Rd. · Haiku · Hana Hwy · 36 · Huelo

Paia Bay · Lower Paia · Kokomo Rd. · Kailinoa Rd. · Twin Falls · 360 · Kailua · Makaiwa Bay · TO HANA (22mi)

Kahului Bay · Kanaha Beach Park · Kahului Airport · Spreckelsville · Paia · 365

32 · 340 · 36A · Kala Rd. · Baldwin Ave. · 390 · 398 · Kokomo · Waikamoi Ridge Trail Nature Walk · Waikamoi Falls

350 · Kahului · 36 · Puunene · Hansen Rd. · Haliimaile Rd. · 37 · Haliimaile · 371 · Makawao · 365 · Kailiili Rd. · Waiohiwi Falls · Puohokamoa Falls

380 · Pulehu Rd. · Haleakala Hwy · Pukalani Bypass · Makawao Ave · Olinda Rd. · Makawao Forest Reserve

Spanish Rd. · Keahua Rd. · 370 · Pukalani · Haleakala Hwy · Koolau Forest Reserve

311 · Mokulele Hwy · Pulehu Rd. · Omaopio Rd. · Lower Kula Rd. · 372 · 37 · Omaopio · Olinda

Upper Kihei Rd. · Waiakoa Rd. · 370 · 377 · Kimo Dr. · Keanae Valley

S. Kihei Rd. · 31 · MAKAWAO DISTRICT · Pulehu · Kamehameiki Rd. · Haleakala Crater Rd.

Kalepolepo Beach Park · Kihei · Kalama Beach Park · Waiakoa · Copp Rd. · 378 · Park Headquarters · Leleiwi Overlook

Kamaole I · Kamaole II · Kula · Kekaulike Ave · Kalahaku Overlook · Haleakala National Park

Kamaole III · Piilani Hwy · Waiohuli · Waipoli Rd. · Haleakala Visitor Center · Haleakala Valley

Keawakapu Beach · TO ULUPALAKUA RANCH (5mi), KAUPO (20mi) · Keokea · Polipoli State Park · Kula Forest Reserve · Puu Ulaula Summit 10,023'

TO WAILEA (1.5mi); MAKENA (4mi) · Kula Hwy · Thompson Rd. · 37

N · LG

0 ____ 2 miles

0 ____ 2 kilometers

Paia lies Haiku, which goes unnoticed a few miles inland of the highway. Twin Falls, on the east end of Haiku near Huelo, offers a taste of the innumerable waterfalls along Hana Hwy. A few small towns lie between Huelo and Hana, including the taro root farming town of Keanae, but for the most part the road is surrounded only by unspoiled tropical forest. Hana, a peaceful town with beautiful beaches and parks, warrants more than a glance from the car, though it might be worth hurrying a bit to make time for Oheo Gulch, where you can swim in freshwater pools and hike to waterfalls.

! HANA HIGHWAY DRIVING TIPS. Many residents commute several times a day on this road. Use your rearview mirror, and use the pull-outs along the road to let cars pass you. Do not stop on the road to look; this is dangerous and inconsiderate. On one-lane bridges, obey the yield signs. On steep downhills, switch to a lower gear rather than riding your breaks.

MAUI

PAIA

Surfing and healthy living are the twin pillars of happiness in zen Paia (pop. 2529), where organic food stores and yoga studios abound and the North

Shore's biggest waves crash beachside. Its waters are renowned for windsurfing in summer, while staggering waves chant siren calls to the most daring of surfers in winter. At any time of year, Paia attracts surfer dudes, bikini-clad Maui chicks, and aging hippies. With a mix of restaurants and beach bars, Paia is arguably the best town on Maui for good, cheap food. It's also a wonderful place to experience the laid-back attitude of Maui without the lofty price tag.

◼✦🛈 ORIENTATION AND PRACTICAL INFORMATION

Paia is at the intersection of **Highway 36 (Hana Highway)** and **Baldwin Avenue,** which runs from Paia to **Makawao** (p. 323). This is the commercial center of the town, called Lower Paia. Actual Paia is farther inland on Baldwin Ave.

There are three **gas stations** in Paia along Hana Hwy. It's a good idea to fill up here on the way to Hana; the only gas station after Paia is in Hana itself, and gas there is significantly more expensive. Other services include **Bank of Hawaii,** 35 Baldwin Ave., with a **24hr. ATM** (☎888-643-3888. Open M-Th 8:30am-4pm, F 8:30am-6pm), and a **laundromat,** 129 Baldwin Ave. (wash $1.75, dry $0.25 per 5min. Open daily 4am-7pm). For **Internet access,** head to **Haz Beans,** 113 Baldwin Ave. (☎808-268-0149. Open daily 6am-3pm. Free Wi-Fi), or **Morning Glories,** 137 Hana Hwy., which has eight computers. (☎808-579-3336. $3 per 30min. Open daily 7am-9:30pm.) The **Paia Post Office** is at 120 Baldwin Ave. (☎808-579-8866. Open M-F 8:30am-4:30pm, Sa 10:30am-12:30pm.) **Postal Code:** 96779.

🛏 ACCOMMODATIONS

Paia is one of the few places on Maui where good beaches, restaurants, and bars converge. It's easy to find a cheap place to stay and many places offer long-term rates. Travelers interested in vacation rentals can look for postings on bulletin boards or contact **Hookipa Haven,** 62 Baldwin Ave., for a wide range of studios, apartments, and cottages in Paia. (☎808-579-8282; www.hookipahaven.com. Open M-F 9am-4pm. Rentals range $70-1000 per night, often with cleaning fees for stays shorter than a week. 5% reservation fee. AmEx/D/MC/V.)

▨ **Rainbow's End Surf Hostel,** 221 Baldwin Ave. (☎808-579-9057), turn at Panini Pl. Probably the best hostel on Maui. Well-maintained and friendly, it's usually filled with windsurfers and young backpackers and is only a short walk from the beach. Every bed comes with its own portion of the pantry and fridge. Free Wi-Fi. 4 dorms and 3 private doubles share a living room with TV/VCR, DVD, 2 kitchens, and 3 bathrooms. Parking available. Quiet hours after 10pm. Reserve far in advance with $20 deposit. 1-month max. stay.. Dorms $25 per night, $135 per week, $375 per month; doubles $55/300/750. Rates higher Dec.-June. Cash only. ❶

▨ **YMCA Camp Keanae,** 13375 Hana Hwy. (☎808-248-8355; www.mauiymca.org), about halfway between Paia and Hana, before mi. marker 17. Pitch a tent on the gorgeous property, or stay in one of the co-ed dorms or cabins. Dorm guests and campers share toilets and single-sex shower rooms, grill pit, and gym. 2 4-person cottages, each with full bathroom, kitchenette, *lanai,* and grill. Linens not included in dorms. Coin-op laundry. Camp is rented to large groups in the summer; call for availability. Check-in 3pm. Check-out noon. Camping and dorms $17; family tent $35; cottages $125. MC/V. ❶

The Inn at Mama's Fish House, 799 Poho Pl. (☎808-579-9764; www.mamasfishhouse. com), turn left on Kaiholo Pl., which dead ends into Poho Pl. A vision of old Polynesia, cottages have A/C, full kitchen, TV/VCR, DVD, Wi-Fi, stereo, grill, and beach access. 3-night min. Check-in 3pm. Check-out 11am. Reserve with 1-night credit card deposit. Singles from $60, cottages $175-575. AmEx/D/MC/V. Singles ❷/cottages ❺

FROM THE ROAD

BANANA NUT BINGE

When undertaking Hana Hwy., there's one thing aside from one-lane bridges and meandering tourists that you can't avoid: banana nut bread (BNB). The unofficial headliner of this notorious drive is available at most pit stops along the way. To see if the drive could be made on BNB and a tank of gas alone, Let's Go initiated the first-ever banana nut bender, on a return trip from Hana:

1. 11:15am, Hana Farms: The BNB here comes baked in several varieties, from pineapple to rum raisin. Some selections are $7. Is it worth the expense?

2. 11:38am, mi. marker 28: Aware of a looming tummy ache, I scarf down only a few moist crumbs of Sarah's Famous ($3).

3. 11:45am, Nihiku street: My stomach reaches full capacity.

4. Noon, Upper Nihiku: Free sample of the special, normally $4. The traveler's tongue approves.

5. 1:15pm, Keanae: I ask for a scraping of Aunt Sandy's classic and soon, sir, I want some more.

6. 2:30pm, Twin Falls: Not sure if the taste buds will hold up. I look for a piece low on the nuts and throw down another few bucks.

7. 3:15pm. Toward Kapalua, there are two dueling BNB stands, operated by a pair of women who—according to locals—despise each other. Both were scrumptious. Total spent: $22.

Favorite variety: the 🡆**chocolate-chip BNB at Hana Farms**—$7 well-spent.

—*Danielle O' Keefe*

🡆🡆 FOOD AND NIGHTLIFE

There are plenty of excellent places to dine out in Paia. In addition, **Mana Foods,** 49 Baldwin Ave., a health-food haven, sells bulk food, organic produce, and packaged groceries at some of the island's lowest prices. (☎808-579-8078. Open daily 8:30am-8:30pm. AmEx/D/MC/V.) For beer, wine, and liquor, stop by **Paia Pit Stop,** 181 Baldwin Ave. (☎808-579-8967. Open daily 8am-9pm. MC/V.)

RESTAURANTS

🡆 **Paia Fishmarket,** 100 Hana Hwy. (☎808-579-8030; www.paiafishmarket.com), at the corner of Baldwin Ave. A Paia stand-by, this eatery fills with people from Upcountry and beyond, sitting at long wooden tables, eating good food, and sipping their favorite beers (Hefeweizen $4.50; Bikini Blonde lager $4.50; domestics $4.50). The *mahi mahi* burgers ($8.50) are the best on the island. Sashimi appetizer $14. Fries, fish tacos, salads, and seafood entrees $13-16. Open daily 11am-9:30pm. D/MC/V. ❷

Charley's Restaurant and Saloon, 142 Hana Hwy. (☎808-579-9453; www.charleyspaia.com). With swinging wooden doors and lazy ceiling fans, this old-time saloon serves 3 meals a day with massive pancakes ($4-7) and *ono* eggs benedict ($12). Dinner features standard pub food, as well as more Hawaiian fare like the papaya *ono* panfry ($14). One of the few places in town that stays open past dinner for hit-or-miss nightlife: W Ladies' Night and DJ; Th Coyote Ugly; F and Sa live music. Cover $5-10. Open daily 7am-2am; food served until 10pm. AmEx/D/MC/V. ❸

Jacques Northshore, 120 Hana Hwy. (☎808-579-8844). A windsurfer hangout with surf paraphernalia and a carefree vibe, Jacques offers creative appetizers (spicy *ahi* roll, $9.50) and frequent live music (M nights are your best bet). While many entrees are on the steep side (up to $27), curries and pastas are easier on the wallet ($13-18). Most locals skip the food altogether and head straight for the beer. F nights bring a DJ (bar open until 1am). Happy hour daily 5-6pm (bar only). Sushi bar open Tu-Sa 5-10pm; ½-off sushi rolls Th and Sa 5-6:30pm. Dinner daily 5-10pm. MC/V. ❹

Milagros Food Co., 3 Baldwin Ave. (☎808-579-8755), at the intersection of Baldwin Ave. and Hana Hwy. If margaritas and people-watching are your thing, then grab a table at this bustling cornerstop and touch your lips to the cool salt-crusted glasses ($2.50, plus the price of tequila), not to mention flavorful hand-rolled taquitos ($7) and fish tacos ($10). Enjoy a healthy midday salad

($13), or hunker down in the evening with a dinner burrito ($14-20). Open daily 8am-10pm. AmEx/MC/V. Lunch ❷/dinner ❸

Flatbread Company, 89 Hana Hwy. (☎808-579-8989; www.flatbreadcompany.com). Families, friends, and visitors sit in long wooden booths as they nibble on Flatbread's wood-fired, clay-oven pizza. The spacious indoor/outdoor setting only adds to the delight in each bite of the Pele pesto, homemade sausage, and vegan pies. Finish up with homemade banana bread or a delectable brownie sundae (each $7). 12-in. pizzas $9.50-13; 16-inch pizzas $16-21. Open M-Th, Su 11:30am-10pm, F-Sa 11:30am-11pm. AmEx/MC/V. ❷

Fresh Mint, 115 Baldwin Ave. (☎808-579-9144). If you don't mind folding chairs and extension cords, then take a load off at this vegetarian Vietnamese joint. Chef's specials include the shiitake wonder and citrus soy spare ribs (each $13); tried-and-true favorites like *chow fun* ($9) are also available. Open M-Sa 5-9:30pm, Su 5-9pm. MC/V. ❷

CAFES AND BAKERIES

▨ **Cafe des Amis,** 42 Baldwin Ave. (☎808-579-6323), across from Mana Foods. The scrumptious crepes at this intimate, sunny cafe are just as popular with the morning latte crowd as they are with Merlot-toting diners. Savory crepes (served with a small salad, $8.50-11.50) are substantial enough for a full meal, while sweet crepes finish things off nicely (try the cane sugar and lime juice, $4). Curries pack a tasty punch, too. Open daily 8:30am-8:30pm. MC/V. ❷

Moana Bakery and Cafe, 71 Baldwin Ave. (☎808-579-9999). Breakfast is a treat for the eyes as well as the stomach, with homemade pastries, Belgian waffles, and hearty omelets all kookily decorated. Dinner is a decadent tour of cuisine (island pesto pasta with macadamia nuts and ginger $14). Lunch includes some of the same dishes at a better value (pasta $12-14, lamb and hummus wrap $13). The daily lingering brunch (8am-3pm) is Moana's specialty, when you can enjoy a Moana Mamma (3 rums, 3 juices; $7.50) while munching on crab cake eggs benedict ($15). M open mic night, W Benoit Jazzworks, and F live music. Open M-Sa 8am-9pm, Su 8am-3pm. MC/V. ❹

Anthony's Coffee Co., 90 Hana Hwy. (☎808-579-8340). Oversized pastries, a merry staff, and 19 flavors of coffee greet regulars and newbies as they enter this shiny spot. A great place for ice cream or a smoothie; try an ▨**Anthuccino** for a real pick-me-up (ice, ice cream, espresso, and milk blended; $5). Open daily 5:30am-6pm. AmEx/MC/V. ❶

Aloha Island Shave Ice, 77 Hana Hwy. (☎808-579-8747), across from Shell gas station. Regular ($3.50), large ($4.50), or jumbo ($5.50) shave ice in 25 tropical and not-so-tropical (root beer or cotton candy) flavors makes this store a great place to stop by on a hot afternoon. Also offers a few plate lunches ($7.50) and the Hobo special (½ main dish and 2 scoops of rice, $5.50). Open daily 11am-5pm. Cash only. ❶

◪ BEACHES

HOOKIPA BEACH. *(Snorkeling. Surfing. Wind sports. Open daily 5:30am-7pm. Lifeguards 8am-4:30pm.)* Hookipa Beach is famous for the windsurfers who race along the west end of the water in the summer; relatively small waves attract longboarders and beginning surfers to the east end. The east end also has some coral that's great for snorkeling if the wind isn't too strong. The entrance is rocky, making it less ideal for swimming; the best place to swim is the far west end in front of the lifeguard stand. In winter, the bay is rocked by giant waves, and only experienced surfers should paddle out. Hana-bound tourists often stop at the east side bluff to catch a glimpse of the action. *(Drive 2 mi. east of Paia on Hana Hwy. Look for the sign for Hookipa Lookout; turn left before the lookout area for beach parking. Porta-potties, pay phones, and picnic tables are available.)*

MAUI

SPRECKLESVILLE TOWN BEACH (BABY BEACH). *(Open daily 24hr.)* West of H.A. Baldwin, the beach turns into Sprecklesville Town Beach. The beach is also known as Baby Beach for the protected swimming area to the right of the parking perfect for *keiki* (kids). Both Baby and Baldwin Beach are subject to strong winds that can kick up brutal sandstorms or make the water too rough for swimming. *(Turn right onto Nonohe Pl. off Hana Hwy. and then turning left onto Kealakai Pl. Parking is in the red sand lot at the end of Kealakai Pl.; do not leave valuables in your car.)*

▣ SHOPPING

Alice in Hulaland, 19 Baldwin Ave. (☎808-579-9922; www.aliceinhulaland.com) Like its name, this bohemian shop is full of character. Much of the clothing can be expensive, but SPF 50 hats ($30) and the store's own line of T-shirts ($15-20) are as stylish as they are well-priced. Open M-F 9:30am-8pm, Sa-Su 9:30am-6pm. AmEx/MC/V.

Aloha Bead Company, 43 Hana Hwy. (☎808-579-9709), behind the Maui Crafts Guild. The 2 rooms here have a wider variety of beads than you'll find in most craft warehouses. Open daily 11am-6pm. AmEx/D/MC/V.

Da Kine Hawaii (☎808-575-2495). This famous surfboard manufacturer sells surf and windsurf accessories. Open M-F 9am-1pm.

Maui Girl, 12 Baldwin Ave. (☎808-579-9266; www.maui-girl.com). Burn up the sand in one of Maui Girl's original bikinis (around $75) and seduce everyone else on the beach! You can mix and match separates' size and style, or choose a sassy number from the oodles of designer items ($30-300). Open daily 9am-6pm. AmEx/D/MC/V.

HAIKU

At first glance, sleepy Haiku (pop. 6578) may not live up to its lyrical namesake (in fact, Haiku means "broken hills" in Hawaiian, a namesake it depicts aptly). However, while its downtown cluster of stores, small restaurants, and a post office lack a certain dreaminess, the sprawling outskirts that spill down the North Shore along Hana Hwy. exemplify its more poetic qualities. Ginger speckles the verdant landscape with brilliant color, while plumeria and soft orange *puakenikeni* flowers infuse the air with heavy fragrance.

◢ ORIENTATION

Hana Highway defines the northern edge of Haiku, Paia is to the west, and Huelo is to the east. **Haiku Road** loops inland from Hana Hwy., intersecting **Kokomo Road, W. Kuiaha Road, Hog Back Road,** and **E. Kuiaha Road,** before reconnecting with Hana Hwy. The intersected roads run southeast to **Kaupakalua Road,** which connects Haiku to Makawao. Kaupakalua ends at Hana Hwy. just before Twin Falls. The center of Haiku is at the intersection of Haiku Rd. and Kokomo Rd., where Haiku Rd. makes a turn to the left and Kokomo Rd. continues inland.

ℹ PRACTICAL INFORMATION

Almost everything you'll need in Haiku you'll find in the **Haiku Marketplace,** 810 Haiku Rd., in the old cannery building, including an **ATM** in both supermarkets, the **medical clinic** (☎808-575-7531. Open M-F 7am-noon and 2-6pm. AmEx/D/MC/V), **pharmacy** (☎808-575-7522. Open M-F 9am-6:30pm, Sa 9am-1pm. AmEx/D/MC/V), and **laundromat** (☎808-575-9274. Open daily 7am-9pm. Last wash 8pm. Wash $2.00, dry $0.25 per 7min.). **Internet access** is available at **1 Stop Postal Shop,** 810 Haiku Rd., in the Haiku Marketplace, which has four computers and copiers. (☎808-575-2049. Internet $0.15 per min., $2 min. Copies

$0.12 per page. Open M-F 9am-5pm, Sa 9am-2pm. AmEx/MC/V.) If you're start-ing the road to Hana from here, you can get gas at **Hanzawa's,** 1833 Kaupakalua Rd. (☎808-572-8337), or at **Toma Garage,** 1073 Haiku Rd. (☎808-575-2652.) The Haiku **Post Office** is at 770 Haiku Rd. in the Haiku Town Center. (☎808-575-2614. Open M-F 8am-4pm, Sa 9-11am.) **Postal Code:** 96708.

TOW-IN SURFING AT JAWS. Every year in Dec. and Jan., there is a grand *pohai na keiki nalu* ("gathering of the surf kids") to witness one of the biggest spectacles in the islands: tow-in big-wave surfing at **Jaws surfbreak.** When the waves break just right off the coast below a pineapple field in Haiku, surfers have jet skis tow them into waves that reach heights of 100 ft. from crest to trough (though the average height is 25-40 ft.). Surfers are strapped into their boards, allowing them to rip nasty tricks on their way down the wave—it's like skiing down an avalanche. After the ride, surfers hold their breath and wait for the jet ski to tow them back to safety before the next wave. Surfers train for years, holding onto heavy rocks below the surface to increase their lung capacity, which they'll need to survive the powerful wave breaking above them. Lifeguards wait outside the impact zone should they be needed. The event also has a hefty price tag, as the cost for the tow-in is a few thousand dollars, unless the surfer is backed by a sponsor or a movie company trying to make a film. News of surfing at Jaws spreads by word of mouth—keep your ears open for a chance to see this crazy event.

ACCOMMODATIONS

Accommodations in Haiku are severely limited due to the number of private B&Bs waiting on permit confirmation from the county of Maui (read more about the B&B situation on p. 284). You'll be best off staying in neighboring towns. Still, many privately rented cottages are listed at **www.vrbo.com.**

Aloha Maui Bed and Breakfast, 101 Loomis Rd. (☎808-572-9820; www.alohamauicot-tages.com). Turn off Hana Hwy. right before mi. marker 2 onto Ulalena Loop. Follow the gravel road over a small bridge, and at the fork stay left onto Loomis Rd. Veer right at the next fork at the sign "Private Rd., Invited Guests Only." Set in a beautiful rainforest, Aloha Maui provides a relaxing and removed getaway. Tropical flowers surround 3 cot-tages, which use solar energy and run filtered rainwater. Continental breakfast included. All cottages have full kitchen and private bath. Sauna, laundry, and mountain bikes available to guests. 3-night min. stay. Reserve with 50% deposit; balance due on arrival. Cottages $70-120; prices slightly higher Dec.-Apr. Weekly rates available. D/MC/V. ❸

FOOD

For groceries, visit the **Haiku Grocery Store,** in the Haiku Marketplace (☎808-575-9291. Open daily 7am-9pm; MC/V). **Hanzawa's Variety Store,** 1833 Kaupakalua Rd., has been serving the area since 1915. (☎808-572-8337. Open M-Sa 7am-8pm. AmEx/D/MC/V.)

Colleen's at the Cannery, 810 Haiku Rd. (☎808-575-9211; www.colleensinhaiku.com), in the Haiku Marketplace, offers flaky pastries, hearty sandwiches (with a fresh cookie, $8-9), salads, and fish and burgers ($8-11). Breakfast offers the Hangover Cure: sau-teed potatoes, cheddar cheese, ham, onions, and mild green chiles, along with sides of salsa and sour cream ($10; with 2 eggs $1). Young locals flock here for the food, jazzy music, and casual, urban atmosphere. Happy hour daily 3:30-5:30pm (slice of pizza and a beer $5). Open daily 6am-9:30pm. AmEx/D/MC/V. ❷

Veg Out, 810 Kokomo Rd.(☎808-575-5320), in the Haiku Town Center. From their homemade falafel ($9) and pesto pizza ($7) to an international array of sandwiches ($5-6), tacos ($5), and smoothies ($3), this casual, fun place is the perfect spot for veggie-lovers to satisfy their palates or simply enjoy a piece of vegan piña colada cake ($4.25). Open M-F 10:30am-7:30pm, Sa-Su 11:30am-7:30pm. MC/V. ❶

Hana Hou Cafe, 810 Haiku Rd. (☎808-575-2661; www.hanahoucafe.com). Although it's in the middle of a parking lot, patrons are happy to fill their stomachs in this charming, screened-in courtyard. Chow down on a burger or plate lunch ($8-13). M and W-Sa live local music. Open daily 4:30-9pm; Th-Su lunch at noon. AmEx/MC/V. ❷

HANA

Hana means "work" in Hawaiian, a name you might understand upon finally reaching town. Since Hana Highway's 617 hairpin turns and 54 bridges were paved in 1984, Hana (pop. 739) has undergone a considerable tourist boom. Yet the town remains relaxed; visitors still stop to smell the plumeria and take a vacation from their vacation, exploring caves, strolling along red and black sand beaches, or joining the entire town to cheer on the local baseball team.

TRANSPORTATION

Hana Airport is on Alalele Pl., off of Hana Hwy. 4 mi. north of Hana. Pacific Wings (☎808-873-0877 or 888-575-4546; www.pacificwings.com) offers regular non-stop service to Honolulu and Kahului; other airlines fly less frequently.

A **gas station** at 5170 Hana Hwy. charges more per gallon than elsewhere on Maui. (☎808-248-7671. Open daily 7:30am-7:30pm in summer, 7:30am-7pm in winter.) For 24hr. emergency road service and repair between Keanae and Kaupo, call **East Maui Towing and Mechanics,** 4228 Hana Hwy. (☎808-248-8085).

ORIENTATION AND PRACTICAL INFORMATION

Approaching Hana from the north, **Hana Highway** splits at the **Hana Police Station,** 4610 Hana Hwy. (☎808-248-8311). Hana Hwy. continues down the right of the fork, past the Hotel Hana-Maui. Left of the police station, **Ua Kea Road** leads to Hana Beach Park and accommodations on Hana Bay. The **fire station,** 4655 Hana Hwy. (☎808-248-7525), is also at the intersection, and the **Hana Community Health Center,** 4590 Hana Hwy., is just before it. (☎808-248-8294. Open M-Tu 7am-8pm, W-Th 7am-5pm, F 8am-5pm, Sa 8am-noon. AmEx/MC/V.) Ua Kea Rd. ends after the **Hana Ball Park;** turn right on **Hauoli Street** to return to Hana Hwy. Hauoli St. crosses Hana Hwy. by the Wananalua Congregational Church, north of Hana's business district. **Internet access** is available at the **Hana Public & School Library,** 4111 Hana Hwy., with the purchase of a 3-month visitor's card ($10). (☎808-248-4848. Open M and F 8am-4pm, Tu 9am-4pm, W and Th 11am-7pm.) A **Bank of Hawaii** is in the **Hana Ranch Center,** at the center of town. (☎808-248-8015. Open M-Th 3-4:30pm, F 3-6pm.) **ATMs** are located in both the **Hasegawa General Store,** 5165 Hana Hwy. and the **Hana Ranch Store.** The **post office,** is at 1 Mill St. (Open M-F 8am-4:30pm.) **Postal Code:** 96713.

OUT OF TOUCH? No matter where you stay in Hana, you'll likely be without Wi-Fi. To remedy this, try your luck by the ballpark. Here, you should be able to connect with the network of the town's posh Hana-Maui Resort.

🏠 🏕 ACCOMMODATIONS AND CAMPING

For an extensive list of accommodations in Hana, look under "lodging" on the local website (www.hanamaui.com).

Aloha Cottages, 73-79 Keawa Pl. (☎808-248-8420). Each unit comes with a full kitchen and bath. The cottages have cable TV, ocean views, and sleep 6 comfortably. A minute's walk from Hana Beach Park, these no-frills lodgings are a great value. Check-in noon. Strictly enforced check-out 10:45am. 2-person studio $65; 2-bedroom cottages $90; 3-bedroom $100. Cash only. ❷

Joe's Place, 4870 Ua Kea Rd. (☎808-248-7033; www.joesrentals.com), offers the cheapest private rooms in town, though it looks like it's seen better days. The spartan rooms are kept neat enough, though the place (especially the kitchen) suffers from both a dust and an insect problem. Guests share a living room with cable TV. Check-in 3pm. Check-out 10am. Quiet hours after 10pm. 7 rooms with shared bath $50; 1 with private bath $60. MC/V. ❷

Napualani O'Hana, 95 Kalo Rd. (☎808-248-8935). A bit out of the way, these cheap quarters subsidize the trek with their private baths, microwaves, and coffeemakers. The larger units have 2 baths, 2 *lanai*, and a full kitchen. Check-in 2pm. Check-out 11am. Studios $75; 2-bedroom units $150; each additional guest $10. Cash only. ❸

Waianapanapa State Park (☎808- 248-4843), 2 mi. north of Hana, on Honokalani Rd. Campsites are steps from the park's lava tube caves and coastal hiking trails. Facilities include restrooms, picnic tables, outdoor showers, and grills. Campsites and a limited number of 6-person cabins available. Cabins come with bedding, towels, electricity, hot water, bath, kitchen, and cooking utensils. Reserve cabins far in advance. Campsites $5; 4-person cabins $45; each additional guest $5. See **Camping in Hawaii,** p. 82. ❶

🍴 FOOD

Bring groceries if you are staying for more than a day or two. The two general stores in town have a limited selection of produce, meat, and fish, and other items are expensive. The **Hasegawa General Store,** 5165 Hana Hwy., (☎808-248-8231; open M-Sa 7am-7pm, Su 8am-6pm) has everything. There's also the **Hana Ranch Store,** 1 Mill Rd. (☎808-248-8617. Open daily 7am-7:30pm). There are numerous fruit stands on Hana Hwy. If you want fresh fish, try fishing off the pier in **Hana Bay,** or if you see a boat trailer parked at the pier, wait until the fishermen return and politely ask if they will sell to you.

Tutu's Snack Shop (☎808-248-8224), at Hana Beach Park, sells burgers ($4), ice cream ($4), plate

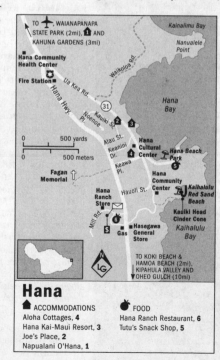

Hana

🏠 ACCOMMODATIONS
Aloha Cottages, **4**
Hana Kai-Maui Resort, **3**
Joe's Place, **2**
Napualani O'Hana, **1**

🍎 FOOD
Hana Ranch Restaurant, **6**
Tutu's Snack Shop, **5**

HOUNDDOGGING IN HANA

A high-school uniform of bobby socks and saddle-shoes, along with a penchant for vanilla milkshakes, has made me unfit for modern times. So, when I chance upon the equally era-challenged Sharon on the side of the road past Hana, it is a meeting of kindred spirits. Her life's work, I soon learn, is to carry on the spiritual beliefs of Elvis Presley.

"Truth is like the sun," she says, quoting him. "You can shut it out for a time, but it ain't goin' away." She adjusts a picture of Presley propped up against her wares and recalls meeting his daughter, a highlight of her long undertaking. I admire her handiwork, as she explains Elvis's lesser-known philosophies and the meaning of each necklace to me—one represents the water's edge, another is to be given only to true love. I buy a thick white cord that would have gone well with the jumpsuit that Presley wore on his Hawaiian TV special, *Aloha from Hawaii.*

After hailing the merits of the King, I ask how long Sharon has lived in Hana. "All my life," she reveals. However, when her husband retires, she is willing to move elsewhere. "Where?" I ask without a thought. "Well, Memphis."

—Danielle O'Keefe

Sharon is on the Wailua bridge in the mornings and early afternoons M-F. The bridge is about 7 mi. south of Hana town.

lunches ($8-9), cold drinks, and a handy map of Hana ($1) for your day in the sun. Open daily 8:30am-4pm. ❶

The Hana Ranch Restaurant (☎808-270-5280), left of the Hana Ranch Store, is open for lunch and dinner, but it's a bit overpriced (ranch bacon cheeseburger, $15). Lunch daily 11:30am-4pm. Dinner W and F 6-8:30pm; reservations highly recommended. AmEx/D/MC/V. ❹ For a better deal, try the take-out window for plate lunches, burgers, and *saimin* (most under $10). Open daily 6:30-10am, 11am-4pm. AmEx/D/MC/V. ❷

🐚 BEACHES

HANA BEACH PARK. *(Open daily 6am-10pm. Lifeguards in summer 8am-4:30pm.)* Hana Beach Park, off of Ua Kea Rd., occupies a stretch of dark sand along Hana Bay. The bay is protected, and the calm water makes it popular for families with small children. Facilities include picnic tables, restrooms, and Tutu's Snack Shop (p. 309). The beach is set against the red cliffs of Kauiki Head. Because of the steep grade and exotic plant life, hiking on Kauiki Head is discouraged, though watching the sunset from the beach is spectacular.

KAIHALULU RED SAND BEACH. *(Snorkeling. Open daily 24hr.)* On the south side of Kauiki Head, a crescent, red sand beach has been carved from the cliffs above. The deep turquoise water that abuts the beach is incredibly clear and ideal for snorkeling. Although an outcropping of rock keeps larger waves out, there is still a surprisingly swift current. According to local lore, it is from this spot that the sun was born. Whether or not that's true, this is a beach that you have to find, as locals are tight-lipped about giving directions to it. Upon arrival, you'll find both locals and nude sunbathers (though nudity is illegal on Hawaii's beaches) delighting in the beauty of this retreat. *(Follow Ua Kea Rd. to the end and park on the left side before the lot for Hotel Hana-Maui guests. Parking in the private lot or on the street may get you ticketed or towed. At the south end of the Hana Community Center, you'll see the start of the trail. As you begin the 10min. hike, think down—not up—and walk toward the shoreline first. If you find yourself in the old Shinto cemetery, which is on private property, turn around. Continue left on the path along the water. Overuse has eroded part of the trail; so you'll have to climb over the coastal rocks very briefly. Rejoin the path and continue up around the corner toward the beach. The final part of the trail is the most dangerous; be sure to wear sturdy shoes.)*

KOKI BEACH. *(Bodyboarding. Surfing. Open daily 24hr.)* Koki Beach is one of Hana's two best swimming and surfing beaches; Hamoa is the other (see below). Red cliffs rise above the rocky sand on the left, while Alau Island, a seabird sanctuary, lies to the right. Koki can be busy at the height of the day, so go in the morning or evening, when it's calmer. Ask locals about hazards, be wary of a potentially dangerous shorebreak, and never swim alone. A grill and picnic tables are available by the parking lot. *(2 mi. south of Hana toward Kipahulu; turn left off Hana Hwy. onto Haneoo Rd., where there is a sign to Koki Beach.)*

HAMOA BEACH. *(Bodyboarding. Surfing. Open daily 24hr.)* Down a path of stone steps, you'll find Hamoa Beach, a beautiful stretch of soft sand open to the public and maintained by the Hotel Hana-Maui. Surfing and bodyboarding are popular here, and although the strong currents make the water rough at times, swimming is generally safe. Hamoa Beach gets crowded in the afternoons but is virtually empty in the mornings and evenings. Public restrooms and an outdoor shower are available. *(Follow the directions to Koki and continue 0.7mi. down the road.)*

ACTIVITIES AND SIGHTS

WAIANAPANAPA STATE PARK. Two miles north of Hana, Honokalani Rd. turns off Hana Hwy. on the *makai* (ocean) side to Waianapanapa (red water) State Park. In addition to the campsite and cabins (p. 309), the park encompasses several miles of shoreline along the rocky lava coast. The **King's Highway Coastal Trail** is a well-defined path that runs parallel to the coast all the way to Hana town, past ancient Hawaiian burial sites and *heiau* (temples). The captivating view and lava rock formations make any part of the trail a joy to hike. The 1 mi. of the trail from the park headquarters to the Ohala Heiau and back is surrounded by *hala* tree groves on one side and the turbulent sea crashing through arches and blowholes on the other. Left of the campsite, a short loop leads through the lava tube caves. Though the caves are steeped in poetic myth about the murdered Princess Popoalaea (her death inspired the name of the park), the mosquitoes and stagnant water may be a disappointment. Below and to the right of the caves is a black sand beach. The shore area is small, and the surf can be strong; watch out for rip currents and jellyfish. Popolana Beach, a more substantial black sand beach, is closer to town in the cove north of Hana Beach Park. *(☎ 808-248-4843. Pick up park maps and camping information at the park office, located in the caretaker's cottage. Office open M-F 7am-6pm, Sa-Su 8am-4pm.)*

BRING ON THE POPCORN. There's not much in Hana in terms of evening entertainment. When faced with a free night, a video might be your best bet. The cheapest rentals are at the Hana Public Library (7 days, $1) but require the purchase of a visitor's card first ($10). Videos and DVDs can also be found on the low at Hasegawa's General Store. For only $2.50, you can rent many recent flicks for a 5-day period.

KAHANU GARDENS. This ethnobotanical treasure is one of five gardens that make up the **National Tropical Botanical Garden (NTBG)**. On its 465 trim acres, visitors will find an *ulu* (breadfruit) grove, the elegant Wishard coconut collection, and the Canoe Garden, filled with 26 plants brought by Polynesians on ancient voyaging canoes. However, the starring role at Kahanu is taken by Piilanihale Heiau, a sacred temple that is both the largest remaining ancient structure in Hawaii and a registered National Historic Landmark. Built by Maui chiefs in the 15th century, its walls rise a sheer 42 ft. over nearly 4 acres. *(On Hana Hwy., 3 mi. north of Hana, turn left on Ulaino Rd. Drive 1½ mi. Proceed slowly; after ½ mi., the street becomes a bumpy 1-lane road. ☎ 808-248-8912; www.ntbg.org. Open M-F 10am-2pm. $10.)*

KAYAK AND SNORKEL TRIPS. Hana-Maui Sea Sports leads kayak and snorkel trips that benefit from guides' knowledge and experience. People paddle in tandem out into Hana Bay and slide into the water to see fish, coral, other marine life, and sometimes even a sea turtle. Consider taking an afternoon trip, as the winds tend to be calmer and you are more likely to catch a glimpse of wildlife. (☎ 808-248-7711; www.hana-maui-seasports.com. 2hr. trips daily 11am and 2:30pm; $120. 8 person limit. Private charters available. Call for reservations. AmEx/MC/V.)

HANA CULTURAL CENTER. On a small hill overlooking Hana Bay, the Hana Cultural Center runs a tiny museum and gift-shop with *kapa* (barkcloth) tapestries, woodcarvings, artifacts, thatched *hale* (huts), and native Hawaiian plants. Peruse over 240 posters of important Hana personalities, or read about the town's warrior culture and the history of the Hotel Hana-Maui. (4974 Ua Kea Rd. ☎ 808-248-8622; www.planet-hawaii.com/hana. Open M-F 10am-4pm. Free tours available. $3.)

KIPAHULU VALLEY AND OHEO GULCH (HALEAKALA NATIONAL PARK)

Unlike the lonely, barren summit of Haleakala Volcano (p. 318), its sea-level alter-egos, Kipahulu Valley and Oheo Gulch, are a lush incarnation of paradise. Dense foliage, swimming pools, and waterfalls welcome visitors.

ORIENTATION

Ten miles south of Hana on Hana Hwy., a swath of **Haleakala National Park** stretches down to the coast through **Kipahulu Valley** and **Oheo Gulch,** home to the famous and delightful **Seven Sacred Pools of Oheo.** If you want to avoid the masses and truly experience the area, consider staying in Hana overnight to get an early start and have more time for the outdoor activities available. Note that this part of the park is not connected to the rest of Haleakala.

PRACTICAL INFORMATION

The road to Kipahulu is narrow but negotiable in any vehicle. Maps and information about the park can be obtained at the **Kipahulu Rangers' Station,** located in the main parking lot. The rangers' station offers free 15min. natural and cultural history talks and guided hikes. (☎ 808-248-7375 for schedule and to confirm that pools are open. Open daily 9am-5pm. $10 per vehicle, for 3 days.) **Camping** (3-night max. stay) in the park does not require a permit. Campground facilities include porta-potties, picnic tables, and grills, but no drinking water.

HIKING

POOLS OF OHEO. (½ mi. 10-15min. Easy.) The trail starts next to the parking lot and leads to the Pools of Oheo, the Hawaiian name for the freshwater pools (also called the Seven Sacred Pools). A stony set of stairs just before the pools leads to the Kuloa Point bluff. From here, you can usually see clear across the channel to the Big Island. Take a few pictures; then descend to the real treat. Keep in mind that algae can make the underwater rocks slippery! Once at the pools, stretch out on a sunny slab or go for a cool dip. Under no circumstances should you swim in the ocean beyond the pools; sharks gather around the mouth of the stream. The path continues up on the left and connects with the

MAUI

road. A one-lane bridge, the last before the sign that tells you to honk your horn, offers a great view of the pools, though traffic can be hazardous.

PIPIWAI TRAIL. *(4 mi. 2-4hr. Moderate.)* The first half-mile of this trail, which starts next to the parking lot, follows the path of the Pipiwai Stream. At the Makahiku Overlook at half a mile, you can usually spy a 185 ft. waterfall. However, the upper part of the trail is more rewarding, as it crosses over many pools, passes a banyan tree, and boasts two bridges. After the Palikea Str. Crossing 1 mi. in, you will enter the lush hallway of the Bamboo Forest. From there, several sets of stony steps and wooden boardwalks will gradually bring the grand finale— the 400 ft. Waimoku Falls—into view. Return the way you came.

THE ROAD FROM HANA

The road from Hana along **Highway 31 (Piilani Highway)** from Kipahulu to Kula couldn't be more different from Hana Hwy. Gone are the lush rainforests and roadside waterfalls. In their place, arid plains and stark, desolate valleys give a sense of the vastness of Haleakala Volcano. In some ways, this drive is even more spectacular than the fabled Hana Hwy., and it's certainly the road less traveled. The road around the backside of Haleakala has been closed since the earthquake of October 15, 2006. Two bridges were damaged and only one has been replaced. Check online and in town for updates on the road—tentative plans suggest it might be open in late 2009. You can, however, make it a mile south of Oheo Gulch, where a narrow road on the *makai* (ocean) side just past mi. marker 41, leads to Palapala Hoomau Church, the incredible site of **Charles Lindbergh's grave. Kipahulu Point Park** and its picnic tables are a nice place for lunch and are accessible from the church property.

UPCOUNTRY MAUI

Upcountry Maui loosely encompasses the rural townships built on the slopes of the ancient Haleakala Volcano. Although the region is only minutes from the busy commercial center of Kahului, you'll feel a world away in Upcountry's quaint villages, rolling landscapes, and cool temperatures. In the heart of Upcountry's pastoral hills, Kula grows much of the island's produce, from sweet corn and greens to tomatoes, avocados, and papayas. Kula is home to magnificent floral gardens, many of which include the unique protea flower. South of Kula along Rte. 37 (Kula Hwy.), the tiny hamlet of Keokea has a coffee shop, art gallery, general store, gas station, and thousands of acres of ranch land. *Paniolo* cowboys ride and hog-tie every year at the Fourth of July rodeo in Makawao, the only town in Upcountry with a proper main street. This old cowboy town is also home to a string of charming shops and galleries. North of Makawao, serene Haiku connects Upcountry to the North Shore.

KULA

Driving through Kula (pop. 9729) is a treat—every side road you venture down reveals something unexpected. The countryside is patched with rural hillside, eucalyptus patches, and fields of exotic flowers. You'll have spectacular views of the Central Maui Valley spreading 4000 ft. below. Feathery clouds that hug the slope of the volcano cast shadows on roaming cattle herds. Of course, there is Haleakala itself (p. 318), rising majestically to 10,023 ft. and occupying a full range of climate zones, from cloud forest to craterous desert.

◧ 🔁 ORIENTATION AND PRACTICAL INFORMATION

To reach Kula from Kahului, take **Route 36** east to **Route 37 (Haleakala Highway)**, which becomes **Kula Highway**, the main north-south road through Kula. Kula Hwy. runs south through Kula and Keokea all the way to the Ulupalakua Ranch, where it becomes **Highway 31** and runs along the southern coast all the way to Hana (p. 308). **Route 377 (Kekaulike Avenue)** strays from Rte. 37 (becoming **Haleakala Highway**) and makes for a very scenic drive past flowering jacaranda trees. **Route 378 (Haleakala Crater Road)** heads up the side of Haleakala from Rte. 377. Stop in the **Ching Store**, 9212 Kula Hwy. in Keokea, for flowers, candy, and some of the island's cheapest gas. (☎808-878-1556. Open daily 7am-6:30pm. MC/V.) Less than a mile away, there is a **24hr. emergency room** and **primary care clinic** at **Kula Hospital**, 204 Kula Hwy. (☎808-878-1221, clinic 808-876-4331; www.kula.hhsc.org.) The **Kula Post Office** (☎808-876-1056. Open M-F 8am-4pm, Sa 9:30-11:30am) is located on Rte. 37, after the sign for the Holy Ghost Church. **Postal Code:** 96790.

🔏 ACCOMMODATIONS

Several cottages and B&Bs in Kula provide Upcountry peace and solitude. Nights are cool at these high altitudes, so pack sweaters and long pants. The beach is at least 30min. from here, but Haleakala's right in your backyard.

◙ Star Lookout, 622 Thompson Rd. (☎907-346-8028; www.starlookout.com). Drive up Rte. 37 past mi. marker 16 in Keokea, turn left at the fork across from Grandma's Coffee House, and make an immediate right onto Thompson Rd. Take this 1-lane road for ½ mi.; Star Lookout will be on your right. The perfect setting for a peaceful retreat, the front of Star Lookout's isolated cottage looks down onto the Central Maui Valley. 6-person cottage with full kitchen. Landscaped gardens, bonfire pit, gas grill, hot tub, and telescope. Cable TV/VCR, Wi-Fi, fresh fruit and vegetables from the garden (when in season), and a wood-burning stove. Washer/dryer available. 2-night min. Reserve well in advance. $200 per night. AmEx/D/MC/V. ❺

Kula Lodge and Restaurant, 15200 Haleakala Hwy. (☎808-878-1535; www.kulalodge. com), on Rte. 377, 1 mi. north of the intersection with Haleakala Crater Rd. As close to Haleakala National Park as you can get without camping. Popular with older guests and families, rooms have lofts, fireplaces, and private *lanai*. Excellent on-site restaurant (see below). Check-in 3pm. Check-out 11am. Reserve with full payment; cancel 30 days in advance with a $25 fee. 2-person chalets $150-230; each additional person $20. AmEx/MC/V. ❹

Upcountry Bed & Breakfast, 4925 Lower Kula Rd. (☎808-878-8083; www.upcountrybandb.com). This big red house on a hill has 4 rooms—3 with king-size beds and 1 with 2 twins. Each has a private bath and *lanai* overlooking West Maui. Wet bar, fridge, coffeemaker, TV/DVD, and Wi-Fi in all rooms. Continental breakfast provided. There is a large kitchen and a living room with fireplace and library available to all guests. Check-in 3pm. Check-out noon. 2-person rooms $150; 1-night stays $200. D/MC/V. ❹

◖ FOOD

Curiously, given how much the area has grown, Kula has few restaurants; some of the best are located within accommodations. **Morihara Store**, 4581 Lower Kula Rd., is the closest thing to a grocery store in Kula; it also sells beer, wine, and liquor. (☎808-878-2578. Open M-Sa 7am-8pm, Su 8am-8pm. MC/V.) **Kula Marketplace**, 15200 Haleakala Highway, is a gift shop with gourmet food and wine sections; they also offer sandwiches and picnic lunches to-go. (☎808-878-2135. Open daily 7am-7pm. D/MC/V.)

Grandma's Coffee House, 9232 Kula Hwy. (☎808-878-2140), in Keokea, is an Upcountry institution that serves excellent coffee, hearty breakfast (eggs, sausage, and toast; $6.50), sandwiches ($6-8), a daily hot special, and decadent cakes and pastries. Take home a helping of macadamia nut pesto ($6.85 per lb.) and a piece of cinnamon coffee cake ($3.50). Open daily 7am-5pm. AmEx/MC/V. ❶

La Provence, 5355 Lower Kula Rd. (☎808-878-1313; www.laprovencekula.com) Maui foodies flock to this hidden gem for crepes ($10-13), waffles ($9), quiches ($10), and other French fare. The enticing pastries, made fresh daily, are sure to provide a sweet escape (try the *lilikoi* merengue tart $4), but this family-run joint's signature dish is "eggs beni" ($10-12), served all week and spotlighted on Sundays (try one with *mahi mahi!*). Open W-Su 7am-3pm. Cash only. ❷

Kula Restaurant, 15200 Haleakala Hwy. (☎808-878-1535; www.kulalodge.com), in Kula Lodge. The perfect (and popular) place to stop for breakfast before or after a summit trek. Great views of West Maui supplement heaping plates of delicious pancakes, all served with coconut and maple syrups (try the bananas foster pancakes, $11). Also serves excellent lunch ($11-19) and dinner ($22-36). AmEx/MC/V. ❸

ACTIVITIES

Explore the Kula countryside on horseback just like the *paniolo* (cowboys) with **Thompson Ranch and Riding Stables** on Polipoli Rd. From Rte. 37 in Keokea, turn left onto Polipoli Rd. before Grandma's Coffee. (☎808-283-6209. 1hr. ride $75. 200 lb. weight limit. 8-person max. Reserve in advance.) For a high-powered look at Maui's countryside, **Maui ATV Tours,** offers tours of Upcountry Ranchland on one- and three-passenger ATVs. (☎808-878-2889; www.mauiatvtours.com. 2hr. tour 2-4pm $90, 4hr. tour 8am-noon $125.)

SIGHTS

ALII KULA LAVENDER FARM. Explore over 45 varieties of lavender at this enthralling and peaceful 11-acre farm at the base of Polipoli. With over 40,000 plants to wander through and five daily 30min. walking tours ($12) in which to partake, you're sure to find this a magical spot. Savor some lavender tea and scones on a veranda with a view, or go on an exclusive tour ($25) of the field with Ali'i himself. Wreath-making workshops and special teas arranged by request. *(1100 Waipoli Rd.* ☎*808-878-3004. Open daily 9am-4pm. AmEx/MC/V.)*

MUSHROOM CHEESE LAVENDER WINE

When you're staying in cozy and slightly-more-affordable Upcountry Maui, you'll likely find yourself with access to a kitchen. Cooking for yourself and friends is not only economically advantageous but also satisfying and delicious. Moreover, this is a great opportunity to combine finds from the many saliva-spurring tours this countryside has to offer.

While more avid cooks may want to tackle mushroom ravioli or goat-cheese stuffing, a simple way to exploit your bounty is the omelet. To start, melt some butter and olive oil in a pan. Sauté some of **Makawao Mushrooms'** (p. 316) oyster mushrooms until brown, and season them with **Alii Kula's** (p. 315) lavender gourmet seasoning. Whisk four eggs and pour them into a pan, adding pepper and lemon to taste. Sprinkle half of the omelet with cheese from **Surfing Goat Dairy** (p. 316). While this is melting, add in the mushrooms and fold the omelet over. Top it all off with more mushrooms, fresh basil, and another smattering of goat cheese.

For an extra luscious finish, ask the fine folks at **Tedeschi Winery** (p. 316) what spirits they'd recommend to accompany your dish. If you're not feeling quite so handy, just stop by Makawao's **Komoda Bakery** (p. 325) for some of their famous cream puffs instead.

BITE ME. If you're tired of pesky bug bites, pick up some lavender spray, as it repels various insects. Deer and goat won't feed on it either, but hopefully, that's not a concern.

MAUI AGRICULTURAL RESEARCH CENTER. The University of Hawaii operates this 35-acre center in Kula for proteas and other flora of the southern hemisphere. The center includes a colorful spectrum of unique protea hybrids and an impressive rose garden, and visitors are invited to stroll around the grounds for free. Just check in at the main office before entering. *(424 Mauna Pl. To reach the Center from Rte. 37, take a left onto Copp Rd. between mi. markers 12 and 13. After 1 mi. on Copp, turn left onto Mauna Pl. ☎808-878-1213. Open M-Th 7am-3:30pm. Free.)*

SURFING GOAT DAIRY. *(Yes, you read that correctly.)* Learn the ropes of life on a goat farm at this 42-acre dairy where the staff mantra is "Da' Feta Mo' Betta." Producing over 20 award-winning cheeses, the Surfing Goat Dairy is dedicated to providing an interactive tour experience. Try their creamy chèvre, or go on a dairy tour. Grand tours allow guests to feed, pet, and even milk the goats. On Sundays, walk with the herd through the pastures at 11am or tour the orchard at noon. *(3651 Omaopio Rd., from Kula Hwy. turn on Pulehu Rd. When Pulehu Rd. splits, veer left to Omaopio Rd. Entrance is 2mi. down on the right. ☎808-878-2870; www.surfinggoatdairy.com. Open M-Sa 10am-5pm, Su 10am-2pm. Dairy tours $7. Guided tours every other Sa 9am, $25.)*

KULA BOTANICAL GARDEN. Kula Botanical Garden, established in 1969, is a family-run operation showcasing native Hawaiian plants, as well as unique specimens from around the world. Laminated maps direct you along several paths as you wind your way past the koi pond, bird cages, aviary (with love birds), fuchsia and orchid "houses," and the tiki exhibit. *(638 Kekaulike Ave., about 1 mi. from the intersection of Kula Hwy. and Rte. 377. ☎808-878-1715; www.kulabotanicalgarden. com. Open daily 9am-4pm. $7.50, ages 6-12 $2. AmEx/MC/V.)*

MAKAWAO MUSHROOMS. If you're curious about Maui's agricultural production, take a walking tour ($5) of the only commercial mushroom farm on the island. Peruse the flowery clusters of the Chenelle family's oyster mushroom specialty. Learn about preparation in the processing and growing rooms; and if your timing is right, bring some home to snack on. *(530 Kealaloa Ave., on the Haleakala Ranch. From Rte. 37, turn left onto Rte. 377. After 1 mi., turn left on Kealaloa Ave. On the left after ½ mi. ☎808-298-8480; www.makawaomushrooms.com. Open W-Sa 10am-2pm.)*

ULUPALAKUA RANCH AND TEDESCHI WINERY AND VINEYARDS. Ulupalakua is a 25,000-acre ranch on the site of a former sugar plantation and rose garden. The ranch's gem, **Tedeschi Vineyards,** is a winery that produces local vintages from grapes, pineapples, and raspberries. The road to the ranch is stunning, but the ■**free wine tasting** certainly doesn't detract from the journey. Samples are served on an 18ft. bar cut from the trunk of a single mango tree. Inside, another room exhibits history from the *paniolo* (cowboy) tradition on Maui and provides interesting food for thought as you decide between the Ulupalakua red or passion fruit-sweetened Maui Blush. The cowboy-themed gift shop is across the street at the **Ulupalakua Ranch Store and Deli ❶,** where you can pick up a juicy ranch burger ($7) or some elk bratwursts marinated in Maui beer ($6.50) to throw on the grill. *(Take Hwy. 37 south from Kula for 5 mi., past Grandma's Coffee in Keokea, or on the way back from Hana via Rte. 31. ☎808-878-6058; www.mauiwine.com. Tasting room open daily 9am-5pm. Free 30-40min. guided tours 10:30am, 1:30, and 3pm. Gift shop open daily 9:30am-5pm. Deli open daily 11am-2:30pm. Grill open daily 11am-2pm. D/MC/V.)*

POLIPOLI SPRING STATE RECREATION AREA

Polipoli Spring State Recreation Area is secluded high above Kula and lies 6200 ft. above sea level on the western slope of Haleakala. The park's damp forest of redwoods and eucalyptus is used mainly by locals for wild boar-hunting and camping. Views from the park look down across the rolling upcountry hills.

Polipoli's trails are excellent for hiking or mountain biking, though only some trails allow biking; check the signs at each trailhead. The trails have been reconstructed by Na Ala Hele, a group committed to preserving and maintaining Hawaii's state and county parks. Their work is evident in the clean trails, marked with lucid signs. Head to a local bookstore for a hiking guide that includes maps of the park. *Day Hikes on Maui* by Robert Stone (Day Hike Books Inc., 2001) will do the trick.

■ ORIENTATION

Visitors access the park via **Waipoli Road,** off Rte. 377. Follow a series of steep switchbacks for 5 mi. (about 30-40min.), until you reach a hunter check-in station that also serves as a trailhead for a few Polipoli hikes. To reach the campground, continue on Waipoli Rd. Full of rocks, mud, and potholes, the road forks a grueling 4 mi. from the check-in station; bear right and continue for a little over 1 mi. to the parking, picnic, and camping area. If the road is impassable, bring a mountain bike for a muddy ride to the campground. Park is open 24hr.

■ CAMPING

Since the hikes are long and it takes a while to get to Polipoli in the first place, camping in the park makes sense. The campground is very basic, with restrooms and picnic tables but no drinking water. The temperature can drop below freezing at night, and the ground is a damp place to pitch a tent. Other than a few pig-hunters, you might be the only person at the campground; think twice before camping by yourself. Another option is to reserve the 10-person rustic cabin from the Division of State Parks. See **Camping in Hawaii,** p. 82, for more information on the cabins and permits. Polipoli's cabin doesn't have cooking utensils or dishes, but there is both a gas stove and a wood-burning stove. Reservations can be made at ☎808-984-8109.

GIVING BACK

OH BABY, BABY, IT'S A WILD WORLD

Whether they're pulling armored catfish out of the Manoa Stream or working on an organic farm, residents and visitors alike are compelled to sustain Maui's offer of paradise. One of the best groups committed to such measures is **Wild Hawaii Learning Adventures,** a nonprofit organization that provides outdoor experiences for Maui's high school students.

Co-founded by Hike Maui, the Hawaii Wildlife Fund, and concerned citizens, Wild Hawaii collaborates with the island's top naturalist organizations in order to educate young people about environmental stewardship. By participating in its interactive field study programs, students can connect with unspoiled habitats and learn about the Valley Isle's coasts, rainforests, and living streams.

While Wild Hawaii's efforts to highlight delicate ecosystems and encourage protective action are themselves inspirational, the public charity could not do its work without the aid of public grants, individual contributions, and everyman volunteers. It's a great organization with which to pitch in your time. If only a few of the students are moved to join the environmental task force, Maui will have *aina* (land) caretakers for many years to come.

For more information about Wild Hawaii, check out their website at www.wildhawaii.com.

HIKES

WAIAKOA LOOP TRAIL. *(4 mi. 1-2hr. Elevation gain: 600 ft. Moderate.)* To reach the trailhead, walk 1 mi. down the grassy road at the hunters' station (5 mi. down Waipoli Rd.) to the large sign marking the trail. Remember to shut the gate behind you. The loop is a 2 mi. trek through pine forests and open hills. The pine needles which blanket the ground can be slippery, so watch your step.

BOUNDARY-WAIOHULI LOOP. *(5 mi. 3-4hr. Elevation gain: 850 ft. Moderate.)* To get to the Boundary Trailhead, head 1 mi. up Waipoli Rd. from the hunter check-in station. About 1 mi. after the paved road becomes a dirt road, you'll pass through a cattle gate, and the trailhead will be on your right. This hike, which passes through stands of redwood, ash, and cedar trees, is a great option for those unable to reach the top of Waipoli Rd. From the trailhead, take the Boundary Trail for 2 mi. until it ends at the junction of the Waiohuli and Redwood Trails. For a longer hike, take the Redwood Trail to the campground at the top of Waipoli Rd., adding another 2 mi. round-trip. Otherwise, turn left and take the Waiohuli Trail for a 1 mi. hike back to Waipoli Rd. When you reach the road, turn left. From there the loop continues another 2 mi. down Waipoli Rd.

> **TIP** **NEED A KNEAD?** After a long day of hiking, soothe any aching muscles with a $25 student massage at **Spa Luna** (810 Haiku Rd.; ☎808-575-2440) or the **Maui School of Therapeutic Massage** (1043 Makawao Ave., #207; ☎808-572-2277).

HALEAKALA NATIONAL PARK

The gradually sloping volcano of Haleakala ("house of the sun") dominates the island of Maui. The National Park stretches from the upper slopes of the volcano down to Kipahulu (p. 312), on the southeast coast past Hana. The extreme landscape of Haleakala is an incomparable site of striking diversity; from the Kipahulu coast to the 10,023 ft. summit, there are as many climate zones as there are between Central Mexico and Alaska. The park was established to preserve the fragile ecosystems of Haleakala's summit, and park rangers are still actively involved in the protection of the rare native Hawaiian species that live here. The most impressive feature of Haleakala is the "crater" at the top; geologists have since determined that the gigantic depression was actually formed by erosion instead of a volcanic explosion. Watching the sunrise from above the cloud line atop the summit has become a customary pilgrimage for visitors to the island. ◪**Sunset** is also beautiful and usually much less crowded.

AT A GLANCE: HALEAKALA NATIONAL PARK	
AREA: 30,183 acres.	**FEATURES:** Haleakala Volcano, Kipahulu Valley (p. 312), Oheo Gulch (p. 312).
HIGHLIGHTS: Hiking the huge crater at Haleakala's summit; observing endangered wildlife such as the silversword plant and *nene* goose; watching the sun rise and set from the slopes.	**CAMPING:** Free camping available at 2 drive-in campgrounds, 2 wilderness campgrounds, and 3 cabins (p. 321).
GATEWAY TOWNS: Kipahulu (p. 312); Kahului (p. 280); Kula (p. 313).	**FEES:** Entrance fee $10 per vehicle, good for 3 days. $10 per motorcycle. $5 for walkers, cyclists, or hikers.

MAUI

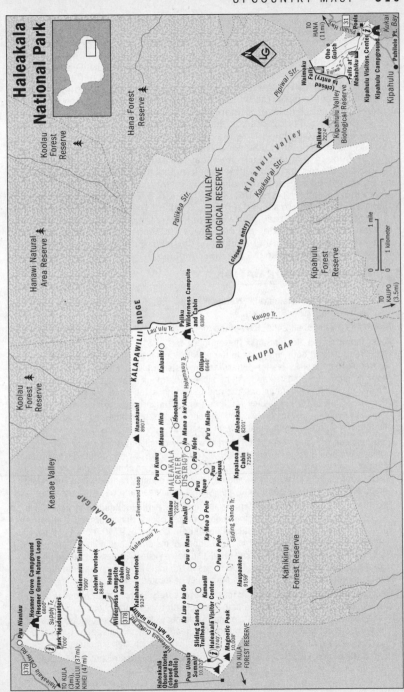

Haleakala National Park

MAUI

Hana Forest Reserve

Koolau Forest Reserve

Hanawi Natural Area Reserve

Keanae Valley

Koolau Forest Reserve

Kipahulu Valley

KIPAHULU VALLEY BIOLOGICAL RESERVE

Pipiwai Str.

Waimoku Falls

Oheʻo Gulch

Falls at Makahiku

Kipahulu Visitors Center

Kipahulu Campground

Kipahulu

Puhilele Pt. Bay

Kukui

TO HANA (11mi.)

Pipiwai (closed to entry)

Kipahulu Valley Biological Reserve

Palikea 2224'

Kaukauʻai Str.

Palikea Str.

KALAPAWILI RIDGE

Lauʻulu Tr.

Paliku Wilderness Campsite and Cabin 6380'

Kaupo Tr.

KAUPO GAP

Kaluaiki

Olilipuu 6646'

Kipahulu Forest Reserve

TO KAUPO (3.5mi)

1 mile

1 kilometer

Hanakauhi 8907'

Mauna Hina

Honokahua

Ka Mana o ke Akua

Halemauu Tr.

Puʻu Maile

Puʻu Kumu

HALEAKALA CRATER DISTRICT

Puʻu Nole

Haleakala Cabin 8201'

Kapalaoa Cabin 7250'

Silversword Loop

Kawilinau 7252'

Halalii

Puʻu Naue

Kaiqua

Ka Moa o Pele

Sliding Sands Tr.

KOOLAU GAP

Halemauu Tr.

Puʻu o Maui

Puʻu o Pele

Haupakea 9159'

Halemauu Trailhead 7990'

Leleiwi Overlook

Holua Wilderness Campsite and Cabin 6940'

Kalahaku Overlook 9324'

Haleakala Crater Rd. (no left turn uphill)

378

Ka Luu o ka Oo

Kamaolii

Haleakala Visitor Center

Kahikinui Forest Reserve

FOREST RESERVE

Puʻu Nianiau

Hosmer Grove Campground (Hosmer Grove Nature Loop)

Supply Tr.

Park Headquarters 7000'

Haleakala Crater Rd.

378

TO KULA (3mi), KAHULUI (37mi), KIHEI (47mi)

Sliding Sands Trailhead 9740'

Magnetic Peak 10,008'

TO KULA

Haleakala Observatories (closed to the public)

Puʻu Ulaula Summit 10,023'

TRANSPORTATION

Don't say we didn't warn you—the drive to the summit can be straight-up harrowing. Especially for those with a fear of heights, the sharp drop-off to the right of the road and the criminal number of hairpin turns are nerve-wracking. If you do take the drive slowly (and you should) other regular commuters to the top may want to pass you, which can be tricky due to the narrow road; use turnouts to let cars by. Never attempt to pass. Be well-rested if you do decide to make the trip, and bring along a friend. Many lone drivers do not get enough sleep, as they try to make sunrise on Haleakala. Consider going for the sunset (which is just as stunning) instead to ensure that you have plenty of shut-eye. Another option is to organize a tour so that you don't have to take the wheel. If you do get to the top and find yourself shaken, talk to a park ranger; sometimes the rangers will arrange for someone to drive your car down for you.

From Kahului, allow 1½ hr. Take Rte. 37 to Rte. 377 to Haleakala Crater Rd. It takes a good 45min. to ascend the final 22 mi. off Haleakala Crater Rd. Once you enter the park, the road is a series of steep switchbacks; take your time and watch for bikers, cattle, and other hazards. Stop at overlooks instead of trying to see everything from behind the wheel. On the way down, switch to a lower gear to prevent brake overheating and failure.

PRACTICAL INFORMATION

Tourist Information: Haleakala National Park, P.O. Box 369, Makawao, 96768. ☎808-572-4400; www.nps.gov/hale.

Hours: The park is open 24hr., though the road may be closed in extreme weather.

Fees, Permits, and Regulations: The entrance fee is $10 per vehicle or motorcycle, good for 3 days at both entrances to the park (the other entrance is in Kipahulu, south of Hana). There is a $5 fee for pedestrians, cyclists, or hikers. Permits are required for camping at wilderness sites and can be picked up at Park Headquarters after a 10min. orientation. Camping permits are free and issued on a 1st come, 1st served basis on the day of the trip (though they rarely run out). 3-night max.; 2-night max. stay per campsite. Hunting, in-line skates, and skateboards are prohibited. Pets and bikes are not allowed on trails. Hikers must stay on the trails.

Weather: Call ☎808-877-5111 for current weather conditions and time of sunrise and sunset, or check http://banana.ifa.hawaii.edu/crater for a webcam of the crater and current weather data. Weather conditions at the summit can change rapidly. For sunrise, prepare for the cold (30-50°F) by wearing layers and bringing blankets. If you are hiking, prepare for hot, cold, wet, and windy conditions. Sunscreen and water are essential.

Facilities: There are 3 **Visitors Centers** in the park. **Park Headquarters,** at 7000 ft., issues permits and has phones, restrooms, maps, books, and information about the park. Open daily 8am-4pm. The **Haleakala Visitors Center,** at 9740 ft., has bathrooms, geologic and environmental displays, an overlook of the crater, and a helpful staff. Open daily 6:30am-3pm. **Kipahulu,** at sea level, also has a Visitors Center and public phones. Open daily 9am-5pm. There is no food or gas in the park. There is no water in Kipahulu. Water from sources in the wilderness area must be treated before drinking.

Emergency: Visitors are responsible for their own safety. There is a pay phone in front of Park Headquarters and at the Kipahulu Visitors Center. The nearest hospital is 1hr. away, and in bad weather, helicopter rescues may be impossible. The summit is over 10,000ft. above sea level; people with respiratory and heart conditions, pregnant women, and young children should consult a doctor before hiking at such high altitudes.

Guided Hikes and Events: 15min. talks on natural and cultural history are held at the Summit building daily; check with the Visitors Center for details. Park rangers lead guided hikes. The Waikamoi Cloud Forest Hike meets M and Th at 9am at the Hosmer Grove shelter. Advance reservations recommended (☎808-572-4459). The 3hr., 3 mi. hike is moderate, with a 500 ft. elevation change. Ask at the Visitors Center or call ☎808-572-4400 for information about other guided hikes.

KNOW YOUR LIMITS. If you decide to tackle Haleakala via bicycle, keep in mind your own physical fitness. Maui Memorial Hospital reports seeing at least 2 to 5 injured cyclists in their emergency room each week with broken bones or facial injuries from downhill rides.

Activities: Dozens of companies offer activities in the park, including biking down the volcano, ziplining over gulches, and horseback riding in the crater. Bike tours range from about $50-150 per person, depending on the company and the time of day.

Maui Sunriders (☎808-579-8970) offers sunrise bike rides for $70 and trips at 9am for $50-65.

Maui Downhill (☎808-877-8787; www.mauidownhill.com) also has a sunrise bike tour for $155 and an early morning tour for $115. Online discounts are available. Tours generally include hotel pickup, breakfast, windbreakers, pants, gloves, helmets, and equipment. Check-in for sunrise rides is usually around 2-2:30am.

Skyline Ecoadventures (☎808-878-8400; www.skylinehawaii.com) provides an educational ziplining course at Haleakala. The company's goal is to teach about the bird ecosystems of Haleakala and each of its 5 zips are named after a different bird ($90, $80 with online booking).

CAMPING AND CABINS

Overnight facilities include two drive-up campgrounds, two wilderness campgrounds, and three wilderness cabins. The two drive-in campgrounds do not require any permits. The wilderness campgrounds require free permits that are issued on the day of the hike at Park Headquarters (8am-3pm); the wilderness cabins have an advanced reservation lottery organized by the Park Service.

Hosmer Grove Campground, near Park Headquarters at 6800 ft. in the cloud belt. Accessible to cars. Tables, grills, drinking water, and porta-potties. Conditions are often cool, windy, and rainy; temperatures can reach near freezing at night. No permit required.

Kipahulu Campground. A 10 mi. drive from Hana on the coast, Kipahulu is located at a 20 ft. elevation, 15 mi. beyond Waianapanapa State Park and a close walk to Oheo Gulch. Kipahulu is not connected to the rest of the park by trails or roads. Accessible to cars. Tables, grills, and porta-potties. No water. Conditions are often warm and wet (with lots of mosquitoes). Flash floods do occur. No permit required.

Holua Wilderness Campground. A 4 mi. hike down the Halemauu Trail (or 7.4 mi. from Sliding Sand Trailhead), Holua is the most accessible wilderness site. Pit toilets; water must be boiled or treated before drinking. No open fires. Free permit required.

Paliku Wilderness Campground, at the base of a rainforest cliff, accessible by a strenuous 10 mi. hike up either Sliding Sands or Halemauu Trail. Paliku is the last campsite before the descent into the Kaupo Gap. Pit toilets; water must be boiled or treated before drinking. No open fires. Free permit required.

Wilderness Cabins. There are rustic cabins at Holua, Paliku, and Kapalaoa, 6 mi. down the Sliding Sands Trail. Each has a wood burning stove, propane stove, cooking utensils and dishes, 12 padded bunks, pit toilets, limited non-drinking water, and firewood. Cookware removed in times of drought. No electricity. Cabin reservations are awarded by monthly lottery. Applications must be submitted in writing at least 3 months prior to requested date. A flexible request improves your chances of getting a cabin. No phone, email, or fax requests. Calls regarding vacancies and cancellations are accepted daily 1-3pm (☎808-572-4459). Full payment must be received 3 weeks ahead or your reservation will be cancelled. Cabins $75 per night per group (1-12 people). Mail applications to: Haleakala National Park, P.O. Box 369, Makawao 96768.

HIKING

The drive to Haleakala, scenic overlooks along the road, and summit itself give visitors a sense of the range of landscapes the park has to offer. However, to truly experience these diverse biomes, you must hike them. The park offers hikes of all levels with trails of various lengths and elevation changes. There are two main trails from the summit area—**Halemauu** and **Sliding Sands**—which connect on the crater floor. Be sure to bring the map provided upon entrance to the park or buy the more detailed hiking guide ($5) from the Visitors Center. The times listed below should be used only as a guideline; be sure to plan for extra time and bring plenty of food and water.

HALEMAUU TO VALLEY RIM. *(2 mi. 1-2hr. Elevation change: 800 ft. Easy.)* The first leg of the Halemauu trail, to the valley rim and back, is a short, fairly level hike. Follow the signs off Haleakala Crater Rd. for the Halemauu trailhead (8000 ft.), 3 mi. above Park Headquarters. The trail begins with a clearly defined path and winds through an eolian meadow before opening to the mist-filled Keanae Valley. About 1 mi. in, you reach the rim of the vast crater, with 300 ft. reddish cinder cones rising from the crater floor. You can turn back here or continue down the switchbacks to the valley floor, adding about another 3 mi., 1200 ft. elevation change, and some sweat to your hike.

FLORA AND FAUNA. The extreme conditions on Haleakala make the diversity of life there even more incredible. The extremely rare and endangered *ahinahina*, or **silversword plant**, is endemic to the volcanic uplands of Maui and the Big Island of Hawaii and only grows on the slopes of Haleakala. Its silvery spines grow for 10 to 50 years and then blossom once (between June and September) with hundreds of purplish blooms, after which the plants shrivel and die. **Silver geraniums** are easy to identify along the Halemauu Trail, with white, five-petal flowers blossoming in summer and early fall. Not too many creatures live in the summit lava fields, so the inch-long **black wolf spider** is at the top of the food chain. This spider carries its young on its back and hunts for food on the ground instead of building a web. The **nene** (the Hawaiian goose and state bird) is nearly extinct but frequently makes an appearance in the park. Never feed a wild *nene* or any fauna in the park. It is illegal to pick flowers or disturb plants.

SLIDING SANDS TO THE FIRST CINDER CONE. *(5 mi. 2-4hr. Elevation change: 2800 ft. Moderate to challenging.)* Sliding Sands is a steep and windswept descent through the dramatic landscape of the crater. The trailhead is at the bulletin board in the Visitors Center parking lot (9740 ft.). After the winding descent, the trail forks; the left fork leads to **Ka Luu o ka Oo,** the first cinder cone. Because of the altitude and steep grade, hiking back up takes twice as long as it does on the way down. Even if you don't have much time, doing the first half-mile of the trail will reward you with an incredible view of the desert crater.

HALEMAUU TO SILVERSWORD LOOP. *(10 mi. 5-7hr. Elevation change: 2500 ft. Moderate to challenging.)* Follow the directions for the first leg of the Halemauu trail. After reaching the valley rim, continue down the series of switchbacks to the valley floor. The view of the crater from the trail is phenomenal. About 4 mi. from the trailhead, past the Holua cabin, a spur trail loops around past a field of the rare *ahinahina* (silversword) plant.

MAUI

SLIDING SANDS TO HALEMAUU TRAILHEAD. *(11 mi. 6-10hr. Elevation change: 4600 ft. Moderate to challenging.)* If you've come to Haleakala for the hiking, this is the trail to do. This combination allows you to experience drastically different terrain. After the steep descent to the crater floor (a little under 4 mi. from the Sliding Sands trailhead), you'll see the intersection with the Halemauu Trail, which leads off to the left. After another 3 mi., you'll reach Holua cabin; from the cabin, it's a 3 mi. uphill trail along switchbacks to the Halemauu parking lot. The trailheads are 6 mi. apart on the steep Haleakala Crater Rd., so before hiking into the crater, many hikers leave cars at the Halemauu Trailhead and hitchhike to the Sliding Sands Trailhead. **Let's Go does not recommend hitchhiking.**

MAKAWAO

Makawao (pop. 6752) is the only Upcountry town with shops, restaurants, and a discernible main street. The storefronts hint at Makawao's cowboy past, but aside from the annual rodeo, it's a tourist town. Stores of aloha wear line up next to a plethora of local art galleries. Nightlife isn't totally desolate either: Casanova's features live music and DJs. And, as you would expect from the heart of *paniolo* (cowboy) country, the steak here takes the cake.

ORIENTATION AND PRACTICAL INFORMATION

The central district of historic Makawao is located where **Makawao Avenue** intersects **Baldwin Avenue**, which continues 7 mi. northwest to **Paia. Kaupakulua Road** continues north to **Haiku** from the end of Makawao Ave. and eventually connects with **Hana Hwy.** There's a public parking lot on Makawao Ave. close enough to walk to all of Makawao's shops, galleries, and restaurants.

The **Makawao Public Library,** 1159 Makawao Ave., is next to Down to Earth Natural Foods. (☎808-573-8785. Open M and W noon-8pm; Tu, Th, and Sa 9:30am-5pm. Copies $0.20 per page.) For **Internet access** and copy services, head to **1 Stop Postal Shop,** 1135 Makawao Ave., just past the library. (☎808-572-3088, fax 808-572-3671. Internet $0.15 per min., $2 per min. Copies $0.12 per page. Open M-F 8am-5:30pm, Sa 9:30am-3:30pm. AmEx/D/MC/V.) Internet access is also available at the public library with a 3-month visitor's card ($10). The **Makawao Post Office** is a little farther down at 1075 Makawao Ave. (☎808-572-0019. Open M-F 8:30am-4:30pm, Sa 8:30-11am.) **Postal Code:** 96768.

ACCOMMODATIONS

Makawao is a convenient base from which to explore Upcountry Maui and the North Shore; the galleries and shops downtown will fill only an afternoon.

Peace of Maui, 1290 Haliimaile Rd. (☎808-572-5045; www.peaceofmaui.com). From Kahului, take Haleakala Hwy.; Haliimaile Rd. will be on your left. Surrounded by pineapple fields and an incredible view of Haleakala, Peace of Maui has a homey lodge with 6 rooms that share toilets, showers, a common living room, and a kitchen. 4 rooms have queen-size beds; 2 have 2 twins. All have TV, fan, fridge, pantry, and access to the hot tub, and free Internet access. A 2-bedroom cottage sleeps 2-4 people, with kitchen and *lanai*. Somewhat flexible 7-night min. stay for cottage. Full payment due 30 days in advance. Singles $50; doubles $55; cottage $120. MC/V. ❷

Banyan Tree Vacation Rentals, 3265 Baldwin Ave. (☎808-572-9021), 1 mi. from Makawao. The grounds of Banyan Tree Rentals are lush, luxurious, and feature a large swimming pool and a spacious yoga and meditation studio. The bungalows offer "a taste of Old Hawaii," and a bit of peeling paint only adds to the rustic charm. Studio cottages $145-190; a luxurious and spacious 3-bedroom, 3-bath house with living room and full

RODEO DRIVE

Even if you don't know a darn thing about uncorkin' a bronc, you're sure to have a hog-killin' time at the Makawao Rodeo and Paniolo Parade, one of Maui's most enduring Fourth of July traditions.

Since the late 19th century, horseback-riding *paniolo* (Hawaiian cowboys) have been wrangling the cattle in Makawao's grassy fields, where today a vivacious art and yoga community also prospers. Instead of barkin' at a knot, mosey on down to the rodeo grounds and elbow in amongst locals, tourists, and alfalfa desperados (farmers) as they watch the *paniolo* rope and ride. The rodeo includes four days of bareback bronc and bull riding, calf roping, team roping, barrel racing, and *po'o wai u*, a Hawaii-specific and timed roping challenge.

Join in the spirit and throw back some wild mare's milk (whiskey) or whistle berries (beans), as the audience screams, "What in tarnation?" when their favorite ranch hand falls off a bucking horse. However, don't forget to stop yer yammerin' long enough to line up along Baldwin Ave. for the celebratory Paniolo Parade. Boots, bonnets, and spurs not required.

The Annual Makawao Rodeo, presented by the Maui Roping Club, takes place at Oskie Rice Arena, Olinda Rd., Makawao. (☎808-572-0356.) Qualifying runs are free admission. Bull Bash $15. Rodeo $10. (Info 808-572-9565; volunteers 808-573-0422.)

kitchen $390. Rates are for 2-person occupancy; each additional person $30. Cleaning fee. Check-in 2pm. Check-out 11am. AmEx/D/MC/V. ❹

🍴 FOOD

There are several good places for a light lunch on Baldwin Ave., in addition to Mexican and steak house options for dinner. For more selection, **Paia** (p. 302) is only a 10-15min. drive away. Natural food store **Down to Earth,** 1169 Makawao Ave., next to the library, has healthy groceries. It also sells the food left in the hot bar for half-price daily 6-7pm. (☎808-572-1488. Open daily 8am-8pm. AmEx/MC/V.) **The Rodeo General Store,** 3661 Baldwin Ave., is a market stocked with basic groceries, local meat, and super-cheap pre-packaged salads, sushi, and sandwiches. It also has a comprehensive wine room and a deli. (☎808-572-2404. Open M-Sa 6:30am-10pm, Su 6:30am-8pm. AmEx/MC/V.) For an extensive selection of cheap spirits, try **Liquor Shack & Grinds,** 1143 Makawao Ave. (☎808-572-7775. Open daily 9am-10:30pm. MC/V.)

RESTAURANTS

Casanova's Italian Restaurant and Deli, 1188 Makawao Ave. (☎808-572-0220; www.casanovamaui.com), at the intersection of Baldwin Ave. Both halves of Casanova's provide reasonably priced, hearty helpings of delicious food. The wooden counter out front provides Makawao's best spot to people-watch and enjoy a "vulcano" (baked eggplant and smoked mozzarella, $7). The restaurant maintains a similarly funky atmosphere and prices just as divine (*fettucine portofino,* $16). Also serves as the best nightlife option in Upcountry (p. 325). Open M-Sa 7:30am-6pm, Su 8:30am-6pm. AmEx/D/MC/V. ❶/❸

Haliimaile General Store, 900 Haliimaile Rd. (☎808-572-2666; www.bevgannonrestaurants.com). Nestled in a refurbished sugarcane plantation store, this award-winning restaurant is a sure-fire way to a satisfied stomach. The eclectic menu (*paniolo* barbecue ribs, $25; coconut seafood curry, $30), stylish desserts, and Bev's famous crab pizza keep both locals and resort-bound tourists coming. Open M-F 11am-2:30pm, daily 5:30pm-9:30pm. AmEx/D/MC/V. ❺

Polli's, 1202 Makawao Ave. (☎808-572-7808), at the intersection of Baldwin Ave. Polli's offers heaping Mexican dishes, most under $12. The setting is intimate, the staff spunky, and the margaritas free-flowing. Entrees are hearty. Vegetarian-friendly. The bar fills with locals, especially during happy hour (M-F 4-5:30pm; beers $2.50, margaritas $4, *pupu* and nachos $5). Open daily 11am-10pm. AmEx/D/MC/V. ❷

CAFES AND BAKERIES

▨ **Komoda Store and Bakery,** 3674 Baldwin Ave. (☎808-572-7261), is famous for its *malasadas* (Portuguese doughnuts, $0.75), cream puffs ($1.35), and enormous doughnuts on a stick ($1). The bakery's unremarkable large brown building is easy to miss, so just follow the scent of mouth-watering pastries. Open M-Tu and Th-F 7am-5pm, Sa 7am-2pm. Cash only. ❶

Cafe del Sol, 3620 Baldwin Ave. (☎808-572-4877), in the plaza behind Maui Hands, next to Hot Island Glass. Serves local greens, sandwiches (roasted chicken salad on a croissant, $8), and freshly baked muffins and pastries. The atmosphere is relaxed and playful; local artwork hangs on the walls. Shady outdoor patio dining is removed from busy Baldwin Ave. Breakfast M-Sa 8-10:45am. Lunch M-Sa 11am-3:30pm. MC/V. ❶

Makawao Sushi & Deli, 3647 Baldwin Ave. (☎808- 573-9044) Enjoy a jolt of caffeine on the pleasant outdoor *lanai* while the staff overstuffs their artful sushi rolls ($6-8.50) and sashimi ($17-21). If you're feeling extra bold, try the 007 roll (spicy tuna with eel, avocado, and unagi sauce; $18). Open M-Th 11:30am-3pm and 5-9pm, F-Sa 11:30am-3pm and 5-10pm, Su 3:30-9pm. MC/V. ❷

◉ ⌂ SIGHTS AND GALLERIES

Galleries line Baldwin Ave. and sell handmade bowls, jewelry, paintings, and prints. Although they aren't cheap, you may find a trinket that suits you.

▨ **Hui Noeau Visual Arts Center,** 2841 Baldwin Ave. (☎808-572-6560; fax 808-572-2750; www.huinoeau.com). This beautiful estate offers 6 exhibits per year of pieces by contemporary local artists. Hui Noeau also sponsors visiting artists, offers classes, and leads painting, photography, printmaking, jewelry, woodworking, and ceramics workshops for all ages. The house and landscaped grounds, once part of the Baldwin estate, are themselves worth a stroll. While the art is expensive, the gift shop offers lovely handmade items starting around $10. Open M-Sa 10am-4pm; closed Sa in June. Suggested donation $2. Email info@huinoeau.com for volunteer info.

Hot Island Glass, 3620 Baldwin Ave. (☎808-572-4527), behind Maui Hands. Visitors come in droves to marvel at Maui's only hand-blown glass gallery with glassblowing onsite (observable most days 10:30am-4pm, call to confirm). Most budget travelers will just come to look (glass starfish $45 and up), but slightly flawed unsigned seconds and small souvenirs are more affordable ($30 and up). Open daily 9am-5pm. AmEx/MC/V.

David Warren Gallery, 3625 Baldwin Ave. (☎808-572-1288). This family-owned gallery was Makawao's first. It has since evolved into a co-op that displays the work of the talented Warrens, including unusual and reasonably priced woodwork (the father-son duo's ever-popular barksia pens, $38), funky creations made from forks and spoons, and other crafts. Framing is also available. Open M-Sa 10am-5pm. AmEx/D/MC/V.

The Sacred Garden of Maliko, 460 Kaluanui Rd., (☎808-573-7700; www.sacredgardenmaui.com), 2 mi. below Makawao Town. A place of interest for peace-seekers and hippies, the Sacred Garden offers a 10,000 sq. ft. greenhouse of prayer-blessed orchids, exotics, and aquatics; a labyrinth in a kukui grove; a gift gallery; and classes on everything from gardening to creativity and spiritual growth. Open 10am-5pm. Free.

▨ NIGHTLIFE

Both **Polli's** (p. 324) and the **Stopwatch Sports Bar and Grill** house bars that attract a local crowd of devotees, but upscale Italian restaurant ▨**Casanova's** is the real pulse of Upcountry nightlife. Wednesday's ladies' night ("Wild Wahine Wednesday"), billed as the best late-night entertainment in Maui, packs the place by 10:30pm. Thursdays occasionally feature salsa/Latin music and dancing. Fridays and Saturdays also attract a crowd for live bands or DJs at 10pm. Pizza is served until 11:30pm. Check the free publication *Maui Time Weekly* for entertainment schedule. (☎808-572-0220. 21+ after 10pm. Cover $5-15.)

MOLOKAI

Amid Hawaii's many resorts and tourist traps, Molokai is the closest you can get to old Hawaii. Fishponds dating from the 14th century, several of which are still operational today, line the southern coast, and some residents choose to spend a portion of the year living in true Hawaiian fashion—at beach campsites. Over half the island's population has Native Hawaiian ancestry, and these residents continue to fight to preserve the island's traditional state. Within the island, there is a divide between members of the community over issues of development and the expansion of tourism. Cruise ships are not allowed to stop on Molokai, and the recently inaugurated Hawaii Superferry has no plans to stop here either. Development-averse locals may find their wishes granted for the time being.

At one time, Molokai was revered for its many powerful *kahuna* (priests). Visitors from all over made pilgrimages to the island to seek the priests' counsel. The island was called Pule Oo (powerful prayer), and was considered a refuge place for *kapu*-breakers (taboo-breakers). For a time, the island was free from armed conflict because it was considered sacred. Now, however, Molokai retains little of its former influence, and the island struggles economically. Jobs are scarce and unemployment rivals some of the mainland's most depressed counties. Subsistence fishing and farming are not uncommon.

Nonetheless, Molokai's laid-back residents maintain a positive outlook on life. The birthplace of both the aloha spirit and hula, Molokai is known as "The Friendly Isle" for a reason, and drivers often smile and wave amiably at passers-by. Molokai's roads are traffic light-free, although the slow pace of some of the island's 7000 inhabitants sometimes causes a bit of a backup. Nobody seems to mind, however, since there's no reason to be in a hurry. A sign that greets visitors at the airport says it all: "Aloha! Slow down: this is Molokai." With some of the state's least-developed coastal areas, Molokai's beaches and the warm personalities of her residents are not to be missed.

HIGHLIGHTS OF MOLOKAI

STAND IN AWE at the Iliiliopae Heiau, the second-largest traditional Hawaiian temple in the islands (p. 344).

BASK IN THE SUN on a deserted beach cove at Make Horse Beach, one of Hawaii's most beautiful white sand beaches (p. 349).

GET BACK TO NATURE at the rugged Kamakou Preserve, home to 219 endemic plant and animal species (p. 336).

SOJOURN to the sobering former leper colony at Kalaupapa Peninsula (p. 334).

ROPE A STEER in *paniolo* lessons at the Molokai Ranch in Maunaloa (p. 347).

✈ INTERISLAND TRANSPORTATION

Molokai is most easily accessible by short **plane** flights (about 20min.) from Maui and Oahu, though there is also a **ferry** service from Maui. Flights to Molokai generally arrive at the **Hoolehua Airport** (6.5 mi. northwest of Kaunakakai, 10 mi. east of Maunaloa), although there is also an airport at Kalaupapa.

Molokai

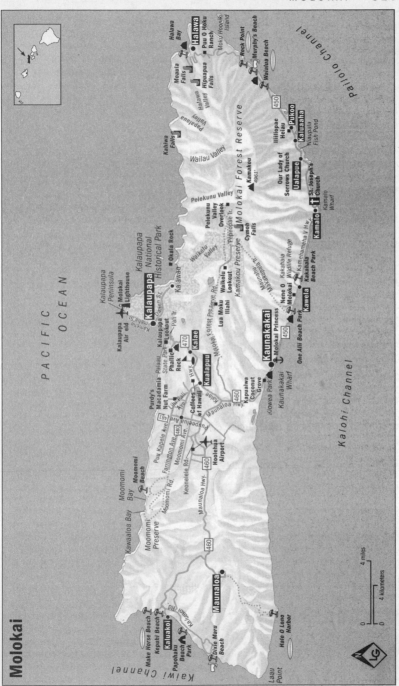

PACIFIC OCEAN

Kaiwi Channel

Kalohi Channel

Pailolo Channel

Molokai Forest Reserve

Kamakou Preserve

Kalaupapa National Historical Park

Halawa
Halawa Bay
Puu O Hoku Ranch
Moku Hooniki Island
Rock Point
Murphy's Beach
Waialua Beach
Hipuapua Falls
Moaula Falls
Halawa Valley
Papalaua Valley

Pukoo
Kaluaaha
Wiaupala Fish Pond
Hiilopae Heiau
Our Lady of Sorrows Church
Ualapue
Kamakou 4961
Kamalo
St. Joseph's Church
Kamalo Wharf

Kahiwa Falls
Wailau Valley

Pelekunu Valley
Pelekunu Valley Overlook
Pepeopae Tr.
Hanalilolilo Tr.
Oloupena Falls

Waikolu Valley
Waikolu Lookout
Lua Moku Iliahi
Kakahaia Wildlife Refuge
Kamehameha V Hwy
Kakahaia Beach Park
Nene O Molokai
One Alii Beach Park
Kawela

Kalaupapa Peninsula
Molokai Lighthouse
Kalaupapa
Kalaupapa Air eld
Kalaupapa Lookout
Kalawao
Okala Rock
Kauhako Crater

Kamehameha Hwy
Waikolu Lookout
Molokai Forest Preserve Rd.
Kaunakakai
Molokai Princess
450
Kaunakakai Wharf
Kapuaiwa Coconut Grove
Kiowea Park

Phallic Rock
Palau State Park
Kalae
Uiu Pali
Moa
Purdy's Macadamia Nut Farm
Coffees of Hawaii
Kualapuu

Puu Kapele Ave
Farrington Ave
Moomomi Rd.
180
490
Maunaloa Hwy
Hoolehua Airport
Keonelele Rd.
460

Kawaaloa Bay
Moomomi Bay
Moomomi Beach
Moomomi Preserve

460

Maunaloa

Make Horse Beach
Kepuhi Beach
Kaluakoi
Papohaku Beach Park
Dixie Maru Beach
Hale O Lono Harbor
Laau Point
Kaluakoi Rd.
Kaunaloa Rd.

470
Pali Tr.
Green St.
Kamehameha St.

0   4 miles
0   4 kilometers

N

MOLOKAI

Go Airlines, (☎888-435-9462; www.iflygo.com). A dependable airline with flights to every island. Flights from Kona (8 daily from $68), Honolulu (6 daily from $59) and Kahului (4 daily from $59); most are in 8-10 seat airplanes. Book early for lower rates.

Pacific Wings Express, (☎888-866-5022; www.flypwx.com). Flights from Honolulu and Kahului ($49-95 each way). Flies to the Kalaupapa Peninsula ($49-95 each way).

Island Air, 99 Kapalulu Pl. (☎800-652-6541; www.islandair.com), on Lagoon Dr., behind the airport in Honolulu. From Honolulu (6 flights per day) or Maui (2 flights per day); one-way from $61, round-trip from $122. 5% discount online.

The Molokai Princess, (☎808-661-8397 or 808-667-6165; www.molokaiferry.com) at Kaunakakai Wharf. Passenger-only ferry to **Lahaina, Maui** (90min.; departs Maui daily 7:15am and 6pm, departs Molokai daily 5:30am and 4pm; $42.40, ages 4-12 $21.20, under 4 free.) Two bags allowed; additional bags, surfboards, or bikes $15 each.

⧉ LOCAL TRANSPORTATION

Once on the island, **renting a car** is a necessity, as there is no public transportation. A single highway stretches 50 mi. from one side of the island to the other, making Molokai Hawaii's easiest island to navigate.

Budget has an office in the Molokai Airport (☎808-567-6877 or 800-527-0700; www.budget.com. Open 6:30am-7pm) as does **Dollar** (☎808-567-6156; www.dollar.com. Open 6am-7pm). Check for Internet specials. **Island Kine Auto Rental,** 242 Ilio Rd. (☎808-553-5242 or 866-527-7368; www.molokai-car-rental.com), is just north of Ala Malama Ave. This local outfit rents cars, trucks, vans, and ATVs from its lot south of town on Ala Malama Ave. It will pick you up from the airport and orient you to the island. ($45-70 per day. Open daily 7am-7pm.) Try **Molokai Outdoors** (☎808-553-4477; www.molokai-outdoors.com) for bargain car rentals negotiated directly with Dollar, as well as a cheap shuttle service from the airport ($14 per person one-way to Kaunakakai). **Taxis** are expensive, but are available from early morning to 8pm from **Molokai Off-Road Tours & Taxi** (☎808-553-3369), which operates all over the island (airport to Kaunakakai $26.80). **Hele Mai Taxis** (☎808-336-0967), also operates island-wide, (airport to Kaunakakai $27, airport to Maunaloa $32). No rental cars are technically permitted off paved roads. Even in a 4WD vehicle, never drive off-road in the rain; getting stuck on Molokai is a major inconvenience. Gas prices on Molokai are often substantially higher than on Oahu or Maui. Always drive with your fuel level in mind, as there are only **three gas stations** on the island—none east of Kaunakakai or near the airport. If you need assistance, call a full-service station in Kaunakakai. **Shirley Rawlins' Chevron,** 20 Maunaloa Hwy. (☎808-553-3214), is a good bet. (Open M-Th 6:30am-8:30pm, F-Sa 6:30am-9pm, Su 7am-6pm.)

 SAVING MOOLA IN MOLOKAI. Because of Molokai's higher gas prices and scarcity of budget accommodations (which means you can't necessarily stay where the beaches are), you will likely be spending lots of money at the pump. The best bet is to rent a compact car; better gas mileage will soften the financial blow.

⧉ ACCOMMODATIONS

Molokai isn't an easy place to find budget accommodations. There are no hostels and most of the less expensive options are condos or beach houses that are better suited for longer stays. Couples can find great deals at the various B&Bs

on the island; try them before staying at a hotel or condo. For a list of nearly all the accommodations available, pick up the **Molokai: Hawaiian by Nature** brochure at the **Molokai Visitors Association,** 28 Kamoi St., in Kaunakakai.

Molokai Vacation Rentals, at the intersection of Hwy. 460 and 470, rents houses, condos, and cottages for a wide range of prices. Most two- or three-bedroom houses go for $100-150 per night. (☎808-553-8334 or 800-367-2984; www. molokai-vacation-rental.com. Open M-F 8am-4:30pm. AmEx/MC/V.) **Friendly Island Realty,** 75 Ala Malama Ave., leases dozens of properties all over the island, from studio apartments ($75-125) to one-bedroom condos ($95-150) to full beach houses for $135 and up. (☎808-553-3666 or 800-600-4158; www. molokairesorts.com. Open M-F 8am-5:30pm, Sa 8am-3pm. MC/V.)

KAUNAKAKAI

Located in the middle of the South Shore, Kaunakakai (pop. 2726) is a mellow, easy-going town. The leisurely amble of cars along Ala Malama Ave. might initially frustrate anxious travelers, but after adjusting to Molokai's slow pace, those same travelers will appreciate the take-it-easy ambience of this island center. It takes less than an hour to walk all of Kaunakakai's paved roads, and after 9pm, you may have them to yourself. Kaunakakai is also home to the majority of Molokai's grocery stores, restaurants, and shops, as well as its police station, hospital, and banks.

ORIENTATION AND PRACTICAL INFORMATION

To get to Kaunakakai from Hoolehua Airport, turn immediately right, and then left on **Route 460 (Maunaloa Highway) East.** Kaunakakai center begins at the intersection of **Route 460** and **Ala Malama Avenue.** There's a gas station in the northwest corner of the intersection, and both of the town's banks are located across the street in the **Molokai Center,** a business complex that stretches north along the first block of Ala Malama. At the end of the block, Ala Malama turns east for another four blocks; most of the town's shops and restaurants are located here. Rte. 460 continues east, but its name changes to **Route 450 (Kamehameha V),** or **"Kam 5,"** as it leaves town. The easiest way to navigate is by the highway mile markers, which begin at mi. 0 in Kaunakakai and ascend in both directions.

Tourist Office: Molokai Visitors Association, 2 Kamoi St., Ste. 200 (☎808-553-3876; www.molokai-hawaii.com), just north of the highway, offers brochures and recommends the island's activity centers and accommodations, but has less information about non-commercial attractions. Open M-F 8am-4:30pm.

Banks: Bank of Hawaii, 20B Ala Malama Ave. (☎808-553-3273), in the Molokai Center on the right side of the street as you turn on Ala Malama from the main highway. Open M-Th 8:30am-4pm, F 8:30am-6pm. **24hr. ATM** out front.

Library: The Molokai Public Library, 15 Ala Malama Ave. (☎808-553-1765), in the Civic Center across from the banks. Knowledgeable staff, well-stocked Hawaiiana book section, 6 computers with **Internet access** and printing with 3-month visitor's card ($10). Open M-Tu and Th-F 9am-5pm, W 12:30-8pm.

Internet Access: The fastest Internet connection is at **Stanley's,** 125 Puali Pl. (☎808-553-9966), the island's only Internet cafe; $1 per 10min. **Kaunakakai Elementary School,** 30 Ainoa St. (☎808-553-1730), has a computer lab with set hours for public use a few days a week (not during the summer), though this time is generally reserved for the local community members. Call ahead for schedule.

Laundry: A self-service **laundromat** is located just off Ala Malama on Makaena Pl., behind the Natural Foods Outpost. Wash $1-2, dry $0.25 per 5min. Change and detergent available at **Kalama's Gas Station** 2 stores down. Open daily 7am-9pm.

Recreation: Mitchell Pauole Center, 90 Ainoa St. (☎808-553-3204), 1 block south of Ala Malama. Free facilities open to the public. The **Cooke Memorial Pool,** 20 Kolapa Pl. (☎808-553-5775), is open in summer M-Tu and Th-Sa 9am-4:30pm, W 10am-4:30pm. Summer W and F night swim 6-8:30pm. Lap swim M, T and Th 7-9am. Closes daily 11:45am-1pm. The **gym** (☎808-553-5141) is open for basketball M-F 11am-3pm, Sa 10am-3pm. Weight room open M-F 10am-9pm. Tennis courts, a skateboarding park, and baseball fields. Also sells camping permits M-F 8am-1pm, 2:30-4pm.

Police: 110 Ainoa St. (☎808-553-5355), south of Ala Malama between the Mitchell Pauole Center and the fire department.

Pharmacy: Molokai Drugs, 28 Kamoi St., Ste. 100 (☎808-553-5790), in the Kamoi Professional Center, behind the post office. Wide selection of Hawaiian CDs, magazines, and souvenirs. Open M-F 8:45am-5:45pm, Sa 8:45am-2pm.

Hospital: Molokai General Hospital, 280 Home Olu Pl. (☎808-553-5331), 4 blocks north of Ala Malama; blue signs clearly indicate the way from Ala Malama on the eastern end of downtown. 24hr. emergency room.

Post Office: 120 Ala Malama Ave. (☎808-553-5179). Open M-F 9am-4:30pm, Sa 9-11am. **Postal Code:** 96748.

🎒 🏕 ACCOMMODATIONS AND CAMPING

While there are no accommodations within walking distance of Kaunakakai, the first 5 mi. east of town along Hwy. 450 have a range of quality places to stay, including hotels, condos, B&Bs, and campgrounds.

🏨 **Ka Hale Mala Bed & Breakfast,** 7 Kamakana Pl. (☎808-553-9009; www.molokai-bnb. com). Before mi. marker 5 east of town on Hwy. 450, turn left on Kamakana Pl. On the left near the end of the small cul-de-sac. Ka Hale is one of Molokai's nicest B&Bs, a spacious suite with a master bedroom, dining room, full kitchen, living room, and a private *lanai*. Sleeps 4. Affable owners will pick you up at the airport. Snorkels, beach towels, and picnic gear are free to borrow. Hawaiian-style breakfast for an additional $5 per guest. Suite $80 (1-2 people); additional guests $15. Cash only. ❸

Aahi Place Bed & Breakfast, 215 Aahi Pl. (☎808-553-8033; www.molokai.com/aahi), located 1 mi. east of town, on the left side of Aahi Pl., at the top of the steep hill and right before the road swings to the east. This B&B's lofty location offers an ocean view and a mixed bag in terms of sleeping quarters: a roomy cottage, a flimsy 1-bedroom trailer (called the "backpacker's cabin"), and a small room off the main house with its own entrance. Guests have access to the outdoor kitchenette, washing machine, grill, phone, and cable TV on the porch. Reserve the cottage months in advance in high season. Trailer $40; room $40; cottage $80. Cash or traveler's checks. ❷

Hotel Molokai, Kamehameha V Hwy. (☎808-553-5347, fax 808-553-5047; www.hotel-molokai.com), before the marker 2mi. east of town. Set on tiny Kamiloloa Beach with a great view of Lanai, Hotel Molokai is a cluster of 2-story Polynesian bungalows. Rooms have phone, *lanai*, TV, fridge, and laundry access. They aren't the island's best value, but guests have access to a small pool next to the hotel restaurant and bar, which hosts F night Hawaiian music jam sessions. $159-249. AmEx/D/MC/V. ❺

One Alii Beach Park I, just past the marker 3mi. on the *makai* (ocean) side of Kamehameha Hwy., was once a favorite beach spot for *alii* (Hawaiian royalty). One Alii is actually 2 parks, One Alii I and One Alii II, located next to each other. One Alii I, the only park available for camping, has lights, outlets, restrooms, and showers. Both parks are hot and windy during the day and, because of silty water near-shore, are not great places to

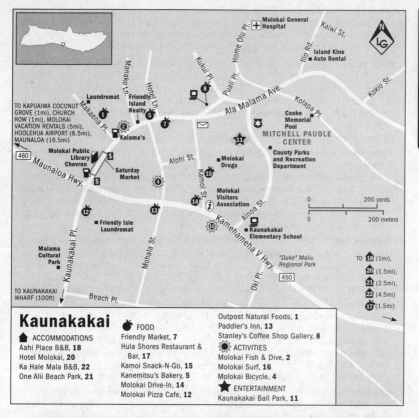

Kaunakakai

🏠 **ACCOMMODATIONS**
Aahi Place B&B, **18**
Hotel Molokai, **20**
Ka Hale Mala B&B, **22**
One Alii Beach Park, **21**

🍴 FOOD
Friendly Market, **7**
Hula Shores Restaurant &
    Bar, **17**
Kamoi Snack-N-Go, **15**
Kanemitsu's Bakery, **5**
Molokai Drive-In, **14**
Molokai Pizza Cafe, **12**

Outpost Natural Foods, **1**
Paddler's Inn, **13**
Stanley's Coffee Shop Gallery, **8**
☀️ **ACTIVITIES**
Molokai Fish & Dive, **2**
Molokai Surf, **16**
Molokai Bicycle, **4**
⭐ **ENTERTAINMENT**
Kaunakakai Ball Park, **11**

swim or snorkel. 3-night max (waived if demand is low). Camping permits required and can be obtained at the Mitchell Pauole Center. $3 per night per camper, children $0.50. See **Camping in Hawaii,** p. 82, for more info. ❶

🍴 FOOD

Molokai is not the place to go for gourmet or healthy dining, and Kanaukakai is no exception—if your palate isn't picky and your cholesterol isn't high, then eating out here should be no problem. Lunch counters and fast-food eateries are the main options, though two of the island's three restaurants are located nearby. Organic, local produce (like papayas and passion fruit) and bulk cereals abound at ◙**Outpost Natural Foods,** 70 Makena Pl., just block off Ala Malama, where it turns east. The mini-warehouse store has a decent vegetarian lunch counter, though erratic hours (ostensibly M-F 10am-3pm) can make it difficult to snag a garden burger ($5-6) or smoothie ($4.50). Wi-Fi is available from the back parking lot for a $1 donation. (☎808-553-3377. Open M-Th 9am-6pm, F 9am-4pm, Su 10am-5pm. AmEx/D/MC/V.) Locals flock to **Friendly Market,** 90 Malama Ave., the largest grocery store on the island. (☎808-553-5821 or 808-553-5595. Open M-F 8:30am-8:30pm, Sa 8:30-6:30pm. AmEx/MC/V.) On Saturday mornings, local merchants set up a **farmers' market** on the sidewalk in front of the Molokai Center on Ala Malama Ave. Vendors start setting up and selling as early as 6am. Sample tropical fruits and look for vintage aloha shirts (from $5), locally-made drums, and letter openers carved from the antlers of the local axis deer. Arrive early if you want fresh produce.

Hula Shores Restaurant & Bar, Kamehameha Hwy. (☎808-553-5347), in Hotel Molokai. One of the few full-service restaurants on the island, Hula Shores serves a variety of quality island-style entrees for dinner, like coconut shrimp ($22) and mac-nut *lilikoi* chicken ($18). Lunch consists of burgers and sandwiches ($8.25-10.25), while the breakfast menu features egg combo plates ($6) and french toast ($8.50). Live music nightly. F Hawaiian music jam sessions 4-6pm. Open daily for breakfast 7am-11am, lunch 11am-2pm, dinner 6pm-9pm. Bar open 1-10:30pm. ❸

Kanemitsu's Bakery, 79 Ala Malama Ave. (☎808-553-5855). For a unique experience, venture down Hotel Ln. (1 block east of the bakery), and then turn down the colorful alley on your left. Loaves of warm French bread with fruit toppings ($4-5) sold fresh Tu-Su 10:30pm-2am, from the window marked "knock here." Standard French bread ($2.20) sells out fast. The dimly-lit cafe in the back of the store is filled with locals wolfing down eggs and meat ($7) for breakfast or a bowl of *saimin* ($5.75) for lunch. Open M and W-Su 5:30am-6:30pm. AmEx/D/MC/V. ❶

Paddler's Inn, 10 Mohala St. (☎808-553-5256), on the corner of Mohala and Kam 5 Hwy. Decorated with canoe gear in honor of Molokai's paddling past, this joint offers rib-eye ($20.50) and *mahi mahi* ($21). Lunch consists mostly of burgers and sandwiches ($8.50-11.50). Happy hour daily 3-6pm (Bud Light draft $1.50, Kona draft $2.50). Breakfast served M-F 7-11am, Sa-Su 9am-noon; lunch and dinner served daily 11am-8:30pm. Bar open until 1am. Th-Sa local bands play until 2am. AmEx/D/MC/V. ❸

Stanley's Coffee Shop Gallery, 125 Puali Pl. (☎808-553-9966), north of Ala Malama on the eastern end of town. The best place to have a latte ($2.75) on Molokai, Stanley's offers vinyl booths, chrome bar stools, and hard-to-come-by A/C for its clientele. No drip coffee here, only espresso from a vintage Italian Elektra machine. High-speed Internet access available. ($1 per 10min.) Monster-sized muffins ($1.85), a breakfast sandwich ($4), and the "best *saimin* in town" ($4). M-F 6am-2pm, Sa-Su 6am-noon. MC/V. ❶

Molokai Pizza Cafe, 15 Kaunakakai Pl. (☎808-553-3288), 1 block south of Rte. 460 on the wharf road. Kaunakakai's popular family restaurant looks like a diner on the inside. Pizzas named after each Hawaiian Island (small, $11.40-20.60, large $16.50-29.50). Subs ($11), burgers ($8-10), pasta ($8-11), *hulihuli* chicken ($12), fresh fish, and on W a Mexican menu with burritos and fajitas ($11). Su dinner prime rib ($16). Open M-Th 10am-10pm, F-Sa 10am-11pm, Su 11am-10pm. Cash only. ❷

Molokai Drive-In, 15 Kamoi St. (☎808-553-5655), on the corner of Rte. 460. Fast food island-style—greasy, good, and dirt cheap. 2 eggs, meat, hash browns, and drink $5.30. Plate lunches $8.50-9.25. Hamburgers ($2.25), tacos ($2), and *saimin* ($4). Serves fish caught daily. Very little seating available so takeout is the norm. Open M-Th and Su 6am-10pm, F-Sa 6:30am-10pm. Cash only. ❶

Kamoi Snack-N-Go, 28 Kamoi St. (☎808-553-3742), in the same complex as Molokai Drugs, behind the post office. Molokai's only ice cream parlor offers 32 unique flavors from green tea to Hawaiian mud pie (single scoop $2.65, double $3.65). No food is served, but malts, milkshakes, and sundaes are available for those with more of an appetite. Open M-F 10am-9pm, Sa 9am-9pm, Su noon-9pm. MC/V. ❶

GOT THE MUNCHIES? Because Molokai doesn't have many places to eat, especially for dinner, it is a good call to stay somewhere that has a kitchen or kitchenette. The grocery stores are stocked with all the essentials, so you'll be able to be creative.

☆ ACTIVITIES

Molokai offers a range of outdoor activities; some of the most popular are hiking, kayaking, and snorkeling. Surfing and golf are also possible, but the surfing spots and golf course are not on par with those found elsewhere in Hawaii. A few outfits near Kaunakakai offer rentals and guided trips of all kinds. Almost all of Molokai can be explored on your own, but you may find it more rewarding to go with a local guide. **Molokai Outdoors,** which currently only has a virtual office, is a great source of information about everything outdoors, including trips to the **Kalaupapa Peninsula** (p. 334), and hiking in Halawa Valley. Their only rentals are kayaks by the week (singles $113, doubles $167, $25-50 delivery fee). They also offer a few half-day and full-day guided tours of the island ($96-167) for those who want to see everything in a short period of time. Most popular is the **Alii Tour** which covers Kaunakakai, St. Joseph's Church, the fishponds, Kalaupapa Lookout, Coffees of Hawaii, and Purdy's Macadamia Nut Farm. (☎808-553-4477; www.molokai-outdoors.com. Open M-F 7am-6pm, $96.) **Molokai Fish and Dive,** 61 Ala Malama Ave., in Kaunakakai, also offers tours and rentals. They rent kayaks (singles $30 per day, doubles $50), snorkel gear ($10 per day), bodyboards ($8 per day), and surfboards ($25-35 per day), and employ full-time guides who lead tours to Halawa Falls ($40-75), a coffee plantation ($35), snorkeling reefs ($69), as well as surfing lessons ($75 per hr., 2 hr. min.). Ask also about their whale-watching, kayaking, fishing and scuba diving adventures. (☎808-553-5926; www.molokaifishanddive.com. Open daily 7:30am-6pm.) Serious surfers should check out **Molokai Surf,** 130 Kam. V, Ste. 103, for surf clothing, equipment, and advice from the 30-year Molokai surf veteran and store owner, Jerry Leonard. (☎808-558-8943. Open M-Sa 9:30am-5pm.) Molokai is easily navigable on two wheels, so try **Molokai Bicycle,** 80 Mohala St. The owner will drop off and pick up a bike to any location on the island and all rentals include a helmet, lock, map, and water bottle. (☎808-553-3931 or 800-709-2453; www.bikehawaii. com/molokaibicycle. $15-20 per day, discounted weekly rates available.)

⬡ SIGHTS

Although the main attractions on Molokai are the beaches on the east and west ends of the island and the Kalaupapa Peninsula, there are also several pleasant things to see around Kaunakakai. About a mile or two west of town lies the **Kapuaiwa Coconut Grove.** An 11-acre expanse of coconut trees is on the south side of the highway. It was originally planted in the 1860s by Prince Lot, a Molokai resident who became King Kamehameha V, to provide shade for visiting royalty as they bathed in the sea. It is one of the few remaining royal coconut groves in the state and has been renovated as a **campground** (p. 82) by the Hawaiian Home Lands Department.

Across the highway from Ala Malama Ave., the road becomes Kaunakakai Pl. and leads out to **Kaunakakai Wharf,** a ¼ mi. stretch from the highway. The longest wharf in Hawaii offers great views of the mountains. This is also the arrival and departure point of the **Molokai Princess.** The wharf's main activity is still fishing; the **Molokai Ice House,** a fishermen's cooperative established in 1988, makes its home. In winter, when the barge can only make it a few times across the dangerous channel, locals gather here to help unload necessities like toilet paper and beer. Many fishing, snorkeling, and whale-watching expeditions leave from the wharf. See **Molokai Fish and Dive** or **Molokai Outdoors.**

During June and July, every other Saturday morning, from 9am to *pau* (finish), a raucous crowd gathers to watch outrigger canoe races and sip cold

THE LOCAL STORY

KALAUPAPA'S STORY

The first documented case of leprosy on the Hawaiian Islands was in 1835; the disease caused a serious epidemic in the 1860s. At the time, little was known about the disease except that it was introduced by Westerners. In 1866, King Kamehameha V decided to exile the most advanced cases to a cove called Kalawao on the southeastern part of the Kalaupapa Peninsula. The infected would be put on a ship and dumped into the water near Kalawao, sometimes hundreds of yards offshore. Until around 1890, when the survivors moved from Kalawao to the more hospitable village of Kalaupapa, death was so common that the colony was described as a living cemetery.

By 1870, a few Christian missionaries were tending to the sick in Kalaupapa. The missionaries built grass huts for themselves even as most patients lived outdoors. Hardly any missionaries remained on the peninsula for more than a few months until a Belgian Catholic priest named Joseph De Veuster, also known as Father Damien, arrived. Damien, originally sent to Kalaupapa for his carpentry skills to fix a church, saw the suffering of Kalaupapa's residents, knew how badly he was needed, and decided to stay. Devoted to improving the lives of the residents, he built houses and dug graves by day, and worked to finish an addition to the church by night. Although he never finished the church, he did build nearly

drinks from concession stands run by local canoe clubs. Anyone 12 and up can participate in one of Molokai's clubs, which start training in spring for the summer races. Just before the wharf on the west side of Kaunakakai Pl., a stone platform is all that remains of King Kamehameha V's vacation home. Although it looks more like an overgrown parking lot than a park, the area is designated **Malama Cultural Park,** and archaeologists believe it was once a *heiau* (temple).

ENTERTAINMENT

The best of local Molokai nightlife takes place at **Paddler's Inn** (p. 332), which has live local bands Thursday to Saturday until 2am. The **Hula Shores Lounge** at Hotel Molokai often attracts hundreds of islanders and tourists to watch the weekly **Na Kapuna jam session** on Friday from 4-6pm. Locals play ukuleles and slack key guitars, and there is informal singing and sometimes hula dancing as well. A live band usually comes on after the jam session and plays until the bar closes. During the rest of the week, the Hula Shores Lounge offers live island music; ask the front desk for a schedule. (Bar open daily 10am-10:30pm.)

Across from the Mitchell Pauole Center at the intersection of Ala Malama Ave. and Ainoa St. is the **Kaunakakai Ball Park,** where the Molokai Farmers have a substantial home field advantage over the other-island competition. The locals take their Little League very seriously: almost the entire town comes out for the Maui County Championship game. The Little League schedule is available at the Mitchell Pauole Center. Basketball leagues also run in the nearby gym, where stands afford visitors a chance to catch a game.

CENTRAL MOLOKAI

KALAUPAPA PENINSULA

Kalaupapa is a flat, leaf-shaped land formation on Molokai's North Shore. It is separated from the "topside" (the rest of Molokai) by a 2000 ft. wall of mountains passable only by a steep switchback trail or plane. A volcanic eruption created the peninsula and the Kauhako Crater, which is one of the deepest lakes in the US at 800 ft. Dubbed "the grotto" by locals, the crater is marked by a cemetery and large white cross, visible from sea.

Kalaupapa's history is painful. Its many stone walls attest to the area's past as a fertile farming land, until 1866, when it was converted into an infamous quarantine colony for leprosy patients by decree of King Kamehameha V. The quarantine was finally lifted in 1969, although a few ex-patients continue to live here; the isolated settlement is the only home they've ever known. The hundreds of graveposts emerging from its green grasses, standing silent testament to the suffering of the peninsula's residents, make the beauty of the peninsula all the more evocative.

⌐ TRANSPORTATION

There are three ways to get to Kalaupapa: you can hike down the strenuous but magnificent cliff trail, fly to an airstrip on the far side of the peninsula, or ride a mule down the trail. Advance reservations are required for all three. You must be 16 years or older to enter the peninsula as part of the tour.

BY FOOT. Hiking the challenging 3 mi. **Pali trail** is by far the cheapest and most rewarding option. It descends over 1600 ft. along 26 numbered switchbacks until it finally reaches sea level. It then continues east for 1 mi. to the end of the road, where tours begin. To get there from Kaunakakai, take Hwy. 460 west, then turn right at Hwy. 470. The trail entrance is 15min. down the highway, past the mule stables, on the right at a metal gate with a sign warning not to enter without a permit. Although the laws requiring permits to hike the trail have expired, you must have an advance reservation with **Damien Tours** (see below), or you'll be turned away at the bottom of the trail or arrested. If you plan to hike, be certain to start before the mules leave at 8:30am to avoid the worst of their droppings on the way down (it's unavoidable on the way up) and bring plenty of water. The hike down can take anywhere from 45 to 90min. if you allow time to appreciate the view. At the base of the trail, walk right toward the settlement. You'll pass a black sand beach (one of the island's most dangerous due to insane currents, large waves, and submerged rocks), and as you enter an open area, you'll see the bleachers where you wait for the tour. The hike will tax your aerobic capacity, but is doable for those in moderately good shape.

BY AIR. If you prefer to fly, you will need to arrange both a flight and a tour reservation with Damien Tours, unless your airline explicitly states that they will handle the tour reservation. The prices listed here are for the flight only. Consider hiking down and flying back, as the hike is very enjoyable. This

300 box-like houses and dug, on average, one grave per day.

Damien was diagnosed with leprosy in 1884 and died in 1889, at the age of 49. Of the over 1000 workers on the peninsula since 1870, Damien is the only documented case of infection. He continued giving church service until just a few days before he died, although his hands and legs were so diseased he could not walk or hold his prayer book. Damien had never forbade any of the patients from entering his house and regularly shared dishware with them.

In 1995, Damien was beatified by Pope John Paul II and sainthood became imminent when in 2008, his second miracle was approved by the Vatican.

Others continued his legacy. Mother Marianne Cope remained in Kalaupapa for nearly 30 more years. Members of her order, the Sisters of St. Francis, still work on there today. Brother Dutton carried on Damien's work for 44 years, never once leaving the island.

The quarantine on Kalaupapa was lifted in 1969. Over 7000 people had been sent to the Kalaupapa colony. Fewer than 30 are left today, most in their 70s or 80s. The area is a National Historical Park, are maintained by the National Park Service, while treatment is provided by the Hawaii Department of Health. Once the last patient dies, the park will be entirely dedicated to preserving and memorializing the past.

option can be booked through **Molokai Fish and Dive** for $159 (round-trip $199). Flights can be booked directly through **Pacific Wings,** which flies from Honolulu and Hoolehua. (☎808-873-0877 or 888-575-4546, $45-$95 each way.)

BY MULE. The third option, **Molokai Mule Ride,** offers rides that include both brown-bag lunch and a tour (☎808-567-6088; $165 per person; AmEx/D/MC/V). The trip begins at 8:30am (plan to arrive by 8) at the stables across the street from the Pali Trailhead. The trailhead is at the entrance to Palaau State Park, 5 mi. up Hwy. 470 from its intersection with Hwy. 460. Although many people enjoy the ride, it is very bumpy, and some may prefer to hike. Nevertheless, mule riders are safely above the mule doodie that hikers otherwise encounter below. Bring long pants and lots of water; in addition, riders must be in good health and weigh no more than 250 lb. Book at least two weeks in advance because space is limited (no more than 18 mules on the trail per day) and fills up quickly. Molokai Mule also offers package deals that include flights from Maui or Honolulu ($300-400). You can book package deals (flight, mule, hike, tour) through Molokai Fish and Dive. A cheaper option is to book the trip and tour together through Damien Tours. (☎808-567-6171. Open daily 4-8pm. Tours M-Sa 10am-1pm. Flight $90; hike $40. Cash only.)

TOURS OF KALAUPAPA. The only way to travel through the Kalaupapa Peninsula is as part of an organized tour. It is against the law to explore the peninsula on your own and disrespectful to the area's residents.

ACTIVITIES

Damien Tours (☎808-567-6171) operates all the tours of Kalaupapa. If you hike, bring your own lunch; once you arrive at the bleachers near the mule corral, wait for the big blue bus and your tour guide (sometimes a former patient or resident) to pick you up at 10am. The tour stops at Kalaupapa's only bar, **The Docks,** where residents gather once a year to receive supplies, and at **St. Francis Church,** whose walls are fixed with images of Father Damien, who ministered to the lepers on Molokai. There is also a stop at the Visitors Center, which is filled with books about Damien and Kalaupapa. *Yesterday at Kalaupapa* or *The Lands of Father Damien* are excellent choices for their photography, *Holy Man: Father Damien of Molokai* for its biographical detail. *No Footprints in the Sand* is a compelling memoir written by a patient who still lives at the settlement. The tour then goes around the **Old Kalawao settlement,** where the first castaways lived and where Father Damien conducted his ministries. From the park, you can see dome-shaped **Okala Rock,** the only place in the world where miniature *okala* palms grow in the wild.

The most poignant part of the tour is the history of Father Damien's life, which is recounted at **St. Philomena Church.** Damien had such little fear of leprosy that he would smoke from the same pipe and eat from the same bowl as the patients. Though his remains were moved to Belgium in 1936, his original grave is located outside. In order to protect the privacy of the residents during the tour, no stops are made at residential establishments and residents stay indoors. Photography of residents is strictly prohibited.

KAMAKOU PRESERVE

The 3000-acre preserve next to **Kamakou Peak,** the last patch of native rainforest in Molokai, is home to more than 250 species of plants, 219 of which can be found only in Hawaii. The plants feed indigenous insects and snails, which in turn support the local bird population. Look for the happy-faced spider, distinguished by its yellow body and bright red grin. Pine, eucalyptus, and *kukui* trees envelope the area, and the bright red native *apapane* (honey creeper) feeds from the same-colored flowers of the *ohia lehua* tree. You will also find the *hapuu*, a tall endemic fern used in the past for mattress stuffing and roof thatch, and *pukiawe*, a short shrub with non-edible, pinkish berries, used by Hawaiian chiefs for ceremonial purposes. The preserve owes its existence to the generosity of the company behind Molokai Ranch, which sold the land rights to the Nature Conservancy in 1982; the rights to the Moomomi Preserve were sold six years later. The **Nature Conservancy** (☎808-553-5236) encourages visitors to call before visiting the preserve.

The destruction of the sandalwood forests and the subsequent overgrazing of cattle caused severe erosion in this area in the mid-19th century. In the 1930s, Molokai, like many of the Hawaiian islands, was reforested with non-native eucalyptus, ironwood, and Norfolk island pines in an effort to stabilize the soil and protect Molokai's watersheds. Today the activity of feral pigs, goats, and axis deer in the area destroys delicate native plant ecosystems and is a further source of erosion. Red soil washes down the slopes of Kamakou to the ocean where it can choke the coral reef. In an effort to control this devastation, the Nature Conservancy builds and maintains fences around preservation areas. They also sponsor monthly hunting trips into Pelekunu, Kamalo, and Kawela. Resident hunters are given first priority to go on the hunts, but anyone can reserve a spot. In general, hunting is permitted on weekends and holidays, so it is a good idea to wear blaze-orange clothing and stay on marked trails.

GETTING THERE. If you're not on a guided tour and are trying to drive to the preserve yourself, a 4WD vehicle is essential. Turn around at the first sign of rain. In the event that you get stuck, you'll have to hike all the way back to one of the gas stations in Kaunakakai. Keep in mind that the last few miles of the road are at high elevation; they can be rainy even when it is sunny below. Use first gear and go slowly, driving around (not over) the man-hole covers along the road. If you lose traction and start to slide, ease up on the gas and turn into the skid. Lastly, avoid stopping if your vehicle is on an upward incline—many parts of the road are passable only with momentum.

 ORIENTATION AND PRACTICAL INFORMATION. The road that leads to the preserve begins west of Kaunakakai on **Highway 460.** Turn right before mi. marker 4; there is a sign that says "Homelani Cemetery." The pavement ends and the dirt road begins just past the cemetery. The first 5 mi. of this road are fairly easy-going, and it does not get difficult until you pass the entrance sign for the **Molokai Forestry Reserve.** Even 4WD may encounter traction problems while trying to climb the steep grades after this point.

This part of the island was a popular place to live back in the days of Kamehameha the Great, but the only people you'll see today are hikers, locals checking on remote *pakalolo* (marijuana) plants, and a woodcutter, who sells carvings slightly past the forest reserve entrance. Ring the bell by the gate if you want a tour of the woodshop. There's a primitive restroom outside. After around 10 mi., you will be able to make out **Lua Moku Iliahi,** or the Sandalwood Measuring Pit, on the left. This 75 ft. long pit was used to ensure that the trees harvested would fit in the ships' hold; the wood was hauled to the wharf.

After 1 mi., you will reach the entrance to the Kamakou Preserve and the **Waikolu Lookout.** Waikolu, or "three waters," refers to the many waterfalls that run over the mountains and into the region's streams. At 3700 ft., the lookout has staggering views of the surrounding valleys, as well as **Okala Rock,** which visitors to Kalaupapa see when stopping at Kalawao. With squat toilets and a picnic area but no drinking water, this camping site is popular with pig hunters and preserve explorers, though it can be chilly. Free camping permits are available through the Maui District's State Forestry and Wildlife Office. You must notify the state of your stay (2-night max.) and have bring your permit when you camp. For more information, see **Camping in Hawaii,** p. 82. Camping is only permitted in the state forest reserve, not the preserve.

GUIDED TOURS. If you are concerned about getting to and hiking through the preserve yourself, or if you'd simply like to avoid the long walk from the Waikolu Lookout, consider arranging a guided hike with the **Nature Conservancy** (p. 336). Because you are driven directly to the trailheads, guided hikes are generally less time-consuming. The tour leaders often have worthwhile background knowledge about the region. The Conservancy runs an eight-person trip, usually on the first Saturday of the month. Hikers meet at the airport at 8:30am for the 3 mi. hike and return by 4pm. A $25 donation is suggested and advance reservations (with a $25 refundable deposit) are required. Another option is to go with locals. Richard, at **Hale Malu Guesthouse** (☎808-567-9136), occasionally takes guests up to the preserve. Call for more information.

HIKING. The Nature Conservancy asks that you stay on the roads and marked trails in the preserve to avoid damaging the surrounding vegetation or hurting yourself. From the Waikolu Lookout, the road is impassable in anything but 4WD, and you'll have trouble even then. Unless you have extensive off-road driving experience—or people to get out and push— the safest course of action is to park at the lookout and walk to the trailheads. Before you leave the lookout, you can sign in on the Nature Conservancy's log sheet, which often has information about road conditions. The main trail in Kamakou Preserve is the **Pepeopae Trail.** Its trailhead is 2¼ mi. down the main road, past the Waikolu Lookout, and is clearly marked. The trail is a 6-8 in. wide boardwalk that is covered in chicken wire for better traction. It winds for slightly over a mile through one of Hawaii's wettest regions. There are no handrails, so you may want to bring a walking stick. The substantial rainfall (over 170 in. annually) and acidic soil have stunted the plant population and maintained the 10,000 year old **Pepeopae Bog.** The bog is humid and cool and the surrounding landscape is brilliantly green. At the end of the boardwalk is a tiny patch of grass on the edge of a cliff known as the **Pelekunu Valley Overlook.** The overlook offers truly arresting (you have the right to remain silent) views of high grassy cliffs towering over the Pelekunu River and the turquoise waters of the Pacific. On a good day, wispy clouds just barely wreath the tops of the cliffs. The 5760-acre Pelekunu Valley is closed to the public, as it is one of the few remaining breeding grounds for several species of marine and terrestrial life.

KALAE AND KUALAPUU

Kalae, the area toward the end of Hwy. 470, 5 mi. up the road from Hwy. 460, is blessed with a lot of sun and a cooler climate than most of the island due to its elevation (1500 ft.). Three miles further up the road, the tiny agricultural town of Kualapuu (pop. 1936), at Farrington Ave. and Hwy. 470, was the island headquarters of the Del Monte Company in the 1930s. When they closed shop in 1982 headed for more profitable pineapple lands in the Philippines and Thailand, the town's economy suffered. In recent years, the coffee bean has replaced the pineapple—the town's main attraction is now a coffee plantation.

ACCOMMODATIONS AND CAMPING. One of the only places to stay in central Molokai is the **Hale Malu Guesthouse ❷**, 23 Kalama Rd., after mi. marker 4 on Kalae Hwy. The unassuming green guesthouse is on the left near the bottom of the hill. Located in cooler and wetter upcountry, Hale Malu consists of a quirky dome cottage and two separate guest rooms in the main house, which is clean and comfortable, but short on space. For backpackers, two furnished "tentalows" and camping facilities are available in the garden next door. All guests have access to the kitchen, living room with cable TV and VCR, washer/dryer, phone, and Internet in the main house. Campers have access to hot outdoor shower, cooking facilities, and Wi-Fi. (☎808-567-9136; www.halemalu-molokai.com. 2-night min. Cottage with A/C, TV, fridge, shower, and *lanai* $80. Rooms with communal bathroom and shower, $50; tentalow $40; tent with bedding $25, bring your own tent $15.) For more bare bones camping, take Hwy. 470 north to **Palaau State Park ❶** (☎808-587-0300). With picnic tables, restrooms, outdoor showers, and a surrounding forest, this peaceful state park is a great bet. Palaau suffers from frequent drizzles and a lack of drinking water, but it is one of Molokai's best camping spots. If you don't mind getting a little damp, bring your own water and pitch a tent on the soft needles on the ground—chances are you'll have the park to yourself. No need for an alarm; wild roosters will ensure you are up at dawn. Camping permits are necessary from the state parks office in Honolulu, and have to be applied for in person or by mail. $5 per night per campsite. See **Camping in Hawaii**, p. 82, and **www.hawaiistateparks.org** for more information.

FOOD. Next door to Kualapuu Cookhouse on Farrington Ave., the **Kualapuu Market,** a well-stocked grocery store (one of two west of Kaunakakai) carries periodicals and magazines, and rents DVDs and VHSs ($3.50/4.50) if you become a member for $10. (☎808-567-6243. Open M-Sa 8:30am-6pm. AmEx/MC/V.) **Coffees of Hawaii Espresso Bar and Cafe ❶**, P.O. Box 37, 1630 Farrington Ave., at Hwy. 470. They serve 100% Molokai coffee (as well as island blends) any way you like it. Cool off with the shop's signature frozen drink, the Mocha Mama (vanilla ice cream, espresso, and chocolate, $4). Sandwiches and other light fare ($3-6) are also available. (☎808-567-9490. Cafe open M-F 6am-4pm, Sa 8am-4pm, Su 8am-7pm.) **Kualapuu Cookhouse ❸**, P.O. Box 1715, is a few doors down from Coffees. The original cookhouse for pineapple plantation workers and the only restaurant west of Kaunakakai, Kualapuu may not look impressive, but it is rightly considered by many locals and visitors to be the best place to eat on the island. The lemon chicken ($10.50) is superb, and the stir-fry (chicken or pork $10.50) is delicately flavored without being drowned in its own sauce. Double the size of any meal by ordering it "Kanaka size" (add $5). Breakfast until 11am. Dinner specials Tu-Sa $18-25. Dine on the outdoor tables or in the tropical-themed interior, or take your food to go. BYOB. (☎808-567-9655. Open M 7am-2pm, Tu-Sa 7am-8pm. Cash only.)

SIGHTS. There are plenty of things to see in this side of molokai, whether it's culinary (macadamia nuts and coffee), cultural, or outdoorsy.

PURDY'S MACADAMIA NUT FARM. Tuddie Purdy runs what may very well be the most hospitable macadamia nut farm in the world, and certainly one of Molokai's best-known tourist attractions. Visitors are welcomed by the man himself and given a full tour of the miniature-sized working farm. When acquired by Purdy in 1980 as a homestead (from land set aside for Native

Hawaiians), the mac-nut-filled property had been neglected for decades. Within two years, he had cleaned it up, learned the ins and outs of mac-nut production, and turned the place into a charming little enterprise. Because Purdy does not prune his trees or use irrigation, fertilizer, pesticides, or chemicals of any kind, visitors have the privilege of wandering freely and taste-testing throughout the property. The 50 trees on his tiny farm are 85 years old, producing nuts year-round. Purdy will insist you crack your own nut before helping yourself to samples of macadamia honey on slices of fresh coconut. A small gift shop stocks treasures like rare macadamia woodworking ($5-55), macadamia blossom honey ($6.50), and the nuts themselves ($6-7). *(On the right side of Lihi Pali Ave., mi. from the intersection with Farrington Ave. From Hwy. 470, turn left on Farrington Ave., then right on Lihi Pali after 1 mi. ☎808-567-6601. Open M-F 9:30am-3:30pm, Sa 10am-2pm, weather permitting. Tours on the hr. Park on the road outside. Free.)*

COFFEES OF HAWAII. This 600-acre coffee plantation, owned by Coffees of Hawaii covers upcountry slopes once used for pineapple cultivation. Even though the entire process, from plant to cup, is done on site, nifty machines (like giant harvesters that deftly shake the cherries off their branches) ensure that the plantation requires surprisingly few employees—a stark contrast to the hundreds that once labored in the pineapple fields. Visitors are able to get a glimpse of all stages of the production through moderately priced tours. The **Morning Espresso Tour** is a walking tour of the processing facilities. The **Mule-Drawn Wagon Tour** covers the same places as the walking tour, but includes a wagon ride through the fields themselves, and a visit to the 1.4 million gallon reservoir that irrigates the crops. A well-stocked gift shop allows visitors to sample and buy the various roasts and blends that the plantation produces. Even if you don't take a tour, there is an informative display on the back of the gift shop that is worth a look. There is a popular Hawaiian music jam session on Sundays from 4-6pm. *(1760 Farrington Ave. Turn onto Hwy. 470 from Hwy. 460, continue for about 2 mi, and turn right onto Farrington Ave. The cafe and gift shop, from which tours depart from, will be on your right. Gift shop open M-F 8am-5pm, Sa 8am-4pm, Su 8am-7pm. Morning Espresso Tour (45 min. to 1hr.) M-F 10am and Sa 9am, $20, ages 5-15 $10. Mule-Drawn Wagon Tour (1¾ hr.- 2hr.) M-F 8am & 1pm, Sa 8am, $35, ages 5-15 $10. Tour reservations required.)*

PALAAU STATE PARK. Daytime visitors will find a large pavilion and lawn near the entrance of the park before reaching the campsite road turn-off; a smaller picnic area with tables and trash cans is farther down on the right. At the end of the road, a display describes the park's two main attractions. The first, **Kaule o Nanahoa (Phallic Rock),** deserves a visit. By foot, the unmistakably-shaped rock is 5min. from the end of the highway along a marked trail down the left fork in the path. A sign claims that the rock is a natural formation which has only been carved "to some extent" by humans. Legend has it that a woman who brings offerings to the rock and sleeps next to it will wake up pregnant. Two minutes down the right fork is the **Kalaupapa Lookout,** with an excellent view of the peninsula of the same name. If you don't hike down to the colony p. 334), at least check out the view—it's one of Molokai's best, especially in the morning before clouds shroud the peninsula. The lookout is perched on nearly vertical cliffs at an elevation of 1500 ft., so stay behind the rock wall and be prepared for high winds. *(At the end of Hwy. 470, about 5 mi. from Hwy. 460.)*

IRONWOOD HILLS GOLF COURSE. Ironwood Hills is a pleasant nine-hole course set in a rustic upcountry venue. This local golf course remains the island's only place to tee-off. While the fairways are not perfectly manicured, Ironwood Hills is a great place to enjoy a casual afternoon of golf. The unpretentious pro shop is run out of a trailer by a good-natured caretaker. This is golf Molokai-style, and the course's laid-back attitude is a refreshing change from the game's often glitzy varnish. *(About 3 mi. from the intersection of Hwy. 460 and Hwy. 470, down a long dirt road on the left, before the Molokai Museum and Cultural Center. ☎808-567-6000. Open daily 7:30am-6pm. Green fees: 9 holes, $18; 18 holes, $24. Club rental: 9 holes, $8; 18 holes; $14.)*

MOLOKAI MUSEUM AND CULTURAL CENTER. It took 16 years to restore the smallest sugar mill in Hawaii to full working condition, but it now sits proudly on a hill. The mill, built by R.W. Meyer, a German immigrant to Molokai, churned out cane sugar over 100 years ago, though it went out of business in just a decade due to the low price of sugar and cane disease. In addition to the mule-driven cane crusher and other authentic mill parts, the museum has an ever-changing display of Molokai artifacts and photos. Be sure to stop at the information desk for advice on local activities, seminars, hiking tours, exhibits, and festivals. *(On Kalae Hwy., turn left at the sign, just past the Ironwoods Golf Course and before mi. marker 4. ☎808-567-6436. Open M-Sa 10am-2pm. $3.50, ages 5-18 $1. Cash only.)*

HOOLEHUA

This large, dry area west of Kalae divides eastern and western Molokai. Most of the land in the area is under the auspices of the department of Hawaiian Home Lands, which provides homesteads to Native Hawaiians.

🛈 PRACTICAL INFORMATION. The 📮**Hoolehua post office** (☎808-567-6144), at Puupeelua Ave. (Hwy. 480) and Farrington Ave., is home to the Post-A-Nut service—you can send a Molokai coconut to your friends back home for the price of postage (US $8-12, international $12-20). The smiling postmaster provides the nuts along with a few felt pens to write on their husks. If you want to get an idea of the cost of your souvenir, ask to weigh the coconut before you decorate. (Open M-F 8:30am-noon and 12:30-4pm.) **Postal Code:** 96729.

◐ SIGHTS. One of the only coastal sand dune ecosystems left untouched by development in Hawaii, the 📮**Moomomi Preserve** is home to a half-dozen endangered plants that cannot be found anywhere else on the planet. Its pristine coast is a breeding ground for green sea turtles, rare on other parts of the island, and the many white sand beaches are expansive and perpetually empty. Most beaches are rocky, however, and in many cases have nasty offshore currents, making them ill-suited for swimming or other aquatic activities.

The **Moomomi Preserve** is one of two Molokai preserves that are managed by the **Nature Conservancy** (p. 336) and open to the public (the other is **Kamakou Preserve,** p. 336). Maps and information are available at the Conservancy's office, where the staff encourages visitors to stop in to get up-to-date information before they visit the preserve. The office is in the second cul-de-sac on the right in the Molokai Industrial Park. Turn down Oha St., which leads south from Hwy. 460. (☎808-553-5236; www.nature.org/hawaii. Open M-F 7:30am-3pm.)

There are three ways to access the preserve. The first is by hiking a trail to the east from the Moomomi Pavilion. To get to the trail, take Hwy. 460 from Kaunakakai, turn left onto Hwy. 480 (Farrington Ave.), and continue straight until the asphalt ends. The dirt road straight ahead is smooth most of the way, and generally passable in good weather, although a few monster ruts may tilt your vehicle at odd angles. The road runs for about 2 mi. and passes through a gate about halfway down before it reaches the **Moomomi Recreation and Cultural Park** on the eastern edge of Moomomi Bay. The pavilion here is owned and maintained by the Hawaiian Home Lands Department (as is all the land in the area) and has restrooms, an outdoor shower, picnic tables, and parking.

Camping by non-Native Hawaiians is not permitted here. From the parking area, the trail leads left along the shore of Moomomi Bay and Kawaaloa Bay until it reaches the preserve. Be absolutely certain to hike only on trails or roads. The trail stays along the coast for 1 mi., and offers magnificent views of untouched beaches and sand dunes. The trail ends at a beach and sandstone cliff. Look for the endangered Hawaiian monk seal or a *pueo* (Hawaiian owl).

The two other ways to enter the preserve are by car or on a guided tour. The Nature Conservancy occasionally grants visitors permission to use the 4WD roads through the preserve with advance notice. Instead of turning right at the fork in the road, keep left; there are two grassy parking lots at the end and the preserve trail begins near the first. Guests must contact the Conservancy and ask for a key to the various gates along this road. Finally, the Conservancy leads guided hikes on the second, third, or fourth Saturday of each month for a suggested donation of $25. Hikers are picked up at the Hoolehua airport at 8:30am and returned by 2:30pm. A $25 refundable deposit is required to reserve a spot on the hike; try to reserve well in advance as these trips are popular. The hike is not difficult, only 2 mi. round-trip, but the heat and lack of shade can take a toll. Bring lunch and plenty of water.

Beyond Moomomi Bay, **Kawaaloa Bay** is characterized by a similar but much longer stretch of sandy beach. Again, the surf is strong, and rocks make swimming difficult and dangerous, but the beach is long, beautiful, and secluded.

EAST OF KAUNAKAKAI

The drive east from Kaunakakai becomes progressively more rural, and the road narrower and less-traveled. The towns listed here are really nothing more than houses clustered along the road. Other than the **Iliiliopae Heiau** (p. 344), most sights worth visiting are visible from the road, making this a great stretch to sightsee with the windows down. The highway is dotted with tiny beaches. After many hairpin turns, the end of the road reveals one of Molokai's most stunning scenes—the **Halawa Valley and Falls** (p. 345).

A variety of private cottages, beach houses, and condos are found along Molokai's southeast shore. There are some great deals, especially if traveling in a larger group; most are easily booked via **Molokai Vacation Rentals** (☎808-553-8334) or **Friendly Isle Realty** (☎808-553-3666, p. 329). Recent enforcement of Maui County zoning laws (Molokai is part of Maui County) have caused some owners to cease renting their houses. Technically, only land designated for resorts/hotels is allowed to host visitors for short-term stays; properties on land zoned for other purposes require special permits. Groups of home owners are trying to obtain exemptions from the restrictions. The owners of ⊠**Kamalo Plantation Cottage** ❸, located at mi. marker 11, and of the **Moanui Beach House** ❹, situated across the road from Murphy's Beach, have had to halt rentals altogether. Visitors can try calling to see if the situation has changed. One place unaffected by the zoning law changes is **The Wavecrest Resort** ❸, located at mi. 13. A condo complex, the resort sits on a lagoon with a good view of Maui. There are two tennis courts, a shuffleboard, and a putting green. Because the units are privately owned, some have been upgraded with stainless steel appliances and flatscreen TVs, while others have more modest furnishings. The condos vary in price; they can be found on www.vrbo.com, www.molokai.com or through local real-estate agencies—often for under $100 per night. (☎808-558-8101.)

Besides **Puu O Hoku Ranch** (p. 346), the only place to grab groceries or lunch on the east side of the island is **Manae Goods & Grindz** ❶ (☎808-558-8186), just before mi. marker 16. In addition to the small but well-stocked market, the food counter (☎808-558-8498) serves up light lunch items such as tuna melt sandwiches on whole wheat bread ($3.30) and fresh *mahi mahi* burgers ($4.60), as well as larger plates like pork stir-fry ($8.75) and chicken nuggets ($6). Video rental is also available for $3.50. (Store open M-F 6:30am-6pm, Sa-Su 6:30am-5pm; food counter open M-F 8am-4pm, Sa-Su 8am-5pm.)

KAWELA

A small residential development between mi. markers 4 and 6, Kawela is notable for its views and memorable history. Kawela is home to **Pukuhiwa battleground,** where Kamehameha I defeated Molokai's warriors on his way to uniting all the islands. It is said that in the hills above Kawela is a *puuhonua,* an ancient place of refuge for the defeated warriors. For a great view of Lanai, drive up any of the streets on the mountain side of the road. The views are especially sweeping from the top of Onioni Dr. (turn just past mi. marker 5, before the "Kawela Plantation I" sign). **Kakahaia Beach Park,** at mi. 5, is a narrow stretch of picnic tables with rather unenviable beach access (the water is silty and the sand scarce). Across the street is the **Kakahaia National Wildlife Refuge,** an ancient fishpond that is now a bird sanctuary for the endangered Hawaiian state bird, the *nene.* It is generally closed to the public, but the wetlands are visible from the highway. You can see the birds and get information about other bird-watching spots at **Nene O Molokai,** a nonprofit facility for breeding and releasing *nene,* at mi. marker 4, on the *makai* (ocean) side. There is usually a tour once a week; ask for details about getting permission to explore the Wildlife Refuge. (☎808-553-5992; http://aloha.net/~nene. Call ahead to visit.)

 NENE NO-NO! If you see a wild *nene,* do not approach or try to feed the bird. The state of Hawaii enforces a $50,000 fine for harassing *nene.*

KAMALO

Between mi. markers 10 and 11, Kamalo (pop. 147) was once the economic and civic center of the island. The **Kamalo Wharf** can be accessed via the dirt road on the right at the major bend in the highway, about 100 yd. after mi. marker 10. Once the main port for Molokai's old pineapple industry, the wharf, now reduced to stones, is home to a few semi-permanent campers and an occasional outrigger canoe race. Due to the sharks, this area is not a popular destination for swimmers. However, the wharf is a great place for fishing and also provides a spectacular view of the inland mountains; look for the highest point on the island, **Mt. Kamakou** (4,961 ft.) which will be slightly to your right when facing the mountains. About 1 mi. farther down the road is **St. Joseph's Church,** built in 1876 and the second oldest church on Molokai. It is one of two remaining churches that Father Damien constructed on "topside"—Molokai slang for anything outside and above the Kalaupapa peninsula. Outside the church, a small statue of Father Damien adorned with leis, pearls, and a plaque commemorate his selfless work among the lepers of Kalaupapa, which resulted in his own death in 1889 after he contracted leprosy (p. 334). The church no longer holds weekly services. About 1 mi. farther, an obscured wooden sign on the right denotes the **Smith-Bronte Landing Site,** where the first civilian flight from the mainland to Hawaii ended in a "safe" crash landing in 1927. The flight took 25 hours and was originally intended to touch down in Honolulu.

UALAPUE AND KALUAAHA

The village of Ualapue (pop. 4702) is clustered just past mi. marker 13, and about 1 mi. later, on the *mauka* (mountain) side of the highway in Kaluaaha,

THE MUSIC OF THE UKULELE

Save surfing and hula, the most well-known symbol of Hawaiian culture is the ukulele. This musical instrument's ancestor, the *cavaquinho,* was first brought to the islands by Portuguese explorers in 1879. As with most legends in Hawaii, there are a few accounts of how it was named. According to Queen Liliuokalani, it was "the gift that came here," from the Hawaiian words *uku* (gift) and *lele (*to come). However, its name also translates to "jumping flea." When Native Hawaiians saw how the fingers of the Portuguese sailors skipping all over the fretboard, the only word they could use to describe the enchanting object was *"ukulele."* It became a standard part of the culture when King David Kalakaua began incorporating it into royal gatherings.

The ukulele only has four strings: G, C, E, and A. Unlike the guitar, the strings are strummed over a fretboard, rather than an open soundboard. There are soprano, concert, and tenor ukuleles as well as a larger baritone.

To absorb as much of the Hawaiian experience during your travels as possible, try catching a free live performance at one of the resorts or listening to the famous ukulele stylings of such artists as Troy Fernandez, Raiatea, or Israel "Iz" Kamakawioole, best known for his otherworldly combination of "Over the Rainbow" and "What a Wonderful World."

is the old **Kaluaaha Church,** built in 1835 by the first missionary to the island. Only the church's 3 ft. thick concrete outer wall remains, but monthly services are still held under a tarp inside the great walls of the worn church. If the gate is padlocked, park outside, off the road and walk in. Just 1 mi. farther is the well-known **Our Lady of Sorrows Church.** A 10 ft. tall wooden cross makes the parking lot for the church unmistakable. Today's building is the 1966 reconstruction of the original, which was built by Father Damien in 1874. Mass is held Sundays at 7am, but visitors are welcome to visit on other days. A bit past and across the street from the church is the **Niaupala Fishpond,** one of the easiest ancient fishponds to see on the South Shore. The fishponds contained gates that permitted small fish to swim inside, but kept them from escaping once large. This early form of aquaculture was a crucial food source for the inhabitants of Molokai.

PUKOO

Located within the tiny village of Pukoo, the colossal ◾**Iliiliopae Heiau** is not to be missed. To reach the *heiau* (temple), watch for the small Mapulehu bridge, about 1 mi. past mi. 15 marker on Rte. 450. The path to the *heiau* is the first dirt road on the left, marked by mailbox #488 and faded signs that read "No Hunting" and "Private Property, Keep Out," immediately past the bridge. Fortunately, in recent years, the site has been opened to the public. The gate is no longer there, so the road is easy to access and could be driven in a 4WD but it is short enough to walk. Limited parking is either right off the highway or at the beginning of the dirt road. Follow the dirt road for almost 1 mi., until you get to a clearing. A house is located straight ahead beyond the chain. A narrow path leads into the forest on the left, crossing the dry creek bed. Fortunately, it is not far from the parking lot, about 100 yards west of the house.

This is an awesome and holy place. Legend has it that this *heiau* was built in one marathon night by a massive human chain that snaked its way inland over the mountain to Wailau Valley. In reality, it was built in the 13th century at a time when Molokai was famed for its religious clout. The flat stone surface rivals a football field in size, over 3000 sq. ft. and almost 22 ft. tall. The surface is remarkably level, and, as with many *heiau*, it is widely believed that Iliiliopae was two or three times its present size when it was in use. Iliiliopae is the second-largest *heiau* in Hawaii and was used as a temple for human sacrifice, as well as a training ground for *kahuna* (priests) from all the islands. It is an astounding reminder of a mighty civilization that has all but disappeared.

EAST TO HALAWA BAY

From roughly around mi. marker 20 onward, the road is nearly one lane and has a fair number of cliff-edge hairpin turns. The views are justly earned after braving the ride; sea cliffs, secluded beach coves, and wide-open pastures await. The road is paved and smooth all the way to Halawa Bay, but use caution nonetheless. Don't hesitate to honk your horn as a warning when you approach tight corners, and drive very slowly. There is a string of various unnamed and unmarked tiny beaches along this road—if you see a small place to pull off the road and park, chances are there is beach access nearby.

WAIALUA BEACH. *(Snorkeling. Surfing. Open 24hr.)* Two hundred yards before mi. marker 19, Waialua Beach is a popular place among locals who gather here to sunbathe, snorkel, and socialize. Legend has it that Kamehameha I was raised here solely on taro leaves. The narrow beach, stretching west a couple hundred yards from where Waialua Stream meets the ocean, is a good spot for swimming and beginner surfing. In the summer, children jump from Honouli Wai Bridge into the stream to rinse off before heading home. Limited parking is available on the side of the road. To access the beach, enter near the western end of the beach, where the highway runs along the beach. There is a patch of grass between the highway and the beach that people often cross by climbing through a rusted gate with signs that say "No Trespassing." Many other secluded beaches await; you should be able to find a place all to yourself.

⚐ MURPHY'S BEACH (20 MILE BEACH). *(Snorkeling. Open 24hr.)* Murphy's Beach is the East Shore's most popular swimming and snorkeling spot. Murphy's Beach is at the eastern end of the 28 mi. barrier reef that extends along the south shore of Molokai. The snorkeling off Murphy's is notable for its ease of entry and the spectacular diversity of fish and local turtle population. The shallow reef connects right to the shore, so be wary of sharp coral when wading in the surf. Plenty of parking is available in the grassy lawn on the south side of the highway beyond mi. marker 20.

⚐ HALAWA VALLEY AND BAY. *(Bodyboarding. Snorkeling. Surfing. Open 24hr.)* About 1 mi. past mi. marker 26, a mesmerizing lookout over Halawa Valley has views of Moaula, Hipuapua Falls, and two beach coves below. As you descend into the valley, be mindful of the stone wall on the edge of the highway and drive slowly, especially when passing oncoming traffic.

Thought to be the site of Molokai's first settlement in AD 700, Halawa Bay typifies the untouched essence of Molokai. Although the area had quite a few taro-harvesting residents at one time, tsunamis left so much salt behind that the farmland became fruitless and all but half a dozen residents moved out. At the bottom of the highway is a small green church, Jerusalem Hou, and a little farther on the right is **Halawa Park,** which has a bathroom and an outdoor shower (though the water here is not safe to drink). When the paved road ends, follow the dirt road to a grassy area where you can park. The main beach is accessible by wading across a stream by the parking area, and is a great place for all water sports. Be careful, as the waves break over shallow rocks, and it can be difficult to see sharks in the murky water. To the right, a smaller beach is a more sheltered place to sunbathe or swim.

An enchanting place to visit while in the valley is the **Halawa Tropical Flower Farm.** The farm's owner and operator, Kalani Pruet, grows floral beauties of all shapes and hues, from gingers to heliconias. He often leaves a bucket of freshly cut flowers by the small church, which visitors are free to take for a small dona-tion. Most days he offers tours of his little slice of paradise (and leads tours up to the falls), but it is best to call before showing up. For a novel place to sleep, Kalani offers a large yurt ($100 per night) that can sleep up to 6 people. Guests have access to a kitchenette and an outdoor shower. Call well in advance for reservations. The farm is located about 1 mi. down the dirt road next to the church, but parking for the tours is next to the church (☎808-336-1149).

POHAKULOA POINT (ROCK POINT). *(Surfing. Open daily 24hr.)* Past Murphy's Beach and around a bend before mi. marker 21 is a rocky area ironically named Rock Point. To access the break, park next to the lone 10 ft. boulder on the ocean side of the road. Natives call this the **Whispering Rock;** legend has it that if you whisper the right question, the rock will whisper back your answer. The area is one of the island's most popular surf spots, especially in winter, but it can be dangerous not least because the paddle-out requires dodging giant boulders. Beginning surfers should look elsewhere, as the steep wave faces and sharp coral bottom are also treacherous. Check with local surfers for the best entry points along the rocky outcropping and arrive before noon, when the break frequently becomes blown out by the onshore trades. Right at mi. marker 21 is a small strip of sand across from a couple of houses.

PUU O HOKU RANCH. After mi. marker 21, the road winds its way upward into the cattle pastures of the Puu O Hoku Ranch. Around mi. 24, the road levels and widens, and you should be able to see **Moku Hooniki Island.** Origi-nally used for target practice during WWII, the island is now protected as a bird sanctuary. This 14,000-acre ranch contains a certified organic farm which grows papaya, avocado, sugarcane, asparagus, and kava, a plant that has been used as a ceremonial drink in the Pacific for centuries. At mi. marker 25, the main office of the ranch doubles as the **Last Chance Store,** where you can pick up snacks. (☎808-558-8109; www.puuohoku.com. Open daily 9am-5pm. MC/V.)

The ranch also has two delightful **vacation cottages ➍.** The ⬛**Grove Cottage** is a 2100 sq. ft., four-bedroom, three-bath house for nine with a fireplace, a master bedroom, and spectacular views of Maui. The **Sunrise Cottage** is a two-bedroom, two-bath house for six with a kitchen and covered *lanai.* Guests have access to the ranch's produce and beef and can go hiking. (2-night min. 1-2 person cottages $140-160; additional guests $20. Weekly stays based on 6 nights.)

MOAULA AND HIPUAPUA FALLS. Halawa's real attraction, aside from its overall grandeur, is the hike up Halawa Stream to two magnificent waterfalls: Moaula and Hipuapua Falls. The hike crosses private property and is closed to visitors except as part of a guided tour. Intermittent fighting between local landowners and the state parks department has resulted in a recent increase of local land-owner vigilance. Hire a tour guide through **Molokai Outdoors** or **Molokai Fish & Dive** (p. 347) to get to these incredible falls, though deals are also available through a less-advertised (and usually cheaper) local service, like **Kalani Pruet.**

PRIVATE PARTS. Don't try to hike to the falls unaccompanied by a guide. Most of the land you must cross to arrive at the falls is private, and nothing irritates Halawa locals more than tourists brazenly trespassing.

Depending on the weather and recent rainfall, the hike to Moaula Falls takes at least 1hr.; you'll need another 30min. to get up to Hipuapua Falls. The total round-trip distance for the hike to both falls is 4 mi. Though the falls are the trip's real payoff, the hike itself is fascinating, as *heiau* (temples) are interspersed among the thick tropical vegetation along the trail. The Moaula Falls hike is gentle the whole way, but getting to Hipuapua Falls involves scrambling over river rocks and through muddy patches—it might be difficult for the inexperienced. Nevertheless, the obstacles are worth the trouble. The pool below Moaula Falls is deep and swimmable (be careful of falling rocks) and the waterfall itself (250 ft. tall) is two-tiered. Hipuapua Falls (500 ft. tall) is narrower and single-tiered.

NORTH SHORE SEA CLIFFS AND WAILAU VALLEY

The north shore of Molokai is home to the world's tallest sea cliffs (4000 ft.). The cliffs were formed when the **Makanalua Peninsula,** a large chunk of the island created by the Kauhako Volcano, sank into the sea after thousands of years of pounding surf eroded its foundation. Masses of rock and earth left behind are spotted with swaths of grass and the occasional herd of mountain goats. In wet weather, dozens of waterfalls spill over the cliffs into the ocean.

Four major valleys span the 12 mi. of coastline from Halawa to the Kalaupapa Peninsula: from east to west they are **Papalaua, Wailau, Pelekunu,** and **Waikolu.** Papalaua Valley is the smallest of the four, but home to one of the most impressive waterfalls visible from the sea, Papalaua Falls. The cliffs just beyond Papalaua Valley are home to **Kahiwa Falls,** the longest waterfall in the state. This thin stream of water spills down the face of the cliffs from an elevation of 1750 ft., eventually plunging into the sea. You might recognize Wailau Valley from Hollywood's *Jurassic Park 3.* It is about an hour boat ride from Halawa Bay and where many locals go to escape the hustle and bustle of Kaunakakai.

The sea cliffs are only accessible by boat. The ocean below the cliffs is a popular spot for advanced sea kayaking: the current flows swiftly away from Halawa, so kayakers must arrange a boat in advance to retrieve them before they reach the restricted area of Kalaupapa Peninsula. Boat tours of the North Shore are an easier way to get a look at Molokai's sea cliffs. **Molokai Action Adventures** (☎808-558-8184) makes excursions from Halawa two to five times per week for sightseeing, fishing, diving, snorkeling, and whale watching. Try calling early morning or late night, and be flexible—the weather can make it hard to pin down an exact date for a tour. The standard North Shore boat tour runs 6hr. and costs $135 per person, but prices are negotiable and family rates are offered. **Molokai Fish and Dive** (☎808-553-5926) also offers sea cliff tours, though primarily on a charter basis; six people are required for a trip ($150).

WESTERN MOLOKAI

The beaches on this side of Molokai are by far the best on the island and, given that western Molokai is for the most part uninhabited, you can find at least one to yourself—to either swim or watch the brilliant western sunsets. The Molokai Ranch, established in the 1850s by King Kamehameha V, was once roamed by Molokai's *paniolo* (cowboys) but closed in early 2008. The company behind the Ranch still owns almost one third of the land in this region, but has sold off its herd of 800 cattle. Aside from the small town of Maunaloa and the condo developments around the now-defunct Kaluakoi Hotel, the area is mostly empty pasture land. Dry and dusty, the west gets 12 in. of rain or less each year, and water has to be piped in from the wetter eastern side to support life.

MAUNALOA

To reach Maunaloa (pop. 230), take Hwy. 460 West to mi. marker 17, where it becomes the town's main road. The **Maunaloa Post Office** is located across from the general store. (☎808-552-2852. Open M-F 8am-noon and 12:30-4:30pm. **Postal Code:** 96770.) Once home to Molokai's only luxury accommodations—

the Lodge at Molokai Ranch and the Beach Village—Maunaloa has become a ghost town virtually overnight. Every property and business owned by Molokai Ranch ceased operating in April 2008. As a result, the West End no longer has a gas station or a restaurant. Molokai Properties, the company behind Molokai Ranch, points the finger at locals who made their operations financially unviable by prohibiting development. Locals, on the other hand, see the closures as a vindictive move by the company, meant more as punishment for their opposition than hard-nosed downsizing. Round two of this legal and political boxing match has already begun, as the responsibility for providing water to the west end's residents is shunted back and forth between the county and the ranch. Meanwhile, the ranch's some 120 former employees are surviving on government assistance while they search for new jobs. With employment prospects abysmal on Molokai, the town is unlikely to recover soon. Still around is the **Molokai Komohana Bed and Breakfast ❸**. This airy four-bedroom plantation home has a wraparound *lanai*. The two guest rooms include cable TV. Owners Tom and Karyl cook up a hot breakfast and open their book collection to guests. There is a mini-fridge and a microwave. (☎808-552-2210; www.vrbo.com/115564. Rooms $75-85 per night. 50% deposit required for reservations. Cash or personal checks only.)

For groceries, try the **Maunaloa General Store,** 200 Maunaloa Hwy., though Kaunakakai has a better selection. The store is also the only place to grab lunch in town; a concession stand offers sandwiches ($6), hamburgers ($2.50) and plate lunches ($7.50-8). (☎808-552-2346. Open M-Sa 9am-6pm. MC/V.)

The only reason to visit Maunaloa, a one-block town, is to buy a kite and fly it. If you're headed to the West End beaches the 🏝 **Big Wind Kite Factory,** 120 Maunaloa Hwy., is well worth the side-trip to Maunaloa. Don't be confused by the name: The Factory is a store with an artisan workshop, not a plant with an assembly line. Hand-painted kites ($25-250) of all colors and styles hang from the walls. Beyond kites, the store connects to the Plantation Gallery next door, which offers an array of merchandise ranging from Indonesian jewelry, intricately-carved coconut light covers ($25), and woodworking to one of Molokai's most substantial collections of Hawaiiana books, CDs, and knick-knacks. (☎808-552-2364. Open M-Sa 8:30am-5pm, Su 10am-2pm. AmEx/D/MC/V.)

KALUAKOI

Much of this area is grassland dotted with a few millionaire estates and miles of sandy and secluded beaches. So far, tourism on Molokai has not proven to make further development of Kaluakoi profitable, and with Molokai Ranch's recent closure things are unlikely to turn around soon. In the meantime, several condo developments offer vacation rentals. About 1 mi. before Maunaloa, just before mi. marker 15, a turnoff from the highway on the right leads 4 mi. down Kaluakoi Rd. to condominiums, as well as most beaches of the west side.

Turn right at Kakaako Rd. and then left at Lio Pl. to find **Paniolo Hale ❹**, a beautiful 77-unit condominium complex. Condos are available there or through **Friendly Island Realty** (☎800-600-4158), **Molokai Vacation Rentals** (☎800-367-2984), **www.vrbo.com,** or the directory at the **Molokai Visitors Association** (p. 329). Most are well-furnished condos that feel like houses, all with full kitchens, living rooms, and some with screened *lanai*. The grounds include a swimming pool, barbecue grills, and access to Make Horse and Kepuhi beaches. ($95-175 per night depending on season and occupancy.) Across the street from the Kaluakoi Villas, on your right heading down Kepuhi Pl. from Kaluakoi Rd., is **Ke Nani Kai ❸**, another condo complex with slightly smaller rooms. Friendly Island Realty or Molokai Vacation Rentals (see above) have rental information, and many owners list their properties on www.vrbo.com. (Condo manager ☎808-552-0945.

Office open daily 1:30-5pm. 1-bedroom $90 and up; 2-bedroom $110 and up.)
Kaluakoi Villas ❹, on the left just down from Ke Nani Kai, has frequent Internet
specials that can save you 20% or more. Try booking through Friendly Island
Realty or www.vrbo.com for discounted prices. (☎808-552-2721, reservations
808-545-3510. Units $75 and up depending on size and agency.

WEST END BEACHES

PAPOHAKU BEACH. *(Open 24hr.)* Over 2 mi. long, Papohaku Beach is the king of
West End beaches. It has the most surface area of any beach in Hawaii (up to
60 yd. in width, depending on the time of year and the tide) and has so much
sand, in fact, that some of it was sent to Oahu during the mid-1950s to create
Waikiki Beach. The water isn't good for snorkeling, but it's perfect for a dip in
the summer. The water is known for an undertow—exercise caution.

Papohaku Beach has three main access points from Kaluakoi Road, all with
outdoor showers and faded signs reading "Beach Access, Public Right of Way."
From north to south, the first is **Papohaku Beach Park,** which is the only campground on the West End. The site has restrooms, picnic tables, grills, and parking. Camping permits can be purchased at the Department of Parks and Recreation (p. 82). The second access point, **Lauhue,** has the most pleasing setting.
Located about 1mi. from Papohaku Beach Park, it's surrounded by taller dunes
and is one of the wider sections of the beach. It has more beach area than the
third access point, **Papapa.** Look for "Papapa Pl." written on a stop sign pole and
turn right. Papapa Beach is the site of **Ka Hula Piko,** a hula festival held in May.

⚑ DIXIE MARU BEACH. *(Snorkeling. Open 24hr.)* Dixie Maru is a dazzlingly beautiful, protected cove that is almost circular. The surrounding rocks and vegetation give the place an aura of privacy, and the water is calm and good for swimming and snorkeling. Locals and visitors soak up sun, swim, and picnic in the
pleasant setting of the beach. While the surf is inconsistent, there is a dredging
left reef point break that has smaller waves. The bay just before Dixie's is a better place to surf on a larger swell. *(At the southern end of Kaluakoi Rd., turn right when the
road comes to a T; the beach is on the right off the cul-de-sac at the end of the road.)*

⚑ MAKE HORSE BEACH. *(Surfing. Open 24hr.)* For far better sand and sun, walk
down the dirt road. Follow the arrow sign that says "beach," at the parking lot
before turning into Paniolo Hale to Make (pronounced "mah-kay") Horse. It
is not recommended, but you can also drive down. Make Horse spans three
crescent-shaped bays of white sand, separated by high rocks that obscure the
other bays from sight. If it's too crowded at the first bay, try the others to the
right. The beach is a favorite local fishing spot and has good surf in the winter,
but it's not the place to snorkel. Make means "dead;" the beach earned its name
when locals slaughtered horses during the 19th century by running them off the
high plateau to the right of the beach. Despite its grisly past, the beach is one
of the most beautiful and sheltered on the island.

HALE O LONO HARBOR. *(Surfing. Open 24hr.)* The only part of the southwest shore
that is open to the public, the harbor is accessible via a dirt road beyond the
Molokai Ranch Lodge in Maunaloa down Mokio St. Following signs to Kaupoa,
you'll eventually pass the locked gate to Molokai Ranch's Kaupoa beach on
your right (access is unavailable since the Ranch's closure). The road goes
east as it nears the water with various access points and ends at a quiet beach
which has a picnic table and primitive restrooms. A surf break on the left side
of the beach shows its colors during summer south swells.

LANAI

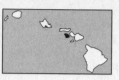

Travelers in search of peaceful serenity, friendly locals, and outdoor adventure should head to Lanai. A quiet, slow-paced paradise, with just one small town and few paved roads, Lanai isn't known for glitz and glamor. Much more so than other destinations, Lanai is a state of mind. Though its industry now centers on two remote luxury resorts, the island was once home to the world's largest pineapple plantation. Its 15,000 acres accounted for over 90% of total US pineapple production, and many of the island's older residents are former field laborers. The community is small and close-knit, and people are genuinely amiable—it is considered common courtesy to wave to all oncoming drivers and pedestrians. Prices on Lanai are a bit higher than those on other islands, but if an escape from dense tourism is what you're looking for, you'll find it on Lanai.

Lanai has been under the control of nearby Maui since before recorded history. It is still part of Maui County, but with just over 3000 residents, it has too

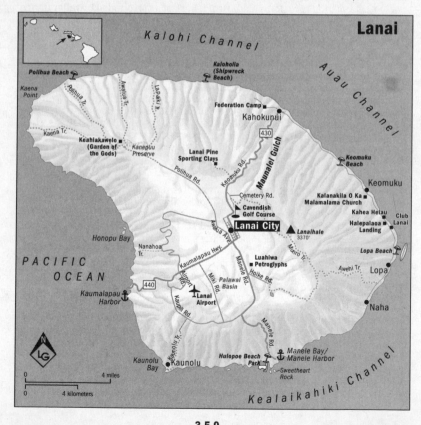

few voters to hold much sway in local politics. Castle & Cooke, a private company, owns 98% of the island, and Castle & Cooke resorts employ and house 80% of the population. Lanai hasn't always enjoyed such a peaceful, simple existence. Maui chiefs believed that evil spirits inhabited the island. During his exile on Lanai, Prince Kaululaau, the unruly son of King Kakaalaneo, is said to have used trickery to rid the island of its spirits. As a reward, Kaululaau was given control of the island. Life on Lanai remained relatively calm until King Kamehameha took control and began slaughtering islanders. His wrath was so fierce that when Captain George Vancouver sailed past the island in 1792, he didn't bother to land because of Lanai's apparent lack of population.

Deterred by treacherous ocean swells and the lack of natural harbors, travelers to Lanai were scarce until 1861, when a group of Mormon missionaries led by Walter Murray Gibson arrived and began to build a holy city in the Palawai Basin. In 1864, it was discovered that Gibson had been using church funds to acquire land for himself, and he was excommunicated. Unfazed, he befriended King Kalakaua, who eventually appointed him Prime Minister (apparently in order to establish links with the US). As such, Gibson effectively controlled the entire kingdom. After his death in 1888, Gibson's daughter and her husband acquired more land to form the Lanai Company, and they tried their hands at cattle ranching. New Zealander George Munro was hired as foreman in 1910, and he is credited with planting the tall pine hallways that still shade the central portion of the island. In 1917, the Baldwin Brothers bought the Lanai Company and sold it five years later to James Dole.

At Harvard University, Dole had studied agriculture and specialized in canning. He built Kamalapau Harbor and Lanai City and is also responsible for much of the island's infrastructure. Thanks to his business savvy, the exotic pineapple became an American staple. By the late 1930s, the Great Depression and the availability of cheap land and labor in Southeast Asia lured Dole overseas, and the Castle & Cooke Company bought out his interest in the island. David Murdoch is the current CEO of Castle & Cooke, and the two Lanai resorts are his brainchildren. Murdoch himself owns the biggest house on the island, just a moment's drive from the Four Seasons at Manele Bay.

In recent years, the hotels have experienced steady growth. Most locals doubt that Lanai's character will change and hope that the resorts will continue to provide jobs without jeopardizing the island's charm and hospitality.

HIGHLIGHTS OF LANAI

OFF-ROAD on the rugged Munro Trail and experience untamed Lanai (p. 357).

TRAVEL BACK IN TIME in the Garden of the Gods, with its ancient stone formations and mythical history (p. 357).

COMMUNE WITH NATURE at Manele Bay, home to Lanai's best beach and only official campsite (p. 359).

JOIN THE WHOLE ISLAND for its weekly barge delivery or simply enjoy a sublime sunset solo at Kaumalapau Harbor (p. 360).

✈ INTERISLAND TRANSPORTATION

The easiest and least expensive way to reach Lanai is on the **Expeditions Ferry** (☎808-661-3756; www.go-lanai.com), which runs from Lahaina and Maalaea on Maui to Manele Harbor (one-way $25, children $20). From Lahaina, the trip takes 45min. (5 per day 6:45am-5:45pm; 5 returns 8am-6:45pm). Out of Maalaea Harbor, there are two daily trips (7am and 3:30pm; returns 9am and 5:30pm).

The only other way to get to Lanai is by **flying.** Schedules change frequently and rates vary by availability, so check with the airline for departure cities, times, and prices. Island Air (from the US ☎800-652-6541, from Oahu 808-484-2222; www.islandair.com. Reservations open daily 7am-7pm) flies from Honolulu (30min., 7 per day, cheapest flight approx. $61 one-way). Hawaiian Airlines (☎800-367-5320; www.hawaiianair.com) also flies to Lanai City.

OH, THE GROAN OF SEAFOAM. Most people arrive on Lanai via the ferry from Lahaina. If you have a tendency to get seasick, sit on the lower level of the ferry and as far back as possible. The ride will be much smoother from this vantage point, though you'll miss the open-air deck up top.

LANAI CITY

Lanai City—less a city than a quaint town—is the social and cultural center of the island, though the distinction is not hard to come by, as it is also the only town on Lanai (pop. 3164). Built by Jim Dole in 1922 to house plantation workers and their families, Lanai City was the first planned community in Hawaii. Almost all of Lanai's inhabitants live in the brightly painted houses here. At an elevation of nearly 1700 ft., Lanai City is cooler than the beaches below. Visitors won't see a single stoplight or fast-food joint, but they will find a charming community of restaurants, shops, and art galleries.

⊞ ORIENTATION

Lanai City surrounds **Dole Park,** a large, rectangular grassy area that runs basically east-west. It is bordered by **7th Street** to the north and **8th Street** to the south. Most of the town's stores and eateries are located along these streets. The boundaries of town are marked roughly by **Fraser Avenue** to the west and **Lanai Avenue** to the east. All streets are at right angles, and those running east-west are numbered 3rd-13th, with 3rd St. the farthest north. Those running north-south start with Fraser in the west and end with Queens in the east.

▣ LOCAL TRANSPORTATION

From the Lanai Airport, you'll need to rent a **car,** as there is no local transportation other than hotel shuttles and Rabaca's Limousine Service. (☎808-565-6670. Open 24hr. From the airport to town $95; to Manele Bay $143. 6-person max per car.) The island's dirt roads require 4WD. Lanai is covered in loose red dirt, so get a hard top and close your windows unless you want to end up coated in it. The only **gas station** on the island is Lanai City Service, on the Dollar property. Gas is pricey, often $1 per gallon more than the rest of the archipelago.

▨ **Adventure Lanai Ecocentre** (☎808-565-7373; www.adventurelanai.com), is a laid-back operation run by the affable Michelle. The gang at Adventure Lanai rents 2- and 4-door safari-style and hard-top 4WD Jeep Wranglers and Land Rovers, starting at $104 per day. Unlike the competition, they let you take their vehicles to all of Lanai's spectacular off-road spots. Reservations are highly recommended. Free airport pickup for renters. Adventure Lanai also rents every kind of outdoor equipment you can imagine. They offer a variety of private tours, including ATV adventures, safari Jeep tours, a kayak/snorkel trip, a mountain bike trek, and surfing safaris. Their most popular guide is Kayak John,

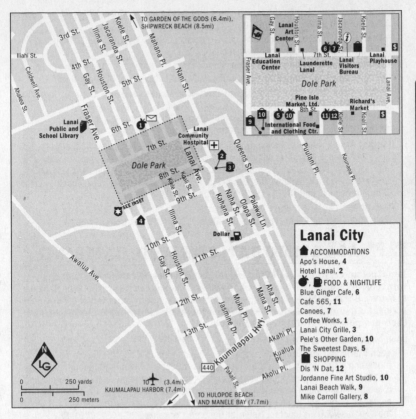

Lanai City

🏠 ACCOMMODATIONS
Apo's House, **4**
Hotel Lanai, **2**

🍎, 🍴 FOOD & NIGHTLIFE
Blue Ginger Cafe, **6**
Cafe 565, **11**
Canoes, **7**
Coffee Works, **1**
Lanai City Grille, **3**
Pele's Other Garden, **10**
The Sweetest Days, **5**

🛍 SHOPPING
Dis 'N Dat, **12**
Jordanne Fine Art Studio, **10**
Lanai Beach Walk, **9**
Mike Carroll Gallery, **8**

a.k.a. "Mikey," a relaxed and helpful islander with an uncanny knowledge of all Lanai has to offer. Also the only place on the island that offers bike rentals ($29 per day). Call anytime; tours everyday. Ask for a Let's Go discount. AmEx/D/MC/V.

Dollar Rent A Car, 1036 Lanai Ave. (☎808-565-7227), south of Dole Park, has a fleet of brightly colored Jeep Wranglers ($139 per day). Minivans, which are restricted to paved roads by the rental agreement and the terrain, run $129 per day. Dollar also has daily updates on road conditions and a shuttle that runs customers to and from the ferry and the airport. Be sure to stay on the proper roads; otherwise, you could pay hundreds to get towed. 21+. Under-25 fee $15 per day. Open daily 7am-7pm. AmEx/D/MC/V.

🛈 PRACTICAL INFORMATION

Tourist Information: Lanai Visitors Bureau, 431 7th St. Ste. A (☎808-565-7600; www.visitlanai.net), near the post office, about 20 ft. from 7th St. The knowledgeable staff here carries brochures for many popular island activities and will help you make the most of your time on Lanai. Open M-F 8am-4:30pm.

Banks: Bank of Hawaii, 460 8th St. (☎808-565-6037), and **First Hawaiian Bank,** 644 Lanai Ave. (☎808-565-6969). Both open M-Th 8:30am-4pm, F 8:30am-6pm (Bank of Hawaii is closed daily 1-2pm). Both have **24hr. ATMs.**

Laundromat: Launderette Lanai, at 7th St. and Houston St. Wash $2, dry $0.25 per 5min. No change machine. Open daily 5am-8:30pm.

Police: Lanai Police Department, 855 Fraser St. (☎808-565-6428). Office open 7:45am-4:30pm. On duty for emergencies 24hr.

Hospital: Lanai Community Hospital, 628 7th St. (☎808-565-6411), east of Lanai Ave. Emergency room open 24hr., administrative office open M-F 7:30am-4pm.

Copy Services: At the **Lanai Education Center of Maui Community College,** 329 7th St. (☎808-565-7266), at the corner of Gay St. Copies $0.10 per page. Open M-F 9am-3pm. Also at the **Lanai Public and School Library,** 555 Fraser Ave. (☎808-565-7920), for $0.20. Open M-W and F 9am-4:30pm, Th 2-8pm.

Internet Access: Coffee Works, 604 Ilima St. (☎808-565-6962; www.coffeeworkshawaii.com), has 1 computer with Internet access. $0.20 per min. $2 min. for cash; $5 min. for credit card. Open M-Sa 6am-5pm, in summer M-Sa 6am-4pm. AmEx/D/MC/V. Internet is also available at the Lanai Public and School Library (see above) with a 3-month visitor's card ($10); 1hr. time slots begin at the top of each hr.

Post Office: Lanai City Post Office, 620 Jacaranda St. (☎808-565-6517), north of Dole Park. Open M-F 9am-4pm, Sa 11:30am-1:30pm. **Postal Code:** 96763.

ACCOMMODATIONS AND CAMPING

Lanai is famous for its five-star resorts: **Lodge At Koele ❺** (☎808-565-4000; www.fourseasons.com/koele), north of town, and its sister resort, the **Four Seasons at Manele Bay ❺** (☎808-565-7700; www.fourseasons.com/manelebay). Though a room at either of these spots ($345-7000) might break the bank, a walk through their grounds is free and worth the time.

Hulopoe Beach Park. There are 6 official campsites that can accommodate 6 people, each with a grill and access to restrooms. The showers that line the beach have sunlit pipes and warm water. There are often groups of locals in semi-permanent campsites on the beach. If all the campsites are booked (not uncommon on weekends), try to find a local sponsor, which may allow you to camp for free. For any price, Hulopoe Beach is simply gorgeous. $5 registration fee, plus an additional $6 per person per night. 3-night max. For reservations, contact Helen at Castle & Cooke (☎808-565-3979). ❶

Apo's House (☎808-565-7373; www.lanaicityrental.com/aposhouse.htm), at the corner of 9th and Gay St. With 5 beds and 2 futons, Apo's has enough room for a small traveling circus, though single travelers will feel just as at home. Well-kept and within walking distance of Dole Park, this is the best place to genuinely and privately experience life in Lanai. Guests enjoy cable TV, a full kitchen, 2 bathrooms, laundry access, and even some feline protectors—Sprout, Deja Vu, and Transient Cat. Since it's run by the folks at Adventure Lanai, discounts are also available on Jeep and equipment rentals. A 25% deposit is required. $175 per night; $1050 per week. AmEx/D/MC/V. ❺

Hotel Lanai, 828 Lanai Ave. (☎808-565-7211; www.hotellanai.com), next to the hospital, at the top of a semicircle driveway. Fantastic value for the service: the staff is warm and friendly, and 10 welcoming rooms showcase elegant furniture, honey-colored floors, and immaculate bathrooms. Complimentary continental breakfast and shuttle to the beach. Check-in 2pm. Check-out 11am. A 50% deposit is required for reservations. 1-2 person rooms $159-179; private cottage $209. Additional guests $50. AmEx/MC/V. ❺

FOOD

The hotel restaurants are all exorbitantly priced with the exception of **Lanai City Grille ❺,** at Hotel Lanai, which serves superb American-Hawaiian fusion cuisine with prices that are within reach of a budget traveler's splurge. (Appetizers $12-14; entrees $28-39. Open W-Su 5-9pm. AmEx/D/MC/V.) On Saturday morning, there's a **swap meet** in Dole Park where locals sell homemade dishes.

GROCERY STORES AND MARKETS

Pine Isle Market, Ltd., 356 8th St. (☎808-565-6488). Equal parts grocery store, hardware store, and drug store, Pine Isle is the closest thing to a supermarket on Lanai. It has a deli counter with fresh meat and fish and also carries beer and wine. Open M-Sa 8am-noon and 1:30-7pm. AmEx/MC/V.

Richard's Market, 434 8th St. (☎808-565-3780). Castle and Cooke's own grocery/ hardware store combo has a decent selection of produce and sells ice, coolers, and the requisite beer, wine, and liquor. Open M-Sa 8:30-noon and 1:30-7pm. AmEx/D/MC/V.

International Food and Clothing Center, 833 Ilima St. (☎808-565-6433), behind Pine Isle Market. This small store has only 5 aisles, but it fills basic food and hardware needs. With a nice wine and liquor selection, it offers generally lower prices and is the only market open on Su. Open M-Tu 9am-7pm, W-F 9am-9pm, Su 8am-4pm. AmEx/D/MC/V.

RESTAURANTS

Cafe 565, 408 8th St. (☎808-565-6622), on the corner of Ilima St, is renowned for its hefty calzones ($10-12), stuffed to the gills with beef, chicken, vegetables, and more. They also sell pizza (slices $2; pies $13), sandwiches ($7-9), salads ($5.75-9), and entrees, including the popular Korean katsu chicken ($9.50). For a sweet escape, try 565's Reese's chocolate dessert calzone, topped with whipped and ice cream ($7.25). Lunch M-Sa 10am-3pm, dinner M-F 5-8pm. D/MC/V. ❷

Coffee Works, 604 Ilima St. (☎808-565-6962; www.coffeeworkshawaii.com), north of Dole Park, serves the best coffee in town, according to locals. They ship their grinds across the country as well, but you can enjoy yours on the large deck out front. There are 7 flavors of bubble tea ($4) to choose from, including taro, avocado, and mango, and the house special espresso milkshake ($8) is worth every penny. Ice cream, pizza bagels, sandwiches, cinnamon buns, and other fare $2-8. Open M-Sa 6am-5pm, in summer M-Sa 6am-4pm. AmEx/D/MC/V. ❶

Blue Ginger Cafe, 409 7th St. (☎808-565-6363). Blue Ginger is Lanai's all-purpose eatery and a good place to grab a cheap meal any time of day. Morning visitors can get 2 eggs, choice of meat, rice, and toast for $7; with 2 pancakes $9. Known for its fresh fish, usually *ono* or *mahi mahi*, dinner specials run $14-16, while lunch specials will only put you back $8-14. Plate lunches $8-10, burgers $3.50-9, and the biggest pigs-in-a-blanket in Hawaii are just $2. Open daily 6am-8pm. Cash only. ❷

Canoes Lanai, 419 7th St. (☎808-565-6537). Open for breakfast and lunch, Canoes is a popular gathering place for locals in the morning. Best known for its juicy Tanigawa burger ($2.25), a Canoes staple since 1957, this simple joint also serves up sandwiches ($2-6), plate lunches ($7-10), and buckets of fried chicken and *ume musubi* ($16-23). Open daily 6:30am-1pm. Cash only. ❶

The Sweetest Days, 338 8th St. (☎808-565-9569), at the corner of Gay St. The sugar-wild laughter of local kids fills the sunny picnic tables outside this candy shop. Perfect for a sundae ($4), smoothie ($5.75), or candy-bar fix, the crowded counter also serves up chocolate-dipped bananas with macadamia nuts ($2.50) and corn dogs ($1.75). Open M-Sa 11:30am-8pm. AmEx/D/MC/V. ❶

Pele's Other Garden, 811 Houston St. (☎808-565-9628; www.pelesothergarden.com), on the corner of 8th St. By day, Pele's is a deli-style eatery that serves decent sandwiches ($7.75-8.50) and "hot stuff" ($8-11). By night, the staff changes the lighting, tablecloths, music, and menu to create an Italian bistro catering mainly to resort types.

The bruschetta ($6.25) is popular, and pasta dishes ($17-19) are satisfying but pricey. Dinner reservations recommended. Happy hour daily 4:30-6:30pm (½-priced drinks and *pupu*). Open daily 11am-3pm and 5-8pm. AmEx/D/MC/V. ❸

🎵 🎭 ENTERTAINMENT AND ACTIVITIES

There isn't much to do on Lanai after dark other than see a first-run movie at the **Lanai Playhouse**, 465 7th Ave. (☎808-565-7500. $8, ages 4-12 and seniors $5, under 4 free.) This one-screen theater shows one movie twice a night (except W and Th). The only bar in town is at **Henry Clay's Rotisserie** in Hotel Lanai (beer $2.75-4.50, mixed drinks about $6). An agreeable way to spend the evening is to wander the streets and park just before sunset, when locals tend their gardens and children play freely in the streets.

For daytime excitement, head north of town on Keomuku Rd. toward Shipwreck Beach, and turn left after 1½ mi. at the **Lanai Pine Sporting Clays** sign, where you can blast compressed fertilizer discs with a 12-gauge shotgun on a gorgeous range. Dollar Rent A Car provides a voucher for 10 free shots, and it's worth taking advantage of the offer. (☎808-559-4600; www.islandoflanai.com. Reservations highly recommended. 25 clays $80, 50 $110, 100 $150. Open daily 9am-4:30pm. First seating 9am, last seating 2:30pm. AmEx/D/MC/V.) If shooting clay discs isn't your bag, try archery ($50 per 45min. session). If you're a sharpshooter, or just feeling lucky, ask about the **Pineapple Challenge.**

To play the nine-hole, par-36 **Cavendish Golf Course** (on Nani St., off Fifth St., north of town), a public course on the grounds of the Lodge at Koele, simply show up and tee off. ($5-10 donations appreciated in the box by the first tee.)

🛍 SHOPPING

The calm pace of life in Lanai City provides an inspiring and creative forum for the arts on the island. The few art galleries and shops that have opened around Dole Park allow visitors to peruse the work of local artists and craftsmen.

Dis N' Dat, 418 8th St. (☎808-565-9170; www.suzieo.com). A charming shop with hundreds of wind chimes ($19-500) and an eclectic mix of bric-a-brac, including "slippah" jewelry (miniature flip-flops that hang from necklaces and earrings, designed by the store's owner, Suzie), bubble string lights ($85), and stained glass lamps. Features local artists' work and a variety of exotic antiques. Open M-Sa 10(ish)am-5:30pm.

Mike Carroll Gallery, 443 7th St. (☎808-565-7122; www.mikecarrollgallery.com). This cozy gallery, which also serves as the artist's studio, features island-inspired paintings, photography, and prints created by local artists and complemented by the Chinese furniture on display. While original works sell for $1300-17,500, decent-sized prints are reasonable ($18-125). Open M-Sa 10am-5:30pm or by appointment.

Lanai Art Center, 333 7th St. (☎808-565-7503), at the corner of Houston St. Artists of all ages take lessons, exhibit work, and sell art at this community center. Postcards $2-5. Paintings, photos, and prints $15-35. Shipping available. Open M-Sa noon-4pm.

Jordanne Fine Art Studio, 850 Fraser Ave. (☎808-563-0088; www.jordannefineart. com.), near Gay and 9th St., showcases lively paintings, murals, and candles inspired by Lanai. The petite gallery also has an in-house studio for the artist and outdoor seating well-suited for artistic debates. Open M, W, F, and Sa noon(ish)-4(ish)pm or by chance.

Lanai Beach Walk, 850 Fraser Ave. (☎808-216-6246), at the corner of 9th St. and Fraser Ave. With better prices than the shops right on the park, souvenir-hunters can stop in here for a mixed offering of cover-ups, knick-knacks, and Crocs. Open M-Sa 10am-6pm, Su noon-4pm. AmEx/D/MC/V.

SIGHTS

CENTRAL LANAI

 MUNRO TRAIL. If you only have time for one off-road trek while on Lanai, this is the way to go. Named for the New Zealand naturalist who planted the island's magnificent pines, the Munro trail offers ethereal views of Maui, Molokai, Kahoolawe, the Big Island, and Oahu throughout its breadth, in addition to high-rise glimpses at the many former pineapple fields far below.

Be certain to stay on the main road. Side roads are often very muddy because they only exist for water drainage purposes. Two miles from the start of the trail, there's a turn-off to the left that leads visitors to a lookout over the gigantic **Maunalei Gulch,** the island's original source of drinking water. The main road bears right, and it takes you as close as you can get to **Lanaihale,** Lanai's highest point (3368 ft.). After another mile or two, the road affords a great view of **Hookio Gulch,** the site of the Lanaian warriors' defeat by King Kamehameha.

At the end of the trail, an exit sign points to the left. Continue down the road and then veer right at the first major fork (if you reach a large orange pipe, then you've gone too far). Follow the steep road until it ends, then turn left and proceed until reaching Manele Rd. Turn right to return to Lanai City. *(To reach the trail from town, take Lanai Ave. toward the Lodge at Koele. Past the Lodge, take Keomoku Rd. toward Shipwreck Beach, and then take a right onto Cemetery Rd. With the cemetery on your right, veer left after the pavement ends and look for a sign that marks the trailhead. The trail is about 13 mi. long with a 1600 ft. elevation change and can take anywhere from 2-4hr. to complete with 4WD, depending on road conditions. Also expect to spend about 30min. making your way from the end of the trail back to the highway. The trail is also good for a 4-8hr. hike or mountain biking.)*

 THE ROAD LESS TRAVELED. Munro Trail is generally in good condition but can only be tackled with 4WD. Do not to attempt the trail if it has rained in the last 48hr., and watch out for mud puddles and fallen boulders. There are several places where an inopportune skid could send your vehicle over the edge of the road and into a deep ravine. Check with a rental agency for an update on the conditions. Drive slowly, and use 1st gear.

THE NORTH SIDE

GARDEN OF THE GODS (KEAHIAKAWELO). Keahikawelo, or Garden of the Gods, is a vast, desert-like expanse of red earth marked by thousands of rock towers. The rolling topography of the wind-swept terrain is both surreal and awe-inspiring. The towers are concentrated at the beginning of the garden, but to fully appreciate the splendor of the place, drive all the way through. Late afternoon is the best time to visit, when the towers cast long shadows and the warm tones of the setting sun complement the colors of the landscape.

TIP OFF-ROADING OFF CHANCES. Many of the best sights on Lanai are accessible only by driving over rough, unpaved terrain. 4WD vehicles are best suited to this activity, and even then, getting stuck in sand or mud is possible. Cell phone coverage is spotty at times, so pack some food and water before you go, and be prepared to wait for rescue if your excursion gets mired.

Some claim that Hawaiians believed that the towers were created by the gods and that locals followed suit with their own man-made versions. However,

ROMPING AROUND LANAI

All-terrain vehicles (ATVs) are four-wheeled, gas-powered quads that can go just about anywhere. If you want to romp around the vast terrain of Lanai, talk to the folks at Adventure Lanai Ecocentre, the pineapple isle's prime resource for outdoor exploits.

Adventure Lanai offers 2-4hr. ATV treks and will take you to any place on the island you wish to go. They'll outfit you in a helmet and goggles, and if you want to drive, they'll teach you. Otherwise, enjoy the most diverse terrain of any Hawaiian isle as you cruise on the back of your guide's ATV.

One of their adventures goes through the Palawi Basin and down the whole length of the Awehi Trail, a steep and bumpy downhill ride with killer views of the Maunalei (mountain lei) Gulch. Another trip traverses the Garden of the Gods and on to the remarkable Polihua Beach, the perfect chance to see the wide, pure sand without sinking your car into it. The gorgeous trek that traverses the Munro Trail is ideal for anyone who prefers cool, high elevations and the shade of trees. All tours promise a light snack, witty banter, and mud splatter at your discretion.

Prices vary depending on the route and duration of the trip. Contact Michelle at Adventure Lanai Eco-centre (☎808- 565-7373; www. adventurelanai.com). If you're an experienced rider, inquire about renting one for the whole day, and don't forget to mention the Let's Go discount.

the larger towers were actually created by natural forces, and it was tourists who built imitative structures. Hawaiian legend has it that Kawelo, a young sorcerer, challenged his master on Molokai to a contest. Each had to build a bonfire, and the person whose bonfire lasted longer would have their island blessed with prosperity. Kawelo, it is said, burned everything in sight, leaving the beautiful, though dry, terrain seen today in the Garden. *(Approx. 25min. from town, 1 mi. beyond the Kanepuu Preserve. The drive requires 4WD, but the road is in decent condition if it hasn't been raining. The drive is less challenging than most.)*

KANEPUU PRESERVE. A road leading over three sets of cattle grates enters the silvery ironwood and pine forest of this 460-acre preserve. After 1 mi., you'll see a sign for a self-guided trail on the right. The walk takes about 15min., and plaques along the path provide information on the rare vegetation in the preserve. Some 48 native species can be found in the largest native Hawaiian dry forest on the island, including endangered Lanai sandalwood and rare Hawaiian gardenia. *(Take Lanai Ave., north toward the Lodge at Koele. Just past the Lodge, turn left onto the dirt road between the tennis courts and the stables. Past the stables, turn right at the intersection onto Polihua Trail. After, you'll see the fence and sign announcing the preserve.)*

POLIHUA BEACH. After the Garden of the Gods, unflappable drivers can continue on to the gorgeous Polihua Beach, a 2 mi. stretch of white sand where sea turtles lay eggs and humpback whales can be spotted December through April. Road conditions are sometimes very unfavorable; but if you make the trip, you'll likely have this conservation beach to yourself. Park on the dirt area off to the right of the end of the road. Do not approach or disturb any species. *(Approx.y 45min. from town. After the Garden of the Gods, continue on Polihua Trail until it ends. The drive requires 4WD. You should not drive on the beach itself—doing so is illegal and you will likely get stuck.)*

THE EAST SIDE

SHIPWRECK BEACH (KAIOLOHIA). Enjoy the simple beauty of the drive to Shipwreck Beach—short dune grass flows along Keomuku Rd., winding to the blue Pacific. The narrow road offers arresting views of both Molokai and Maui as well as the forsaken, rusting hulls of two large ships that give the 4 mi. stretch of white sand beach its name. This part of the island gets less than 12 in. of rain per year, and the vegetation is sparse enough that the burnt red dirt shows through, creating a rough-hewn patchwork of contrasting colors.

The first sight along the dirt road is Federation Camp, about 1 mi. from Keomuku Rd. The deserted fishing shacks were built as vacation homes in the early 20th century by the island's Filipino pineapple plantation workers. A few minutes beyond the houses is a turn-around area with picnic tables. Park here and continue walking along the road over bumpy rocks for about 50 yd. On the left you will see a small straw house and patio tucked into a cove of bushes and a rock that says "Shipwreck Beach." Continue towards your right where you will find the cement foundation that once supported a lighthouse. Walk down the small ramp of the lighthouse foundation and continue away from the sea (toward a boulder that warns "Do Not Deface"). Climb down the rocks to the right of this boulder to reach the well-preserved **Kukui Point petroglyphs.** Look carefully on the undersides of the large rocks to see these ancient drawings of warriors and animals, believed to date back to AD 500-900.

Once on the beach, walk along the coast toward the shipwreck, which becomes visible almost immediately, though you'll have to walk over rocks for about 15min. to reach it. As you continue, keep your eyes peeled for dozens of piles of sand next to holes in the ground; the holes are crab homes. Sea turtles have also been known to lay eggs on this beach at night. After about 15min. of walking, you'll reach the closest point to Liberty Ship, a WWII-era frigate that became stuck on the reef due to navigational error. There are nearly a half-dozen other shipwrecks along the beach. *(Take Keomoku Rd. until it ends. Turn left onto a dirt road at the end of the highway. Be careful not to drive into any of the large ruts in the road. The road is usually passable, but do not attempt it with 2WD or in the rain. Under no circumstances should you drive on the beach itself—doing so is illegal and you may get stuck.)*

KEOMUKU BEACH AND ENVIRONS. From the end of Keomuku Rd., the beach road heads southeast to Halepalaoa Landing. The ocean next to the road is shallow, rocky, and rife with marine life. A mile past the fork is Kalaehi (White Rock), known historically as the spot where Kaululaau vanquished the *akua* (ghosts) from Lanai. After about 5 mi. you will reach Keomuku Village, a former sugar plantation that operated from 1899 to 1901. The only noteworthy sight is **Kalanakila O Ka Malamalama,** an abandoned wooden church built after the collapse of the industry. About a mile out from the village, a walking trail on the right leads inland to **Kahea Heiau,** a temple once the site of human sacrifices, which was partially dismantled to build a railroad. The Buddhist shrine near the wharf was constructed to commemorate workers killed by a 1900 plague.

Lopa Beach, a good surfing beach and home to four ancient Hawaiian fishponds, lies another 5 mi. down the road. Naha, over 12 mi. from the end of the highway, is also the site of an ancient fishpond and probably not worth the trek, though Maui residents sometimes charter boats that drop them at the beach there for the day. *(To get to Keomuku Beach from the end of the highway, go straight on the dirt road at first and then veer right. The village is about 5 mi. down. The road is very bumpy and impossible to navigate in poor weather. Do not drive along the beach—you might get stuck. Check with your rental agency to see if the road has been re-graded before heading out.)*

THE SOUTH SIDE

MANELE BAY AND HULOPOE BEACH PARK. Dominated by the luxurious Manele Bay Hotel, Manele Bay is home to Lanai's most popular beach, only official campground, and a small harbor where you can catch the ferry to Maui (see **Interisland Transportation,** p. 351). From town, take Manele Rd. south. As the road straightens, you'll be driving through the caldera of an extinct volcano. This tree-lined Palawai Basin was once the center of the Dole Plantation.

At the very end of the highway, after a series of sloping switchbacks down to the shore, the road forks. To the left is Manele Harbor, the ferry landing and the island's principal port until the 1926 construction of the commercial harbor at Kaumalapau. To the right is **Hulopoe Beach Park,** the island's best beach for swimming and snorkeling. Although the surf is nothing remarkable in the summer, the beach gets much busier in the winter (but the sandy white expanse is large enough that it won't seem crowded). Hulopoe also has the island's only campsite, with picnic tables, grills, showers, and restrooms (p. 354).

From the beach, you can walk uphill and to the left along the bay. At low tide, take the green steps on the right down to the vibrant tide pools. Continue along to reach **Puu Pehe Rock,** more popularly known as **Sweetheart Rock.** According to Hawaiian legend, a local fisherman decided to build his home in a cave to prevent other men from laying eyes on his beautiful wife, Pehe. One day, a sudden storm swept his home into the sea, taking his wife with it. Her family recovered the body and brought it back to town. Late that night, the fisherman stole her body and, with the help of the gods, scaled the 150 ft. rock tower and buried her on top. Overcome with grief, he jumped off the rock to his death. The tomb structure, **Kupapau Puu Pehe** (tomb of Puu Pehe), is visible on top of the tower. This southeastern lookout is a romantic spot to watch the morning sunrise. The waters that lay below the area are known as Sharks' Cove, although none of its namesake creatures actually inhabit the wonderfully iridescent waves.

While at Hulopoe Beach, you can stroll around the grounds of the Manele Bay Hotel. If you face the water and stand toward the back of the beach, you'll see a path off to the right that takes you up to the resort. At night this passageway is illuminated with tiki torches. You'll pass the luau grounds on your right and arrive at Manele Bay's pool area. If you prefer not to visit the resort, follow the path that starts on the resort end of the beach. The path starts out on the sand, guided by a line of rocks and supplemented by plaques with historical information. If you cross the low point of the path and climb up and slightly toward the right, you'll see a sign for the "Lanai Fisherman's Trail," which crosses in front of the resort. The views from the trail are exceptional.

KAUMALAPAU HARBOR. Though there isn't much here, you'll probably make the quick trip to Kaumalapau Harbor simply because it's connected to town by a paved road. The drive itself is worth the trip, with remarkable views of the Pacific Ocean and the western slopes of the island. At one time, over a million pineapples a day were sent to canning plants on Oahu via the harbor, but today it's the drab commercial facility of an oil company. It's also the landing site for the weekly barge that supplies Lanai with goods such as cars, furniture, industrial equipment, and wholesale products retailed at grocery and hardware stores. The Thursday delivery is an all-day affair, with public access limited and restaurants, shop owners, and hotels all stopping by for provisions. When the shipment is late, the whole island reels in its wake. The area is rarely populated after 5pm, and the glacial sea wall next to the road is a superb place to watch the sunset. *(From town, take Kaumalapau Hwy. After 6 mi., you will reach the harbor area. Slow down to 5mph at the entrance—there may be men at work or locals fishing.)*

KAUNOLU. Once the summer retreat of Kamehameha the Great, Kaunolu remains one of Lanai's most remarkable archaeological sites. The *heiau* (temple) here, called **Halulu,** was used until 1819. One of its altars bears a stone image of the fish god Kunihi, representing Kuula, the patron of fishermen. To the left of Halulu is **Kahekili's Leap.** Also known as Warriors' Leap, Kamehama's warriors would prove their worth by leaping from this 63 ft. natural platform into the waters below. While Kaunolu remains a must-see, the unpaved road to the valley is rather treacherous; the few tourists who do decide to make the trip generally do so via an ATV tour. *(From town, take Kaumalapau Hwy. After 3 mi., just past the airport, turn left. Follow this road for 5 mi. until it ends.)*

KAUAI

In the family of Hawaiian Islands, Kauai would be known as the "pretty one." Kauai's shores, cliffs, and forests give the island its stunning good looks and mysterious aura. Kauai's 65,000 residents stand tall on their gem of a homeland. Locals are fiercely proud of their heritage and Kauai's lack of commercial development (law prohibits any buildings taller than a palm tree). The oldest and northernmost major island, Kauai is at the lonely end of the chain, next to only Niihau and the tiny Northwest islands. Aptly nicknamed "The Garden Isle," Kauai's plentiful rainfall nurses the verdant land and supports local agriculture, including coffee, sugar, and taro root production. Kauai's rainforest jungle is best described as primordial (*Jurassic Park* was filmed here), and markers of the island's six million years of weathering are visible in its impressive landscape. The Na Pali Coast cliffs and the jagged Waimea Canyon were carved by millennia of rainfall, and Waialeale Mountain is the wettest spot on earth, receiving over 450 in. of rain per year. Kauai's tranquil isolation, untamed landscape, and opportunities to commune with nature once lured hippies from the mainland. Today, Kauai still draws a more rugged and independent traveler than Maui or Oahu. Many visitors who come here blaze their own paths through the "real Hawaii" of the Na Pali Coast and its spectacular Kalalau Trail. Regardless of activity, anyone who visits Kauai is likely to leave with lingering images of its splendor and memories of a land timeless in its beauty.

HIGHLIGHTS OF KAUAI

STEP onto the shimmering sand of remote Polihale Beach (p. 422) as you watch the fiery sunset paint the sky with a vibrant palette.

SWIM WITH SEA TURTLES at PKs, one of many beautiful beaches by Poipu (p. 400).

SCALE DOWN into the Waimea Canyon (p. 416), the "Grand Canyon of Kauai."

TAME the Kalalau Trail, the hardcore hiker's mecca on the Na Pali Coast (p. 395).

⬛ INTERISLAND TRANSPORTATION

All commercial **flights** fly into **Lihue Airport (LIH).** Direct flights to Kauai from the mainland are rare—most passengers connect in Honolulu. However, American Airlines (☎800-433-7300; www.aa.com) has daily nonstop service to Kauai from Los Angeles, and United Airlines (☎800-241-6522; www.united.com) flies direct daily from Los Angeles and San Francisco. Hawaiian Airlines (☎800-367-5320; www.hawaiianair.com) flies to: Honolulu, Oahu; Hilo, the Big Island; and Kahului, Maui. Flights from Honolulu begin around $130 round-trip. Prices change frequently; be sure to check online or call for the most current information.

EAST SHORE

Anchored by Lihue, the county seat, the East Shore is Kauai's center of government and commerce. Most of the island's population is concentrated up and down the East Shore, and a multitude of restaurants and shopping centers cater to tourists and visitors. Drop your bags and buy your groceries here, but

Kauai

KAUAI

PACIFIC OCEAN

Kauai Channel

Kaulakahi Channel

Na Pali Coast State Park

Haena
Princeville
Kilauea
Hanalei
Kapaa
Waipouli
Wailua
Lihue
Koloa
Poipu
Kalaheo
Eleele
Hanapepe
Waimea
Kekaha

HANALEI DISTRICT
KAWAIHAU DISTRICT
MAKAWEHA MTNS
ANAHOLA MTNS
NAMOLOKAMA MTNS
LAAU RIDGE
WAINIHA RIDGE
LIHUE DISTRICT
KOLOA DISTRICT
WAIMEA DISTRICT

Waimea Canyon
Alakai Swamp

Nihili Lighthouse

4 miles
4 kilometers

seek beauty and adventure elsewhere. The area north of Lihue, also known as the Coconut Coast, provides an easily accessible sample of many of Kauai's attractions, from *heiau* (temples) to boat rides on the Wailua River.

LIHUE

Welcome to the big city—for Kauai that is. Despite a decade of tourist influx to the island, this county seat remains relatively tranquil and untouched by development projects. Expect no-frills shopping, good food, and relatively inexpensive accommodations in Lihue (pop. 5674); you can find posh resorts and popular sights elsewhere on the island. Though plenty of tourists come to Lihue for its historical sights and decent beach, few stay the night. For travelers on a budget, Lihue's affordable hotels and its central location make it a convenient launching pad for excursions to the southern and eastern coasts. Lihue restaurants usually serve local fare in large portions at a low price.

⌐ TRANSPORTATION

Flights: Lihue Airport, 3901 Mokulele Loop (☎808-246-1400), 2 mi. east of town.

Bus: The Kauai Bus (☎808-241-6410) runs 6 bus routes M-Sa around the island, offering affordable, but infrequent (every 30min.-4hr., depending on route and day of the week) transportation. Rte. 700 runs M-F within Lihue. The other main routes stop at every town as they run across the south shore to Kekaha and up and across the North Shore to Hanalei. Carry-ons are limited to 10x17x30 in. and oversized bags and surfboards are prohibited—this rule is generally not enforced, especially if the item will fit on your lap. Bikes are permitted. In addition to the regularly scheduled stops, riders can request on-call pick-up at a number of locations. Schedules are available at the **Kauai Visitors Bureau** and most of the larger stores in town (Lihue Big Save and Walmart) or at www.kauai.gov/transportation. $1.50, seniors and ages 7-18 $0.75, 6 and under free; monthly pass $15, available for purchase from the **Kauai Transportation Agency** at 3220 Hoolako St. Bus runs M-F 5:15am-7:50pm, Sa 6:20am-5:50pm.

Taxis: All cabs on the island charge the same prices: $3 initially, and $3 for each additional mi. Most companies add $0.50 per bag and $5 per surfboard and can provide vans upon request. The following companies service the entire island: **Akiko's Taxi** (☎808-822-7588), **City Cab** (☎808-245-3227), **North Shore Cab** (☎808-826-4118), and **South Shore Cab** (☎808-742-1525).

WHEELIN' AND DEALIN'. Under 25 and renting a car in Hawaii? Avoid young driver surcharges by booking online through discount providers, which have pre-negotiated contracts with all major rental companies. Visit www.hawaiidrive-o.com or www.discounthawaiicarrental.com

Car Rental: Island Cars, 2983 Aukele St., Ste. 2 (☎808-246-6000), in the industrial park. Go 1 mi. from airport on hwy. 50 toward Lihue, turn left onto Haoa, go around the bend, and continue for a block until reaching Aukele St. Island rents out a selection of older sedans, vans and mini-vans. Rates (including taxes) for drivers under 25 are around $200 per week, while ages 25+ are $150 per week. Personal car insurance is mandatory, though optional liability coverage can be added ($3/day for minimal coverage; $10/day for full coverage). Will stay open for arrival of any flight, and will provide pickup for $7, depending on staff availability. In addition, **Alamo** (☎808-246-0646 or 800-327-9633), **Avis** (☎808-245-3512 or 800-831-2847), **Budget** (☎808 245-9031 or 800-527-0700), **Dollar** (☎866-434-2226 or 800-800-4000), **Hertz** (☎808-245-3356 or 800-654-3131), **National** (☎808-245-5636 or 800-227-7368),

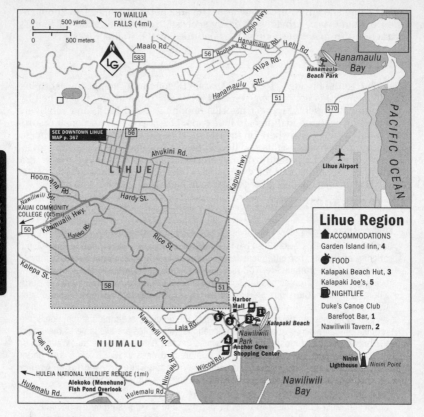

and **Thrifty** (☎877-283-0898 or 800-847-4389), all at the airport, charge similarly higher rates. Package deals and AAA membership can usually swing a discount.

⊹ ORIENTATION

There are two main streets in Lihue: **Rice Street** runs through downtown and **Nawiliwili Road** meanders near the coast. Most of the cheaper accommodations are downtown, while luxurious hotels and **Kalapaki Beach** line the waterfront. From the beach, Nawiliwili Rd. heads north to Kauai's largest shopping center, **Kukui Grove,** and ends at its intersection with **Highway 50. Highway 56 (Kuhio Highway)** leaves town heading north on the way to Wailua and Kapaa.

⑦ PRACTICAL INFORMATION

Tourist Information: Kauai Visitors Bureau, 4334 Rice St., Ste. 101 (☎808-245-3971; www.kauaivisitorsbureau.com), in the Watamull Plaza. Open M-F 8am-4:30pm.

Banks: Bank of Hawaii, 4455 Rice St. (☎808-245-6761), next to the post office. Open M-Th 8:30am-4pm, F 8:30am-6pm, Sa 9am-1pm 24hr. ATM.

Library: 4344 Hardy St. (☎808-241-3222). Internet access is available with a 3-month visitor's card ($10). Use of 8 computers is limited to 1 session per day per person. Printing $0.15 per pg. Also has a wide selection of DVDs ($1 per rental) for library members. Open M and W 11am-7pm, Tu and Th-F 9am-4:30pm.

Laundromat: Lihue Laundromat, in Rice Shopping Center. 25 washers and 28 dryers handle a ton of duds. Wash $1.75, dry $0.25. Open 24hr.

Weather Forecast: ☎808-245-6001.

Police: Kauai Police Department, 3990 Kaana St., Ste. 200 (☎808-241-1711).

Hospital: Wilcox Memorial Hospital, 3420 Kuhio Hwy. (☎808-245-1100).

Internet Access: Cox Internet Cafe in Harbor Mall, Ste. 100 (☎808-632-0192). Take Nawiliwili Rd. or Rice St. toward the harbor. $4 per 15min., $6 per 30min., $10 per hr. Wi-Fi $5 per 30 min. or $10 per day. There's another Internet cafe, **Cyber Connection,** 3366 Waapa Rd., Ste. 508 (☎808 246-3831), across the street in the Anchor Cove Shopping Center. Internet access is $3 per 15min., and Wi-Fi $4 per 30min. or $8 for 24 hr. Alternatively, you can try your luck at **Kauai Community College** library, 3-1901 Kaumualii Hwy. (☎808-245-8233), on the right of Kaumualii Hwy. heading out of Lihue toward Poipu, about ½ mi. past Kilohana's. 15min. per day of free Internet access to the public, although students have priority. No printer. Library open M-F 8am-4pm.

Post Office: Lihue Post Office, 4441 Rice St. Open M-F 8am-4pm, Sa 9am-1pm.

Postal Code: 96766.

▐ ACCOMMODATIONS

Anyone looking for luxury and spectacular surroundings should peel right out of Lihue for the resorts on the North Shore and southern coast. But for penny-pinchers and independent travelers alike, Lihue's central location and affordable accommodations make it a great choice.

▨ **Kauai Palms Hotel,** 2931 Kalena St. (☎808-246-0908; www.kauaipalmshotel.com), one block off of Rice St. This 2 fl. hotel with outdoor entrances for its 28 rooms strikes the perfect balance between budget and homey comfort: they all sport comfy mattresses and flatscreen TVs. The basic rooms have ceiling fans rather than A/C, but windows allow the island's nighttime breezes to act as a natural coolant. Coin-op laundry ($1.50) and ▨**free Wi-Fi** in the lobby, though some rooms might pick up the signal. Reception 7am-9pm. Ask about late night check-in, if necessary. Basic room with king bed or 2 singles $75; with A/C and kitchenette $100. AmEx/D/MC/V. ❸

Garden Island Inn, 3445 Wilcox Rd. (☎808-245-7227; www.gardenislandinn.com), across from Nawiliwili Harbor. Tropical-themed door murals and bright, Gauguin-like paintings by local artist Camile Fontaine,enliven the hotel's 21 rooms. Convenience and comfort are not neglected, as all units have A/C, cable TV, refrigerator, microwave, wet bar, coffee maker with complimentary Kona coffee, and fresh flowers. Nicer rooms lie on higher floors and have private *lanai* and ocean views. Complimentary continental breakfast and beach gear for nearby Kalapaki Beach. Reception 7:30am-9pm. Rooms $99-$145; 6-person condo from $180, with 4-night min. AmEx/D/MC/V. ❸

Motel Lani, 4240 Rice St. (☎808-245-2965). Tidy and centrally located, Motel Lani is a deal. Lots of plants brighten up the courtyard that sits next to 6 basic rooms with beds, a bath, mini-fridge, and A/C. 2 larger rooms with 3 beds in each come with TV but no A/C. Reception 7am-9pm. Discount of around $10 per night for multi-day stays. Rooms with double bed or 2 singles $45/$55, with 3 beds $65/$70. Cash only, though credit card (no debit) is required upon check-in as insurance against damages. ❷

▐ FOOD

Lihue's diverse assortment of restaurants reflects the city's residual plantation-era demographics. A typical restaurant for locals features Asian, Hawaiian, or

American cuisine (or a mix of all three), offers heaping portions and homey decor, and might insist on cash only. Such eateries are located at the upper end of Rice St. and in the Kukui Grove Shopping Center, while those geared toward tourists are nestled next to Kalapaki Beach. For something fancier, save up for a splurge in Poipu. **Vim 'n Vigor**, 3122 Kuhio Hwy., Ste. A9, is one of Lihue's only health food stores, carrying vitamins, packaged sandwiches on local bread ($6-7), and organic salads ($6-7). (☎808-245-9053. Open M-F 9am-7pm, Sa 9am-5pm.) For groceries, try **Star Market** in Kukui Grove Center. (☎808-245-7777. Open daily 6am-11pm. MC/V). **Walmart**, 33300 Kuhio Hwy., north of town, has a pharmacy. (☎808-246-1599. Open daily 6am-11pm. Pharmacy open M-Sa 9am-7pm, Su 9am-6pm.) Lihue holds weekly **"Sunshine Markets,"** sales of Kauai-grown fruit, vegetables, and flowers, Fridays at 3pm behind Vidinha Stadium.

■ **Pho Kauai**, 4303 Rice St. #B-1 (☎808-245-9858), in Rice Shopping Center. Occupying an unassuming corner of an austere stripmall, this is a not-to-be-missed eatery for famished travelers. Customize the flavor of your pho soup ($7) with an array of savory sauces, or try the exquisite stir-fried tofu and vegetables in a spicy lemongrass sauce ($6.75). Bubble tea addicts will be delighted with their selection of flavors (from taro to mango, $3). Open M-Sa 10am-9pm. MC/V. ❶

Kalapaki Beach Hut, 3474 Rice St. (☎808-246-6330), across from Harbor Mall. Juicy, flame-broiled burgers ($4-6.50), generous toppings, and a prime location make the Beach Hut very popular for lunch. Try the Classic (teriyaki glaze, pineapple, and cheese; $6.25). The charred Ono Fish Sandwich ($6.50) is a must-have. Although seating is available, many people take their burgers to Nawiliwili Beach Park for an entertaining view of beginning surfers. Breakfast includes omelets ($5.75-$7.75), pancakes, french toast, or an egg sandwich ($4.75). Kids meals ($4.50) come with a burger, fries, and drink. Open M and Sa-Su 7am-4pm, Tu-F 7am-8pm. AmEx/D/MC/V. ❶

Kalapaki Joe's, 3051 Rice St. (☎808-245-6266). This new arrival offers innovative grub from its breezy open-air perch on the 2nd fl. of Harbor Mall. Joe's takes advantage of the Pacific's bounty with a selection of *mahi mahi*, mackerel, snapper, and *ahi*, all of which can be prepared fried ($12), grilled ($13), or in tacos ($10, Asian- or island-style). Beefy burgers ($8-9) and giant salads ($6-15) round out their menu. Happy hour daily 4-6pm on the covered-balcony bar (Bud Light drafts $2.50, Heineken $3). The rear of the restaurant hosts **Block Sushi**, a small bar that offers premium rolls ($8-13) and standard 2-piece *nigiri* ($4-6). Open daily 11am-11pm. AmEx/D/MC/V. ❸

Deli and Bread Connection (☎808-245-7115), next to Macy's in Kukui Grove Shopping Center. A deli, bakery, and kitchenware store in one, the Connection is a popular lunch stop for famished shoppers. The sweet bread, delightful variety of sandwiches, and rock-bottom prices make the wait worthwhile. A number of vegetarian selections (veggie burger $6) and fresh daily soups ($3) round out the usual meat-and-cheese offerings (BLT $5.50; crab and shrimp, or "Crimp," $5.50). Open M-Th and Sa 9:30am-5:30pm, F 9:30am-9pm, Su 10am-4pm. MC/V. ❶

Genki Sushi (☎808-632-2450), in Kukui Grove Shopping Center, Ste. A10-11. Genki is the only outpost of the Tokyo-based boat-sushi chain on Kauai. Chopstick-wielding diners slide into family size booths where they have the option of either custom ordering prepared maki rolls and nigiri or helping themselves from the selection that passes by on the conveyor belt at the end of the table. Dishes are color coded according to prices (avocado roll or miso $1.55, vegetarian roll $2.20, spicy tuna $3, *ahi* $4). Open M-Th 11am-9pm, F-Su 11am-10pm. AmEx/D/MC/V. ❷

Kauai Bakery and Cinnamons (☎808-246-4765), in Kukui Grove's outdoor mall, between Sears and Star Market. This hole-in-the-wall has a steady flow of eager customers and a staff of bantering bakers hard at work. All the goods are fresh out of the oven or fryer, including doughnuts ($0.75) and pastries ($1-3). Don't miss the divine banana

ENTERTAINMENT
Kukui Grove Cinemas, 6
Lihue Bowling Center, 8

NIGHTLIFE
Duke's Canoe Club
  Barefoot Bar, 12
Nawiliwili Tavern, 14
RipTydz, 2
Rob's Good Times Grill, 4

Downtown Lihue

ACCOMMODATIONS
Motel Lani, 7
Kauai Palms Hotel, 11

FOOD
Deli and Bread Connection, 10
Genki Sushi, 1
Kalapaki Beach Hut, 13
Kalapaki Joe's, 15
Kauai Bakery and Cinnamons, 9
Oki Diner and Bakery, 3
Pho Kauai, 5
Kalapaki Joe's, 15

bread, flaky apple turnovers ($1-3), sumptuous pigs in a blanket ($1.65), or the chocolate, cream, or red bean-filled *malasadas* ($1), a Portuguese import. Open M-Th and Sa 6am-7pm, F 6am-9pm, Su 6am-6pm. Cash only. ❶

Oki Diner and Bakery, 4491 Rice St. (☎808-245-5899), on the corner of Haleko Rd. Plenty of parking in back. Pastel walls and floral-patterned chairs warmly invite patrons to dine on either Hawaiian staples ($10-14) or breakfast favorites ($6-10), which are served all day. Go upmarket and try their new snazzier offerings like snapper in a sun-dried tomato sauce ($17) at dinner. The selection, amiable service, and prices make Oki an easy and reliable place for a bite, and it's just about the only late-night option in town. Open M-W and Su 6am-midnight, Th-Sa 6am-3:30am. AmEx/D/MC/V. ❸

BEACHES

KALAPAKI BEACH. (*Bodyboarding. Surfing. Open daily sunrise to sunset.*) Given the commercial development around it, Kalapaki is a surprisingly gorgeous beach, drawing eager beachgoers to its quarter mile of fine white sand. The bay, one of Kauai's historic surfing sites, creates gentle waves ideal for swimming, sailing, bodyboarding, and learning to surf. Though the beach is often littered with abandoned catamarans, volleyball nets, and the beach chairs of Marriott guests you won't have trouble finding an empty spot. West of the beach, **Nawiliwili Park**

provides tables, grills, bathrooms, outdoor showers, and grass perfect for picnicking aficionados. Public parking is available on the far east side of the Marriott via its main entrance; follow the beach access signs. Parking is also available behind Anchor Cove Shopping Center in the Nawiliwili lot, though take note of the towing notices aimed at non-shoppers.

 BEACHY KEEN. All beaches in Hawaii must be open to the public. So don't limit yourself to the public (and often crowded) beach parks. Anywhere you see a resort, look for the public access signs and you might just enjoy a stretch of beach to yourself.

HANAMAULU BEACH PARK. *(Bodyboarding. Surfing. Open daily sunrise to sunset.)* Two miles east of Lihue, a trip to the dusty town of Hanamaulu will yield prime beachfront campsites. Plenty of silt makes the water's color rather uninviting as it laps Hanamaulu Beach's narrow crescent of fine sand. However, gentle swells, an all-sand bottom, and a few small breakers make this beach great for swimming, bodyboarding, and beginner's surfing. The slightly battered facilities include crumbling stone grills, picnic tables, trash cans, showers, and a pavilion. Locals comprise the majority of those who take advantage of the beach's weekend-only camping; for more information, see **Camping in Hawaii**, p. 82. *(After driving 2 mi. east of Lihue on Hwy. 56, take a right onto Hanamaulu Rd. at the "Welcome to Hanamaulu" sign, then take the third right onto Hehi Rd. for parking.)*

👁 SIGHTS

Long before Walmart's arrival in town, Lihue had already established itself as the thriving commercial center of Kauai. The town's location next to the island's main port, Nawiliwili Harbor, supported the sugar plantations that directed the course of Kauai's history. Today, remnants from this age promise to give visitors a glimpse into the resplendent lives of its great sugar kings. Other sights include those with ceremonial import to the Native Hawaiians.

ALEKOKO (MENEHUNE) FISHPOND OVERLOOK. This overlook is no more than a pull-off in the road, but it offers a quick view of a small pond steeped in island lore. According to legend, the pond owes its origins to the Menehune, a mythical race of mischievous, pot-bellied, elf-like creatures who lived in the forest and built impressive structures overnight. The story goes that a Hawaiian king asked the Menehune to build a fishpond (a body of water encircled by walls made of lava rock) and they happily complied. Yet despite their prodigious effort, the Menehune were unable to finish, and left the walls half-built. As the sun began to rise, they hurriedly washed their hands (scratched and bleeding from the rough lava rock) in the pond before disappearing. *Alekoko* ("rippling blood") filled the pond with fish and provided the Hawaiian Royalty with their main source of protein from that point on. Today *amaama* (striped mullet) and *awa* (milk fish) continue to thrive in the freshwater pond, laying their eggs amid the tangled roots of mangroves that have taken hold along the walls. *(From Nawiliwili Rd., turn onto Wilcox Rd. at Hale Kauai or onto Niumalu Rd., farther to the northwest. Both eventually lead over a 1-lane bridge, after which you turn right onto Hulemalu Rd. Drive about 1 mi. up to a small lookout on the left.)*

GROVE FARM HOMESTEAD MUSEUM. Visitors can enjoy an informative 2hr. walking tour of the 22,000-acre estate of George "G.N." Wilcox, Kauai's first and greatest sugar baron. The tour, capped at six people, begins in G.N.'s office with a brief biography of the industrious man (he funded his Yale education by gathering guano). The tour's next stop is Wilcox's austere cottage and the spectacular house he gave his brother and family. Gleaming ohia floors, a grand koa staircase, beautiful paintings, and a vast library are just a few of the luxuries inside. A devout Christian, Wilcox preferred to spend his hard-earned money helping others—he furnished both the land and funds for Nawiliwili Harbor, which became the island's central trading port. (*Northbound on Nawiliwili Rd., turn right at the small sign onto a private dirt road about 1 mi. from the harbor. ☎808-245-3202. 2hr. tour M and W-Th 10am and 1pm; may be cancelled on rainy days. Reservations are necessary to guarantee a place on the tour, and are strongly recommended. Requested donation $10, ages 5-12 $5.*)

KILOHANA. Built in 1935 by G.N. Wilcox's youngest nephew, Gaylord Parke Wilcox, and his wife, Ethel, Kilohana was once the most elegant and expensive house on Kauai. When Wilcox and his Grove Farm Plantation were the height of the sugar era on Kauai, the lavish dinner parties thrown by Gaylord and Ethel were famous throughout Hawaii. The word *kilohana* translates as "not to be surpassed," which was Gaylord's intent when he built it. Today, the 15,000 sq. ft. Tudor-style mansion's eight bedrooms and bathrooms have been converted into shops retailing art, jewelry, and collectibles. Unlike other historic homes, Kilohana encourages guests to truly experience the house—you can even sit on the furniture. Guests are also free to wander 35 acres of flowering gardens, cottages, and the working farm around the main house, which provide a spectacular view of the inland mountains. A Clydesdale-drawn carriage tour is an opportunity to learn more about Kilohana's history while the upscale steak-and-seafood restaurant in the main house, **Gaylord's,** invites guests to dine like the sugar baron himself (dinner entrees $24-40). A recent addition is a working train of four shiny mahogany passenger cars (enough to carry 140 people) and steam engine that encircles the entire plantation. Kilohana also boasts one of the island's best luaus, a commercial reproduction of a traditional Hawaiian feast that features roast pig, singing, and hula dancing. (*1 mi. west of Lihue on the mauka, or mountain, side of Hwy. 50. ☎808-245-5608. House and galleries open M-Sa 9:30am-9:30pm, Su 9:30am-2:30pm. 20min. carriage rides Tu-W and F 10am-6pm; M, Th and Sa 10am-4pm; Su 10am-3pm; $12, under 13 $6. 1hr. wagon rides M-Tu and Th 11am and 2pm; reservations required, call ☎808-246-9529; $29, under 13 $15. Luau Kalamaku Tu and Th 5pm; ☎808-245-9333; $95; ages 12-18 $65, ages 3-11 $45, under 3 free. Gaylord's ☎808-245-9593; dinner M-Sa from 5:30pm, lunch M-Sa from 11am, breakfast M-Sa 7:45-10am,*)

THE LOCAL STORY

SILVER SCREEN FLIRTATION

In front of the camera, Kauai has been marvelously versatile. Its jagged coastline, shimmering beaches and steamy jungles have doubled as Skull Island (in *King Kong*), Bali Hai (in *South Pacific*) and Isla Nublar (in *Jurassic Park*). In total, Kauai has played host to over 50 box-office productions since 1933. Its tropical beauty notwithstanding, Kauai's popularity with Hollywood producers is somewhat curious: there are hundreds of other tropical locations around the world; and production expenses on Kauai are high.

Part of the appeal might just be the comfort of longstanding relationships. From 1992 to 2002, Kauai film commissioner Judy Drosd hobnobbed with Hollywood's biggest producers—with impressive results, landing all three *Jurassic Park*s as well as *Six Days, Seven Nights*, which starred Harrison Ford. After Drosd's tenure, Kauai experienced a few sagging years. In response, the islands unveiled a tax-credit program, which came into effect in 2006, offering film companies up to a 20% write-off of their production costs. Shortly thereafter, Kauai was able to land a couple mega-productions, including the $100-million Ben Stiller film *Tropic Thunder*. Don't be surprised if you find yourself feeling déjà vu in the hills of Kauai: you might have indeed just seen it!

brunch Su from 9am. Reservations recommended. Kauai Plantation Railway, (☎808-245-7245), 40min. train ride M-Su 40 min. 10, 11am, noon, 1, and 2pm; $18, ages 2-12 $14.)

KAUAI MUSEUM. Small but informative, the Kauai Museum gives you a run-down of the natural and anthropological histories of the island. A self-guided tour begins in the Wilcox building (one of two that comprise the museum) with a sweeping aerial video of the island. Comprehensive displays illustrate Kauai and Niihau's indigenous and immigrant histories as well as the geology and ecology of the Hawaiian islands. *(4428 Rice St. ☎808-245-6931; www.kauaimuseum.org. Guided 1hr. tours M-F 10:30am; included in admission. Open M-F 9am-4pm, Sa 10am-4pm. $10, over 65 $8, ages 13-17 $6, ages 6-12 $2, under 6 free. 1st Sa of every month free.)*

WAILUA FALLS. Hawaiian *alii* (royalty) would dive from the cliffs overlooking the pool at Wailua Falls to prove their courage; many did not survive. Today, classic television fans may recognize the falls from the opening scenes of *Fantasy Island*. The south fork of the Wailua River flows to the falls where the magnitude varies with rain and the river's flow. Come early to avoid the crowds and watch the morning sun sparkle against the falls. The convenience of the lookout leaves you feeling a bit like a cheater; one should have to work for such sights. There are trails to the pool at the bottom, but they are dangerous and signs attempt to dissuade potential hikers. *(From Lihue, drive 1 mi. east on Hwy. 56 and turn left at Hwy. 583 or Maalo Rd. The road ends 4 mi. later at the falls.)*

HULEIA NATIONAL WILDLIFE REFUGE. The undeveloped wetlands, fertile hills, and verdant valleys west of the overlook form part of the Huleia National Wildlife Refuge, established in 1973 to protect the habitats of endangered waterbirds—including Hawaii's largest population of koloa ducks. The refuge is closed to the public with the exception of a few guided boat and kayak tours up the river. However, the road that passes through it (an alternative route to Poipu) affords some decent views of the flora, if not the protected fauna. Movie buffs may recognize the valley as the site of Indiana Jones's rope-swinging escape in the opening scene of *Raiders of the Lost Ark*.

NININI LIGHTHOUSE. A good place to watch for humpback whales in the winter, the 86 ft. Ninini Lighthouse also offers a fantastic and incredibly windy view of the ocean and Nawiliwili Bay. Patches of grass and volcanic rocks can provide the setting for an unforgettable picnic. If you're lucky, an attendant may be around to take visitors to the top of the lighthouse. *(Entrance off Hwy. 51 between the airport and Rice St. About 1 mi. north of Rice St., turn toward the sea at the road with a gatehouse. Drive for 1 mi. and follow the road as it makes a sharp left at the stop sign. Take the right fork and stay on the paved road. Past a "Shoreline Access-Ninini Point" sign, keep left at the "Running Path" sign; cross the golf cart path. The last stretch of the road is tricky for 2WD and roughly follows the fence of the airport on the left until it comes to a dirt parking lot.)*

🎵 📷 ENTERTAINMENT AND NIGHTLIFE

Lihue is the place to be after dark; nightlife here is as thick as it gets on Kauai. A few places are near the harbor while the rest are closer to the town center.

🏆 **Rob's Good Times Grill,** (☎808-246-0311), in Rice Shopping Center. Happy hour draws familiar *pau hana* (literally "quit work time") faces to this casual neighborhood bar. Rob and his wife, Lolly, pour drinks and mingle while customers kick back in booths or battle it out on the foosball table. Pool tables, 17 flatscreen TVs, and the only dance floor in town keep things going until closing. Enjoy local *pupu* ($5-9), typical bar food ($7-8), or heartier fare (steak and shrimp $14.50, *mahi mahi* $8) while dancing to Top 40 hits blasted from a state-of-the-art sound system. Happy hour daily 3-7pm (draft and domestic beers $3.25). Open daily 11am-2am. MC/V.

Duke's Canoe Club Barefoot Bar, 3610 Rice St. (☎808-246-9599), at the west end of Kalapaki Beach; enter from the beach or the Marriott Courtyard. Only a sidewalk and a neat lawn from the beach, Duke's serves *pupu* ($3-10) and drinks (Mai Tais $7.25; local draft beer $5). The stunning view of Kalapaki Beach can't be beat during the day and tiki torches light up the place at night. Patronized by tourists, Duke's prices are a hair higher than other bars. Taco Tu (4-6pm) features $3.25 draft beer and $2.50 fish tacos; Tropical F (4-6pm) delivers $6 tropical drinks. F live music 4-6pm and 9-11pm. Serves pricey entrees ($20-29) in the restaurant upstairs. Bar open daily 11am-midnight; food served 11am-11pm. Restaurant open daily 5-10pm. MC/V.

Nawiliwili Tavern, 3488 Paena Loop (☎808-245-1781), in the old Hotel Kuboyama next to Kalapaki Beach Hut. Wall-to-wall neon beer signs and the occasional pin-up make Nawiliwili Tavern a frat-boy fantasy. Darts, billiards, shuffleboard, video games, and beer welcome a diverse crowd; TVs are always tuned to ESPN. Locally brewed Keoki on tap ($5). Practice for the F karaoke contest in the back room with Kauai's largest karaoke collection. Karaoke every night except Th. Happy hour M-F 11am-6pm (Mai Tais and Pina Coladas $5, beer $2). Open daily 11-2am, food served Th-Sa 6pm-1am. MC/V.

RipTydz, 2978 Umi St. (☎808-241-7447), 1 block off of Rice St. near the town center. This local watering hole is the latest project of the owners of Tradewinds, the popular Wailua nightspot. It offers patrons dart boards, pool tables and lots of seating in which to grab a quick meal with friends. Karaoke lyrics appear in mesmerizing flashes on nearly a dozen plasma screens scattered around the bar. Last call for entrees ($9-14) is at 9pm, while sandwiches and burgers ($6.50-$8.50) are available for an hour longer. *Pupu* ($3.50-9.50) 'til midnight. Open daily 11am-2pm. D/MC/V.

Lihue Bowling Center, (☎808-245-5263), in the Rice Shopping Center. What could be better than 28 lanes, video games, and cheap food (*pupu* and meals, $2.25-6.25)? A lounge that taps cheap beer (15 oz., $2.75) and serves decent wine ($3.75). $3.75 per game, seniors and ages 18 and under $2.75; shoe rental $2. "Rock 'n Glow" F-Sa 9-11:30pm, $10 (includes shoe rental). Open M-Th 9am-11pm, F-Sa 9am-11:30pm, Su noon-10pm. Lounge open daily from 4pm to close. D/MC/V.

WAILUA

The first Tahitian settlers of Hawaii landed in Wailua (pop. 2083) where the convergence of the north and south forks of the Wailua River became the center of the Tahitians' new community. Ever since, Wailua, where "two waters become one," has been one of Kauai's most popular locales. Today, Wailua is characterized by the aquatic activities on the Wailua River, white sand beaches, and the resorts around town. Travelers can make a day of exploring the beach, the river or the foothills of Mt. Waialeale.

▟ ACCOMMODATIONS

Wailua is home to a number of hotels, small B&Bs, and mid-level resorts, most of which advertise on the Internet.

▩ **Magic Sunrise,** 139 Royal Dr. (☎808-821-9847; www.magicsunrisehawaii.com). From Lihue, turn left just past the Wailua River at "Coco Palms"; after going for about 3 mi. turn left on Royal Dr. right before the Wailua Country Store (the street sign is hidden), and go to the end of the road. A gate with a painted sun will be on your right. A fantastic B&B set in a tropical garden that ends in a dramatic overlook of the valley and river far below. Besides an apartment and a cottage, there are 3 rooms each of which have their own aloha color scheme, bamboo trimmings, and 4-poster beds. Guests have access

KAUAI

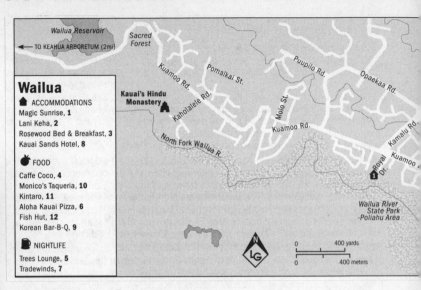

Wailua

🏠 ACCOMMODATIONS
Magic Sunrise, **1**
Lani Keha, **2**
Rosewood Bed & Breakfast, **3**
Kauai Sands Hotel, **8**

🍎 FOOD
Caffe Coco, **4**
Monico's Taqueria, **10**
Kintaro, **11**
Aloha Kauai Pizza, **6**
Fish Hut, **12**
Korean Bar-B-Q, **9**

🍺 NIGHTLIFE
Trees Lounge, **5**
Tradewinds, **7**

to a kitchen, living room, dining area, outdoor patio, swimming pool, office with Internet access and fax, and fresh avocados and mangos from trees on the property (when in season). Singles $66-76; doubles $72-$82. 2-story, 1-bedroom apartment $120; 2-bedroom cottage $130; 5-night min. for apartment and cottage. ❸

Kauai Sands, 420 Papaloa Rd. (☎808-822-4951; www.kauaisandshotel.com) A moderately priced option, this 200 room establishment is part of a family-owned hotel chain that also operates on Maui and the Big Island. Bordering the Coconut Marketplace, it features immaculate rooms with one king-size bed or two twin beds, a fan, cable TV, mini-fridge, and private *lanai*. The oceanfront location boasts two swimming pools, laundry room, exercise facilities, and restaurant. Rooms start at $98. AmEx/D/MC/V. ❸

Rosewood Bed and Breakfast, 872 Kamalu Rd. (☎808-822-5216; www.rosewoodkauai. com). Continue on Kuamoo Rd. for 2 mi., take a right onto Kamula at Wailua Country Store, and go for 1 mi. Flower beds and a white picket fence demurely foreground the yellow colonial houses at this classic Wailua Homestead establishment. In operation for over 25 years, Rosewood's owners graciously accommodate all types of travelers, from swooning honeymooners to hardcore backpackers. The Bunk House is the best deal, with 3 private double-occupancy rooms ($50-60 with a $25 cleaning) that share a nifty outdoor heated shower. The cottage and the 2- and 3-bedroom houses ($135-$200) afford more privacy and include laundry service. 3-day min. Cash only. ❸

Lani Keha, 848 Kamalu Rd. (☎808-822-1605; www.lanikeha.com). A sloping grass lawn doubles as a parking lot for guests staying at this simple B&B. With views of Mt. Waialeale and a yard of 3 acres, the ranch-style home contains 4 rooms with king-sized beds. In the luminous living room, well-thumbed books line the wall and rustic straw mats cover the floor. Amenities include fully-equipped kitchen, covered *lanai*, and Wi-Fi. Breakfast is MYO, but the ingredients are supplied. No cleaning fee. 3 night min. Reservations require 50% deposit. Double-occupancy $75. Cash only. ❸

🍴 FOOD

Wailua Shopping Plaza and **Kinipopo Shopping Village,** across from each other on Kuhio Hwy. north of the Wailua River bridge, both hold a number of excellent

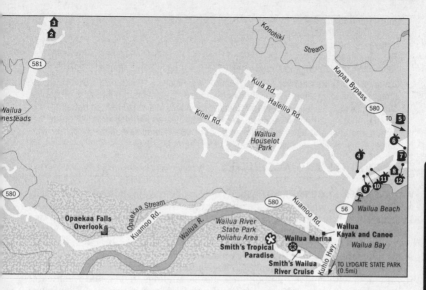

restaurants. A ¼ mi. further down the highway is the **Coconut Marketplace,** which serves as a home to many decent fast food joints.

Caffe Coco, 4-369 Kuhio Hwy. (☎808-822-7990), on the *mauka* (mountain) side of the highway past Kinipopo Shopping Village. Diners enjoy breezy open-air seating when choosing from the small but tried-and-true menu, which includes black sesame *ahi* ($20), Pacific-rim tofu ($18), and mushroom gorgonzola penne ($16). BYOB, corkage fee $5. Live music nightly, featuring local singer-songwriters and the occasional patron-cum-musician. Coffee, tea ($2), homemade appetizers, and desserts (samosas $4; vegan mango-date bar $4.50) are available for those who would like to hear the music without splurging on dinner. Open Tu-Su 5-9pm. MC/V. ❹

Kintaro, 4370 Kuhio Hwy. (☎808-822-3341), opposite Caffe Coco. Kintaro's upscale dining room serves Kauai's best Japanese food. Try the tempura combination of local fish, shrimp, and vegetables ($14), which comes with miso soup, rice and tea. They have a refreshing bowl of *zaru soba* (chilled buckwheat noodle soup $18). Extensive sushi (*maki*, $4-13). Hibachi seating or regular tables. Reservations strongly recommended. Open M-Sa 5:30-9:30pm. AmEx/MC/D/V. ❹

Monico's Taqueria, 4-356 Kuhio Hwy., Bldg. D (☎808-822-4300), in the Kinipopo Shopping Village. Not a roadside taco stand, but a full-service restaurant offering an inexhaustible selection of Mexican favorites. An effusive staff ensures that every part of your meal, from the complimentary bowl of tortilla chips to your burrito smothered in spicy tomatillo sauce (choice of meat $11; vegetarian or vegan upon request $10), is to your liking. The sizzling plates of fajitas ($15-17), served with all the fixings, are large enough for 2. Open daily for lunch 11am-3pm, dinner 5pm-9pm. AmEx/MC/V. ❸

The Fish Hut, 4-484 Kuhio Hwy. (☎808-821-0033). This stand prepares fish—freshly caught—every way you can imagine: in a burger, wrap or salad ($8), or in plate form ($10) or with a combo of oysters, scallops, or shrimp (pick 2), with fries. Freshly baked foccacia bread sandwiches ($8) are a treat. Another highlight is their 40+ flavors of shave ice ($3.50). Open M-Sa 11am-9pm, Su 11am-8pm. AmEx/MC/V. ❷

Aloha Kauai Pizza, 4-484 Kuhio Hwy, #29. (☎808-822-4511), in the Coconut Market-place. This small stand serves familiar Italian dishes to hungry shoppers lured in by the tantalizing aromas. Pizzas come in 7 in., 12 in., and 16 in. pies (cheese, $6/14/17). The house specialty, "Artichoke Eddie," (12in., $18) comes highly recommended. Cal-zones, lasagna ($7-8), and sandwiches ($7). Open daily 11am-9pm. MC/V. ❶

Korean Bar-B-Q Restaurant, 4-356 Kuhio Hwy., Bldg. E. (☎808-823-6744), in the Kinipopo Shopping Village. A local favorite, this small restaurant offers Korean staples. The menu's pictures help people unfamiliar with dishes like *katsu* (a fried battering) and *bibimbap* (steamed rice mixed with meat, vegetables and a fried egg). Plate lunches (marinated beef and barbecue chicken combo, $9) include rice, miso soup, macaroni salad, *kimchee*, and veggies. Open daily 11am-9pm. MC/V. ❷

👁 🎏 SIGHTS AND ACTIVITIES

WAILUA RIVER STATE PARK. The locus of most activity in the area is the majes-tic Wailua River, which flows 21 mi. from Mt. Waialeale to the north end of Lydgate Park. It is known as the only navigable river in Hawaii. Split into two branches for much of its path, the river converges to a single powerful water-way as it descends to sea level, mixing with the ocean in a brackish environ-ment that supports a healthy fish population.

In the time of the *alii* (royalty), the Wailua River basin was the home of royal chiefs who enjoyed its beaches, canoe landings, fields, and freshwater and saltwater resources. Known as the King's Highway, in honor of Kauai's last king, Kamehameha, the river is joined by a line of *heiau* (temples), that parallel the water's path from mountain to ocean. Six of the *heiau* that form this sacred path are visible today, while the seventh sits atop the Waialeale summit. Nearly all of the sights below fall within the boundaries of the 1000-acre Wailua River State Park, which encompasses the Wailua River, the town of Wailua (p. 371), Opaekaa Falls, Kuamoo Rd., Fern Grotto, and Lydgate Park.

Although tourist-filled riverboats dominate the Wailua River, it is also a favor-ite of kayakers who launch on the north bank. Turn from Kuhio Hwy. onto Kuamoo Rd. (north of the bridge) and take the second left into Wailua River State Park. There are over a dozen companies in the area that rent kayaks for trips on the river, some of which launch from the marina on the south shore (accessed by taking a left before the bridge that crosses the river). A convenient place from which to rent is **Wailua Kayak and Canoe,** next to the Smith's Tropi-cal Paradise shack, on the north bank close to Kuhio Hwy. just off Kuamoo Rd. The river is only a short walk from here. All rentals come with a map, dry bag, cooler, and brief orientation for first-time kayakers. Set out early to beat the blustering trade winds. (☎808-821-1188. *Single $45 per day; double $75. 4 hr. tours 8am, 12:30pm; $55-90. Open M-Sa 7am-5:30pm.*) Alternatively, you can rent from the relatively cheaper **Wailua Kayak Adventures,** 4-1596 Kuhio Hwy., just a few miles north of the river. Rentals come with dry bags, cooler, map, and a roof rack. They also offer kayak and hiking tours in the Wailua River area. (☎808-822-5795 or 808-639-6332. *Open daily 9am-6pm. Singles $25 per day; doubles $50. Tours $85.*)

LYDGATE STATE PARK. Picnic tables dot Lydgate's popular, long, grassy lawn. A few trees provide shade along the modest beach and the two wonderful salt-water pools. Man-made walls enclose the large pools and shelter swimmers from unpredictable surf, creating a beginning snorkeler's paradise. The larger pool is great for relaxed snorkeling, while the shallower adjoining pool is more appropriate for younger *keiki* (children). The stretch of beach immediately next to the pools tends to get crowded with boisterous families, but the areas north and south of them are often empty. Exercise caution when swimming in the ocean outside of the pools. Restrooms, showers, a lifeguard stand (manned 9am-5pm), and a pictorial fish-finder are located at the north end of the park.

Hikina Akalaheiau ("rising of the sun"), at the north end of the park, is the first of seven *heiau*. The stacked rock walls, built as early as 1300 and originally 11 ft. tall, form a large rectangle, within which the *kahuna* (priests) celebrated dawn with prayer and chant. At one end of the *heiau*, criminals sought sanctuary in Hauola, the City of Refuge. Untouchable within its boundaries, the offenders could stay until purified by a *kahuna* and absolved of their crimes. Camping is currently unavailable at the park; the former campsites are only open to daytime picnicking and grilling. *(Turn off Leho Dr. onto Nehe Rd., before Nalu Rd. The sites are right on the ocean and offer a shower, restroom, picnic tables, and grills. From Kuhio Hwy., turn toward the ocean onto Leho Dr. at the Lydgate State Park sign just north of mi. marker 5, a few hundred yards south of the bridge over Wailua River. About 1 mi. down, turn right on Nalu Rd. to the parking lot.)*

SMITH'S TROPICAL PARADISE. The Smith family has helped to introduce visitors to the beauty and culture of the island for three generations. Walter Smith, Sr., the son of an English immigrant who worked as a postman on Oahu before settling on Kauai, began taking tourists up the Wailua in a rowboat. Today's tours, run by Walter's descendants, are a little more industrial, employing large barges, but they feature many of the same elements as the originals. The 1hr. boat tours to Fern Grotto include a 30min. stop at the cave, an informative walk up the trail, and some history. Musicians serenade below, taking advantage of the grotto's perfect acoustics. Hula dancers and a Hawaiian band perform on the outbound cruise; local stories and legends are told on the return.

West of the marina, the Smiths have a 30-acre garden, home to over 20 types of fruit and wandering peacocks. The garden is divided into themed areas connected by 1 mi. of pathways. They also host Kauai's most authentic luau three nights a week in winter, five in summer. *(174 Wailua Rd., past the marina. ☎ 808-821-6895. Open daily 8:30am-4pm. Self-guided walking garden tour $6, ages 2-12 $3.)*

KUAMOO ROAD (HIGHWAY 580). Running from Coco Palms Resort, where Elvis tied the knot in *Blue Hawaii*, all the way past Opaekaa Falls, the highway runs along the northern bank of the river following the path the *alii* (royalty) walked from one religious site to another. The **Poliahu Heiau** held religious ceremonies here until the abolition of the Hawaiian religion in 1819. The *heiau* (temple) ruin

THE LOCAL STORY

KFC: KAUAI'S FERAL CHICKENS

A chicken contently clucking and feeding itself is a charming sight; thousands of them nesting in flower gardens and crowing at 5am, however, is a bloody nightmare. Any visitor to Kauai will quickly see that the island is plagued by the latter scenario.

Feral roosters, hens, and their chicks are so used to human presence that they stand poised to gobble up the crumbs from any careless diner. An absence of natural predators and wide availability of food have allowed the chickens to propagate unchecked.

The most popular rumor for their pestilential presence is that Hurricane Iniki, which ravaged the island in 1992, destroyed a chicken farm and released its inhabitants all over the Garden Isle. Yet an amateur historian will quickly point out that it was plantation workers who brought chickens over in the 19th century and allowed some to escape into a welcoming subtropical ecology.

Locals have mounted various proposals to deal with these survivors, including a widespread cull (which only elicit howls from animal rights activists) or the introduction of a predator, such as the mongoose. Other island residents, though, express a fondness for the fowl, having adopted a small family of chicks to feed. For the interim, be patient when you see a chicken crossing the road. It just wants to get to the other side.

has walls 3 ft. high and thicker than they are tall. A scenic lookout of the Wailua River from the same turnout provides parking for the *heiau* visitors, and signs explain the significance of the river. This site is sacred to Hawaiians: show respect for the *heiau* and avoid touching the rocks. *(On the south side of the road, about 1 mi. up Kuamoo Rd. from Kuhio Hwy. 1 mi. downhill from the Opaekaa Falls overlook.)* **Opaekaa Falls** is a popular scenic viewpoint: a lofty waterfall, surrounded by dense green vegetation, flows in a number of dramatic streams to the pool below. An unofficial trail leads to the top of the falls from a dirt turnout on the north side of the road about 200 yd. past the parking lot, right where the guardrail ends. Keep to the right when you reach the river and follow the steep trail leading to the pool below the falls. *(The viewpoint is located along a sidewalk that runs west from a parking lot 1 mi. up Kuamoo Rd. on the right.)* Further up the road are the **Wailua Homesteads,** a residential development that is home to many budding B&B's and **Kauai's Hindu Monastery** (see below).

This verdant area boasts views of cloud-covered Waialeale and protection from the tourist convoys and trucks that clog Kuhio Hwy. The road officially ends after 7 mi. and arrives at the **Keahua Arboretum,** a leafy clearing perfect for lazy afternoons picnicking. A parking lot will be on your left and a stream flows over the road. Only a 4x4 should attempt to cross. Further along, a muddy stretch of road leads to the trailhead for the **Powerline Trail,** an arduous 11mi. poorly maintained trail that follows the electric transmission lines that span the island. An easier, but still rewarding, hike is the **Kuilau Trail;** the trailhead is on the right-hand side of the road before the arboretum.

KAUAI'S HINDU MONASTERY. Paradise is not a bad place to live as an ascetic. That might have been one of the reasons that the revered teacher Satguru Sivaya Subramuniyaswami, or "Gurudeva," (a Hindu convert originally from Oakland) founded a monastery in the idyllic foothills next to the Wailua River State Park. Part of the Saiva Siddhanta Church based in Sri Lanka, the monastery is home to 20 devotees of Saiva (one of three major deities in Hinduism), all of whom follow a strict regimen of prayer, chanting, and fasting. Fortunately, these monks don't find respectful guests to be an impediment to their goal of spiritual purification. During designated hours, visitors are welcome to walk around, meditate, and pray in the **Kadavul Temple,** home to the world's largest crystal, a 700-pound, 3-foot tall obelisk. Four days a month, the monks offer a guided tour of the sprawling 458-acre complex, where an even loftier project is afoot—the **Iraivan Temple.** First conceived in 1975 when Gurudeva received a vision from Saiva, the temple is being built from hand-carved blocks of granite shipped from a village in Bangalore, India. When complete (sometime around 2012, pending successful fundraising) it will be the only all-granite Hindu temple in the Western hemisphere. Even if you cannot make it for a tour or during visitor hours, the **Ganesha Shrine** at the Visitors Center and the **Sacred Forest** further up Kuamoo Rd. are a real treat. (*107 Kaholalele Rd., from Kuhio Hwy. turn onto Kuamoo Rd., turn left onto Kaholalele and go to end of road; ☎808-822-4351. Call for tour days and to reserve a spot, as tours invariably fill up. Kadavul Temple open daily 9am-noon. Sacred Forest, 7345 Kuamoo Rd., 5 mi. on Kuamoo Rd from Kuhio Hwy. on the left, open daily 6am-6pm. Visit www.himalayanacademy.com to see what some tech-savvy 21st century monks can do.)*

ENTERTAINMENT AND NIGHTLIFE

Wailua rivals Lihue as the center of Kauai's modest nightlife. The small dance floor at **Tradewinds,** in the Coconut Marketplace, fills with giddy locals and sunburned tourists on weekends. Arcade games, satellite sports, and dart boards entertain the less rhythmically inclined. Although Tradewinds does not have its own kitchen, guests are welcome to order from of any of the restaurants in the shopping center. (☎808-822-1621. 21+. Happy hour daily 3-6pm; Mai Tais $4.50, domestic beers $2.50. Open daily 10am-2am.) **Trees Lounge,** 440 Aleka Pl., adjacent to the Islander Resort, attracts a trendier crowd of locals and tourists, drawn by the plush red lounge chairs, reliably good musical talent (usually jazz, blues, or Hawaiian) and innovative *pupu* ($3-10). By halting the live music at 11pm every night and closing the bar sometime thereafter, Trees avoids the rambunctious, late-night crowd while ensuring that patrons can order their last Jamaican-inspired cocktail or pint of Keoki beer ($4). Owners feature work of local artists. (☎808-823-0600. Open daily 5-11pm. Check website www.tree-sloungekauai.com for upcoming music. AmEx/D/MC/V.)

◪ **Smith's Tropical Paradise** hosts the island's most spectacular luau. Gates open at 5pm, and guests are welcome to take a self-guided tour of the gardens or a guided tram tour ($1). Following the *imu* ceremony (the unearthing of the pig which has been cooking for hours in an underground pit), cocktails and music accompany the buffet dinner, before the party moves to the lagoon amphitheater. Twenty-five dancers and entertainers perform in a fantastic show highlighting the diverse culture of Hawaii. (☎808-821-6895. In summer M-F 5pm; in winter M, W, and F 5pm; 7:30pm show only. $75, ages 7-13 $30, ages 3-6 $19; show only $15, ages 3-12 $7.50.)

WAIPOULI

The short stretch of highway between Wailua and Kapaa, known as Waipouli, is infamous for its horrendous traffic, which can be bypassed by going through Kapaa. Public beach access is available at the many resorts that line the highway (just follow the signs). There is little of note in this area of glorified strip malls, save for some of the island's best prices on groceries and other non-durable goods. Waipouli's many restaurants do not rival the quality of ritzier North and South Shore establishments, but there are plenty of places to grab a tasty meal after an exhausting day at the beach.

🖬 **PRACTICAL INFORMATION.** Those with piles of dirty clothes will love the triple-load washers and dryers at the **Kapaa Laundry Center,** 1105J Kuhio Hwy., in Kapaa Shopping Center. (☎808-822-3113. Wash $3, dry $0.25 per 4min. Open daily 7:30am-9:30pm.) Across from Safeway is **Longs Drugs**. (☎808-822-4915. Open M-Sa 7am-10pm, Su 8am-8pm. Pharmacy open M-Sa 9am-8pm, Su 8am-5pm.) The **Kapaa Post Office,** 1101 Kuhio Hwy., is in the back of Kapaa Shopping Center. (Open M-F 8am-4pm, Sa 9am-2pm.) **Postal Code:** 96746.

◨ **FOOD.** You can buy the most affordable groceries on the island from **Safeway,** 831 Kuhio Hwy. (*☎808-822-2464. Open daily 24hr.*) Waipouli's extensive shopping centers contain a wide variety of dining options. ◪**King and I Thai Cuisine ❷,** 4-901 Kuhio Hwy., in Waipouli Plaza, has a long menu of reasonably priced meals ($9-13) and a section devoted to vegetarian dishes. (☎808-822-1642. Open daily 4:30-9:00pm. D/MC/V.) ◪**Papaya's ❶,** 831 Kuhio Hwy., in Kauai Village Shopping Center, is a delight to health- and budget-conscious diners, selling fresh fruits, veggies, and a host of other organic and vegan food. The popular deli counter caters to a loyal lunchtime clientele. Take your food outside to tables on the grass lawn. (☎808-823-0190. Soup/salad/hot bar $7.50/lb. Sandwiches $6.50. Open M-Sa 9am-8pm, Su 10am-5pm; food served until 1 hr. before closing. AmEx/D/MC/V.) North of Waipouli Plaza, on the *mauka* (mountain) side of the road, **Coconuts ❸,** 4-919 Kuhio Hwy., has a funky, modern dining room with coconut wood furniture, and a partially shaded patio, but a somewhat pricey menu. Organic green salads ($8.50), teriyaki-dipped Atlantic

KAUAI

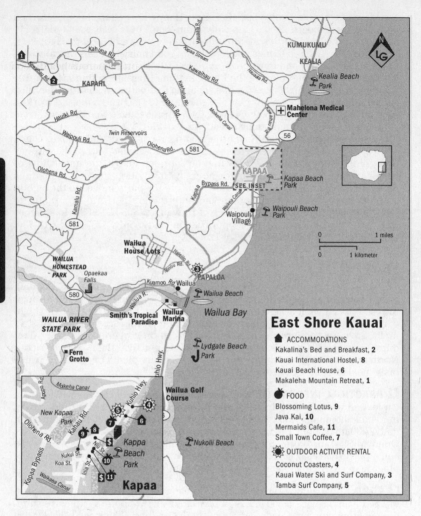

East Shore Kauai

♠ ACCOMMODATIONS
Kakalina's Bed and Breakfast, **2**
Kauai International Hostel, **8**
Kauai Beach House, **6**
Makaleha Mountain Retreat, **1**

🍎 FOOD
Blossoming Lotus, **9**
Java Kai, **10**
Mermaids Cafe, **11**
Small Town Coffee, **7**

☀ OUTDOOR ACTIVITY RENTAL
Coconut Coasters, **4**
Kauai Water Ski and Surf Company, **3**
Tamba Surf Company, **5**

salmon ($26), coconut shrimp turnover appetizer ($11), and vegetarian pasta dishes ($17-18) can usually be found on the menu. (☎808-823-8777. Open M-F dinner 5-9pm. Happy hour 4-6pm; $2 off *pupu* and salads.)

🎸 NIGHTLIFE. Sandwiched between Blockbuster and Pizza Hut, **Lizard Lounge Bar and Grill ❸,** in Waipouli Town Center, outshines its corporate-owned neighbors in their respective entertainment and food departments. Talkative regulars down good draft beer ($3.75) around the pool tables, dartboards, and jukebox. The kitchen cooks a number of entrees like barbecue ribs ($15) and shrimp sauteed in tequila ($18) to satisfy late-night munchies. (☎808-821-2205. Sandwiches and burgers $7-9.50. Happy hour daily 2-6pm. Open daily 11am-1am; food served M-Th and Su until midnight; F-Sa until 12:30am. AmEx/D/MC/V.)

KAPAA

Kapaa (pop. 9472) is the hub of the East Shore, the most populous town in Kauai, and a convenient distance from the shopping centers of Waipouli. Young, independent, and free-spirited travelers support numerous health food stores, and Kapaa is one of few towns where it's easier to find a fresh fruit smoothie than an ice-cold beer. Affordable restaurants populate the historical wood buildings along Hwy. 56, and unspectacular but family-friendly beaches stretch the length of the town, only blocks east of the highway. Although the surfing scene is nothing to write home about, Kapaa does have a number of places that rent boards for testing out the waters.

ORIENTATION AND PRACTICAL INFORMATION

Downtown Kapaa occupies a few blocks of **Kuhio Highway,** and while tourists tend to hug the coast, most residents live farther inland.

Bank of Hawaii, 1407 Kuhio Hwy. (☎808-822-3471), on the *mauka* side of the highway at the north end of downtown, and **First Hawaiian Bank,** 1366 Kuhio Hwy. (☎808-822-4966), on the *makai* (ocean) side in the center of town, each have a 24hr. ATM. (Both banks open M-Th 8:30am-4pm, F 8:30am-6pm.) A 3-month visitor's card ($10) provides **Internet** access at the **Kapaa Public Library,** 1464 Kuhio Hwy., in the red building on Hwy. 56 south of the stream crossing. (☎808-821-4422. Open M and W-F 9am-5pm, Tu noon-8pm.) Travelers can also surf the web at **Business Support Services,** on the *mauka* (mountain) side of the highway, in the southern part of town. (☎808-822-5504. Open M-Sa 8am-6pm, Su 10am-4pm. $2.50 per 15min.) For freshwater swimming, there's the **Smokey Louie Gonsalves Jr. Swimming Pool,** a public oceanfront **pool** at the end of Kou St. (Open in summer Tu-F 11am-3pm, Sa 10am-4:30pm, Su noon-4:30pm. Free.)

ACCOMMODATIONS

Some of the lodgings below are within a block of downtown Kapaa and have some of the cheapest rooms on the island. Lodging in the Wailua area is suitable for Kapaa because the two towns are virtually next to each other; driving from one to the other rarely takes more than 10min. The same goes for the B&Bs located in the surrounding foothills.

Kauai Beach House, 4-1552 Kuhio Hwy. (☎808-822-3313; www.kauai-blue-lagoon. com), on the north side of town, across from Kojima's Supermarket; on the *makai* (ocean) side of the road. There's plenty of parking in back. A freewheeling hang-out for both weekend sojourners and long-term itinerants. Guests of the rambling, 3-story Beach House share an outdoor kitchen, comfortable patio-style common area, a fantastic view of the Pacific from the rooftop shower, and laundry facilities. Some dorms are more spacious and have better ocean views than others; double beds for couples are bunked with curtains for "privacy." Very friendly management. Linens included. Dorms $30; doubles $45; private rooms $65-70. Reservations recommended. Cash only. ❷

Kauai International Hostel, 4532 Lehua St. (☎808-823-6142; www.kauaiinternationalhostel.com), behind Bubba's Burgers. Steps from downtown Kapaa, the cinderblock International Hostel hosts backpackers from around the world. Guest-initiated music shows and communal meals are encouraged. Facilities include laundry, shared kitchen, and lounge with cable TV. Manager requires proof of return flight; no indefinite stays. Linens included. Key deposit $10. Lights-out 11pm. Dorms $25, without reservation $30; private double $60-75. Reservations recommended. MC/V. ❶

Kakalina's Bed and Breakfast, 6781 Kawaihau Rd. (☎808-822-2328; www.kakalina. com). Turn toward the *mauka* (mountain) side on Kawaihau Rd. from Hwy. 58, at the

START: Kapaa.
FINISH: Kilauea.
DISTANCE: 13 mi.
DURATION: 2-3hr.
SEASON: Any.

1. KEALIA BEACH. Just past mi. marker 10, this long, golden sand beach—teeming with surfers—is visible from the highway. A dirt parking lot at the northern end, past a lifeguard stand, provides access to the most sheltered part of the beach. Swimmers are advised to stay within the protective breakwater. Only seasoned bodyboarders and surfers should attempt to battle the giant waves.

2. DONKEY BEACH. Named after the pack animal once used in the nearby plantations, this beach was once Kauai's most popular unofficial nude beach, but has since lost that status due to police crackdowns. A half-mile past mi. marker 11, a short, unmarked driveway leads to a small parking lot. From here, the beach is a 10min. walk. Trees provide a bit of shade. The waves come fast, so swimmers stay close to shore; incredibly strong breaks challenge even experienced surfers.

3. ANAHOLA. A sleepy little community inhabited mostly by Native Hawaiians, Anahola's major attraction is its mile-long stretch of family-friendly surf. **Duane's Ono-Char Burger ❶**, is a popular roadside burger stand on the *makai* (ocean) side of the highway just south of mi. marker 14. A huge variety of toppings complement the famous ¼ lb. burgers (plain "ono" burger $4.45, "local boy" with teriyaki sauce, cheddar cheese, and pineapple $7); (808-822-9181. Open daily 10am-6pm.) Immediately after mi. marker 14, the first Aliomanu Rd. (southern branch) leads to the northern half of Anahola Beach Park. Most residents favor the more protected waters of the southern end, accessible from Anahola Rd. between mi. markers 13 and 14. Camping is available here with a permit ($3) every day except Thursdays.

4. KOOLAU RD. Turn right onto Koolau Rd. when you see the sign for **Moloaa's Sunrise Fruit Stand ❶**, a perfect place to get smoothies. (808-822-1441. Open M-Sa 7:30am-5pm). A narrow country road flanked by working farms and leafy plantations, Koolau Rd. forms a loop whose ends connect to Hwy. 56; two of the area's prettiest beaches await. On the south end is **Moloaa Beach,** which hides behind a wall of secluded homes. To get there, turn right on the first Koolau Rd., between mi. marker 16 and 17. Turn onto Moloaa Rd. toward the beach and drive mi. Keep to the left, and park on the left near the end of the road. Walk to the right, to the southern end, where the daunting waves give way to gentle swells. **Larsen's Beach** can be reached from a road about 1 mi. south of the point at which Koolau Rd. intersects Hwy. 56, heading toward the ocean. A "beach access" post marks the turn onto the dirt road which leads to a trail to the beach. Snorkelers will enjoy clear waters during the calm summer months; at other times, a strong rip current can make the waters unsafe.

Kapaa to Kilauea Scenic Drive

KAPAA TO KILAUEA

northern end of Kapaa, just before the road leaves town. Kakalina's is 4 mi. down Kawaihau Rd. on the left side; drive down to the house in the back. In a remodeled building on a tropical flower farm, the studio or the 1-bedroom is the best bet for a couple on a budget. Rooms overlooking a sugarcane era reservoir have coffee maker, microwave, refrigerator, and access to laundry facilities. Beach towels, mats, and coolers are free for guests to borrow. Continental breakfast included. 2-night min. $40 cleaning fee. Studio $85; 1-bedroom $90; 2- to 4-person suites with kitchen $155-175. ❸

Makaleha Mountain Retreat, 7124A Kahuna Rd. (☎808-822-3142; www.makaleha. com), toward the *mauka* (mountain) side on Kawaihau Rd. from Hwy. 58 at the northern end of Kapaa, just before the road leaves town. After about 4.5 mi., turn left on Kahuna Rd. and drive another mi.; Makaleha will be on your right. Surrounded by banana trees and ti leaf plants, the Makaleha Mountain Retreat is backed dramatically by the lush green foothills of rainy Mt. Waialeale. Guests are welcome to use the hammock, pick citrus or papaya in the private garden, or borrow snorkel equipment, body boards, beach chairs, and mountain bikes. 3-night min. Cleaning fee $40. Garden studio with kitchen $60; 2- to 6-person home with wrap-around deck $165; each additional guest $15. Discounts for longer stays available. ❷

🞄 FOOD

🞑 **Small Town Coffee Co.,** 4-1495 Kuhio Hwy. (☎808-821-1604), in the aqua blue 2-story house on the *mauka* (mountain) side. Filled with shirtless hippies, musicians, wanderers, and even the occasional parrot, Small Town Coffee Co. serves a whole lot of local, friendly atmosphere with every cup of organic coffee. Laptop users also flock here for free Wi-Fi. Kauai chai ($3-4), lemonade with real raspberries ($3.50), and macchiatos ($3.50) satisfy the thirsty, and the turkey pesto sandwich ($7) the peckish. Th night open mic. Open M-W 5:30am-9pm, Th-Sa 5:30am-10pm, Su 5:30am-4pm. ❶

🞑 **Mermaids Cafe,** 4-1384 Kuhio Hwy. (☎808-821-2026), on the *makai* (ocean) side. Eating at this unassuming mural-covered cafe feels refreshingly personal. Watch the duo behind the cashier toss freshly-grated ginger into your sizzling peanut satay plate (tofu or chicken $11). Ask the local artist with whom you're sharing an outdoor table why she swears by the *ahi nori* wrap ($9.50). Though the menu is limited, all offerings retain that homemade, must-have-the-recipe quality. Open daily 11am-9pm. MC/V. ❷

Blossoming Lotus, 4504 Kukui St. (☎808-822-7678), in the Historic Dragon Building, just off the main highway through town. The award-winning and uber-New-Age place has a menu with focus on "live" food—vegetables that have not been processed. The vegan dishes include Super Shakti's Spanikopita (marinated tofu in a phyllo-dough pastry $18) and Vishnu's Tempeh Vindaloo (spicy tempeh curry with cucumber-ginger raita $17). Its juice bar and cafe, **The Lotus Root,** is located across the highway next to Java Kai. Live entertainment nightly 7-9pm. Brunch Sa-Su 10am-2pm. Open daily 5-9pm. Lotus Root open daily 7am-6pm. AmEx/D/MC/V. ❸

Java Kai, 4-1384 Kuhio Hwy. (☎808-823-6887), in the large green building downtown. Good coffee drinks from $4. Smoothies from $4.50. Big muffins and yummy aloha bars ($2-3) baked on premises. Free Wi-Fi. Open daily 6am-5:30 pm. MC/V. ❶

🞄 BEACHES

If you're tired of fighting traffic on the way to North or South Shore beaches, swim and sunbathe along Kapaa's continuous stretch of sand. Neither Kapaa Beach or Waipouli Beach Park is as rivetingly beautiful or secluded as any of the beaches north of Kapaa but both are family-friendly and very accessible.

WAIPOULI BEACH PARK (BABY BEACH). *(Open daily sunrise to sunset.)* Better known as Baby Beach, Waipouli Beach Park is on Moana Kai Rd. along the oceanfront south of downtown. A long stone jetty runs north from the end of Makaha Rd. and forms a shallow pool perfect for a leisurely dip at the south end of this golden sand beach. A local *pau-hana* (after work) favorite for a barbecue or fishing, the beach is often lined with pick-up trucks and locals kicking back in camp chairs. A shower and good-sized parking lot lie farther north by the mouth of the river, where the sandy beach all but disappears. *(Turn down Makaha Rd. off Kuhio Hwy., then turn left on Moana Kai Rd. and continue to the parking area.)*

KAPAA BEACH PARK. *(Open daily sunrise to sunset.)* On the other side of the canal, Kapaa Beach Park parallels downtown Kapaa. The long, narrow beach is popular with local fishermen and kiteboarders, who usually stick to the south end or the occasional retiree hitting golf balls into the ocean. Restrooms, a soccer field, and a big parking lot back the sandy shore. A recent addition is a scenic 2½ mi. paved path along the ocean connecting Kapaa Beach to Kealia Beach. Enjoyed by cyclists and joggers, the path is also perfect for an afternoon amble. *(Turn toward the ocean just before the soccer fields.)*

🪂 ACTIVITIES

Although the East Shore of Kauai isn't as well known for surfing as the North and South Shores of the island, Kapaa, Wailua, and Waipouli are all home to a number of shops that rent surfboards, bodyboards, kayaks, and other equipment. Surfboards usually rent for $10-20 per day and $50-100 per week, depending on the type of board. Roof racks typically cost an additional $5 per day, or $15 per week. Bodyboards and snorkel gear are much cheaper, renting at about $5 per day or $15 per week. Bicycle rentals are a good call for cruising along the coastal path between Kapaa and Kealia beaches. Prices for bikes are set such that it is usually worthwhile to take them out for the day.

🏄 **Tamba Surf Company,** 4-1543 Kuhio Hwy. (☎808-823-6942), on the west side of Kuhio Hwy., at the northern end of Kapaa, across the street from the Kauai Beach House. The very friendly management sets competitive rates for surfboards and bodyboards that

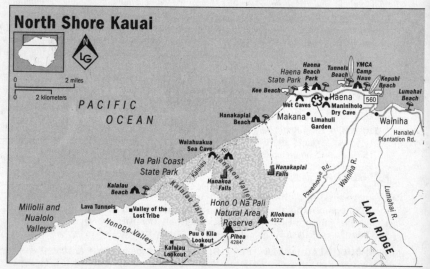

North Shore Kauai

make renting them a solid deal. Longboard rentals $20 per day, $75 per week; includes roof rack. ½hr. surf lessons $40. Open daily 9am-5pm.

Kauai Water Ski and Surf Company, 4-356 Kuhio Hwy. (☎808-822-3574), in Wailua, just north of the Kinipopo Shopping Village, has a good selection of snorkel gear, bodyboards, and surfboards at exceptionally low rates. Shortboards $10 per day, $50 per week; long boards $20/75. Roof rack $5. Kayak tours $55. Open daily 8am-6pm.

Coconut Coasters, 4-1586 Kuhio Hwy. (☎808-822-7368), on the *makai* (ocean) side of Kuhio Hwy., at the northern end of Kapaa, is one of a handful of bike rental places to spring up with the opening of the coastal path. They offer stylish wide-handlebar cruising bikes, in classic ($8.50 per hr or $20 per day), 3-speed ($9.75 per hr or $25 per day) and tandem versions ($16 per hr or $45 per day). Locks included. Reservations accepted. Tu-Sa 8am-6pm, Su 10am-4pm.

NORTH SHORE

The north side of Kauai is the wettest and greenest part of an island known for its rainfall and verdance. The region is remote; the locals and wealthy mainlanders with second homes that inhabit this part of the island live at a leisurely pace surrounded by beauty. Recent years have accelerated development and sent land values skyrocketing. In winter, surf's up on the North Shore, transforming its beaches and bay from swimming and snorkeling coves to the hardcore surfer's paradise. Some of the best surfers in the world spent their childhood enjoying the big wave breaks here and come home hungry for more.

KILAUEA

Sprawling pastures, organic farms, and grassy bluffs shape Kilauea (pop. 2092). Many of Hawaii's former plantation towns have embraced tourism after agriculture's decline, but not Kilauea. This eclectic, peaceful North Shore community is home to a motley collection of Hawaiian families, wandering surfers, and dreadlocked hippies, and is best known for its seabird refuge and lighthouse.

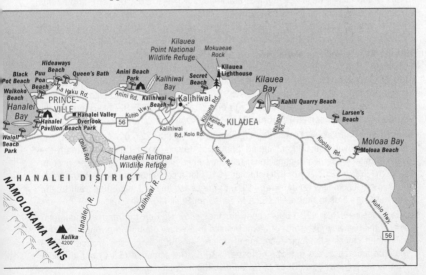

⚡🔢 ORIENTATION AND PRACTICAL INFORMATION

Kilauea is centered on **Kilauea Road,** which begins 100 yd. down **Kolo Road,** 1 mi. north of mi. marker 23. Kilauea Rd. runs 2-3 mi. northeast to Kilauea Point, the northernmost point in the major islands. The **Kong Lung Center,** on Kilauea Rd., at Keneke Rd., has restaurants and shops. Shell, on the right as you turn off the highway into Kilauea, is the only highway gas station between Kapaa and Princeville. (Open daily 6am-7pm.) Next door, the **Menehune Food Mart** has groceries and an ATM inside. (Open M-F 5:30am-7pm, Sa-Su 6am-7pm.)

🔦 ACCOMMODATIONS

There aren't many places to stay in Kilauea. Vacation rentals are available through **www.vrbo.com,** where a search can be done for Kilauea. An old sugar plantation house from the 1920s, **Aloha Plantation** ❸, 4481 Malulani St., is a charming B&B complete with vintage posters and appliances. Turn onto Kolo Rd. from the highway and turn right onto Malulani after 1mi.; Aloha Plantation is the third house on the left. Guests can use the outdoor kitchen, shower, jacuzzi, and communal dining area. (☎877-658-6977 or 808-828-1693; www.alohaplantation.com. Doubles $69-99; additional guest $10. Cash or check only.)

🍴 FOOD

Kilauea's few restaurants aren't ideal for the budget conscious traveler. But by featuring incomparably fresh ingredients from the surrounding fertile valleys, some might warrant the expense. You can also do it yourself by buying organic herbs at the **Sunshine Market** (Th 4:30pm), in the Neighborhood Center parking lot next to **Kilauea Town Market and Deli.**

> **Lighthouse Bistro,** 2484 Keneke St. (☎808-828-0480), in Kong Lung Center. This open-air bistro serves delicately flavored dishes including pineapple pork medallions ($19), filet mignon ($34), fresh fish (grilled, blackened, or ginger crusted; $26), and salads featuring local produce ($10-15), with an extensive wine list and mixed drinks (Mai Tais $7, martinis $6.50-7.50). Live music nightly, M-W and F-Su. All-you-can-eat pasta ($15). Open M-Sa noon-2:30pm and 5:30-9pm, Su 5:30-9pm. MC/V. ❹

> **Kilauea Bakery and Pau Hana Pizza** (☎808-828-2020), in Kong Lung Center. A wide selection of coffees and teas complements gourmet pastries. Pizzas topped with healthy tofurella, spinach, local fish, or good old Italian sausage and pepperoni delight customers (3 toppings, 12" $20, 16" $27.50). Try their Hawaiian sourdough bread with soup or the Big Kilauea salad made with organic veggies ($8.50). Bakery open daily 6:30am-9pm. Pizza served 10:30am-9pm. MC/V. ❸

> **Kilauea Fish Market,** 4270 Kilauea Lighthouse Rd. (☎808-828-6244), in the rear of the Kilauea Plantation Center. Signed photos of Kauai's grateful surf pros adorn the walls of this hidden health-conscious deli. Brown rice and organic veggies can accompany grilled fish ($12-15) or BBQ chicken ($10) for a contemporary twist on the traditional plate lunch. Take an ahi wrap ($10) to the beach and you might just want to add your gushing words to their wall. Open M-Sa 11am-8pm. MC/V. ❷

> **Banana Joe's** (☎808-828-1092). Look for the yellow sign on the *mauka* (mountain) side of the highway, just north of town. Housed in a yellow plantation-era building, this fruit stand stocks island produce, locally-made jams, dressings, and granola ($3-6) You'll be amazed at the pineapple frostie ($3.75). The smoothie ($3-4) hits the spot after a long highway drive. Open M-Sa 9am-5:30pm. Cash only. ❶

BEACHES

Winding mountain roads hide spectacularly secluded beaches and beguiling waterfalls. Most of the best beaches lie west of Kilauea in the town of Kalihiwai. Kalihiwai Rd., once a U-shaped loop bridging the **Kalihiwai River,** was split when its bridge was destroyed by a tsunami in the 1950s. The split in the road is at the base of Kalihiwai Bay, on the shore of Kalihiwai Beach, leaving nearby Hanapai Beach inaccessible save from the other direction.

SECRET BEACH. *(Surfing. Open daily 24hr.)* Officially Kauapea Beach, this formerly hidden spot has outgrown its mysterious nickname, and the parking area can barely hold the rows of shiny rental cars. Secret Beach's magnetic appeal is in its irresistible scenery: a vast expanse of powdery golden sand with lava rocks surrounded by bluffs and a fetching view of Kilauea Point. The beach, one of the widest on the island, also features strong breaks enjoyed by surfers and bodyboarders alike. *(From the base of the trail, the sands stretch to the east where a sheltered cove and gently sloping shore provide safer swimming. From Hwy. 56 North, turn right on the first Kalihiwai Rd., just before mi. marker 24; turn right again at the first dirt road. After 1 mi., the road ends in a parking area. From here, follow a steep, well-marked trail for 5min. to the beach.)*

> **TIP** **SPINNING SECRETS.** Between 6 and 10am, drive out to Kalihiwai or Secret Beach. There are often spinner dolphins playing in the waters near these beaches during the early morning hours. If you decide to jump in with them, remember to swim at a respectful distance!

KALIHIWAI BEACH AND HANAPAI BEACH. *(Bodyboarding. Surfing. Open daily 24hr.)* Bodyboarders and surfers enjoy the right point break wave, while local families favor the beach for weekend picnics. A wide sandy crescent continues to the west on the other side of the river mouth, which can be a chore to cross in high surf. The smaller, western portion of the beach, known as Hanapai Beach, is also accessible from Anini Rd. The sandy river provides a nice place to splash around, and a short rope swing keeps kids entertained. It is more secluded than the main section of Kalihiwai Beach; a trip to this section is probably not worth the trouble unless you're very curious or in need of quiet. Take the first Kalihiwai Rd. to the end and park under the trees facing the beach, or the second Kalihiwai Rd. and park in the small lot at the end on the left before wading across the shallow river to the beach.

ANINI BEACH PARK. *(Snorkeling. Surfing. Wind sports. Open daily sunrise to sunset.)* The golden sand of Anini Beach is stretched thin as it covers the coastline for almost 2 mi. around a wide, shallow lagoon of clear, reef-protected water. Swimmers and snorkelers frolic at the east end, while boat owners, surfers, and windsurfers occupy the water to their left. County campgrounds (closed Tu) with spacious beachfront sites, restrooms, and showers, are available at the east end. (See **Camping in Hawaii,** p. 82.) The lawn behind the park has pavilions, picnic tables, and grills. The flat shore and incredibly calm summer water make Anini one of Kauai's safest swimming beaches.

Shallow turquoise waters and the warm offshore breeze are so inviting that everyone will want to try windsurfing. A veteran with almost 20 years of teaching experience, Celeste at **Windsurf Kauai** takes small groups (up to six) out on the lagoon. A 3hr. introductory lesson, open to competent swimmers ages 5 and up, includes 1hr. on a land simulator before 2hr. on the water. Those who catch the windsurfing bug can take a second 3hr. lesson that focuses on advanced skills and qualifies students for certification. Rentals ($25 per hr.; $65 per 3hr.) are also available. 3hr. windsurfing lesson $85, including equipment; students meet Celeste at the beach. (☎808-828-6838 *To reach the beach, head toward the ocean on the west Kalihiwai Rd., between mi. markers 25 and 26, and turn left on Anini Rd., which runs north to the shore and then west along the length of the beach.*)

👁 🎵 SIGHTS

KILAUEA POINT NATIONAL WILDLIFE REFUGE. The historic Kilauea Lighthouse and the wild bird population are featured in the Kilauea National Wildlife Refuge. Built in 1913, the Kilauea Lighthouse guided commercial boats on their way to Asia. Although decommissioned in 1976, the 52 ft. tall lighthouse retains its giant clamshell lens, the largest in the world, and an unbeatable view of the frothing blue ocean from 217 ft. above sea level. Today, a small beacon light next to the lighthouse offers guidance to local boaters and aircraft. Though visitors are only allowed into the first floor of the lighthouse, the old communications building has a historical display, a video, reference books, and articles about the lighthouse and refuge for those interested.

The various birds that inhabit the refuge include red-footed boobies (the most visible species in the refuge; visible year-round), great frigatebirds with distinctive long forked tail (visible year-round), the endangered nene (the official state bird; visible year-round), the enormous laysan albatross (Dec.-July), pacific golden plovers (Aug.-Apr.), and wedge-tailed shearwaters (summer). Humpback whales (Nov.-May), spinner dolphins, endangered monk seals, and sea turtles are commonly seen from shore.

Inaccessible to man and a favorite roosting spot for birds, **Mokuaeae Rock** forms an island about 100 yd. north of the point. An old story claims that Mokuaeae Rock was the first American possession in Hawaii, lost by King Kalakaua in a poker game to an American ambassador long before Hawaii became the 50th state. The visitor-accessible part of the refuge consists of a Visitors Center and a quarter-mile sidewalk from the parking lot to the lighthouse. Those who want a closer look at birds can sign out binoculars from the Visitors Center. Guided hikes up Crater Hill are available through the Kilauea Point Natural History Association. (*At the end of Kilauea Rd. ☎808- 828-0168; www. kilaueapoint.org. Refuge open daily 10am-4pm. $5, under 16 free. Tours $20.*)

🎵 ENTERTAINMENT

Paina O Hanalei Luau is the Princeville Hotel's extravagant beachside luau. The feast offers 6 main courses of Hawaiian favorites, but a show-only option like **Smith's** (see p. 377) is a better bet. (☎808-826-2788. M and Th 6-9pm. Dinner and show $99, seniors and ages 13-19 $90, ages 6-12 $45.) Instead, head to **Happy Talk Lounge**, 5380 Honoiki Rd., which offers live entertainment Tuesday through Sunday. Coconut shrimp ($11), pizza ($13.50-16.50), Caesar salad ($9), and fresh sashimi (market price) are all reasonably priced. (☎808-826-6522. Hawaiian M-F 6:30-9. Jazz or Blues Sa 7-9:30. Jazz Su 4-7pm. Happy hour F-Sa 4-6pm, discounted drinks vary. Kitchen open daily 2-9pm. AmEx/MC/V.)

HANALEI

Set in a deep green valley surrounded by sheer cliffs and cascading waterfalls, Hanalei (pop. 278) is marked by natural splendor and a welcoming, relaxed vibe. Within the diverse community, local taro root farmers mingle with affluent mainland tourists in the colorful shopping centers. The name Hanalei can be translated as "lei valley" or "crescent-shaped bay" because rainbows often

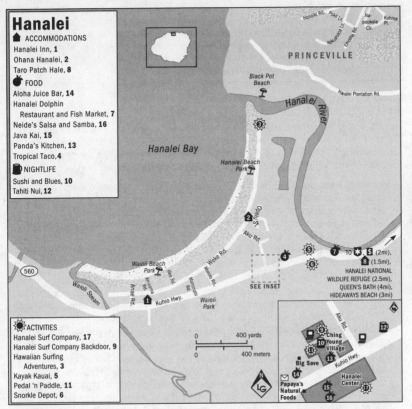

Hanalei

🔺 ACCOMMODATIONS
Hanalei Inn, **1**
Ohana Hanalei, **2**
Taro Patch Hale, **8**

🍴 FOOD
Aloha Juice Bar, **14**
Hanalei Dolphin
  Restaurant and Fish Market, **7**
Neide's Salsa and Samba, **16**
Java Kai, **15**
Panda's Kitchen, **13**
Tropical Taco, **4**

🌃 NIGHTLIFE
Sushi and Blues, **10**
Tahiti Nui, **12**

🔆 ACTIVITIES
Hanalei Surf Company, **17**
Hanalei Surf Company Backdoor, **9**
Hawaiian Surfing
  Adventures, **3**
Kayak Kauai, **5**
Pedal 'n Paddle, **11**
Snorkle Depot, **6**

drape the rain-heavy sky—and look like leis. The pristine bay is the ocean playground of experienced wave riders and a wonderful backdrop for photographs.
Its sparkling shore also served as the inspiration for Peter, Paul, and Mary's
classic song about ▨**a dragon named Puff.**

▨ ▨ ORIENTATION AND PRACTICAL INFORMATION

Hanalei lies a few miles west of Princeville's manicured lawns and condominiums. Two large retail centers, brimming with choice restaurants and shops,
face each other across the highway in the center of town. On the *mauka*
(mountain) side is the **Hanalei Center,** whose expansive lawn is dotted with picnic tables. Across the way, the **Ching Young Village** shops line both sides of an
outdoor sidewalk where there are restrooms and pay phones.

Internet is available at **Discount Activities,** on the corner of Hwy. 56 and Aku St.,
across from Kalypso's. (☎808-826-1913. $2.50 per 10min. Open daily 9am-6pm.)
Bali Hai Photo in the Ching Young Center has Internet also. (☎808-826-9181.
$5 per 20min. Open M-F 8:30am-5pm, Sa 9am-5pm, Su 10am-5pm). The **Hana-
lei Post Office,** 5226 Kuhio Hwy., is immediately west of Ching Young Center.
(☎808-826-1034. Open M-F 9am-4pm, Sa 10am-noon.) **Postal Code:** 96714.

TIP

WI-FI IN HI. If you're looking for free Wi-Fi in Hanalei, go to the two-story brown building on the right, which is next to Java Kai and houses Bar Acuda and Neide's. In order to get good reception, you need to sit down on the benches next to the stairs to the second floor. Connect to the network helpfully called "FreeWifiKauai."

ACCOMMODATIONS

Because of the surrounding taro fields, Hanalei has little room for expansion. Most of the available real estate is snatched up by mainlanders looking for a vacation home. Thus, very few B&Bs have emerged to meet the surging demand for non-resort lodging, and prices are steep. There are some good bets.

Taro Patch Hale, 5475 D-Ojiki Ohiki Rd. (808-826-9828; www.hanaleivalley.kauaistyle. com.) Turn left on Ohiki Rd. after the first bridge upon entering Hanalei and right as the bend in the road straightens out. Go 2 mi. up; Taro Patch Hale is on your left 50 yards before a stop sign and a gate marking the beginning of a private road. A peaceful place to sleep in the middle of taro-filled Hanalei Valley. Rooms are located next to a murmuring stream and have kitchenettes, covered *lanai*, and private outdoor baths. 3-night min. stay. Cleaning fee $35. $45 Rooms from $85 $100. ❸

The Hanalei Inn, 55468 Kuhio Hwy. (☎808-826-9333), has simple, clean studio rooms with kitchens, flatscreen TVs, Wi-Fi, A/C and bath. Common facilities include a covered *lanai*, barbecue, hammocks, and a coin-operated washer/dryer. Ask about week-long discounts and online specials. Rooms $139-149. Rooms right across from Hanalei Bay, at 5404 Weke Rd, with twin bed, $69; private rooms $159-199. AmEx/MC/V/D. ❹

Ohana Hanalei, Pilikoa Rd., (☎808-826-4116). From Kuhio Hwy., turn onto Aku, then right on Weke, then right on Pilikoa. Ohana has an enviable location down by the beach and consists of just 1 secluded studio next to the owners' home. With a king bed, bath, and kitchenette, the room is comfy, if a little unadorned by Hanalei standards. Outdoor shower and beach chairs are provided, as well as bikes. Rates, including tax, $115 per day or $750 per week. 50% of total due for reservation. Cash only. ❸

FOOD

Nearly all of the North Shore restaurants take full advantage of the surrounding landscape's dramatic beauty. For a healthy snack or wholesome groceries, visit **Papaya's Natural Foods and Cafe,** 5-5121 Kuhio Hwy. The food window at the back serves salad, soup, and quinoa ($7.50 per lb.), along with apple-cinnamon muffins ($3), and organic smoothies ($5.50). (☎808-826-0089. Grocery open daily 9am-8pm. Food stand open M-Sa 9am-5pm.) At the west end of Ching Young Village, **Big Save** also sells groceries and has an ATM. (☎808-826-6652. Open daily 7am-9pm.) For fresh fruit and crafts, go to the **Hanalei farmers' market,** on the south side of Hwy. 56, 1 mi. past the Hanalei Center, at the Neighborhood Center and ballpark (Sa 9:30-11:30am).

Hanalei Dolphin Restaurant and Fish Market, 5-5016 Kuhio Hwy. (☎808-826-6113), in the 1st building past the 1-lane Hanalei Bridge coming from the east. Beautiful wood-working and tradewind-friendly design might not soften the financial blow for those on a budget. Local catches (from $30) are the signature of this popular seafood restaurant. Outdoor seating on the grassy banks of the Hanalei River, perfect for kayak-watching, and lower prices make lunch a good option. Salads (fish salad $12) and dishes (charbroiled fresh fish of the day $14) grace the still-stellar lunch menu. Open daily 11:30am-9:00pm. MC/V. Lunch ❸/Dinner ❺.

Tropical Taco (☎808-827-8226), in the long green Halelea building past Kayak Kauai. A Hanalei institution for over 25 years, this former food truck had to move indoors to accommodate the lunchtime demand for its corn tortillas and beer-battered fish burritos ($10).¹Veggie burrito $8. Beef taco $10. Be prepared for a wait during peak hours. Open M-Sa 11am-5pm. Cash only. ❶

Neide's Salsa and Samba (☎808-826-1851), in Hanalei Center. Enjoy spicy Mexican *antojitos* or authentic Brazilian cuisine in the cozy dining room or on the *lanai*. Locals rave about the *muqueca* (fresh catch with coconut sauce, shrimp, and Brazilian rice). Mexican dishes like fish tacos ($13) nachos grande ($9), *huevos rancheros* ($9), deliver flavors without the grease. Open daily 11:30am-2:30pm and 5-9pm. MC/V. ❸

Java Kai (☎808-826-6717), in Hanalei Center. Java Kai's impressive array of coffee drinks is unsurpassed on the North Shore. In the morning, try a fresh-brewed cup of 100% Kona coffee ($3). Savor fabulous aloha bars (shortbread, coconut, macadamia nuts, and chocolate; $3) with your caffeine fix on the *lanai*. Open daily 6:30am-6pm. Internet access available (p. 386). AmEx/D/MC/V. ❶

Panda's Kitchen (☎808-826-7388), in Ching Young Center. A popular option is create-your-own: choose the sauce (spicy garlic or sweet and sour), the meat (fish, $11; chicken, beef, pork or tofu $8), and steamed rice ($.75) or noodles ($1.50). No MSG is used in its generous portions. Open M-W and F 11am-9pm, Th 4-9pm. MC/V. ❶

Aloha Juice Bar (☎808-826-6990), on the west side of the Ching Young Center. This seemingly mobile juice bar doesn't stray from its parking lot location, blending smoothies (from $5) for crowds of parched tourists. The Hanalei Passion smoothie (a mix of mango, papaya, banana, and passion fruit; $5) is especially yummy. Local tropical fruit is also available. Open daily 9am-5pm. Cash only. ❶

🌊 BEACHES

Disarmingly beautiful, Hanalei Bay attracts dozens of beachgoers who lie out on its soft, sandy shore; be advised that if you join them, you may never be able to tear yourself away. Swimming is only safe during the summer; currents and large waves make the water dangerous in winter. Winter surf also draws experienced wave riders who charge the huge peaks breaking inside the bay, while novice surfers attempt the baby swells which gently graze the shallow shoreline from June to August. The first three beaches below are all on Hanalei Bay and the last two can be found in Princeville, just a mile northeast.

BLACK POT BEACH. *(Open daily 24hr.)* Black Pot's sturdy pier and picnic tables provide great sunset views and a pleasant place for an evening picnic. Locals often leap off the pier, but make sure you know where to jump before following them. Named for the communal cooking pot used by campers, the flat beach blends into the sandy parking lot and slopes gradually into murky water. Camping is only available on weekends and holidays. See **Camping in Hawaii,** p. 82. *(From the highway, turn toward the ocean on Aku Rd. Take a right where Aku ends at Weke Rd. and continue to the end of the road. There are restrooms, picnic tables, and grills.)*

HANALEI PAVILION BEACH PARK. *(Bodyboarding. Open daily 24hr. Lifeguards 9am-5pm.)* Shady trees and wood benches dot the wide lawn, and a pavilion shelters a few picnic tables at this beach park on the eastern side of Hanalei Bay. In summer, *keiki* (children) play in the gentle waves that break along the sandy shore, and young bodyboarders slide through the water. Winter's larger surf makes swimming unappealing, but some still go for it on more mellow days. *(From Aku Rd., turn right on Weke. The parking area will be on the left. Restrooms and showers.)*

KAUAI

WAIOLI BEACH PARK. *(Surfing. Wind sports. Open daily 24hr.)* Nicknamed "Pinetrees" by the local surfers who chill beneath the tall ironwoods, Waioli is a long, wide beach at the base of Hanalei Bay. The east end of Waioli Beach is less crowded than Hanalei Pavilion but sees similar waves. The west half is more exposed to ocean swells and is popular with surfing and kiteboard instructors. Summertime waves provide the perfect learning environment, but in winter it's strictly for the experienced; it's the training ground of two-time world-champion surfer Andy Irons and his brother Bruce. *(From Aku Rd., turn left on Weke and then right down Hee Rd. or Anae Rd. to small dirt parking areas. Facilities at the east end of the beach.)*

⬛ QUEEN'S BATH. *(Snorkeling. Open daily 24hr.)* A deep lava rock pool filled by aquamarine ocean water, Queen's Bath is a unique swimming and snorkeling spot. Along a half mile stretch of shoreline in Princeville, waves splash ocean water over black rock walls, and a series of pools and inlets provide swimming holes for visitors, fish, and sea turtles. The largest pool is known as Queen's Bath, but when the surf is down in the summer, other pools and inlets are sometimes swimmable, too. In good weather, visiting the bath is one of the most enjoyable experiences on the whole island. A hike west along the lava rocks yields pool after beautiful pool. The high tide and heavy surf in the winter can make it too dangerous to swim in the pools; at any time of year, swimming in the open ocean beyond the pools is extremely dangerous. Bring shoes for the walk from your car to the bath. When hiking around the lava rocks, be mindful of endangered monk seals who doze there. It is illegal to approach them and violators are fined. Arrive early to beat the crowds. *(From Ka Haku Rd., turn toward the ocean on Punahele, which curves to the right to form a loop with Kapiolani. Just past the base of the loop, there is room to park, and a trail leads down toward the ocean. At the end of the trail, turn left and walk across the rocks for another 5min. to Queen's Bath.)*

HIDEAWAYS BEACH (PALI KE KUA BEACH). *(Snorkeling. Open daily 24hr.)* This beautiful, secluded, short expanse of coarse gold sand has amazingly clear water and exceptional snorkeling. Although swimming is usually safe, be careful in the high surf and unpredictable tides of winter. The steep trail and scant parking deters a lot of people so you just might have the beach to yourself. *(Park on the right just before you get to the Princeville Hotel, in the tiny public lot between the hotel and Puu Poa condos. From there, Hideaways is 10min. down the steep trail between the lot and the tennis court. Wet weather can make the walk dangerous; go in something sturdier than sandals.)*

🔻 ACTIVITIES

Many ocean activities on the North Shore do not run during the winter, but conditions vary so checking with these places doesn't hurt, even in December.

⬛ Learn to Surf (☎808-826-7612; www.learntosurfkauai.net). Wannabe surfers looking for the best value should call Learn to Surf. Lessons are taught by their very friendly, knowledgeable staff of local surfers, who will meet students at whichever beach has that day's best surf. Their flexibility and friendly attitude make a great intro to surfing. 2 person 1hr. lesson $40 per person; 3 or more $30 per person.

Hawaiian Surfing Adventures (☎808-482-0749; www.hawaiiansurfingadventures.com), on the far north end of Black Pot Beach, where the Hanalei River enters the bay, offers surfing lessons and rentals. 2hr. lesson $65, private lesson $95. Lessons available daily 8am-2pm. Rentals $5 per hr., $20 per day. 5hr. surfing safari to the best surf spots on the island $150; each additional person $50.

Kayak Kauai (☎808-826-9844; www.kayakkauai.com), on the *makai* (ocean) side of the highway on the way into town from the east. Spring through fall, Kayak Kauai offers kayak and hiking tours (including a 17 mi., 13-14hr. kayak trip along the Na Pali Coast; $205). They also offer surfing and kayak lessons and rent out beach and camping equipment. Reserve 24hr. in advance. Surfing lessons ($50) in Hanalei Bay daily 10am and 2pm. Tent $8 per day, stove $6, snorkel gear $8, surfboards $20, bikes $20, and kayaks for Hanalei and Wailua Rivers $28-75 per day. Rent any equipment for 5 days, and get 2 additional days free. Open daily in summer 8am-8pm; in winter 8am-5:30pm.

Hanalei Surf Company Backdoor (☎808-826-1900, reservations 808-826-6924), in the Ching Young Village, has surfing lessons with Australian pro Russell Lewis and others. Two hr. lesson daily 10am and 1pm. Private lesson $150, group lesson $65 per person. Surfboard rentals $20 per day or $95 per week. Open daily 9am-9pm.

Hanalei Surf Company (☎808-826-9000), in Hanalei Center, across the street from their Backdoor outlet, stocks lots of gear. Snorkel equipment ($6 per day), bodyboards ($6 per day), surfboards ($20-25 per day, $95-110 per week). Open daily 9am-9pm.

🎵 ENTERTAINMENT

The best place to kick back with a drink and enjoy live entertainment is **Sushi and Blues,** in Ching Young Village. Thursdays through Saturdays, patrons can expect almost anything—from DJs to jazz bands to blues guitarists. During the high season acts may come in on other nights. Order fresh sushi (hand rolls $7-10; *maki* rolls $9-15), along with entrees such as pineapple teriyaki chicken and coconut shrimp ($23). The entrees come with miso soup and a mini-sushi roll. (☎808-826-9701; www.sushiandblues.com. MC/V.) Another nightspot, one with a bit more history and character, is **Tahiti Nui,** 5-5134 Kuhio Hwy., down the road. Founded over 45 years ago, the place wears its aging thatched walls and kitschy Polynesian decor with a time-tested nonchalance. Tourists love the stiff Mai Tais ($7.50). Locals crowd in to hear live Hawaiian music M-Sa 6-8pm (Th until 9pm). Late-night programming includes karaoke (M and Th after 9pm) and rock or reggae (F-Sa after 9pm). Bar food ($10-15) varies nightly. Open daily 11am-2am. (☎808-826-6277; www.thenui.com.)

📷 SIGHTS

HANALEI NATIONAL WILDLIFE REFUGE. Many years ago, Hawaiians settled Hanalei, cultivating taro root in the fertile wetlands. Today, part of that tradition is preserved in the 917-acre refuge, visible from a highway overlook slightly west and to the *mauka* (mountain) side of the Princeville Shopping Center. The turnout provides a bird's-eye view of the meandering Hanalei River and the patchwork of taro ponds and fields scattered across the valley. The refuge was established in 1972 to protect the endangered native waterbirds, including the gallinule, coot, koloa duck, and black-necked stilt, and it also shelters wintering migrant birds. Local Hawaiian farmers work the taro root ponds on a rotating cycle. Less than 5% of the original taro patches remain, as much of the crop has been replaced with sugarcane. While public access to the wildlife refuge is restricted, a tour includes bird-watching, exploring the taro patches, and a stop at the Haraguchi Rice Mill. (☎ 808-651-3399; www.haraguchiricemill.org. Tours W at 9am. 3hr. tour $65, includes a picnic lunch.)

HAENA

While Haena has few services or shops, it's home to some of the most beautiful beaches in the state and a handful of intriguing natural sights. Its one-lane bridges carry thousands of cars every year to and from Kee Beach, and the beginning of the Kalalau Trail. Popular activities include fishing, diving, snorkeling, hiking, and surfing. The town is home to a mix of Hawaiian taro root farmers, mainlanders vacationing in fantastic beachfront homes, and visitors intent on exploring the area's unspoiled beauty.

ORIENTATION

Leaving Hanalei, **Route 560** ascends parallel to the western shore of Hanalei Bay before going through the miniscule town of **Wainiha** and following the coast through Haena to its end at Kee Beach.

ACCOMMODATIONS AND CAMPING

A number of vacation rentals line the streets of Haena, and those with cash to burn can enjoy their luxury. An online search or a call to a rental agent will yield many appealing—and certainly pricey—options. In summer, staying elsewhere may be your best bet. However, budget-conscious travelers bent on staying in Haena need not despair, as Haena is also home to one of the North Shore's only budget accommodations, **YMCA Camp Naue ❶**, on Kepuhi beach. Turn *makai* (towards the ocean) onto the west end of Alealea Rd., right before mi. marker 8. The not-for-profit camp, equipped with hot showers, sleeps 56 people in five bunkhouses and can accommodate tents on its lawn. During the summer the camp is typically reserved for large groups from youth organizations and schools and is closed to the public. The best time to find a bunk here is from mid-September to mid-April. Reservations aren't accepted; to check availability, call or visit the campsite. A sign on the front gate will indicate whether the camp is open for drop-in travelers. (☎808-826-6419 or 808-246-9090. No linens. Tents and bunks $15 per person. Arrive before dark. Cash only.)

FOOD

The only convenience store west of Hanalei is the **Wainiha General Store,** at mi. 6.5, on the left after the Wainiha Bridge. In addition to stocking drinks, snacks, and sunblock, it's also the last place to rent snorkel gear ($7 per day) on the way to the beaches. The store also store bikes ($5 per day) and bags ($3 per day) for hikers heading to the Kalalau Trail. (☎808-826-6251. Open daily 10am-7pm.) **Red Hot Mama's ❷**, a bustling food window next to the general store, serves a variety of Mexican-style dishes, including taco salad ($10) and popular "The Mama," a burrito with rice, lettuce, cheese, corn, beans, and choice of protein or veggie ($7-9). (☎808-826-7266. Open daily 11am-5pm. Cash only.) A coffee shop and decent restaurant are located in the Hanalei Colony Resort past mi. marker 7. The **Na Pali Art Gallery and Coffee House ❶** serves up fresh-brewed cups of 100% Kona ($2.75) as well as a dependable house blend ($1.75). Don't think of sitting down to the morning paper here—it's standing room only in what is an island-themed art gallery first and a coffee counter second. (☎808-826-1844. Open daily 7am-4pm, gallery until 5pm.) Next door, **Mediterranean Gourmet** (Lunch ❸/ Dinner ❺) offers ocean-view dining to the resort crowd, and fancier versions of Middle Eastern favorites like kebabs, falafels, and hummus. As usual, lunch dishes ($12-17) are a better deal than dinner dishes ($23-30). Though pricey, the restaurant might be a refreshing change in a place with little gastronomic diversity. (☎808-826-9875. Open M-Sa 11am-9pm.)

BEACHES

From the stark black lava rocks of Lumahai to the green vegetation on the cliffs at Kee, Haena's beaches are strikingly beautiful. These glorious golden beauties outshine their soft-sanded cousins to the east in Hanalei Bay, offering everything from hardcore surfing to child-friendly wading pools. These beaches are listed in order from east to west along Kauai's North Shore.

■ LUMAHAI BEACH. *(Bodyboarding. Snorkeling. Open daily 24hr.)* Considered by many to be Kauai's most beautiful beach, a picture of Lumahai sits in every postcard rack on the island. Divided into two stretches of sand by a mass of volcanic rock halfway down the beach, Lumahai is a joy to explore. The west half of the beach, bounded by a stream, is one of the widest beaches on Kauai. Devastating surf and powerful currents make swimming here unsafe year-round; the ocean has claimed more than one life. On the far west side of the beach, there are excellent barrel waves for bodyboarding. Sunbathers and fans of the musical *South Pacific* (it was Nurses' Beach) frequent this captivating stretch of sand, and families with children sometimes take a dip in the stream. However, due to the occasional flash flood, swimming is not advised. The east half of Lumahai, also known as **Kahalahala Beach,** is even more exquisite than its western counterpart and a better place to swim and snorkel; however, it is consequently more crowded. Powerful winter waves and tides can also make the sometimes placid water quite dangerous. Stay away from the lava rocks on either side of the beach—freak waves twice the size of others are common and can be deadly. Both halves of Lumahai are accessible from the other; simply climb over the giant rocks that separate the sands or walk on a path behind them. *(Leaving Hanalei, the highway takes a U-curve toward the sea between mi. markers 4 and 5. Long turnouts lined with parked cars hug the base of the curve, and a short marked trail leads down to the beach from the 2nd turnout. To access the west beach, an opening in the trees leads to a large dirt parking lot 1 mi. after mi. marker 5. The east end is accessible via a short but steep 100 yd. trail that leads from a turnout down to the beach; ignore the misleading "no beach access" signs, which only refer to the trail going up on the right and not the one going down on the left.)*

■ TUNNELS BEACH (MAKUA BEACH). *(Snorkeling. Surfing. Open daily 24hr. Lifeguards daily.)* A wide horseshoe reef encloses the fine, and often hot, sand of the North Shore's premier snorkel and shore dive locale. On calm summer days, Tunnels' crystalline waters and intricate reef are a sight to behold. Despite its fame for complex underwater topography, the beach's name actually describes the hollowness of its winter surf. With the right wind and swell direction, the right-breaking Tunnels is arguably the best surf location on the island. Trees back the long sandy beach, providing much-appreciated shade. The coral reef is close to shore and shallow in parts; take extra care not to touch or step on the coral. There are no facilities, but Haena Beach Park (see below) is only a 10min. stroll along the beach to the west. *(Two unmarked dirt roads provide access. The first is 1 mi. west of mi. marker 8, just before a "Weight Limit 10 Tons" sign, and the second is 1 mi. farther. The second dirt road is longer, offers a few more parking spaces, but also ends at a steeper slope to the beach. Due to the popularity of Tunnels, spots tend to fill up quickly. It may be necessary to park at Haena Beach Park, 1 mi. down the road.)*

HAENA BEACH PARK. *(Open daily 24hr. Lifeguard 9am-5pm.)* Popular with Kalalau Trail backpackers, Haena boasts a grassy, if sparsely shaded, lawn that welcomes a multitude of tents. A huge expanse of sand and picnic, bathrooms, camping, and shower facilities, along with the **Maniniholo Dry Cave** (p. 395) across the street, make the beach park a nexus of North Shore activity. Kayakers venturing off to explore the Na Pali Coast often launch here. The beach park is closed to camping on Mondays for maintenance. Due to its exposure to ocean currents and the steepness of the beach itself, Haena is dangerous for swimmers, especially in the winter, though beachgoers pushed off Tunnels will spill over into Haena's patch of sand and water. The surf break, Cannons, on the west end of the beach, is exceptionally dangerous due to crazy currents and a sharp, shallow reef. *(The park is easily accessible. Two parking areas are located on the highway just before mi. marker 9 and across from Maniniholo Dry Cave.)*

KAUAI

THE LOCAL STORY

SAC-RIFICIAL RITES

While the moral status of the human embryo is the centerpiece to many debates in the US, the moral status of the placenta usually is not. According to the National Conference of State Legislatures, there has historically been no law in place in regards to the legal status of the placenta post-partum either. This changed in 2006, when Hawaii became the first state to legislate on the tissue, passing a bill allowing hospitals to release placentas to mothers under certain conditions.

The unconventional ruling came down as a result of the placenta's historic role in Hawaiian culture. According to ancient Hawaiian folklore, the placenta, or *lewe*, is believed to connect a child to its birthplace. Traditional ceremonies are held to honor its status, involving burial of the placenta under a tree, whose growth then mirrors the growth of the child.

With growing concern over infectious disease and HIV transmission among health care workers, the Hawaii State Department of Health had declared the placenta "infectious waste," which should not be returned to the mother. The issue rose to the public spotlight after a couple sued in federal court after being denied the return of the mother's placenta.

The state legislature, succumbing under public pressure, passed the bill allowing the release of the placenta under the condition that it test negative for HIV and hepatitis. There were trees waiting.

KEE BEACH. *(Snorkeling. Open daily 24hr.)* Kee attracts beachgoers with soft sand, exceptionally clear sapphire-blue water, and towering cliffs which mark the beginning of the Na Pali Coast. Kalalau Trail (p. 396) day-hikers, beachgoers, and cave explorers share the sprawling parking lot, which forks right to restrooms and pay phones. Families noisily fan out across the hot sand with their coolers, beach chairs, and mini armadas of flotation devices. During the summer, experienced snorkelers can explore the area just beyond the reef. In winter, rip currents and waves make snorkeling impossible outside the protected reef. The sandy shore stretches east to Haena Beach, but most visitors stick to the area west of the parking lot, where a jumble of lava rocks leads around the bend to stunning views of the Na Pali cliffs, a very popular spot for sunset photographers. *(The beach is at the end of the highway, and additional parking can be found about 1 mi. before the end, on the ocean side of the highway.)*

KEPUHI BEACH. *(Snorkeling. Surfing. Wind sports. Open daily 24hr.)* This long, narrow ribbon of sand provides the venue for a secluded day at the beach, hidden from the highway by a series of residential roads. Few visitors ever come to Kepuhi, and even locals tend to pass it over in favor of Tunnels to the west. The sloping beach provides good snorkeling during calm surf, but beware of occasionally strong currents. During low tide, a long wading pond forms along the rocky shore, which is perfect for kids. Local surfers and kiteboarders also frequent the windier west end of the beach during the summer. *(From the highway, turn right on Oneone Rd. just after Hanalei Colony Resort. Turn left on Alealea and then right on Alamoo Rd., which curves left to parallel the beach for about 1 mi. Access is provided by unmarked pathways on both ends of Alamoo Rd., right at the bend in the road where it loops back out to Alealea; park on the grass along the side of the road.)*

◉ SIGHTS

LIMAHULI GARDEN. The final of the three National Tropical Botanical Gardens on Kauai, Limahuli Garden features a comprehensive collection of native plants and traditional lava rock wall terraces that date back over 700 years. Nestled in the foothills of the Na Pali cliffs, the garden aims to educate the public and re-establish native plants among more aggressive, recently introduced flora. Limahuli's focus on conservation complements the art and science themes of its sister gardens, the **McBryde** and **Allerton Gardens** (p. 404), in the Lawai Valley. An uneven 1 mi. trail meanders through the terraces and climbs a bluff to a perch with outstanding views of the soft green mountains and bright blue ocean. *(Toward the mountain, between mi. markers 9 and 10. ☎ 808-826-1053; www.ntbg.org. Open Tu-Sa 9:30am-4pm. 2hr. guided tours at 10am by reservation only, $25. 90min. self-guided tours $15, under 13 free. Guide book included.)*

MANINIHOLO DRY CAVE. Maniniholo Dry Cave is a large crevice carved out of the soaring rock walls behind Haena Beach Park. Legend attributes the cave to the Menehune (a tribe of deity-like troublemakers) and a fisherman named Maniniholo who dug into the rock to capture an evil spirit that was stealing their catches. In reality, thousands of years of pounding surf carved the gaping hole out of the cliffs. The sea's creative (and destructive) power was evident once again when, in the 1950s, a tsunami closed much of what was a huge cave. Even at its current size, it remains an impressive sight. Stop for a picture to remember and walk around the cavern if you're headed to Kee Beach. *(Across from Haena Beach Park. Parking available in the beach lot.)*

WET CAVES. Just west of the dry cave lies the boundary of Haena State Park, which encompasses Kee Beach and the nearby wet caves. Scientists estimate that the caves were formed 4000 years ago, during an earlier geological period that was marked by a higher sea level. Hawaiian lore offers a different story, crediting the fire goddess Pele with creating the two water-filled caverns. Scouring the islands for a hot, dry home to suit her needs, Pele came across the North Shore of Kauai but quickly left when her subterranean explorations yielded water. Linked to the ocean below ground, the level of the two fresh-water caves fluctuates with the tide, and scuba divers sometimes explore Waikanaloa. Signs request that visitors don't swim and warn of leptospirosis and falling rocks, though there are usually people wading around anyway. Those with cuts should definitely refrain from taking a dip. *(A grassy visitor parking lot on the ocean side of the highway shortly past Limahuli Garden provides access to the trail, which begins a little farther down and across the street. There is also limited parking right at the trailhead. Waikanaloa is farther up the highway, just before the Kee parking lot.)*

NA PALI COAST

The Na Pali Coast refers to a rugged 15mi. of jagged cliff and pristine coastline that stretch from Kee Beach (p. 394) in the north to **Polihale State Park** (p. 422) in the south. There is no way to drive through this unmarred part of Kauai; visitors can journey either by foot or by boat. Those who do visit the concealed coast will encounter steep lava rock walls, fertile green valleys, secluded sandy beaches, and cascading waterfalls.

The steep *pali* (cliffs) tower 4000 ft. above the ocean. At one time, however, the terrain sloped gradually from the ancient volcanic dome to the sea. Powerful winter surf and constant runoff from Mt. Waialeale combined to sculpt the coast, eroding its foundations and causing massive landslides. Slowly, the coast's prominent cliffs, narrow canyons, and furrowed valleys took shape.

The five large valleys strung between Kalalau and Milolii have rich agricultural lands that once sustained hundreds of inhabitants. Reliable water sources from the highlands of Kokee provided easy irrigation for taro root farms where the valley residents cultivated their staple food. Native fishermen reaped abundant catches in the waters offshore, and the moist soil proved perfect for cultivating Polynesian crops such as bananas, sweet potatoes, coconuts, and *ulu* (breadfruit). Today, these trees continue to flourish alongside the more recently introduced mangos, passion fruit, guava, and plums. The simple life of farming and fishing was the standard in the Na Pali valleys for hundreds of years, until the beginning of the 20th century, when many residents began to abandon their remote settlements for the booming plantation towns of Waimea and Hanalei. By the 1920s, the coast's few remaining inhabitants were only grazing herds of cattle. Hippies, drawn by the coast's primal ruggedness, took over in the late 1960s. In response, the state worked to control the burgeoning tent cities and protect the wild coast from a sanitation disaster. Beginning with the Kalalau Valley, the establishment of the Na Pali Coast State Park has strictly regulated human access. Even though there are those who flout the rules and live out there on a more extended basis, over the years the restrictions have allowed the coastline to regain most of its original splendor.

KALALAU TRAIL

Long ago, a series of trails stretched all the way from Polihale to Haena, but hundreds of years of wind and waves erased the fragile dirt paths until only the **Kalalau Trail** remained. Cleared by Hawaiian traders who traveled the coast by canoe and on foot, the trail was widened in 1860 to allow for the transportation of coffee, oranges, and cattle from Na Pali's valleys to Hanalei's markets.

Today, adventurers from around the globe come to Kauai to experience the Kalalau Trail, traveling 11 mi. southwest along the Na Pali Coast. It crosses five major valleys (from northeast to southwest: Hanakapiai, Hoolulu, Waiahuakua, Hanakoa, and Kalalau) and at least half a dozen streams before it is stopped by the impassable, fluted green cliffs of Kalalau Valley. The trail alternates between exposed oceanside ridges with outstanding views of the coastline and sheltered, quiet stretches through shady valleys and streams. Mile markers are posted throughout the trail, though they are often difficult to spot. There are three shorter side trails that branch off the Kalalau Trail: the **Hanakapiai Falls Trail** (2 mi.), the **Hanakoa Falls Trail** (1 mi.), and the **Kalalau Valley Trail** (2 mi.).

The condition of the Kalalau Trail varies greatly with the season and, more importantly, the current weather conditions. The trail is 1 to 2 ft. wide, and is neither flat nor steep. Gradual switchbacks make the steep valleys more tractable. Other parts of the trail cross cliff faces where there is poor footing and a dizzying drop to rocks and surf below. Acrophobes or anyone with less than sure footing should not hike to Kalalau Beach. It's wise to wait until high waters recede before attempting to cross streams, as flash floods are common. Always check weather conditions before you head out on the trail.

In ideal weather, a physically fit hiker can make it from Kee Beach to Kalalau Beach without any stops or side hikes in 7-8hr. Nevertheless, be ready for wet and hot weather, flooded streams, or any number of other obstacles that can slow things down. By leaving early in the morning, you stand a chance of avoiding day-hiker traffic on the first 2 mi., and you can afford to rest more often as you hike the last few dry, exposed miles under the scorching midday sun. The two campsites (**Hanakapiai Beach,** at mi. marker 2, and the **Hanakoa Stream,** at mi. marker 6) are equipped with outhouses and a sheltered picnic table or two, though the state often limits one or the other to day use. All water must be treated before drinking. Some hikers cover the entire 22 mi. round-trip in two days, but most people allow up to five days to enjoy the arresting vistas and pristine beaches along the way there and back. Even if staying in the Na Pali Coast for several days, those who are in top physical shape often try to make it to Kalalau Beach in one day, where the best campsites and views are located. Obviously, if the trail is in poor condition, then spreading the hike over two days will be necessary. It's best to call the state parks office (☎808-274-3444) or visit websites like **www.kauaiexplorer.com** to find out the most up-to-date trail info and campsite closures before departing.

PERMITS. A state park camping permit is required of all campers and dayhikers who go beyond Hanakapiai Beach. Permits cost $10 per night per person, up to 5 people per group, with a 5-day max. stay. Permits can sell out up to a year in advance. During summer, one third of permits are issued for 1 week periods, 4 weeks in advance at the **Division of State Parks Office.** Pick them up on Wednesdays at 8am. Check with the office for last-minute cancellations even a few days before a potential hike. See **Camping in Hawaii,** p. 82 for more information.

HIKING

There are four basic types of hikes on Na Pali Coast: a day hike from Kee Beach to Hanakapiai Beach and back, a multi-day hike to the end of the Kalalau Trail, a hike all the way to Kalalau Beach in one day, and several side hikes.

KEE BEACH TO HANAKAPIAI BEACH. *(2 mi. 1-2hr. Moderate.)* Relatively wide, the hike from the Kee Beach parking lot to Hanakapiai is the part of the trail least likely to induce vertigo.The initial part of the trail, laden with rocks, climbs steadily uphill, affording panoramic views of Kee and the green, thickly vegetated cliffs. Less ambitious hikers can walk a short but strenuous mile and still enjoy the view. The trail gradually descends from its 400ft. perch after 1½ mi. A few hundred yards before reaching Hanakapiai, a striped pole marks the elevation below which hikers would be in danger during a tsunami—it is surprisingly high above sea level. A wide, glorious stretch of sand in summer, **Hanakapiai Beach** all but disappears during the winter. Totally exposed to the forces of the ocean, it might be Kauai's most dangerous beach, a fact to which hikers are alerted by a memorial sign on the side of the trail carved with a tally mark for every recent drowning victim—there are over 80. Powerful currents moving along the coast to the west and pounding surf make winter swimming here extraordinarily dangerous. Swimmers are should evaluate ocean conditions before diving in. Besides swimming, Hanakapiai Beach and the surrounding area offer campsites, an outhouse, and plenty of boulders on which to sunbathe. The beach is accessible by bearing right after crossing a stream; the trail continues to the left after the crossing.

HANAKAPIAI FALLS SIDE HIKE. *(4 mi. 2-3hr. Challenging.)* Many day-hikers combine this side trail with the hike from Kee, forming a strenuous 8 mi. round-trip. From Hanakapiai Beach, allow 3hr. to make the 4 mi. round-trip hike to the falls and back, which covers terrain more challenging than most of the Kalalau Trail itself. The side hike splits off from the Kalalau Trail about 30 yd. past the stream crossing; go straight for the campsite and side hike; the Kalalau Trail veers right. The waterfall trail is unmarked until you are past the campsite. There is a sign just beyond a cleared helicopter landing site on the far side of the camping area that reads "trail" with the words "waterfall" etched above. After taro root farms, bamboo groves, the remains of an old coffee mill once operated by *haole* (Caucasian) planters, and three stream crossings, weary hikers are rewarded with an astonishing 120 ft. waterfall. Due to the potential danger of falling rocks, swimming is not recommended.

HANAKAPIAI BEACH TO HANAKOA VALLEY. *(4 mi. 2-3hr. Challenging.)* An endless series of steep switchbacks that leads 800 ft. uphill, the grueling ascent out of Hanakapiai Valley is arguably the hardest part of the Kalalau trail. About 3 mi. in from Kee, the trail passes between a cliff on the left and a huge boulder on the right, opening up to a staggering view of Hoolulu Valley, the second of the five major valleys that the Kalalau Trail crosses. Having left behind Hanakapiai

Valley and the day-hikers that crowd it, **Hoolulu Valley** introduces hikers to the real Kalalau Trail: wild, isolated, and awe-inspiring. The trail is gentle as it passes mi. marker 4, proceeding to the other side of Hoolulu and into the next valley, Waiahuakua. Around mi. 5, the trail suddenly leaves the ocean behind and takes hikers from windy, exposed cliffs into the quiet, shady, and lush **Hanakoa Valley**, where wild mangoes, if in season, can be gathered from the forest floor. Mi. marker 6 is about 100 yd. shy of Hanakoa Campground. The outhouse on the far side of the river and sheltered picnic table are a nice convenience, and those who wish can stay for the night. The trail then crosses Hanakoa Stream at the point where two branches of the stream meet; the crossing can be tricky when the water level is high. Just across the stream and up the trail to the left are more campsites, another picnic table, and a restroom.

HANAKOA FALLS SIDE HIKE. *(1 mi. 30-40min. Easy.)* The Hanakoa Falls Trail branches off the Kalalau Trail near the stream crossing on the Kalalau Beach side, continuing up the left fork of the valley about 1 mi. A small sign on the shelter points the way to the trail. The first 100 yd. of the trail are the most difficult to follow, as it crosses back over the right branch of the stream and winds through a few campsites. Bear left and you will stay roughly on track; eventually all paths lead to the main trail, which is marked by pink and orange ribbons every 50 yd. for most of its length. You must navigate two side streams to continue onto a ridge that has a stunning view of a larger stream below. Continue along this stream for a few hundred yards to reach the falls. The cliffs surrounding the falls form a 270° arc that puts Hanakoa Falls in the middle of a natural amphitheater, making it one of the most eye-opening views on the entire coast. You'll probably have the place all to yourself.

HANAKOA VALLEY TO KALALAU BEACH. *(5 mi. 3-3½hr. Challenging.)* After ascending the ridge out of Hanakoa Valley, the lush lowland valleys and flourishing trees give way to spindly shrubs and barren cliff faces. The dry heat of the West Shore and the lack of shade make this segment of the trail a very sweaty experience, but views of the surrounding cliffs and coast alleviate some of the discomfort. After the trail exits Hanakoa Valley, it winds down a series of steep switchbacks into one of the more nerve-rattling sections of the trail. Narrow and rocky, the trail between mi. markers 7 and 8 traverses a number of cliff edges that require extra concentration to pass safely, as a misstep on these dangerously steep cliffs could cause serious injuries. This section of the trail also affords the first, though distant, view of Kalalau Beach during the summer (in winter high surf obscures the beach). Shortly after mi. marker 9, hikers officially enter the majestic Kalalau Valley, whose impossibly steep walls make other valleys look like roadside drainage ditches. Mi. marker 10 is at the crossing of Kalalau Stream, and the final mile is a nearly flat footpath to the beach.

KALALAU VALLEY SIDE HIKE. *(4 mi. 2-2½hr. Easy.)* This spur trail is an enjoyable way for multi-day campers to escape the midday sun. The trail begins slightly past mi. marker 10, a few yards up the slope on the southwest bank of the Kalalau Stream, where the Kalalau Trail forms a "T." To the left is the valley trail, which gently climbs for 2 mi. until it reaches a series of pools in the stream known as "Big Pools." The valley trail passes through quiet, shady country dotted with guava and mango trees, bamboo, and agricultural terraces originally built by Native Hawaiians. The trail makes two easy stream crossings and offers at least one unforgettable view of the valley from a rocky clearing. The trail ends when it runs into the stream at Big Pools. The lower pool is about 6 ft. deep and makes a wonderful spot for a dip.

WEST OF KALALAU

From Kalalau Valley south to Polihale, the cliffs of the Na Pali Coast are far
too steep for hikers. Those who wish to explore this part of the coast must
do so by boat or helicopter, and countless companies of both types advertise
all over the island. More adventurous travelers can tour the coast by kayak,
either alone or with a guided trip; **Kayak Kauai** (p. 390) leads 14hr. sea tours
that include transportation back from Polihale. Those who want to do it alone
and camp overnight on one of the beaches along the way, must secure landing
permits from the Division of State Parks. Most kayakers travel only one way—
launching at Kee, following the currents from north to south, and finishing at
Polihale. Paddling against the currents would be impossibly difficult, and the
trip either way is too dangerous outside the summer months.

By sea, the 1hr. hike to Hanakapiai Beach from Kee becomes a quick 5min.
paddle, but boat landings are prohibited. Cruising past the trail-accessible section of the shoreline, boaters and kayakers pass Kalalau Beach and arrive at
Honopu, the second of five major valleys stretching from **Kalalau** in the northeast
to **Miloli** in the southwest. Although the verdant valley of Honopu lies far above
ocean travelers, its scenic beach, divided by an arch, makes for breathtaking
photographs, even though boat landings are prohibited there. Continuing west
for a mile, **Awaawapuhi Valley** winds through a deep canyon 3000 ft. below sheer,
green cliffs. A strenuous trail in **Kokee State Park** (p. 417) ends at a steep ridge
overlooking the same valley. Nine miles west of Kee Beach, the beach at **Nualolo**
is sheltered by a wide reef, which makes landings much easier than along the
exposed coast, and offers some of the best snorkeling on the island (a fact
many tour boat operators stress when touting their trips). The Nualolo Valley
has ancient taro terraces. Another reef provides safe landing at the secluded
beach 2 mi. further at Milolii (see **Camping in Hawaii**, p. 82). A few more miles of
plunging cliffs and clear water separate the Na Pali Coast from **Polihale State
Park** (p. 422), where kayakers from the North Shore, exhausted and dizzy from
resplendent views, can crash on the beach.

Not surprisingly, most visitors to Kauai forego kayaking and skim beside the
Na Pali Coast in power catamarans that cruise the waters or helicopters that
crisscross the Na Pali sky. Countless tour boat operators leave from the West
Shore—and a few from the North Shore—most on half-day snorkeling and
sightseeing trips. Most of the tours only operate fully in the summer months;
in the winter, many companies switch to a limited schedule. **Catamaran Kahanu**
is a Native Hawaiian-run operation based out of Port Allen that provides a 5hr.
morning tour of Na Pali including swimming and snorkeling at Nualolo beach
and lunch (M-Sa 7:30am-12:30pm) and an afternoon tour (M-F 1:30-6:30pm)
without lunch or swimming. (☎808-645-6176; $135, ages 4-11 $75.)

SOUTH SHORE

The southern shore of Kauai draws the greatest concentration of tourists who
come for the sun and sand of its unbeatable beaches. The south shoreline jux-
taposes the calmest water of the island year-round—it's the only place where
swimming is safe throughout the winter. However, the South Shore is not just
a homogeneous region of resorts and beach-bound tourists; Koloa is still home
to a diverse set of locals proud of their small-town's plantation past.

POIPU

The southernmost town on Kauai, Poipu (pop. 1075) is known for sunny skies, white sand beaches, stellar surfing, accessible snorkeling, and huge resorts. Luxurious hotels and expensive restaurants sit mere feet from the water's sandy shore, but budget travelers can find cheaper B&Bs and guesthouses in the area. Sea turtles and colorful fish also favor the warm southern waters, which offer excellent opportunities for both free diving and scuba diving. The town is overshadowed by the stunning coast; downtown is little more than a shopping center facing a wall of condominiums.

ORIENTATION AND PRACTICAL INFORMATION

From Lihue, **Highway 50** runs 7 mi. until **Highway 520** branches off to the south. The intersection is marked by the **Tree Tunnel,** made from hundreds of eucalyptus trees donated by Walter Duncan McBryde, a sugar and pineapple baron. The trees shade cars for a full mile along Hwy. 520, which travels south toward Poipu and Koloa. For the sake of simplicity, all the sights and beaches on the ocean will be listed in Poipu. Three miles after leaving Hwy. 50, Hwy. 520 passes through Koloa and continues south on **Poipu Road,** passing Poipu Plaza before forking east where the area's resorts and condominiums are concentrated, and west to **Lawai Road,** PK's, and Spouting Horn. Composed of resorts and beaches, Poipu has limited services for non-resort guests. Not to worry—nearby Koloa can supply anything Poipu lacks. A small **Bank of Hawaii,** 2360 Kiahuna Plantation Dr., in Poipu Shopping Village, has a **24hr. ATM.** (☎808-742-6800. Open M-Th 8:30am-4pm, F 8:30am-6pm.)

ACCOMMODATIONS

Countless condominium developments and a few pricey resort hotels line Lawai and Poipu Rd.; an online search will yield many options. To save a few hundred dollars a night, you may want to focus on privately owned and listed condos or vacation homes, or stay in nearby Kalaheo.

Poipu Beach SurfSong, 5135 Hoona Rd. (☎808-742-2331; www.surfsong.com). The bright salmon-colored building contains 3 well-furnished studios and a 1-bedroom unit with full kitchen. Right across from Baby Beach, but without the steep price tag. The tropical garden around back has bananas and a gas grill for barbecues, and all units come with free Wi-Fi. Units $85-160 for double occupancy; additional guests $15. Cleaning fee $60-75. Discounts for longer stays available. AmEx/MC/V. ❸

Kauai Cove Cottages, 2672 Puuholo Rd. (☎808-742-2562; www.kauaicove.com), on the left after turning south from Lawai Rd. Just blocks from the water, these 3 romantic studios come complete with 4-poster bamboo beds and beautiful tiling. Wood-paneled walls give the interior a sturdy, luxurious feel. The kitchenettes include 2-burner hotplates and full-size fridges. The views aren't to die for, though—a street on 1 end, and a high fence on the other. Cleaning fee $50-85. Units $99-175. MC/V. ❸

CLEANING UP YOUR WALLET. When booking accommodations, pay attention to the cleaning fee, a one-time charge for preparing the unit for the next occupants. If the cleaning fee is high, it makes more sense to stay in one locale for a longer period of time. Some places will actually waive the fee if you stay for a week or longer.

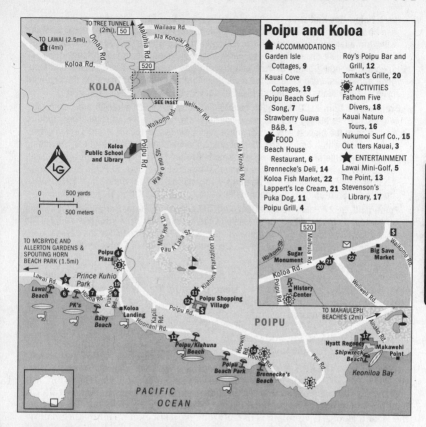

Poipu and Koloa

ACCOMMODATIONS
Garden Isle
  Cottages, **9**
Kauai Cove
  Cottages, **19**
Poipu Beach Surf
  Song, **7**
Strawberry Guava
  B&B, **1**

FOOD
Beach House
  Restaurant, **6**
Brennecke's Deli, **14**
Koloa Fish Market, **22**
Lappert's Ice Cream, **21**
Puka Dog, **11**
Poipu Grill, **4**

Roy's Poipu Bar and
  Grill, **12**
Tomkat's Grille, **20**

ACTIVITIES
Fathom Five
  Divers, **18**
Kauai Nature
  Tours, **16**
Nukumoi Surf Co., **15**
Out tters Kauai, **3**

ENTERTAINMENT
Lawai Mini-Golf, **5**
The Point, **13**
Stevenson's
  Library, **17**

KAUAI

FOOD

Despite being geared towards big-spenders, Poipu does have its own grocery store, the **Kukuiula Store**, 2827 Poipu Rd. (☎808-742-1601.) Besides the basics, Kukuiula has a great selection of organic produce and a small, but decent salad bar ($7 per lb.); lunch specialities like vegetarian lasagna are also available. Eating out at Poipu's many steak-and-seafood restaurants can be a costly habit, but thankfully sandwich shops and burger stands serve as cheap alternatives.

Beach House Restaurant, 5022 Lawai Rd. (☎808-742-1424), next to Lawai Beach. Wall-to-wall windows at this Poipu landmark ensure surfers and sunsets are never more than a glance away. The menu is elegant and never dull. The fish nacho appetizer ($13) is graced with Thai rice and mango chipotle salsa. Entrees include wasabi-crusted snapper ($30) and mint coriander rack of lamb ($36). Reservations recommended. Open daily 5-10pm. AmEx/MC/V. ❺

Puka Dog, 2360 Kiahuna Plantation Dr. (☎808-742-6044), in Poipu Shopping Village. A puka dog is a hot dog in a roll, topped with garlic lemon sauce and a range of relishes including Polihale Sunset (papaya) and Waimea Canyon (banana). Polish or veggie sausage $6.25. Lemonade $2.25. Open M-Sa 11am-6pm. Cash only. ❶

Roy's Poipu Bar and Grill (☎808-742-5000), in Poipu Shopping Village. The place to see and be seen—Hawaii's celebrity chef, Roy Yamaguchi, has attracted a loyal following with "Hawaiian-fusion" cuisine. Those willing to splurge will be treated to chic patio seating and exquisite dishes. The menu, constantly in flux, features an entire page of nightly specials, including plenty of fresh island fish (jade pesto whitefish $31.50), dim sum-style appetizers, fresh local salads, and pizzas baked in an *imu* (Hawaiian underground oven). Reservations recommended. Open daily 5:30-9:30pm. AmEx/MC/V. ❺

Brennecke's Deli, 2100 Hoone Rd. (☎808-742-1582), serves made-to-order deli sandwiches ($6) to hungry beachgoers, picnickers, and adventurers who take their food to go. Some of the biggest servings of shave ice on the island ($3.50), and a small convenience store with a limited selection of snacks, drinks, and beach essentials (including sunscreen). Upstairs is **Brennecke's Beach Broiler** (☎808-742-7588), a steak and seafood restaurant with open-air seating that offers sunset views of Poipu Beach. Happy hour daily 3-5pm (pitchers of daiquiris and coladas $12, drafts of Bud $2.75). Deli open daily 8am-9pm. Broiler open daily 11am-10pm. MC/V. Deli ❶/Broiler ❹

Poipu Grill, 2827 Poipu Rd. (☎808-742-1707), in Poipu Plaza. The parking lot in front of this food counter fills up with locals in their pickups. It serves burgers ($6-7), fish and chips ($8), and unexciting dinner plates ($7.25-9.50). The fish of the day is usually ono. There is no seating, only takeout. Open daily 11am-9pm. Cash only. ❶

◢ BEACHES

Once recognized as "America's #1 Beach," sunny Poipu Beach and the neighboring sandy coves that line Kauai's southern coast possess excellent snorkeling sites, safe swimming, crystal-clear waters, and remarkable sea cliffs. Some beaches are a bit rocky, so caution is advised when swimming. Summertime swells are excellent for bodyboarding and surfing. The beaches below are listed from west to east, and all lie on or just off Lawai or Poipu Rd.

LAWAI BEACH (BEACH HOUSE). *(Bodyboarding. Snorkeling. Surfing. Open daily 24hr.)* Close-by condos and the occasional monk seal sighting make this short and narrow stretch of sand and rock a daytime hot spot. Bodyboarders ride the beachbreak, while experienced surfers favor the larger offshore waves behind the Beach House. Swimming is usually safe, and snorkelers enjoy the shallow, clear water just west of the restaurant. High tide covers nearly all of the sand, but the manicured lawn around the Beach House provides sanctuary for sunbathers and great views of sunsets. *(On Lawai Rd., 1 mi. west of the fork, next to the Beach House Restaurant. A public parking lot is in front of the Lawai Beach Resort.)*

PK'S. *(Bodyboarding. Snorkeling. Surfing. Open 24hr.)* This tiny patch of sand surrounded by rocks is the birthplace of Prince Kuhio ("PK") who witnessed the US overthrow of the Hawaiian monarchy in 1893 and went on to become Hawaii's delegate to Congress for 19 years. Early risers take advantage of relatively calm water to snorkel or see the big sea turtles that visit the cove. PK's is also an excellent place for non-snorkelers to watch turtles as they bob in and out of the water. Further offshore, surfers and bodyboarders revel in the South Shore's best waves but will have to cope with everyone else who's doing the same. *(Past Lawai Beach, across from Prince Kuhio Park.)*

KOLOA LANDING. *(Snorkeling. Open daily 24hr.)* Once the largest port on Kauai, Koloa Landing is now the South Shore's premier scuba diving spot. Moray eels, sea turtles, and schools of angel fish huddle around to the nearshore reef. Local dive shops, including **Fathom Five** and **Kauai Aquatics Scuba,** often bring entry-level shore divers here, and the water can get downright crowded with flopping snorkelers. An old boat ramp provides very easy access to the slightly cloudy near-shore water that clears up farther away from land. *(From Lawai Rd. eastbound, turn right on Hoonani Rd. and park in the dirt clearing half a block up on the right. More parking is down the driveway to the left, but space is limited and often filled with diving vans. The landing is down a very rough 1-lane driveway on the right; it is best to walk.)*

POIPU/KIAHUNA BEACH. *(Bodyboarding. Snorkeling. Surfing. Open 24hr.)* Running from the Sheraton to the Kiahuna Plantation Resort, this long crescent beach is backed by resorts and a neat row of tall, swaying palms along its entire length. Surfers crowd the crisp breaking waves a short paddle offshore. If you thrive on activity, wedge your towel into an available patch of sand or join the throng of bodyboarders or snorkelers. Surfers can use Kiahuna Beach or Poipu Beach Park to paddle out to the waves that break over a shallow reef point between the two beaches. The first of two public parking lots on Hoonani Rd. sits just west of the entrance to the Sheraton, a 5min. walk from the beach. The other, more crowded lot is at the eastern end of the road, directly behind the beach.

⬛ POIPU BEACH PARK. *(Snorkeling. Surfing. Open 24hr. Lifeguards 9am-5pm.)* Extensive facilities, including picnic tables, grills, showers, restrooms, playgrounds, a large lawn, and a lifeguard station, attract a diverse crowd to Poipu's—and probably Kauai's—most popular beach. At low tide, sunbathers can walk all the way out to the point along a thin sandy peninsula; high tide submerges the path and turns the tip of the point into an island. Swimming is safe on both sides of the isthmus, but snorkelers prefer the shallow protected area west of the point. Poipu Beach is also home to one of the South Shore's better surf breaks, especially for beginner- and intermediate-level surfers, and it's a cinch to rent a board across the street at the **Nukumoi Surf Company** (p. 404). Sand space is at a premium, and late arrivals will probably be relegated to the western end. *(On Hoowili Rd. From eastbound Poipu Rd., turn right at the sign a few blocks past Poipu Shopping Village. Two large parking lots lie at the end of the road directly across from the beach.)*

⬛ MAHAULEPU BEACHES. *(Wind sports. Open daily 7:30am-6pm.)* These two pretty, relatively deserted beaches offer great kiteboarding, peaceful sunbathing, limited swimming, plenty of pole-fishing, and a wonderful place for a stroll. From the west section of Mahaulepu to the east, the first stop on the road is long, narrow **Gillin's Beach,** which has little shade and wild waves. The eastern end of Gillin's provides some swimming, and ideal winds for kiteboarders. The road to the western end of Gillin's is private, so you'll have to walk there from the parking lot. For slightly calmer waters, either drive or walk along the coast to **Kawailoa Bay,** a pleasant half-crescent of white sand most often visited by picnicking locals. The rocky outcroppings just east of the bay are a popular pole-fishing spot. The area also has a few shady trees and some of Mahaulepu's best swimming. An eastbound stroll from Kawailoa Bay to the fence along the shore rewards walkers with grassy fields, beautiful views, and a very small, secluded stretch of sand where the water is frequently choppy. Access to the Mahaulepu beaches is over privately owned land, so please respect the surroundings and refrain from giving the owners any reason to suspend access. *(Continue down Poipu Rd. as it turns into dirt past the Hyatt, and turn right 1 mi. later at the "T;" stay right at the 2nd fork. The parking area for Gillin's Beach is another mi. down. The beach is a short walk down any of the overgrown trails from the lot. To reach Kawailoa Bay, continue down a dirt road on the left of the Gillin's Beach parking lot until it runs along the ocean. The parking area is on the right.)*

SHIPWRECK BEACH (KEONILOA BAY). *(Bodyboarding. Surfing. Open 24hr.)* Poipu's widest beach fronts the grand Hyatt Regency. Surprisingly few hotel guests venture onto this beautiful—but slightly windy—beach, preferring the artificial sand-ringed pools and comfy lounge chairs behind the hedge. Mostly populated by locals, the beach is big enough that visitors will not feel like they are

THE BIG SPLURGE

OFF THE DEEP END

Koloa Landing is home to several dive companies, but **Kauai Aquatics Scuba** specializes in first-timers, foregoing the typically obligatory pool dive. Divers are treated to a 40min. on-land lesson which covers the basics, a short training session in shallow water, followed by a 1hr. offshore dive. Damion is the experienced, wisecracking dive master with Kauai Aquatics (over 15,000 dives under his belt), and he often leads first-time dive trips. He keeps groups small at around 4-6 divers, with 1-2 other instructors helping out. An instructor will be with you the whole time, checking your air pressure and pressing all the right buttons on your 40 lb. suit and tank (which feels weightless underwater). First-time divers are only about to go down to a depth of 40 ft. Even at this depth, you may see giant green sea turtles, ink-squirting octopi, snapping dragon moray eels, and striped butterflyfish.

Before your journey, instructors teach about certain rare species—many exclusively found on Hawaii, some found only on Kauai—with scuba-specific sign language. Kauai Aquatics Scuba is most often based in the south at Koloa Landing, which is among the best dive sites in the state, but also offers dives at Tunnels on the North Shore and offshore boat dives around the island.

☎ *808-645-6815; www.kascuba. com. First dive $110, subsequent dives $69.*

intruding. Look out to Makawehi Point, the striking cliff to the east, which made its Hollywood debut as a diving platform for Harrison Ford in *Six Days Seven Nights*. Large waves frequently crash here in the summer, especially on the eastern end, making it ideal for bodyboarding and surfing, but beware of the rocky floor. Those without boards will need to be strong swimmers. *(Turn right on Ainako from Poipu Rd. immediately after the Hyatt, at Poipu Bay Golf Course. A parking lot is located right behind the sand. Bathrooms and outdoor showers are adjacent to the Hyatt.)*

🎿 ACTIVITIES

Kauai Nature Tours, 1770 Pee Rd. (☎808-742-8305; www.kauainaturetours.com). Geologist Chuck and his son Rob lead small group adventures to most of Kauai's standout natural sites. Tours range from easy coastal walks along Mahaulepu to strenuous hikes along the Na Pali Coast, Waimea Canyon, and Sleeping Giant. Full-day hikes include lunch, water, snacks, and transportation. $100-130; ages 5-12 $75-85.

Nukumoi Surf Company (☎808-742-8019; www. nukumoi.com), on Hoone Rd. across from Brennecke's Beach. Good spot for reasonably priced snorkel and beach gear. Snorkel sets or bodyboards $6 per day, $20 per week. Surfboards $6-8 per hr., $25-30 per day. Open M-Sa 7:45am-7pm, Su 10:45am-6pm. Rentals close 30min. before store.

Outfitters Kauai, 2827A Poipu Rd. (☎808-742-9667; www.outfitterskauai.com), in Poipu Plaza, rents bikes ($25-45 per day) and offers a selection of tours, including a downhill bicycle ride from the rim of Waimea Canyon ($98, ages 12-14 $78), a 1-day sea kayak along the Na Pali Coast in summer ($200), and a zipline tour of Kapu Falls (4 or 8hr.; $125-175, ages 3-14 $99-135). Open daily 8am-5pm.

🔵 SIGHTS

MCBRYDE AND ALLERTON GARDENS. A verdant valley surrounded by steep cliffs, Lawai Valley shelters two of the **National Tropical Botanical Garden's** five gardens dedicated to protecting endangered native plants (the last on Kauai is Limahuli, p. 394). A tram, the only way to get to the gardens, transports guests from the Visitors Center and parking lot to the valley. Winding along a private road, it stops at a high coastal vista, offering views of pristine Lawai Kai Beach. Dedicated to science, the McBryde Garden is divided into four short walking tours, featuring native Hawaiian plants, palm trees, food and spice plants, and canoe plants. Butterflies, wild chickens, and croaking frogs may be your only company on the walk along the 1 mi. loop that links the four areas together. The only way to see the equally beautiful Allerton Garden is on a guided walking tour. Volunteer naturalists share their knowledge and admiration of the garden, laid out by Robert Allerton in a series of outdoor "rooms." Fans of *Jurassic Park* will appreciate a stop at the three towering Moreton Bay fig trees that hid the giant cracked eggshell. The tour ends at the Allerton Family home on Lawai Kai, where a cottage once inhabited by Queen Emma faces a beach now populated by sea turtles. For those not taking a tour, the Visitors Center by the parking lot contains informative displays and a gift shop, and the nearby grounds offer tropical trees, flowers and some ferns to at which to gawk. (*4425 Lawai Rd., 2 mi. west of the fork, across the street and just before Spouting Horn. ☎808-742-2623; www.ntbg.org. Visitors Center open daily 8:30am-5pm. Trams leave the Visitors Center to the gardens every hr. on the ½hr.; check-in 15min. in advance. Self-guided tours for McBryde Garden daily 9:30am-2:30pm; $20; all ages welcome; no reservations required. Guided tours of McBryde Su at 9am; $40; reservations required. Allerton Garden 2hr. guided tours daily M-Sa 9, 10am, 1, 2pm; $40; only ages 10+. Guided combo tour of both gardens, 4½ hr.; $85, ages 10-12; $55; reservations required.*)

SPOUTING HORN BEACH PARK. Beneath a securely fenced viewing area, a thin shelf of rock extends from the coast. Waves breaking below the shelf move water into the narrow spaces between the rocks, forcing a giant plume of sea spray skyward to the delight and applause of camera-toting tourists. Mini-spouts surround the central plume, while another lava opening contributes the "horn," sounded by a gush of air. High tide or large swells usually cause the most dramatic spouting, when the plume can reach more than 60 ft. high. The overlook provides a pretty view of Kukuiula Harbor to the east. The park also has a small lawn dotted with picnic tables, and a row of outdoor gift shops near the restrooms. (*On the makai, or ocean, side of Lawai Rd., immediately west and across the street from the National Tropical Botanical Garden's Visitors Center.*)

🎵 🎭 ENTERTAINMENT AND NIGHTLIFE

Pub crawlers and dancing queens may be disappointed with Poipu's mellow evening scene—those looking for a late night should book the next flight to Honolulu. After a long day at the beach, most travelers are simply happy to slather on aloe and crawl into bed. If you've still got energy, **The Point,** at the Sheraton, offers fantastic views of Poipu Beach to the east and the setting sun to the west. (☎808-742-1661. M 9-11pm Karaoke. Th 9:30pm-midnight DJ, F-Sa 9pm-1am. Local band comes in Su 6-9:30pm. Open M-Th and Su 11am-midnight, F-Sa 11am-1am.AmEx/D/MC/V.) **Stevenson's Library,** an opulent room at the Hyatt, features a *koa* wood bar, pool and chess tables, and a pleasant terrace. Tourists patronize this overpriced bar (with $7 domestic drafts), but some locals come for the eclectic live music. (☎808-724-1234. Live music nightly 8-11pm. Sushi night M and F-Su 6-9pm. Bar open daily 6-11:30pm.) The 🥁**Drums of Paradise Luau,** 1571 Poipu Rd., also hosted by the Hyatt, is one of two luaus on the South Shore. (☎808-240-6456; grandhyattkauailuau.com. Open bar. Reservations recommended 1 week in advance. Th and Su 5:15-8pm, $94, ages 13-20 $84, ages 6-12 $57, under 5 free.) The Sheraton offers a similar Surf to **Sunset Oceanfront Luau.** (☎808-742-8200; www.sheraton-kauai.com. M and F 5pm. $75, ages 6-12 $37.) Kauai's only **minigolf** course can be found at the **Lawai Beach Resort,** 5017 Lawai Rd., across the street from Lawai Beach and the Beach House Restaurant. Built as part of the Lawai Beach Resort's recreation center, the 18-hole course sits atop the resort's four-story parking garage, a long way from natural grass but a little closer to the stars. Use of the tennis facilities is also available to nonguests for the same price. (☎808-240-5350; www.lawaibeach.org. Public parking for golfers available on 3rd fl. of garage. Open 8am-7pm. $5.)

KOLOA

Koloa (meaning "long cane") is Hawaii's oldest sugar town (pop. 1942), and its plantation past has undergone quite a face lift in response to neighboring Poipu's steady stream of tourists. Historic buildings that once housed barbershops and bathhouses have been spruced up and filled with souvenirs and beachwear. A charming, raised wooden boardwalk now runs out front along the main street. Underneath its tourism-lacquered facade, however, Koloa retains a comfortable small-town feel and a strong sense of pride in its past.

ORIENTATION AND PRACTICAL INFORMATION

Koloa is about 10 mi. southwest of Lihue—7 mi. west on **Highway 50** and 3 mi. south on **Highway 520 (Maluhia Road)**, which leads to the center of town. Most of the town's shops and restaurants center around Old Koloa Town, at the intersection of Poipu and Koloa Rd., while others lie up the street to the east of Poipu Rd. Koloa ends a few miles north of the coast, where Poipu begins. To bypass Koloa and head straight for the sun and sand of Poipu, turn left on **Ala Konoiki Road** before reaching Koloa. Once in Koloa, head south on **Poipu Road.**

Services include: **First Hawaiian Bank,** 3506 Waikomo Rd. (☎808-742-1642; open M-Th 8:30am-4pm, F 8:30am-6pm); **Koloa Public and School Library,** on the west side of Poipu Rd. about 1 mi. south of the Chevron station, which offers high-speed **Internet access** with a 3-month visitor's card ($10) and a huge video and music collection (☎808-742-8455; open M-Tu and F 8:30am-5pm, W noon-8pm, Th 9am-5pm); the **South Shore Pharmacy,** 5330 Koloa Rd. (☎808-742-7511; open M-F 9am-5pm); and the **Koloa Post Office,** 5485 Koloa Rd. (☎808-742-1319; open M-F 9am-4pm, Sa 9-11am). **Postal Code:** 96756.

ACCOMMODATIONS

Most of the South Shore's accommodations are found closer to the beaches of Poipu. Near Koloa is the **Strawberry Guava Bed and Breakfast ❸,** 4896 Z Kua Rd., across the highway in Lawai. Turn right on Kua Rd. from Hwy. 50. After 1 mi., turn right up a steep unmarked hill and continue for 1 mi. to the third driveway on the right; turn in and bear right at the fork. Strawberry Guava has petite suites are tastefully furnished and come with refrigerators but no kitchenette. Two of the rooms have a gorgeous valley view. Breakfast varies daily, featuring locally grown fruit as well as hot dishes, like eggs or pancakes. (☎808-332-0385. Breakfast included. Cleaning fee $10. Rooms $75-95. Cash only.)

FOOD

Stock up at the **Big Save Market,** next to First Hawaiian Bank on Koloa Rd. (☎808-742-1614. Open daily 7am-11pm.) Koloa's weekly **Sunshine Market** is held Mondays at noon at the Koloa Ball Park, north of downtown.

Koloa Fish Market, 5482 Koloa Rd. (☎808-742-6199), across from the post office. A popular local stop for fresh fish (*poke* $9.50 per lb., seared *ahi* $14 per lb.). Lunch specials change daily ($8) and frequently include kalua pork and *lau lau* chicken. Take-out only. Open M-F 10am-6pm, Sa 10am-5pm. MC/V. ❷

Lappert's Ice Cream, 5424 Koloa Rd. (☎808-742-1272), in the middle of downtown. A bright ice cream parlor with a classic coffee shop feel offers 25+ flavors. Island-inspired flavors such as Kauai pie (Kona coffee base with fudge and coconut flakes) and Kilauea guava sorbet. A coffee and espresso bar, and good selection of baked goods (macadamia nut shortbread cookies $2, coconut pineapple muffins $3.50) make a tasty breakfast. Ice cream $3.50. Open daily 6am-1pm. MC/V.❷

Tomkats Grille, 5404 Koloa Rd. (☎808-742-8887), near the middle of the downtown storefronts. Sheltered tables surround a sunken outdoor garden, which infuses the place with the soft scent of plumeria. Appetizers include Kalua pig quesadillas ($9) and seared *ahi poke* ($9). Entrees include mac-nut crusted fish, steak, and grilled sandwiches ($10-25). Happy hour daily 3-6pm (Mai Tai $3, beer $2). Open daily 10am-10pm, bar until midnight. MC/V. ❸

🎿 ACTIVITIES

The knowledgeable folks at **Fathom Five Divers,** 3450 Poipu Rd., behind the Chevron station, offer scuba diving, snorkel rentals, and a variety of dives. The location of dive meeting points varies seasonally and on request; call for more info. (☎808-742-6991; www.fathomfive.com. 2-tank shore dive $85; boat dive $120; 4-5 day certification course for ages 10 and up, $495 for single, $395 per person for groups of two or more. Boat dive tours of Niihau $330. Snorkel equipment $6 per day, $30 per week. Open daily 7am-5pm.) For high-quality snorkel gear at low prices, head to **Snorkel Bob's,** 3236 Poipu Rd., 1mi. south of Koloa Chevron. Rentals have free interisland and 24hr. gear return. (☎808-742-2206; www.snorkelbob.com. Basic snorkel sets from $2.50 per day or $9 per week, deluxe sets $5.50-8/22-32; bodyboards $6.50/26. Open daily 8am-5pm.)

📷 SIGHTS

Koloa's **History Center,** at the corner of Koloa Rd. and Hwy. 520, presents a life-size diorama of plantation life with instructional plaques. Koloa was established in 1834 as a commercial center for the plantation community. Home to a sugar plantation and the major Koloa Landing sea port, the town soon became a hub of activity, growing oranges, sweet potatoes, and sugar. Across the street, a grassy field immortalizes this plantation tradition. Koloa's **Sugar Monument** is a registered historical landmark, and features a white, circular, concrete sculpture that represents a millstone opened to show seven bronze figures, one for each of the main ethnic groups—Hawaiian, Puerto Rican, Chinese, Korean, Japanese, Filipino, and Portuguese—who played a role in the formation of modern Hawaii. A plaque facing the monument describes an eighth figure as well, a Caucasian overseer on horseback, whose statue was omitted at the last minute in response to heavy criticism about the role white planters have played in Hawaiian history. Across the field, the crumbling stone tower is all that remains of the first successful sugar mill in Hawaii from the 1830s.

WEST SHORE

The West Shore maintains a sense of small-town community that is more insular than other parts of the island. Largely untouched by development projects, it is home to many descendents of the multi-national workforce that labored in area's sugar plantations. Its more arid climate may come as a surprise to visitors accustomed to afternoon showers from their visits to the island's North Shore. Its small towns serve mainly as gateways to the parks farther north—Waimea Canyon State Park, Kokee State Park, and Polihale State Park—though there are a few good beaches on the way.

West Shore Kauai

KALAHEO

Tourists often bypass Kalaheo (pop. 3913) on their way to Poipu or the state parks. But its proximity to some great beaches (on the South and West Shores) and solid budget accommodations make it an ideal homebase for extended stays. Bonus: this quiet, one-light town offers some first-class pizza.

■ ⑦ ORIENTATION AND PRACTICAL INFORMATION. Kalaheo is located 11 mi. west of Lihue on **Highway 50**. If you turn toward the ocean at the light, you will find **Papalina Pharmacy**, 4469 Papalina Rd. (☎808-332-9130. Open M-F 8:30am-5:30pm, Sa 8:30am-12:30pm.) **Kalaheo Post Office**, 4489 Papalina Rd., is behind Ohana Cafe on the highway. (☎800-275-8777 or 808-332-5800. Open M-F 8am-4pm, Sa 9-11:30am.) **Postal Code:** 96741.

⑦ ACCOMMODATIONS. Kalaheo, hands down, has the best budget accommodations on the island. We're talking king-size beds, cable TV, and spotless floors for as low as $45 per night. While many of these places fill up far in advance, you can often snag a room on the spot if you're flexible. The first place check is the **◼Classic Vacation Cottages ❷**, 2687 Onu Pl. Turn right on Puuwai Rd. just after entering Kalaheo, and stay to the right. Follow the winding road until you see the Onu Pl. cul-de-sac on your left; go up the driveway with the "Classic" sign. Tucked away from the main road yet still just a minute or two from the center of Kalaheo, the 8 unique units range from studios (some have kitchenettes, some full kitchens) to a three-bedroom house. The owners have stocked enough picnic gear, beach toys, and sporting equipment (including bikes, tennis racquets, bodyboards, snorkel gear, and golf clubs) in their garage to make Walmart jealous. Grills, a hot tub, and free use of the Kiahuna Tennis Club facilities are also included. (☎808-332-9201. Coin-op laundry on-site. Reserve well in advance with a 50% deposit, though walk-ins are welcome space permitting. Studios from $45; cottages and houses $55-100; Dec. 15-Jan. 15 prices $15-$50 more per night. Weekly and monthly rates available. Cash only.)

Get a lot of bang for your buck at **Aloha Estates ❷**, 4579 Puuwai Rd. Turn right just past the Chevron on Puuwai Rd. and continue 1 mi. to Aloha Estates on the left. James, the Aloha's owner, keeps his six floral-themed rooms clean and well-stocked. (☎808-332-7812; www.kalaheo-plantation.com. 2-night min. stay. Reserve with 50% deposit. 2-person studios with kitchenette $55-69; 4-person $69-75. Weekly rates are around $10 per night less. Cash only.) Another good value is the **Kalaheo Inn ❸**, 4444 Papalina Rd. Turn south onto Papalina Rd. at the stoplight where it intersects Hwy. 50; the inn will be one block up on the left. Simple but sparkling clean, the 15 suites with full kitchens or kitchenettes are arranged in tidy rows. There is laundry on-site, a small collection of beach equipment, and free use of the Kiahuna Tennis Club. (☎808-332-6023; www.kalaheoinn.com. 2-night min. stay. Reserve with $100 deposit; balance due 30 days before arrival. Units $80-120. $20 cleaning fee. MC/V.)

❒ FOOD. Outstanding Italian food, a friendly coffee shop, juicy hamburgers, and the island's best pizza make Kalaheo the hidden gem of Kauai dining. ❧**Kalaheo Cafe & Coffee Company ❶**, 2-2560 Kaumualii Hwy., on the *makai* (ocean) side of the road just past Papalina Rd., is a popular local meeting spot. Try the garden burger ($9.50) or the hot pastrami sandwich ($9.25) at lunch. Dinner entrees ($16-30) include an island seafood wrap with fish, scallops, and shrimp ($24). Park in the back, off Papalina Rd. (☎808-332-5858; www.kalaheo.com. Open daily 6:30am-2:30pm. Dinner W-Sa 5:30-8:30pm. MC/V.) Locals rave about **Brick Oven Pizza ❷**, on the *mauka* (mountain) side of the highway at the east end of town. Baked in a hearth, these thin-crust pizzas ($15-35) are delightfully crispy and are served on red-checkered table coverings. Hot sandwiches ($8) and salads ($4-8.50) are also available. (☎808-332-8561. Open M 4-10pm, Tu-Su 11am-10pm. MC/V.) More Italian cuisine can be found across the highway on the left at **Pomodoro ❹**, on the 2nd fl. of Rainbow Plaza. The specialties, including veal sauteed in marsala sauce with fresh mushrooms ($25) and lasagna ($18), have a loyal following. (☎808-332-5945. Open M-Sa 5:30-9:30pm. V.) The **Camp House Grill ❷**, just past Papalina Rd., on the *mauka* side, is set in a house from the days of the sugar plantation. Camp House offers fresh fish (market price), teriyaki chicken ($11), salads ($3-10), and burgers ($5-7). They also have free Wi-Fi. (☎808-332-9755. Open daily 6:30am-9pm. AmEx/D/MC/V.)

◪ SIGHTS. Just west of Kalaheo, Hwy. 540 runs south from Hwy. 50 to **Kauai Coffee.** Though the thousands of acres of oceanfront fields were once filled with sugarcane and macadamia nuts, adverse weather conditions prompted the switch to coffee about a decade ago. Check out the video highlighting the coffee-making process and sample more than a dozen flavors of freshly brewed coffee. For a full cup, check out the adjacent coffee bar, which has a window that opens to the *lanai.* Ice cream, smoothies ($3.25), and pastries ($0.85-2.50) are available. The self-guided tour around the visitors center gives an up-close overview of coffee cultivation and processing, which proves to be a fascinating 15min. (☎808-335-0813; www.kauaicoffee.com. Gift shop and museum open daily in summer 9am-5:30pm; in winter until 5pm. Coffee bar open 9am-4:45pm.) A short drive west of Kalaheo, at mi. marker 14, a newly paved turnout provides a place to park for the **Hanapepe Valley Lookout.** The well-maintained vista offers a wide, impressive view of Hanapepe Valley.

KALAHEO TO WAIMEA

ELEELE

A residential community on the west shore of the Hanapepe River, across from mi. marker 16, Eleele (pop. 2040) affords visitors a surprisingly comprehensive cluster of establishments and a beautiful out-of-the-way beach.

◼◪ ORIENTATION AND PRACTICAL INFORMATION.

The Eleele Shopping Center houses a **Big Save** (Open M-Sa 6:30am-10pm, Su 6:30am-9pm. AmEx/MC/V), a **First Hawaiian Bank** with a **24hr. ATM** (☎808-335-3161. Open M-Th 8:30am-4pm, F 8:30am-6pm), a **24hr. laundromat** (wash $1.75, dry $11.50), and a small **post office** (☎808-335-5338. Open M-F 8am-4pm, Sa 9am-11am). There is also a **24hr. ATM** in the **Port Allen Marina Center** on the right side down Waialo Rd. **Postal Code:** 96705.

◖ FOOD.

At the far end of the shopping center, ◧**Grinds Cafe and Espresso ❶,** offers a basic menu of baked goods ($2-3), pizza (from $14), and breakfast all day (from $5). Dinner is pricier but still affordable (*mahi mahi* $10, chili and rice $6). The delightful combination of diner-style booths, a warm staff, and hearty portions wins over locals and tourists alike. (☎808-335-6027; www.grindscafe.net. Free Wi-Fi. Open daily 6am-9pm. AmEx/D/MC/V.) ◧**Toi's Thai Kitchen ❷,** in the shopping center, features a huge menu of curries (red, green or yellow) and stir-fries, all served with papaya salad, a choice of rice, and (at dinner) dessert ($11-14 for lunch, $14-17 for dinner). Diners with a shy

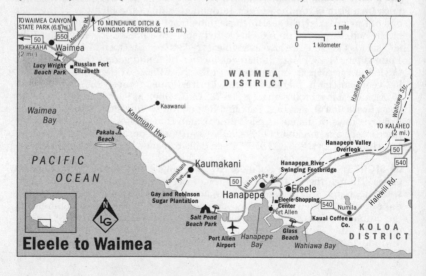

Eleele to Waimea

palate can order from the "American plate" section, which includes batter fried fish and french fries. (☎808-335-3111. BYOB corkage fee: $6 for wine, $3 for beer. Open Tu-Sa 10:30am-2pm and 5:30-9pm. Lunch is takeout only. AmEx/MC/V.)

N OUTDOOR ACTIVITIES. Straight ahead at the fork is **Port Allen,** a favorite local fishing spot where many adventure outfits are located. The tour companies include **Holo Holo Charters,** 4353 Waialo Rd., #5A, which boasts the fastest service on the largest boat to the Na Pali Coast and Niihau. (☎808-335-0815; www.holoholocharters.com. 7hr. Na Pali/Niihau tour with snorkeling $164, ages 5-12 $114.) **Captain Andy's,** in the shopping center, offers sailing and snorkeling trips. (☎808-335-6833; www.napali.com. 5hr. Na Pali sailing/snorkeling expedition $139, children $99.) **Captain Zodiac** is similar to Andy's, but riders get a closer view from a motor-powered rubber raft. (www.napali.com. 6hr. Na Pali rafting expedition $159, ages 5-12 $109.)

HANAPEPE

The self-proclaimed "biggest little town" on Kauai, Hanapepe (pop. 2153) attracts visitors in search of art galleries, gourmet vegetarian cuisine, and the inspiration for Lilo's hometown from Disney's *Lilo and Stitch.* Hanapepe means "crushed bay," perhaps due to the flattened appearance of the surrounding landscape from sea. Every Friday evening, the town hosts an "Art Night," when all of the town's galleries open their doors.

⊞ ⁊ ORIENTATION AND PRACTICAL INFORMATION. Less than 1 mi. past the Eleele Shopping Center, a welcome sign on the right side of the highway marks the turn for **Hanapepe Road.** The road swings north of Highway 50 and creates a mile-long loop that circles Hanapepe's historic downtown area. This horseshoe-shaped downtown area is lined with storefronts featuring the works of local painters, artisans, and designers. In the middle of town, on the corner of Hanapepe Rd. and Kona Rd., is an **American Savings Bank** with a **24hr. ATM.** (Open M-Th 8am-5pm, F 8am-6pm.) **Westside Pharmacy,** 3845 Kamualii Hwy., is well-stocked and decorated with antique bottles and a vintage dentist chair, which certainly evince its claim as Kauai's oldest pharmacy. (Open M-F 8:30am-5:30pm, Sa 8:30am-1pm.) **Internet access** can be found at the **Hanapepe Public Library,** directly across from the pharmacy. (☎808-335-8418. Tu, W, and F 9am-5pm, Th noon-8pm, Sa 8:30am-4pm. 3-month visitor's card $10.) A good selection of new and used books is available

THE ART CAPITAL OF KAUAI

Friday night is when most of Hanapepe's galleries open their doors. With over 16 galleries, these picks don't mind curious browsers.

1. Giorgio's Fine Art Gallery, 3871 Hanapepe Rd. Some of Giorgio's paintings are reminiscent of a tropical Van Gogh. (☎ 808-335-3949)

2. Island Art Gallery, 3878 Hanapepe Rd. Featuring the oil-works of Angela Headley, with paintings of Polynesian women, floral close-ups and tree-covered bungalows (☎808-335-0227). Ceramics and sculptures from other local artists are also featured (☎ 808-335-0591).

3. Arius Hopman Gallery, 3840 Hanapepe Rd. This photographer's gallery has incredibly vivid giclee prints of ecstatic nature shots: waves, red lava, and sunlight (☎808-335-0227).

4. Timespace Contemporary Art, 4545 Kona Rd. Cycles the works of the most talented Hanapepe artists (☎808-335-0094).

at **Talk Story Bookstore,** 3785 Hanapepe Rd. (☎808-335-6469). Visitors to Hanapepe can park in the gravel lot on the mountain side of Hanapepe Rd.; turn at the swinging footbridge sign. **Hanapepe Park** offers additional parking, along with restrooms and picnic tables. Turn off Hanapepe Rd. onto Kona Rd.; the park is immediately on your right. The **Hanapepe Post Office,** adorned with a mural, is behind the bank. (Open M-F 8:30am-4pm, Sa 9:30-11:30am. **Postal Code:** 96716.)

☐ FOOD. A darling of earth-crunchy food connoisseurs island-wide, the ▨**Hanapepe Cafe ❸,** 3830 Hanapepe Rd., satiates veggie and seafood cravings with light lunches (grilled vegetable sandwich, $9), refreshing salads ($7-10), and scrumptious pastas (vegetable lasagna, $9.75). The town's only bakery, the Cafe pumps out fresh loaves of bread ($3-6). Dinner is served on Friday to coincide with Hanapepe's Art Night (reservations are necessary) and the menu changes regularly (entrees, $18-25). For a $5 corkage fee, bring your own bottle of wine. (808-335-5011. Cafe open M-Th 11am-3pm, bakery 7am-3pm. Dinner F-Sa 6-9pm. Closed for 2 weeks in June or July. MC/V.) Besides Hanapepe Cafe there are no restaurants of note here, just a few places to fill the belly. For plates of cheap salty Chinese food there is **Wong's Restaurant ❶,** 1-3450 Kaumualii Hwy. The dining room has closed—now only rented for private parties—but a pay-by-serving bar is open throughout the day. Dishes include orange chicken, beef broccoli, and tofu with vegetables (☎808-335-5506; 1, 2 or 3 selections, $6.25/$6.75/$7.25). For a delectable dessert, look no further than the **Kauai Kookie Kompany Factory ❶,** 3959 Kaumualii Hwy. (Hwy. 50), on the north side of Hwy. 50, in Hanapepe Place. A small gift shop offers visitors free samples of the cookies, many with flavors like macadamia nut shortbread. Friends from back home probably wouldn't mind receiving cookies ($2-12) that are famous throughout the islands. (☎800-361-1126; www.kauaikookie.com. Open M-F 8am-4pm, Sa-Su 9am-4pm.) Try **Tahina's Fish and Chips ❷,** 4505 Puolo Rd., on the *mauka* (mountain) side of the highway, for bubble tea ($4.25), smoothies ($4.75), shave ice ($3.50), seafood and chicken sandwiches ($6.75-7.75), and fish and chips ($7.75). Organic salads ($6-8) are available for those who want to skip the fries. The food isn't memorable, but it works for a quick lunch. (☎808-335-0260. Open M-F 11am-5pm. AmEx/D/MC/V.)

IN TOUCH WITH NATURE: Don't worry about your cell phone or camera running out of battery while you're camping. Most campsites have pavilions with electrical outlets. Just don't leave them there charging overnight.

◙ SIGHTS. A slightly unsteady yet thrilling view of the surrounding hills and fields can be had from the middle of Hanapepe's swinging footbridge. The bridge is near the east end of town; turn at the gravel parking lot west of a big green building, about 100 yd. after the road through downtown curves to the left. The footbridge replaces the one that was swept away during Hurricane Iniki in 1992. Right along Hanapepe Rd., the town's surfeit of galleries (which normally have erratic hours) open their doors on Friday from 6pm-9pm for ▨**Art Night.** Most of those milling around are tourists looking for a deal on some island art, but the weekly event draws a fair number of curious locals as well. The area of interest is not more than two blocks long. **Talk Story Bookstore** on the west end of the strip brings live music, and a scrumptious taco stand, called **Heapin' Helpings,** sets up shop on the east end. Heading west of Hanapepe, past mi. marker 17 and left onto Lele Rd., reveals one of Kauai's best-kept secrets. *Kamaaina* (Native Hawaiians) of all ages treasure **Salt Pond Beach Park** for its wide, curving bay and soft sand. The park gets its name from the salt flats behind the east end of the beach, where locals still harvest salt from the ocean water. The salt ponds are thought to be among the most ancient in Hawaii; salt has supposedly been harvested here for over 1000 years. Its gentle swells and enclosed, uncrowded waters are perfect for swimming, though not for snorkeling. The rocky spit creates two protected bays where endangered monk seals sometimes bask in the sun. Restrooms, showers, and grills make this a great picnic site. The grassy field by the east end of the beach lacks shade, but it remains one of the better places to camp on the island. For more information, see **Camping in Hawaii,** p. 82. To get to the beach, turn south onto Lele Rd. from Hwy. 50 just west of mi. marker 17, and follow signs to Lolokai Rd.

KAUMAKANI AND MAKAWELI

Most drivers cruise right by the small dirt roads that lead into the sugar plantation towns of Kaumakani (pop. 607) and Makaweli (pop. 635), and the Robinson family probably prefers it that way. The close-knit plantation community of Makaweli, which is home for more than a few immigrants from secretive Niihau, keeps tourists away with a number of "Private Property" signs. The sugarcane fields that dominate this stretch of highway belong to **Gay and Robinson,** the only family-run sugar plantation still in operation on the islands. The Visitors Center on Kaumakani Ave. has since closed, but to drive down the canopied street is to step into another century. Small plantation cottages and aging electric street lamps, all covered in layers of rust-red dirt, lead to the still-operating factory. You can turn around at a small parking lot at the end of the road. Turn left off westbound Hwy. 50 after mi. marker 19.

Also along this stretch of highway is the famous **Pakala Beach,** one of the West Shore's best surf spots. The break has been dubbed **"Infinities,"** because the waves are some of the longest on the island. The muddy water, narrow beach, and nonexistent facilities make this almost exclusively a surfing destination (for the experienced only). Swimmers and sunbathers are uncommon. The murky water and long paddle over a deep bay to the offshore reef (where the waves break) have given Infinities a reputation as a "sharky" spot. Exercise caution and paddle out with a friend. A 5min. walk along a short path leads from Hwy. 50 to the beach. The path is on the south side of the highway, immediately west of mi. marker 21. There is room to park on both sides of the road. When you get to the beach at the end of the trail, go left to the best surf spot.

WAIMEA

Once an important agricultural port, Waimea (pop. 1787) was the first stop for many visitors to Hawaii, including Christian missionaries, Russian emissaries, and the western "discoverer" of Hawaii, Captain Cook (p. 416). The sandalwood trade of the early 1800s, along with the whaling and sugar industries, made Waimea an important port. The historic wooden buildings that line Waimea Rd. downtown are evidence of the town's colorful past, and Waimea's dusty streets recall the high-noon showdowns of silver screen notoriety. There's no shortage of genuine hospitality; the few tourists who take a picnic to Hofgaard Park or watch a movie at the fabulous Waimea Theater are warmly welcomed.

ORIENTATION AND PRACTICAL INFORMATION

The biggest town on the West Shore, Waimea lies 23 mi. west of Lihue on **Highway 50.** After heading west across the Waimea River and leaving Fort Elizabeth behind, the highway runs through the center of town. Most businesses and restaurants lie along the highway or on the adjacent **Waimea Road.**

Tourist Office: The West Kauai Technology and Visitors Center, 9565 Kaumaualii Hwy. (☎808-338-1338), is a good place to pick up a map or use the free Internet. The center also offers a 90min. historic walking tour every M at 9:30am. Tour reservations ☎808-338-1332. Open M-F 9:30am-5pm.

Bank: The stately **First Hawaiian Bank,** 4525 Panako Rd. (☎808-338-1611), has a **24hr. ATM.** Open M-Th 8:30am-4pm, F 8:30am-6pm.

Library: Waimea Library, 9750 Kaumualii Hwy. (☎808-338-6848), across from the sports field, is a good place to catch up on the news or surf the Internet. The library has six computers with speedy cable connections. Open M and W noon-8pm, Tu and Th 9am-5pm, F 10am-5pm. 3-month visitor's card $10.

Internet Access: Aloha-n-Paradise Espresso Bar, 9905 Waimea Rd. (☎808-338-1522). $4 per 30min. Open M-F 7am-5pm, Sa 8am-1pm. Also at the Visitors Center.

Laundry: Wishy Washy Laundry Center, 9889 Waimea Rd. (☎808-338-1522), is across from the Captain Cook Monument. Wash $1.25, dry $1.50 per 45 min. Open 24hr.

Police: Waimea Police Substation (☎808-338-1831), on the *mauka* (mountain) side of the highway, across Menehune Rd. from Big Save.

Hospital: West Kauai Medical Center, 4643 Waimea Canyon Dr. (☎808-338-9431), located just outside of town on Waimea Canyon Dr.

Post Office: Waimea Post Office, 9911 Waimea Rd. (☎808-338-9973), across the street from the bank. Open M-F 8:30am-4pm, Sa 9-11am. **Postal Code:** 96796.

ACCOMMODATIONS AND CAMPING

If you are camping, don't forget about attaining a **permit.** For permit information, see **Camping in Hawaii, p. 82.**

Inn Waimea, 4469 Halepule Rd. (☎808-338-0031; www.innwaimea.com), turn *makai* (toward the ocean) from the hwy. at Wrangler's Steakhouse. A beautifully restored 2-story yellow house in the heart of Waimea. The 4 spacious rooms and gracious staff welcome guests with complimentary juice and granola bars. $110; with hot tub $120. $25 surcharge for one-night stays. Vacation cottages also available $150 per night. ❸

ResortQuest Waimea Plantation Cottages, 9400 Kaumualii Hwy., (☎808-338-1625; www.waimeacottages.com). Originally built to house plantation workers at the beginning of the 20th century, the cottages have been restored and filled with the modern amenities of a Hawaiian hotel. Each has its own *lanai*. 2-person room $155-175. Cottages with kitchenettes with 1 bed/1 bath $220-360, 2 bed/2 bath $275-425, 3 bed/2 bath $325-475. 5-bedroom estate $800. AmEx/D/MC/V. ❺

Lucy Wright Beach Park, on the east edge of town. Traveling west on Kamualii Hwy., take the first left onto Ala Wai Rd. after crossing the Waimea River Bridge. This small, dusty, and predominantly local park has campsites which double as a sports field during the day. Restrooms, a pavilion, picnic tables, and a boat launch are available. ❶

FOOD

Waimea offers a plethora of *ono kine* (delicious food) grinds and the largest choice of restaurants on the West Shore. Grab groceries at the **Big Save,** on the corner of Hwy. 50 and Waimea Rd. (Open M-Sa 6am-10pm, Su 6am-9pm.)

Ishihara Market, 9894 Kaumualii Hwy. (☎808-338-1751), on the *makai* (ocean) side, across from the Cook Monument. Stock up for a big day of hiking with everything from cold plate lunches ($5-7) to sushi ($3-6), sandwiches ($4-5), and a variety of seafood

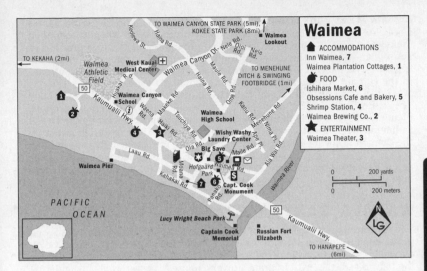

Waimea

🔺 ACCOMMODATIONS
Inn Waimea, **7**
Waimea Plantation Cottages, **1**

🍴 FOOD
Ishihara Market, **6**
Obsessions Cafe and Bakery, **5**
Shrimp Station, **4**
Waimea Brewing Co., **2**

⭐ ENTERTAINMENT
Waimea Theater, **3**

salads. Ishihara's is also a great place to pick up groceries. No indoor seating. Open M-F 6am-8pm, Sa 7am-8pm, Su 7am-7pm. AmEx/D/MC/V. ❶

Shrimp Station, 9652 Kaumualii Hwy. (☎808-338-1242), on the *makai* (ocean) side, across from Barefoot Burgers. The crustaceans come in baskets of 9 or 10, beer or coconut battered, with ginger-papaya dipping sauce and fries ($11). For the grease-averse, there is shrimp sauteed in either garlic, cajun spices (both $11) or Thai coconut sauce ($12), accompanied by 2 scoops of rice. Non shrimp-lovers are stuck with a hot dog and fries ($3.75). Open daily 11am-5pm. MC/V. ❷

Obsessions Cafe and Bakery, 9875 Waimea Rd. (☎808-338-1110), on the left heading up Waimea Rd., just past Big Save. This place has some vegetarian options and is home to Waimea's only bakery. Order breakfast (asparagus-mushroom omelet $7), salads ($5-7), a vegetarian wrap ($6.25), or Obsessions Club Sandwich (bacon, turkey, and ham; $7.25). Open W-Su 6am-2pm. D/MC/V. ❶

Waimea Brewing Company, 9400 Kaumualii Hwy. (☎808-338-9733). This brewery saves itself from culinary purgatory by delivering a tasty selection of in-house lagers and ales ($5.25). Try one of their rotating selection of locally-inspired beers, like West Side Wheat or Waialeale Ale, on the breezy outdoor patio. And if you must eat something, stick with the pupus ($7-14) or salads ($10-13); you might have a long wait if you order an entree ($18-23). Free Wi-Fi. Open daily 11am-9pm. AmEx/D/MC/V. ❹

👁 🎵 SIGHTS AND ENTERTAINMENT

🎬 **WAIMEA THEATER.** Housed in an Art Deco building that boasts the first electric marquee on Kauai, the restored theater is a local landmark. It's also an excellent place to cool your sunburn one afternoon. The large screen and modern sound system don't detract from the charm of the "loge" seating—two rows of roomy, cushioned armchairs that put standard movie theater seats to shame. The theater primarily shows Hollywood blockbusters (one film for weekdays, another one for the weekend) with the occasional surfing movie or cool special-interest film; call in advance to see what's playing. (*9691 Kaumualii Hwy. ☎ 808-338-0282, box office 808-338-2027. Films M-Th 7:30pm, F-Sa 5:15pm and 8:15pm, Su 3pm and 7:30pm. $7; students and over 55 $6; ages 4-10 $5.*)

CAPTAIN JAMES COOK MEMORIALS. Two sites commemorate Captain James Cook, the British explorer who first "discovered" Hawaii when he landed at Waimea in 1778. Neither site will tell you much about the captain's life or subsequent death at the hands of the Hawaiians. The triangle of grass that separates Waimea Rd. from the highway is **Hofgaard Park,** home to a sculpture of the captain, a replica of the British original. At the southern end of Ala Wai Rd., a small dirt parking lot faces the mouth of the Waimea River in Lucy Wright Beach Park. The park also has a baseball field, showers, restrooms, picnic tables, and a pavilion. The beach is small and clouded by the river's sediment. While great waves frequently break, the river mouth is primarily the domain of local surfers and bodyboarders. You can see the **Waimea Pier,** built in 1865 to transport sugar from Waimea, it was abandoned in the 1930s and is now used recreationally. Turn onto Kahakai Rd. from Alawai Rd. and continue straight until you see the pier on your left.

WAIMEA CANYON STATE PARK

The view from the iron-rich soil of the Waimea Canyon State Park's cliffs is one of the most magnificent on the island. Brilliant red cliffs plunge into a valley carved by streams and faults millions of years ago, while birds sweep through the blue sky, flirting with fragrant flowers, impressive waterfalls, meandering streams, and broad green valleys. The canyon's characteristic red dirt, from rusted ancient lava, is reflected in its name: Waimea literally means "reddish water." Though the canyon owes its existence to the water that flows through it, many of its river beds run dry, save when it rains heavily, because the sugar plantation draws heavily on the water above. Arrive early for a better chance of a cloudless view, and after your visit, you'll understand why Waimea Canyon State Park has been nicknamed "The Grand Canyon of the Pacific."

👁 LOOKOUTS

There are several stunning lookouts to stop at on your way up the canyon. From central Waimea, Waimea Canyon Dr. (Hwy. 550) slowly winds up to the rim of the canyon, joining the less windy—but not nearly as scenic—Kokee Rd. after seven glorious miles. Every canyon-facing bend in the road's sinuous path has a car-slowing, neck-craning view. But keep your eyes on the road: about 1 mi. past mi. marker 10, is the official **Waimea Canyon Lookout.** Here you can see the intersection of all the canyon's tributaries as they form an expansive river of eroded bluffs and water-chiseled grooves. Back on the road, the next official lookout is **Puu Hinahina,** between mi. markers 13 and 14, where you stare down from the beginning of a steep gulch to its eventual union with the main canyon. Another lookout lies at the end of a short path past the restrooms, where you can see Niihau on clear days. Between these two lookouts are a few smaller lookouts accessible by several dirt turnoffs along the highway.

🥾 HIKING

A way down to the base of Waimea Canyon does exist, as implausible as it may look. From the edge of the canyon between mi. markers 8 and 9, the **Kukui Trail** begins an over 2000 ft. descent into the canyon, ending at the Waimea River. The 2 mi. trail is strenuous because of its steepness, but it is well defined and marked every mile (watch out for markers that have been obscured by plant growth). The trail rapidly descends down the side of the canyon through shrubs and low vegetation for 1 mi. If you look up here across the canyon to the top of the eastern edge, you can see **Waialae Falls.** After heading straight for about 1 mi., the trail turns back down toward the Waimea River and enters a wooded area. As the trail approaches the river, it flattens out and the outhouse and sheltered picnic table of **Wiliwili Campground** appear on the left. The Kukui Trail hits a T here: to the right lies the **Waimea Canyon Trail,** which leads 8 mi. downriver all the way to Waimea town, while to the left a path heads upriver to the start of the **Koaie Canyon Trail.** This trail tiptoes along the western shore of the Waimea River until it crosses the river 1 mi. upstream and passes a picnic table and outhouse marking the **Kaluahaulu Camp,** 100 yd. from the trail. The 3 mi. Koaie Canyon Trail terminates at Lonomea Camp, used mostly by hunters during open season. Be careful: the Koaie Canyon trail is vulnerable to flash flooding in wet weather. Take a break before you head back up the Kukui Trail; under a scorching sun it seems twice as long on the way up.

KOKEE STATE PARK

Continuing up the road, past mi. marker 14, Waimea Canyon State Park gives way to Kokee State Park. The cool upland forests of Kokee present a marked contrast to the arid climate of Kekaha; temperatures are often 10-15F° cooler than at sea level. The sprawling trails of Kokee present accessible and spectacular hiking territory. Most of the trails feature stunning vistas and peaceful forests, but Kokee also has a boardwalk through the muddy, fascinatingly unique Alakai Swamp. Here Kauai's own *mokihana* berry can be found, along with a host of native birds that are rarely seen elsewhere.

⁊ PRACTICAL INFORMATION

For **trail information** and advice, head first to the **Kokee Natural History Museum,** on the left after mi. marker 15. Comprehensive (though somewhat aging) displays present general information about Kauai's ecology, hunting and fishing opportunities, and the indigenous birds and plants of the park. Historical photographs depict the park as it appeared to early explorers, and an absorbing one-room display details the Hurricane Iniki's wrath in 1992 as well as the park's slow but encouraging recovery. Museum staff also knows which park roads are closed and can offer hiking advice based on interests and fitness. Books, short guides to popular trails, maps, and gift items are for sale. The simple **Kokee Trails Map** ($1.50) will satisfy the needs of most casual hikers. The comprehensive ⬛**Earthwalk Press Northwestern Kauai Recreation Map** ($9), encompassing the region between Hanalei, Polihale State Park, and Mt. Waialeal, is a good buy for anyone planning to stay a few days. (☎808-335-9975; www.kokee. org. Museum open daily 10am-4pm. Donations accepted.)

Next door, the **Kokee Lodge** stocks souvenirs and snacks and maintains public restrooms. The **restaurant ❶**, 3600 Kokee Rd., offers surprisingly good food. Although crowded at lunch time, the lodge's long windows provide a rustic setting for a hearty meal. The breakfast menu includes quiche ($7), Kokee cornbread ($3.50), and fruit ($3.25). Lunch features sandwiches ($7), hot dogs ($3.50), meat chili, or Portuguese bean soup with sausage ($7), *lilikoi* (passionfruit) or guava chiffon pie ($3.75), and plenty of alcohol for celebrating the completion of a tough hike. (☎808-335-6061; www.kokee-lodge.com. Lodge restaurant and gift shop open daily 9am-4pm. AmEx/D/MC/V.)

⌂ ⛺ ACCOMMODATIONS AND CAMPING

Kokee Lodge acts as the rental office for the 12 wooden **cabins ❷** scattered along the road to the south. The cabins, ranging from studios to two-bedrooms, some of which can accommodate up to six people, come with kitchens, hot showers, linens, and wood-burning stoves. (☎808-335-6061. 5-day max. stay. Reservations recommend 2-4 month in advance; 1 year for holiday weekends. $65 per night for double occupancy. $5 per person per night for each additional person. D/MC/V.) Across the meadow from the museum, Kokee **campground ❶** is a series of spacious, grassy sites along a dirt road, with restrooms, cold showers, questionable drinking water, and picnic tables. The best sites are located behind the restrooms in alcoves cut out of the surrounding vegetation. Three forest reserve campgrounds—**Kawaikoi, Sugi Grove,** and **Camp 10**—lie to the east, on the muddy (and 4WD-only) Mohihi-Camp 10 Rd. The campgrounds have pit toilets, picnic shelters, and firepits, but no drinking water. The grounds are designed for backpackers, not car campers. Campers must stay for a minimum of three nights. For permit information, see **Camping in Hawaii**, p. 82.

YWCA Camp Sloggett ❶ has affordable indoor accommodations, although the bunkhouse often fills up with large groups. Two bathrooms are provided for guests; camping facilities are limited to hot showers. Bring a sleeping bag for the bunkhouse ($25 per person). The 15-person lodge has two bedrooms and a living room and a kitchen (2-night min. stay, $125 mid-week, $200 weekend; $25 per additional person if more than 5 during week, if more than 8 on weekend). The two-person cabin (2-night min. stay, $85 mid-week, $120 weekend) has a kitchen, fireplace, and sheets, but bring your own towels. Tents ($10 per person) are another option. (☎808-335-6060, reservations 808-245-5959; www. campingkauai.com. Down Mohihi-Camp 10 Rd., directly opposite the lodge. Keep left at the first fork and turn right at the second, following the signs to the camp. 2WD can make it if driven slowly. MC/V.)

🄖 SIGHTS

The Kokee lookouts provide expansive views of the wild, untouched Na Pali Coast and the endless Pacific Ocean. Across from mi. marker 18, the **Kalalau Lookout,** over 4100 ft. above sea level, presents a mind-blowing view of the verdant cliffs of Kalalau Valley. Veterans of the Kalalau Trail will get an extra kick out of seeing the valley they crossed on foot from thousands of feet above. With less tour buses and chatty guides than its neighbor, the **Puu o Kila Lookout** has another magnificent outlook over Kalalau's cliffs and lush river basin. A sign to the east points toward Mt. Waialeale (the rainiest spot on the planet, averaging more than 460 in. per year). Puu o Kila also serves as the trailhead for the Pihea trail into Alakai Swamp.

🄗 HIKING

The singular network of trails is the highlight of Kokee State Park. About 45 mi. of trails crisscross the park, encompassing everything from short forest walks through groves of Methley plums to heart-pounding balancing acts across narrow, rocky ridges. A few trails begin from **Highway 550,** but the majority of the trailheads are located along the handful of 4WD dirt roads that degenerate quickly from road to mud bog when it rains. Fortunately, the ones that are accessible from Hwy. 550 are among the park's best (and are listed below). The main dirt roads are the **Mohihi-Camp 10 Road, Kumuwela Road,** and **Halemanu Road.** The longest 4WD dirt road, Mohihi-Camp 10 Rd., contains the most trailheads. It begins across from the Kokee Lodge and extends about 4 mi. east of the highway until it reaches its final destination, forestry reserve Camp 10. A sign at the beginning of the road says "Kumuwela Rd." because it eventually splits into Kumuwela Rd. Although Mohihi-Camp 10 Rd. is officially considered a 4WD-only road, the stretch from the highway to about a mile past the Kumuwela Rd. intersection is frequently passable in 2WD in dry weather. Kumuwela

Rd. itself branches to the right about 1 mi. in and heads south for over 2 mi. The third road, Halemanu Rd., branches east of Hwy. 550 near mi. marker 14 and meanders about 1 mi. into the forest. On dry days, the first mile or so of Halemanu Rd. is technically passable in 2WD, providing access to a couple popular trailheads. However, without 4WD it is wiser to park on the shoulder of Hwy. 550 where Halemanu Rd. begins.

Another option is to take advantage of the park's ✴**Wonderwalks,** informative and accessible guided hikes led by park employees or local naturalists. State vehicles transport the 4WD-less to otherwise unreachable trailheads, and knowledgeable guides lead hikers through a wide range of hikes. (☎808-335-9975; www.kokee.org/wonderwalks.html. Reservations recommended. Weekends in summer, most walks leave at 12:30pm and return by 4pm. In winter, call for custom hike for a fee. Donations appreciated.)

Anyone hiking in the park should carry sufficient water or iodine tablets; leptospirosis, a bacterium that can sneak through most water filters, is a constant concern. Hikers should also avoid attempting the trails during rainy weather; many of the canyon and Na Pali view hikes include extremely steep drops and narrow ledges that are treacherous when wet.

✴ **CANYON TRAIL.** *(1 mi. 2-3hr. Moderate.)* The trailhead is 1 mi. down Halemanu Rd. from Hwy. 550, and then 500 ft. down the dirt road that branches to the right off Halemanu Rd. Kokee Park's most popular hike, and with good reason, the Canyon Trail skirts the edges of the Waimea Canyon and reveals breathtaking views of the forested valley below at every corner. After taking travelers through dense native forest brimming with *koa* trees and blackberry bushes, the trail passes over an old sugar plantation ditch. A quick climb out of the forest leads to a broad ridge with an exhilarating view of the valley below. From here, the trail descends to **Waipoo Falls,** a spectacle that varies with the amount of recent rainfall, about 1 mi. from the trailhead. Most hikers turn back at this point, but continue on to escape some of the crowd. To the left, a short spur takes adventurers to a small swimming hole that is only safe when the water is not stagnant. Another magnificent view awaits atop Kumuwela Ridge, before the trail ends at the lower end of Kumuwela Rd.

✴ **NUALOLO-NUALOLO CLIFF-AWAAWAPUHI LOOP.** *(8 mi. 4-7hr. Challenging.)* The trailhead is 100 yd. south of the lodge road, and the Awaawapuhi trailhead is past mi. marker 17, on the left. The Nualolo-Awaawapuhi Loop is a combination of three relatively strenuous hikes. Together, they form a grueling trek that loops from the highway to and from the majestic Na Pali Coast, and should satisfy any hardcore hiker's hunger for adventure. Start early on a sunny day—wet weather can make a few stretches of trail extremely treacherous. The **Nualolo Trail** gradually descends 3 mi. from the highway toward the ocean through dry upland forests dominated by lofty trees, flowering shrubs, and a grassy meadow. Shortly after mi. marker 2 comes the first good view of the shimmering Pacific Ocean. After about 3 mi., you'll reach a junction where you can continue on the loop by turning right onto the 2 mi. **Nualolo Cliff Trail,** or hike mi. more toward the ocean to ✴**Lolo Vista,** which is the end of the Nualolo Trail. Lolo Vista is a must-see along the hike, with one of the best views of the Na Pali Coast in an area that is inaccessible except by boat. Do not go beyond the railing at the end of the trail—the ground is unstable and the drop to the valley floor is over 2000 ft. The Nualolo Cliff Trail tiptoes precariously atop the rim of Nualolo Valley for about 2 mi. and connects the Nualolo Trail and the **Awaawapuhi Trail.** It reaches an area with picnic tables and a stream near its intersection with Awaawapuhi Trail. The cliff trail crosses another stream and passes by a l waterfall 1 mi. from the intersection of the Nualolo Cliff Trail and the Awaawapuhi Trail. The Awaawapuhi Trail extends 2 mi. from the highway to its junction with the Nualolo Cliff Trail, and then an additional mi. to another lookout on the Na Pali Coast. Awaawapuhi, meaning "valley of ginger," boasts fragrant yellow ginger, blackberries, thimbleberries, and passionfruit. Because the loop does not begin and end at the same trailhead, there is another 1 mi. hike along Hwy. 550 to get back to your car. Thus, in total, hikers could be in for an 11 mi. journey. Bring lots of water and be prepared for a 1600 ft. climb from the Nualolo Cliff Trail back to your car.

PUU KA OHELO-BERRY FLATS LOOP. *(2 mi. 1hr. Easy.)* Take Mohihi-Camp 10 Rd. about 1 mi. and then another 1 mi. down a dirt trail fork to the left that leads to a small group of private cabins; a sign at the trailhead says "State Park Area." The **Berry Flats** trailhead is 1 mi. farther down Mohihi-Camp 10 Rd., past Kumuwela Rd., about 100 yd. before a wide section of the road and a left turn. The constant struggle between indigenous and introduced plants is evident— flowering alien honeysuckle, beautiful but destructively invasive, grows along either side of the path. Along the loop, two trails branch off to the side. Take a left onto the forested **Puu Ka Ohelo Trail.** About 1mi. into this trail, the **Water Tank Trail** forks to the right (or to the left if you've started at the Puu Ka Ohelo trailhead) and leads about 1 mi. back to Hwy. 550, across the street from the Kokee campground. The loop is a gentle hike that is great for families.

KALUAPUHI TRAIL. *(1 mi. 1hr. Easy to moderate.)* Kaluaphui Trail starts a little less than 1 mi. past the Awaawapuhi trailhead, slightly beyond mi. marker 17; park at the Awaawapuhi lot. The well-maintained trail travels inland through upland forest, ending a couple hundred yards past the Kalalau Lookout. With a change in elevation of only 120 ft., the peaceful stroll can be enjoyed by all. The trail is particularly susceptible to rain, however. Native Hawaiian flora and fauna prevail here: birds swoop down from above the canopy of *ohia* trees, and strawberry guava grows in abundance. At the T-intersection in the grove, take the left fork—the right fork leads to a dead-end hunting trail. The trail ends in an orchard of Methley plums, harvested by locals in early summer. If you choose to walk back to your car via the highway, it's about 1 mi. to the trailhead.

PIHEA TRAIL TO ALAKAI SWAMP TRAIL. *(3 mi. 3-4hr. Challenging.)* The Pihea trailhead is to the right of the Puu o Kila Lookout, at the end of Waimea Canyon Dr. The only way to get to the Alakai Swamp without 4WD is via the **Pihea Trail,** which is memorable in its own right. The first section of the Pihea Trail features sweeping views of the Na Pali cliffs and valleys. Hovering around 4000 ft., this stretch follows the course of an old, abandoned road across the top of Kalalau Valley. Parts of this section of trail are shaded by ohia trees that form a leafy roof overhead and attract a steady stream of chirping native birds. Bring binoculars if you are an avid bird-watcher—this area of the park is frequented by many different species. The Kauai honey-creeper, *Iliwi*, and bright-red Apapane are common, while the handful of critically endangered birds in this area, including the beautiful yellow Kauai Akialoa, are rarely seen. After about 1 mi., the trail forks, and a steep offshoot to the left leads to **Pihea Vista.**

The Pihea Trail turns right at the fork and leaves the Na Pali Coast behind, heading to a very steep section where you must grapple up a tough hill with exposed tree roots and slick puddles of mud. After 1 mi., the trail becomes a narrow boardwalk, descending gradually for another mi. until it reaches a junction with the **Alakai Swamp Trail.** Straight ahead, the Pihea Trail continues for almost 2 mi. until it ends at Kawaikoi Camp, along Mohihi-Camp 10 Rd., 3 mi. from Puu o Kila Lookout. To the right are the first 1 mi. of the Alakai Swamp Trail, which also terminates along Mohihi-Camp 10 Rd. To the left are the last

2 mi. of the Alakai Swamp trail, which ends at the Kilohana Lookout, where there is a fantastic view of a few North Shore beaches and the verdant valleys of Hanalei and Wainiha. These last couple miles of the Alakai Swamp trail are a level hike along a boardwalk through havens for endemic birds. Make sure to stay on the boardwalk; the bog is frequently much deeper than it appears.

KEKAHA

Although Kekaha (pop. 3175) doesn't have much to offer in the way of shopping or nightlife, its miles of remote, uncrowded beaches and spacious public park-lands make it a decent place to relax and get away from the crowds and traffic of other west shore towns. Once a sugar town where life centered around the big—and now rusting—mill, modern-day Kekaha is interesting mainly as a gateway to **Waimea Canyon** (p. 416), **Kokee State Park** (p. 417) to the north, and **Polihale State Park** (p. 422) to the west.

ORIENTATION. The westernmost town in the United States, Kekaha lies 26 mi. west of Lihue on **Highway 50. Kekaha Road** branches right from Hwy. 50 between mi. markers 24 and 25 (follow the "Alternate Kekaha" sign) and runs parallel to the highway for 2 mi. west, past the old sugar mill, to **Waimea Canyon Plaza** at the base of Kokee Rd., which heads north to the canyon. The plaza has a few standard tourist shops with aloha shirts and beach towels, and the last few places to fill your tummy or picnic basket. Take advantage of the "Last Chance Restroom" before heading north to Kokee or west to Polihale.

FOOD. Kekaha doesn't have any restaurants per se, but there are a few last-resort lunch spots and a convenience store to stock up on snacks. The **Menehune Food Mart** has a good selection of the basics as well as food to-go: large Icees ($1.50) and prepared sandwiches ($3.50-4.50). There is also an **ATM.** (☎808-337-1335. Open daily 5am-6pm, Su 5am-4pm. AmEx/MC/V.) The **Waimea Canyon Snack Shop** is probably your best bet for reasonably tasty food, selling fresh-made sandwiches and wraps ($5.50), local favorite Lappert's ice cream (2 scoops $3.50, 3 scoops $4.50), and various chili bowls ($4-5). (☎808-337-9227. Open daily 8am-4:30pm.) A few hundred yards before reaching the plaza, on the ocean side of Kekaha Rd., is the **Thrifty Minimart,** 8240 Kekaha Rd., which offers lunch and dinner plates of pork or chicken, among other Hawaiian favorites, for around $7. They also sell delicious ahi *poke* for $9 per lb. or smoked salmon *poke* for $10 per lb. (☎808-337-1057. Open daily 8am-9pm. MC/V.)

BEACHES. Across Kekaha Rd. from the Plaza, between the elementary school and ocean, the aging **Faye Park**—featuring a track, baseball field, tennis courts, basketball court, playground, picnic tables, pavilion, and grills—has hosted many a neighborhood luau. There are restrooms behind the Neighborhood Center and near the baseball field as well as an outdoor shower at the far end of the park (right on the highway facing the beach). Every Saturday at 9am, a modest farmers' market sets up shop next to the tennis courts. Kekaha's main attraction is the glistening white **Kekaha Beach Park,** one of the West Shore's best beaches. Far enough away from the silt dumped into the ocean by the Waimea River, the water at Kekaha has that familiar azure hue. Though, like at other West Side beaches, strong rip currents tug the waters of Kekaha, it is sometimes safe enough for strong swimmers or bodyboarders to play in the surf. Locals often use the beach for shore fishing. Families with young *keiki* (children) favor the eastern end of the beach. The western end benefits from being close to a lifeguard tower and an outdoor shower. A little further along, just before mi. marker 29, there is a lawn with four day-use picnic shelters and grills. The beach's short breaks drive experienced surfers east to an area of water right around mi. marker 27; there is no beach on this rocky shore, but they can be watched from a pull-out along the highway.

POLIHALE STATE PARK

Outside of Kekaha, Polihale State Park is well worth at least one trip, if not more. Hwy. 50 ends 5 mi. to the northwest out of Kekaha; follow the signs to Polihale, eventually turning left on a wide dirt road (a yellow gate will be open if the park is open). While trucks full of local teenagers careen merrily down miles of potholes, bumps, and rocks to the park, visitors in modest rental cars may have a more difficult and bumpy—but definitely worthwhile—ride. Ease off the gas and shift into low gear as you navigate through the cane fields. About 3 mi. later, the road forks to the right at a big monkeypod tree, becomes somewhat narrower, and continues for 1 mi. to the north end of **Polihale Beach.** Along this road a dirt loop branches off to the left toward the ocean and is the access road for a number of campsites. There are a few more campsites and plenty of beach access points beyond the loop toward the northern end of the road, and the whole area has restrooms, showers, water fountains, grills, and pavilions. Camping **permits** are required. Permits can be purchased at the **Division of Forestry and Wildlife Office,** 3060 Elwa St., #306, in Lihue. (☎808-274-3444. 5-night max. Open M-F 8am-3:30pm. $5 per person per group.) For more information, see **Camping in Hawaii,** p. 82. The left fork at the monkeypod tree leads south about 1 mi. to a small parking area on the northern edge of Polihale's famous dunes and provides access to the southern end of Polihale Beach. A relatively calm place to swim is **Queen's Pond,** the only section of Polihale protected by a reef. It is a small bay about 100 yd. north of the parking area. The rest of the Polihale beach is usually pounded by surf; swimming is possible (not for children) but requires caution. Be aware of dangerous shorebreaks, currents, and high surf. The beach itself is an absolute wonder; up to 50 yd. wide, the white sands stretch for 3 mi. along Kauai's western coast, from the military base on the south to the steeply jutting cliffs of the Na Pali Coast to the north—often with only a handful of visitors. On a clear day, Niihau can be seen to the southwest.

 STUCK IN THE MUCK. When the Polihale State Park road reaches the beach it quickly becomes less hard-packed dirt and more loose beach sand. Do not proceed without 4WD; you will get stuck! If you do, try using a low gear, reverse, and step lightly on the gas. If all else fails, get out and push.

Even without entering the water, Polihale will leave a strong impression. At the northern end of the beach, past the campsites, the ruins of an ancient *heiau* (temple) are barely detectable at the base of Polihale Cliff. According to legend, the souls of the dead used the cliff as a departure point, springing away from the earth and into the glorious setting sun. As one stands at Polihale, isolated from the rest of Kauai, gazing out over the unbroken Pacific, it's not hard to imagine why Hawaiians considered this a spiritual place. The incredible Polihale 🌅sunset is best seen from the northern end, where the sun paints the clouds a fiery coral pink as it sinks below the waves, a sublime conclusion to a day spent relaxing on the beach.

APPENDIX

CLIMATE

Hawaii manages to exceed the expectations of even a typical tropical climate; the **average temperature** in Hawaii is 85°F (29°C) in summer and 78°F (26°C) in winter. Northeasterly trade winds and varying elevations limit the extremes of temperature and humidity seen at other tropical locales, giving the Hawaiian islands, in our opinion, one of the best climates in the world. Though weather reports in Hawaii often sound like broken records proclaiming "warm and sunny," we've included a climate chart below. Always remember that the weather conditions can vary depending on whether you are on the leeward or windward sides of the islands. Most of Hawaii has only two seasons: winter from November to April and summer from May to October.

AVG. TEMP. (LOW/ HIGH), PRECIP.	JANUARY			APRIL			JULY			OCTOBER		
	°C	°F	in.	°C	°F	in.	°C	°F	in.	°C	°F	in.
Honolulu	18/24	65/80	4.1	20/26	68/78	1.9	23/28	73/82	0.9	22/28	71/82	1.9
Hilo	17/26	63/78	12.1	18/26	63/78	10.1	20/28	68/82	9.5	20/28	68/82	9.9
Kahului	17/24	63/80	3.7	19/28	66/83	1.8	22/30	71/87	0.5	20/30	69/87	1.1
Lihue	18/26	65/78	4.6	20/26	69/79	3.0	23/29	74/84	2.1	23/28	73/83	4.3
Lanai City	15/22	60/72	5.1	16/23	61/74	2.6	18/25	65/77	1.7	18/25	65/77	2.5
Kaunakakai	17/26	63/78	3.7	18/24	65/80	2.1	22/30	70/85	0.6	22/30	70/85	1.8

To convert from degrees Fahrenheit to degrees Celsius, subtract 32 and multiply by 5/9. To convert from Celsius to Fahrenheit, multiply by 9/5 and add 32.

°CELSIUS	-5	0	5	10	15	20	25	30	35	40
°FAHRENHEIT	23	32	41	50	59	68	77	86	95	104

MEASUREMENTS

Like the rest of the US, Hawaii uses the English system. The basic unit of length is the foot (ft.), which is divided into 12 inches (in.). Three feet make up one yard (yd.), and one mile (mi.) is made up of 1760 yards. Fluids are measured in US gallons (gal.), each divided into 128 US fluid ounces (fl. oz.). The basic unit of weight is the pound (lb.), which is divided into 16 ounces (oz.). One short (US) ton is 2000 lbs. Gallons in the US and those in Britain are not identical: one US gallon equals 0.83 Imperial gallons. Pub aficionados will note that an Imperial pint (20 oz.) is larger than its US counterpart (16 oz.).

MEASUREMENT CONVERSIONS	
1 inch (in.) = 25.4mm	1 millimeter (mm) = 0.039 in.
1 foot (ft.) = 0.305m	1 meter (m) = 3.28 ft.
1 yard (yd.) = 0.914m	1 meter (m) = 1.094 yd.
1 mile (mi.) = 1.609km	1 kilometer (km) = 0.621 mi.
1 ounce (oz.) = 28.35g	1 gram (g) = 0.035 oz.
1 pound (lb.) = 0.454kg	1 kilogram (kg) = 2.205 lb.

MEASUREMENT CONVERSIONS	
1 fluid ounce (fl. oz.) = 29.57mL	1 milliliter (mL) = 0.034 fl. oz.
1 US gallon (gal.) = 3.785L	1 liter (L) = 0.264 gal.

LANGUAGE

Hawaii has two official languages, **English** and **Olelo Hawaii.** English is spoken universally on the islands. The Hawaiian language, *Olelo Hawaii,* is spoken largely by Native Hawaiians. *Olelo Hawaii* is a Polynesian language distinctive for its reduplication, apparent in words like *wikiwiki* (fast). Hawaii's unofficial language is **Hawaiian Creole English (HCE).** A byproduct of Hawaii's tremendous diversity, HCE, commonly known as **"pidgin,"** is an other-than-standard English which developed as a means of communication for business transactions. The dialect integrates elements from Hawaiian, English, Chinese, Japanese, and several other languages. Although it is primarily used by teenagers, pidgin is incorporated in many Hawaiians' daily conversation. While Hawaiians often appreciate attempts by visitors to speak *Olelo Hawaii,* it is inadvisable for visitors to speak pidgin unless fluent, as it is usually considered condescending.

ALPHABET. The *Olelo Hawaii* **alphabet** *(piapa),* was written by 19th century missionaries. The alphabet contains 12 letters: 5 vowels (a, e, i, o, u) and 7 consonants (h, k, l, m, n, p, w). *Olelo Hawaii* is considered unique by linguists due to its prolific use of vowels and its single guttural letter (k).

PRONUNCIATION. The key to pronouncing all things Hawaiian is to sound consonants as in English and break up words so they are easy to say. For example, *Waianapanapa* sounds like "Wai-a-napa-napa." The Hawaiian language often utilizes two symbols, the **glottal stop,** ', (or *'okina* in Hawaiian) and the **macron** *(kahakō).* The glottal stop is sometimes utilized in Hawaiian words like *Hawai'i* and *O'ahu,* indicating a short break in pronunciation. English orthography does not use the glottal stop and often many Native Hawaiians also omit it from their writing. It is advocated mainly by teachers of Hawaiian as a second language and by linguists. The macron marks that a vowel is a double or long vowel in phonetic terms. Similar to the *'okina,* the *kahakō* is only used sporadically in written Hawaiian and is often not pronounced in conversation. Pronounce vowels marked by a glottal stop (') quickly, that is, *o'o* sounds like "oh-oh!" in English. Stress rising dipthongs (ae, ai, ao, au, oi, ou, eu, ei) on the first letter and end with a short e, i, o, or u. Thus, *oi* sounds like "oy" in "boy," ending with a short "i." These are the basic vowel pronunciations:

PHONETIC UNIT	PRONUNCIATION
a	a, as in "above"
e	e, as in "bet"
i	ee, as in "see"
o	o, as in "sole"
u	oo, as in "moon"

PHRASEBOOK

HAWAIIAN	PRONUNCIATION	ENGLISH
aina	eye-nah	land, earth
alii	ah-lee-ee	Hawaiian chiefs, royalty
aloha	ah-low-ha	love, hello, goodbye

HAWAIIAN	PRONUNCIATION	ENGLISH
aole	ah-oh-lay	no, not, never
hale	hah-lay	house, hut
haole	how-lay	Caucasian, stranger
hauoli	how-oh-lee	happiness
heiau	hey-ee-au	temple
hui	hoo-ee	club, association, group
hula	hoo-lah	Hawaiian dance
imu	ee-moo	underground oven
inu	in-new	drink
kahakai	ka-hak-ay	beach
kahuna	ka-hoo-na	priest
kaikamahine	kay-kah-ma-hee-nay	daughter
kala	kah-la	money
kalua	kah-loo-ah	baked shredded meat
kamalii	kah-mali-ee-ee	children
kane	kah-nay	man, masculine
kapu	kah-poo	taboo, forbidden
kaukau	kow-kow	food
keiki	kay-kee	child
keikikane	kay-kee-kah-nay	son
kokua	ko-koo-ah	help, aid, relief
kumu	koo-moo	teacher, tutor
kupuna	koo-poo-nah	grandparent, ancestor
lanai	lah-nye	porch
lei	lay	necklace of flowers
lomilomi	low-me low-me	massage
lua	loo-ah	bathroom
luau	loo-ow	Hawaiian feast
mahalo	mah-hah-low	thank you
mahina	ma-hee-nah	moon
maikai	mah-ee-kah-ee	good, fine
makaainana	mah-kah-ay-nah-nah	common people
makai	mah-kye	toward the ocean
makamaka	mah-kah mah-kah	close friend
makua	mah-koo-ah	parent, parent generation
malama	mah-lah-mah	to take care of, attend to
mauka	mah-ow-kah	toward the mountains, inland
mauna	mow-nah	mountain
mele	meh-leh	song, chant, or poem
Menehune	meh-neh-hoo-neh	legendary race of little people
muumuu	moo-moo	loose gown, dress
nalu	nah-loo	wave, to surf
nani	nah-nee	beautiful
nui	noo-ee	big
ohana	oh-hah-nah	family
olelo	oh-lay-low	language, word, quotation
ono	oh-no	delicious
pali	pah-lee	cliff
paniolo	pah-nee-oh-low	Hawaiian cowboy
pau	pow	finished
pule	poo-leh	prayer, incantation
pupu	poo-poo	hors d'oeuvre
pupule	poo-poo-lay	crazy
wahine	wah-hee-nay	woman, girl, female
wai	why	freshwater, liquid, liquor
wikiwiki	wee-kee-wee-kee	very fast, speedy

HAWAIIAN	PRONUNCIATION	ENGLISH
aloha aina	ah-low-hah eye-nah	love of the land
aloha ahiahi	ah-low-hah ah-hee-ah-hee	good evening
aloha kakahiaka	ah-low-hah kah-kah-hee-ah-kah	good morning
aloha kakou	ah-low-hah kah-koo	aloha to all, hello everyone
aloha au ia oe	ah-low-hah ow ee-ah oh-ay	I love you
aole pilikia	ah-o-lay pee-lee-kee-ah	no problem, no trouble
hauoli la hanau	how-oh-lay la ha-now	happy birthday
kamaaina	kah-mah-ay-nah	"child of the soil," native-born or long-time resident
kanaka maoli	kah-nah-kah mah-oh-le	full-blooded Hawaiian person
kipa mai	kee-pah mah-ee	you're welcome
mahalo nui loa	mah-ha-low new-ee low-ah	thank you very much
mai kai	mah-ee kah-ee	I am fine
okole maluna	oh-ko-lay mah-loo-nah	bottoms up
owai kau inoa?	oh-why kah-oo ee-no-ah?	What is your name?
pau hana	pow hah-nah	end of the work day
pehea oe?	pay-hay-ah oh-ay?	How are you?

LOCAL FOOD AND DRINK

adobo: Filipino pork or chicken cooked in vinegar, soy sauce, and garlic

ahi: yellowfin tuna

azuki: sweetened red or black beans

crack seed: popular snack of dried fruits with salt, sugar, and seasonings

dim sum: Chinese brunch of appetizer-size food, often served with tea

haupia: coconut pudding

huli huli chicken: chicken barbecued on spits over an open grill

laulau: pork, butterfish, beef, or chicken wrapped in taro leaf and then baked or steamed in an *imu*

li hing mui: preserved plum, a type of crack seed

lilikoi: passion fruit

limu: edible seaweed

loco moco: a fried egg on top of a hamburger, served with rice and gravy

lomi salmon: cold diced salmon, tomatoes, and onion

kalua pig: barbecued pork, cooked whole in an *imu* (underground oven)

katsu: pork or chicken dipped in bread crumbs and deep-fried

kimchee: Korean spicy pickled cabbage seasoned with garlic, chiles, and other spices

kona coffee: coffee from beans grown in the Kona District of the Big Island

kulolo: dessert made of baked taro root mixed with coconut milk and honey or sugar

mahi mahi: dolphinfish that can be broiled, grilled, baked, or poached

malasadas: sweet Portuguese doughnuts without a hole

mochi: cakes made out of rice

musubi: rice ball wrapped in dried seaweed (often made with Spam)

nori: dried, compressed seaweed

onaga: red snapper

ono: fish similar to mackerel or tuna

opihi: island limpets (a shellfish delicacy)

plate lunch: two scoops white rice, macaroni salad, and a local-style meat or seafood entree

poi: purple paste-like food made of pounded taro root

poke: appetizer consisting of cubed raw fish, served with seaweed

saimin: Japanese ramen-like noodle soup

shave ice: shaved ice topped with syrup, flakier than a snow cone

shoyu: Japanese word for soy sauce

ulu: breadfruit

INDEX

A

accommodations 60
advocacy 70
Ahihi-Kinau Natural Area Reserve 299
AIDS/HIV. See health
airmail 60
airplanes. See flights
airports
    Hilo International 188
    Honolulu International 96
    Hoolehua 326
    Kahului International 260
    Keahole-Kona International 187
    Lanai 352
    Lihue 361
Ala Moana 103
Ala Moana Shopping Center 124
Alekoko Fishpond Overlook 368
Alii Kula Lavender Farm 315
Aliiolani Hale 117
aloha attire 28
Aloha Stadium 147
Aloha Theater 204
animals
    box jellyfish 88
    green sea turtles 81
    Hawaiian hoary bat 81
    Hawaiian monk seal 81
    humpback whales 81
    humuhumunukunukuapuaa 81
    mongoose 82
    nene 82
    portuguese men-of-war 88
    sharks 81, 88
    toothed dolphins 81
Aquarium 299
Arizona Memorial 144
ATV tours 93
Awaawapuhi Valley 399

B

Battleship Missouri Memorial 146
beaches
    20 Mile 345
    69 256

Ala Moana 116
Alanuihaha Park 224
Anaehoomalu 255
Anini 385
Baby, Kauai 402
Baby, Maui 267
Baby Queen's 138
Beach House 402
Bellows Field 155
Big 298
Black Pot 389
Black Rock 276
Canoe 276
Charley Young 294
Dig Me 276
Dixie Maru 349
D.T. Fleming 279
Duke Kahanamoku 137
Ehukai 170
Five Caves 298
Five Graves 298
Fort DeRussy 137
Gillin's 403
Haena 393
Halawa Bay 345
Haleiwa 177
Haleiwa Alii 176
Hale o Kapuni 257
Hale O Lono Harbor 349
Hamoa 311
Hana 310
Hanakaoo 276
Hanakapiai 397
Hanalei Pavilion 389
Hanamaulu 368
Hanapai 385
Hapuna 256
Hauula 164
Hideaways 390
Honolii 232
Honolua Bay 279
Hookena 203
Hookipa 305
Hulopoe 354, 359
Infinities 413
Ironwoods 279
Isaac Hale 224
Kaanapali 276
Kahaluu 195
Kahana 278, 285
Kahekili 276
Kaihalulu Red Sand 310
Kailua 160
Kaimana 138
Kaiolohia 358
Kakahaia 343
Ka Lae 209
Kalama 160, 294
Kalapaki 367
Kalihiwai 385
Kamakahonu 195
Kamaole 294

Kapaa 382
Kapalua 278
Kawaaloa Bay 342
Kawailoa 177
Kawailoa Bay 403
Kealakekua Bay 203
Keawakapu 297
Keawaula Bay 186
Kee 394
Kehena 224
Kekaha 421
Kekaha Kai 196
Keomuku Beach and Environs 359
Keoniloa Bay 403
Kepuhi 394
Kiahuna 403
Kiholo Bay 196
Koki 310
Koloa Landing 402
Kuhio 138
Lanikai 160
Launiupoko Wayside Park 267
Laupahoehoe Point 240
Lawai 402
Little 298
Lopa 359
Lucy Wright 414
Lumahai 393
Maalaea Harbor 289
Mahaulepu 403
Mailekini 257
Maili 185
Makaha 185
Makapuu 153
Make Horse 349
Makena Landing 298
Makua 393
Manele Bay 359
Mauna Kea 256
Milolii 203
Mokapu 297
Mokuleia 180
Mokuleia Bay 279
Moomomi Recreation and Cultural Park 341
Murphy's 345
Nanakuli 185
Napili Bay 278
Nualolo 399
Old Kona Airport Park 195
Onekahakaha 231
Oneloa 279
Outrigger Canoe Club 139
Paako 299
Pakala 413
Paki Ke Kua 390
Papakolea Green Sand 208
Papohaku 349
PK's 402
Poipu 403
Polihale 422

Polihua 358
Poolenalena 298
Puamana 267
Punaluu Black Sand 209
Puu Kekaa 276
Puu Olai 298
Queen's Bath 390
Queen's Pond 422
Richardson Ocean Park 232
Royal Moana 138
Salt Pond 412
Sandy 152
Sans Souci 138
Secret 385
Secret Cove 299
Shark's Cove 171
Shipwreck, Kauai 403
Shipwreck, Lanai 358
South Point 209
Sprecklesville Town 306
Sprouting Horn 405
Sugar 289
Sunset 170
Swanzy 164
Tunnels 393
Ukumehame 267
Ulua 297
Wahikuli 267
Waialua 345
Waikiki 137
Waikoko 390
Wailea 297
Waimanalo 155
Waimanalo Bay 155
Waimea Bay 171
Waioli 390
Waipouli 381
Wawaloli 196
White Sands 195
Yokohama Bay 186
Beyond Tourism 67–77
    studying 71
    volunteering 68
    working 73
Big Island 187–252
    Hamakua Coast 238
    Hawaii Volcanoes National
        Park 210
    Hilo 226
    Kailua-Kona 189
    Kau and Ka Lae 205
    North Kohala including Hawi and
        Kapaau 249
    Puna 218
    Saddle Road 234
    South Kohala 255
    South Kona 199
Big Wind Kite Factory 348
Blaisdell Center 141
bodyboarding 92
Boiling Pots 233
boogie boarding. See body-
    boarding
botanical gardens
    Allerton Gardens 404
    Amy Greenwell Ethnobotanical

Garden 204
    Enchanting Floral Gardens 316
    Foster Botanical Garden 118
    Hawaii Tropical Botanical Garden
        238
    Hoomaluhia Botanical Gardens
        166
    Kahanu Gardens 311
    Kula Botanical Garden 316
    Limahuli Gardens 394, 404
    Lyon Arboretum 119
    McBryde Gardens 404
    National Tropical Botanical
        Gardens 404
    Rainbow Gardens 239
    Sacred Garden of Maliko 325
    Senator Fong's Plantation and
        Gardens 165
    Wahiawa Botanical Garden 149
    World Botanical Gardens 239
Bowfin Park 145
buses 53
    Hele-On 188
    Kauai Bus 363
    Maui Bus 260
    TheBus 98, 130

C

caldera 215
calling cards 59
camping 82
Captain Cook (town) 199
car assistance 56
car rental 53
    insurance 54
    local agencies 54
    national agencies 54
Castle & Cooke 351
cell phones. See phone
Chain of Craters Road 214
Chinatown 105
churches
    Kaluaaha 344
    Kawaiahao 118
    Liliuokalani Protestant 178
    Mokuaikaua Chruch 197
    Our Lady of Sorrows 344
    St. Andrew's Cathedral 117
    St. Augustine 140
    St. Benedict's Painted Church
        205
    St. Francis 336
    St. Joseph's 343
    St. Philomena 336
Civic Center 116
Coffees of Hawaii 340
community outreach 70
consulates
    abroad 38
    in the US 39

Cook, Captain James 15
    Captain Cook Monument and
        Trail 204
    Captain James Cook Memorials
        416
county parks 85
crack seed 26
Crater Rim Drive 213
cultural preservation 70
currency exchange 42
customs 41

D

Damien Tours 336
demographics 21
DFS Galleria 142
Diamond Head 139
dietary concerns. See specific
    concerns
Dillingham Airfield 181
disabled travelers. See spe-
    cific concerns
diseases. See health
Dole, James D. 17, 351
Dole Park 352
Dole Plantation 149
Doris Duke Theater 121
Dragon's Teeth 280
driving permits 55
Duke Kahanamoku Statue
    138

E

earthquakes 90
Eleele 410
email. See Internet
Essentials 38–66
    accommodations 60
    getting around Hawaii 53
    getting to Hawaii 45
    keeping in touch 53
    other resources 66
    planning your trip 38
    safety and health 45
    specific concerns 63

F

Faye Park 421
ferries 55
    Expeditions Ferry 260, 351
    Hawaii Superferry 260
    Molokai Princess 260, 328

INDEX

festivals 35
First Fridays
  Hanapepe, Kauai 412
flights 50
  airfares 50
  interisland 53
  standby 52
  ticket consolidators 52
Flumin' da Ditch 253
Forest Reserves 87

G

galleries
  Celebrités 274
  David Warren 325
  Higgins Harte International
    Gallery 274
  Hot Island Glass 325
  Peter Lik 274
  Tennet Foundation Gallery 120
  Vintage European Posters 274
  Volcano Art Center 213
Ganesha Shrine 376
Garden of the Gods 357
Gay and Robinson 413
Gibson, Walter Murray 351
GLBT travelers. See specific
concerns
Great Outdoors 78–95
  camping in Hawaii 82
  flora and fauna 80
  land 78
  organized adventure trips 94
  outdoor activities 91
  useful resources 94
  wilderness safety 87

H

Haena 391
Haiku 306
Halawa Valley 345
Haleakala National Park
317–321
Haleiwa 172–177
Halona Blowhole 151
Hamakua Coast 238–247
Hana 308–311
Hana Cultural Center 312
Hanakoa Valley 397
Hanalei 386–389
Hanalei National Wildlife
Refuge 391
Hanapepe 411
Hanapepe Valley Lookout

410
Hanauma Bay 150
Hawaiian Creole English
(HCE) 22
Hawaii Maritime Center 116
Hawaii Nature Center
  Oahu 119
Hawaii Regional Cuisine 27
Hawaii's Plantation Village 147
Hawaii State Capitol 117
Hawaii Theater Center 122
Hawaii Volcanoes National
Park 210–219
  accommodations and camping
    211
  hiking 216
  orientation 210
  practical information 211
  sights 212
  transportation 210
Hawi 249
health 45
  AIDS/HIV 48
  altitude sickness 89
  dengue fever 90
  food- and water-borne diseases
    90
  heat exhaustion 88
  hypothermia 89
  immunizations 48
  insect-borne diseases 89
  insurance 48
  leptospirosis 90
  MedicAlert 49
  sexually transmitted infections 49
  sunburn 89
  women's 49
heiau 23, 29
  Ahuena 197
  Halekii 286
  Halulu 360
  Iliiliopae 344
  Kahea 359
  Kaneaki 186
  Keaiwa 148
  Mookini Luakini 252
  Pihanakalani 286
  Poliahu 375
  Polihale 422
  Puukohola 257
  Puu o Mahuka 172
  Ulupo 161
hiking
  Aihualama Trail 127
  Alakai Swamp Trail 420
  Alea Loop Trail 148
  Awaawapuhi Trail 419
  Berry Flats Trail 420
  Canyon Trail 419
  Captain Cook Trail 204
  Devastation Trail 214
  Gulch Rim Trail 242
  Halemaumau Trail 217

Halemauu Trail 322
Hanakapiai Falls Side Hike 397
Hanakoa Falls Side Hike 398
Hauula Loop and Maakua Ridge
  Trails 167
Hiilawe Falls 244
Hilina Pali Trail 218
Honolanenui Valley Trail 254
Honolulu Mauka Trail System 127
Judd Trail 128
Kaena Point Trail 180
Kaiwa Ridge Trail 161
Kalalau Trail 396
Kalalau Valley Side Hike 398
Kalauahine Falls 244
Kalaupuhi Trail 420
Kau Desert Trail 218
Kaunala Loop 172
Kealia Trail 181
Keauhou Trail 217
Kilauea Iki Trail 216
Koale Canyon Trail 417
Kolowalu Trail 128
Kuilau Trail 376
Kukui Trail 416
Lahaina Pali Trail 272
Maiwalu Trail 244
Makiki Valley Loop 127
Manoa Cliff Trail 128
Manoa Falls Trail 127
Mauna Kea Observatory Trail 238
Mauna Kea Trail 237
Mauna Loa Trail 218
Maunawili Ditch Trail 161
Maunawili Trail 161
Munro Trail 357
Napau Trail 217
Native Forest Nature Trail 242
Nualolo-Awaawapuhi Loop 419
Nualolo Cliff Trail 419
Nualolo Trail 419
Nuuanu Trail 128
Pepeopae Trail 338
Pihea Trail 420
Pipiwai Trail 313
Polulu Valley Trail 254
Pools of Oheo 312
Powerline Trail 376
Puna Coast Trail 217
Pupukea 172
Puu Huluhulu Trail 217
Puu Ka Ohelo Trail 420
Silversword Loop 322
Sliding Sands Trail 322
Waikama Falls 255
Waimea Canyon Trail 417
Waimea Valley 171
Waipio Valley Beach Trail 244
Water Tank Trail 420
Hilo 226–233
  accommodations 229
  beaches 231
  food 230
  intercity transportation 226
  local transportation 226
  nightlife and entertainment 233
  orientation 228
  practical information 228
  sights 232

Hipuapua Falls 346
history. See Life and Times.
hitchhiking 57
Hofgaard Park 416
Hokulea 20
holidays 35
Holualoa 199
Honaunau 199
Honokaa 240
Honokaa People's Theater 243
Honokowai 276
Honolohau Marina 193
Honolulu 98–124
  accommodations 108
  arts and entertainment 122
  beaches 116
  food 110
  hiking 127
  local transportation 98
  museums 120
  nightlife 125
  orientation 102
  practical information 105
  shopping 123
  sights 116
Honolulu Symphony 123
Honolulu Zoo 140
Hoolehua 341
Hoolulu Valley 398
horseback riding 93
Hui Noeau Visual Arts Center 325
hula
  Hulihee Palace 197
  Kuhio Beach Torch Lighting and Hula Show 141
  Lahaina Cannery Mall 272
  Royal Hawaiian Shows and Lessons 141
  Waikiki hotel hula shows 141
Huleia National Wildlife Refuge 370
Hulihee Palace 197
hurricanes 91
Hyatt Shops 142

I

Iao Needle 286
Iao Theater 287
identification 41
Imiloa Astronomy Center 232
International Marketplace 142
Internet 58
Iolani Palace 116

Iraivan Temple 376
Ironman Triathlon 34

K

Kaanapali 274
Kadavul Temple 376
kahako 22
Kahakuloa 280
Kahana 276
Kahekili Highway 279
Kahekili's Leap 360
Kahilu Theater 249
Kahiwa Falls 347
Kahoolawe 23
Kahului 280
Kahuna profile 286
Kailua 155–161
Kailua-Kona 189–198
  accommodations 192
  activities 196
  beaches 195
  food 193
  nightlife 197
  orientation 190
  practical information 190
  transportation 189
Kailua Pier 193
Kaimuki 105
Kakahaia National Wildlife Refuge 343
Ka Lae 205–209
Kalaheo 408
Kalakaua, David 17
Kalakaua Park 233
Kalalau Lookout 418
Kalalau Trail 396
Kalapana 225
Kalaupapa Peninsula 334
Kalihiwai River 385
Kaluaaha 343
Kaluakoi 348
kalua pig 28
Kamakou Preserve 336
Kamalo 343
Kamehameha I 15
Kamehameha's birthplace 252
Kamehemeha Statue 253
Kaneohe 162–168
Kanepuu Preserve 358
Kapaa 379
Kapalua 278

Kapauu 249
Kapualwa Coconut Grove 333
Kau 205–209
Kauai 361–420
  East Shore 361
  Na Pali Coast 395
  North Shore 383
  South Shore 399
  West Shore 407
Kauai Coffee 409
Kauai's Hindu Monastery 376
Kaumakani 413
Kaumalapau Harbor 360
Kaumana Caves County Park 233
Kaunakakai 329–332
Kaunakakai Ball Park 334
Kaunakakai Wharf 333
Kaunollu 360
Kawela 343
Keahiakawelo 357
Keahua Arboretum 376
Kealakekua 199
Kealakekua Bay 203
Kekaha 421
Kennedy Theater 122
Keomuku Village 359
Kihei 290–296
Kilaauea 383
Kilauea Point National Wildlife Refuge 386
Kilohana 369
Kipahulu Valley 312
Koko Crater 152
Koko Head Regional Park and Environs 150
Koloa 406
Koloa History Center 407
Koloa Sugar Monument 407
Kona. See Kailua-Kona
Kona Boys 196, 203
Kona Pacific Farmers Cooperative 202
Kualoa Ranch and Regional Park 167
Kuamoo Road 375
Kuan Yin Temple 118
Kula 313
Kula Kai Caverns 209
Kumukahi Lighthouse 225
Kupapau Puu Pehe 360

L

Lahaina 261–272
   accommodations and camping 264
   activities 267
   beaches 266
   entertainment 272
   food 265
   galleries 274
   hiking 272
   nightlife 273
   orientation 262
   practical information 262
   shopping 274
   sights 269
   transportation 261
Lahaina Restoration Foundation 269
Lanai 350–359
   Central Lanai 357
   East Side 358
   Lanai City 352
   North Side 357
   South Side 359
Lanai City 352
language 22
language schools 72
La Pérouse Bay 299
Laupahoehoe 243
lava 79
Life and Times 14–37
   additional resources 36
   culture 26
   history 14
   holidays and festivals 35
   people 21
   the "other" islands 23
Lihue 363–370
Lolo Vista 419
luaus 27
   Drums of Paradise 405
   Island Breeze Luau 199
   Kona Village Resort 199
   Old Lahaina Luau 272
   Paina O Hanalei 386

M

Maalaea 288
Magic Island 116
Makalawena 196
Makanalua Peninsula 347
Makapuu Point 152
Makawao 323
Makawao Mushrooms 316
Makaweli 413
Makena 298

Mamala Bay 116
Maniniholo Dry Cave 395
Manoa 105
Manoa Marketplace 114
Maui 258–322
   Central Maui 280
   Lahaina 261
   North Shore 299
   South Maui 288
   Upcountry Maui 313
   West Maui 260
Maui Agricultural Research Center 316
Maui Arts and Cultural Center 287
Maui Bowling Center 287
Maui Film Festival 287, 297
Maui Nei 272
Maui Ocean Center 289
Maui Swap Meet 287
Maunakea Marketplace 113
Maunaloa 347
Mauna Loa 237
Mauna Loa Rd. 215
McCoy Theater 287
Menehune Ditch 415
Menehune Fishpond Overlook 368
Merrie Monarch Festival 232
Moaula Falls 346
Mokuaeae Rock 386
Moku Hooniki Island 346
Mokuleia 178
Molokai 326–349
   Central Molokai 334
   East of Kaunakakai 342
   Kaunakakai 329
   Western Molokai 347
Molokai Forestry Reserve 337
money 42
Moomomi Preserve 341
mopeds 57
movie theaters
   Kaahumanu 6 Theaters 287
   Kress Cinemas 234
   Lanai Playhouse 356
   Maui Mall Megaplex Cinemas 287
   Movie Museum 123
   Palace Theatre 234
   Prince Kuhio Stadium Cinemas 234
   Ward 16 123
Munro, George 351
Munro Trail 357

museums
   Contemporary Museum 121
   Grove Farm Homestead Museum 368
   Hawaii State Art Museum 121
   Honolulu Academy of Arts 120
   Jagger Museum and Hawaiian Volcano Observatory 213
   Kauai Museum 370
   Kokee Natural History Museum 417
   Laupahoehoe Train Museum 240
   Lyman Museum and Mission House 232
   Mission Houses Museum 121
   Molokai Museum and Cultural Center 341
   Movie Museum 123
   Old Lahaina Courthouse Museum 269
   Pacific Aviation Museum 146
   Pacific Tsunami Museum 232
   Parker Ranch Historic Homes 248
   Parker Ranch Museum and Visitors Center 248
   Tropical Gardens of Maui 286

N

Nakalele Blowhole 280
Na Pali Coast 395–400
Napili 276
Natatorium 138
National Parks 84
Native Hawaiian rights 70
nature conservation 69
Nechung Dorje Drayang Ling 209
Nene o Molokai 343
Niaupala Fishpond 344
Niihau 24
Ninini Lighthouse 370
North Kohala 249
North Shore Country Market 170
North Shore Sea Cliffs 347
Northwest Hawaiian Islands 25
Nuuanu Pali Lookout 166

O

Oahu 96–182
   Central Oahu 144
   Honolulu 98–124
   Leeward Coast 181
   North Shore 168
   Southeast Oahu 150
   Waikiki 129–143
   Windward Coast 155

Oahu Market 113
Oheo Gulch 312
'okina 22
Olelo Hawaii 22
Onizuka Center for International Astronomy 235
Opaekaa Falls 376
Outrigger Canoe Club 34

P

Pacific Whale Foundation 289
Pahoa 221
Paia 302–305
Panaewa Rainforest Zoo 233
Papaiko Road 238
Parker Ranch 245
passports 40
Pearl Harbor 144
Pearlridge Shopping Center 147
Pelekunu Valley Overlook 338
People's Open Markets 123
Pepeekeo Scenic Drive 238
petroglyphs
  Kukui Point 5, 359
  Olowalu 272
  Puu Loa 215
phone
  cell phones 59
  from Hawaii 58
  in Hawaii 59
  phone cards 58
pidgin 22
Pihea Vista 420
pineapple industry 16
planes. See flights
plate lunch 26
Pohakuloa Point 346
poi 27
Poipu 400
Pololu Valley Lookout 253
Polynesian Cultural Center 166
Port Allen 411
Puck's Alley 114
Puff the Magic Dragon 387
Pukalani 323
Pukoo 344
Pukuhiwa Battleground 343
Puna 218–223
Punchbowl National Memorial

Cemetery 119
Purdy's Macadamia Nut Farm 339
Puu Hinahina Lookout 416
Puuhonua O Honaunau National Historical Park 205
Puukohola Heiau National Historical Site 257
Puu O Hoku Ranch 346
Puu O Kila Lookout 418
Puu Pehe Rock 360

Q

Queen Emma's Summer Palace 120
Queen Kaahumanu Center 287
Queen Liliuokalani 17

R

Rainbow Falls 233
religion 23
rental cars. See car rental
Restaurant Row 111
Road from Hana 313
Rock Point 346
Royal Hawaiian Shopping Center 142

S

Sacred Forest 376
Saddle Rd. 234
safety 45
saimin 26
Sandwich Islands 15
scuba 92
Sea Life Park 152
shave ice 27
Smith-Bronte Landing Site 343
Smith's Tropical Paradise 375
snorkeling 92
South Kohala 255
Spam 27
specific concerns
  dietary concerns 65
  disabled travelers 65
  GLBT travelers 64
  minority travelers 65
  solo travel 64

sustainable travel 63
terrorism 46
women travelers 64
state parks 84
  Akaka Falls 239
  Iao Valley 286
  Kaena Point 186
  Kalopa State Recreation Area 242
  Keaiwa Heiau State Recreation Area 148
  Kokee 417
  Kolekole 233
  Lapakahi State Historical Park 252
  Lava Tree 225
  Lydgate 374
  Mackenzie State Recreation Area 225
  Mauna Kea State Recreation Area 235
  Maunka State Natural Area Reserve 209
  Palauu 340
  Polihale 422
  Polipoli Spring State Recreation Area 317
  Waianapanapa 311
  Wailua River 374
  Waimea Canyon 416
Stones of Life 138
study abroad 71
sugar industry 16
Sunset Beach 168
surfing 33, 91
Surfing Goat Dairy 316
sustainable travel. See specific concerns
Sweetheart Rock 360

T

taxes 44
Tedeschi Winery and Vineyards 316
temples. See heiau
time differences 59
tipping 44
tourist offices 39
trails. See hiking
traveler's checks 42
Tropical Farms Outlet 167
tsunamis 91
Twain, Mark 30

U

Ualapue 343
Ulupalakua Ranch 316

Umauma Falls 239
universities 72
USS Arizona 144
USS Missouri 146
USS Oklahoma 146
USS Utah 146

V

Valley of the Temples 165
Victoria Ward Centers 124
visas 40, 71
volcanoes 91
Volcano Village 219
volunteering 68

W

Wahiawa 149
Waialae Falls 416

Waialea 256
Waialua 178
Waialua Shopping Center 180
Waikiki 129–143
  accommodations 134
  activities 139
  beaches 137
  entertainment 141
  food 135
  local transportation 130
  nightlife 143
  orientation 132
  practical information 133
  Shopping 142
  sights 139
Waikiki Aquarium 140
Waikiki Historic Trail 137
Waikiki Shell 141
Wailau Valley 347
Wailea 297
Wailua Falls 370
Wailuku 280

Waimanalo 153
Waimea, Big Island 245
Waimea Canyon Lookout 416
Waimea, Kauai 413
Waimea, Oahu 168
Waimea Theater 415
Waimea Valley 171
Waipahu 147
Waipio Valley 243
Waipouli 377
Warrior's Leap 360
Wet Caves 395
Whispering Rock 346
wilderness safety 87
wildlife conservation 69
Wonderwalks 419
working abroad 74
work permits 73
World War II 18

ABOUT LET'S GO

NOT YOUR PARENTS' TRAVEL GUIDE

At Let's Go, we see every trip as the chance of a lifetime. If your dream is to grab a machete and forge through the jungles of Costa Rica, we can take you there. If you'd rather bask in the Riviera sun at a beachside cafe, we'll set you a table. We write for readers who know that there's more to travel than sharing double deckers with tourists and who believe that travel can change both themselves and the world—whether they plan to spend six days in Bangkok or six months in Europe. We'll show you just how far your money can go, and prove that the greatest limitation on your adventures is not your wallet but your imagination.

BEYOND THE TOURIST EXPERIENCE

To help you gain a deeper connection with the places you travel, our fearless researchers scour the globe to give you the heads-up on both world-renowned and off-the-beaten-track attractions, sights, and destinations. They dive into the local culture only to emerge with the freshest insights on everything from festivals to regional cuisine. We've also opened our pages to respected writers and scholars to hear their takes on the countries and regions we cover, and asked travelers who have worked, studied, or volunteered abroad to contribute first-person accounts of their experiences. In addition, each guide's Beyond Tourism chapter shares ideas about responsible travel, study abroad, and how to give back while on the road.

FORTY-NINE YEARS OF WISDOM

Let's Go got its start in 1960, when a group of creative and well-traveled students compiled their experience and advice into a 20-page mimeographed pamphlet, which they gave to travelers on charter flights to Europe. Almost five decades later, we've expanded to cover six continents and all kinds of travel—while retaining our founders' adventurous attitude. Laced with witty prose and total candor, our guides are still researched and written entirely by students on shoestring budgets, experienced travelers who know that train strikes, stolen luggage, food poisoning, and marriage proposals are all part of a day's work.

THE LET'S GO COMMUNITY

More than just a travel guide company, Let's Go is a community. Our small staff comes together because of our shared passion for travel and our desire to help other travelers see the world the way it was meant to be seen. We love it when our readers become part of the Let's Go community as well—when you travel, drop us a postcard (67 Mt. Auburn St., Cambridge, MA 02138, USA), send us an e-mail (feedback@letsgo.com), or sign up online (http://www.letsgo.com) to tell us about your adventures and discoveries.

For more information, visit us online: www.letsgo.com.

Hostelling International USA:
Comfort, fun and great value across the USA!

From picturesque lighthouses to bustling cities, Hostelling International USA offers the largest network of quality hostels across the USA. Enjoy fantastic destinations like New York, Boston & Cape Cod, Chicago, Washington, the Pacific Northwest, San Francisco and Los Angeles, or adventures in Hawaii or Alaska.

Wherever you stay, you'll love our great rates and warm HI welcome!

Information & reservations:

hiusa.org

MAP INDEX

Ala Moana and University Area 104
Big Island (Hawaii) 188
Central Oahu 145
Chinatown and Downtown 112
Downtown Honolulu 101
Downtown Lihue 367
East Shore Kauai 378
Eleele to Waimea 410
Haleakala National Park 319
Haleiwa 173
Hamakua Coast 240
Hana 309
Hanalei 387
Hawaii X
Hawaii: Chapters VIII
Hilo 227
Honolulu and Vicinity 99
Honolulu Mauka Trails 129
Kaanapali Area Beaches 275
Kahului and Wailuku 283
Kailua 157
Kailua-Kona 191
Kauai 362
Kaunakakai 331
Kihei 291
Kohala Coast 251
Lahaina 263
Lanai 350

Lanai City 353
Leeward Coast 183
Lihue Region 364
Maui 259
Molokai 327
North Shore and Upcountry Maui 302
North Shore Kauai 382
North Shore Oahu 169
Oahu 97
Poipu and Koloa 401
Puna 219
Saddle Road 236
Southeast Oahu 151
Southern Kau District 205
South Kona 199
Waikiki 130
Wailua 372
Waimea 245, 415
West Shore Kauai 408
Windward Oahu 154

SUGGESTED ITINERARIES:

Back to Nature 10
The Big Island 6
Hawaiiana and More 12
Kauai 7
Maui 7
Oahu 6
Off the Tourist Beaten Path 8

MAP LEGEND

- Point of Interest
- Accommodations
- Activities
- Camping
- Entertainment
- Food
- Nightlife
- Shopping
- Airport
- Bank/ATM
- Beach
- Botanical Garden
- Cave

- Church
- Cinder Cone
- Ferry Landing
- Golf Course
- Hospital
- Internet Cafe
- Library
- Lighthouse
- Mountain
- Park/Forest
- Parking Lot
- Pharmacy
- Police Station

- Post Office
- Shelter
- Snorkeling Site
- Surfing Site
- Tourist Office
- Volcano Crater
- Waterfall
- Federal Highway H1
- State Highway 78

- Beach
- Building
- Cemetery
- Military Base
- Lava Flows
- Park
- Water

- 4WD Road
- District Boundary
- Ferry Line
- Hiking Trail
- Pedestrian Zone
- Railroad/Station

The Let's Go compass always points NORTH.